CHILDREN'S
BOOK-A-DAY
ALMANAC

DISCARD

W9-BVH-014

CHILDREN'S
BOOK-A-DAY
ALMANAC

ANITA SILVEY

ROARING BROOK PRESS
New York

For Gordon Perry, John Schumaker,
and Vicki and Steve Palmquist—
in gratitude for all their support on this project

Text copyright © 2012 by Anita Silvey
Published by Roaring Brook Press
Roaring Brook Press is a division of Holtzbrinck Publishing Holdings Limited Partnership
175 Fifth Avenue, New York, New York 10010
mackids.com
All rights reserved

Library of Congress Cataloging-in-Publication Data

Silvey, Anita.
   Children's book-a-day almanac / Anita Silvey. — First edition.
      pages cm
   Summary: "An Almanac with information about famous events and celebrations for each day of the year
and related children's book recommendations"—Provided by publisher.
   Includes bibliographical references.
   ISBN 978-1-59643-708-1
   1. Children's literature—Bibliography.   2. Children's literature—Stories, plots, etc.   3. Children—
Books and reading—United States.   4. Best books—United States.   5. Almanacs.   I. Title.
   Z1037.S578 2012
   011.62—dc23

                                                                                              2012013301

Roaring Brook Press books are available for special promotions and premiums.
For details contact: Director of Special Markets, Holtzbrinck Publishers.

First edition 2012
Book design by Roberta Pressel
Printed in the United States of America

10   9   8   7   6   5   4   3   2   1

INTRODUCTION

In October of 2010 the Children's Book-a-Day Almanac website was launched (childrensbookalmanac.com); each day since then one essay showcasing one of the gems of children's literature has been published. Day after day I have been able to connect with readers—to lead them to books that they need and to remind them of the books that have made a difference in the lives of children. I have responded to questions and critiques. I have also had children comment on the Almanac, through their parents and teachers, to inform me how they felt about my choices. All critics need to keep in touch with what happens when the rubber meets the road! As I prepared the final pages for the printed book, I kept thinking about how much my daily Almanac readers have made it a better resource.

Although I love the immediacy of cyberspace, I am thrilled to have this book in print. Now readers can easily thumb through and make plans for celebrating their own favorite days in advance. Every day of the calendar year I discuss an appropriate title and then provide information about how it came about, the author, the ideal audience, and how the book has connected in a meaningful way with young people from babies to age fourteen. For 365 days—or with a leap year 366—I provide a reliable guide to the classics and to new books on their way to becoming classics. On March 12 I talk about Madeleine L'Engle's road from rejection to her award-winning book *A Wrinkle in Time;* on June 11 I relate how Hans and Margret Rey saved *Curious George* and themselves from the Nazis; on July 18 I focus on the beginning of the Spanish Civil War and its impact on Munro Leaf's *The Story of Ferdinand.*

For each day of the year I also include a sidebar that lists other events and contains children's books related to these events. Because the sidebar covers books for different age ranges than the essay itself, this material extends the usefulness of the *Children's Book-a-Day Almanac.* Various indexes round out the book—making it easy to find the right book for the right child at the right time.

When working on these essays, I have always tried to make them as accessible and lively as possible—but keep them inspiring as well. Basically, by using the calendar as an organizing device, the *Children's Book-a-Day Almanac* shines the spotlight on the best books for young readers. Just as we want to get children the best food for their bodies, they need the best nourishment for their minds. My entire career, now spanning over forty years, has been devoted to a statement by Walter de la Mare: "Only the rarest kind of best in anything can be good enough for the young." For each day of the year, I provide insight into that "rarest kind of best."

JOHNNY TREMAIN

By Esther Forbes

On January 1, 1735, Paul Revere, patriot, silversmith, and engraver, was baptized in Boston's North End. Although made famous by Henry Wadsworth Longfellow in "The Midnight Ride of Paul Revere," Revere's story has attracted many fine writers over the years, including one of the descendants of Samuel Adams, the organizer of the Sons of Liberty: Esther Forbes.

Although Esther Forbes would become a brilliant writer for both adults and young people, she suffered from a type of dyslexia. She could not spell words and used the dash as her only form of punctuation. These problems did not deter her from writing a biography of Paul Revere, *Paul Revere and the World He Lived In*, that won the Pulitzer Prize for history in 1943. An editor suggested that Forbes try her hand at writing history for young readers. Because American soldiers were going into World War II, Forbes reflected on how in peacetime adolescents are protected but in wartime they are asked to fight and die. Remembering the story of a young boy who delivered a critical message to Paul Revere, she produced the first draft of *Johnny Tremain*.

Normally, publishing a great story by a Pulitzer Prize winner would have been a "no brainer" for an editor—but Grace Hogarth at Houghton could not help but notice Forbes's issues with spelling and punctuation. Hogarth gathered her courage to tell Forbes that although she loved the book, she would have to standardize the spelling! Forbes merely said, "My editors always do that!" So a very messy manuscript got transformed into the greatest work of historical fiction for children in the first part of the twentieth century. According to editors on staff at the time, Forbes drove two aging proofreaders almost out of their minds in the process.

This complex and brilliant novel spans two years in the life of Johnny Tremain, an orphan and silversmith apprentice. While casting a sugar basin for John Hancock, he burns his right hand and must abandon his position. But he finds work as a messenger for the Sons of Liberty, becoming swept up in the American Revolution. Forbes brought an amazing amount of historical detail to life and takes young readers behind the scenes as the colonists decide to rebel against the British. As the *New York Times* said of her, she was "a novelist who wrote like a historian and a historian who wrote like a novelist."

I can think of no better way to begin a new year than rereading *Johnny Tremain*. It reminds all of us just how great fiction for young readers can be.

JANUARY 1

Happy Birthday Jeanne DuPrau (*The City of Ember*).

It's the birth date of Maria Edgeworth (1767–1849), *Moral Tales for Young People*; J. D. Salinger (1919–2010), *The Catcher in the Rye*; and E. M. Forster (1879–1970), *A Room with a View, A Passage to India*.

It's also the birth date of Betsy Ross (1752–1836), credited with crafting the first American flag for the fledgling United States. Read *Betsy Ross* by Alexandra Wallner.

In 1788 *The Times*, London's oldest running newspaper, published its first edition.

On this day in 1863 President Abraham Lincoln issued the Emancipation Proclamation, freeing the slaves in the Confederacy.

It's National Soup Month. Read *Soup* by Robert Newton Peck, *Mouse Soup* by Arnold Lobel, *Stone Soup* by Marcia Brown, and *Chicken Soup with Rice* by Maurice Sendak.

It's National Book Blitz Month, an opportunity to promote books we love.

JANUARY 2

Happy Birthday Jean Little (*From Anna*) and Lynda Barry (*The Good Times Are Killing Me*).

It's the birth date of Crosby Bonsall (1921–1995), *The Case of the Scaredy Cats*, *Piggle*; and Isaac Asimov (1920–1992), Foundation series.

Happy Birthday Georgia, which became the fourth U.S. state on this day in 1788. Read *Fame and Glory in Freedom, Georgia* by Barbara O'Connor.

 In 1959 **Luna 1**, the first spacecraft to reach the vicinity of the moon, was launched by the U.S.S.R. Read *Beautiful Moon: Bella Luna* by Dawn Jeffers, illustrated by Bonnie Leick, and *The Moon Is La Luna* by Jay M. Harris, illustrated by Matthew Cordell.

THE ADVENTURES OF CAPTAIN UNDERPANTS

By Dav Pilkey

Today is set aside to "Run it up the flagpole and see if anyone salutes." The concept behind the day, and the phrase, is to get people to try out a new idea. But often for children, these sayings take on literal meanings, such as in Jerry Spinelli's *Who Ran My Underwear Up a Flagpole*.

For me, today, January 2, is a day for a new idea—a day of surrender. I have avoided talking about *Captain Underpants* for over ten years. Male friends have teased me about the book. Male journalists decried the fact that I did not include it in *100 Best Books for Children*. Even when I borrowed the book from my local library, one of the staff said, "I never thought I would see you check this out."

But while I have been avoiding this book, the books in the Captain Underpants series have sold more than forty million copies; they have made children who think they hate books become readers; and they have made the author a household name. One of the standing jokes in publishing is that if you want to create a bestseller for children you should include underwear in the title. Comedic genius Dav Pilkey knew this a long time before publishers discovered it. Still in touch with the kind of child that he was—"getting into trouble for pulling pranks, cracking jokes, and making silly comic books"—he invented his famous character in second grade. Fortunately, he didn't listen to the teacher who told him to straighten up "because you can't spend the rest of your life making silly books." As an adult he returned to that character, and the rest is history.

In the first book in the series, *The Adventures of Captain Underpants,* published in 1997, readers meet the two anti-heroes George Beard and Harold Hutchins. The two BFFs find endless ways to create mayhem and end up spending more time with the principal, Mr. Krupp, than their teachers. After buying a 3-D Hypno-Ring, they hypnotize Mr. Krupp, causing him to run around town in his underpants and cape because he believes himself to be Captain Underpants.

The book contains so much silly, gross-out humor and action-filled drawings that young readers finish an entire book without meaning to. If you know a young reader, ages six through ten, who thinks books have to be boring, you might as well surrender. Your solution will be the ever-growing series—"lots of fun, lots of laffs"—that was first created in the mind of a prank-playing second grader. Today I am running Captain Underpants up the flagpole. We'll see if anyone salutes him.

DIAMOND WILLOW

By Helen Frost

Today marks Alaska's statehood day, when in 1959 Alaska became the forty-ninth state in the Union. Of the myriad books for children that have been set in Alaska, my favorite, *Diamond Willow* by Helen Frost, appeared in 2008. Frost lived and taught for three years in a small Athabascan community in interior Alaska. Many years later she found the appropriate story, and poetic form, to pay tribute to those she had encountered there.

In this contemporary story Diamond Willow's father is a science teacher whose ancestors migrated across Canada and the United States for about 160 years before they settled in Old Fork. Her mother is of Athabascan descent, people who have lived in Alaska for centuries. The spirits of their dead relatives inhabit the birds and animals living around them. Most of the story is narrated from the point of view of twelve-year-old Diamond Willow. She loves her community and particularly the sled dogs that the family uses. Convincing her father and mother that she is old enough to handle them alone, she heads out to her grandparents' home, only to have tragedy strike. Their prize dog Roxy suffers an accident that renders him blind. Naturally, Diamond Willow feels responsible. So when her parents decide to euthanize the dog because he will never run and lead sleds again, the girl takes matters into her own hands. She sets out, on the night of a terrible storm, to beg her grandparents to protect the dog.

Diamond Willow's story, which is written in diamond-shaped poems alternating with prose pieces, is told by the animals themselves. Their comments provide context for some of the events happening to Diamond Willow. On its most basic level, *Diamond Willow* tells the love story between a girl and her dog: she is willing to risk her own life to save this animal. But this is one of the rare books for children that also explores the spiritual realm. In it the love and longing of those now dead intersect with the struggles of the living. Imagine Thorton Wilder's *Our Town* set in Alaska, and you have an idea of the power of this brief text, only 110 pages long.

As with everything Helen Frost writes, poetic form lies at the heart of her structure. Each diamond-shaped poem contains a message, hidden in darker ink. The form of this work was inspired by diamond willow bark, which reveals reddish-brown diamonds that have a dark center, the scar of a missing branch. As Helen writes in the introduction, "The scars, and the diamonds that form around them, give diamond willow its beauty, and gave me the idea for my story."

In this rare look at a small town in interior Alaska, *Diamond Willow* provides a haunting, impossible-to-forget story—that lingers long after the reader closes the book.

JANUARY 3

Happy Birthday Patricia Lee Gauch (*The Knitting of Elizabeth Amelia*), Tony Chen (*A Child's First Bible Storybook*), J. Otto Seibold (*Olive the Other Reindeer, Mind Your Manners, B.B. Wolf*), and Chris Soentpiet (*So Far from the Sea*).

It's J.R.R. Tolkien Day, in honor of the birthday of J.R.R. Tolkien (1892–1973), *The Hobbit, The Lord of the Rings*.

It's also the birth date of Carolyn Haywood (1898–1990), *"B" is for Betsey*.

In 1870 construction began on the **Brooklyn Bridge**. Read *Brooklyn Bridge* by Karen Hesse and *Brooklyn Bridge* by Lynn Curlee.

Happy Birthday Alaska, which became the 49th U.S. state on this day in 1959.

JANUARY 4

Happy Birthday Phyllis Reynolds Naylor (Shiloh trilogy, Alice series) and Robert Burleigh (*Hoops, One Giant Leap*).

It's the birth date of Jakob Grimm (1785–1863), *Grimm's Fairy Tales*.

Happy Birthday Utah, which became the 49th U.S. state on this day in 1896.

It's World Braille Day. Louis Braille (1809–1852), the creator of braille, a system enabling blind and visually impaired people to write and read, was born on this day. Read *Louis Braille: A Touch of Genius* by C. Michael Mellor, *A Picture Book of Louis Braille* by David A. Adler, illustrated by John and Alexandra Wallner, and *Out of the Darkness* by Russell Freedman, illustrated by Kate Kiesler.

THE GREAT AND ONLY BARNUM: THE TREMENDOUS, STUPENDOUS LIFE OF SHOWMAN P. T. BARNUM

By Candace Fleming

On January 4, 1838, Charles Sherwood Stratton, probably the most famous small person in history, was born in Bridgeport, Connecticut. He was discovered in 1842 by another resident of the city, P. T. Barnum, and named "General Tom Thumb." Because the General performed for years for Barnum, the two men are inextricably linked in history. A showman, con man, great humbug, philanthropist, Barnum learned early on that "When entertaining the public, it is best to have an elephant."

Barnum's larger-than-life personality and his willingness to lie to his customers create a challenge for any biographer. Fortunately one of our most creative writers of narrative nonfiction, Candace Fleming, tackles this complex individual in a book for ten- to fourteen-year-olds, *The Great and Only Barnum: The Tremendous, Stupendous Life of Showman P. T. Barnum*.

All aspects of the book are adapted to be entertaining; even the acknowledgments have been written in the language of the circus. Readers first meet Barnum's joke-loving family who taught him that people love to be "humbugged" or fooled. As one of his first acts, Barnum toured Joice Heth as "the world's oldest living woman"—a hoax done at the expense not only of the public, but also of this aged African-American. Fleming's authorial voice is impeccable as she describes Barnum's dubious actions. While she acknowledges the moral issues involved, she still manages to show events from Barnum's perspective. Although he exhibited the unusual or misshapen—bearded women, Siamese twins, a giantess, or General Tom Thumb—Barnum also provided housing, care, food, and employment for people who otherwise would have been shunned in nineteenth-century America.

Besides creating circus acts, Barnum purchased John Scudder's American Museum and built one of the great showplaces of his time, redefining the idea of an American museum. Readers go on a room-by-room tour of Barnum's creation. The American Museum became so popular that Barnum needed to find a way to get people to leave. So he created a sign that said "To the Egress." Customers eager for the next exhibit hurried on, only to find themselves on the street.

A devout churchgoer and someone who gave generously to Bridgeport, Connecticut, Barnum seems like a contemporary American celebrity—a bit of fraud and a bit of genius, energetic and driven, capable of great cruelty and generosity.

Candace Fleming's superb biography can help us celebrate the birthday of Tom Thumb, the beginnings of the Barnum & Bailey Circus, or just the life of this quintessential American.

THE RACE TO SAVE THE LORD GOD BIRD

By Phillip Hoose

Today marks a relatively new holiday on the calendar, National Bird Day—to think about the birds we keep as pets and how owning them affects the bird population on earth. Our attitudes toward animals and birds and how we treat them has changed dramatically over time.

No one has ever captured the changing mores about birds better than Phillip Hoose, in his masterpiece *The Race to Save the Lord God Bird*. In this intelligent photo-essay for fifth to eighth graders, Hoose focuses on the Ivory-billed Woodpecker, sometimes called the Lord God Bird, "a majestic and formidable species," and its struggle for survival. In a book that covers two hundred years of bird history, readers first see those bird lovers of the 1800s, who shot, drew, and preserved their specimens. Then Audubon, another hunter, comes on the stage, but he preserves details of his prey through art. Some years later women's hat fashions devastate the bird population. Everyone wanted a distinctive plume to wear in her chapeau. Consequently, the Audubon Society was created—to try to convince those with a fashion sense to leave out the birds. Hoose moves with grace and dexterity through American history—the need for timber, the shrinking habitat of the Ivory-bill, and the wanton collectors.

Hoose weaves the Ivory-bill in and out of his tale during this history, as the bird fights for survival while its habitat shrinks. Eventually the Cornell University ornithology crews head out into the swamps, with video cameras and microphones, to try to capture the sound of this bird. They are a different kind of hunter, seeking a scientific record.

By this point, anyone reading the book wants one thing—to actually see and hear one of these woodpeckers. How do you make people love something that no longer can be found? That, of course, has been the problem when it comes to all vanished species. If a child has never seen a passenger pigeon, how can he or she care what they were like? But Hoose manages to make readers care in this book. Through *The Race to Save the Lord God Bird* they can watch others come under the spell of this species and witness these creatures dwindle in number.

Shortly after *The Race to Save the Lord God Bird* appeared in print in 2004, a sighting of the Ivory-bill was reported and made national news. The sighting was never verified; but Phillip Hoose has made all his readers hope that some day, one will be seen again. Great for discussion, brilliant in its execution, *The Race to Save the Lord God Bird* should be read by everyone who loves winged creatures.

JANUARY 5

Happy Birthday Lynne Cherry (*The Great Kapok Tree*) and Betsy Maestro (*How Do Apples Grow?*, *Why Do Leaves Change Color?*).

It's the birth date of King Camp Gillette (1855–1932), the inventor of the safety razor, and Herbert Bayard Swope (1882–1958), the journalist who coined the term "Cold War."

On this day in 1759 George Washington married Martha Dandridge Custis. Read *George and Martha* by James Marshall.

In 1781 British naval forces led by **Benedict Arnold** burned Richmond, Virginia. Read *The Notorius Benedict Arnold* by Steve Sheinkin.

Construction of the Golden Gate Bridge began in San Francisco Bay in 1933. Read *Pop's Bridge* by Eve Bunting, illustrated by C. F. Payne.

JANUARY 6

Happy Birthday Vera Cleaver (*Where the Lilies Bloom*) and Wendelin Van Draanen (*Flipped*).

It's the birth date of Carl Sandburg (1878–1967), *Rootabaga Stories*.

Happy Birthday to the fictional character Sherlock Holmes. Read *The Extraordinary Cases of Sherlock Holmes* by Arthur Conan Doyle.

Happy Birthday New Mexico, which became the 47th U.S. state on this day in 1912.

In 1929 Mother Teresa arrived in Calcutta to begin her work among India's poorest people. Read *Mother Theresa* by Tracey Dils.

In one of the closest presidential elections in U.S. history, George W. Bush was finally declared the winner of the bitterly contested 2000 presidential elections on this day in 2001.

It's Cuddle Up Day. Read *I Love to Cuddle* by Carl Norac, illustrated by Claude K. Dubois, and *Daddy Cuddles* by Anne Gutman and Georg Hallensleben.

THE STORY OF JOAN OF ARC
By Maurice Boutet de Monvel

On January 6, or close to it, in 1412, a peasant girl destined to become a saint was born in Domrémy-la-Pucelle, France. As a teenager, Joan of Arc experienced visions, heard voices, and set out to save the King of France. She delivered Orléans from a siege during the Hundred Years War and paved the way for Charles VII to be crowned. Burned at the stake by the English, she was canonized in 1920. Joan became one of the first military maids, a symbol for countless women who wanted to take up weapons and fight.

The first brilliant biography for children of the Maid of Orléans was written by another resident of the city, Maurice Boutet de Monvel (1850–1913). A student at Ecole des Beaux-Arts in Paris, Boutet de Monvel, an academy painter, needed to augment his income. Hence he began to create children's books and contribute illustrations to *Century* and *Scribner's*, as well as the French edition of *St. Nicholas*, the famous magazine for boys and girls. But his interest in French history led him to write and illustrate his masterpiece, first published in Paris in 1896, *The Story of Joan of Arc*. Normally, I am a whole book critic—text and art have to work equally well for me to love a book. No one can possibly defend Boutet de Monvel's text. He was neither a writer nor a historian—but he was one of the great French artists of his period. The illustrations in this book are best used alone to present Joan of Arc's life.

What incredible images they are. Gerald Gottlieb, in the introduction to the book, argues that the rich detail in the book is reminiscent of early fifteenth-century illuminated manuscripts. They contain muted tones and the flat color found in Japanese prints. As Boutet de Monvel himself said about his art: "It is not color really, it is the impression, the suggestion of color." As the artist depicts Joan, he blends modern elements with the medieval. Even on the title page, she leads French soldiers wearing the uniform of 1896. This artwork displays processions and vast panoramas, stirring scenes of battles and of Joan's bravery.

Only a few first editions of the book exist, and the copy owned by The Morgan Library & Museum was used to create the paperback volume of the book now available. Anyone who loves children's book illustration—and wants a dramatic way to introduce Joan of Arc to children ages six to ten—should pick up a copy of Boutet de Monvel's *The Story of Joan of Arc*.

PICTURE BOOK, CLASSIC, BIOGRAPHY, All Ages

ZORA AND ME

By Victoria Bond and T. R. Simon

Born on January 7, 1891, Zora Neale Hurston become one of the most renowned black writers of the twentieth century, part of the Harlem Renaissance, and pioneer of collecting regional black folklore. During her lifetime she was often compared to, and sometimes competed against, Richard Wright, but for a period of time her work vanished, while his became a staple of high school and college curricula. In the 1970s Alice Walker became Hurston's champion, and because of the generosity of one living writer to one dead, Hurston and her 1937 classic *Their Eyes Were Watching God* once again became part of the adult literary canon.

How does any author for children take a well-known adult writer, whose books stand outside of the comprehension of a young audience, and make the person come alive? In one of the best debut novels of 2010, two young writers, Victoria Bond and T. R. Simon, set out to make Hurston a real person for young readers ages eleven to fourteen. The two, who had worked together in publishing, discovered they shared a passion for Hurston's work. Simon had studied anthropology, Bond, writing, so they combined their talents to create *Zora and Me*, a novel that explores the childhood of Zora Neale Hurston.

JANUARY 7

Happy Birthday Kay Chorao (*Shadow Night*), Rosekrans Hoffman (*Pignic*), and Ethel Kessler (*Stan the Hot Dog Man*).

It's the birth date of Eleanor Clymer (1906–2001), *The Trolley Car Family*.

It's also the birth date of **Millard Fillmore** (1800–1874), the 13th President of the United States.

Help! The distress signal "CQD" was established in 1904 only to be replaced two years later by "SOS." Read *The SOS File* by Betsy Byars, Betsy Duffey, and Laurie Myers; and *The Watch that Ends the Night* by Allan Wolf.

It's Old Rock Day. Read *Everybody Needs a Rock* by Byrd Baylor, *If You Find a Rock* by Peggy Christian, and *Rocks In My Pockets* by Marc Harshman and Bonnie Collins.

In the book, readers see Zora from the point of view of her best friend, Carrie, as the two grow up at the beginning of the twentieth century in Eatonville, an all-black town in Florida. Zora excels in storytelling; she takes real incidents and either "lies" about them as some of her classmates believe or embroiders them to make a good tale. Zora's father rejects her for being educated or "acting white." When a murder occurs in the town, the girls watch and eavesdrop as town members find a way to solve this crime. What the authors do best is bring two ten-year-old girls to life, in all of their excitement and wonder, without softening the types of racism and prejudice both face. In the end, Carrie realizes that Zora has places to go: "One day her mother's arms and best friend would not be enough to contain her."

Excellent endnotes, an annotated bibliography, and a time line provide added background to Hurston's life. Adults sharing it will see some of the characters and themes of Hurston's work developed in the book. For children, this character-driven work presents two very appealing young girls. The only book not written by Hurston herself to be endorsed by the Zora Neale Hurston Trust, *Zora and Me*, written with love and passion, will create young readers eager to read Hurston's books when they are old enough to do so.

JANUARY 8

Happy Birthday Stephen Manes (*Be a Perfect Person in Just Three Days!*), Nancy Bond (*A String in the Harp*), Floyd Cooper (*The Blacker the Berry*), and Marjorie Priceman (*Zin! Zin! Zin! A Violin!*, *How to Make an Apple Pie and See the World*).

Happy Birthday to the Chicago Public Library system, begun with the Blackstone Library, dedicated in 1904. Read *The Library* by Sarah Stewart, illustrated by David Small.

In 1963 Leonardo da Vinci's Mona Lisa was exhibited in the U.S. for the first time, at the National Gallery of Art in Washington, D.C. Read *The Mona Lisa Caper* by Rick Jacobson and Laura Fernandez.

It's Bubble Bath Day. Read *Squeaky Clean* by Simon Puttock, illustrated by Mary McQuillan.

THE MIDWIFE'S APPRENTICE
By Karen Cushman

In Greece January 8 has been designated Midwife's Day or Women's Day, to honor midwives. Midwifery, of course, has a long and important history throughout the world. Drawing on her extensive knowledge of medieval times, Karen Cushman chose the practice of helping women deliver babies as the subject for her second novel, *The Midwife's Apprentice*, winner of the Newbery Medal.

The book opens with an intriguing scene: an unwashed, unloved, unnourished young girl climbs into a dung heap to seek shelter for the night. Awoken in the morning by noisy boys calling her "dung beetle," the girl begs for food from a woman who comes by, offering to do any work for it. That woman, Jane Sharp, happens to be the midwife of the area, plying her craft with herbs and drawing on vast experience delivering babies. So Beetle, as she is now called, becomes her apprentice, soaking up the schooling that Jane provides.

Living up to her name, Jane is truly sharp in manner and style, always cursing the young apprentice; Beetle has a softer, gentler manner. One day a villager only wants to hire the young girl—for a case that Beetle cannot handle. Feeling guilt and remorse, Beetle runs away—but ultimately has the courage to face Jane and ask for another chance.

The Midwife's Apprentice is filled with the sights, sounds, and smells of a medieval village. Beetle, who has a single companion, a cat named Purr, makes a great protagonist. She has the liveliness, the spirit, and the determination to make a better place for herself. Ideal for fourth and fifth graders, the book has frequently been taught in classrooms and naturally leads to discussions of medieval villages and life—the fairs and inns and customs.

Many authors long to find an editor who will appreciate their work. In the case of Karen Cushman, she entrusted her first novel, *Catherine, Called Birdy*, to a friend in New York. He lived in the same apartment building as Dorothy Briley, one of the great children's editors of the twentieth century, and he stalked her, always with manuscript in hand. One day he jumped into the elevator with Dorothy and thrust the manuscript at her. Without missing a beat, Dorothy took the package to her apartment. The next morning she brought it in for editor Dinah Stevenson to look over. Fortunately for young readers, Karen found a sympathetic and skilled midwife in Dinah, one who has helped bring all of her books into the world.

FREDDY THE DETECTIVE

By Walter R. Brooks

On January 9, 1886, Walter R. Brooks was born in Rome, New York. Orphaned at an early age, he was sent to a military academy and then attended the University of Rochester. An interest in homeopathic medicine brought him to New York City, where he worked for the Red Cross. He then turned his hand to writing, at first stories for *The New Yorker* and *Scribners*.

Many of his short stories for adults, which appeared in *Saturday Review* and *Esquire*, featured Ed the Talking Horse—the inspiration for a 1960s television series. But Brooks's novels for young people centered on a very unlikely protagonist who overeats, sleeps too much, daydreams, and is very lazy. Not the usual characteristics of a heroic figure. But Freddy is a pig, and he starred in twenty-six books that began in 1927 with *Freddy Goes to Florida*. Freddy, however, does possess virtues; he is even something of a Renaissance pig. He writes poetry, paints, edits the *Bean Home News*, and most important, runs a successful detective agency that has been based on the solid principles established by Sherlock Holmes. Freddy is also a balloonist, a magician, a campaign manager, and a pilot. He and the other barnyard characters—Mrs. Wiggins the cow, Jinx the cat, Hank the horse, and Charles the bragging rooster—have a lot of interesting adventures together.

JANUARY 9

It's the birth date of Clyde Robert Bulla (1914–2007), *A Lion to Guard Us*.

It's also the birth date of Richard Milhous Nixon (1913–1994), the 37th President of the United States.

Happy Birthday Connecticut, which became the fifth U.S. state on this day in 1788. Read *A Connecticut Yankee in King Arthur's Court* by Mark Twain.

Before Barnum & Bailey or Ringling Brothers, Philip Astley staged the first modern circus in London, 1768. Read *Henrietta Hornbuckle's Circus of Life* by Michael de Guzman.

The **United Nations headquarters** officially opened in New York City in 1951.

It's Positively Penguins Day. Read *Mr. Popper's Penguins* by Richard and Francis Atwater or *My Season with Penguins* by Sophie Webb.

Brooks brought American homespun humor and a profound understanding of children to his books. As he said, "Children are people; they are just smaller and less experienced [than adults]. They are not taken in by the smug playfulness of those who write or talk down to them as if they were dull-witted and slightly deaf."

Extremely popular for years, the Freddy books began to go out of print in the 1980s, although they were never out of favor with an avid "Friends of Freddy" fan club. In the 1990s, Overlook Press began reprinting these funny, gentle stories, bringing them to a new generation of readers. In *Everything I Need to Know I Learned from a Children's Book*, writer Adam Hochschild wrote about his fascination with Freddy and the entire series of books: "the moral center of my childhood universe, the place where good and evil, friendship and treachery, honesty and humbug were defined most clearly, was not church, not school, and not the Boy Scouts. It was the Bean Farm. . . . Essentially, [the books] evoke the most subversive politics of all: a child's instinctive desire for fair play."

JANUARY 10

Happy Birthday Remy Charlip (*Arm in Arm*) and Max Grover (*The Accidental Zucchini*).

It's the birth date of both Charles Ingalls (1836–1902), father of Laura Ingalls Wilder, and of her sister Mary Ingalls. Read any of the Little House books by Laura Ingalls Wilder.

 In 1776 **Thomas Paine** published *Common Sense*. Read *Thomas Paine: Common Sense and Revolutionary Pamphleteering* by Brian McCartin.

John D. Rockefeller incorporated Standard Oil in 1870. Read *Oil Spill!* by Melvin Berger.

It's Peculiar People Day. Read *The Kneebone Boy* by Ellen Potter.

10 LITTLE RUBBER DUCKS
By Eric Carle

On January 10, 1992, a cargo of around 29,000 rubber toys—including ducks, beavers, turtles, and frogs—fell overboard from a container ship in the northern Pacific Ocean. Some eventually landed on a remote coast of Alaska. In *Tracking Trash: Flotsam, Jetsam, and the Science of Ocean Motion,* author Loree Griffin Burns explains what actually happened to these objects; she explains the work of Dr. Curtis Ebbesmeyer, who tracked the toys around the world.

But our book of the day, and author/artist of the day, is a bit more whimsical in his approach to the events of January 10, 1992. Eric Carle has always said that he is never happier than when he is painting the collage papers that he uses to build his artwork. In *10 Little Rubber Ducks,* he once again shares his joy with readers as he imagines what the journey of the rubber ducks on that container ship might have been like. He shows the ducks being built, put into boxes, loaded on the ship, and getting dumped into the big wide sea.

Drawing on what he does best—the depiction of fish, birds, and mammals; all creatures great and small—Eric shows each of the ten ducks encountering different creatures, from a polar bear to a flamingo. A whale sings to the ninth rubber duck. But he saves for the tenth the best fate of all, being adopted by a mother duck and becoming part of a family. I know I feel a lot better about the world after reading this reassuring book. It shows that difficult situations can be survived and have happy endings. If for any reason you need further entertaining, a squeak device for the rubber duck has been built into the last page of the book. He certainly sounds happy.

Few have ever shown the joy and enthusiasm about life on this planet as brilliantly as Eric Carle. After a brief childhood in the United States, he was taken with his German parents back to Hitler's Germany. Brutally disciplined in school, Eric knew personally what it meant to move from joy to difficulty. But much like his rubber ducks, he found a happy ending, a home back in the United States, painting and drawing his collage masterpieces that give both adults and children so much joy.

With Rubber Duckie Day occurring on the thirteenth of this month, you might want to get out yours and read *10 Little Rubber Ducks*. For me the world always seems a kinder, gentler place after I finish any book by Eric Carle.

MRS. FRISBY AND THE RATS OF NIMH
By Robert C. O'Brien

Today marks the birthday of one of the most reclusive children's book authors of all time. He was not so, however, because of his personality or because he did not want to engage with children. Robert Leslie Conly was born in Brooklyn in 1918; he studied English at the University of Rochester. Working for magazines his entire life, he wrote for *Newsweek* before joining the staff of *National Geographic*.

But in the late 1960s, Conly wrote three books for children. His work arrangement with *National Geographic*, however, forbid him from publishing with any other company. So he did what many authors have done before: he printed his books under a pseudonym—Robert C. O'Brien, based on his mother's name. He also made no appearances on behalf of his books, to protect his true identity. His second book, *Mrs. Frisby and the Rats of NIMH*, combines talking-animal fantasy with science fiction. When dear Mrs. Frisby, a widowed mouse, learns that her own home may soon be destroyed by a plow, she attempts to move her sick son to safety. As a last resort, she consults the rats that live under the rosebush. These superintelligent laboratory rodents had been fed mind-enhancing drugs. One of them, Nicodemus, narrates how he and the other rats, part of an experiment in the National Institute of Mental Health, learned to read and finally escape to form a brave new rat world. "By teaching us how to read, they taught us how to get away." This story works both as adventure but also as an exploration of what constitutes intelligence and community.

Mrs. Frisby and the Rats of NIMH often lingers in the mind of its readers. British journalist Lucy Mangan read the book when she was nine, and in *Everything I Need to Know I Learned from a Children's Book* wrote, "It rocked my world. Everything I took for granted only existed because it was built or organized by us, because we were here first. But it could have been so different."

When *Mrs. Frisby and the Rats of NIMH* won the Newbery Medal in 1972, O'Brien faced a real dilemma. As part of winning the award, he was expected to appear at the annual ALA conference and give a speech. In the end, he sent his editor Jean Karl with his comments and remained anonymous until his death in 1973. Then his wife and his daughter Jane finished his last book, *Z for Zachariah*; only after he died did his readers learn his true identity.

I always think Robert C. O'Brien should be the patron saint of shy children's book authors and illustrators. Without book tours, media interviews, talking to children, or any form of personal marketing, O'Brien gained his following simply through writing one of the great fantasy/science fiction stories of the modern era.

JANUARY 11

Happy Birthday Mary Rodgers (*Freaky Friday*) and Ann Tompert (*Grandfather Tang's Story*).

Milk was first delivered in bottles in 1878. Read *The Milk Makers* by Gail Gibbons.

In 1922 insulin was used for the first time to treat diabetes in a human patient. Read *The Truth About Stacey* by Ann M. Martin.

It's Step in a Puddle and Splash Your Friends Day, but only if you live in an ice- and snowless place. Read *Splish, Splash* by Sarah Weeks, *Splash* by Ann Jonas, and *The Problem with Puddles* by Kate Feiffer.

JANUARY 12

Happy Birthday Nina Laden (*Peek-A Who?*) and Margaret Rostkowski (*After the Dancing Days*).

It's the birth date of Laura Adams Armer (1874–1963), *Waterless Mountain*; Clement Hurd (1908–1988), *Goodnight Moon*; **Jack London** (1876–1916), *White Fang, Call of the Wild*; and fairy-tale writer Charles Perrault (1628–1703).

It's also the birth date of John Singer Sargent (1856–1925), the American artist considered the greatest portrait painter of his era.

A long-distance radio message was sent from the Eiffel Tower for the first time in 1908. Read *Dodsworth in Paris* by Tim Egan.

THE CALL OF THE WILD
By Jack London

On January 12, 1876, Jack London was born in San Francisco, California. But the event that shaped London's life occurred in 1896 when he was twenty. Three men who were fishing for salmon—Shookum Jim, Dawson Charlie, and George Carmack—found gold in Rabbit Creek, a small tributary of the Klondike River in Alaska. Because of their discovery, tens of thousands came over the Chilcoot Pass, swept up in the mass hysteria of the Klondike Gold Rush. Since sled dogs provided the only reliable transportation in this uninviting climate, dogs were stolen from owners throughout America and worked to death by those hunting for their fortune.

At the age of twenty-one, Jack London also became part of the gold rush, not as a prospector but as a laborer, carrying bags and packages. This experience allowed him to make observations about the men and these dogs, which turned into his great masterpiece, *The Call of the Wild*.

London chose to tell the story from the point of view of a dog, Buck. Weighing 140 pounds, Buck begins his life as a pampered pet. Kidnapped for service in the gold rush and beaten by his master, Buck struggles to survive. Although mistreated by humans, Buck is saved by a man and becomes devoted to him. In the end, however, Buck becomes part of a wolf pack, determined to live in the wild on his own terms. Although first published as an adult novella in 1903, the book quickly became part of the childhood canon, often read in school.

As reading guru Jim Trelease says in *Everything I Need to Know I Learned from a Children's Book*, "*The Call of the Wild* . . . [was] my home run book. . . . Like one's first big kiss or first home run—they're unforgettable, and we spend the rest of our lives trying to duplicate or surpass them." For Jim, and so many children ages ten to fourteen, this piece of virtual reality has brought the Klondike gold rush to life.

My favorite edition of the book is the Scribner Classic, illustrated by Wendell Minor. His Buck looks exactly like I imagine him to be—although I may be partial. Wendell used a Bernese mountain dog as his model, and I share my life with members of this breed.

But whatever version you decide to pick up, there is still no better way to understand what happened over a hundred years ago in the Yukon than Jack London's brilliant classic *The Call of the Wild*.

LETTERS FROM A DESPERATE DOG

By Eileen Christelow

The second week of January is designated as National Letter Writing week, celebrating the art of writing and receiving a hand-written letter. Certainly in the age of computers, letter writing on paper has suffered in popularity. Even the protagonist of our book of the day, Emma, uses the keyboard to send off her letter. Possibly Emma can be forgiven for not using pen and paper because she happens to be a dog. In Eileen Christelow's humorous masterpiece, *Letters from a Desperate Dog*, illustrated in the comic-book style that endears the artist to her readers, Christelow demonstrates a keen understanding of canine behavior.

From Emma's point of view, her owner George, an artist, seems completely unreasonable. He gets upset if she sleeps on the couch or explores the trash. He tells her "no" or that she is a "bad dog." So, in despair, Emma writes to the new canine advice column "Ask Queenie!" Fortunately her local public library provides computer access to all. Queenie tells Emma to keep her tail wagging and everything will work out well in the end—certainly brilliant advice for any dog. Unfortunately when Emma tries it, she dips her tail into George's red paint can and the results are disastrous. "I would have been better off taking a nap on the couch," Emma complains.

On Queenie's advice Emma goes out to get work. After she applies for a part in a play, Emma rides away on the bus that takes the performers on tour. Eventually, George sees the errors of his ways because he misses her. But even as all ends well, Emma confides to Queenie, "this probably won't be my last e-mail. You know how unpredictable George can be!"

Eileen Christelow has been enchanting children for years with her Five Little Monkeys series. For *Letters from a Desperate Dog*, she drew from personal experience—watching some exchanges between her husband and their dog, Emma. Emma had been a real challenge as a puppy, and they had even returned her to the Humane Society only to bring her home again. In the book, Eileen certainly supports Emma's point of view—or at least she knows it makes the funnier story.

I have always been grateful that my dogs don't have access to a keyboard; no doubt they'd sound a bit like Emma. For all who love dogs, love humor, and want to see a letter-writing exchange that will keep them laughing, pick up *Letters from a Desperate Dog* and its sequel *The Desperate Dog Writes Again*.

JANUARY 13

Happy Birthday Michael Bond (Paddington Bear series).

It's the birth date of Horatio Alger (1832–1899), *Ragged Dick, Struggling Upward*; and Albert Lamorisse (1922–1970), *The Red Balloon*.

Happy Birthday to Britain's daily paper, *The Times*, first published in 1785 as *The Daily Universal Register*.

In 1910 the first public radio broadcast was a transmission from the **Metropolitan Opera House** of a live performance. Therefore, it's Public Radio Broadcasting Day. Read *Radio Fifth Grade* by Gordon Korman.

Celebrate the bathtub icon on Rubber Ducky Day. Read *It's Useful to Have a Duck* by Isol and *Ducky* by Eve Bunting, illustrated by David Wisniewski.

JANUARY 14

It's the birth date of Thornton W. Burgess (1874–1965), *Mother West Wind's Neighbors*; Hugh Lofting (1886–1947), *Doctor Dolittle*; and Hendrik Willem van Loon (1882–1944), *The Story of Mankind*.

The Human Be-In took place in San Francisco's Golden Gate Park in 1967, the prelude to "the Summer of Love." Read *The Young Oxford Book of the Human Being* by David Glover.

In 1972 Queen Margrethe II of Denmark ascended the throne, the first queen of Denmark since 1412 and the first Danish monarch not named Frederick or Christian since 1513.

On this day in 1784 Congress ratified the treaty of Paris officially ending the Revolutionary War. Read *Will You Sign Here, John Hancock?* by Jean Fritz.

It's Dress Up Your Pet Day, though we don't know how the outfitted animals really feel about this. Read *Fancy Nancy* by Jane O'Connor.

SORCERY & CECELIA
By Patricia Wrede and Caroline Stevermer

If any book might inspire young readers ages eleven to fourteen to pick up their pens and start composing during National Letter Writing Week, it will be the book of the day, Patricia Wrede and Caroline Stevermer's *Sorcery & Cecelia*.

Although this title is most often found in young adult collections, absolutely nothing in the content makes it outside the range for fifth through seventh grade fantasy fans. Anyone who can devour an eight-hundred-page Harry Potter novel possesses the necessary reading skills. Set in Regency England, the story might have been coauthored by Jane Austen and J. K. Rowling. Told as an epistolary novel between two cousins, Kate and Cecelia, the saga begins in April of 1817, as the girls write about what happens when one goes to London for the season and the other stays in the country. Powerful wizards battle in this world, and Kate, at her first major London event, is mistaken for one of them and narrowly escapes being poisoned. Cecelia dabbles in making charm bags, particularly to help her goose-witted brother, Oliver. But he manages to get himself turned into a tree anyway. As they chatter on about balls and gowns and boys, picnics and mysterious men, both of them get swept up in this war of wizards—and they find love in the process. For Letter Writing Week, *Sorcery & Cecelia* naturally suggests the activity of pairing two writers together to write their own novel in letters.

This novel with delicious language, settings, and plot twists, first appeared in 1988, went out of print, and was then reissued with an attractive jacket in 2003. It began as a letter game played by the two authors. One would write a letter, and then the other responded. Neither knew where the story was headed, and the book reads like a literary tennis match—readers learn what is happening at the same time that the authors do. For anyone who loves English romance and fantasy—even for adults who read Georgette Heyer—this book holds great charm and humor. It often gets adopted for mother/daughter book discussion groups, because it delights all the participants. In this book readers have just as much fun turning the pages as the writers did creating it.

CAPS FOR SALE
By Esphyr Slobodkina

Today we celebrate National Hat Day. I love wearing hats. What shoes did for Imelda Marcos—hats do for me. Given this propensity, I have always hunted for good books featuring my favorite apparel. Yet the one that still pleases me the most first appeared in 1940. Esphyr Slobodkina's *Caps for Sale* reinforces my fantasy of wearing several hats at a time.

Born in Siberia into a family of considerable artistic talent, Slobodkina fled Russia because of the Revolution, and in 1928 at the age of twenty, arrived in New York. She quickly became involved with a group of painters and sculptors called American Abstract Artists that included Josef Albers, Willem de Kooning, and Jackson Pollock. Much inspired by Henri Rousseau, she began showing her work with Arshile Gorky, Stuart Davis, and Mondrian.

But she needed to supplement her income and sought out Margaret Wise Brown, who at that point worked as an editor for William R. Scott, the independent, experimental publisher that would also release the work of Gertrude Stein for children. Dressed in a swirling Bohemian black cape and beaded skullcap, Slobodkina may have impressed Brown as much by her outfits as she did with the storyboards she delivered. Certainly Slobodkina's fine sense of style was preserved in her nattily dressed peddler featured in *Caps for Sale*. Brown offered her a contract, and eventually the two created several books together, including *The Little Fireman*.

Finally, when Slobodkina got to write and illustrate her own book, she turned to a story passed on to her by her nephew: *Caps for Sale: A Tale of a Peddler, Some Monkeys and Their Monkey Business*. A peddler, with all of his wares stacked on his head, advertises his caps for sale. When he takes a nap, some monkeys steal the hats, put them on their heads, and climb into trees. When he asks for the hats back, the monkeys reply, "Tsz, tsz, tsz." The repetitive refrain and the well-paced text make the book absolutely perfect for group sharing. For over seventy years children have loved acting out the part of the mischievous animals in this spirited tale of monkeys and their monkey business.

I have never been able to resist the caps in the story. It makes me want to pile up my own hats and wear several at a time. Maybe I will do so for National Hat Day.

JANUARY 15

Happy Birthday Ernest J. Gaines (*The Autobiography of Miss Jane Pittman*).

It's the birth date of Martin Luther King Jr. (1929–1968). Read *Martin's Big Words* by Doreen Rappaport, illustrated by Bryan Collier.

Elizabeth I was crowned Queen of England in Westminster Abbey, London, in 1559. Read *Good Queen Bess* by Diane Stanley.

James Naismith published the rules of basketball in 1892. Read *My Basketball Book* by Gail Gibbons.

A lethal mess! In 1919 a large molasses tank in Boston, Massachusetts, burst and a wave rushed through the streets, killing 21 people and injuring 150 others. Read *The Great Molasses Flood* by Deborah Kops.

JANUARY 16

Happy Birthday Robert Lipsyte (*Center Field*), Kate McMullan (*I Stink!*), Andrew Glass (*Mountain Men*), Marla Frazee (*All the World*), and Rebecca Stead (*When You Reach Me*).

The 18th Amendment to the Constitution, forbidding the manufacture and sale of alcohol in the United States, was ratified in 1919. Read *Bootleg: Murder, Moonshine, and the Lawless Years of Prohibition* by Karen Blumenthal.

The first edition of *El Ingenioso Hidalgo Don Quijote de la Mancha* (Book One of Don Quixote) by Miguel de Cervantes was published in Madrid in 1605.

It's Appreciate a Dragon Day. Identify your favorite dragon in children's literature. Read *My Father's Dragon* by Ruth Stiles Gannett.

On National Nothing Day, don't celebrate, observe, or honor anything. Unless you want to. Read *Nothing* by Jon Agee and *Tales of a Fourth Grade Nothing* by Judy Blume.

BLACK DUCK
By Janet Taylor Lisle

On January 16, 1919, the ratification of the 18th Amendment to the Constitution was certified. The 18th Amendment forbids the manufacture and sale of alcohol in the United States. In many areas of the country, people felt justified breaking this particular law. In *Black Duck,* published in 2006, Janet Taylor Lisle spins a fascinating tale for fifth through eighth graders that revolves around rum-running and Prohibition. Lisle sets the book along the Rhode Island coast near Newport, a place of small beaches and landing spots. In the Narraganset Bay, small vessels made contact with alcohol-carrying boats from Canada, Europe, and the West Indies, moored outside of U.S. territorial limits. Then these boats brought the liquor to the coast, where it was unloaded in the middle of the night and often stored in cellars. Key to the story is the notorious *Black Duck*, a vessel that continually outruns the Coast Guard.

The protagonist of this contemporary story, David Peterson, has just finished eighth grade. He becomes intrigued by this part of Rhode Island's past and sets out to record the story of Ruben Hart, now an old man, who as a boy had become involved with rum-running. Slowly Ruben opens up, about his own involvement and that of his best friend Jeddy. By the late 1920s everyone in the town—including the constables—was getting involved one way or another in this illicit trade. But so much money was being made that gangsters from first Boston and then New York begin to take over the territory. When Ruben and Jeddy find a dead man on the beach, and Ruben takes his pipe and tobacco pouch, they get swept into the alcohol trade. They change from innocent boys to willing accomplices of criminals. In this time period, it is difficult to tell the good guys from the bad ones. Ruben gets kidnapped several times, and fortunately survives the last mission of the *Black Duck*, when three members of the crew are killed.

This mystery/adventure is so exciting, readers barely notice they are learning a good bit of local and national history about the Rhode Island coastal community and the Prohibition era. If you want to explain the 18th Amendment or just entertain young readers, pick up *Black Duck*.

MARTIN'S BIG WORDS: THE LIFE OF DR. MARTIN LUTHER KING, JR.

By Doreen Rappaport
Illustrated by Bryan Collier

Happy Birthday Janet Stevens (*Tops & Bottoms*).

It's the birth date of John Bellairs (1938–1991), *The House With a Clock in Its Walls*; Robert Cormier (1925–2000), *The Chocolate War*; and A. B. Frost (1851–1928), *Stuff and Nonsense*.

It's the birth date of both Benjamin Franklin (1706–1790) and Al Capone (1899–1947). Read *Ben and Me* by Robert Lawson and *Al Capone Does My Shirts* by Gennifer Choldenko.

When we come to the third Monday in January, I am often reminded that I did not celebrate Martin Luther King Day as a child. But I did have an opportunity to witness the incredible life and amazing accomplishments of Dr. King. I still remember exactly what I was doing when I heard the news of his assassination.

For those who did not watch the unfolding drama of Dr. King's life, how does an author convey his amazing charisma? How do you show the way one human being can become larger than life and move into the conscience of those who watched him live? Particularly, how can you do this for young readers, ages four to ten, who want to know why we are celebrating Martin Luther King Day?

In 2001 veteran author Doreen Rappaport and then-novice illustrator Bryan Collier published *Martin's Big Words: The Life of Dr. Martin Luther King, Jr.*, one of the best picture books of the decade. Everything in this book was executed with care—all of it contributes to a feeling of the grandeur of the subject.

To begin, there are no words on the front jacket. Bryan Collier has used all of the space for his warm, animated painting of Dr. King, larger than life, ready to come off the page. The endpapers, which look like stained-glass windows, welcome readers into the story. As Bryan Collier wrote, "When I close my eyes and think about Dr. King's life, the main image that comes to me over and over again is the stained-glass windows in a church." The story, narrated only in double-page spreads, relates a few incidents from Dr. King's life, but all seem vitally important. Collier uses collage to build each scene. Rappaport alternates between segments of King's life and important phrases of his speeches. These phrases have been set in large type conveying the feeling that these words are indeed "big."

The author seamlessly moves from King's childhood, where he sees signs that say "White Only," through his early professional years. The book presents the Montgomery Bus Boycott, the Civil Rights Movement, and the awarding of the 1964 Nobel Peace Prize to Dr. King. Although, inevitably, the narrative takes readers to the day in Memphis, Tennessee, when Dr. King was shot, the last line proclaims, "His big words are alive for us today."

Both author and illustrator have rendered a complex set of circumstances understandable for children. They convey the power and charisma of Dr. King. And they have introduced to young readers some of the words of one of our most eloquent leaders. Remarkable achievements for a forty-page picture book.

On Martin Luther King Day I am grateful not only for the life of Dr. King but also for this brilliantly executed book.

BIOGRAPHY, PICTURE BOOK, Preschool, Elementary School

JANUARY 18

Happy Birthday Catherine Anholt (*Chimp and Z*), Raymond Briggs (*The Snowman*), and Alan Schroeder (*Ragtime Tumpie*).

It's the birth date of A. A. Milne (1882–1956), *The House at Pooh Corner*.

It's the birth date of lexicographer Peter Roget (1779–1869), *Thesaurus of English Words and Phrases*. It's also Thesaurus Day.

In 1903 **President Theodore Roosevelt** sent a radio message to King Edward VII, the first transatlantic radio transmission originating in the United States. Read *The Radio* by Gayle Worland.

On this day in 1943 sliced bread was banned in the United States as part of the World War II conservation effort. But because of public outery the ban was lifted just two months later.

Jazz goes mainstream! In 1944 the Metropolitan Opera House in New York City hosted a jazz concert for the first time. Louis Armstrong, Benny Goodman, Lionel Hampton, Artie Shaw, Roy Eldridge, and Jack Teagarden played. Read *If I Only Had a Horn* by Roxane Orgil.

WINNIE-THE-POOH
By A. A. Milne
Illustrated by Ernest H. Shepard

Today has been designated Winnie-the-Pooh Day. On October 14, 1926, a British playwright, who also liked to dabble in poetry and prose for children, published a book named after a stuffed toy bear: "Here is Edward Bear, coming downstairs now, bump, bump, bump on the back of his head, behind Christopher Robin."

Milne's son Christopher Robin had been, with the help of his mother, making up stories about his toys. Eventually Alan Milne joined in, writing an occasional poem and scene about Pooh and Christopher's other toys—Piglet, Eeyore, Owl, Kanga and Roo, and Tigger, the tiger who liked to bounce. Milne spun these tales out, adding his own blend of whimsy and creative imagination to the material that Christopher had already provided. In the wonderful Hundred Acre Wood, these animals and Christopher Robin build a trap for a Heffalump, plan an "exposition" to the North Pole, and engage in a variety of exciting activities.

Then, one Saturday morning, the artist Ernest Shepard, who did not have an appointment, called on Milne at home to show a portfolio of his sketches. Milne loved these drawings, and consequently Shepard provided drawings for Milne's poetry volume, *When We Were Very Young,* and also *Winnie-the-Pooh*.

Today at New York Public Library's Children's Center at 42nd Street, the old and now battered toys of Christopher Robin Milne have found a permanent home. Preserved in cases for the delight of other children, they stand stiff and lifeless in place. Like all toys, they needed the care and imaginative power of their owner—and in this case, his father—to bring them to life.

I'm glad a Winnie-the-Pooh Day exists; the world is a better place because of this book. It has made children and families laugh, recite poetry, and even sing together for decades.

THE MAN WHO WAS POE

By Avi

On January 19, 1809, Edgar Allan Poe was born in Boston, Massachusetts. At some time or another during childhood or adolescence, almost every child in America falls under his spell. I remember the first time my mother read me "The Raven;" later I became obsessed with his dark mysteries and macabre short stories. Poe lived only for a brief forty years, but he was the first well-known American writer who attempted to live on proceeds from his works as an author—resulting in a difficult, erratic financial life. Things haven't changed much in two hundred years!

In 1989 Avi wrote a multilayered, haunting tribute to this literary master, *The Man Who Was Poe*. When working on the book, Avi resided in Providence, Rhode Island, and focused the novel on the brief period of time Poe also lived there, November 1848, while he was courting Mrs. Sarah Helen Whitman. From this period comes the daguerreotype of Poe most frequently reproduced, and at one point in Avi's book, Poe goes to the studio to have this picture taken.

JANUARY 19

Happy Birthday Nina Bawden (*Granny the Pag*) and Pat Mora (*Book Fiesta*).

In 1840 **Captain Charles Wilkes** completed circumnavigating Antarctica, claiming what became known as Wilkes Land for the United States. Read *Antarctica: Journeys to the South Pole* by Walter Dean Myers.

It's National Popcorn Day. Read *The Popcorn Book* by Tomie dePaola; *Popcorn* by Alex Moran, illustrated by Betsy Everitt; and *The Ghost of Popcorn Hill* by Betty Ren Wright, illustrated by Karen Ritz.

It's also Tin Can Day. Read *The Tin Forest* by Helen Ward and Wayne Anderson, and *Gregory, The Terrible Eater* by Mitchell Sharmat.

The story opens with Edmund and his twin, Sis, living alone in a tenement room without food. Their caretaker, their aunt, has been gone for two days. Ignoring his aunt's explicit instruction, Edmund leaves to find something for them to eat. When he returns, he faces his worst possible nightmare—his sister has vanished.

Running into a man who calls himself Dupin (Edgar Allan Poe), Edmund enlists his aid to find his aunt and sister. In fog-shrouded streets of Providence, with villainous creatures who haunt the docks, a tale of mystery and deception ensues. It is, in fact, just the type of tale Poe himself might have spun out of his fevered brain, involving trysts in a cemetery, ghosts, and a bank robbery.

It is unclear, as can often be the case in postmodern novels, whether Poe himself is simply writing this story, or if events are happening and Poe is trying to make a story out of them. Either way, readers learn about Poe's life, the death of his beloved wife, Virginia (Sis), and his attempt to find a new wife and stabilize himself in Providence. Often taught to fifth through seventh graders, the book definitely gives young readers the background they need if, and when, they become Poe addicts. Historical fiction, mystery, and horror, *The Man Who Was Poe* dishes them all out in equal measure.

Happy Birthday Edgar Allan Poe. As a child, I thought that the phrase "Quoth the Raven, 'Nevermore,'" was one of the coolest lines written in the English language. I still do.

JANUARY 20

Happy Birthday Tedd Arnold (*Hi! Fly Guy*) and Mary Anderson (*The Rise and Fall of a Teenage Wacko*).

It's the birth date of Joy Adamson (1910–1980), *Born Free*; and Helen Hoover (1910–1984), *A Place in the Woods*.

In 1885 L. A. Thompson patented the roller coaster. Read *Roller Coaster* by Marla Frazee.

The first official basketball game was played in 1892 at the YMCA in Springfield, Massachusetts. Read *Basketball (Or Something Like It)* by Nora Raleigh Baskin.

It's Inauguration Day. On this day in 2009, Barack Obama was inaugurated as the 44th president of the United States, making him the first African-American president. Read *Barack Obama: Son of Promise, Child of Hope* by Nikki Grimes, illustrated by Bryan Collier.

365 PENGUINS
By Jean-Luc Fromental and Joëlle Jolivet

Today marks Penguin Awareness Day. And who doesn't appreciate penguins? They look so wonderful in their tuxedos, so well turned out and charming. But, then, I have never lived with any. If I did, possibly I'd feel differently—I'd be more circumspect about them, like the family in our book of the day, *365 Penguins* by Jean-Luc Fromental and Joëlle Jolivet.

In this oversize book—with a 1950s retro style and a palette of black, orange, and blue—a young boy narrates a strange saga. On New Year's Day the doorbell rings, "Ding dong!" and a package arrives. It contains a penguin, with the note: "I'm number 1. Feed me when I'm hungry." The young narrator's father, mother, and sister, Amy, try to determine who sent the package, and then the next day, "Ding dong!" another penguin arrives. A resilient group, the family sets out to master the situation—naming the penguins and feeding them. By the end of January, 31 penguins live in their home. Rather well behaved, the birds watch television as an orderly group—except for a couple who help themselves to food. By the end of February (31 + 28 penguins), the family needs to figure out how to organize them. So father and Amy start stacking penguins. By the time they have three-digit penguins, they admit the problems have escalated—cost of feeding per day, cleaning the penguins, and housing them. To solve the issue of living space, the family builds file cabinets and keeps their charges in order by number. When a blue-footed penguin, Chilly, appears, the drawings provide young readers with opportunities to locate him in masses of penguins. The whole idea, of course, is preposterous, but in this story the family never flinches. They just keep doing the math, making decisions, and trying to keep penguins in order.

Finally, the mystery of the penguins is solved: Uncle Victor, the ecologist, has sent them from the South Pole, where their habitat is being threatened. Now he will now take them all to the North Pole to start a colony (the science in the book is not quite as good as the math). So he leaves just Chilly, and a very relieved family. That is until the next day, "Ding dong!" when polar bear number one arrives.

For group or family participation, *365 Penguins* offers all kinds of opportunities. The bold drawings can be seen across a room. Outside of Jon Scieszka's *Math Curse*, books that teach math have rarely been so much fun. The frequent "Ding dong!" lends itself to responsive reading. Winner of a Boston Globe–Horn Book Honor Award, *365 Penguins* definitely strikes the funny bone of children and adults alike.

On Penguin Awareness Day, I am relieved that I don't have to organize 365 penguins. I'll take writing about 365 great childrens books instead!

SCAREDY SQUIRREL

By Mélanie Watt

Today has been designated Squirrel Appreciation Day. Like many city dwellers, I don't appreciate squirrels. My dogs basically believe that all squirrels deserve to be driven up trees. The squirrels in my backyard retaliate by making fun of these lumbering, large creatures.

I have liked these bushy-tailed creatures more since I read Mélanie Watt's *Scaredy Squirrel*. As a young author, Mélanie was told to put down on paper what she knew. In her case, she had been plagued by fears since childhood. Hence, she created an alter ego, a small squirrel who lives in a tree and is too afraid to set out from his home.

Even the endpapers of *Scaredy Squirrel* warn readers to clean their hands with antibacterial soap before opening the book. Scaredy Squirrel has so many things that make him afraid—green Martians, killer bees, and even sharks. He spends time drawing out elaborate exit plans in case of a crisis and maintains a well-stocked emergency kit. Every day he does the same things, at the same time. Of course, a crisis happens, and suddenly all his plans fail to work. When he's forced to jump from the tree, he discovers that he is a flying squirrel and the pages fold out to show him in flight. Now he can add a little adventure to his days—although he still keeps to a schedule.

On the surface the book allows everyone to laugh at the antics of a small squirrel, trying to keep tragedy at bay. But, of course, human beings are all subject to rational and irrational fears, and in its gentle way *Scaredy Squirrel* allows children and adult readers to examine their own worst fears. In her author's notes, Canadian author Mélanie Watt lets people know that she shares a lot of traits with Scaredy Squirrel—she herself is afraid of sharks.

The book naturally lends itself to activities with children. They can draw pictures of what they fear, map out an exit strategy from school or home, or plan an emergency kit for their own needs. Since its publication, children ages three to eight have absolutely loved this title. The book has won awards chosen by children, such as the Red Clover Award selected by the children of Vermont and the Monarch Award by young readers in Illinois. It has several superb sequels, including *Scaredy Squirrel at Night* and *Scaredy Squirrel Has a Birthday Party*.

Even if you don't want to appreciate squirrels today, you will definitely enjoy reading *Scaredy Squirrel*. As I look out in my backyard, I can see one of those squirrels taunting my dogs. Maybe we have a different species in New England than Mélanie observes in Canada.

JANUARY 21

Happy Birthday Carol Beach York (*Good Charlotte*).

The first American novel, *The Power of Sympathy* by William Hill Brown, was printed in Boston, Massachusetts, in 1789.

In 1977 President Jimmy Carter pardoned nearly all American Vietnam War draft evaders, some of whom had emigrated to Canada. Read *Summer's End* by Audrey Couloumbis.

It's National Hugging Day. Read *Hug* by Jez Alborough, *Hug Time* by Patrick McDonald, *Giant Hug* by Sandra Horning, and *Hugging the Rock* by Susan Taylor Brown.

JANUARY 22

Happy Birthday Brian Wildsmith (*ABC*, *Saint Francis*) and Rafe Martin (*The Rough-Face Girl*).

It's the birth date of Blair Lent (1930–2009), *Tikki Tikki Tembo*; Arkady Gaidar (1904–1941), *Timur and His Gang*; and the poet George Gordon Byron also known as Lord Byron (1788–1824).

The Central Intelligence Group, forerunner of the Central Intelligence Agency, was created on this day in 1946. Read *The Real Spy's Guide to Becoming a Spy* by Peter Earnest, illustrated by Suzanne Harper, in association with The International Spy Museum, Washington, D.C.

It's also National Blonde Brownie Day. Blondies are basically brownies without the chocolate. Read *The Triple Chocolate Brownie Genius* by Deborah Sherman.

HOW TO TALK TO YOUR CAT

By Jean Craighead George
Illustrated by Paul Meisel

Today has been designated Ask Your Cat Questions Day. I know a lot of cat owners, and pet owners, who admit that they talk to their animals all the time, as if the pets could answer. "How are you feeling today, Lancelot?" I just said to my dog before sitting down to write. Therefore, it may be unnecessary to designate a day that encourages people to talk to or question their pets.

However, what if you really wanted to communicate with a cat—beyond meaningless questions such as, "Why did you bring the dead vole into the house?"—is there a way to become a cat whisperer? In 2000, Jean Craighead George, a woman who knew how to communicate with all things wild, published *How to Talk to Your Cat*, with illustrations by Paul Meisel. Jean grew up in a family of naturalists. The Craigheads were always doing exciting things: tracking grizzly bears, banding bald eagles, or paddling kayaks down Western white waters. As Robert Kennedy Jr. said in *Everything I Need to Know I Learned from a Children's Book*: "I thought the Craigheads might be the only family in America having more fun than the Kennedys."

When Jean began to write her books in 1959 (*My Side of the Mountain*), she engaged in a type of research far outside the norm in children's books. For *Julie of the Wolves*, she stayed with a wolf pack in Alaska and allowed a wolf to greet her—he put her face in his mouth. Talk about going the extra mile to get an accurate book! But such dedication was always typical for Jean Craighead George.

Jean begins *How to Talk to Your Cat* with an exploration of the typical cat personality: they are loners who don't like company, even other cats, and are generally self-sufficient. Then she traces the origins of *Felis Catus*, the domestic house cat. "If you speak to your cat first, it probably won't speak back. Cats initiate conversation." Certainly, one of the funniest things about this book is the juxtaposition of real photos of Jean next to Paul Meisel's illustrations of cats. Readers see Jean saying hello by rubbing the cat's head with her own head. But the book is also filled with illustrations of cat postures, tails, and facial expressions along with great advice. If you want to read uninterrupted, put a brown paper bag on the floor for the animal to investigate; Jean says you will be free to enjoy your book for a long time.

I'm just grateful that for over fifty years, Jean Craighead George explained the animal kingdom to children, writing fascinating books and sharing her wisdom.

ANGELINA BALLERINA

By Katharine Holabird
Illustrated by Helen Craig

Today we celebrate Measure Your Feet Day. But why?

Well, one reason youngsters might measure their feet would be for special shoes, say ballet shoes. Since this also happens to be the birthday of Katharine Holabird, author of *Angelina Ballerina*, our book of the day features a very special mouse, Angelina, who loves to dance. Published in 1983 and now a classic, *Angelina Ballerina* presents a mouse heroine who doesn't want to straighten her room or get ready for school—she only wants to dance. So she dances her way to school and lands in a pansy patch. Angelina can't stop dancing. She twirls on the playground; she even executes a beautiful arabesque in the kitchen. Driven to exasperation, her mother Mrs. Mouseling buys pink ballet slippers and sends Angelina off to Miss Lilly's Ballet School.

Katharine Holabird's text presents this sequence lightly and with a touch of humor. And illustrator Helen Craig's enchanting drawings show this winsome mouse prancing around. When Angelina attends Miss Lilly's Ballet School, Craig pulls out all the stops and depicts grand scenes of mouse ballerinas together. Her artwork is animated and vital—she delineates character and expression with the lightest of touch. Full of movement and life, the artwork pulls the reader's eye across the page and on to the next spread.

In the end Angelina becomes a famous ballerina—living out the dream of her childhood. This anthropomorphic mouse represents the feelings, behavior, dreams, and actions of many four- to eight-year-olds.

Angelina Ballerina begins a series that became very popular with young readers. These books feature Angelina engaged in a variety of activities that might be experienced by any child: going to a fair (*Angelina at the Fair*), getting a bike (*Angelina's Birthday Surprise*), or ice skating (*Angelina Ice Skates*). She even participated in a royal wedding in 2010 (*Angelina and the Royal Wedding*). But the original book still makes the best introduction to Angelina. Like a great performance, you can return to it again and again.

A standing ovation to Katharine Holabird on her birthday and Helen Craig on Measure Your Feet Day. I may not measure my feet, but I will reread this gem one more time.

JANUARY 23

It's the birth date of **John Hancock** (1737–1793), signer of the U.S. Declaration of Independence and the first governor of Massachusetts. On a related note, it's National Handwriting Day.

Elizabeth Blackwell was awarded her M.D. in 1849, by the Medical Institute of Geneva, New York, becoming the United States' first female doctor. Read *Doctor Meow's Big Emergency* by Sam Lloyd.

On this day in 1973 President Richard Nixon announced a peace accord had been reached in Vietnam. Read *Vietnam: A Traveler's Literary Companion* edited by John Balaban and Nguyen Qui Duc.

It's National Pie Day. Read *How to Make an Apple Pie and See the World* by Marjorie Priceman.

JANURY 24

It's the birth date of Charles Boardman Hawes (1889–1932), *The Dark Frigate*.

In 1848 James Marshall found gold in Sutter's Mill in Coloma, California, an event that ignited the California Gold Rush. Read *Gold! Gold from the American River!* by Don Brown.

In 1922 Christian K. Nelson of Iowa patented the Eskimo Pie, America's first chocolate-covered ice cream bar.

It's Global Belly Laugh Day. Read *A Barrel of Laughs, A Vale of Tears* by Jules Feiffer.

Say something nice! Today is National Compliment Day.

MARTHA SPEAKS
By Susan Meddaugh

January is appropriately named National Soup Month. Inevitably, when the weather turns chilly, I gravitate toward warm soup, a fire, and a good book.

Susan Meddaugh began her career as a graphic designer in the children's book department of Houghton Mifflin. She worked with James Marshall, Bill Peet, Bernard Waber, and David Macaulay, among others, to design some of their classic titles. But she longed to create books of her own and in the 1980s began publishing her own work.

Susan came from a family of dog nuts and in turn became a dog owner herself. A stray dog adopted by the family, Martha, would become Susan's muse. In *Martha Speaks,* Susan developed a fabulous premise for a book. What if, after being fed alphabet soup, a dog could actually talk? How would that affect the people in the family? After all, if dogs are unhappy, they can't verbally list their grievances. But Martha the dog can comment on everything.

Susan sets up the book according to a child's sense of logic—the letters from the alphabet soup go to Martha's brain rather than her stomach, an idea suggested to Susan by her son. In the story, Martha begins talking with her family. They ask her why she drinks out of the toilet. She tells them she dreams about chasing meat loaf. Because Martha uses language the way a child does—honestly and with no sense of what might be appropriate or inappropriate—she causes both a lot of laughs and a lot of trouble: "Mom said that fruitcake you sent wasn't fit for a dog. But I thought it was delicious."

Then the family teaches her how to use the telephone—and Martha begins to think for herself. Eventually, Martha simply talks too much, and her family gets mad at her. Dejected, she stops eating alphabet soup—that is, until the moment that she needs to speak to save the house from a burglar.

Martha Speaks and its sequels, ideal for two- to eight-year-olds, contain all the elements of great picture books: a story arc with a great ending, illustrations that extend the humor of the text, and exquisite pacing and timing. Martha has come up in the world since her humble beginnings in 1992 and now has her own PBS television series. So if you like this dog, you can follow her adventures in many different forms.

I myself will celebrate National Soup Month by rereading *Martha Speaks*—it makes me even happier than soup itself.

THE DARING NELLIE BLY: AMERICA'S STAR REPORTER

By Bonnie Christensen

On January 25, 1890, stunt newspaper reporter Nellie Bly arrived in New Jersey, after managing to travel around the world in seventy-two days. She had set out to beat the record of Jules Verne's imaginary hero, Phineas Fogg in *Around the World in Eighty Days*. This feat was only one of Bly's accomplishments. In *The Daring Nellie Bly: America's Star Reporter*, Bonnie Christensen creates an exciting portrait of the journalist who at the age of twenty-five captured the world's fancy.

Christensen is particularly good at creating context for Nellie Bly in just a few sentences. "In an age when women were not entitled to vote, when few women could attend college, and when fewer held jobs, Nellie Bly dared to defy convention." At sixteen, Nellie began to search for work but for five years she found nothing. Finally a letter to the editor of the *Pittsburg Dispatch* landed her a spot on the paper. There she began a series of on-the-scene exposés; at one point she had to flee Mexico before the Mexican government arrested her.

When she joined the staff of the *New York World*, she really began to make waves. The newspaper liked to place undercover, or, as they were called, "stunt," reporters in different places. In Bly's case, she managed to get herself committed to the Women's Lunatic Asylum—where she observed conditions and wrote about life inside the madhouse. Soon she came up with the idea of a round the world trip designed to imitate Verne's story. In a mere two days Bly prepared a wardrobe and set out from Hoboken, New Jersey, on the *Augusta Victoria*. Bonnie Christensen describes the journey, the places, and some of the sights that Bly saw. As both writer and illustrator Bonnie records fascinating details of Bly's trip and traces her route on a world map, depicting some of the scenes that Bly witnessed.

After Bly reached San Francisco, she received aid from her employer, who sent a special train to make the rest of the trip. Along the way, Americans greeted Nellie with fanfare—fireworks, telegrams, fruit, and candy. Arriving on time in the Jersey City train station, Bly demonstrated that Jules Verne had been right—and that a real woman could do things better than his male protagonist.

The great historian David McCullough once told me that American history was filled with stories that young people should know about, such as the exploits of Nellie Bly. Fortunately, in 2003 Bonnie Christensen made her story accessible to readers ages six to ten. In an era when women can run for president, it is still good to remind young readers of their triumphs along the way.

JANUARY 25

It's the birth date of James Flora (1914–1998), *The Day the Cow Sneezed*.

It's also the birth date of Virginia Woolf (1882–1941), *Mrs. Dalloway, To The Lighthouse, A Room of One's Own*. And it's A Room of One's Own Day. Read *My Very Own Room/Mi Propio Cuartito* by Amada Irma Pérez, illustrated by Maya Christina Gonzalez.

In 1858 "The Wedding March" by **Felix Mendelssohn** became a popular wedding recessional after it was played on this day at the marriage of Queen Victoria's daughter, Victoria, and Friedrich of Prussia. Read *Uncle Bobby's Wedding* by Sarah S. Brannen and *Alligator Wedding* by Nancy Jewell, illustrated by J. Rutland.

JANUARY 26

Happy Birthday Jules Feiffer (*The Phantom Tollbooth*), Shannon Hale (*The Princess Academy*), and Ashley Wolff (*Miss Bindergarten* books).

It's the birth date of Mary Mapes Dodge (1831–1905), *Hans Brinker, or the Silver Skates*; and Charles Mikolaycak (1937–1993), *Babushka*.

Happy Birthday Michigan, which became the 26th U.S. state on this day in 1837.

In 1863, during the American Civil War, Governor of Massachusetts John Albion Andrew received permission from the Secretary of War to raise a militia organization for men of African descent. Read *Which Way Freedom* by Joyce Hansen, *Riot* by Walter Dean Myers, and *From Slave to Soldier* by Deborah Hopkinson, illustrated by Brian Floca.

THE RUINS OF GORLAN
By John Flanagan

Today we celebrate Australia Day, when in 1788 the first European settlement was established at Port Jackson, now part of Sydney. The Australian writing and illustrating community seems to me to be the most vibrant and original group of children's book creators working any place in the world. In a few short years Australian writer Marcus Zusak has distinguished himself as the premier writer for young adults with titles like *The Book Thief* and *I Am the Messenger*.

Our Australian author of the day, John Flanagan, wrote the Ranger's Apprentice series, which first appeared in the United States five years ago. I picked it up because it was consistently recommended as a no-fail book for fourth through sixth graders by both booksellers and teachers. If you are hunting for a book for this age group that will engage boys and girls, readers and nonreaders, the series contains pure magic.

At the beginning of the series in *The Ruins of Gorlan* readers meet Will, who was left as an orphan in the care of Baron Arald. Raised in this European medieval society by the baron, Will and the rest of the wards become apprentices if they are chosen by a person who wants to train them for a profession. All of Will's companions receive the placements they long for—cooking, diplomacy, or battle school. But Will finds himself the apprentice of a shifty, strange Ranger, called Halt, who begins to teach the boy how to serve the kingdom. Since a huge war is brewing, the Rangers will be needed, as they have been before, to combat the evil Morgarath.

Both Will and Halt emerge as fabulous characters. Readers cheer on the boy as he learns his craft and helps his fellow ward Horace turn the tables on some battle school bullies. In the final scenes, the stakes are raised as Will and Halt take on the almost invincible Kalkara. Epic fantasy, an orphan boy longing for his unknown father, the conflict of good and evil, and training for a special place in society—all these components have been used many times before. But because Flanagan has a genius for storytelling, by building tension and creating dramatic scenes, the book is much greater than the sum of its parts. Both character and action driven, it compels readers to finish this story and continue the series.

The series has sold over two million copies worldwide, and a movie has been in development for some time. Rather than wait for it to appear in a theater near you, pick up these books to celebrate Australia Day. And don't just pass them to the children in your life. Just like Philip Pullman and Stephanie Meyer, John Flanagan has as many devoted readers among adults as he does children.

SAM AND THE TIGERS

By Julius Lester
Illustrated by Jerry Pinkney

On January 27, 1939, Julius Lester was born in Saint Louis, Missouri. Son of a Methodist minister, he lived in Kansas City and Nashville, where he attended Fisk University. Later Lester embraced the Jewish religion, which he wrote about in *Lovesong: Becoming a Jew.* One of those rare multitalented individuals who can do many things well, Lester worked as a musician, an editor, a photographer, a college professor, and a radio and television host, as well as a writer. In the 1960s he wrote books for adults including *Look Out, Whitey! Black Power's Gon' Get Your Mama!* Then his adult editor suggested that he try his hand at children's books.

Like Jerry Pinkney, Walter Dean Myers, and John Steptoe, Lester became one of the first group of extraordinarily talented black writers and illustrators to integrate the all-white world of children's books. His first book, *To Be a Slave,* published in 1968, contains first-person narratives of former slaves, originally collected by the Federal Writers' Project. This Newbery Honor Book remains one of the most powerful indictments against slavery published for children.

JANUARY 27

Happy Birthday Jean Merrill (*The Pushcart War, The Girl Who Loved Caterpillars*), Harry Allard (*Miss Nelson is Missing!*), and Julius Lester (*To Be a Slave*).

It's the birth date of Lewis Carroll (1832–1898), *Alice's Adventures in Wonderland, Through the Looking-Glass*; and composer **Wolfgang Amadeus Mozart** (1756–1791).

In 1825 the U.S. Congress approved Indian Territory (in what is present-day Oklahoma), clearing the way for forced relocation of the Eastern Indians on the Trail of Tears. Read *Only the Names Remain: The Cherokees and the Trail of Tears* by Alex W. Bealer, illustrated by Kristina Rodanas.

Happy Birthday to The National Geographic Society, founded in Washington, D.C., in 1888.

Certainly one of the most felicitous pairings in children's books has been Julius Lester and artist Jerry Pinkney. The two became collaborators, friends, and over the years have inspired each other to do their best work. Their first rendition of the Uncle Remus tales began in 1987 with *The Tales of Uncle Remus: The Adventures of Brer Rabbit.* Lester's lively text and Pinkney's spirited artwork bring the stories alive for a modern audience—and remove any material that would seem offensive.

Lester did much the same for his retelling of *Little Black Sambo.* In *Sam and the Tigers: A New Telling of Little Black Sambo* he retains the charm of the story that always enchanted young readers but removes the racial sting that became associated with the tale. Sam lives in the land of Sam-sam-sa-mara, where everyone is named Sam. A savvy hero, Sam learns to anticipate the tigers' actions and outwits these animals who want to eat him. Lester's beautifully written text makes the perfect read-aloud.

Articulate, passionate, dedicated to preserving African-American folklore, often acting as a spokesperson for the African-American community, Julius Lester has served as the conscience of the children's book community for over four decades.

JANUARY 28

Happy Birthday Vera B. Williams (*A Chair for My Mother*, *"More More More" Said the Baby*).

Pride and Prejudice by Jane Austen was first published on this day in the United Kingdom in 1813. Read the mind-bending *Pride and Prejudice and Zombies*, by Jane Austen and Seth Grahame-Smith.

In 1855 the first locomotive ran from the Atlantic Ocean to the Pacific Ocean on the Panama Railway. Read *The Last Train* by Gordon M. Titcomb.

ACTION JACKSON

By Jan Greenberg and Sandra Jordan

Illustrated by Robert Andrew Parker

Today marks the birthday of Jackson Pollock, the American painter born in 1912 in Cody, Wyoming. Killed in an automobile accident in 1956, Pollock struggled with alcoholism and depression and has been the subject of hundreds of adult studies, biographies, and movies. Given his lifestyle, he does not seem a natural subject for a picture book for the six to ten set.

But Jan Greenberg and Sandra Jordan's *Action Jackson* demonstrates how great narrative nonfiction writers for children can take an unlikely subject and make it fascinating. They do so, in part, by focusing on the process Pollock used to create his artwork. Process is something that children can understand, because they themselves enjoy creating art and thinking about interesting ways to make things.

The book focuses on the two months in 1950 when Pollock painted *Lavender Mist*, now in the National Gallery of Art. Drawing from primary source material, particularly interviews of those who knew Pollock well, the lyrical text shows him taking a canvas, placing it on the floor of his barn, and using his entire body to create a masterpiece. "His eyes move up and down, back and forth. With light steps, he follows the sweep of his brush . . . 'The painting has a life of its own. I try to let it come through.'" An excellent bibliography, footnotes, and source notes round out this volume, illustrated with the vigorous watercolors of Robert Andrew Parker. In them Pollock dances and swoops and fashions his art with energy and passion.

Sandra Jordan worked for many years as a children's book editor. While at Farrar, Straus and Giroux she published a book by Jan Greenberg, who taught art appreciation to children. The two became friends. When Sandra left publishing to create her own books, they began their collaboration. Both do extensive research. They argue through the fine points of the text. Both have a passion for getting details right and still telling a compelling story. In the case of *Action Jackson*, they had written the story about another painting—only to discover while the book was being vetted that this canvas had not been created in Jackson's barn, even though many eye-witness accounts claimed so. They went back and redid the text to make it accurate. Sometimes a Greenberg/Jordan text can undergo forty to fifty revisions.

The results, however, are well worth it. You can trust their books—for the accuracy and child-centered approach. Not only will children get educated about art and the creative process, but adults using this book will learn a lot as well.

BILL PEET: AN AUTOBIOGRAPHY

By Bill Peet

For several decades January 29 has been a birthday dear to me. In the last week of January, during Bill Peet's lifetime, thousands of cards and greetings arrived from children across America at his publisher's office in Boston. He never wrote for, nor cared much about, critics. But he loved his audience—and they loved him in return.

Born in 1915 in Grandview, Indiana, Bill Peet attended the John Herron Art Institute in Indianapolis, where he met his wife Margaret. Recruited by Walt Disney for his new film company, Bill moved to Los Angeles and worked for twenty-seven years on classic Disney films like *Fantasia*, *101 Dalmations*, *Peter Pan*, *Sleeping Beauty*, and *Alice in Wonderland*. In 1959 he wrote and illustrated *Hubert's Hair-Raising Adventure*—his first of many children's books with great storytelling, cartoon-style illustrations, and animal characters engaged in fantastic adventures. Eventually, he was able to work on the books full-time and leave his often conflicted relationship with Disney. Although Bill's stories can be read for their lighthearted nonsense and memorable verse, he created characters who experienced universal problems—fear, loneliness, and self-doubt. Bill also tackled timely issues—both *The Wump World* and *Farewell to Shady Glade* address environmental concerns.

In 1989 Bill created one of the best autobiographies published by a children's book author, *Bill Peet: An Autobiography*. In it he honestly addressed the personal issues of his life and filled the pages with his spirited and extremely funny drawings. It explores his work at Disney and the children's books he created.

I was fortunate to work with Bill for many years. At one conference, when Bill was about to appear for an autographing, I was alone in a booth setting up stacks of books. Two eager seven- or eight-year-old boys approached the table. "Is Mr. Peet here yet?" they asked. I said he would be right along. "And will he have his bodyguard with him?" they inquired. "Oh, no," I said. "Well why not?" came the quick retort. "The president has a bodyguard, and Mr. Peet is more important than the president." To these children and to so many others Bill Peet has truly been much more important than the president. His books—filled with humor and action and an understanding of childhood—continue to make young readers laugh as they turn the pages.

JANUARY 29

Happy Birthday Rosemary Wells (Max and Ruby books) and Christopher Collier (*My Brother Sam Is Dead*, written with his older brother James Lincoln Collier).

It's the birth date of Sylvia Cassedy (1930–1989), *Lucie Babbidge's House*.

It's also the birth date of William McKinley (1843–1901), the 25th president of the United States.

In 1845 "The Raven" was published in the *New York Evening Mirror*, the first story printed with the name of the author, Edgar Allan Poe.

Happy Birthday Kansas, which became the 34th U.S. state on this day in 1861.

In 1891 Lili'uokalani is proclaimed Queen of Hawaii, its last monarch. Read *The Last Princess: The Story of Princess Ka'iulani of Hawai'I* by Fay Stanley, illustrated by Diane Stanley.

It's National Puzzle Day. Read *The Puzzling World of Winston Breen* by Eric Berlin.

JANUARY 30

Happy Birthday Polly Horvath (*Everything on a Waffle*).

It's the birth date of Michael Dorris (1945–1997), *Morning Girl, A Yellow Raft in Blue Water*.

It's also the birth date of Franklin D. Roosevelt (1882–1945), the 32nd President of the United States and the longest-serving U.S. president. Read *A Boy Named FDR: How Franklin D. Roosevelt Grew Up to Change America* by Kathleen Krull, illustrated by Steve Johnson and Lou Fancher, *FDR's Alphabet Soup: New Deal America 1932–1939* by Tonya Bolden, and *Breakfast at the Liberty Diner* by Daniel Kirk.

And it's the birth date of Richard Theodore Greener (1844–1922), the first African American to graduate from Harvard University.

In 1933 Adolf Hitler is sworn in as Chancellor of Germany. Read *The Book Thief* by Markus Zusak.

THE BOOK OF THREE
By Lloyd Alexander

On January 30, 1924, Lloyd Alexander was born in Philadelphia. He knew from the age of fifteen that he wanted to be a writer, and for seventeen years he wrote for adults. Then in 1963, this charming, erudite author published his first children's book, *Time Cat*. *The Book of Three*, his second book, appeared in 1964. His editor, Ann Durell, believed both in the book itself and the author—two judgments that would be justified over time—and she printed 20,000 copies with confidence. Never out of print and never out of favor with young readers, this volume introduces the fascinating set of characters in the Chronicles of Prydain series.

Alexander worked in U.S. Army intelligence in Wales during World War II. To write his new series he began intensive research into the mythology and history of that country, reading Lady Charlotte Guest's *Mabinogion* at least a dozen times. For the next seven years of his life, he spun out the story that he started in *The Book of Three*—one that introduces as its main character Taran, a hero who serves as an assistant pig keeper but longs for great adventures. However lowly this position seems, Taran fiercely guards a white oracular pig named Hen Wen.

When Hen Wen escapes, Taran sets out to find her and ends up on a quest with a strange group of companions—Gurgi, a Golem-like figure, Fflewddur Fflam, a bard with a harp whose strings break when he tells a lie, Princess Eilonwy, an independent young woman who uses magic and cunning to keep them all alive, and Doli, a dwarf who tries to make himself invisible. It doesn't look much like a heroic band, but in their case looks turn out to be deceiving. Although *The Book of Three* works perfectly well as a single volume, it also sets up the rest of the series. Millions of children have fallen under its spell over the decades. Perfect for eight- to eleven-year-olds, the Chronicles of Prydain provide exciting fantasy for those a bit too young for Harry Potter or J.R.R. Tolkien.

Alexander lived to be eighty-three, won the Newbery Medal for the final book in the series, *The High King*, and received multiple National Book Awards. His rise to fame began with a dinner with Ann Durell, when he beguiled her with the idea of the Chronicles of Prydain series. Then he went on to write the book that would completely capture the hearts of young readers.

THE NEW WAY THINGS WORK

By David Macaulay

On January 31, 1930, 3M began marketing Scotch Tape, an invention of Richard Drew. The familiar plaid design, an adaptation of the Wallace tartan, did not come along for another fifteen years. But Scotch Tape, like so many other simple inventions, changed everyday life.

If I were to recommend to parents a single reference source to have in their home library it would be one of my favorite books of all time, David Macaulay's *The New Way Things Work*. Even if you are mechanically handicapped as I am, the clear and precise way that Macaulay presents how machines work—from levels to lasers, windmills to websites—engages even the most initially reluctant readers for four hundred pages and encourages young people to think about inventions.

For a recent essay I was writing, I had to sort out nuclear fission, nuclear fusion, and the atomic bomb. Who did I turn to for help? Macaulay, of course. My can opener doesn't work. Consult David. Page after page, he makes the incomprehensible seem easy to understand.

Born in the Manchester area of England, David grew up in a household where everyone created things. His father fashioned wood carvings and toys; in the evening the family sat around the coal stove in their kitchen. Macaulay recalls, "By the time we got out of that kitchen, we actually believed that creativity and craftsmanship were desirable—even normal." When he was eleven years old, Macaulay came with his family to America and made a place for himself in this new land. As a student at the Rhode Island School of Design and later as a faculty member there, he pursued his love of drawing and architecture—one that eventually led to his series of very successful children's books about how architectural structures are created—*Castle, Cathedral*, and *Mosque. Built to Last* combines all three titles.

David Macaulay is one of the hardest-working practitioners in the field of children's books. All of his books take enormous amounts of research; the drawing time alone for each page is daunting. But his early books seem a cake walk compared to *The New Way Things Work*. Here he describes, and shows in the art, hundreds of objects—holograms, helicopters, airplanes, bits and bytes, even the stapler. And he manages to do this with humor. The book features a woolly mammoth as a protagonist, who always provides a laugh when he demonstrates how the inventions are used.

In short, the book provides endless hours of enjoyment for young readers. I firmly believe that in the future, when some new young inventor is interviewed, he will say with pride, "I got my early inspiration from David Macaulay."

JANUARY 31

Happy Birthday Gerald McDermott (*Anansi the Spider, Arrow to the Sun*), Denise Fleming (*In the Tall, Tall Grass*), and Bryan Collier (*Rosa, Martin's Big Words*).

It's the birth date of baseball player Jackie Robinson (1919–1972). He was the first black Major League baseball player. Read *Testing the Ice: A True Story About Jackie Robinson* by Sharon Robinson, illustrated by Kadir Nelson.

Guy Fawkes was hanged, drawn, and quartered for his part in the Gunpowder Plot, an attempt to blow up the English Parliament, on this day in 1606.

It's Inspire Your Heart with Art Day. Visit a museum and read *A Nest for Celeste: A Story about Art, Inspiration, and the Meaning of Home* by Henry Cole.

FEBRUARY 1

Happy Birthday Jerry Spinelli (*Stargirl*), James Preller (*A Pirate's Guide to First Grade*), and Meg Cabot (*The Princess Diaries*).

 It's the birth date of **Langston Hughes** (1902–1967), *Poetry for Young People*.

On this day in 1861 President Abraham Lincoln signed the 13th Amendment, abolishing slavery.

The first volume of the *Oxford English Dictionary* (A to Ant) was published in 1884.

Four African-American students from a North Carolina college staged the first Greensboro lunch counter sit-in at a Woolworth's in 1960. Read *Freedom on the Menu: The Greenboro Sit-Ins* by Carole Boston Weatherford, illustrated by Jerome Lagarrique.

BETSY-TACY
By Maud Hart Lovelace

The first week of February has been designated as a week to celebrate children's authors and artists. In keeping with this holiday I'll focus on some fabulous children's book creators, beginning with Maud Hart Lovelace. Born in 1892 in Mankato, Minnesota, Lovelace began to write at an early age. She once asked her mother, "How do you spell 'going down the street'?" She kept scrapbooks and diaries and later used this material for her books. At a time when women rarely received a college education, Lovelace attended the University of Minnesota, and she married another writer. Then she began to publish historical novels for adults such as *Early Candlelight*, which is set in Minnesota, and *Gentleman from England*, written with her husband.

Had she simply written adult novels, Lovelace would be forgotten today. But she enjoyed telling her daughter Marien stories about her own childhood—about growing up in Mankato and her best friend Bick Kenney, whom she met at her fifth birthday party. Lovelace drew on these memories for a series of books presenting the adventures of three friends, Betsy, Tacy, and Tib, in Deep Valley, Minnesota.

When a new family moves into Betsy's neighborhood, she finally has a friend her age to play with. In fact, they do so much together that everyone simply refers to them as Betsy-Tacy. Lovelace aged her protagonists from ages five to twelve in the first four books. The Betsy-Tacy series explores childhood and adolescence at the turn of the twentieth century in a small Midwestern community. The last six books in the series take the girls through high school and adult years.

In these lighthearted, very enjoyable books for seven- to ten-year-olds, Lovelace introduces difficult issues. In *Betsy-Tacy*, published in 1940, Tacy's baby brother dies, and as a five-year-old she must cope with her grief. In later Betsy-Tacy books and in a novel, *Emily of Deep Valley* (1950), the characters must deal with small-town prejudice against the ethnic community Little Syria.

Acclaimed children's writer Mitali Perkins expressed her enthusiasm for Lovelace in a new edition of *Emily of Deep Valley*: "Maud Hart Lovelace's classic novels served as a superb orientation for a young newcomer from India eager to understand the history and heritage of a new world. They took me back to 1912, a time when America shared many of the values that resonated in my old-world home, but they also sparkled with timeless humor that made me laugh out loud in the library."

Like many of our classics, the Betsy-Tacy books went out of print for a short period. But the Betsy-Tacy Society and the Maud Hart Lovelace Society kept the fans organized and managed to get the titles back in print. Long after other books have been forgotten, adults cherish their memories of reading about Betsy, Tacy, and Deep Valley.

ALEXANDER AND THE TERRIBLE, HORRIBLE, NO GOOD, VERY BAD DAY

By Judith Viorst
Illustrated by Ray Cruz

Today marks the birthday of Judith Viorst, author, poet, and journalist. She became known as a writer through her *Redbook* columns, full of witty and stylish prose. They led to a series of children's books addressing childhood psychological issues. *The Tenth Good Thing About Barney*, for instance, helps children process grief about the death of a beloved cat.

Viorst was born in Newark, New Jersey, and married Milton Viorst in 1960. She always knew she wanted to be an author and at age seven her work got her into a bit of hot water; she had constructed odes to her dead parents though they were still very much living—and annoyed. That experience, however, did not stop Viorst from using those near and dear to her as the subject matter for essays or books. Her three sons, Anthony, Nicholas, and Alexander, gave her ideas and protagonists for her stories.

Her most famous character first appeared in 1972 in *Alexander and the Terrible, Horrible, No Good, Very Bad Day*. Viorst's real son Alexander had lots of bad days—he fell out of trees and off chairs, knocked out his front teeth and broke bones. She used this emotional material and created a five-year-old protagonist who tells us in the first line, "I went to sleep with gum in my mouth and now there's gum in my hair and when I got out of bed this morning, I tripped on the skateboard . . . I think I'll move to Australia." The day proves to be just as bad as Alexander thinks it will.

The book presents a common human experience—a day where things just seem to go wrong from the moment you get up. Because it occurs in only one day, it suggests these problems can be contained. It allows readers to laugh about themselves and their own situations, while they are laughing at Alexander. The book has been adapted for theater and millions of copies are now in print. Often, when I ask young men in their twenties about their favorite picture books, they respond with two titles—*Where the Wild Things Are* and *Alexander and the Terrible, Horrible, No Good, Very Bad Day*.

I hope Judith Viorst isn't having one of Alexander's days on her birthday. For her generous help in getting so many of us over bad days, she definitely deserves some very good ones. After all, she has given us a refrain to use from time to time when things are going awry—"I think I'll move to Australia!"

FEBRUARY 2

Happy Birthday Eve Rice (*Sam Who Never Forgets*), Deborah Hopkinson (*Under the Quilt of Night*), Mary Casanova (*One-Dog Canoe*), and Lin Oliver (Hank Zipzer series).

It's the birth date of Pura Belpré (1899–1982), *Firefly Summer*, the first Latina librarian in the New York Public Library System. The Pura Belpré Award, named in her honor, recognizes books that celebrate Latino culture.

Also born on this day was Rebecca Caudill (1899–1985), *A Pocketful of Cricket*. Illinois children vote to determine the recipient of the Rebecca Caudill Young Reader's Books Award.

In 1925 dog sleds carrying diphtheria serum reached Nome, Alaska, and inspired the Iditarod race. Hence, it's Sled Dog Day. Read *Winterdance* by Gary Paulsen.

In 1876 the National Baseball League was founded with eight teams.

It's Groundhog Day.

FEBRUARY 3

Happy Birthday John Wallner (*Hail Stones and Halibut Bones*).

It's the birth date of Walt Morey (1907–1992), *Gentle Ben*; Joan Lowery Nixon (1927–2003), *Nightmare*; poet and novelist Gertrude Stein (1874–1946), *Three Lives*, *The Autobiography of Alice B. Toklas*; and painter **Norman Rockwell** (1894–1978). Read *Norman Rockwell: Storyteller With a Brush* by Beverly Gherman.

In 1690 the Massachusetts colony issued the first paper money in America. Read *A Smart Girl's Guide to Money: How to Make It, Save It, and Spend It* by Nancy Holyoke, illustrated by Ali Douglass.

Boy Scout Anniversary Week begins today. Read *The Official Handbook for Boys: The First Boy Scout Handbook*, originally published in 1911.

WHERE THE MOUNTAIN MEETS THE MOON

By Grace Lin

As you know if you live in a city with a thriving Chinatown, the Chinese New Year gets celebrated at the end of January or the beginning of February, depending on the year. While modern China follows the Western Gregorian calendar, or "common calendar," for day-to-day business, the ancient traditional Lunisolar calendar, or "agricultural calendar," is still observed for holidays. If you want to honor this event, a recent book is perfect for this holiday: Grace Lin's *Where the Mountain Meets the Moon*.

What does it mean to be a Chinese American, particularly if most traces of your native culture have vanished from your life? When writer Grace Lin traveled to Hong Kong, Taiwan, and China to answer this question, she immersed herself in the legends and folktales of the country. Just as other authors before her, such as Jean Fritz and Allen Say, hunted for their roots by creating children's books, Grace took her own personal journey and wrote one of the best books of the twenty-first century.

Where the Mountain Meets the Moon stands as good a chance of becoming a classic as any book published in the last few years. A Newbery Honor book that adults and children adore, the story works for independent reading or for reading aloud in both families and second through sixth grade classrooms. It is a particularly good choice for sharing because the short chapters can be enjoyed just one or a few at a time. Wherever you end the narrative, young readers want it picked up again.

In a land conjured up from Chinese folklore, a young girl, Minli, lives in poverty with her parents in the dull, brown village where Fruitless Mountain and the Jade River meet. Although poor in possessions, her father is rich in imagination, telling her wonderful stories of folklore and adventure. In a plot that perfectly follows the pattern of the hero quest, Minli sets off to find the Old Man in the Moon and ask him for good fortune for her family. Her journey brings her the friendship of a dragon, a visit with the king, the help of a family that has learned the formula for perfect happiness, and, finally, a chance to make one request of the Old Man. In the end, all of the stories intersect to provide a completely satisfying and touching conclusion.

For this exciting, lyrical, and well-crafted text, the publisher has gone the extra mile to produce a beautiful book. Thick ivory paper, full-color artwork, and elegant typography add to the enjoyment of reading. Not only does the book seem timeless in both story and content, it looks like an object that can be kept on a bookshelf, proudly, for a long, long time.

FLAT STANLEY

By Jeff Brown
Illustrated by Tomi Ungerer

In this age of the Internet, tweets, Facebook, and e-mail, we may not take time for today's celebration: Thank the Mailman Day. Even titles like James Cain's *The Postman Always Rings Twice* seem a bit arcane. Mine doesn't even ring once. But there is at least one classic children's book that owes everything to postal services around the world. Rather than going quietly out of print as it might have, the mail carriers of the world saved this book from oblivion.

Jeff Brown began *Flat Stanley* as a bedtime story to his sons. He had discovered that one of them feared that a bulletin board in the bedroom would fall down during the night and crush him while sleeping. Of course, one of the best ways to face fears, childhood or otherwise, is to laugh at them. So Jeff made up stories about what would happen if the bulletin board fell, and suddenly one little boy was squashed flat. Jeff's son J. C. named the character Stanley Lambchop, a name he found wildly funny. Being flat didn't prove to be such a problem for Stanley. He could go places that other children could not. He could fly like a kite. He could take vacations in an envelope.

Although *Flat Stanley* received mixed reviews when it was published in 1964 with Tomi Ungerer's quirky drawings, it stayed in print because children loved the idea. In *Everything I Need to Know I Learned from a Children's Book*, Professor Phil Nel wrote about its appeal to young readers: "In first grade, *Flat Stanley* was my favorite book. Bolstering my six-year-old's willingness to believe in stories, illustrator Tomi Ungerer rendered Stanley nearly two-dimensional—'half an inch thick,' just as Brown says. This slight concession to a third dimension made Stanley's flatness seem not just plausible, but possible. Maybe I could become like Flat Stanley."

In 1995, an inspired third-grade teacher in Canada thought Stanley perfect for a letter-mailing project. She had her class place a Stanley drawing in an envelope and send him to family, pen pals, and friends, keeping a journal of all the places he traveled. A great idea, the project took off internationally, and he began to gain entrance into pretty fancy places. After security clearance, he visited the White House. He traveled on the *Discovery* space shuttle. He made an appearance at the 2006 Olympic Games, and Clint Eastwood proudly displayed him at the Academy Awards. Not bad for a character who began his journey as a way for a father to put young boys to sleep.

So, for the triumphant journeys of Stanley Lambchop, we can thank the mailman. And for this delightful book we can thank Jeff Brown and his sons. If you want to participate in Thank the Mailman Day, just send Stanley to someone who'd like to hear from you!

FEBRUARY 4

Happy Birthday Barbara Shook Hazen (*Tight Times*) and Pat Ross (M & M series).

It's the birth date of Russell Hoban (1925–2011), *Bread and Jam for Frances*; and civil rights activist Rosa Parks (1913–2004), *Rosa Parks: My Story*.

It's also the birth date of Charles Lindbergh (1902–1974), the first man to fly solo across the Atlantic.

In 1789 **George Washington** was unanimously elected the first United States president. Read *George Washington's Socks* by Elvira Woodruff.

Happy Birthday Facebook, founded in 2004. Read *A Smart Girl's Guide to the Internet* by Sharon Cindrich, illustrated by Ali Douglas.

FEBRUARY 5

Happy Birthday Joan Elma Rahn (*Plants That Changed History*), Mona Kerby (*Owney, The Mail-Pouch Pooch*), and David Wiesner (*Tuesday, Art and Max*).

It's the birth date of Patricia Lauber (1924–2010), *Volcano: The Eruption and Healing of Mount St. Helens*.

Happy Birthday to baseball legend Hank Aaron. Read *Hank Aaron: Brave in Every Way* by Peter Golenbock, illustrated by Paul Lee.

Those of us with a little chocolate-hazelnut spread addiction will be happy to celebrate World Nutella Day. Read *After the Wreck, I Picked Myself Up, Spread My Wings, and Flew Away* by Joyce Carol Oates.

HARRY THE DIRTY DOG

By Gene Zion
Illustrated by Margaret Bloy Graham

Today for children's authors and artists week, I'd like to honor a nonagenarian who published her first children's book over sixty years ago, Margaret Bloy Graham. Born in Canada, Margaret moved to New York in the 1940s to work as a commercial illustrator. During that time she became good friends with two other U.S. immigrants, Hans and Margret Rey, creators of *Curious George*. Because Margaret wanted to illustrate children's books, Hans showed her how to put together an art portfolio, and Margret encouraged legendary Harper & Row editor Ursula Nordstrom to take a look. Nordstrom liked what she saw. So did the rest of the children's book community, because Margaret's first two picture books, one written by her husband Gene Zion (*All Falling Down*) and one by Charlotte Zolotow (*The Storm Book*) both won Caldecott Honors.

Margaret and Gene would become known for another text that he wrote in a short period of time, one he gave to Margaret when she came back from shopping one day. Margaret read it and exclaimed, "This will keep us." She knew immediately that not only was the text for *Harry the Dirty Dog* delightful, but it naturally suggested very compelling visual material. It is still hard for me to believe that one of the doggiest dogs in the cannon of children's books was created by someone who did not live with one—but such was the case. Graham's aunt, however, had both Aberdeen and Sealyham terriers, and Graham developed Harry—short legs, long body, big head, and white dog with black spots—as a combination of these two dogs.

In the beginning of *Harry the Dirty Dog*, we meet our hero, Harry, scurrying down the front steps, carrying his scrubbing brush out of the house because he hears the bathwater running in the tub. Like many dogs, Harry hates taking a bath. So Harry buries the brush in the backyard and sets out for a day of mischief, even sliding down the coal chute. This turns him into a dirty dog, one unrecognizable to his family. But the book has a happy ending, and in the final scene we see Harry, clean, with his scrubbing brush hidden under his pillow—he may not have reformed all that much.

The book was followed by sequels, *No Roses for Harry!* and *Harry by the Sea*, and in 2002 Graham went back to her classic and created new artwork for the book that retains all the charm of the original but provides more color than the printing process made possible in the 1950s. Tastefully executed, this new edition reminds everyone who reads it why the book has been in print for fifty-five years.

ISLAND OF THE BLUE DOLPHINS
By Scott O'Dell

For children's authors and artists week, I'd like to talk about the most impressive author I ever worked with, Scott O'Dell. Scott was in his mid-seventies and I was in my late twenties when we first met. A tall man, large in body, spirit, and charisma, he excelled at telling stories. Probably even more important to me, Scott genuinely paid attention to and appreciated junior publishing staff members. Whatever you did for him, he thanked you and encouraged you personally.

By that point he had become one of America's most accomplished writers for children. In his home Scott displayed on a mantel the treasures he'd gathered—the Newbery Medal, the Hans Christian Anderson Medal, and the Regina Medal. As someone who came late in his life to writing for children, perhaps he valued his profession more than he would have if it had come easier.

Born in Los Angeles in 1898, Scott attended a number of colleges and eventually worked in the motion picture industry. He was on set for the first filming of *Ben Hur*. Eventually he became the book review editor for the Los Angeles *Daily News* and wrote some books for adults. But a true story about a young Native American who spent eighteen years alone on an island off the California coast had always haunted him. There was no record of how she spoke, and because Scott wanted to give this character, Karana, great dignity, he wrote in iambic pentameter, the language of Shakespeare. He had no idea who might want to read this story and entrusted it to his friend Hardwick Mosley, West Coast sales representative for Houghton Mifflin. Houghton thought *Island of the Blue Dolphins* a children's story, published it in 1960, and Scott won the Newbery Medal for his first book.

Married to children's librarian Elizabeth O'Dell, who would be his lifelong supporter and first-reader of his books, Scott loved no group of people more than librarians—they read his books, they could tell him what children said, and they appreciated his stories. Although *Island of the Blue Dolphins* was published when Scott was in his sixties, he lived and wrote for another thirty years and crafted other superb novels: *Zia*; *Black Star, Bright Dawn*; *The King's Fifth*; *The Black Pearl*. Always personally generous with the money from his books, Scott set up the Scott O'Dell Award for Historical Fiction to help other authors receive recognition for their efforts.

How I wish I could have dinner with Scott and Elizabeth again. When I was a young woman trying to find her way in the publishing profession no one was ever kinder to me. Instead I pick up *Island of the Blue Dolphins* from time to time—just to hear the sound of Scott's eloquent storytelling voice.

FEBRUARY 6

Happy Birthday Jerome Wexler (*Venus Flytraps*) and Betsy Duffey (*How to Be Cool in the Third Grade*).

It's the birth date of Berta Hader (1891–1976), *The Big Snow*.

It's also the birth date of Ronald Reagan (1911–2004), the 40th president of the United States.

Baseball legend **George Herman "Babe" Ruth** (1895–1948) was born on this day. Read *Home Run: The Story of Babe Ruth* by Robert Burleigh, illustrated by Mike Wimmer.

Happy Birthday Massachusetts, which became the sixth U.S. state on this day in 1788.

It's Lame Duck Day. This does not refer to injured waterfowl, but to those whose political tenure is about to expire. However, go ahead and read the Duck & Goose books by Tad Hills, *The Story of Ping* by Marjorie Flack, and *I Can Help* by David Costello.

FEBRUARY 7

Happy Birthday Shonto Begay (*The Mud Pony*).

It's the birth date of Charles Dickens (1812–1870), *A Christmas Carol, The Adventures of Oliver Twist*; Fred Gipson (1908–1973), *Old Yeller*; and Laura Ingalls Wilder (1867–1857), Little House series.

Blacksmith John Deere (1804–1886), founder of the tractor-making company, was born on this day. Read *Katy and the Big Snow* by Virginia Lee Burton.

It's Ballet Day. Read *Ballerino Nate* by Kimberly Bradley, illustrated by R. W. Alley; *Dancing to Freedom: The True Story of Mao's Last Dancer* by Li Cunxin, illustrated by Anne Spudvilas; *Josephine Wants to Dance* by Jackie French, illustrated by Bruce Whately; and *Angelina Ballerina* by Katharine Holabird.

THE ADVENTURES OF PINOCCHIO
By Carlo Collodi

On February 7, 1940, RKO Radio Pictures released the second of the Walt Disney animated classics, *Pinocchio*. As a child who fell under the spell of the film, I remember many of its virtues—cutting-edge animation, Academy Awards for the Best Original Score and Original Song, "When You Wish Upon a Star," and the delightful Jiminy Cricket. Hence, imagine my surprise, and the shock of many readers, when I actually picked up Collodi's *The Adventures of Pinocchio* twenty years later and discovered that the film and the book share a title but little else.

They were closer in conception, but Walt Disney felt that no one could sympathize with Collodi's antihero, the wooden puppet with sawdust for brains and a penchant for getting into trouble. Disney wanted a hero plus comic relief, and so Pinocchio's sidekick Jiminy Cricket entered the script. If you have not read this book, you will find some amazing surprises.

Pinocchio first appeared as a magazine serial and became a book in 1883. As Italian writer Umberto Eco has stated, "Though it's written in very simple language, *Pinocchio* is not a simple book." Even as the toy marionette is being carved out of wood, he creates havoc in Master Cherry's studio. After Geppetto brings the puppet back to his home, the long-suffering saint of a father gets nothing but grief for his pains. Just like Curious George the monkey, Pinocchio delights young readers precisely because of the scrapes he manages to get into.

Collodi initially ended the story after Chapter 15, when Pinocchio dies by hanging. The author had no intention of bringing this scamp back to life, but his editor begged him to write more. So the blue-haired fairy intercedes and resurrects Pinocchio—she also turns him into a real boy at the end. As originally published, the puppet had no desire to become good—Collodi only added those elements as an afterthought. Even so Pinocchio remains a subversive character—when he should work, he plays; when he can do the right thing, he always does the wrong thing.

The *New York Review of Books* provides an excellent translation of this classic by Geoffrey Brock with notes by Eco and Rebecca West, but my favorite version for children remains the Creative Editions 2005 *The Adventures of Pinocchio*, with Roberto Innocenti's dark and haunting illustrations. The master of unforgettable picture-book illustrations, Innocenti does not flinch away from the dark side of this story—rather he gives meaning and substance to Collodi's sometimes disturbing text.

What surprised me the most in rereading *Pinocchio* was how little time is spent on the idea of Pinocchio's nose growing when he lies. That detail has haunted me from childhood. However you remember the story, you will be amazed when you actually pick it up in either of these excellent translations.

STUCK ON EARTH
By David Klass

If you live in New Mexico, today you can celebrate Extraterrestrial Culture Day—established by a congressman from Roswell, New Mexico, to celebrate and honor all past, present, and future extraterrestrial visitors. And if you don't live in New Mexico, the day sounds so cool that you probably want to celebrate it anyway. No matter where you are, you can read a fabulous book, featuring the perfect hero for this day.

If you believe the narrator of David Klass's *Stuck on Earth*, you have just met Ketchvar III, a snaillike intergalactic traveler who has been dropped in New Jersey. He has been sent on an important mission: he must determine if the people on earth should be allowed to live. To understand earthlings, Ketchvar III invades the brain of a fourteen-year-old boy, Tom Filber, someone whose nickname on earth just happens to be "Alien." A normal teenage boy, Tom deals with a crush on the girl next door, a difficult mother, a drunken father, and a sister who does constant battle with him. Ketchvar III, who comes from a peaceful planet, finds all of Tom's life—including the daily bullying he undergoes—horrific. But the longer our alien stays on earth the more he grows to appreciate its residents.

The school psychologist and Tom's peers at the school believe that Tom has created an empowerment fantasy to make his difficult life bearable. Because *Stuck on Earth* is told from Tom's perspective, you join them in wondering: Has Tom really been taken over by an alien or is he inventing it all? How in the world is Tom, and for that matter Ketchvar III, going to survive on earth even for a short period of time? These questions, and our hero's attempts to uncover serious ecological damage occurring in his town, form the basis of a very funny, fast-paced, and totally convincing story of a young boy's adolescent struggles. This book can be enjoyed by ten- to fourteen-year-olds—particularly if on some days they feel like aliens themselves.

Unfortunately, Ketchvar III landed in New Jersey. If he had touched down in New Mexico, he'd be celebrated and honored today. Welcome to earth, Ketchvar III—and we do hope you recommend that the people of this beautiful planet not be exterminated. The rest of us will have to read *Stuck on Earth* to find out what our honored visitor decided.

FEBRUARY 8

Happy Birthday Anne Rockwell (*Apples and Pumpkins*) and Adrienne Adams (*A Woggle of Witches*).

It's the birth date of **Jules Verne** (1828–1905), *A Journey to the Center of the Earth, Twenty Thousand Leagues Under the Sea, Around the World in Eighty Days*.

In 1692 a doctor in Salem, Massachusetts, suggested that two girls may be suffering from bewitchment. Read *Wicked Girls: A Novel of the Salem Witch Trials* by Stephanie Hemphill.

Happy Birthday to the Boy Scouts of America, incorporated in 1910. It's Boy Scouts Anniversary Day. If you didn't get to it last week, read *The Official Handbook for Boys: The First Boy Scout Handbook*, originally published in 1911.

In 1587 Mary, Queen of Scots was beheaded in Fotheringhay Castle for her alleged part in the conspiracy to usurp Elizabeth I, and in 1952 Elizabeth II became the Queen of England after her father, King George VI, died.

FEBRUARY 9

Happy Birthday Dick Gackenbach (*Harry and the Terrible Whatzit*), Stephen Roos (*The Gypsies Never Came*), and Alice Walker (*The Color Purple*).

It's the birth date of Hilda Van Stockum (1908–2006), *The Winged Watchman*; and George Ade (1866–1944), *Fables in Slang*.

It's also the birth date of William Henry Harrison (1773–1843), the ninth president of the United States.

In 1950 Senator Joseph McCarthy accused the U.S. State Department of being filled with communists. Is it a coincidence that today is National Stop Bullying Day? Read *The Hundred Dresses* by Eleanor Estes.

Happy Birthday to the United States Weather Bureau, established in 1870. Read *Weather* by Seymour Simon.

In 1994 Nelson Mandela was elected the first black president of South Africa.

It's Read in the Bathtub Day. Read *The Tub People* by Pam Conrad, illustrated by Richard Egielski.

SNOWFLAKE BENTLEY

By Jacqueline Briggs Martin
Illustrated by Mary Azarian

On February 9, 1865, close to the end of the Civil War, Wilson Bentley was born in Jericho, Vermont. As a young boy he loved snow and began to keep a record of the weather. Studying snow crystals under a microscope, he discovered that each one was unique, with its own shape and design. He set out to find a way to photograph snow crystals, to record the beauty of individual drops of snow. Many of Bentley's photographs, along with more information about him, can be found at the Jericho Historical Society website.

Few children or adults knew about Wilson Bentley in the early 1990s. Initially, publishing house after publishing house turned down a manuscript about him by Jacqueline Briggs Martin. After all, not only did it focus on an obscure subject but it also did not have a child protagonist. Most of the book recounts Bentley's struggles as an adult.

Fortunately, Ann Rider of Houghton Mifflin had read the text again and again and believed it would make a fine picture book, one that she felt would be perfect for Vermont artist Mary Azarian. After a lot of work on the part of Ann, Jackie Martin, Mary Azarian, and designer Bob Kosturko, *Snowflake Bentley* became one of those books where everything comes together in a superb package. The text was beautifully paced and written; Mary Azarian's woodcuts provided an extension of the words; Bob's design was understated and elegant. When the book won the Caldecott Medal, the committee praised all three elements. Great picture books never belong only to the artist or to the writer—they always combine art, text, and design.

One of the first reactions to the book came from the editor's daughter Molly. She liked the text and even wanted to photograph snowflakes. But she added, "I don't want to do it for my whole life." Still the book's underlying theme about following your passion, or dream, in spite of adversity resonates with thousands of children.

Some teachers use *Snowflake Bentley* around this time of year for a month-long unit on snowflakes. I myself read it every year because it reminds me that we all need to follow our passion, no matter where it takes us. In the end, love, dedication, and perseverance triumph.

HENRY'S FREEDOM BOX

By Ellen Levine

Illustrated by Kadir Nelson

Since 1976 Black History Month has been celebrated in the United States during February. We'll look at a couple of superb titles this month, beginning with one of the best nonfiction picture books of the decade, *Henry's Freedom Box: A True Story from the Underground Railroad* by Ellen Levine, illustrated by Kadir Nelson. Ellen was an historian's historian; she loved research—and had a nose for a superb story. While reading an eight hundred-page book, William Still's *The Underground Railroad* (1872), she came across the story of a man who mailed himself to Still's Anti-Slavery Society office. Slave Henry Brown built himself a box, less than three feet square, and mailed himself to freedom, a journey that took twenty-seven hours in a tight space with tiny air holes. Levine knew this true incident should be available for children, a perfect way to describe the lengths to which slaves would go to be free.

In *Henry's Freedom Box* Ellen tells Henry's story—his work and brutal treatment on the plantation, the selling of his wife and children into slavery. With the help of a white abolitionist doctor, Henry executes his plan. Ellen's spare but effective text has been brilliantly illustrated by Kadir Nelson, one of the most accomplished artists working today. Brilliant in his portraits, Nelson brings us Henry as a young boy and then a young man falling in love. He shows him trapped inside the box, steeled for whatever happens in those twenty-seven hours. And in this Caldecott Honor book, he shows us the final triumphant scene: Henry emerging from the box with a birthday (his first freedom day) and a new name, Henry "Box" Brown.

To the children's book field, Ellen Levine brought more credentials than most—a B.A. in Politics from Brandeis, a master's in Political Science from University of Chicago, and a Juris Doctor degree from New York University School of Law; she even served as a clerk for Judge Joseph Lord's U.S. District Court. As someone who hated injustice, Levine was a passionate speaker about the rights of individuals. In another book, *Freedom's Children*, she recorded the stories of thirty children and teenagers who contributed to the civil rights movement.

Ellen also served as part of the faculty for Vermont College's M.F.A. program. As author M. T. Anderson, who taught with her there, has written: "Everything Ellen writes—fiction, non-fiction, picture books—is written out of passion. Not just passion for the truth, but passion for justice. That's what makes her voice so unique and so defiant." The children's book field was, indeed, fortunate that Ellen gave up the power of law for the power of the pen.

FEBRUARY 10

Happy Birthday E. L. Konigsburg (*From the Mixed-Up Files of Mrs. Basil E. Frankweiler, The View From Saturday*), Stephen Gammell (*The Relatives Came*), Mark Teague (*How Do Dinosaurs Say Goodnight?*), James Rice (*Cowboy Night Before Christmas*), and Lucy Cousins (*Maisy* series).

It's the birth date of Charles Lamb (1775–1834), *Tales from Shakespeare*.

The Postal Telegraph Company of New York City introduced the singing telegram in 1933.

In 1996 the IBM supercomputer Deep Blue defeated Garry Kasparov in chess. Read *Way Down Deep in the Deep Blue Sea* by Jan Peck, illustrated by Valeria Petrone.

FEBRUARY 11

Happy Birthday Jane Yolen (*Owl Moon*), Toshi Maruki (*Hiroshima No Pika*), Holly Keller (*Farfallina & Marcel*), and Mo Willems (*Don't Let the Pigeon Drive the Bus!*).

It's the birth date of Mabel Esther Allan (1915–1998), Wood Street series.

 Thomas Edison (1847–1931) was born on this day, which is now National Inventors' Day.

In 1990 South African antiapartheid activist Nelson Mandela was freed after twenty-seven years in prison. He was elected president of his country four years later. Read *Nelson Mandela: "No Easy Walk to Freedom"* by Barry Denenberg.

In 1805 sixteen-year-old Sacajawea, the Shoshoni guide for Lewis and Clark, gives birth to a son, with Meriwether Lewis serving as midwife.

It's Don't Cry Over Spilled Milk Day. Read *The Moon Might Be Milk* by Lisa Shulman, illustrated by Will Hillenbrand, and *Oops* by Arthur Geisert.

A NEST FOR CELESTE: A STORY ABOUT ART, INSPIRATION, AND THE MEANING OF HOME

By Henry Cole

In February of 1896 the Massachusetts Audubon Society was founded, the beginning of the current national organization. It was established to protect birds and to discourage the women of the era from wearing bird plumes in their hats. The man honored by the name of the organization, John J. Audubon, has been the focus of thousands of children's books over the years.

But Henry Cole's 2010 book, *A Nest for Celeste: A Story About Art, Inspiration, and the Meaning of Home*, presents a slightly different portrait of this iconic figure than normally found in children's books. The story is narrated by a young orphan mouse, Celeste, living in the Oakley Plantation, not far from New Orleans. She manages to find enough food in the dining room to keep alive, but a close encounter with a cat sends Celeste scurrying to the upstairs rooms of the house. There she finds a friend, Joseph, a teenage apprentice to Audubon who helps with the master's painting. Joseph carries Celeste around in his pocket—so she witnesses Audubon killing an ivory-billed woodpecker or sketching a live osprey held in captivity. In Celeste's eyes Audubon looks the way he probably did to the birds that he captured or killed. Swept away in a rainstorm, Celeste manages to convince an osprey to carry her back to the plantation.

Celeste settles into a home of her own in the attic, where she can invite other wild creatures to visit.

Lavishly illustrated with brown pencil drawings, this old-fashioned animal fantasy keeps readers riveted. Celeste charms everyone, including Joseph, and readers cheer her on as she finds a place of her own. Touching without being sentimental, the book has already found an eager audience of second through fifth graders. Even though the art helps the reader comprehend the story better, *A Nest for Celeste* works extremely well—with short chapters, lots of action, and delicious language—as a read aloud for both families and classrooms. If you use it for story time, just make sure that young readers have a chance to savor the artwork as well.

Thank you Henry Cole for this fabulous new book—one ideal for those readers who love *Charlotte's Web* or *The Cricket in Times Square*.

FANTASY, HISTORICAL FICTION, Elementary School

CHARLES AND EMMA

By Deborah Heiligman

Today is the birthday of Charles Darwin. He has the distinction of being not only one of the most controversial figures of his era but also someone who still causes discord two hundred years later. Or more accurately, his theories have been controversial—often obscuring Darwin the human being. Around Darwin's 200th birthday some excellent books began to appear for children and middle school readers, such as Peter Sís's *Tree of Life* and Alice B. McGenty's *Darwin.*

But certainly the most original book about Darwin for young readers appeared in 2009: Deborah Heiligman's *Charles and Emma: The Darwins' Leap of Faith.* Even the cover—a silhouette of a woman holding a cross, looking at a man with a simian form lurking behind him—sets the stage for the contents. In this book, which works for thoughtful readers ages eleven to eighteen, Heiligman focuses on something unexplored in most Darwin biographies: Darwin as a man and his personal life during the period when he set forth his controversial ideas.

The book begins brilliantly—Darwin is conducting a scientific study, "To Marry or Nor Marry," and listing the pros and cons of the idea. At the end of this exercise, he decides that "To Marry" seems the best idea. Charles's choice of wife, his cousin Emma Wedgewood, will be one of his best decisions. Although they do not know each other well until they get engaged, Emma provides just the right balance for Charles. A caretaker and intelligent first critic of his work, she supports him in every way—and raises their large family while Charles works on scientific theory. At the beginning of the courtship, however, Emma has one nagging concern: she is a devout Christian and she fears for Charles's soul because of his religious doubts.

Heiligman walks readers through the publication of *On the Origin of the Species*, and the furor created by the book. But the focus of *Charles and Emma* remains an internal drama—a portrait of the marriage and family of Charles Darwin. Readers see Charles Darwin much as Emma might have viewed him, a loving husband and father, a caring human being who truly did not want to upset his wife because of his scientific writings.

Heiligman herself majored in religious studies; her husband is a science writer. So she understands on a personal level the issues she explores in this book. To get a better sense of Emma, Heiligman read her letters and makes Emma just as much a part of the saga as her more famous husband.

Charles and Emma can be enjoyed by adults just as much as young adults. Come for the science—stay for the romance. This book provides both in equal measure.

FEBRUARY 12

Happy Birthday Judy Blume (*Are You there God? It's Me, Margaret*), Ann Atwood (*Haiku: The Mood of Earth*), David Small (*Imogene's Antlers, Stitches*), Chris Conover (*The Christmas Bears*), and Jacqueline Woodson (*Show Way*).

It's the birth date of **Abraham Lincoln** (1809–1865), the 16th president of the United States. Read *Lincoln Shot: A President's Life Remembered* by Barry Denenberg, illustrated by Christopher Bing.

Illustrator Randolph Caldecott (1846–1886) died on this day. The prestigious Caldecott Medal, awarded annually to the most distinguished U.S. children's picture book, was named in his honor.

In 1554 Lady Jane Grey, the Queen of England for thirteen days, was beheaded on Tower Hill. She was barely seventeen years old.

FEBRUARY 13

Happy Birthday William Sleator (*Interstellar Pig*), Ouida Sebestyen (*The Girl in the Box*), and Janet Taylor Lisle (*The Art of Keeping Cool*).

It's the birth date of Eleanor Farjeon (1881–1965), *Martin Pippin in the Apple-Orchard*.

In 1542 Catherine Howard, fifth wife of Henry VIII, was executed. Read *The King's Rose* by Alisa M. Libby.

On this day in 1914 key players in the music industry founded the American Society of Composers, Authors, and Publishers. The ASCAP protects the rights of composers, songwriters, lyricists, and music publishers and strives to ensure that musicians receive royaltiers for the use of their material.

JOSEPH HAD A LITTLE OVERCOAT

By Simms Taback

Today marks the birth date of one of the most innovative illustrators of the twentieth century, Simms Taback. When Simms won the Caldecott Medal in 2000 for *Joseph Had a Little Overcoat*, so many members of the illustration community delighted in this news not only because they had long admired his work but also because he had worked on behalf of all artists for decades.

Born in New York in 1932, Simms Taback grew up in the Bronx. A graduate of Cooper Union, he served in the army, and then worked at CBS Records, the *New York Times*, and as an advertising art director. A tireless advocate for the rights of artists, Simms founded The Illustrators Guild, which became the New York Graphic Artists Guild. During this period, he designed the first McDonald's Happy Meal Box!

These accomplishments don't even include his more than forty children's books. Even in winning awards, Simms broke new ground. Both his Caldecott Honor book, *There Was an Old Lady Who Swallowed a Fly*, and *Joseph Had a Little Overcoat* were the first books using die-cut holes to be so honored. This technique had begun at the beginning of the twentieth century with Peter Newell's *The Hole Book*, but such books had always been considered "toy books," not worthy of awards.

In *Joseph Had a Little Overcoat*, based on a Yiddish folk song, Simms relied on a childlike folk art style that incorporates watercolor, gouache, collage, and die cuts. With one of the best color senses in the industry, Simms created vibrant and saturated hues that immediately please the eye of a child. In the book Joseph owns an overcoat that he truly likes. As it becomes worn, rather than throwing it away, he makes a vest out of it. The he continues to adapt this piece of clothing into a scarf, necktie, and handkerchief until finally it becomes a button. At its core about reusing and recycling, the story makes a wonderful book to read aloud with children anticipating what will happen next.

Regina Hayes of Viking Children's Books knew Simms for over twenty years. She loved working with him because "we laughed all the time. Simms had a warmth and humor that drew people to him. He had so many interests; he could talk about everything—books, movies, photography. Although Simms did not take himself too seriously, he took his work very seriously. The ultimate professional, he cared about every single detail, down to creating a special typeface for each book."

During his lifetime, Simms Taback made all who worked with him happy; and the books remain, still bringing joy to children.

A DOG'S WAY HOME

By Bobbie Pyron

Today, of course, we celebrate Valentine's Day, and my first Valentines always go to my dogs. This is also the time of year when the famous Westminster Dog Show opens. Certainly, the bond between a dog who participates in dog shows and his or her handler is incredibly loving and complex.

That relationship gets explored in *A Dog's Way Home* by Bobbie Pyron. In the first chapter, we watch Abby, age eleven, and Tam, a Shetland sheepdog, win an agility contest. They work together so well as a team that Abby does not even need to use hand signals. But on their way home to the small town of Harmony, North Carolina, a horrible car accident sends Abby to the hospital and Tam sailing out of the truck in his crate.

Now, if you are like me, you will skip ahead and read the last chapter. I do not need to read a book to cry over the death of dog. So here's the last line of *A Dog's Way Home*: "Finally, everything was as it should be." And that means, of course, Abby and Tam reunited. Pryon alternates this heart-touching book, one that will remind readers of *Lassie Come-Home* or *The Incredible Journey*, between the narrative voices of Abby and Tam. Tam's voice seems particularly brilliant; he emerges as a real dog, with one concern—to find the girl he loves. But to do that he will almost drown, nearly starve, bond with a coyote, get rescued by a dog shelter, and dodge bullets. His odyssey, as he travels four hundred miles to come home to Abby, has all the elements of an epic quest.

FEBRUARY 14

Happy Birthday George Shannon (*Tomorrow's Alphabet*), Phyllis Root (*One Duck Stuck*), and Paul O. Zelinsky (*Rapunzel*).

It's the birth date of Jamake Highwater (1942–2001), *Anpao*.

Happy Birthday Oregon, which became the 33rd U.S. state on this day in 1859.

George Washington Gale Ferris Jr. (1859–1896), inventor of the **Ferris wheel**, was born on this day. Read *Ferris Wheel: George Ferris and His Amazing Invention* by Dani Sneed.

Happy Birthday Arizona, which became the 48th U.S. state on this day in 1912. Read *My Great-Aunt Arizona* by Gloria Houston, illustrated by Susan Condie Lamb.

In 1962 First Lady Jackie Kennedy takes television viewers on a White House tour. Read *A Family of Poems: My Favorite Poetry for Children* by Caroline Kennedy, illustrated by Jon J. Muth.

It's Valentine's Day. Read *The Valentine Bears* by Eve Bunting, illustrated by Jan Brett.

Abby tries to soldier on. Her father works as a traveling musician and the family lacks the funds necessary for an all-out search for Tam. But Abby stays true to her belief that Tam lives and that he will find her. At one point, the family moves to Nashville. Abby adjusts, slowly, to the new environment. During the same time in the story, Tam has found someone to care for him and nurse him back to health. Yet neither stops thinking about the other.

A good dog story well told is much more difficult to write than most people think. Bringing knowledge gained by being a librarian and an animal rescue worker, Bobbie Pryon has pulled together the necessary elements and makes the book original with her portrait of Abby and Tam. The book works as a read alone or read aloud for third through sixth grades. Short chapters provide just the right amount of material for sharing. Even without a dead dog, this is definitely a three-handkerchief ending.

On Valentine's Day, read *A Dog's Way Home*—a perfect love story.

FEBRUARY 15

Happy Birthday Norman Bridwell (*Clifford the Big Red Dog*), Doris Orgel (*Sarah's Room*), Elaine Landau (*Popcorn!*), Jan Spivey Gilchrist (*The Great Migration*), Sonya Sones (*One of Those Hideous Books Where The Mother Dies*), and Art Spiegelman (*Maus*).

It's the birth date of Richard Chase (1904–1988), *The Jack Takes*.

Susan B. Anthony (1820–1906) was born on this day. Hence, it's Susan B. Anthony Day! Read *Susan B. Anthony: Fighter for Women's Rights* by Deborah Hopkinson, illustrated by Amy June Bates.

It's National Gum Drop Day. Read *The Gum-Chewing Rattler* by Joe Hayes, illustrated by Antonio Castro L.

STARRY MESSENGER
By Peter Sís

Born on February 15, 1564, Galileo Galilei, the Italian physicist, mathematician, astronomer, and philosopher, has often been called the man responsible for the birth of modern science. Even his name indicates his rock star status in the scientific world—he's known by a single name only, just like Cher or Madonna.

In 1996, Peter Sís, an artist with incredible ability to explore history, turned his hand to presenting Galileo's life to young readers, ages eight to twelve, in *Starry Messenger: A book depicting the life of a famous scientist – mathematician – astronomer – philosopher – physicist*. Although every now and then a picture book may be ideal for third- to sixth-grade readers, Sís has always created books—*The Wall, Tibet, The Tree of Life*—that best serve the child who can read novels, but who enjoys exploring complex picture books.

Sís begins his story with the common scientific misperception of the era—people believed the earth was the center of the universe. On a time line throughout the book, he shows busts of the great thinkers like Aristotle and Copernicus. In the city of Pisa, Galileo was born the same year as William Shakespeare. Studying at the University of Pisa, he eventually heard about telescopes and turned these "spy glasses" on the heavens, writing down his findings in a book called *The Starry Messenger*. Galileo became part of the Medici court, a famous author throughout Europe, and a controversial figure. Found guilty of heresy because he presented scientific ideas counter to the teachings of the Catholic Church, Galileo, as Sís notes, was finally pardoned three hundred years later.

Although Galileo's life could be presented in many ways, Sís has focused this story on his persecution for his beliefs. Sís himself grew up in Czechoslovakia under the Soviet regime. Although his parents encouraged his artistic freedom, he found in art school "there was really no space for fantasy or individuality." While creating a film about the 1984 Olympic Games, Sís visited Los Angeles and decided to remain in the United States so that he could explore whatever ideas he wanted to. He once said, "I think children should have choices, and I would like to participate in that growth." Hence Sís brings his own personal experience to this impassioned account of a scientist persecuted for his ideas.

In *Starry Messenger*, Peter Sís makes the life of Galileo attractive and understandable for both children and adults. Exquisitely detailed drawings provide extra information for the reader and are designed to make the book look like an ancient manuscript. Some adults urge children to use a magnifying glass with the book to focus on all the intricate details of the drawings. Anyone who spends time with this Caldecott Honor Book will learn a great deal about science and also about art.

PICTURE BOOK, BIOGRAPHY, Elementary School, Middle School

SMILE

By Raina Telgemeier

February has been designated National Children's Dental Health Month—to increase awareness and stress the importance of regular dental care. In 2010 *New York Times* bestselling author Raina Telgemeier published a graphic memoir, ideal for ten- to fourteen-year-olds, called *Smile*. In 214 pages Telgemeier presents the struggles of her protagonist, Raina, who has two front teeth knocked out in sixth grade. This means lots of time at the dentist and undergoing a variety of procedures and problems—in total, four and a half years of treatment.

In this honest and straightforward book examining the struggles of growing up and dealing with identity, Raina shares all her concerns—getting crushes, finding new friends, and slowly beginning to understand her place in a new school. In the end she finds the solution to her problems: "I threw my passion into things I enjoyed, rather than feeling sorry for myself. I realized that I had been letting the way I looked on the outside affect how I felt on the inside. But the more I focused on my interests, the more it brought out things I liked about myself."

Few writers have given better advice to young readers. Because Raina uses the most popular format of the day, the graphic novel, to tell this story, she has already won over her audience by the time she delivers these lines. Readers come to love Raina and even learn a great deal about what happens in the dentist chair and what various dental procedures entail. For anyone who has had to undergo extensive dental work, whether braces or reconstructive surgery, this book is almost a necessity.

Since publication, *Smile* has been wildly popular with young readers. John Schumacher, librarian at the Brook Forest Elementary School in Oak Brook, Illinois, witnessed a fifth grader put the book in a friend's hand, guide her to the circulation desk, and say, "You must check this out now and tell me your thoughts in the morning!" An interactive website has also been widely used by fifth and sixth graders. Some read *Smile* as a memoir; others simply find themselves fascinated by a story that rings so true to their own experiences. Outside of being easy to comprehend and a very fresh and honest look at common dilemmas among children and teens, *Smile* has been created by someone who remembers, in exacting detail, the concerns of fifth through eighth graders. In the end, whether you are an adult or child, you will find yourself smiling along with the protagonist.

FEBRUARY 16

Happy Birthday Elizabeth K. Cooper (*And Everything Nice: The Story of Sugar, Spice and Flavoring*) and Nancy Ekholm Burkert (*Snow-White and the Seven Dwarfs*).

In 1959 **Fidel Castro** became premier of Cuba. Read *The Red Umbrella* by Christina Diaz Gonzales, *Flight to Freedom* by Ana Veciana-Suarez, and *My Havana: Memories of a Cuban Boyhood* by Rosemary Wells and Secundino Fernandez, illustrated by Peter Ferguson.

The first 911 call was placed on this day in 1968 in Haleyville, Alabama.

FEBRUARY 17

Happy Birthday Robert Newton Peck (*A Day No Pigs Would Die*, *Soup*), Susan Beth Pfeffer (*Life As We Knew It*), and Michael McCurdy (*American Tall Tales*).

It's the birth date of Dorothy Canfield Fisher (1879–1958), *Understood Betsy*; Virginia Sorensen (1912–1991), *Miracles on Maple Hill*; and Chaim Potok (1929–2002), *The Chosen*.

In 1968 the Naismith Memorial Basketball Hall of Fame was founded in Springfield, Masachusetts. Read *The Basketball Hall of Fame's Hoop Facts and Stats* by Alex Sachare. Also, the legendary basketball player Michael Jordan was born on this day in 1963.

It's Random Acts of Kindness Day. Share your favorite book with a friend. Or read *The Kindness Quilt* by Nancy Elizabeth Wallace.

THE LIBRARIAN OF BASRA: A TRUE STORY FROM IRAQ

By Jeanette Winter

February has been set aside as Library Lovers Month to celebrate school, public, and private libraries of all types. In my case, without libraries this book would not exist. My early exposure to a variety of books came at a small school library in Village Elementary School in Fort Wayne, Indiana. An enormous amount of the research for this book took place at my local public library. In my community, and in the United States, libraries circulate materials to every citizen that once might have been only available to the wealthy.

In 2005 Jeanette Winter both wrote and illustrated a book that has made its readers look at libraries in a slightly different way. *The Librarian of Basra: A True Story from Iraq* opens with a line from Alia Muhammad Baker: "In the Koran, the first thing God said to Muhammad was 'Read.'" Alia is the librarian of Basra in Iraq. She worries the fires of war will destroy her collection so without government approval she begins bringing home books every night. When war finally comes and the city is engulfed in flames, Alia, with the help of the citizens of the town, removes the remaining books from the library and hides them in a restaurant. After the fighting stops, she transports thirty thousand volumes to her house and the homes of friends. She waits, dreaming of peace and a new library. "But until then, the books are safe—safe with the librarian of Basra."

My local public library recently moved to glorious new headquarters. Volumes from one library will go to another, without fires or raging wars. *The Librarian of Basra* reminds both children ages four through eight and adults just how lucky we are to have safe libraries at our disposal. We are also fortunate to have people like Alia, librarians who care passionately about books.

I hope everyone will use Library Lovers Month to thank those who, every day, protect our treasures, our books. If you love libraries, you also love the unsung heroes and heroines in this country and Iraq—librarians.

KNUFFLE BUNNY: A CAUTIONARY TALE

By Mo Willems

For about ten years February has been designated Adopt a Rescued Rabbit Month. When I think of a rabbit that needs rescuing in children's books, the first one that comes to mind appeared in 2004—not a living rabbit but a stuffed toy named Knuffle Bunny.

In Mo Willems's *Knuffle Bunny: A Cautionary Tale*, we first see Trixie's parents getting married, her birth, and a scene of this young toddler squishing her beloved toy, Knuffle Bunny. Cartoon characters set against real photographs of the Park Slope neighborhood in Brooklyn show Trixie and her father going to the Laundromat. A typical ebullient child, Trixie runs around in the clothes her father wants to place in the washer, but she helps put the money in the machine before they leave. Adults may be clueless at this point about what is going to happen, but children never miss the detail that Knuffle Bunny now can be seen through the window of the washer. As Trixie and her father head home, she tries to communicate her terrible tragedy to him—" 'Aggle

FEBRUARY 18

Happy Birthday Barbara Joosse (*Mama, Do You Love Me?*) and Toni Morrison (*The Bluest Eye, Song of Solomon, Beloved*).

It's the birth date of Virginia Kahl (1918–2004), *The Duchess Bakes a Cake*.

The Pilgrim's Progress, by John Bunyan, was published on this day in 1678. Read *John Bunyan's Pilgrim's Progress*, retold by Gary Schmidt, illustrated by Barry Moser.

It's also the publication date of *Adventures of Huckleberry Finn* by Mark Twain, first released in 1885.

In honor of the celestial body that was discovered on this day in 1930 and considered a planet until 2006, it's Pluto Day.

flaggle klabble!' Trixie bawled. She went boneless." When they arrive at the house, Mom realizes what has happened, and all ends well with Trixie's first words, "KNUFFLE BUNNY!!!" In this simple story, perfect for the youngest readers, Mo Willems tells a common childhood tale in a way that gets both adults and children laughing.

When researching *100 Best Books for Children*, I discovered that many of our best authors were rejected by publishers as they began their careers—L. M. Montgomery, Dr. Seuss, Kate DiCamillo, and J. K. Rowling, to name only a few. Mo Willems also had his first book manuscript, *Don't Let the Pigeon Drive the Bus*, rejected again and again. In his case, a very persistent and committed agent, Marcia Wernick, simply refused to give up. She believed Mo, with a background in writing for Sesame Street and Cartoon Network, had all the right impulses when it came to creating books for children. Finally, she found a new editor, hunting for projects, who was willing to take a chance.

Like so many of those who struggled before him, Mo Willems discovered that once he got published, wild enthusiasm for his books took over. Some of his titles seem destined to sit on the classic picture book shelf along with Dr. Seuss. With a real grasp of childhood behavior, a sense of what constitutes a good picture book story, and the artistic ability to render his thoughts in simple line and color, Mo Willems has emerged as one of the most popular picture book artists of the twenty-first century.

If by any chance you have missed Mo Willems, *Knuffle Bunny* makes a great place to begin reading his work. If you want to rescue your own Knuffle Bunny today, he can be purchased in stuffed-toy form, a lovely gift for those who have already fallen in love with these books.

FEBRUARY 19

Happy Birthday Jill Krementz (*A Very Young Dancer*) and Amy Tan (*The Moon Lady*).

It's the birth date of Louis Slobodkin (1903–1975), *The Hundred Dresses*; Mildred Lee (1908–2003), *The Skating Rink*; and Carson McCullers (1917–1967), *The Heart Is a Lonely Hunter*.

Renaissance astronomer Nicolaus Copernicus (1473–1543) was born on this day. Read *Nicolaus Copernicus: The Earth is a Planet* by Dennis B. Fradin, illustrated by Cynthia Von Buhler.

The children's television program *Mister Rogers' Neighborhood* premiered in the United States on this day in 1967.

It's Chocolate Mint Day. Read *The Ice Cream Con* by Jimmy Docherty.

BASEBALL SAVED US

By Ken Mochizuki
Illustrated by Dom Lee

Executive order 9066: On February 19, 1942, President Franklin Roosevelt signed an order that would send 110,000 Japanese Americans, two-thirds of them U.S. Citizens, to concentration camps in remote desert areas. Not allowed to return to their homes until January 2, 1945, these families lost an estimated $400 million worth in property—not to mention their own freedom and sense of well-being.

Many children's and young adult writers over the years have chosen to write about the internment of Japanese Americans, including Jeanne Wakatsuki Houston in her touching autobiography *Farewell to Manzanar*. In 1993, writer Ken Mochizuki and illustrator Dom Lee combined their talents in *Baseball Saved Us*, a book that makes this incident understandable for children ages six through ten.

In a brief but passionate opening, Ken Mochizuki sets the stage for this picture book; none "of these immigrants from Japan—or their children, who were American citizens—were ever proven to be dangerous to America during World War II. In 1988, the U.S. government admitted that what it did was wrong."

Then readers meet a young Japanese boy, standing with his father and looking out over the endless desert. In this desolate place, the father decides to build a baseball diamond. In flashbacks the author presents how the residents were taken to the camps and how family members broke down and relationships were strained—the boy's mother cries, his older brother becomes disrespectful to their father. Those forced into the camp decide to take positive action—they sew baseball unifroms, get supplies from friends back home, build bleachers, and clear the land. All the while, they are watched by a guard in the tower. Our unnamed hero, small for his size, becomes a baseball player to contend with—in part because of his anger against the guard in the tower. When he's finally at home again and people call him "Jap," he hits a ball "against the blue sky and the puffy white clouds. . . . over the fence." For this powerful text Dom Lee created art inspired by the Ansel Adams photographs of Manzanar. Applying beeswax to paper, Lee scratched out the images and then added oil paint, providing a strong outline for his illustrations—some of them small vignettes and others panoramas that look like old sepia photographs. Because the story comes from the perspective of a small boy, *Baseball Saved Us* truly relates to children what happened after Executive order 9066 was issued. The book relies on the American passion for baseball, and many can identify with being the weakest member of a team. A powerful and important book, *Baseball Saved Us* has changed the way many children view history.

FROM THE MIXED-UP FILES OF MRS. BASIL E. FRANKWEILER

By E. L. Konigsburg

Today in 1872 the Metropolitan Museum of Art opened its doors for the first time. Founded by a group of businessmen and financiers, the Met was established to bring art and art education to Americans. Over the years, many families, school classes, and children have visited the magnificent collection. But it wasn't until 1967 that an author for children found a way to make this building and its contents really accessible to young readers.

Several elements came together in the mind of E. L. Konigsburg while she was constructing the plot for her ingenious second novel, *From the Mixed-up Files of Mrs. Basil E. Frankweiler*. In 1965, Konigsburg read a *New York Times* article about the Met's purchase of a statue, *The Lady with the Primroses*, possibly the work of Leonardo da Vinci. However, her "aha" moment occurred on a family picnic at Yellowstone National Park. In this gorgeous setting her children kept complaining—about the heat, the ants, the melting icing on the cupcakes. Where, Konigsburg asked herself, could these privileged children ever run away to if they wanted to escape home? Nothing less grand than the Met would be good enough for them! So Konigsburg began her novel, basing the protagonists on her son and daughter—and she tested out what she was writing on them for good measure.

In *From the Mixed-up Files of Mrs. Basil E. Frankweiler*, Claudia Kincaid, bored with suburban life, decides to run away. Bringing her younger brother, Jamie, along with her because he has enough funds to finance the expedition, Claudia picks the Met as their destination. Much better than a desert island, the Met has sumptuous antique canopy beds to sleep in and fountains where they can take baths. During the story the children meet the eccentric Mrs. Basil E. Frankweiler and even discover the secret of a new acquisition of the museum.

In 1968 Konigsburg's first novel, *Jennifer, Hecate, Macbeth, William McKinley, and Me, Elizabeth* won a Newbery Honor and *From the Mixed-up Files* won the Newbery Medal. Talk about a good year for a rookie author! However, our birthday celebrant, the Met, remained dubious about the book for some years. No doubt staff members worried that it would send scores of children hunting for a camping spot. Eventually, the children's responses to the story won the Met over—and they published a guide to the rooms mentioned in the book.

Over forty years after publication, this story still captivates young readers. For many of us, when we look at those canopy beds in the Met or other museums, we can't help but wonder what it would be like to sleep on them, for at least one night. Probably they would be lumpy—but not in our dreams.

FEBRUARY 20

Happy Birthday William MacKellar (*The Silent Bells*), Rosemary Harris (*The Moon in the Cloud*), and Mary Christian Blount (*If Not For The Calico Cat*).

Best birthday wishes to the United States Postal Service, created by the Postal Service Act signed by President George Washington in 1792. Read *Millie Waits for the Mail* by Alexander Steffensmeier and *Mailing May* by Michael O. Tunnell, illustrated by Ted Rand.

In 1962 Mercury astronaut **John Glenn** became the first American to orbit the Earth.

Another example of a special day for something that should really be celebrated every single day—it's Love Your Pet Day.

FEBRUARY 21

Happy Birthday Virginia Driving Hawk Sneve (*The Trickster and the Troll*), Patricia Hermes (*Emma Dilemma and the Soccer Nanny*), and Ruthanne Lum McCunn (*Moon Pearl, Pie-Biter*).

It's the birth date of poet W. H. Auden (1907–1973).

In 1878 the first telephone book was issued in New Haven, Connecticut.

Happy Birthday to *The New Yorker*. The first issue was published on this day in 1925. Cartoons by Roz Chast appear frequently in this notable magazine. Read *The Alphabet from A to Y with Bonus Letter Z* by Steve Martin and Roz Chast and *Too Busy Marco* by Roz Chast.

LINCOLN: A PHOTOBIOGRAPHY
By Russell Freedman

On the third Monday of every February, we celebrate Presidents' Day. On this day I always feel sorry for George Washington. He is, after all, the father of the country, yet he has to share a birthday celebration with Abraham Lincoln. Of the two, Lincoln has received the best treatment in children's books. Of all the hundreds and thousands of books about Lincoln, Russell Freedman's *Lincoln: A Photobiography* remains the standard bearer not only for Lincoln biographies, but all biographies for ages ten through fourteen.

Born in San Francisco, Russell grew up in an ideal household for a future writer. His parents met in a bookstore, and his father worked for years as the West Coast sales representative for Macmillan. This meant that at Russell's house, John Steinbeck and Margaret Mitchell actually came to dinner. Their presence did not impress the young boy as much as it might have. He would have been happier if his favorite children's book authors, Howard Pease and Hendrik van Loon, had come to dinner.

Russell created thirty-three books, many of them about science, before he began work on a biography of Lincoln. At the urging of his editor, Ann Troy, he decided to tackle his boyhood hero as the subject for his next book. When he came upon a sentence describing Lincoln as "the most secretive—reticent—shut-mouthed man that ever lived," he realized this hero might be a bit more complicated than he had ever imagined.

Freedman describes his passionate portrayal of Lincoln this way: "My biography of Abraham Lincoln tells the story of an ambitious, self-educated man who goes from a log cabin to the White House, but at the same time it's also a story about slavery, racism, class privilege, and economic and political forces." Freedman deftly portrays Lincoln, his time, and his place. Since children need heroes and heroines, Lincoln emerges in this book as one they can emulate.

The first time I read this book, I was flying to Washington, D.C., to give a speech. When I came to the end, I was sobbing, and the attendant came to me and said, "Miss, is anything wrong?" "Oh yes," I blurted out, "Lincoln has been shot!" The book made me care so much about this figure that I could cry over his death, even though it had happened around 150 years ago.

When it won the Newbery Medal in 1988, something an information book had not done for thirty-two years, *Lincoln* brought Russell great acclaim and a chance to write other spectacular nonfiction books. He has always kept his sense of humor about his accomplishments. Russell's favorite letter came from a child who wrote, "Did you take the photographs yourself?"

HOOT

By Carl Hiaasen

On February 22, 1819, Secretary of State John Quincy Adams signed the Florida Purchase Treaty, making the Spanish territory part of the United States. In his Newbery Honor book *Hoot*, Carl Hiaasen brings a community in present-day Florida vividly to life.

Roy Eberhardt, new kid in town, has come from Montana to Coconut Grove, Florida. Since his father works for the Department of Justice and moves frequently for his job, Roy knows the routine—eating by himself, isolation, and bullies waiting to push him around. In fact, the book begins with the local bully, Dana Matherson, squashing Roy's face against the bus window. While Dana is holding his head against the glass, Roy sees a towheaded boy recklessly running barefoot through the Florida landscape. When Roy decides to find this boy, nicknamed Mullet Fingers because he can catch the fish with his bare hands, Roy discovers that a new pancake house is about to be built over the dens of some extremely cute and very tiny burrowing owls. To save these small members of the biological community, Mullet Fingers has been engaging in ecoterrorism.

Soon Roy and Mullet Finger's sister, Beatrice, get swept up in Mullet Finger's obsession. Rather than ecoterrorism, Roy decides to rely on the law and convinces his classmates to fight for the life of these owls and their babies. Readers turn the pages breathlessly to see if these three middle school children can successfully challenge the adult community and save some fellow travelers on this planet.

Not only does this engaging story explore the issues of endangered species and biological diversity, it also shows young people taking action. Filled with humor, quirky characters, and suspenseful scenes, the book gives some of the best advice about bullies in contemporary fiction—Roy solves that problem, too, in a very creative way. The book's a perfect choice for eight- to fourteen-year-olds, but fans of Hiaasen's adult mysteries usually find themselves enjoying it as well. A well-written story, with something to say, can appeal to people of many generations.

FEBRUARY 22

It's the birth date of Roma Gans (1894–1996), Let's-Read-and-Find-Out Science series; Harry Kullman (1919–1982), *The Battle Horse*; and Edward Gorey (1925–2000), *The Gashlycrumb Tinies, Old Possum's Book of Practical Cats*.

It's also the birth date of George Washington (1732–1799), the first president of the United States. Read *George Washington's Teeth* by Deborah Chandra and Madeleine Comora, illustrated by Brock Cole.

Senator **Edward M. Kennedy** (1932–2009) was born on this day. Read *My Senator and Me: A Dog's-Eye View of Washington, D.C.* by Edward Kennedy, illustrated by David Small. It's also Walking the Dog Day, though dogs should have the chance to go for a good walk every day!

Today on World Thinking Day, we think about people in different countries and celebrate international friendships. Read *Oh, the Things You Can Think!* by Dr. Seuss and *Half a World Away* by Libby Gleeson, illustrated by Freya Blackwood.

FEBRUARY 23

Happy Birthday C. S. Adler (*Ghost Brother*) and Walter Wick (*A Drop of Water*).

It's the birth date of Erich Kästner (1899–1974), *Emil and the Detectives*.

 W. E. B. DuBois (1868–1963), author of *The Souls of Black Folk*, was born on this day. Read *W. E. B. Du Bois* by Mark Stafford.

In 1927 the Federal Communication Commission begins to regulate radio frequencies. Read *Sounds in the Air: The Golden Age of Radio* by Norman H. Finkelstein.

On this day in 1896 Leo Hirshfeld put out the Tootsie Roll, which was named for his daughter, Clara "Tootsie" Hirshfeld.

THE STORY OF BABAR
By Jean de Brunhoff

Toward the end of February, Reading Is Fundamental, the largest children's literacy nonprofit in the United States, celebrates Read Me Week to highlight the importance and fun of reading. All week long, local businesses and organizations who have adopted schools in their area will send out volunteers to read. The week culminates on Read Me Day in Nashville, Tennessee—where local celebrities flock to Nashville schools. Many Nashville organizations, including the Junior League, get involved.

When I think of books and celebrities, the essays I published in *Everything I Need to Know I Learned from a Children's Book* instantly come to mind. I asked those who have achieved some status in various professions to provide a testimony about a children's book that had a profound influence on their lives. Leslie Moonves, the CEO of CBS, selected a book that has been the favorite of many: *The Travels of Babar*.

First written and published in France, the book began as a bedtime story. Celeste de Brunhoff originally created the adventures of Babar the Elephant for her children as they fell asleep. Her husband Jean turned them into *The Story of Babar* in 1933. In the saga Babar sees his mother killed by hunters and flees. When he arrives in Paris, he is befriended by a rich lady and becomes a Parisian dandy. First printed in oversized volumes, the books have been reissued from time to time in this same format. This is the ideal way to experience the stories—Babar the Elephant belongs on a large canvas.

For Leslie Moonves, the Babar books "provided noticeable life lessons. Babar the elephant is quite sensitive and quite exploratory. He is very interested in everything in the world. Babar goes to new places—Paris, the seashore, mountains—and travels in a balloon and on an ocean liner. I related to him because I wanted to be an adventurer; I was very curious. To this day I remain curious; it helps me every day that I am in my job and that I am on earth." I personally love the idea that a future CEO of one of the world's largest telecommunications companies would delight, as a child, in the image of an elephant sailing over the earth in a balloon.

Do what you can in your community for Read Me Week—no matter what book you might choose. Children's hopes, dreams, ambitions, and life quests come from books shared with them. Read Me Week reminds us that we all have reason to share books with the children in our community; in doing so, we all become part of their lives and their futures.

HONUS & ME

By Dan Gutman

On February 24, 1874, Honus Wagner was born in Pittsburgh, Pennsylvania. Called "The Flying Dutchman" because of his great speed and his German heritage, Wagner played shortstop for the Pittsburgh Pirates, won eight batting titles, and became one of the first five players inducted into the Baseball Hall of Fame. Because Wagner disliked smoking, when a tobacco company manufactured baseball cards with his picture on them, he demanded that the cards be recalled. Only about forty survived, making them one of the most valued collectors' items in the world. In February of 2007, a Honus Wagner baseball card sold for $2.35 million.

In *Honus & Me*, the first book of the Baseball Card Adventures series, Dan Gutman creates a portrait of Wagner, explains a lot of baseball history, and throws in a bit of fantasy. Young Joe Stoshack is an uninspired baseball player. But he has a gift. When Joe touches a baseball card, it takes him back to the time period of the person on the card. When he finds a valuable Honus Wagner 1909 baseball card in a neighbor's attic (who has asked him to throw everything away), he finds himself in a moral dilemma. Should he return it to his elderly neighbor, or use the money it would bring to help his cash-strapped family.

This dilemma gets pushed to the back of his mind when suddenly Honus Wagner is sitting in Joe's bedroom, and they travel back to 1909. Joe gets to watch the 1909 Tigers/Pirates World Series from a box seat, and he actually plays in the game to pitch hit for Wagner. In short, the book draws on several fantasies of almost every baseball devotee—seeing the great players in their times, actually getting to talk to them and play with them, and finding an invaluable baseball card.

Gutman has continued his winning fantasy/reality combination in a series of books—all of them absolutely perfect for eight- to twelve-year-old readers. He has become a hero for those hunting for well-written sports books for this crowd. So, Honus (rhymes with honest), happy birthday. I hope many baseball fans read *Honus & Me* today in his honor. It will truly make him, and the sport he loved, come alive.

FEBRUARY 24

Happy Birthday Uri Orlev (*Run, Boy, Run*) and Matthew Holm (*Babymouse* series).

It's the birth date of Wilhelm Grimm (1786–1859), *Grimm's Fairy Tales*; and Mary Ellen Chase (1887–1973), *Silas Crockett*.

Steve Jobs (1955–2011), Apple cofounder, was also born on this day. Read *Steve Jobs and Steve Wozniak: Geek Heroes Who Put the Personal in Computers* by Mike Venezia and *Oh No! (Or How My Science Project Destroyed the World)* by Mac Barnett, illustrated by Dan Santat.

On this day in 1940 Frances Langford recorded the song "When You Wish Upon a Star" from Disney's adaptation of *Pinocchio*. If you want to understand the real story of the modern puppet, pick up Carlo Collodi's *The Adventures of Pinocchio*.

FEBRUARY 25

Happy Birthday Cynthia Voigt (*Dicey's Song, A Solitary Blue*), True Kelley (*Claude Monet: Sunshine and Waterlilies*), Iain Lawrence (*The Giant-Slayer*), and Woodleigh Hubbard (*C Is for Curious*).

It's the birth date of Frank Bonham (1914–1988), *Durango Street*; and Anthony Burgess (1917–1993), *A Clockwork Orange*.

It's also the birth date of Pierre-Auguste Renoir (1841–1919), French painter and founder of the French Impressionist movement.

THE NOTORIOUS BENEDICT ARNOLD: A TRUE STORY OF ADVENTURE, HEROISM, & TREACHERY

By Steve Sheinkin

In February we celebrate American History Month. When I was a child, I was educated about American history through a series of books, with reddish-orange spines, that told stirring tales about our heroes and heroines. The series was Landmark Books, with titles such as Sterling North's *Abe Lincoln: Log Cabin to the White House*. I still remember how these books smelled and their exact place, two shelves down, in my school library. As an adult I have revisited these titles and found them a bit wanting in terms of accuracy—but these writers knew how to create scenes, drama, and characters. They made history exciting.

When I picked up Steve Sheinkin's *The Notorious Benedict Arnold: A True Story of Adventure, Heroism, & Treachery*, I was reminded of why the Landmark Books worked so well. But in this case, Sheinkin had done his research. He has a fine scholarly grasp, great sources, and effective footnotes. Sheinkin reveals Benedict Arnold as a man of action and adventure.

Now, I admit, I love the bad boys of history. Arnold is a personal favorite, and I have read scores of books about him. Both Jim Murphy and Jean Fritz have written great Arnold biographies for children, but *The Notorious Benedict Arnold* adds something new to what is available. Arnold was always restless when not in the height of action, and so is his biographer. Sheinkin begins his saga with the hanging of another bad boy—John André. He quickly moves through Arnold's early years and follows him out on the battlefield. Readers watch Arnold seize Fort Ticonderoga "in the name of the Great Jehovah and the Continental Congress." He hacks his way through the wilderness in an attempt to capture Quebec. He outsmarts the British fleet in the Battle of Valcour Island. In his greatest moment Arnold defies General Gates's orders and helps the Patriots win the Battle of Saratoga, the turning point in the American Revolution because it brought French aid for the Americans.

Although Sheinkin doesn't try to glamorize Arnold during these triumphs, neither does he demonize him. Readers can see Arnold as his contemporaries viewed him—a man of action, who gave money, his physical health, and everything he had for the American cause. Had Arnold decided to accept Washington's offer to lead half of the Continental army, he would be revered today and might well even have become president. Sheinkin does not dwell on the reasons why Arnold became a traitor, but he plays out in full measure the dramatic scene of Arnold's attempt to hand over West Point, with George Washington present, to the British.

If you have young readers ages ten to fourteen who love American history with military action and adventure, *The Notorious Benedict Arnold* will keep them enthralled from the striking jacket to the final lines. It reminds all of us that history can be exciting. That is what I learned from the Landmark Books—and once again from Steve Sheinkin.

THE WATSONS GO TO BIRMINGHAM—1963
By Christopher Paul Curtis

In February we celebrate Black History Month, and today I want to present one of the finest debut novels of the 1990s, *The Watsons Go to Birmingham—1963*. Although Christopher Paul Curtis has emerged as one of the most brilliant and beloved writers of his era, he went through the usual author struggles to find a publisher. I know at least two people who turned his first book down and lived to regret it.

Narrator Kenny, age ten in 1963 and the middle child, describes the family he dubs the "Weird Watsons" of Flint, Michigan. Wise-cracking, joking, teasing, and sometimes tormenting each other, they form a solid family unit. Kenny rejoices when his thirteen-year-old brother Byron gets in trouble—such as the time Byron kisses a frozen car mirror and his lips stick, making him the "Lipless Wonder." For 120 pages readers follow the antics of this creative group, from one funny scrape to another. Curtis has a pitch-perfect voice for dialogue and develops all his characters brilliantly, including little sister Joetta.

Then, because Mother and Father think that Bryon, who Kenny calls an "official juvenile delinquent," needs to learn some lessons, they set out for Mrs. Watson's family home, believing that Grandma Sands will straighten Byron out in no time. With a record player in the car—and "Yakety Yak, Don't Talk Back" coming from the speakers—the Watsons take a road trip to Grandma Sands's Alabama home.

Readers of this novel, ideal for ten- to fourteen-year-olds, become so used to the bantering and humor-filled story that the final forty pages stand as a shocking juxtaposition to what has come before. On September 15, 1963, Joetta heads out for Sunday school class—and into one of the most famous and tragic events of the civil rights movement. Her life is in grave danger when the church is bombed that day. In *The Watsons Go to Birmingham—1963* Christopher Paul Curtis takes one of the most horrible moments of American history and makes it immediate and accessible for young readers.

This novel works for independent reading, but over the last decade it has moved into the curriculum across the United States. *The Watsons Go to Birmingham—1963* is taught as early as fifth grade or as late as eighth. The tie-in to civil rights events is obvious, but the most compelling aspect of this book remains its portrait of a funny, loving family.

FEBRUARY 26

Happy Birthday Bernard Wolf (*Coming to America: A Muslim Family's Story*), Judith St. George (*So You Want to Be President*), Colby Rodowsky (*Not My Dog*), and Sharon Bell Mathis (*The Hundred Penny Box*).

It's the birth date of Miriam Young (1913–1974), *Miss Suzy*; and Victor Hugo (1802–1885), *The Hunchback of Notre-Dame*, *Les Misérables*.

Also born on this day was frontiersman William F. "Buffalo Bill" Cody (1846–1917). Read *Buffalo Bill and the Pony Express* by Eleanor Coerr, illustrated by Don Bolognese.

In 1848 Karl Marx and Frederich Engels published *The Communist Manifesto* in London.

Ground was broken for the Golden Gate Bridge in San Francisco on this day in 1933.

In 1993 a bomb rocked the World Trade Center in New York City. Five people were killed and hundreds suffered from smoke inhalation.

It's National Pistachio Day. Read *Probably Pistachio* by Stuart J. Murphy, illustrated by Marsha Winborn, and *The Pistachio Prescription* by Paula Danziger.

FEBRUARY 27

Happy Birthday Florence Parry Heide (*Princess Hyacinth*), Uri Shulevitz (*Snow*), and Mary Kay Kroeger (*Paperboy*).

It's the birth date of Laura Richards (1850–1943), *Captain January*; Edna Barth (1900–1981), *Shamrocks, Harps, and Shillelaghs*; Eric Sloane (1905–1985), *A Reverence for Wood*; and John Steinbeck (1902–1968), *The Grapes of Wrath, Of Mice and Men*.

 Also born on this day was the poet **Henry Wadsworth Longfellow** (1807–1882). Read *Paul Revere's Ride* by Longfellow, illustrated by Ted Rand, and *The Midnight Ride of Paul Revere*, illustrated by Christopher Bing.

It's No Brainer Day. Read *The Great Brain* by John D. Fitzgerald.

A NATION'S HOPE: THE STORY OF BOXING LEGEND JOE LOUIS

By Matt de la Peña
Illustrated by Kadir Nelson

In February we celebrate Black History Month; one of the finest picture books to use was published in 2011. *A Nation's Hope: The Story of Boxing Legend Joe Louis* fits for both holidays and combines the talents of Matt de la Peña and Kadir Nelson.

Although Matt de la Peña has concentrated on books for young adults, this text shows his dexterity at writing for a younger audience. He begins the saga: "Yankee Stadium. 1938. / Packed crowds buzzing and bets / banter back and forth / The Bronx night air thick with summer." Here on June 2, at 8:15 p.m., soft-spoken African-American Joe Lewis will take on Max Schmeling, the German boxer considered an example of Hitler's master race.

Joe Lewis did not always look like a hero; as a boy, son of a sharecropper, Joe didn't speak until he was six. With few opportunities open to him, he trained to be a boxer—learning to let his fists speak for him. As he progressed in his career, Joe Lewis became the pride of Harlem. At a time when all of America needed a hero, Joe stepped forth to battle the German fighter in this historic Yankee Stadium match.

Matt de la Peña, who has distinguished himself with sports books like *Ball Don't Lie* and *Mexican WhiteBoy*, brings boxing—with its jabs and stabs—to life in this text. He sets the stage for the match and allows readers to experience the excitement that viewers felt. Kadir Nelson, certainly one of the finest artists working today, expands the story—providing strong and memorable portraits, scenes of action, and athletic bodies put to the test. As he did in *We Are the Ship*, Nelson paints dignified people who engage in sports, capturing their prowess and their finesse. He makes Joe Lewis so engaging that readers are on their feet, cheering with the crowd at the end of the book.

I can think of no other book for children that presents boxing, and a boxer, so vibrantly. *A Nation's Hope* is one of the best sports biographies for young readers in existence. It combines superb writing and brilliant art to bring readers a moment of sports history. And it celebrates the more serious underpinnings of this boxing match—when black and white citizens put aside prejudice and came together as Americans.

APRIL AND ESME: TOOTH FAIRIES

By Bob Graham

On February 28, Tooth Fairy Day commemorates our love and affection for the kindly tooth fairy and her generosity to children. Many retain wonderful childhood memories of placing a tooth under the pillow and finding some coins in the morning.

But does the tooth fairy visit everyone—all over the globe? In *Throw Your Tooth on the Roof: Tooth Traditions from Around the World*, author Selby B. Beeler explores the way different areas of the world celebrate when a child loses a tooth. It would appear that the tooth fairy has a fairly limited geographic range—Australia, Canada, Britain, and the U.S. In Mexico and Guatemala, El Raton, the magic mouse, aids children who lose teeth. Children in El Salvador receive a visit from a rabbit. In Botswana children throw their teeth on the roof. In Mali it goes in the chicken coop, with hopes for a big, fat hen. Divided by areas of the world and moving around the globe, *Throw Your Tooth on the Roof* presents small vignettes for sixty-five different locations; for each of them G. Brian Karas has fashioned a funny, realistic drawing.

In *April and Esme: Tooth Fairies*, published in 2010, Australian comic genius Bob Graham explores the trials and tribulations of would-be tooth fairies. After all, how do they know what to do? April is only seven, but she convinces her parents that she and her younger sister Esme can make their first attempt to rescue a tooth. In this modern family, although April is a "spirit of the air . . . magic," her mother asks her to text if she gets in trouble. The young tooth fairies find the location, follow a line of toys to the bedroom, and remove their first tooth. At the end Mom and Dad hug them "til their wings cracked." *April and Esme: Tooth Fairies* shows a functional family and also demonstrates the pride children feel in a job well done. As delightful as the story itself, the art contains just as many fabulous details—teeth hanging from the ceiling or a fairy taking a bath in a teacup. A perfect combination of pictures and text, this storybook not only delights young readers, it frequently brings requests for just one more reading.

Happy Tooth Fairy Day! I hope you keep all of your teeth today—but if you know children who have just lost one, *April and Esme* will go a long way toward reassuring them and making them feel that something magical could happen tonight.

FEBRUARY 28

Happy Birthday Donna Jo Napoli (*The King of Mulberry Street, Albert*), Megan McDonald (Judy Moody series), and Daniel Handler, pen name Lemony Snicket, (*A Series of Unfortunate Events*).

It's the birth date of illustrator **Sir John Tenniel** (1820–1914), *Alice in Wonderland*; and author Dee Brown (1908–2002), *Bury My Heart at Wounded Knee*.

In 1977 the first killer whale was born in captivity. Read *Killer Whales* by Sandra Markle and *Keiko's Story: A Killer Whale Goes Home* by Linda Moore Kurth.

It's Floral Design Day. Read *Alison's Zinnia* by Anita Lobel and *Planting a Rainbow* by Lois Ehlert.

PICTURE BOOK, FANTASY, Preschool, Elementary School

FEBRUARY 29

It's the birth date of English poet John Byrom (1692–1763) and Dee Brown (1908–2002), *Bury My Heart at Wounded Knee*.

In 45 BC the first Leap Day was recognized by proclamation of Julius Caesar. Under the old Roman calendar, the last day of February was the last day of the year.

In 1916 South Carolina raised the minimum working age from twelve to fourteen for factory, mill, and mine workers. Read *Lyddie* by Katherine Paterson.

In 1972 Hank Aaron became the first baseball player to sign a contract for the amazing sum of $200,000 a year. Read *Hank Aaron's Dream* by Matt Tavares.

In 1988 South African archbishop Desmond Tutu was arrested during a five-day antiapartheid demonstration in Cape Town. Read *God's Dream* by Desmond Tutu and Douglas Carlton Abrams, illustrated by LeUyen Pham.

WITCHES!: THE ABSOLUTELY TRUE TALE OF DISASTER IN SALEM

By Rosalyn Schanzer

The end of February can be brutal in New England. Certainly more than one inhabitant of the region has felt that powers of darkness have seized the barren land. And during the end of February 1692, the Reverend Samuel Parris and other ministers in Salem, Massachusetts, grilled two children, nine-year-old Betty Parris and her eleven-year-old cousin Abigail Williams, about the presence of truly malevolent spirits in the community. Consequently, on February 29, 1692, two Salem town magistrates filed an official complaint against three women accused of witchcraft and set in motion the infamous Salem Witch Trials.

The claiming of innocent lives because of mass hysteria, the miscarriage of justice, and the fact that children and teenagers played key roles in the incident have all made the Salem Witchcraft Trials one of the most popular subjects in children's books over the years. In Sibert Honor Award–winner *Witches! The Absolutely True Tale of Disaster in Salem*, author and illustrator Rosalyn Schanzer adds something new to the discussion.

The book opens with cameo portraits of those accused of witchcraft and the people responsible for persecuting them. She provides background for the story, showing how early New England settlers, the Puritans, believed in witches, witchcraft, and the devil. Then she plays out the events of the story—the accusations, the trials, the deaths of innocent people—in a dramatic way. While doing so, she gives background on the law and courts and the changing nature of allowable evidence under Massachusetts law.

One of the most poignant parts of the book actually comes at the end in sketches about what happened to people after the trial. In 1706, at the age of twenty-nine, Ann Putnam, one of the chief accusers, read the following statement: in her childhood she had been "an instrument for accusing severall persons of a grievous crime, whereby their lives were taken away. I now have good reason to believe they were innocent, and justly fear I have been instrumental with others, though unwittingly, to bring upon myself the guilt of innocent blood."

The book makes a perfect introduction to the Salem Witch Trials for third through fifth graders. Although it focuses on history, it can be used to introduce topics of slander, name calling, and bullying—for such were the weapons of the children of Salem Village. In a small, compact book Schanzer creates an exciting narrative and explores some of the reasons why things spun out of control in Salem Village so many years ago.

BABE: THE GALLANT PIG

By Dick King-Smith

Today marks National Pig Day. There are hundreds, if not thousands, of pig books for me to choose from. Intelligent and humorous, pigs make a naturally intriguing subject for children. I first read the book of the day in 1984, and I have never fallen so hard or so fast for a new title for ages six to ten as I did for *Babe: The Gallant Pig* by Dick King-Smith.

Admittedly, the plot contains a lot of screwball logic. As editor of *The Horn Book*, I first heard the bare bones of the story from a wildly enthusiastic reviewer, and I thought she might have lost her mind—the story sounds so bizarre. Babe, an orphan pig, is adopted by Farmer Hogget and his sheepdog Fly. With intelligence, courage, and determination, Babe trains to become a sheep-herding pig and manages, mainly because he remains extremely polite to the sheep, to win the Grand Challenge Sheep-Dog Trials.

Long before this book was made into a movie, Dick King-Smith's saga began, like *Charlotte's Web*, as a way to save the life of a pig. King-Smith, who had held a variety of occupations—including soldier, farmer, and teacher—happened to be manning a "Guess the Weight of the Pig" stall in an English village summer fair. Realizing that the winner of the animal would probably kill it, he began to think of happier alternatives. What if the pig could go live on a farm instead—maybe even be taken care of by a mother sheepdog. What if the pig was behaviorally imprinted from the dog? Could the dog's young charge become a sheep pig?

To write this saga King-Smith drew on his experiences as a farmer and his raising of a six-hundred-pound porker called Monty. Although an animal fantasy, the book is grounded in animal behavior. Readers learn a lot about sheepdog training and herding competitions as well.

Great writing and imagination have made *Babe: The Gallant Pig* a read-aloud favorite for classrooms and families. Everyone enjoys hearing about Babe and his antics.

MARCH 1

Happy Birthday John Lonzo Anderson (*The Halloween Party*), Ruth Belov Gross (*If You Grew Up With George Washington*), and Barbara Helen Berger (*Grandfather Twilight*).

It's the birth date of Ralph Ellison (1913–1994), *Invisible Man*.

Best birthday wishes to fictional character Ron Weasley from the Harry Potter series.

In 1692 three young women accused of witchcraft were brought before local magistrates in colonial Massachusetts's Salem Village. The ensuing interrogation of Sarah Good, Sarah Osborne, and Tituba is considered the start of the Salem Witch Trials. Read *Tituba of Salem Village* by Ann Petry, and *Tituba* by William Miller, illustrated by Leonard Jenkins.

Happy Birthday to both Ohio and Nebraska. Ohio became the 17th U.S. state on this day in 1803, and Nebraska became the 37th state in 1867.

In 1780 Pennsylvania became the first U.S. state to abolish slavery.

MARCH 2

Happy Birthday Leo Dillon (*Why Mosquitoes Buzz in People's Ears*), Anne Isaacs (*Swamp Angel*), Marjorie Blain Parker (*A Paddling of Ducks*), P. J. Lynch (*The Christmas Miracle of Jonathan Toomey*), and Doug Keith (*The Bored Book*).

It's the birth date of Metta Victoria Fuller Victor (1831–1885), *The Bad Boy at Home and His Experiences in Trying to Become an Editor*; Helen Roney Sattler (1921–1992), *The Book of North American Owls*; Richard Cuffari (1925–1978), *The Perilous Gard*.

In 1807 the U.S. Congress prohibited importing slaves. It was many decades before the "peculiar institution" of slavery was abolished.

The film *King Kong* opened at Radio City Music Hall, New York City, in 1933.

In 1955 Claudette Colvin refused to give up her seat in Montgomery, Alabama, nine months before Rosa Parks's famous arrest for the same offense. Read *Claudette Colvin: Twice Toward Justice* by Phillip Hoose.

AND TO THINK THAT I SAW IT ON MULBERRY STREET

By Dr. Seuss

On March 2, 1904, Theodor Seuss Geisel was born in Springfield, Massachusetts. Seuss won a Pulitzer Prize for lifetime contribution, one of the few children's book creators ever so honored, and his books have sold over 200 million copies.

Like so many of our pivotal children's book creators, Seuss struggled to get his first book published. He had submitted *And to Think That I Saw It on Mulberry Street* to twenty-four to twenty-seven publishers—the number varied as he told the story over the years. During the 1930s, when picture books tended to carry serious messages, Dr. Seuss's lighthearted nonsense went against the tide. According to Seuss, he was walking down Madison Avenue, his last rejection in hand, on the way to his apartment to burn this manuscript. Then the fates intervened. Seuss ran into a Dartmouth classmate on the street and began telling his tale of woe. But the more Seuss talked, the broader the smile on his friend's face became. It turned out his friend had just been hired at Vanguard Press, a small publisher, and as a new children's book editor he needed something to publish. His friend knew nothing about children's books which is why he could simply enjoy Seuss's lighthearted nonsense. Seuss always said that if he had been walking down the other side of the street that day, he would have gone into the dry cleaning business!

Only the title of the book was changed (originally it was called *A Story That No One Can Beat*). In spirited rhyme Seuss tells the story of Marco, who sees a broken-down wagon, drawn by a horse, on Mulberry Street and imagines all kinds of wonderful creatures appearing in the town. When Seuss offered up this madcap nonsense to children, they fell in love with him.

Like so many of our child-friendly authors, Seuss received few adult-selected awards—but his sales and the devotion of readers more than compensated. In later years, he would write *The Cat in the Hat*, launch the Beginner Books series for Random House, and become a household name. In Bennett Cerf of Random House, he found a dedicated editor who once said, "I've published any number of great writers, from William Faulkner to John O'Hara, but there's only one genius on my author list. His name is Ted Geisel."

In honor of Seuss's birthday the National Education Association celebrates Read Across America Day. I personally always spend March 2 being grateful that Dr. Seuss didn't end up in the dry cleaning business.

THE BLUE LOTUS
By Hergé

On March 3, 1983, one of Belgium's most famous citizens, Hergé, died at the age of seventy-five. Over the years his adventure stories have been translated into more than thirty languages and have made the brave and resourceful snub-nosed reporter Tintin and his fox terrier Snowy popular with both adults and children around the world. In twenty-four books, told completely as comic strips, Tintin and Snowy travel to various exotic places, including America, where he takes on the Chicago mobster Al Capone.

Hergé, the pen name of Georges Remi, began creating material for the Catholic newspaper where he worked, *Le Vingtième Siècle*, and in 1929 Tintin and Snowy first appeared in their children's supplement. It printed *Tintin in the Land of the Soviets* a year later. The character of Tintin was partly inspired by Georges's brother Paul Remi, an officer in the Belgian army. After the Nazi occupation of Brussels, when the newspaper was shut down, Hergé produced a new Tintin strip in *Le Soir*. Because of paper shortages, Tintin was published daily in three or four frames. In this short format Hergé had to introduce more cliff-hangers and faster action. That meant the comic strips, when issued as books, kept readers enthralled with chases, narrow scrapes, and page-turning stories.

The Blue Lotus (1936) has always been considered the best of Hergé's offerings. The story had roots in current events and was a clear protest of Japanese expansion into China's mainland. Tintin had many other notable adventures as well, including landing with Snowy on the moon in *Explorers on the Moon*, printed fifteen years before the voyage of *Apollo 11*.

Although these books sold millions of copies worldwide, they did not find an American publisher until the 1970s. The comic book format was considered substandard literature in the United States at that time, and this perception, as well as some of the racial stereotypes in the books themselves, made children's book editors wary. But poet Peter Davidson, then director of the Atlantic Monthly Press, loved the books and decided to take a chance on them.

Intelligent, kindhearted, and fearless, Tintin has beguiled young readers around the world. Even the charismatic French President Charles de Gaulle once remarked, "my only international rival is Tintin."

MARCH 3

Happy Birthday Erik Blegvad (*The Tenth Good Thing about Barney*), Patricia MacLachlan (*Sarah, Plain and Tall*), Suse MacDonald (*Alphabatics*), and Margaret Miller (*Baby Faces*).

It's the birth date of Edward Radlauer (1921–2006), *Dinosaur Mania*; William Kurelek (1927–1977), *A Prairie Boy's Winter*; and Libba Moore Gray (1937–1995), *Miss Tizzy*.

It's also the birth date of George Pullman (1831–1897), inventor of luxury Pullman sleeping car for railroads. Read *The Pullman Strike and the Labor Union in American History* by R. Conrad Stein. And it's the birth date of Alexander Graham Bell (1847–1922), inventor of the first telephone as well as other devices.

Happy Birthday Florida, which became the 27th U.S. state on this day in 1845.

Congress established the U.S. Mint on this day in 1791.

In 1931 the United States officially adopted "The Star-Spangled Banner" as the national anthem. Hence, it's National Anthem Day. Read *The Star-Spangled Banner* by Francis Scott Key.

MARCH

Happy Birthday Miriam Bourne (*Dog Walk*), Helen Frost (*Keesha's House*), Peggy Rathmann (*Officer Buckle and Gloria*), David A. Carter (*Love Bug*), and Dav Pilkey (Captain Underpants series).

It's the birth date of Johann David Wyss (1743–1818), *Swiss Family Robinson*; and Meindert DeJong (1906–1991), *The Wheel on the School*.

 In 1791 **John Adams** was sworn in as the second president of the United States, succeeding George Washington.

Happy Birthday Chicago, incorporated as a city in 1837.

In 1877 Tchaikovsky's ballet *Swan Lake* premiered at the Bolshoi Theater in Moscow. Read *Swan Lake* adapted and illustrated by Rachel Isadora, and *Swan Lake* retold and illustrated by Lisbeth Zwerger.

Happy Birthday Vermont, which became the 14th U.S. state on this day in 1791.

OUT OF THE DUST
By Karen Hesse

On March 4, 1791, Vermont became the fourteenth state admitted to the Union. Certainly at the time, the event did not seemed connected to the children's book community. But by the beginning of the twenty-first century, Vermont had emerged as one of the best environments for those who create books for children and young adults. Part of this seems due to the incredible work going on at Vermont College's MFA program for children's book writers in Montpelier. Life in this still largely rural area encourages time for reflection. A very active library and bookstore community supports Vermont writers and illustrators. The second National Ambassador for Young People's Literature, Katherine Paterson, lives in Vermont, as does Caldecott winner Mary Azarian. The list goes on and on and includes our author of the day, Newbery Medal winner Karen Hesse.

When Karen took a road trip from Vermont to Colorado with author Liza Ketchum (a part-time Vermonter), Karen fell in love with the Kansas plains, a landscape very different from the one she looked at every day. Later she thought about this place when writing the picture book *Come On, Rain!*, about a child longing for rain showers. As she asked herself why a child might want a rain shower, she thought about the Oklahoma Dust Bowl in the 1930s and set her next novel there. The book for eleven- to sixteen-year-olds, *Out of the Dust*, explores the life of fourteen-year-old Billie Jo. Crops blow away like tumbleweeds, tractors get buried under dust drifts, and Billie Jo's mother dies in a tragic accident that physically scars the young girl. In this grief-filled landscape she and her father must make the best of what they have left.

In *Out of the Dust* Karen explores the longing, anguish, and pain of living and shows how people heal from tragedy. Written in free-form poetic verse, Karen polished every word, phrase, and line break with care from the opening sentence to the final one: "And I stretch my fingers over the keys, / and I play."

After Karen wrote the first draft of the manuscript, she went out to find photographs of what her characters might look like, placing them around her studio. But she never admitted to this writing method, because it might seem "hokey." So Karen was amazed when her editor Brenda Bowen chose the photo of Lucille Burroughs by Walker Evans for the cover; it was the same photo that Karen herself had used while writing the book—although she had never told her editor.

Happy Vermont Statehood Day to Karen and all those in the children's and young adult book community in Vermont. So many great books for children have been created there.

HISTORICAL FICTION, POETIC NOVEL, Middle School, High School

STONE FOX

By John Reynolds Gardiner

Around this time of year the Iditarod, "the last great race on earth," begins in Anchorage, Alaska. Dog teams and humans travel 1,150 miles through Alaskan wilderness to Nome. Some families and classes like to encourage children to pick a team and follow it throughout the month, writing about its journey. And for a story to introduce dog racing, no better book exists than John Reynolds Gardiner's *Stone Fox*.

Willy, an engaging young boy, lives with his grandfather on a farm in Alaska. The old man has been declining in health, refusing to leave his bed. He owes $500 in back taxes and soon will lose his home. Willy wants to save both his grandfather and the farm, so he enters his dog Searchlight in the National Dogsled Race, which offers $500 in prize money. Because the race goes past his house, he and Searchlight have the advantage of running on home territory, but they will be pitted against the legendary Native American racer Stone Fox. The details of the tense race keep readers enthralled, all the way to its surprising end.

Of all the writers I have researched over the years, John Reynolds Gardiner seems the least likely to have produced such a powerful and memorable book. As a boy he was very rebellious. Since his parents thought he should learn to read, he refused. He didn't read his first novel until he turned nineteen and struggled with grammar and spelling throughout his life. In college he found that English as a Second Language (ESL) students could write better than he could. After taking up engineering as a career, Gardiner worked for McDonnell Douglas and even holds a patent for a plastic necktie filled with water and guppies.

Still, it is a long way from clever toys to classic literature. Encouraged by his brother, Gardiner took a television writing class from Martin Tahse, a creator of After School Specials. When Harper & Row editor Barbara Fenton wrote to Tahse, asking him if he had a book he might want to write, he sent her instead to Gardiner, who was working on a story based on a Rocky Mountain legend. Fenton took a chance on this unknown writer, teaching him the craft of writing along the way. The book took several years to develop but always seemed worth the time to her. In the end she got a manuscript that combined elements of adventure, sports, Westerns, and dog stories.

If you know any second through fourth-grade reading rebels, *Stone Fox* read either aloud or silently just might convince them that a great story can be found in the pages of a book. It was created by someone like them.

MARCH 5

Happy Birthday Mem Fox (*Time for Bed*) and Gary Hogg (*Scrambled Eggs and Spider Legs*).

It's the birth date of Howard Pyle (1853–1911), *Otto of the Silver Hand*; and Errol Le Cain (1941–1989), *The Twelve Dancing Princesses*.

In 1770 a riot known as the Boston Massacre, one of the key events that turned British colonists against King George III, took place in what would become the capital of Massachusetts. Read *For Liberty: The Story of the Boston Massacre* by Timothy Decker.

Winston Churchill used the phrase "Iron Curtain" in a speech on this day in 1946. Read *The Wall: Growing Up Behind the Iron Curtain* by Peter Sís.

MARCH 6

Happy Birthday Ellen Schecter (*The Warrior Maiden*), Thacher Hurd (*Art Dog*), Kathleen Hague (*Alphabears*), and Christopher Raschka (*Yo! Yes?*).

It's the birth date of Will Eisner (1917–2005), *Will Eisner's Shop Talk*.

The artist Michelangelo (1475–1564) was also born on this day. Read *Michelangelo* by Diane Stanley.

In 1836 after fighting for thirteen days, the Alamo fell.

On this day in 1857 the Supreme Court's Dred Scott decision held that blacks cannot be citizens.

DOCTOR DE SOTO
By William Steig

Today we celebrate National Dentist Day. Suggestions for the day include delivering a thank-you note to your dentist—although I would recommend giving them the book of the day instead. For me, the greatest book ever written about a dentist is also one of the best picture books of the twentieth century: *Doctor De Soto* by William Steig.

In the stock market crash of 1929 Steig's father lost everything, and as a young man Steig had to work to support his family. He could draw with great finesse and believed if he became a commercial artist he would have the best chance of putting food on the table. He sold his first cartoon to *The New Yorker* in 1930 and became their longest running contributor until his death in 2003, crafting scores of covers and more than seventeen hundred drawings.

Steig was a late bloomer when it came to children's books and didn't start publishing them until he was sixty. A fellow *New Yorker* artist, Robert Kraus, founded his own small publishing house, Windmill Books, and began enticing his friends to be authors and artists. With Windmill, Steig published *Sylvester and the Magic Pebble*, which won the Caldecott Medal in 1970. And with that he launched his next career, one that continued for thirty-five years.

In *Doctor. De Soto*, William Steig imagines what would happen if a mouse dentist suddenly had to deal with a fox as a patient. White-smocked and of good cheer, Doctor De Soto treats his larger patients, such as cows and donkeys, by climbing onto a ladder and using a hoist to get into their mouths. No one is more dedicated than the good doctor, although he does refuse cat patients, for obvious reasons. When a fox with a rotten bicuspid shows up, Doctor De Soto uses all his own cunning—and a little modern science—to ensure his own safety. Readers watch with glee as the protagonist and his wife outwit a wily fox.

Steig's work always looks fresh and vibrant, but that spontaneity actually took a great deal of work to achieve. Using Picasso as his model, Steig worked from a loose pen line and began his drawings with a face or an expression. If readers look closely at Steig drawings, they see the drooping mouths, raised chins, or narrowed eyes that reveal what the characters are thinking and feeling. Steig's language matches his artwork to perfection. He always chose the right phrase. The text of *Doctor De Soto*, in fact, won a rare honor for a picture book, a Newbery Honor Award.

I am very grateful for dentists on this day that honors them. But I would go to my own much more enthusiastically if I thought I'd find Doctor De Soto there to greet me.

SPOON

By Amy Krouse Rosenthal
Illustrated by Scott Magoon

Today marks National Cereal Day, so raise a glass of milk or a cup of coffee to your favorite brand. Americans are, as group, addicted to cereal. Our book of the day, *Spoon* by Amy Krouse Rosenthal, features a page with cereal—but its focus rests on the utensil that makes cereal eating possible.

Inanimate objects sometimes make great protagonists for children's books—Mary Anne the steam shovel in *Mike Mulligan* and Little Toot the tugboat, to name a couple stellar examples. It is difficult to pull off a book about nonhuman or nonanimal protagonists successfully. Readers don't naturally identify with a spoon—unless the author and illustrator are very clever.

We first meet Spoon and Spoon's family (who have been patterned after real collectible spoons—wooden, slotted, salt, and souvenir) via a fabulous double-page spread of all kinds of expressive and varied objects. Then the author sets out the dilemma. Although it would seem that the little spoon has a perfect life, he is feeling blue. Jealousy has set in—it seems to him that Fork, Knife, and Chopsticks have a better deal. Chopsticks in particular seem "really cool and exotic." At night Mom gives the needed perspective when tucking the small utensil into bed. His friends never get to dive headfirst into ice cream or clink against a cereal bowl. Later that night, when Spoon can't sleep, he tucks himself into bed with the parents, as they nestle like spoons.

Krouse Rosenthal's text, both spare and sweet, provides just the right amount of room for Scott Magoon to work his illustration magic. From endpapers showing Knife, Fork, Spoon, and Chopsticks to the final page of Spoon dreaming about all the things he can eat, every page has been given character, action, and emotional touches. Long before the end of the book, readers have done something extraordinary—they have grown to love a spoon. An art director in his day job, Magoon is a master at dividing text, keeping the pacing just right, alternating layouts, and moving readers to the next page. Ideal for even the youngest reader, *Spoon* has been used successfully for children nine months through five years.

I know when I pick up my spoon today to celebrate National Cereal Day, I'm going to check and see if it has expressive eyes and mouth. I just wish this spoon family lived in my silverware box. At least they are alive in a very beguiling and satisfying picture book.

MARCH 7

Happy Birthday Joanne Rocklin (*This Book is Haunted*) and Jane Dyer (*Sugar Cookies*).

It's the birth date of Margaret Goff Clark (1913–2003), *Freedom Crossing*.

In 1876 Alexander Graham Bell is granted a patent for the telephone. Read *Telephone* by Kornei Chukovsky, illustrated by Vladimir Radunsky.

Who knew? It's National Crown Roast of Pork Day. Read *The Silver Crown* by Robert C. O'Brien, *Love and Roast Chicken* by Barbara Knutson, and *A Perfect Pork Stew* by Paul Brett Johnson.

MARCH 8

Happy Birthday Edna Miller (Mousekin series), Lore Segal (*The Story of Mrs. Lovewright and Purrless Her Cat*), Peter Roop (*If You Lived with the Cherokees*), Robert Sabuda (*The Night Before Christmas*), and Jackie French Koller (*Nothing to Fear*).

It's the birth date of Kenneth Grahame (1859–1932), *The Wind in the Willows*.

In 1775 Thomas Paine published "African Slavery in America" calling for emancipation of slaves and abolition of slavery.

The New York Stock Exchange founded in 1817. Read *Six Days in October* by Karen Blumenthal.

INDEPENDENT DAMES

By Laurie Halse Anderson
Illustrated by Matt Faulkner

March 8 marks International Women's Day. Fortunately, in the last two decades we have been given scores of books that promote the role of women in history. For some great suggestions you can consult the Amelia Bloomer list compiled by the American Library Association.

Today I'd like to focus on one of the exceptional books in this area, Laurie Halse Anderson's *Independent Dames*. Anderson is one of those writers who may have already created several classic books. Her young adult novel *Speak* has a devoted audience. Her historical fiction for ten- to fourteen-year-olds, *Fever 1793* and *Chains*, has been brought into the curriculum across the country. And her picture book for six- to ten-year-olds, *Independent Dames*, published in 2008 and illustrated by Matt Faulkner, presents a stirring portrait of the women who made America possible.

Beginning with the scene of a school play about the Founding Fathers, Anderson declares that if we look only at them we are missing half of the story. Then she continues with small vignettes of some of our heroines. Sybil Ludington rode longer than Paul Revere and didn't get caught. The Daughters of Liberty make an appearance, along with nine-year-old Susan Boudinot who protested at a tea party of the Royal Governor. Writers (Phyllis Wheatley), soldiers (Deborah Sampson), spies, scouts, nurses, and the wives of the patriots all get their due via a small fact and portrait.

Having written myself about the women soldiers of the Civil War (*I'll Pass for Your Comrade*), I can't help but appreciate how brilliantly Anderson has overcome one of the great problems of women's history. In many cases, we know very little about each person because comprehensive records were not kept about women. Because Anderson uses only one or two arresting facts for each woman, she keeps the text lively and encourages young readers to find out more.

At the bottom of each picture Anderson includes a timeline of events and defines some of the terms, making the book even more information rich. At the end, she adds material on other women and a great bibliography. This short text lends itself to all kinds of activities or can be used as a supplement for more traditional texts. Anderson's research is thorough and her understanding of young readers, as always, is profound. When I conducted an informal poll of teachers, *Independent Dames* emerged as their favorite book for Women's History Month. Writing with passion and humor, Laurie Halse Anderson is on a mission to set the record straight. And she does.

INKHEART
By Cornelia Funke

Today marks a new celebration, World Read Aloud Day. I'd like to commemorate it by talking about my favorite recent read aloud, written by Germany's bestselling author for children, Cornelia Funke. Cornelia was brought to the attention of publisher Barry Cunningham by a devoted fan. The girl wrote to Cunningham, who had discovered J. K. Rowling, and told him that although he published the Harry Potter books, he did not publish the best writer in the world—Cornelia Funke. This letter piqued his interest, and after he read a translation of a couple of chapters of *The Thief Lord*, Cunningham was convinced that Cornelia deserved a chance to beguile English-speaking children. When *The Thief Lord* appeared, it became a *New York Times* bestseller.

Funke both wrote and translated her next book to appear in English, *Inkheart*, our book of the day. By working on her own translation, she was able to get the right sound and timbre to her words, which is one of the reasons *Inkheart* reads aloud so well.

In this book-lover's story, twelve-year-old Meggie lives with her father Mo, a skilled book repairer. Her mother has been gone for nine years. One night a mysterious stranger called Dustfinger appears and in a rush Mo takes Meggie on a frantic flight only to be captured by the evil Capricorn and his henchmen. Eventually they end up as prisoners in his medieval Italian village.

Only then does Meggie begin to learn her true history. Mo can read aloud so brilliantly that he actually coaxes characters from books into the real world. Unfortunately, a real person from this world then goes into the book. So when Mo read Capricorn, Basta, Dustfinger, and other villains from *Inkheart*, Meggie's mother, Theresa, vanished into the book. Now they are causing terror in this world and it's up to Meggie to attempt to set things right for she has discovered that she has inherited this reading gift from her father. Although probably all lovers of literature harbor fantasies about meeting characters that they love in fiction, most of us would not like to encounter some of its villains face-to-face.

Funke sets scenes and creates atmosphere brilliantly. All the chapters are just the right length for reading aloud; they contain a lot of action, cliff-hangers, and beautiful language. The book is perfect for use with nine- through fourteen-year-olds, in class or at home. Reading it aloud, savoring the scenes and the details of the plot, actually makes it more enjoyable than reading it independently.

If you are hunting for a great book for World Read Aloud Day, pick up *Inkheart*. For those who become enthralled, it begins a trilogy continued in *Inkspell* and *Inkdeath*.

MARCH 9

Happy Birthday Ellen Levine (*Henry's Freedom Box*), Margot Apple (*Sheep in a Jeep*), A. LaFaye (*Worth*), Harry Bliss (*Louise, The Adventures of a Chicken*), Joan Lexau (*Crocodile and Hen: A Bakongo Folktale*), and Denise Brunkus (*Junie B. Jones* series).

It's the birth date of chess master Bobby Fischer (1943–2008). Read *Chess: From First Move to Checkmate* by Daniel King.

In 1796 French Emperor **Napoleon Bonaparte** married Josephine. Read *Napoleon: The Story of the Little Corporal* by Robert Burleigh.

In 1841 the United States Supreme Court ruled that the captive Africans who seized control of the ship carrying them had been taken into slavery illegally. Read *Amistad: The Story of a Slave Ship* by Patricia McKissak, illustrated by Sanna Stanley.

The Barbie doll was unveiled at a toy fair in New York City on this day in 1959. Read *The Good, the Bad, and the Barbie* by Tanya Lee Stone.

MARCH 10

Happy Birthday Ilene Cooper (*The Golden Rule*) and B. G. Hennessey (*Because of You*).

It's the birth date of Jack Kent (1920–1985), *There's No Such Thing as a Dragon*.

In 1804 a formal ceremony in St. Louis, Missouri, transferred ownership of the Louisiana Purchase land from France to the United States. Read *The Louisiana Purchase* by Peter and Connie Roop, illustrated by Sally Wern Comport.

In 1922 Mahatma Gandhi was arrested and tried for "sedition" by the British Raj in India, then sentenced to six years. He served only two. Read *Gandhi* by Demi.

On this day in 1876 **Alexander Graham Bell** made the first telephone call to Thomas Watson saying, "Watson, come here. I need you."

It's Middle Name Pride Day. Read *The Girl with 500 Middle Names* by Margaret Peterson Haddix, illustrated by Janet Hamlin.

DAVE THE POTTER: ARTIST, POET, SLAVE
By Laban Carrick Hill
Illustrated by Bryan Collier

March has been designated Arts and Crafts Month, and today I'll be looking at a book about a great but largely unknown American artist and craftsperson. History, as the saying goes, is written by the winners. The disenfranchised, those who struggled for recognition, left few clues for those who read the record of history. That is one of the reasons why Laban Carrick Hill's *Dave the Potter: Artist, Poet, Slave* is such an important book.

In his poetic text, Laban begins Dave's saga: "To us / it is just dirt, / the ground we walk on. / Scoop up a handful. / The gritty grains slip / between your fingers." This slave takes common clay and makes pots to store a season's grain. He also is a poet. He takes simple words and writes powerful poems that express his inner life. He throws his pots, sometimes sixty pounds of clay at a time, and pulls shape out of this material—like "a magician pulling a rabbit out of a hat." He rolls long ropes of clay, pounds in wood ash and sand, and, in the final spread, writes on his pot: "I wonder where / is all my relation / friendship to all— / and, every nation." With only a first name, because slaves were not allowed to have last ones, Dave (c. 1801–c. 1862) was literate at a time when slaves were not allowed to read or write. He comes down through history because some of his 40,000 pots have survived, along with his notations on them. In a final note, Laban explains the primary source materials that can be found about this slave who lived in Pottersville, South Carolina, in the 1800s. This note shows readers the material the author drew upon to re-create the life of this extraordinary artist.

For this lyrical text, Bryan Collier created watercolors, enhanced by collage, showing Dave at work. Although Collier had no pictures or photographs of Dave to work from, he portrayed a figure of great dignity and sympathy. Dave was one of the finest artists of this time period and he crafted objects that have lasted well beyond his lifetime. Collier brings him to life and shows him plying his craft. After seeing Dave at work and reading the simple but profound text, readers feel as if they know this man who was all but lost to the historical record—a true accomplishment on the part of both writer and artist. American history, black history, art—all come together in this tribute. When you want to celebrate Arts and Crafts Month, you can begin with no better book than *Dave the Potter*.

BLIZZARD!

By Jim Murphy

On March 11, 1888, a record blizzard hit the East Coast. Today most areas have snow-removal equipment and constant weather monitoring to lessen the impact of Mother Nature. But such was not always the case, as Jim Murphy relates in his compelling story about the 1888 snowstorm, *Blizzard!*

Drawing on primary sources, newspapers, and accounts written by survivors, Murphy begins the saga on March 10, 1888, a day warmer than normal on the East Coast. The Army Signal Corp, then the weather monitoring unit of the United States government, closed its offices at midnight, to observe the Sabbath. On Sunday, March 11, two air masses began to collide—one moving over the northern part of the country and one swinging up the East Coast from the south. They created one doozy of a snowstorm—almost fifty inches. In this era of snow removal by shovel, no underground transportation, and no underground electricity or wires, the massive storm wreaked a kind of damage unimaginable today.

Trains came to a halt and passengers had to try to walk to safety or die in the storm. Wires came down over the city of New York and electrocuted people. Even farmers heading from their houses to their barns died of hypothermia and exhaustion. Focusing the narrative on the struggles of those braving the elements, Jim Murphy walks readers through the dangers posed by massive snow. Some died trying to get to work the next Monday. Senator Conklin died of a heart attack brought on by battling the elements. Even to walk a few blocks in New York City put people in harm's way. Day laborers, mostly Italians, were solicited to clean the streets. But no municipal government was set up to handle a disaster of this magnitude. In *Blizzard!* readers not only see the elements, they taste and feel the fury of the snow. And they get to know the people affected by the storm.

In this book, ideal for third through seventh grades, Jim Murphy explores the snowstorm that changed America, giving us the United States Weather Bureau and city governments ready to respond to disaster. Many classes use the book in a snow unit this time of year. Otherwise it makes compelling reading in a warm house by a fire. No one describes disasters—fire, snowstorms, or the plague—to children better than Jim Murphy.

MARCH 11

Happy Birthday Jonathan London (Froggy series) and Peter Sís (*The Wall: Growing Up Behind the Iron Curtain*).

It's the birth date of Wanda Gág (1893–1946), *Millions of Cats*; and Ezra Jack Keats (1916–1983), *The Snowy Day*.

In 1824 the United States War Department created the Bureau of Indian Affairs. Read *The Absolutely True Diary of a Part-Time Indian* by Sherman Alexie, illustrated by Ellen Forney.

It's Johnny Appleseed Day. Read *Johnny Appleseed* by Steven Kellogg and *Johnny Appleseed* by Reeve Lindbergh, illustrated by Kathy Jakobsen Hallquist.

MARCH 12

Happy Birthday Arlene Alda (*Did You Say Pears?*), Daniel Cohen (*Real Ghosts*), Naomi Shihab Nye (*19 Varieties of Gazelle: Poems of the Middle East*), Carl Hiaasen (*Hoot*), and Diane Gonzales Bertrand (*The Party for Papá Luis*).

It's the birth date of Virginia Hamilton (1936–2002), *M. C. Higgins, the Great*.

In 1894 Coca-Cola was sold in bottles for the first time in Vicksburg, Mississippi. Read *My Vicksburg* by Ann Rinaldi and *The Drummer Boy of Vicksburg* by G. Clifton Wisler.

Moscow became the new capital of Russia in 1918. Prior to that St. Petersburg was the capital city for 215 years. Read *Eloise in Moscow* by Kay Thompson, illustrated by Hilary Knight, and *Max Moves to Moscow* by Winifred Riser.

Happy Birthday to the Girl Scouts, first named Girl Guides in 1912. Read *Here Come the Girl Scouts!* by Shana Corey, illustrated by Hadley Hooper.

The U.S. Post Office was established on this day in 1789.

A WRINKLE IN TIME
By Madeleine L'Engle

On March 12, 1963, the *New York Times* wrote "A housewife and an artist today won the nation's top awards for the most distinguished children's book published in 1962." This statement doesn't even hint at the truth—that the most courageous committee in the history of the Newbery and Caldecott Awards had just announced its results. In the 1960s a single committee chose both prestigious awards.

The housewife of the headlines, Madeleine L'Engle, married to television actor Hugh Franklin, had won the award for a book rejected by 26–40 publishers, the number changing depending on who is telling the story. She had, in fact, abandoned the idea of ever getting this saga into print. Many claim credit for finally putting the manuscript into the hands of John Farrar—but there is no question that he and editor Hal Vursell decided to take a chance on a book that had no precedent. Part fantasy and part science fiction, *A Wrinkle in Time* features a girl as the protagonist in an era when science fiction clearly belonged to male heroes. Traveling through time and space Meg Murry and her precocious little brother Charles Wallace—along with Mrs Whatsit, Mrs Who, and Mrs Which—try to save their father from a giant pulsing brain, the embodiment of evil.

Reviewers seemed a bit skeptical about this unusual story. However, Ruth Hill Viguers, the editor of *The Horn Book Magazine*, wrote that although the book "will no doubt have many critics, I found it fascinating. . . . It makes unusual demands on the imagination and consequently gives great rewards." A book with a very small first printing, probably 1,500 copies, *A Wrinkle in Time* did not get placed in the hands of many children until it won the Newbery Medal.

Along with Alice in Wonderland, Jo March of *Little Women*, and Anne of Green Gables, Meg has taken her place as one of the most loved and remembered female characters created in children's books. Madeleine L'Engle put a good deal of herself into Meg. "Of course I'm Meg," she once admitted. Her husband thought his wife understood Meg quite well but noted that Madeleine had "never explored outer space"—although he wouldn't put it past her. Now after several decades, the book still draws young readers in and keeps them awake at night to finish the story.

In 1963 the Newbery-Caldecott committee definitely picked an unusual and challenging novel, a story that would both stand the test of time and become one of our greatest classics. The 50th anniversary edition is worth owning, even if you already have a copy. It contains some of the background material for the book and gives readers a deeper appreciation of this magnificent work.

THE WESTING GAME

By Ellen Raskin

On March 13, 1928, Ellen Raskin was born in Milwaukee, Wisconsin. At first she pursued a career in fine arts, graduating from the University of Wisconsin. After she moved to New York, she began designing book jackets and created over one thousand of them.

Raskin was lured into the field of children's books to serve as an illustrator for other people's texts. However, her first solo venture, *Nothing Ever Happens on My Block*—filled with stylized drawings and her quirky, off-beat humor—received rave reviews and encouraged Raskin to do more. In this book a young boy fails to see all of the amazing events going on around him—an artistic reversal of Dr. Seuss's *And to Think That I Saw It on Mulberry Street*.

Having made one great shift in her career, Raskin decided to make another: writing novels. Raskin's ingenious books—*The Mysterious Disappearance of Leon (I Mean Noel)*, *Figgs and Phantoms*, and *The Tattooed Potato and Other Clues*—ideal for third through sixth grade, rely on zany characters, slapstick humor, and clever puzzles created from letters and words.

MARCH 13

Happy Birthday Diane Dillon (*Why Mosquitoes Buzz In People's Ears*), Thomas Rockwell (*How to Eat Fried Worms*), Gail Owens (Encyclopedia Brown series), Lisa Campbell Ernst (*Little Red Riding Hood: A Newfangled Prairie Tale*).

It's the birth date of Dorothy Keeley Aldis (1896–1966), *Hiding*; and Eleanor B. Heady (1917–1979), *Sage Smoke*.

On this day in 1639 Harvard College (now Harvard University) was named after clergyman John Harvard. Read *Of Beetles and Angels: A Boy's Remarkable Journey from a Refugee Camp to Harvard* by Mawi Asgedom and *Judy Moody Goes to College* by Megan McDonald, illustrated by Peter Reynolds.

In 1976, the bicentennial year, Raskin began drafting a novel with a historical background, a mystery, and the death of a millionaire, originally called *Eight Imperfect Pairs of Heirs*. In *The Westing Game* an eccentric millionaire draws up a will that sends his heirs on a search for his murderer. This simple idea grows amazingly complex in Raskin's hands—aliases, disguises, word games, and trickery create a book much more fun than it seems at the beginning. Although Raskin admitted she had always hoped to win a Caldecott Medal, *The Westing Game* received both the Boston Globe–Horn Book Award and the Newbery Medal. In her acceptance speech she talked about her detailed approach to her books: "I write and design my books to look accessible to the young reader. . . . There will be no endless seas of gray type. I plan for margins wide enough for hands to hold, typographic variations for the eyes to rest, decorative breaks for the mind to breathe. I want my children's books to look like a wonderful place to be."

Although many adults thought the book was too much fun to win the Newbery, children have disagreed—it is just what they need. Fortunately all of Raskin's drafts, and an audio of her talking about the book, can be found online. From these drafts, adults and young people can see just how much work Raskin put into creating this elegant and incredibly inventive mystery.

Happy Birthday Ellen Raskin. I hope adults and children will pick up one of her great books today.

MARCH 14

Happy Birthday Malka Drucker (*Jacob's Rescue*).

It's the birth date of Marguerite de Angeli (1889–1987), *The Door in the Wall*; and Hank Ketcham (1920–2001), *Dennis the Menace*.

It's also the birth date of Charles Ammi Cutter (1837–1903), the librarian who developed Cutter Expansive Classification system. Read *Our Librarian Won't Tell Us Anything* by Toni Buzzeo, illustrated by Sachiko Yoshikawa.

And finally it's the birth date of Albert Einstein (1879–1955), who was born on this day in Germany and is best known for his theories on relativity. Read *Odd Boy Out: Young Albert Einstein* by Don Brown.

In 1794 Eli Whitney patented the cotton gin.

LIKE THE WILLOW TREE
By Lois Lowry

In honor of Women's History Month, the book of the day is a title by veteran writer Lois Lowry. *Like the Willow Tree* presents the charismatic figure of Ann Lee who fled persecution in Europe for her religious beliefs and came with eight others to form a colony in New York. Although Lee died at just forty-eight, she set the direction and philosophy of the American Shaker sect.

Lowry had always been fascinated by the Shaker Village of Sabbathday Lake, close to her home in Maine. However, the three elderly Shaker residents there did not seem a likely focus for a children's book. Then Lowry thought about the 1918 Spanish flu epidemic, a time when the Shakers provided homes for many orphaned children, and realized that year provided the historical context she needed.

Eleven-year-old Lydia Pierce loses her mother, father, and baby sister to the Spanish flu. She and her brother ultimately find themselves in the Shaker community at Sabbathday Lake. At first the rules seem harsh to the young girl when she has some of her favorite possessions taken away. But for Lydia, who lost so much, the order, peace, and simplicity of the Shaker life provide the discipline she needs to heal, grow, and ultimately make decisions about her life.

The novel rests on the internal conflict of Lydia who worries about her brother and how unhappy he seems. Although he eventually runs away, he does return to the community and embrace the Shaker lifestyle. Lydia recounts Shaker songs and shows the daily schedule that keeps the community working and praying together. Master storyteller Lois Lowry crafts a totally satisfying saga that unfolds over six months in Lydia's life. Final notes and photographs round out the historical information. Although readers learn a great deal about the flu epidemic and the history of the Shakers, they do so because they want to follow Lydia's story. Ultimately Lois does in this book what she has done in every book that she's written since her debut novel, *A Summer to Die*—delineate compelling, believable characters and their relationships to each other.

Like the Willow Tree is accessible, compassionate, and deals honestly with sorrow and joy. The simplicity of Lowry's style matches the subject matter perfectly. In describing a spare lifestyle, she too has honed away every extraneous word. Not only appropriate for Women's History Month, the book will work with young readers—and adults—any day of the year.

THE SNOWY DAY

By Ezra Jack Keats

In 1963 when Madeleine L'Engle's *A Wrinkle in Time* won the Newbery Medal, an artist who had struggled a long time to find his voice received the Caldecott Medal. Born in Brooklyn, Ezra Jack Keats was the son of Polish immigrants. Although his mother encouraged him to create art, his father admonished him against such a career: "Never be an artist; you'll be a bum; you'll starve; you'll have a terrible life." But Keats persisted in his dream.

With money given to him by his brother, Keats spent a year in Paris and came back ready to work as an illustrator. His career began inauspiciously enough—jackets for adult books, interior art for children's books, all of it workmanlike. Keats himself always maintained that had he died before 1962 he would simply have been viewed as a hack illustrator, doing work for hire. Although this judgment is a bit harsh, it is true that until Keats had a chance to choose his own subject matter for a book, he remained emotionally unengaged from the process.

When Annis Duff asked Keats to write and illustrate his first solo book, he turned to a subject matter dear to him: the children who were playing on the streets of Brooklyn where he lived. In 1962, children's books were dominated by white, middle class characters. But Keats's Peter is a young black boy who dons a red snowsuit and explores his neighborhood during a magical snowfall. He makes snow angels, tracks his feet in the snow, and slides down a mountain of snow.

To illustrate the book, Keats used collage, because of the freedom it provided. He located a piece of Belgian canvas that he turned into bed linen, and, to produce the image of a wall, he spattered India ink with a toothbrush. The artwork's simplicity invites readers to enter into each picture.

After the book won the Caldecott Medal in 1963, it was purchased for library collections throughout the country, and for a period of years *The Snowy Day* was often the only book featuring a person of color in many public and school libraries. Hence it had a profound influence on thousands of children who for the first time could see themselves in a book. In *Everything I Need to Know I Learned from a Children's Book,* National Book Award winner Sherman Alexie talks about encountering this book in the library on his Spokane Indian Reservation: "I vividly remember the first day I pulled that book off the shelf. It was the first time I looked at a book and saw a brown, black, beige character—a character who resembled me physically and spiritually, in all his gorgeous loneliness and splendid isolation."

By creating a successful book with a black protagonist, Ezra Jack Keats encouraged others to publish multicultural books. Both he and the brave Newbery-Caldecott committee of 1963 changed the contents of children's books forever.

MARCH 15

Happy Birthday Sarah Sargent (*Between Two Worlds*), Robert Nye (*Beowulf: A New Telling*), Ruth White (*Belle Prater's Boy*), Adèle Geras (*Time for Ballet*), and Mary K. Pershall (*Two Weeks in Grade Six*).

It's the birth date of Maureen Daly (1921–2006), *Seventeenth Summer*; and Barbara Cohen (1932–1992), *Molly's Pilgrim*.

It's also the birth date of **Andrew Jackson** (1767–1845), the seventh president of the United States.

"Beware the ides of March," wrote William Shakespeare. Roman dictator Julius Caesar was assassinated on this day in 44 BC. Read *Julius Caesar: Dictator for Life* by Denise Rinaldo.

Happy Birthday Maine, which became the 23rd U.S. state on this day in 1820. Read *One Morning in Maine* by Robert McCloskey.

PICTURE BOOK, Preschool, Elementary School

MARCH 16

Happy Birthday Helen Caswell (*Saint Francis Celebrates Christmas*).

It's the birth date of Eric P. Kelly (1884–1960), *The Trumpeter of Krakow*; Joseph Gaer (1897–1969), *Fables of India*; Sid Fleischman (1920–2010), *The Whipping Boy*; and William Mayne (1928–2010), *Hob and the Goblins*.

It's the birth date of **James Madison** (1751–1836), the fourth president of the United States.

In 1995 Mississippi formally ratified the 13th Amendment. It was the last state to approve of the abolition of slavery, though slavery was federally abolished in 1865. Read *Mississippi Bridge* by Mildred D. Taylor, illustrated by Max Ginsburg.

It's National Freedom of Information Day. Celebrate the First Amendment to the U.S. Constitution. Read *First Freedoms: A Documentary History of First Amendment Rights in America* by Charles C. Haynes, Sam Chaltain, and Susan M. Glisson.

A WIZARD OF EARTHSEA

By Ursula K. Le Guin

March has been set aside to recognize the contribution of small presses to our literary heritage. When I wrote *100 Best Books for Children*, I calculated the percentage that had originally been published by small or independent publishing houses. Ten percent! An amazing figure when you realize that most books published appear on the lists of large houses, often owned by media corporations. Small presses, both in the U.S. and internationally, have always taken risks on new authors or unusual books. Dr. Seuss first appeared on such a list, as did J. K. Rowling in England. And so did Ursula K. Le Guin with her classic *A Wizard of Earthsea*.

Le Guin was best known, probably as she still is today, as a writer of adult science fiction and fantasy novels like *The Left Hand of Darkness*. In 1967 the publisher of the small California publishing house Parnassus Press, Herbert Schein, wrote to Le Guin asking her to consider writing a book for children/young adults. Schein had published *Ishi: Last of Her Tribe* by anthropologist Theodora Kroeber, Le Guin's mother. Although Le Guin had not considered writing for this audience, she crafted a coming-of-age story, *A Wizard of Earthsea*, set in a fantasy world.

Taking place on an island community, presented in detailed maps, *A Wizard of Earthsea* shows the struggles of a young goatherd named Sparrowhawk (but called Ged) as he trains to become a wizard. Magic and wizardry are completely embraced by this community, and after some trials Ged earns his place in a school for wizards. Created long before Hogwarts, Le Guin's wizard school tests and tries its members in very exacting ways. Although Ged initially does very well in his classes, his jealousy of another student causes him to engage in magic beyond his reach. Hence a dark shadow emerges, who haunts Ged to the far reaches of the kingdom. In the end, Ged must summon all his courage to face this shadow, name it, and merge with it.

Unlike much fantasy for children that is grounded in the Judeo-Christian tradition, *The Wizard of Earthsea* was inspired by the writings of Carl Jung. The heroes are brown or black skinned, not white. Although there are fabulous battles with dragons and evil sorcerers, much of Ged's struggle comes from mastering the evil inside him—not forces outside of him. It's a mesmerizing book, an important book, a book that does not merely re-create Tolkien but adds something new to the fantasy cannon.

In this age when speculative fiction—fantasy, science fiction, and horror—is often the preferred choice of ten- to fourteen-year-olds, make sure they get a chance to travel to Earthsea. The series can be read in adulthood, but it is so much better if first experienced in childhood.

IF YOU WERE A PENGUIN

By Florence Minor

Illustrated by Wendell Minor

Today illustrator Wendell Minor celebrates his birthday. Wendell possesses one of the strongest work ethics in the children's book field. He has created so many fine books for children that he deserves to have the nation celebrate his birthday!

Someone who suffers from dyslexia, Wendell discovered that he had a particular talent for drawing. He pursued a career in graphic arts and in 1968 illustrated his first cover for an adult book. Over time he crafted fifteen hundred book jackets—including all the works of David Mc-Cullough, Harper Lee's *To Kill a Mockingbird*, James A. Michener's *Alaska*, and Pat Conroy's *The Great Santini*. But that incredible output marked only the beginning stage of Wendell's career.

As Wendell says in *Everything I Need to Know I Learned from a Children's Book*, he believes that children's books "are the last pond in the Serengeti. They are the one place we go to drink for inspiration." In the next stage of Wendell's work, he became a children's book illustrator. His natural love of the land brought him time and time again to depicting wildlife, and he has worked over the years on fabulous books with naturalist Jean Craighead George. A few years ago he and his wife Florence created *If You Were a Penguin*, perfect for the preschool set.

Original information preschool books are hard to come by, and *If You Were a Penguin* distinguishes itself as one of the best. Florence and Wendell help children imagine all the things they might do if they became one of their favorite creatures. A rhymed text introduces the activities of penguins, from flying to tobogganing. Then Wendell plies his craft, featuring large, appealing animals set against the polar landscapes. The book works for one-year-olds and even those up to five enjoy it. But it is definitely one of the first information books that you want to put in the hands of those who would like to read someday.

Wendell will no doubt be working on his birthday. I'm just grateful that he decided to move from the arena of adult books to children's books—that was a great day for young readers.

MARCH 17

Happy Birthday Penelope Lively (*Dragon Trouble*), Zibby Oneal (*The Language of Goldfish*), Keith Baker (*LMNO Peas*), Ralph Fletcher (*Fig Pudding*), and Patrick McDonnell (*The Gift of Nothing*).

It's the birth date of Kate Greenaway (1846–1901), *Under the Window*; Ennis Rees (1925–2009), *Brer Rabbit and His Tricks*; and Lillian Moore (1909–2004), *My First Counting Book*.

It's St. Patrick's Day, first celebrated in the United States in 1756 in New York City at the Crown and Thistle Tavern. Read *Saint Patrick* by Ann Tompert, illustrated by Michael Garland, and *Patrick: Patron Saint of Ireland* by Tomie dePaola.

The city of Boston was liberated from the British in 1776. Read *Henry Knox: Bookseller, Soldier, Patriot* by Anita Silvey, illustrated by Wendell Minor.

MARCH 18

Happy Birthday Barbro Lindgren (*Sam's Cookie*), Susan Patron (*The Higher Power of Lucky*), Diane Siebert (*Heartland*), Douglas Florian (*Insectlopedia*), and Kaethe Zemach (*Ms. McCaw Learns to Draw*).

It's the birth date of Rudolf Diesel (1858–1913), inventor of the diesel engine. Read *Hansel and Diesel* by David Gordon.

 It's also the birth date of **Grover Cleveland** (1837–1908), the 22nd and the 24th president of the United States. He is the only president to serve two nonconsecutive terms.

It's a sad day for those who love art and believe in access for all. In 1990, twelve paintings worth around $300 million were stolen from the Isabella Stewart Gardner Museum in Boston. Works by Degas, Vermeer, Rembrandt, and Manet were among the abducted.

DOWN THE RABBIT HOLE
By Peter Abrahams

The game's afoot. For all Sherlock Holmes fans, around this time of year in Cape May, New Jersey, the Sherlock Holmes Weekend takes place. Everyone attending the event at the Inn of Cape May, preferably in Victorian attire, will be attempting to solve a Sherlock Holmes mystery. For those who can't attend, plan your own sleuthing week or weekend with some good children's mysteries and a couple of Sherlock Holmes stories.

Mystery writers for adults—those like Rick Riordan or Carl Hiaasen—often make the best writers for children, once they decide to create books for this audience. They have already learned to craft enticing plots and develop intriguing characters; all they need to do is find the appropriate subject matter for children. In 2005 mystery writer Peter Abrahams published *Down the Rabbit Hole*, the first book in the Echo Falls Mystery series. In this debut children's novel he demonstrates finesse that would take most other writers for children years to develop.

In this mystery book for ten- through fourteen-year-olds, thirteen-year-old Ingrid takes a wrong turn as she runs through the town of Echo Falls and finds herself in the seedy part of town. There she meets a woman called Cracked-up Kate, right before Kate gets murdered. Because Ingrid has left her soccer cleats at the scene of the crime, she returns to get them at Kate's house. But someone else now roams the neighborhood, probably the murderer. Although Ingrid is good friends with the son of the police chief, she decides to solve the crime herself, drawing on her extensive reading of Sherlock Holmes. That's not all that she accomplishes: she helps her grandfather save land from developers and gets the lead role in the local *Alice in Wonderland* play. She even finds romance!

This mystery works very well for those who want intrigue and excitement but don't want to be scared too much. Everything Ingrid does is totally believable and within the range of any normal thirteen-year-old. She has no superpowers but still solves the crime and narrowly escapes becoming the next murder victim herself. For those who like this modern-day Nancy Drew, there are two more books in the series: *Behind the Curtain* and *Into the Dark*.

THE RUBY IN THE SMOKE

By Philip Pullman

Around this time of year it's Sherlock Holmes weekend in Cape May, New Jersey. Children's mysteries are perennial favorites and one of our best-written ones is Philip Pullman's *The Ruby in the Smoke*, first published in the United States in 1987. With this book, Pullman, a former schoolteacher raised in Rhodesia, Australia, London, and Wales, launched his career as a writer for children and young adults. A few years after the Sally Lockhart mysteries appeared, Pullman became internationally famous for the His Dark Materials series, which began with *A Golden Compass*.

Sometimes we continue to love best the first book we read by an author, and *The Ruby in the Smoke* remains my favorite title by Pullman. In it he explores neither religion nor theology nor any other serious matter; he simply uses his many gifts to tell a good tale. The book is set in Victorian London, with its dark alleys, poverty, and underworld crime. Sally Lockhart, who believes she has just become an orphan at sixteen, shows up at her late father's offices and asks about a mysterious note sent to her with the words "The Seven Blessings." When she mentions the phrase, an office worker, Mr. Higgs, dies on the spot. So Sally's quest begins—to find Major Marshbanks, also mentioned in the note, and ultimately to locate a valuable ruby. The story explores opium dens, Britain's trade in the Far East, the development of photography, and life in London for those with few resources. So completely does Pullman evoke the world of Sherlock Holmes that readers almost expect him to make a cameo appearance. But Sally, as the heroine of the tale, doesn't need him to emerge. With ingenuity, bravery, and some help from people who become her friends along the way, she locates the ruby and unravels other crimes of the past. And, best yet, she receives enough money to set up her own detective business—and future stories as well, including *The Shadow in the North*, *The Tiger in the Well*, and *The Tin Princess*.

Ideal for ten- to fourteen-year-olds, as well as adults, the book demonstrates Pullman's strengths as a writer. Even in his first books, he masterfully weaves a complex and interesting plot that envelops the reader with mystery and suspense. I've always thought that Sir Arthur Conan Doyle himself would love to read *The Ruby in the Smoke*.

MARCH 19

Happy Birthday Robin Brancato (*Winning*).

It's the birth date of James Otis Kaler (1848–1912), *Toby Tyler: or, Ten Weeks at the Circus*; and Lucy Bate (1939–1993), *Little Rabbit's Loose Tooth*.

In 1915 Pluto, considered a planet until recently, was photographed for the first time.

The United States Congress established time zones and approved of daylight savings in 1918. Read *Daylight Runner* by Oisín McGann and *Saving Shiloh* by Phyllis Reynolds Naylor.

It's National Quilting Day. Read *The Keeping Quilt* by Patricia Polacco, *The Quilt* by Gary Paulsen, and *The Quilt* by Ann Jonas.

MARCH 20

Happy Birthday Mitsumasa Anno (*Anno's Counting Book*), Lois Lowry (*The Giver, Number the Stars*), Ellen Conford (*Jenny Archer* series), Pamela Sargent (*Child of Venus*), and Louis Sachar (*Holes*).

It's the birth date of Fred Rogers (1928–2003), *When a Pet Dies*; and Shigeo Watanabe (1928–2006), *Ice Cream Falling*.

 In 1852 **Harriet Beecher Stowe**'s *Uncle Tom's Cabin* was published. It was the bestselling novel of the nineteenth century and is credited for fueling the American Civil War because of its antislavery message.

On this day in 1760 the Great Fire of Boston destroyed 349 buildings.

Edgar Allen Poe's "The Murders in the Rue Morgue," considered the first detective story, was published in 1841.

It's Rotten Sneaker Day. (Ugh!) Read *Rotten Ralph* by Jack Gantos, illustrated by Nicole Rubel.

Today is the first day of spring!

BROWN BEAR, BROWN BEAR, WHAT DO YOU SEE?

By Bill Martin Jr.

Illustrated by Eric Carle

Born on March 20, 1916, in Hiawatha, Kansas, Bill Martin Jr. served as a teacher and textbook editor before he became a children's book writer. Growing up in Kansas, he struggled with reading, but adored listening to his grandmother, who was a storyteller. Also, he was saved from a lifetime of hating books by a fifth grade teacher who read aloud twice a day. Martin discovered that he loved the sound of language. Because Martin understood the difficulties of those who had trouble with the written word, he began to write stories that read aloud beautifully. The fairy godmother of his writing career was none other than Eleanor Roosevelt; in 1945 she praised his self-published book, *The Little Squeegy Bug*, which eventually sold around a million copies.

Bill then received a PhD from Northwestern University and became an editor for the Holt, Rinehart & Winston reading series. In 1967 he wrote a patterned question and answer book, *Brown Bear, Brown Bear, What Do You See?*, and asked the then-unknown illustrator Eric Carle to contribute art. Although the book was successful as part of the series, it became an even greater hit when released in 1991 as an individual book. The text draws on all of Martin's great strengths—rhythm, rhyme, the participation of children—to introduce a variety of animals, amphibians, and birds. Eric Carle fashions all these creatures with brilliant collage papers.

During Martin's lifetime, he and Eric Carle also published *Polar Bear, Polar Bear, What Do You Hear?* and *Panda Bear, Panda Bear, What Do You See?* Carle remembers that Martin once came to him and said, " 'Da, da, Dah, Dah.' Or do you think it should be 'Dah, Dah, Dah.' " Carle was confused but Martin explained, "First I get the rhythm, and then I fill in the words." Small wonder then that Martin's books, created with an understanding of how children learn to read, have been so influential in the education of babies and preschoolers. Martin believed that children do not need to understand every word of the text, they just need to "assimilate the sounds, the music, and the poet's vision."

Children the world over are so lucky that this educator, who had problems reading, dedicated his life to helping children find poetry, rhythm, and rhyme in their stories.

MARCHING FOR FREEDOM: WALK TOGETHER, CHILDREN, AND DON'T YOU GROW WEARY

By Elizabeth Partridge

On March 21, 1965, Dr. Martin Luther King Jr. began the five-day protest march from Selma to Montgomery, Alabama—a triumphant event in the civil rights movement. A few months later the Voting Rights Act was signed into law, outlawing literacy tests and other measures used to keep African Americans from registering to vote.

A remarkable book, *Marching for Freedom: Walk Together, Children, and Don't You Grow Weary* by Elizabeth Partridge, explores in vivid detail the eight tumultuous months in 1965 that ended with the Voting Rights Act. On January 2 Dr. Martin Luther King Jr. spoke at the Brown Chapel African Methodist Episcopal Church in Selma: "We're not on our knees begging for the ballot. We are *demanding the ballot*." On March 7, Bloody Sunday, troopers turned tear gas and billy clubs on peaceful marchers. By the time readers come to the events of March 21, they completely understand what is at stake—and just how brutal the fight for voting rights has been.

Partridge tells this story through the eyes of the children and young adults who participated in these demonstrations. The book begins with the first arrest of ten-year-old Joanne Blackmon, who goes with her grandmother as she tries to register to vote. In photographs and personal stories, Partridge uses a calm, even voice to put a human face on the events of 1965. Although the freedom fighters know they can be beaten, even killed, they persist. Stunning photographs, many rarely seen, along with freedom songs and chants round out the volume.

The book not only presents information but also raises ethical questions. How could American citizens be denied their rights? How could white officials and the Ku Klux Klan be allowed to spread fear and violence in these communities? What groups today fight for their own rights?

A perfect book for family or classroom discussion, *Marching for Freedom* also reminds us that young people can challenge their society and change laws. Partridge ends the saga with these words: "Hundreds of students put themselves at risk to change American voting laws. . . . With only their songs and faith for protection, they believed they could make a difference. And they did."

MARCH 21

Happy Birthday Margaret Mahy (*Bubble Trouble*), Michael Foreman (*War Game*), Peter Catalanotto (*Ivan the Terrier*), and Lisa Desimini (*How the Stars Fell into the Sky: A Navajo Legend*).

It's the birth date of Phyllis McGinley (1905–1978), *The Year without a Santa Claus*; and David Wisniewski (1953–2002), *Golem*.

Composer Johann Sebastian Bach (1685–1750) was also born on this day. Read *Bach's Goldberg Variations* by Anna Harwell Celenza, illustrated by JoAnn E. Kitchel, and *Bach's Big Adventure* by Sallie Ketcham, illustrated by Timothy Bush.

The first United States zoo! In 1859 the charter estabilishing the Zoological Society of Philadelphia was approved and signed. Read *The Trumpet of the Swan* by E. B. White.

On this day in 1928 **Charles Lindbergh** was presented with the Medal of Honor, the highest accolade a United States citizen can receive, in acknowledgment of his trans-Atlantic flight of 1927. Read *Charles A. Lindbergh: A Human Hero* by James Cross Giblin.

MARCH 22

Happy Birthday Virginia Mueller (*Monster Goes to School*), Denys Cazet (*The Perfect Pumpkin Pie*), Sandra Olson Liatsos (*Bicycle Riding*), Karen Lynn Williams (*Galimoto*; *Four Feet, Two Sandals*), and Mike Wimmer (*All the Places to Love*).

It's the birth date of Harry Devlin (1918–2001), The Cranberry Tales series.

Also born on this day was Randolph Caldecott (1846–1886), *The House that Jack Built*. The Caldecott Medal bestowed annually by the American Library Association on the year's most distinguished picture book is named in his honor.

In 1638 Anne Hutchinson was expelled from Massachusetts Bay Colony for religious dissent. Read *Anne Hutchinson's Way* by Jeannine Atkins, illustrated by Michael Dooling.

In 1765 the Stamp Act, the first direct British tax on the American colonists, was passed.

BUSY, BUSY TOWN
By Richard Scarry

Today has been designated International Goof-Off Day—a day to relax, be yourself, and avoid what you are supposed to do. If you are in the position to celebrate International Goof-Off Day, you first might want to read Tony Fucile's *Let's Do Nothing* for tips.

But I myself am happiest when working at something I like to do, and so is our hero of the day, Richard Scarry. Even his biography by Walter Retan and Ole Risom is entitled *The Busy, Busy World of Richard Scarry*. No one ever showed people working, doing things, or going places with such spirit and joie de vivre as Scarry. Born in Boston on June 5, 1919, Scarry thought like an artist even as a child. When his mother sent him to the store, he never wrote out a list—he drew pictures of the items she wanted. He always carried a pad and pencil with him and drew feverishly. Although Scarry's father did not want his son to become an artist, Richard failed at everything else. Eventually, he headed to Boston's Museum of Fine Arts art school for the training he so desperately wanted.

After his service in World War II, he came to New York and established himself as a freelance artist. Scarry got his first big break a couple of years later when he attracted the attention of Lucille Ogle at the Artists and Writers Guild. A publishing legend known for her hats, Ogle served as the creative force behind Golden Books. Printed in huge numbers, distributed in grocery stores, and priced at a quarter, the Golden Books franchise had already sold thirty-nine million copies by the time Ogle looked at Scarry's portfolio. Ogle signed Scarry up for a one-year exclusive contract that paid him $400 a month. Although he quickly became one of Golden's best-selling authors, he never received royalties on his books until 1956. He got them because he finally asked for them.

From the 1950s on, Scarry's books became a staple of preschool and picture book collections. In books like Richard Scarry's *Busy, Busy Town*, he celebrates the work and activities of animals who like to do things. With a vibrant and strong black line, Scarry filled every inch of his double-page spreads with activity, action, and humor; children can pore over the drawings for hours and go back the next day and see different details. Scarry always used animal characters because he wanted all children, no matter what they looked like, to be able to identify with the figures in his books—and children have by the millions.

Even if you want to goof off today, you can pick up *Busy, Busy Town*—or *Cars and Trucks and Things That Go* or *What Do People Do All Day?*—and feel productive.

INTERRUPTING CHICKEN

By David Ezra Stein

On the first Monday of spring we celebrate World Folk Tales and Fables Week, established to encourage children and adults to explore the lessons learned from folk tales and fables. Although folk and fairy tales form the basis of world literature and culture, adults have often questioned introducing them to children. After all, the material in these legends is usually dark and violent. But these are the basic building blocks of literature, that inform and illuminate much adult literature later on.

Folk and fairy tale retellings formed a large portion of books published for children in the 1970s and 1980s, but have since fallen out of favor. Fortunately in the last few years, individual volumes dedicated to the world's most enduring stories have proliferated, giving those who work with children a wide range of choices. Though our book of the day won't teach children any of these tales, it may well pique their curiosity and make them want to go back to the original stories.

The protagonist of David Ezra Stein's *Interrupting Chicken*, a Caldecott Honor Book, is a little red chicken who adores having her rooster father read her a bedtime story. Although he admonishes her not to interrupt his readings of "Hansel and Gretel," she just can't help warning the characters in the story. She tells Hansel and Gretel to stay away from the witch—and immediately proclaims that the story is over. She does the same with "Little Red Riding Hood" and "Chicken Little." Finally this girl makes up her own story, which sends her father to sleep.

Humor, personal relationships, and the loving bond between a father and child all get explored in this funny picture book that can be used for the two- to eight-year-old crowd. Illustrated with vibrant watercolors capturing the action and passion of the young chicken, *Interrupting Chicken* has already become the favorite story of many picture-book readers. Reading this book is a great way to begin celebrating the diversity and the lessons learned from world folk and fairy tales. But do not ignore my warning. Once *Interrupting Chicken* is read to your four-, five-, or six-year-old, you will be asked to read it again, and again—and again!

MARCH 23

Happy Birthday Lynne Barasch (*First Come the Zebra, Hiromi's Hands*).

It's the birth date of Eleanor Cameron (1912–1996), *A Room Made of Windows, The Wonderful Flight to the Mushroom Planet.*

On this day in 1775 American revolutionary hero Patrick Henry, while addressing the House of Burgesses, declared, "give me liberty, or give me death!"

In 1839 the first recorded use of the term "OK" appeared in Boston's *Morning Post*.

It's National Toast Day. Read *Creamed Tuna Fish and Peas on Toast* by Philip C. Stead.

And it's National Puppy Day! Read *Pigeon Wants a Puppy* by Mo Willems.

MARCH 24

It's the birth date of Mary Stolz (1920–2006), *Belling the Tiger* and Bill Cleaver (1920–1981), *Where the Lilies Bloom*.

On this day in 1900 New York City Mayor Robert Anderson Van Wyck broke ground for underground "rapid transit railroad" to connect Manhattan and Brooklyn. The subway is born. Read *Subway* by Christoph Niemann, *Subway* by Anastasia Suen, illustrated by Karen Katz, *The Subway Sparrow* by Leyla Torres, and *The Cricket in Times Square* by George Seldon, illustrated by Garth Williams.

In 1989 the *Exxon Valdez* oil tanker hit a reef in Prince William Sound, Alaska, resulting in one of the nation's worst oil spills.

And it's National Chocolate-Covered Raisins Day. Read *How Do You Raise a Raisin?* by Pam Muñoz Ryan, illustrated by Craig Brown.

ESCAPE! THE STORY OF THE GREAT HOUDINI

By Sid Fleischman

On March 24, 1874, Harry Houdini was born in Budapest, Hungary. Some figures from history remain perpetually interesting to children. Certainly Harry Houdini, magician, escape artist, performer, actor, and film producer, has garnered his share of biographies for children over the years.

Newbery Medal–winner Sid Fleischman, in one of his last and best books for children, *Escape! The Story of the Great Houdini*, crafted a biography ideal for eight- to twelve-year-olds about his childhood idol. During his California boyhood he met and was greatly influenced by Houdini's widow, Bess. Fleischman himself pursued card and magic tricks—although he was most spellbinding in his writing. His biography of Houdini includes information about not only the great magician but also Sid Fleischman himself: "I used to read palms, which is pure bunk, but it gave me a chance to hold a girl's hands."

Born Erhich Weisz, Houdini invented everything about himself—including his name. His happiest years as a child were spent in Appleton, Wisconsin. Later, on the road, he found employment whenever he could—including being "The Wild Man" in a cage. While in Europe, Houdini gained fame as "The Handcuff King." He would go to local police stations, have them lock him in a cell, and then escape. The publicity brought hundreds to theatres to watch him perform.

In 1900, weighed down with chains and manacles, he jumped off a bridge in Dresden, Germany, and in 1912 he premiered his greatest escape act at Circus Busch in Berlin. Lowered into a glass-fronted water-filled cell, upside down, Houdini hung with his ankles in clamps. Then he miraculously freed himself from this water torture cell. As Fleischman describes these incidents, he has a sure sense of Houdini as a man and such an understanding of magic and magic tricks that readers feel as if they have spent a day with Houdini, getting to know who he was and what he did.

Before Fleischman's death in 2010, I was able to sit with him at dinner and watch him perform tricks—with a glint in his eye and a sure feeling for the fun we were all having. Since then, I have been rereading his books to be reminded of his genius. If you haven't read Fleischman's books, *Escape!* is a great place to begin. It will make you, and the children in your life, long for more.

EVERYTHING ON A WAFFLE

By Polly Horvath

Today marks International Waffle Day, a holiday that originated in Sweden. Waffles have a long, glorious history. In Colonial times President Thomas Jefferson brought a long-handled waffle iron from France to the U.S. In 1869 Cornelius Swarthout patented the first U.S. waffle iron. Believe it or not, there is actually a controversy in America about when we should celebrate Waffle Day. Some claim that August 24 would be appropriate, because of the patent. But for the purposes of the Almanac, I've chosen the international holiday—and you can celebrate in August as well if you are so inclined.

I experienced no controversy in selecting the book of the day, Polly Horvath's quirky and funny *Everything on a Waffle*, a Newbery Honor Book. Living in Coal Harbour, British Columbia, Primrose Squarp, an eleven-year-old with hair the color of "carrots in an apricot glaze," loses both parents when a typhoon blows them out to sea. She always believes them to be simply lost; her neighbors and those at school insist they must be dead and that Primrose must live in reality. But reality is not Primrose's strong suit—she excels in imagination and whimsy. Eventually, her bachelor uncle Jack moves to Coal Harbour to care for her. He also seems attracted to the possible real estate development of this sleepy little spot. Under his care

Primrose manages to get into a lot of scrapes in chapters entitled "I Lose a Toe" and "I Lose Another Digit." For a short time she gets placed with a foster family, but she continues to believe in a happy ending to her plight—when her parents return.

In this Garrison Keillor–like take on small-town life, not only do waffles appear in the title, they also play a major role in the book. Primrose's favorite café, The Girl on the Red Swing run by the sympathetic Mrs. Bowser, serves everything on a waffle. Lasagna, steak, and fish and chips all come on a waffle. A bit of a foodie, Primrose provides a recipe at the end of each chapter, showing how to make one of the dishes mentioned in the text. She may not become the next Julia Child (she sets a guinea pig on fire in the kitchen) but she has heart and wit and wins readers over. In the end, Primrose's optimism and dreaming prove to be more realistic than the despair of those around her. *Everything on a Waffle* makes a great book to read aloud for fourth through sixth graders—although some teachers admit that they must stop reading for a moment because they are laughing so hard.

So happy International Waffle Day. Thank you Polly Horvath for your witty and clever book—it is just as satisfying as a stack of waffles, no matter what gets put on them.

MARCH 25

Happy Birthday Alan Arkin (*Tony's Hard Work Day*), Linda Sue Park (*A Single Shard*), Petra Mathers (*Button Up!*), and Kate DiCamillo (*The Tale of Despereaux*).

It's the birth date of Jaap ter Haar (1922–1998), *Boris*.

According to legend, Venice, Italy was born at noon on this day in 421. Read *This is Venice* by M. Sasek, *The Thief Lord* by Cornelia Funke, and *The Merchant of Venice*, a graphic novel based on the Shakespeare play, by Gareth Hinds.

In 1957 U.S. Customs seized all copies of Allen Ginsberg's "Howl" on grounds of obscenity. Read *The Mysterious Howling: The Incorrigible Children of Ashton Place, Book 1* by Maryrose Wood, illustrated by Jon Klassen, and *Night of the Howling Dogs* by Graham Salisbury.

In 1911 a fire at the Triangle Shirtwaist Company, a sweatshop in New York City, claimed the lives of 146 workers.

MARCH 26

Happy Birthday T. A. Barron (*The Lost Years of Merlin*), Julie Danneberg (*First Day Jitters*), and Jerry Pallotta (*Apple Fractions*).

It's also the birth date of **Robert Frost** (1874–1963). Read *Stopping By the Woods on a Snowy Evening* illustrated by Susan Jeffers.

In 1830 *The Book of Mormon* was published in Palmyra, New York. Read *Nauvoo: Mormon City on the Mississippi River* by Raymond Bial.

The groundbreaking ceremony for the Vietnam Veterans Memorial was held in Washington, D.C., on this day in 1982. Read *The Wall* by Eve Bunting, illustrated by Ronald Himler.

It's Make Up Your Own Holiday Day.

MRS. PIGGLE-WIGGLE

By Betty MacDonald

On March 26, 1908, Betty MacDonald was born in Boulder, Colorado. Because her father worked as a mining engineer, she spent many years of her childhood traveling around the West. Eventually settling in Seattle, MacDonald attended the University of Washington and wrote *The Egg and I*, a funny account of her married life on a chicken farm.

As accomplished as her adult books were, MacDonald is remembered and celebrated for her series of books for children ages six through ten about a charming but no-nonsense widow named Mrs. Piggle-Wiggle who lives in a small town. Although experts like to say that children want to read books only about other children and are not interested in adults, Mrs. Piggle-Wiggle is an exception to that rule. She loves children and entertains them in a house she has turned upside down. To these young people she gives sound advice about living with and understanding parents.

The first volume in the series, *Mrs. Piggle-Wiggle,* appeared in 1947; the fourth, *Hello, Mrs. Piggle-Wiggle*, in 1957. At this time most parents got child-raising wisdom from Dr. Spock, but it probably would have been better for them to have consulted Mrs. Piggle-Wiggle instead. The books present a variety of children with different kinds of behavior problems. Mrs. Piggle-Wiggle considers these problems ailments or diseases that, just like the measles, need only to be cured. Although some of her solutions involve magic, most have been grounded in an understanding of children and common sense.

Children enjoy reading about these young monsters in the making, who act out in horrible ways. Adults appreciate the happy resolution of each case study. Mrs. Piggle-Wiggle believes that everyone in the family really wants harmony. So when two girls fight and quarrel, she advises the adults to engage in the same behavior. Genuinely horrified by watching their parents fight, the girls begin to treat each other with respect, and the family heads out for ice cream sodas to celebrate.

An ideal chapter book for children who have just learned to read, each chapter works as a self-contained unit, with a beginning, middle, and end. The pattern of the stories repeats in each chapter, so children quickly feel competent in understanding what will come next. Originally Hilary Knight and Maurice Sendak, illustration superstars, added their interpretations to the stories. The 2007 reissue of these books contains the more modern artwork of Alexandra Boiger. Certainly reflections of their times, the books deal exclusively with the problems of two-parent families and present old-fashioned gender roles. But when I ask people about the most important books of their childhood, someone in the audience always pipes up and says, "*Mrs. Piggle-Wiggle.*"

Happy Birthday Betty MacDonald. Your books, in print for over sixty years, have made many laugh and many want to read more.

ELLA ENCHANTED

By Gail Carson Levine

World Folk Tales and Fables Week has been set up in the first week of spring to encourage children and adults to explore the lessons learned from folk tales and fables. One of the most popular retellings of a folk tale published in the last twenty years, Gail Carson Levine's *Ella Enchanted*, relies on the content and structure of "Cinderella." Although this fairy tale can be traced back to the first century BC, the best-known version in the West was created by French writer Charles Perrault in 1697. For anyone hunting for a folk tale to show children how the same story is told in different cultures, Cinderella remains one of the best—with great cultural adaptations such as *Mufaro's Beautiful Daughters* by John Steptoe, *The Rough-Face Girl* by Rafe Martin, and *Yeh-Shen* by Ai-Ling Louie.

For *Ella Enchanted*, however, Gail Carson Levine took the story and expanded and changed it, making it into something completely new. As a baby, Ella, daughter of a wealthy merchant father and fairy mother, receives a gift from the fairy Lucinda. She is given obedience—something that proves to be a curse. If someone commands Ella to do something, she cannot refuse, even if it would be in her best interest to do so. While her mother lives, Ella can be protected from the worst problems this gift causes. But after her mother's death, she suddenly finds herself in finishing school and at the mercy of an odious student who has discovered her secret. In this vaguely medieval land of giants, elves, and ogres, Ella runs away, searching for Lucinda to get her curse removed.

In the meantime, the prince of the realm, Prince Char, has fallen in love with Ella, and she knows that her condition will cause problems for him. In the end, only her love for the prince and her own determination make it possible for her to overcome her affliction. Like the original fairy tale, Ella participates in a series of balls with the prince—where she rides in a coach pumpkin and wears glass slippers.

Ella emerges as a compelling protagonist, and her curse of obedience seems real and terrible. Fabulous creatures and epic journeys add to the texture of the story. Ella's triumph over her condition creates a totally satisfying read. A favorite of ten- to fourteen-year-olds, *Ella Enchanted* proves that the best folk tales can be retold again and again in different forms. In *Ella Enchanted*, Cinderella has been transformed into an exciting, page-turning, and romantic novel.

MARCH 27

Happy Birthday Patricia C. Wrede (The Enchanted Forest Chronicles) and Julia Alvarez (*Return to Sender, Before We Were Free*).

It's the birth date of Dick King-Smith (1922–2011), *Martin's Mice, The Water Horse*, and *Babe: The Gallant Pig*.

On this day in 1886 **Geronimo**, an Apache warrior and chief, surrendered to the U.S. Government after a thirty-year struggle to protect his tribe's homeland. Read *Geronimo* by Joseph Bruchac and *I Am Apache* by Tanya Landman.

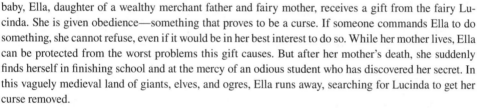

MARCH 28

Happy Birthday Byrd Baylor (*Everybody Needs a Rock*), Steven Lindblom (*How to Build a Robot*), and Doreen Cronin (*Click, Clack, Moo: Cows That Type*).

In 1797 the washing machine was patented by Nathaniel Briggs of New Hampshire.

On this day in 1930 the name of Turkey's largest city, Constantinople, was officially changed to Istanbul, though it had been called Istanbul since 1453 when a conquering Ottoman sultan gave it the moniker based on a Greek phrase meaning "the city." Read *Leyla: The Black Tulip* by Alev Lytle Croutier, illustrated by Kazuhiko Sano.

In 1941 writer **Virginia Woolf** filled her pockets with stones, walked into a river, and drowned. Read *Nurse Lugton's Curtain* by Virginia Woolf, illustrated by Julie Vivas.

CLEMENTINE
By Sara Pennypacker
Illustrated by Marla Frazee

March has been designated Exotic Winter Fruit Month and Leeks & Green Onions Month. When I think of winter fruit, my mind instantly conjures up one of the most engaging heroines developed in the past few years in children's books—a very fresh and cheeky third grader named Clementine. She also has a baby brother, and rather than call him by his real name, she always refers to him with the name of a vegetable—spinach, broccoli, rutabaga, whatever comes to her mind.

The daughter of an artist, Clementine is a true independent spirit. She cuts off all her best friend's hair—and then destroys her own as well. A cyclone, she spends more time in the principal's office than in her classroom. Everyone keeps telling her to "pay attention" and she does—to all the things occurring outside the classroom window. But if you need someone with an out-of-the box idea, Clementine will come to the rescue. Through observation and ingenuity, she even manages to help her father win "The Great Pigeon War," as he attempts to disperse the pigeons that befoul their apartment building.

Books for second- and third-grade readers are about as difficult to write successfully as any in the children's book arena. It is hard to craft a story out of the everyday events of childhood, keep the material within the reading and comprehension range of young children, and include enough action so that they will want to read the book. Hence we adore writers like Beverly Cleary and Judy Blume who can accomplish all these tasks in beautifully crafted books. For my money, Sara Pennypacker is a modern-day Cleary. She manages to make funny and compelling reading out of the trials of a third grader—problems with friends, sibling rivalry, and a pet who has died. Readers laugh at Clementine's antics and misunderstandings as they get swept along in her first-person stream-of-consciousness voice. As an added bonus, Marla Frazee adds energetic and drama-filled illustrations that perfectly round out Clementine's dilemmas.

So today let's celebrate a fresh fruit—Clementine. Once children read one chapter in this series, they will clamor for all of these delightful books.

CHASING VERMEER

By Blue Balliett

March has been designated Youth Art Month, set aside to promote art and art education in the United States. The perfect book to celebrate the month, Blue Balliett's *Chasing Vermeer* contains all the necessary elements to get young people thinking about art and artists.

Set at the University School in Hyde Park, Illinois, *Chasing Vermeer* features two very engaging protagonists, eleven-year-olds Petra and Calder. They have a lot in common: both come from mixed racial backgrounds; both might be characterized as quirky loners. Calder plays with Pentominoes, a mathematical tool, and explores the world in terms of geometry and numbers. Petra has fallen under the spell of Charles Fort and his book *Lo!*, which claims the world is full of strange events that no one witnesses. When Petra and Calder become friends, they bring two divergent and original minds together for a sleuthing team.

From the beginning of the book, readers know that some game is afoot. Three strange letters are delivered to surprised readers: "If you show this to the authorities, you will most certainly be placing your life in danger." Petra and Calder's teacher Ms. Hussey, a free thinker who they adore, begins to act suspiciously. Then the unthinkable happens—a valuable Vermeer painting, "A Lady Writing," vanishes en route from Washington, D.C. to Chicago, where it's been sent for an exhibition. The thief appears to be a total lunatic—for he/she is asking that people examine the career of Vermeer, get to know this genius's paintings, post notes about him on the Internet, and determine which of the works attributed to him in museums are false. If all these things don't happen, the thief will destroy this masterpiece.

Because of the premise, the book presents a lot of information about Vermeer that fits quite naturally into the story. While the world studies Vermeer, Petra and Calder begin to solve the crime. Petra has visions and dreams; Calder works on mathematical patterns. While the police and everyone else remain clueless, these two sleuths build a pattern of clues and coincidences that lead them alone on a dark night into a deserted building to search for the painting's hiding place.

Even Brett Helquist's brooding artwork contains clues to the mystery; there are Pentominoes built into the composition. Just as quirky and original as the protagonists, *Chasing Vermeer* provides delightful, page-turning pleasure, and Petra and Calder reappear in two engaging sequels, *The Wright 3* and *The Calder Game*, exploring Frank Lloyd Wright and Alexander Calder. All these books focus on art and the creative process. Reading them is a great way to celebrate Youth Art Month.

MARCH 29

Happy Birthday Suçie Stevenson (Henry and Mudge series).

It's the birth date of Helen Wells (1910–1986), Cherry Ames series.

It's also the birth date of John Tyler (1790–1862), the tenth president of the United States.

In 1882 the Knights of Columbus was established. Hence, it is Knights of Columbus Founders Day. Named in honor of **Christopher Columbus**, it is the largest Catholic fraternal service group in the world. Read *Where Do You Think You're Going, Christopher Columbus?* by Jean Fritz, illustrated by Margot Tomes.

It's Smoke and Mirrors Day, to celebrate illusions. Read *Smoke and Mirrors* by Neil Gaiman, *The Houdini Box* by Brian Selznick, and *Now You See It, Now You Don't* by Seymour Simon.

MARCH 30

Happy Birthday Charles Keller (*Best Joke Book Ever*).

It's the birth date of Anna Sewell (1820–1878), *Black Beauty*.

Painter Vincent van Gogh (1853–1890) was also born on this day. Read *Vincent's Colors* by The Metropolitan Museum of Art, *Van Gogh: The Touch of Yellow* by Jacqueline Loumaye, and *Vincent van Gogh: Sunflowers and Swirly Stars* by Joan Holub.

In 1858 Hymen Lipman patented a pencil with attached eraser. Hence, it is Pencil Day! Read *The Pencil* by Allan Ahlberg, illustrated by Bruce Ingman, and *Brand-new Pencils, Brand-new Books* by Diane deGroat.

A SICK DAY FOR AMOS McGEE

By Philip C. Stead
Illustrated by Erin Stead

Today marks National Doctor Day, when we should show our personal doctor appreciation with a card or a gift. It commemorates March 30, 1933, the date of first use of anesthesia in surgery. If by any chance you want to give a book as a gift, for yourself or your doctor, I can think of no better title than the 2011 Caldecott winner *A Sick Day for Amos McGee*.

Philip C. Stead's quiet text, illustrated by his wife Erin, has become even more powerful for me with each reading. The palette of this book and distinct but delicate black line cause the reader to slow down, pause, and relax. With retro colors, the book might well have been published in the same time period as some of the Ellen Raskin gems like *Nothing Ever Happens on My Block*. Both the Steads understand you don't have to scream at children—you can whisper.

Amos McGee, a kindly zookeeper, lives an ordered life—every day he eats the same things, rides the number 5 bus to work, and enjoys his day on the job. We watch Amos play chess with the elephant, race the turtle (who has never lost), and sit with a very shy penguin. After he lends his handkerchief to the rhinoceros, he ends his day by reading stories to the owl.

But the next morning he wakes up with a cold and chills—and Amos stays home for the day. A lovely picture shows him cuddling his teddy bear, his rabbit slippers on, and a wee mouse under the bed. Because the animals miss their friend, they take action. In two wordless double-page spreads, they wait for and board the number 5 bus and bring a balloon to their friend Amos McGee. He plays with the animals until they all go to sleep—because they have a bus to catch in the morning.

Whether used as a good-night book or just for story hour, *A Sick Day for Amos McGee* has been winning over one reader after another. A book full of emotion and heart that never becomes sentimental, the story and pictures provide a quiet, gentle world for two- through eight-year-olds and adults. Devotion and friendship between humans and animals has rarely been so well portrayed. The artist shows how strong composition, with only a touch of color, can convey story and character. Using wood blocks and pencil, Erin creates character with the subtlest of line. On Doctor Day, the book reminds us that some of the best healing comes from the love and support of those we care for—even if they happen to be animals.

On any day, it reminds us that our greatest picture books only improve with each visit—until we cannot imagine a time when we did not know them.

HOW TO STEAL A DOG

By Barbara O'Connor

Today I'd like to acknowledge two holidays. March has been designated Ethical Awareness Month, and today is National She's Funny That Way Day, a time for people to list the five ways that the women in their lives make them laugh.

When I thought about a funny, engaging character who faces an ethical dilemma, Georgina Hayes of Barbara O'Connor's *How to Steal a Dog* came instantly to mind. O'Connor moves with grace through this story of a young girl, abandoned by her father and now facing hard times. Her opening line grabs the reader's attention immediately: "The day I decided to steal a dog was the same day my best friend, Luanne Godfrey, found out I lived in a car."

Thrown out of an apartment because the family cannot pay rent, Georgina, her mother, and her younger brother, Toby, all work desperately to keep their lives as normal as possible. Georgina becomes more and more unkempt, begins to fail at school, and loses her friends. But she is a girl with a plan. She wants to help her mother get enough money for a deposit on a place to live, and she sees a sign that offers a five-hundred-dollar reward for finding a dog. Georgina's mind begins working overtime—if she can't find this dog, why not steal another one and then claim the money?

MARCH 31

Happy Birthday John Jakes (*Susanna of the Alamo*) and Junko Morimoto (*Two Bullies*).

It's the birth date of Andrew Lang (1844–1912), *Blue Fairy Book*; and Beni Montresor (1926–2001), *May I Bring a Friend*.

It's the birth date of **Jack Johnson** (1878–1946), the first African-American world heavyweight boxing champion, known as the "Galveston Giant." Read *Black Jack: The Ballad of Jack Johnson* by Charles R. Smith Jr., illustrated by Shane W. Evans.

It's also the birth date of Al Gore, vice president to President Clinton from 1993–2001. Read *An Inconvenient Truth* by Al Gore.

The Eiffel Tower in Paris officially opened on the Left Bank as part of the Exhibition of 1889.

So she keeps a notebook about her ideas—what types of dogs to look for and what kinds of houses to case. Finally she spots the perfect dog in what seems the perfect neighborhood, and then realizes she has no place to hide a stolen animal. However, she and Toby persist in their quest. Only after Georgina takes a dog from its owner does she begin to have qualms about what she has just done. The situation doesn't seem as ethically clear-cut as Georgina first believed (after all, she desperately needs money and other people have more of it than they need), particularly after she befriends the owner.

Rarely has a family struggling with poverty been so brilliantly portrayed in fiction for young readers, and few books for children have ever explored an ethical issue so clearly. Does the poverty of Georgina's family override what a decent human being should do? Basically a caring, good person caught in bad circumstances, Georgina makes the right decision, just as readers hope she will. For any readers concerned about the final outcome or the morality of the book, Georgina makes the lesson she learned quite clear: "DO NOT STEAL A DOG."

Extremely successful as a read aloud for third through fifth grades or for book discussion groups, *How to Steal a Dog* has gained a host of fans, many who believe that it is the best book they have ever read.

APRIL 1

Happy Birthday Anne McCaffrey (*Dragonsong*), Jan Wahl (*Pleasant Fieldmouse*), Edward Myers (*Storyteller*), Karen Wallace (*Bears in the Forest*), and Tad Hills (*How Rocket Learned to Read*).

It's the birth date of Margaret Scherf (1908–1979), *Glass on the Stairs*; and Augusta Baker (1911–1998), *Young Years: Best Loved Stories and Poems for Little Children*.

It's April Fools' Day and the birthday of the fictional pranksters Fred and George Weasley from the Harry Potter series by J. K. Rowling.

Birthday greetings also go to the computer company Apple Inc., formed by Steve Jobs and Steve Wozniak in 1976. Read *Steve Jobs & Steve Wozniak: Geek Heroes Who Put the Personal in Computers* by Mike Venezia.

HENRY AND MUDGE: THE FIRST BOOK

By Cynthia Rylant
Illustrated by Suçie Stevenson

The first week in April has been designated Laugh at Work Week and International Pooper Scooper Week. April 1 is Reading is Funny Day and National Fun Day. April has also been set aside to celebrate National Humor, Pets Are Wonderful, and Dog Appreciation Months. Cynthia Rylant's Henry and Mudge series actually fits all these holidays!

Cynthia Rylant did not have an easy path to crafting lighthearted humorous stories for children. Growing up in the home of her grandparents in Cool Ridge, West Virginia, she faced the divorce of her parents when she was four and lived in poverty. Later, as a young woman in her twenties, she read her first children's book while working in the children's section of a library. She became fascinated with them and read obsessively to find the books she had missed. Rylant has written successfully in many formats, including novels and poetry. But she began by creating picture books like *When I Was Young in the Mountains* and *The Relatives Came* that were about the area of the country where she grew up.

In 1987 she began a series of easy-to-read books, ideal for preschool through third grade, about a boy named Henry and his 180-pound English mastiff Mudge. Essentially, the books contain a love story between a boy and his dog, two friends who stay together all the time. In the first book, Henry convinces his parents to let him get a pet because he has no brothers or sisters. At first a small fluffball, Mudge grows to be three feet tall and delights in sitting on Henry. Although he is larger than Henry, Mudge still loves sleeping in Henry's bed.

Like in all of Rylant's writing, a good deal of her real life has been incorporated into the stories. Henry was based on her son Nate, and her former husband owned large dogs like Mudge. With a strong sense of family, the books about these characters celebrate the everyday pleasures of life—spring, snow, puddles, Thanksgiving. Each book contains several short stories told with a poetic text that captures the cadence of oral storytelling and makes the stories enjoyable to return to again and again. Suçie Stevenson's drawings both bring the characters to life and provide scenes and settings for these sunny, happy books.

Rylant once wrote, "some children who have suffered a loss too great for words grow up into writers who are always trying to find those words, trying to find meaning for the way they have lived." In the Henry and Mudge series Cynthia Rylant has found words for the joy and beauty of being a child—and having a dog as a best friend.

I hope you enjoy April Fools' Day. Mine has been made much more joyful by rereading several Henry and Mudge stories.

RULES

By Cynthia Lord

In 2007, April 2 was designated World Autism Awareness Day by the General Assembly of the United Nations, because of the prevalence and high rate of autism in children. In the past few years several notable children's books have featured a child with autism. My favorite book on the topic remains Cynthia Lord's *Rules*. Not only does she deal with how autism affects a family but she also writes a compelling story with a believable and totally lovable protagonist.

All twelve-year-old Catherine longs for is a normal life and a chance to have a reasonable conversation with her young brother, David. But he suffers from autism, and the family, slowly and inextricably, begins to revolve around his disability and his needs rather than Catherine's. In order to make their life more normal, Catherine tries to help David grow and mature. David's autism makes him a stickler for rules so she makes a list of rules for him that include imperatives like: "Don't stand in front of the TV when other people are watching it." Or "No toys in the fish tank." However, no matter how many rules Catherine can think of, David always manages to careen out of control.

As a twelve-year-old trying to navigate the changing world of middle school, Catherine also struggles to find rules for her own life. She needs to figure out how to make a new friend and how to deal with an attractive boy, Jason, whom she meets at David's clinic. Catherine's key problem centers around her parents. How can she get them to see her needs, rather than just treat her as part of a support system for David?

Like Jodi Picoult in *My Sister's Keeper*, Lord brilliantly shows the dynamic of a family that focuses all its resources on the child who has special needs. Catherine truly cares for David, and because she has the normal aspirations of any twelve-year-old, the effects of an autistic child on a family seem very real to young readers. People, relationships, dealing with life's problems: all these topics are explored with humor and finesse in Cynthia Lord's debut novel. To write it she drew on her own family experience of a son with autism. When her daughter turned ten, she said, "I never see families like mine in books and on TV." Cynthia Lord set out to create that book.

Since its publication in 2008, *Rules* has received numerous awards from adults, including a Newbery Honor, but it also has been selected by children ages eight through thirteen as their favorite book for state children's choice awards. *Rules* combines literary quality with child appeal, making it one of our finest books published in the twenty-first century. I can think of no better way to celebrate World Autism Awareness Day than by sharing *Rules* with the children in your life.

APRIL 2

Happy Birthday Judith Janda Presnall (Animals with Jobs series), Dave Ross (*Book of Hugs*), Amy Schwartz (*Bea and Mr. Jones*), and Mark Shulman (*Scrawl*).

It's the birth date of **Hans Christian Andersen** (1805–1875), *Andersen's Fairy Tales*; and Ruth Heller (1924–2004), *Chickens Aren't the Only Ones*.

In 1902 the first full-time movie theater in the United States opened in Los Angeles—Electric Theatre. Read *Dani Noir* by Nova Ren Suma, *Cam Jansen: The Mystery of the Monster Movie* by David A. Adler, and *If You Take a Mouse to the Movies* by Laura Numeroff, illustrated by Felicia Bond.

It's National Peanut Butter and Jelly Day. Read *Peanut Butter and Jelly: A Play Rhyme* by Nadine Bernard Westcott.

APRIL 3

Happy Birthday Virginia Silverstein (*Life in a Bucket of Soil*) and Sandra Boynton (*Barnyard Dance; Moo, Baa, La La La!*).

Jane Goodall, British anthropologist, known for her work with African chimpanzees, was born on this day in 1934. Read *Me, Jane* by Patrick McDonnell.

 It's the birth date of **Washington Irving** (1783–1859), *The Legend of Sleepy Hollow* and *Rip Van Winkle*; and Edward Everett Hale (1822–1909), *The Man Without a Country*.

In 1860 the Pony Express began its first successful run from Missouri to Sacramento. Read *They're Off!: The Story of the Pony Express* by Cheryl Harness and *Off Like the Wind!: The First Ride of the Pony Express* by Michael D. Spradlin, illustrated by Layne Johnson.

DARK EMPEROR AND OTHER POEMS OF THE NIGHT

By Joyce Sidman
Illustrated by Rick Allen

Inaugurated by the Academy of American Poets in 1996, National Poetry Month takes place in April. The Academy lists a variety of projects, including a Poem-a-Day, where new poetry is e-mailed to those who register. The month of April provides an opportunity to think about poetry and its place in American culture, not to mention its part in the lives of children.

Today I'd like to introduce National Poetry Month with the work of the one of the twenty-first century's best new poets for children. As publisher at Houghton Mifflin, I saw the manuscript for Joyce Sidman's first book of poems, *The World According to Dog*, which was sent to me by her editor Ann Rider. I loved Joyce's voice, and her ability to capture the essence of an animal in a few well-chosen words. Since that time, Joyce's books have won more major awards than most poets for children ever see, including a Newbery Honor for *Dark Emperor and Other Poems of the Night*. When I read this book, and her other title published in 2010, *Ubiquitous: Celebrating Nature's Survivors,* I realized I still love her voice. In ten years, Joyce has moved from a poet of promise to a seasoned, intelligent craftsperson who selects ambitious subjects for books.

Since 99 percent of all the species that have appeared on the planet are now extinct, in *Ubiquitous* Joyce focuses on nature's survivors. This book, illustrated by Beckie Prange, takes readers through 4.6 billion years of history. Joyce presents both a poem and well-crafted paragraph of information to describe bacteria, lichens, beetles, geckos, ants, and in the end, human beings. In a concrete stream-of-consciousness poem about squirrels, she writes, "we dash from limb / to limb sailing out over / the leaves with our para- / chute tails which by the / way also act as umbrella." Never before has a poem made me long to be a squirrel, but that is exactly what this talented author pulls off.

For her Newbery Honor book, *Dark Emperor*, Joyce uses the same format—poem and thoughtful facts—to present the creatures who come out at night while others sleep. Owls, snails, moths, bats, and porcupettes (what a delicious word) emerge. "I am a baby porcupette. / My paws are small; my nose is wet. / But I can deal with any threat; / I raise my quills / and pirouette." Rick Allen's exquisite linoleum cuts add to the pleasure of reading the material. Both of these books present poetry and information of equal value. Both are lovingly designed and illustrated, inviting the reader into the poetry and text. Both testify to the power of a well-chosen word and the artistry of Joyce Sidman.

I hope you have a wonderful month of April celebrating poetry.

THE ENORMOUS EGG

By Oliver Butterworth

April has been designated National Humor Month. Many children tell adults that they just want funny books. One of my favorites in this category, Oliver Butterworth's *The Enormous Egg*, was created in 1956 and concerns a favorite topic of children: dinosaurs.

Nate Twichell, an ordinary boy in Freedom, New Hampshire, helps on the family farm and in his father's printing press for the local paper (circulation eight hundred). One day his chicken lays an enormous egg; Nate and his father carefully tend it for six weeks. And then, surprise! A baby triceratops, which Ned names Uncle Beazley, hatches and begins to eat his way through the Twichell farm, doubling his weight every few days. A visiting scientist from Washington, D.C., gets involved and eventually Congress has its say before Ned's companion finds a permanent home in the National Zoo. I hadn't read this book for years and was struck, as an adult, by Butterworth's cynicism about congressmen. It makes the book seem contemporary.

Butterworth's archives at the Thomas Dodd Center at the University of Connecticut reveal that he hoped to illustrate his own novel, only to have editor Dudley Cloud of the *Atlantic Monthly* put a kibosh on that idea. Butterworth then expressed the hope that Garth Williams, who had so magically illustrated *Stuart Little*, might be employed. In the end Louis Darling was paid the extravagant fee of $1,000 to do the work—causing the publisher to express consternation at the expense. After all, Butterworth himself had only been given $500 in advance for this whimsical story.

A year after the book's release, the publisher was no longer complaining; the book had sold 4,820 copies, "which ain't hay, hooray." In print ever since, the book has gone on to win scores of admirers. At one point Butterworth's editor had hopes for television adaptation, but told his writer: "It wouldn't surprise me if you don't believe in TV."

Well, Butterworth did believe in creating an engaging character that children would admire and emulate. Who wouldn't want to raise a dinosaur from an egg? Although the plot is, of course, nonsensical, Butterworth presents it in such a believable way that young readers and parents are taken along for the ride. Like *Jurassic Park*, *The Enormous Egg* rests on the fantasy that dinosaurs and humans could cohabit this planet. Even if we haven't yet figured out how, it still feels good to laugh at this saga, the perfect read aloud for ages six through ten.

APRIL 4

Happy Birthday Fred Brenner (*The Drinking Gourd*), Maya Angelou (*Life Doesn't Frighten Me*), Johanna Reiss (*The Upstairs Room*), Elizabeth Levy (*My Life as a Fifth-Grade Comedian*), and Joan Leslie Woodruff (*The Shiloh Renewal*).

It's the birth date of Glen Rounds (1906–2002), *The Blind Colt*; and Phoebe Gilman (1940–2002), *The Balloon Tree*.

Happy Birthday Los Angeles, incorporated as a city in 1850. Read *Weetzie Bat* by Francesca Lia Block and *City of Angels* by Tracie Peterson and James Scott Bell.

On this day in 1968 Martin Luthur King Jr. was assassinated by James Earl Ray in a Memphis, Tennessee, hotel.

It's School Librarian Day. Read *Lunch Lady and the League of Librarians* by Jarrett A. Krosoczka.

In 1581 Francis Drake completed circumnavigation of the world. Read *The Girl Who Circumnavigated Fairyland in a Ship of Her Own Making* by Catherynne M. Valente.

APRIL 5

Happy Birthday Helen Hoover (*Another Heaven, Another Earth*) and Lurlene McDaniel (*Heart to Heart*).

It's the birth date of Frank Stockton (1834–1902), *The Bee-Man of Orn*; and Yasuo Segawa (1933–2010), *Sleepy Time*.

Booker T. Washington (1856–1915), author of the autobiographical *Up From Slavery*, was also born on this day. Read *Booker T. Washington* by Thomas Amper, illustrated by Jeni Reeves.

THE TEACHER'S FUNERAL: A COMEDY IN THREE PARTS
By Richard Peck

On April 5, 1934, Richard Peck was born in Decatur, Illinois. He trained to be a teacher and spent years working with students. He did not write his first novel until he was thirty-seven. Then he made up for lost time!

If ever there was a Renaissance figure in the field of children's and young adult books, Richard Peck would certainly qualify. He has written in all genres for children and teens and has consistently produced one book of quality after another since his first, *Don't Look and It Won't Hurt*, published in 1972. After that book he explored some of the toughest issues of teenage life, such as suicide in *Remembering the Good Times* and rape in *Are You in the House Alone?* For this work, Peck received the Margaret A. Edwards Lifetime Achievement Award.

Then Peck distinguished himself as one of the finest humorists writing for fourth through sixth grade readers. In the late 1990s he began to develop a series of books about hard-edged Grandma Dowdel and her two grandchildren who visit her rural Illinois home during the Depression. *A Long Way Home* won the National Book Award. Its sequel *A Year Down Yonder* finally brought a long-deserved Newbery Medal to Peck. I cannot even count the number of adults who have said to me that they believe Grandma Dowdel to be the finest adult character to appear in children's books.

If I had to choose one Richard Peck book (and no one should have to do this), I would select his hysterically funny work of historical fiction, *The Teacher's Funeral: A Comedy in Three Parts*, set in rural Indiana in 1904. Starting with the line "If your teacher has to die, August isn't a bad time of year for it," the novel moves with grace and finesse through the experiences of Russell Culver, who attends a one-room school and has to endure his sister as a teacher. All of Peck's strengths are evident in this book—great characters, smooth and graceful writing, an ear for dialogue, laugh-out-loud humor, and human compassion and insight.

For forty years Richard Peck—witty, urbane, vibrant, and committed—has logged hundreds of miles visiting schools, libraries, and conferences. He has not only written some of our finest books for children and teens, but he has also supported the teachers and librarians who bring books to them.

Happy birthday, Richard! You are a class act. I'd like you to have the final words of your celebration. Here are some signature Peck lines from one of his poems about reading. "Read to your children / Twenty minutes a day / You have the time, / And so do they."

THE LITTLE PRINCE
By Antoine de Saint-Exupéry

On April 6, 1943, one of the most unusual offerings in the children's book canon was published. Whether it was a book for adults or children or more appropriately "all ages" would become an endless debate about *The Little Prince*. But with 80 million copies in print and translations into more than 210 languages, Antoine de Saint-Exupéry's classic has definitely engrossed readers of all ages and become one of the fifty bestselling books of all time.

One of the most eccentric characters ever to appear in a book, the Little Prince from planet B-612 encounters the narrator of the story, a stranded aviator in the Sahara Desert. While the pilot works to repair his engine before he runs out of water, the prince describes his journey from planet to planet and what he has learned about relationships, and life. Containing a mesmerizing story with a great deal of philosophy, the book ends with our space traveler returning to his planet and the rose he left behind.

French aviator Antoine de Saint-Exupéry was living on Long Island while he wrote his masterpiece. Several stories exist about the beginnings of the book. The version I've always liked best claims that Saint-Exupéry, while dining with his publisher Eugene Reynal, sketched out on the tablecloth a cast of invented characters, including a little boy with wings. Eugene suggested that the author write a fairy story that could be published at Christmas.

The book turned out to be a good deal more than a fairy story. To create *The Little Prince*, Saint-Exupéry relied on some of his own experiences, such as his plane crashing in the Libyan desert. In this amazing book, he transforms his life into a view of the universe accessible to both children and adults. Written in French, the book was first released in English in the United States, with the French version coming later. In 2000 poet Richard Howard published a new translation, correcting some of the errors of the first American edition and providing a fresh interpretation of this classic. The book has influenced thousands with its wisdom and whimsy. Fred Rogers of *Mr. Rogers' Neighborhood* kept a quote from the book on his wall: "*L'essential est invisible pour les yeux.*" ("What is essential is invisible to the eye.")

Slightly over a year after the publication of *The Little Prince*, Antoine de Saint-Exupéry died in an airplane crash, while serving as a pilot for the Free French Forces in World War II. But he still lives on for his readers in the guise of his most famous character, the Little Prince from planet B-612.

APRIL 6

Happy Birthday Alice Bach (*Moses' Ark: Stories From the Bible*), Fulvio Testa (*Aesop's Fables*), Jerdine Nolen (*Thunder Rose*), and Graeme Base (*Animalia*).

It's the birth date of Ida Chittum (1918–2002), *The Cat's Pajamas*; and Douglas Hill (1935–2007), *The Dragon Charmer*.

The Italian painter and architect Raphael (1483–1520) was born on this day. Read *Raphael* by Mike Venezia and *Raphael* by Juliet Mofford.

In 1896 the first modern Olympic Games opened in Athens. Read the Percy Jackson and the Olympians series by Rick Riordan.

In 1909 Americans Robert Peary and Matthew Henson became the first explorers to reach the North Pole.

In 1917 the United States declared war on Germany and entered World War I on the Allied side.

It's National Tartan Day, honoring Americans of Scottish descent. Read books from the Tartan Magic series by Jane Yolen.

APRIL 7

Happy Birthday Alice Schertle (*All You Need for a Snowman, Little Blue Truck*) and Cheryl Willis Hudson (*Hands Can*).

It's the birth date of Donald Carrick (1929–1989), *The Wednesday Surprise, Patrick's Dinosaurs*; and poet William Wordsworth (1770–1850).

In 1795 France adopted the metre (meter) as a basic measurement of length. Hence, it is Metric System Day.

Best birthday wishes to the World Health Organization (WHO), established by the United Nations in 1948. And, by chance, it happens to be World Health Organization Day. Read *Horton Hears a Who!* by Dr. Seuss and *Peek-a Who?* by Nina Laden.

LOVE THAT DOG
By Sharon Creech

April 7 has been designated Thank the School Librarian Day. I can think of nothing else I would rather do today than show appreciation for those who run libraries or media centers in schools. For some children the school library may be the only place to access books, particularly books of quality. So on this day, donate a book to your school or write your librarian a note about what he or she means to you. Or even better—write a poem.

April is also Poetry Month, and Sharon Creech's *Love That Dog*, a small volume of one hundred pages, uses free verse to celebrate poetry and the writing of poetry. *Love That Dog* also provides a lesson in modern poetic forms.

Sharon Creech, who grew up outside Cleveland, Ohio, received an education degree and went to teach American and British Literature in England. Consequently, her first book, *Absolutely Normal Chaos*, was first published in England and did not appear until 1995 in the United States. Her second novel, *Walk Two Moons*, won the Newbery Medal. In all of Creech's work, her sure hand as a teacher prevails. After reading any one of them, young readers know they'd love to be in a class with her.

In *Love That Dog* readers meet Jack, a student of Miss Stretchberry's. He tells us simply, "I don't want to / because boys / don't write poetry. / Girls do." But then readers watch Jack make some small attempts and respond to poems being read. (Many of these have been included in the book.) As the school year progresses from September through June, Jack develops as a writer—responding in more sophisticated ways to what has been presented to him. Over time his own poetry grows in complexity and skill. Finally, toward the end of the year, Jack writes to Walter Dean Myers, because he has become a fan of Myers's poetry. Myers actually comes to the school—and Jack writes a poem inspired by his hero.

A book that teachers use in grades three through six, *Love That Dog* can be read in less than an hour. Parents report success in reading the book aloud to children as young as five, six, seven years old. In this love letter to poetry and poets, Sharon Creech demonstrates how powerful a few pages and a few well-chosen words can be. With her background as a teacher, she has a keen grasp of children and of the teaching/learning process.

I would imagine that most children will be able to find a copy of this book in their school library today. If they do, ask them to spread some love to the librarian as well.

MANIAC MAGEE

By Jerry Spinelli

In April 1990, Jerry Spinelli's *Maniac Magee* was released. I first read an advance copy of the book before it was published, and then watched it sweep the prizes, including the Boston Globe–Horn Book Award and Newbery Medal. Still going strong, it has now become a classic, one of the books remembered with great fondness by those in their twenties and thirties.

The book's unconventional approach distinguished it from so much else that had appeared at the time. Jerry Spinelli combined realistic fiction with tall tale, legend, and a dose of fantasy to craft a book unlike any other. In *Everything I Need to Know I Learned from a Children's Book*, singer Tyler Hilton admits that as a child he wasn't much of a reader until he found *Maniac Magee* and was inspired by the hero. "But then I met Maniac Magee," he writes, "a mysterious young wanderlust of a kid, and knew that I had a new role model."

Maniac Magee has both one of the best openings and closings in the children's book canon. "They say Maniac Magee was born in a dump. They say his stomach was a cereal box and his heart a sofa spring. They say he kept an eight-inch cockroach on a leash." An orphan running away from his guardians, Jeffrey Lionel Magee lives by his own rules and in a variety of locations. Legends grow around him as he does one outstanding feat after another. Fearless, he breaks all the rules in the town of Two Mills, Pennsylvania. This young white boy sees no race barriers in a town divided by them. So he lives with families in both the East and West Ends, as well as in the buffalo pen in the local zoo.

But Maniac Magee is always haunted by his past—the death of his parents and the bad things that happen to those he loves. For a time he takes up with Grayson, a failed baseball player in the minors, who sets up a temporary home for the boy in the equipment room of the band shell. But then Grayson dies, and Maniac starts running again.

Slowly, in this town torn by racial hatred, Maniac Magee begins to make a difference. And by running and racing and being involved with the people in the town, he heals himself enough finally to accept an invitation to stay with a black family that he has come to love. The book ends, "He knew that finally, truly, at long last, someone was calling him home."

With humor, heart, and wit, *Maniac Magee* brings to life an unforgettable hero and explores the issues of class and race in a way that a child can understand. Not only did the character of Maniac Magee make a difference in his small Pennsylvania town, but this book has also made a difference in the lives of children everywhere.

APRIL 8

Happy Birthday Susan Bonners (*Edwina Victorious*), Linda Crew (*Children of the River*), and Steven Schnur (*The Koufax Dilemma*).

It's the birth date of Harold Keith (1903–1998), *Rifles for Watie*; Ruth Chew (1920–2010), *The Wednesday Witch*; and Trina Schart Hyman (1939–2004), *Saint George and the Dragon, King Stork*.

In 1904 Longacre Square in Manhattan was renamed Times Square. Reread *The Cricket in Times Square* by George Selden, illustrated by Garth Williams.

It's Draw a Picture of a Bird Day. Read *How to Paint the Portrait of a Bird* by Jacques Prévert, illustrated by Mordicai Gerstein.

APRIL 9

Happy Birthday Gloria Kamen (*Edward Lear: King of Nonsense*) and Margaret Peterson Haddix (*Missing* series).

It's the birth date of Joseph Krumgold (1908–1980), . . . *And Now Miguel, Onion John*; and Leonard Wibberley (1915–1983), *The Mouse That Roared, Flint's Island.*

 In 1865 **Robert E. Lee** surrendered at the Appomattox Court House to Ulysses S. Grant, ending the U.S. Civil War. Read *Marching to Appomattox: The Footrace that Ended the Civil War* by Ken Stark and *A Ballad of the Civil War* by Mary Stolz, illustrated by Sergio Martinez.

In 1939 Marian Anderson sang at the Lincoln Memorial after being denied the chance to perform at the Daughters of the American Revolution's Constitution Hall. Read *The Voice That Challenged a Nation: Marian Anderson and the Struggle for Equal Rights* by Russell Freedman.

BALLET OF THE ELEPHANTS

By Leda Schubert

Illustrated by Robert Andrew Parker

On April 9, 1942, fifty-one elephants performed in a ballet in Madison Square Garden. Although at first this idea seems absurd, the strange but true story is explored in Leda Schubert and Robert Andrew Parker's *Ballet of the Elephants*.

Over the last ten years, picture book texts have grown shorter, and editors today often say they prefer five hundred to six hundred words—allowing ample room for the illustrator to convey the story. In *Ballet of the Elephants*, seasoned picture book author Leda Schubert uses brevity and eloquence to tell a fascinating story. Leda introduces three protagonists—John Ringling North, circus manager who thought of the idea; George Balanchine, ballet master; and Igor Stravinsky, music genius who wrote *The Rite of Spring*. Although appreciated today, when *The Rite of Spring* was first performed "people hissed after the first chord. Fistfights broke out in the audience. Stravinsky said his music was best understood by children and animals." So the three men came up with an amazing plan: produce a ballet for elephants. Balanchine studied how elephants move. Stravinsky crafted *Circus Polka*, which ended with a march. And John Ringling North taught the elephants to learn their paces.

On opening night, the ballet begins with Modoc, the largest Indian elephant in America, dressed in a tutu—a very large tutu—and dancing alone, turning and turning. Then Vera Zorina, world-famous ballerina, danced with him. Fifty elephants, the *corps de ballet*, held one another's tails and danced in an endless chain. "They raised enormous legs to rest on one another's backs, and trumpeted to Stravinsky's odd harmonies." Finally, ballerinas joined in the performance of *Circus Polka*. They did not hiss or fight. It seemed Stravinsky was right: animals understood his music better than people.

After reading *Ballet of the Elephants*, adults and children alike wish they lived in 1942 and could have been one of those four million in the big top. Until time travel becomes possible, the best way to experience *Circus Polka* is simply to read Leda Schubert's magnificent text—and watch Robert Andrew Parker use watercolors to bring this performance to life. Few nonfiction picture books contain such a naturally interesting subject for children. As P. T. Barnum, circus guru himself, said, "When entertaining the public, it is best to have an elephant." *Ballet of the Elephants* has fifty-one!

THIS LITTLE PIGGY: LAP SONGS, FINGER PLAYS, CLAPPING GAMES, AND PANTOMIME RHYMES

By Jane Yolen

Illustrated by Will Hillenbrand

Musical Arrangements by Adam Stemple

The second week of April has been designated the Week of the Young Child (WOYC). More information and a handbook can be found at the National Association for Education of Young Children website.

What are the books to which every young child should be exposed? In the early years we want children to experience poetry and rhythm information about the world around them, cumulative stories, call-and-response books, and bedtime stories.

One of the best baby shower gifts is an attractive nursery rhyme volume. These rhymes, which serve as lap songs or clapping games, are perfect for parents or infant caregivers. Many of these rhymes and chants have been used with infants for hundreds of years, hence they form one of the cultural building blocks of the English language. There are many superb collections, but I favor Jane Yolen's *This Little Piggy: Lap Songs, Finger Plays, Clapping Games and Pantomime Rhymes* with Will Hillenbrand's animated and whimsical drawings and Adam Stemple's musical arrangements.

To create the text for this lavish gift book, Jane Yolen, author of three hundred books, has deftly categorized more than sixty lap songs, finger plays, and clapping games. Each rhyme contains a note on how a parent might use it—a pragmatic and welcome touch. Then Will Hillenbrand's vibrant animal characters act out the words. He has created dynamic pacing for the volume and made sure every page is pleasing to the eye. It is to his credit that a book with so many elements, including on occasion the history of a nursery rhyme, never seems overwhelming but appears clean, clear, and easy to use.

The production of the book makes it even more special. A large format with sturdy paper and binding, readable typeface, and an attractive cover (plus a CD of performances of the material) add to the pleasure that users of this book experience. Just reading *This Little Piggy* will make you long for an infant or toddler to pull on your lap.

APRIL 10

Happy Birthday Harvey Weiss (*Maps: Getting from Here to There*), Martin Waddell (*The Pig in the Pond, Farmer Duck*), David Adler (Cam Jansen mystery series), and Wendy Anderson Halperin (*The Racketty-Packetty House*).

It's the birth date of Eric Knight (1897–1943), Lassie series.

In 1874 in Nebraska, the first Arbor Day was celebrated. Read *The Giving Tree* by Shel Silverstein, *Tell Me, Tree* by Gail Gibbons, and *Our Tree Named Steve* by Alan Zweibel, illustrated by David Catrow. Also, reread *A Tree Is Nice* by Janice May Udry, illustrated by Marc Simont.

On this day in 1912 the *Titanic* began her maiden voyage.

APRIL 11

Happy Birthday Graham Salisbury (*Under the Blood-Red Sun*) and April Pulley Sayre (*Turtle, Turtle, Watch Out!*).

It's the birth date of Felix Hoffmann (1911–1975), *Hans in Luck*.

In 1899 Spain ceded Puerto Rico to the United States. Read *The Golden Flower: A Taino Myth from Puerto Rico* by Nina Jaffe, illustrated by Enrique O. Sanchez; *Shake It, Morena!* by Carmen T. Bernier-Grand, illustrated by Lulu Delacre; and *Juan Bobo Goes to Work* retold by Marisa Montes, illustrated by Joe Cepeda.

In 1954 this was the "most boring day in history," since 1900. Read Tony Fucille's *Let's Do Nothing*.

Fort Sumter was shelled by the Confederacy, starting the Civil War on this day in 1861.

It's Barbershop Quartet Day. Read *Uncle Jed's Barbershop* by Margaree King Mitchell, illustrated by James Ransome.

MR. GUMPY'S OUTING

By John Burningham

For the Week of the Young Child, I want to talk about books for babies and toddlers. As Julie Roach, Manager of Youth Services of the Cambridge (MA) Public Library, has told me on many occasions, the best titles for this age group include a text with few words that encourages participation and simple images and plots that appeal to the very young.

One of the best books for babies and toddlers, *Mr. Gumpy's Outing*, published in 1971, was created by John Burningham, England's premier artist for young children. Although John Burningham attended many schools, including A. S. Neill's Summerhill, he was an indifferent student except when creating art. For periods of time he worked on farms and in hospitals and later enrolled in London's Central School of Arts and Crafts. There he met his wife, the amazingly talented Helen Oxenbury, and was teaching part time in an art school when his first picture book, *Borka: The Adventures of a Goose with No Feathers*, was published. Because it won the prestigious Kate Greenaway Medal, Burningham decided to create other children's books. In *Mr. Gumpy's Outing*, our hero, Mr. Gumpy, travels along a river on a boat, picking up animals and children who promise to make no trouble for him. Of course, they can't help being themselves, and eventually the whole crew ends up in the river. But all ends happily, as everyone heads out to a sumptuous high tea.

Mr. Gumpy's Outing by John Burningham is the ideal participation book for the very young—and can be acted out by a parent or child, or with a group of children, with ease. The story has a predictable sequence—" 'May I come please, Mr. Gumpy?' said the pig. 'Very well, but don't muck about.' " Children want to join in, and gain confidence as they do. For the art Burningham balances brown pen sketches with vibrant full-color art. He has paced the text and art brilliantly. Even after readers know the outcome, they still enjoy watching the story unfold.

The ultimate artist, Burningham remains true to his belief that the best children's books include as much for the parents as they do for children. Hence adults also love this book and its sequel, *Mr. Gumpy's Motor Car*. At the end of *Mr. Gumpy's Outing*, Mr. Gumpy invites us to come again for a ride some other day. I myself have loved every repeat trip on this boat—and so have children.

HENRY HUGGINS

By Beverly Cleary

Today marks the birthday of one of America's most beloved writers for children: Beverly Cleary. Born in McMinnville, Oregon, on April 12, 1916, Beverly Alice Bunn lived for a short time on a farm in Yamhill before moving to Portland when she was six. In *Girl from Yamhill*, Cleary provides one of the most honest and poignant autobiographies that we have of a children's book writer, one that shows how difficult her path to becoming an author has been. As her editor Barbara Lalicki has noted, Cleary emerged from her trials as a person with "a sparkling laugh and a unique, upbeat way of observing the world."

For years Cleary worked as a children's librarian and the children she had contact with on a daily basis became her muses. Those in first, second, or third grades often asked her for books about children, just like themselves, who have everyday adventures. As one said to her, "Where are the books for kids like us?" The books of the time favored foreign settings, wild adventures, or mysteries. Unable to find the type of stories she wanted, Cleary set out to write them. In 1950 she published *Henry Huggins*, a book about a third grader who lives on Klickitat Street in Portland and who believes that nothing much ever happens to him. But then Henry discovers a stray dog, names him Ribsy, and life gets much more interesting. Each episodic chapter stands on its own, an ideal format for those learning to read. The chapters focus on Henry's problems—as when his pet goldfish begin to multiply.

Certainly these books, and those about Ramona and her sister Beezus, keep children laughing and happy, but they also have a great deal of depth. In *Everything I Need to Know I Learned from a Children's Book* Pulitzer Prize–winner Michael Dirda wrote about the final chapter of *Henry Huggins*, in which Ribsy needs to choose between his former owner and Henry. "In those final pages of her novel, Beverly Cleary compels the reader to think hard about conflicting loyalties and obligations, to recognize the necessity of accommodation to circumstances, and to acknowledge one of life's great, sad truths: Nothing that involves people and their feelings is ever plain and straightforward. All of us live with shadow and uncertainty and sometimes with qualms and regrets."

Beverly Cleary has never had a reason for regret. For over sixty years she has made children want to read and enjoy reading.

APRIL 12

Happy Birthday Gary Soto (*Baseball in April and Other Stories*, *Too Many Tamales*).

It's the birth date of C. W. Anderson (1891–1971), *Billy and Blaze: A Boy and His Pony*; Hardie Gramatky (1907–1979), *Little Toot*; Paul Showers (1910–1999), *The Listening Walk*; and Barbara Corcoran (1911–2003), *Wolf at the Door*.

In 1954 musical group Bill Haley and His Comets recorded the song "Rock Around the Clock." Read *Bats Around the Clock* by Kathi Appelt, illustrated by Melissa Sweet, and *Boom Chicka Rock* by John Archambault, illustrated by Suzanne Tanner Chitwood.

It's National Licorice Day. Read *Arthur's Funny Money* by Lillian Hoban.

APRIL 13

Happy Birthday Lee Bennett Hopkins (*Amazing Faces*) and Rita Williams-Garcia (*One Crazy Summer*).

It's the birth date of Genevieve Foster (1893–1979), *George Washington's World*; Marguerite Henry (1902–1997), *Misty of Chincoteague*, *Justin Morgan Had a Horse*; Eudora Welty (1909–2001), *The Shoe Bird*; Erik Haugaard (1923–2009), *The Samurai's Tale*; and Jon Stone (1931–1977), *The Monster at the End of This Book*.

 It's also the birth date of **Thomas Jefferson** (1743–1826), known as the principal author of the Declaration of Independence and the third president of the United States. Then in 1943, the 200th anniversary of his birthday, the Jefferson Memorial was dedicated in Washington, D.C. Hence it is Thomas Jefferson Day.

CHASING LINCOLN'S KILLER

By James L. Swanson

On April 13, 1865, the city of Washington, D.C., celebrated the end of the Civil War by illuminating the city. Both public and private buildings glowed from candlelight, torches, gaslight—even fireworks. Many thought it the most beautiful night ever experienced in the nation's capital. But April 14 would be one of worst days in the history of the country.

Every now and then, an author of a book for adults adapts that work into an important book for young readers, just as John Fitzgerald Kennedy did for *Profiles in Courage*. James L. Swanson revised his bestselling novel *Manhunt: The 12-Day Chase for Lincoln's Killer* to create *Chasing Lincoln's Killer*, a book that reads like a thriller and works perfectly for ten- to sixteen-year-olds.

In a page-turning, exciting narrative he brings readers to the events of 1865 that preceded the assassination of Abraham Lincoln. Readers watch John Wilkes Booth, hour by hour, plot the assassination of Lincoln, the attack on the secretary of state, and the attempted murder of the vice president, Andrew Johnson. They meet his partners in crime—Mary Surratt, David Herold, Lewis Powell, George Atzerodt. And then they watch in detail as Booth pulls off his own part of the master plan before the rest of the events start to go awry—including the attack on the secretary of state. Booth and his coconspirators then escape from Washington and those pursuing them. A twelve-day manhunt ensues, which finally ends in Booth's death and the capture of his team.

Even though the outcome is known, readers breathlessly follow the events, watching how ideology played itself out in the days following the surrender of Lee to Grant. Not everyone who helped Booth believed in the Lost Cause of the South; many struggled with the possible danger to themselves and to their families. Some helped gladly, knowing the consequences. Swanson allows readers to understand why the events happened, but spends almost all of his text on exact details of how events transpired in the days after the assassination. His scenes are so well written that readers feel they are actually traveling along with Booth, desperately trying to get deep into the South for safety. After reading the book, I put on my "must do" list the twelve-hour bus tour organized by the Surratt House Museum that follows Booth's escape route.

For those hunting for a book that can engage young people in history, *Chasing Lincoln's Killer* provides action, true crime, and suspense. I remember as a young reader gobbling up Jim Bishop's *The Day Lincoln Was Shot*. Many will have the same reaction to this book. In *Chasing Lincoln's Killer*, Swanson shows why history, told as a story, makes the most compelling reading of all.

THE NEW KID ON THE BLOCK

By Jack Prelutsky

In April we celebrate National Poem in Your Pocket Day, a day much beloved by school children and poetry enthusiasts. The idea behind the event is quite simple: during National Poetry Month select a poem that you love and carry it with you today to share with classmates, co-workers, family, and friends. Activities have been planned in schools, libraries, workplaces, and bookstores across the country. The Academy of American Poets provides lots of ideas, including finding a poem on a mobile device.

One of the most popular poets for children, the no-fail Jack Prelutsky, has an extraordinary body of work; any one of his poems would be ideal for carrying in your pocket today. When he was young Jack did not think that he would become one of America's best-loved poets for children, much less be selected as America's first Poet Laureate for Children. He hoped to be an illustrator and showed his art with some poems he had written to Greenwillow's legendary editor Susan Hirschman. Then Hirschman did something extraordinary; she offered to take him to lunch in the executive dining room if he brought a good poem to her each week. At this point in his life, Prelutsky drove a cab to make ends meet. Since this might be the only good meal he could count on, Prelutsky started to craft a poem a week.

Eventually, his body of work would make cab driving no longer necessary. I have always thought this story one of the most beautiful editor/author sagas that I know.

Twenty years after first meeting with Hirschman, Prelutsky wrote 107 poems for his best-known compilation of poetry, *The New Kid on the Block*. It features unforgettable creatures such as the Slyne, the Gloppers, and Baloney Belly Billy. Hirschman hired James Stevenson, a *New Yorker* cartoonist, to illustrate the book. The result was a wonderful collaboration between author and artist—and a book that delights the eye and the ear.

Jack Prelutsky—with his strong rhyme, rhythm, and word play—has kept generations of children happy with his poetry.

APRIL 14

Happy Birthday Frank Remkiewicz (Horrible Harry series).

It's the birth date of Anne Sullivan (1866–1936), who worked with Helen Keller and assisted Keller in writing *The Story of My Life*, and Robert Lopshire (1927–2002), *Put Me in the Zoo*.

In 1828 Noah Webster copyrighted the first edition of his dictionary.

The epic and controversial classic *The Grapes of Wrath* by John Steinbeck was published in 1939. Read other John Steinbeck books as well, such as *The Red Pony* and *The Pearl*.

On this day in 1865 President Abraham Lincoln was assassinated in Ford's Theater by John Wilkes Booth. He died the next day. Read *Chasing Lincoln's Killer* by James L. Swanson.

It's National Pecan Day. Read *Pecan Pie Baby* by Jacqueline Woodson, illustrated by Sophie Blackall.

APRIL 15

Happy Birthday Eleanor Schick (*Navajo Wedding Day*) and Jacqueline Briggs Martin (*Snowflake Bentley*).

It is the birth date of Leonardo da Vinci (1452–1519), the Italian Renaissance painter, scientist, inventor, anatomist, and writer.

On this day in 1802 poet William Wordsworth and his sister Dorothy saw a "long belt" of daffodils, which inspired "I Wandered Lonely as a Cloud." Read *Poetry for Young People: William Wordsworth* edited by Dr. Alan Liu, illustrated by James Muir, and *Daffodil* by Emily Jenkins, illustrated by Tomek Bogacki.

In 1912, the day after hitting an iceberg in the Atlantic Ocean, the steamship *Titanic* sank. Hence, it is Titanic Remembrance Day. Read *Titanic: Voices from the Disaster* by Deborah Hopkinson and *The Watch That Ends the Night: Voices from the Titanic* by Allan Wolf.

LIBRARY LION
By Michelle Knudsen
Illustrated by Kevin Hawkes

The second week of April has been designated National Library Week. All kinds of libraries—school, public, and academic—participate in this annual event that celebrates the contributions of our nation's libraries. If you haven't registered a child for a library card recently, you will be pleasantly surprised about the offerings in children's rooms of modern public libraries. Videos, audio books, recordings, and computers can be found there. Story hours and reading clubs help both parents and children find new books that they will enjoy.

But my book of the day, *Library Lion* by Michelle Knudsen, resurrects the old-fashioned library of the 1950s and 1960s. Here the librarian Miss Merriweather worries about rules being broken. When a lion saunters into the library, she realizes, however, that no rules exist about them. As long as he remains quiet and does not roar, he can listen to story hour with the children. Then he learns to dust the shelf with his tail, lick envelopes, and allow himself to serve as a footstool for children. All goes well until Miss Merriweather has an accident—and the lion must roar to get help.

This old-fashioned story is accompanied by acrylic-and-pencil illustrations by Kevin Hawkes. Hawkes is one of the most versatile illustrators working in children's books today. He adapts his style for each new book, shaping his art to the demands of the text. The lion he renders is so charming that anyone would want to curl up with this furry friend. The pacing and timing of the pictures are impeccable. Printed on a creamy, off-white paper, the art and text draw readers in, pulling them along with the tension of the story. Since this book appeared in 2006, many families have decided that *Library Lion* is one of their favorite books, one that they buy and share with their friends—or one that they check out of the library again and again.

So if you go to the library this month you probably won't find a lion—except sometimes as a statue outside. But you will find a lot of books like *Library Lion* that bring you into another world and make you want to stay there for a while. And who knows? I'm headed to the library myself today—maybe, just maybe, that wonderful lion will be there.

THE BOXCAR CHILDREN
By Gertrude Chandler Warner

Today we honor a writer who has inspired millions of children to fantasize about living in a broken-down railroad boxcar. Born on April 16, 1890, in Putnam, Connecticut, Gertrude Chandler Warner lived across the street from the railroad station. Young Warner would talk to the men on the train and peek inside to see the neatly arranged living quarters. And she asked herself what it would be like to live in a caboose or a boxcar.

Due to poor health, Warner spent most of her schooling with a tutor and discovered that she loved to write. During World War I, although she did not have a high school diploma, she was recruited to teach—something that she continued for thirty-two years. While in the classroom, she began to work on a story inspired by her childhood fantasy. Putnam, a mill town, drew a diverse population, and many of her students struggled to learn English as a second language. She developed her tale to help these immigrant children and other slower readers. But she also worked to

provide a fascinating story, one that would appeal to the better students in her class. The resulting book, *The Boxcar Children*, uses simple words and concepts, appeals to a wide range of readers in first and second grades, and contains a very compelling plot line.

In this totally satisfying book, the four Alden children—Henry, Jessie, Violet, and Benny—have become orphans and run away rather than be taken to their grandfather, who they do not know but fear. With only a few dollars in Henry's pocket, the children locate an abandoned railroad boxcar and furnish it with pine branches and plates and cups from a nearby dump. Henry locates work that provides food and money, and they transform their surroundings into a kind a paradise, complete with a swimming hole for hot summer days. A spot behind a waterfall serves to keep butter and milk cold. In short, every small object the resourceful children find is made useful. In the end, their grandfather turns out to be kindly and takes them in, but he transfers the boxcar to his property so they can have more adventures.

Naturally, a few grown-ups protested about children living unsupervised. But this detail has never bothered children. In fact, it taps into a frequent childhood fear—what if children had to live without adults? Once a child reads *The Boxcar Children*, he or she never has to worry again. Readers love the self-reliance of this family and the way they work together for a happy ending.

If you are ever near Putnam, Connecticut, stop by and visit the Gertrude Warner Museum right near the railroad station. They won't let you move into the boxcar—but you can see her home and the environment that inspired her books.

APRIL 16

Happy Birthday John Christopher (*The White Mountains*), Eleanora E. Tate (*Celeste's Harlem Renaissance*), and Eva Moore (*Buddy: The First Seeing Eye Dog*).

It's the birth date of Dorothy P. Lathrop (1891–1980), *Hitty: Her First Hundred Years*; Gunnel Beckman (1910–2003), *Admission to the Feast*; Sir Kingsley Amis (1922–1995), *We Are All Guilty*; Gertrude Chandler Warner (1890–1979), The Boxcar Children series; and illustrator Garth Williams (1912–1996), *Stuart Little*, *Charlotte's Web*, *The Cricket in Times Square*, the Little House series.

In 1963 Rev. Martin Luther King Jr. penned his famous letter from the Birmingham Jail. Read *Walk Together Children* by Elizabeth Partridge.

APRIL 17

Happy Birthday Dora Jessie Saint, pen name Miss Read (*News From Thrush Green*); Roy A. Gallant (*The Ever-Changing Atom*); and Jane Kurtz (*River Friendly, River Wild*).

It's the birth date of Dayal Kaur Khalsa (1943–1989), *I Want a Dog*; and Martyn Godfrey (1947–2000), *Baseball Crazy*.

In 1397 Chaucer told the Canterbury Tales for the first time at court of Richard II. Read *Canterbury Tales* adapted by Barbara Cohen, illustrated by Trina Schart Hyman, *Chaucer's Canterbury Tales* by Marcia Williams, and *Sir Gawain and the Loathly Lady* by Selina Hastings.

It's Bat Appreciation Day. Read *Bats at the Ballgame* by Brian Lies.

BECAUSE OF WINN-DIXIE

By Kate DiCamillo

April has been set aside as "Dog Appreciation Month." The bond between child and dog remains one of the universal experiences of childhood, as does the longing for a dog if the child has been denied one by a parent.

That longing has been beautifully described in our book of the day, *Because of Winn-Dixie* by Kate DiCamillo. Ten-year-old India Opal Buloni lives with her preacher father; they are newcomers in a Florida town. Opal's mother left years ago, and her father has come to take up his calling at the Open Arms Baptist Church. One day, while shopping in the Winn-Dixie store, Opal sees a stray dog with a charismatic smile who has knocked down some groceries into the aisles. She claims him as her own and calls him the first thing that comes to her mind, Winn-Dixie. Opal finds that he follows obediently and fits in perfectly—after a bath and some food.

Then, because of Winn-Dixie, she begins to make friends—the local librarian, an old lady some call a witch, the owner of a pet store, and even some of the boys and girls of the town. At the end of the book, they all have a wonderful party—only to have Winn-Dixie vanish suddenly in a thunderstorm. But all ends well, as readers watch Opal move from a misfit to a member of a community, helping others heal from their own loneliness and heartache.

Ideal for eight- to twelve-year-old readers, *Because of Winn-Dixie*, DiCamillo's first children's book, met with little success when sent to publishers. In fact, DiCamillo is probably the most rejected of our contemporary writers, with 440 rejections, from the time she first started sending work out until the day *Winn-Dixie* was accepted. This manuscript sat in the Candlewick offices for several months until editorial assistant Kara LaReau found it, liked it, and passed it on to Liz Bicknell. Bicknell laughed at the first chapter, and then cried. After finishing it, she thought it the best middle grade novel she had ever read. When Bicknell called to ask if the book might still be available, DiCamillo was faced with something new to her—acceptance. Quickly selling a half million copies and winning a Newbery Honor, the book won over critics and children in equal measure. As one child has said of the story: "If *Winn-Dixie* weren't a book, I'd marry it."

In the twenty-first century Kate DiCamillo has written one fabulous book after another like *The Tale of Despereaux*, winner of the Newbery Medal, and *The Miraculous Journey of Edward Tulane*. Starting as one of the most rejected writers, Kate DiCamillo has become one of this century's most acclaimed authors. If by any chance you have missed her, you can begin with no better book than *Because of Winn-Dixie*. Telling a beautiful story, with great characters, in simple language, Kate reminds all her readers just how satisfying a story of girl and her dog can be when told from the heart.

THE GARDENER

By Sarah Stewart
Illustrated by David Small

April has been designated National Gardening Month. Gardening month reminds me of that desperate plea from Mary Lennox in *The Secret Garden*: "Might I have a bit of earth?" Organizers of National Gardening Month suggest sharing plants with friends and planning a community clean-up. Before you get started, you might want to pick up a book that will inspire you, Sarah Stewart's *The Gardener,* with illustrations by David Small.

Certainly one of the most satisfying picture books of the last fifteen years, the text of this Caldecott Honor book is presented in letters from a young girl, Lydia Grace Finch, circa 1935. Readers first see Lydia on the endpapers, picking tomatoes with her grandmother in a lush country garden. Lydia has been summoned to city to live with her uncle Jim, until things get better for her family hit hard by the Depression. Lydia leaves King Mill on a train, carrying packets of seeds from her grandmother. When she arrives in the city, the dark railroad station looms over her. But Lydia only notices window boxes and beams of light. Although her uncle Jim does not smile, she writes him poetry and learns to work in his bakeshop, kneading bread. But Lydia is a gardener at heart, not a baker. In this impoverished environment, she finds a secret place to ply her craft: the apartment building roof. Vacant lots provide the necessary dirt and cracked teacups and bent cake pans become the vessels for her dreams. Finally, she shows grumpy Uncle Jim her rooftop garden, a once-grimy place now transformed into a beautiful spot. After Lydia's father finds a job, this no-longer unhappy man hugs his niece as he sends her back home.

The Gardener is brilliantly illustrated with watercolors with a strong black line. David Small sets scenes and shows what characters feel, even when those emotions are not described in the text. The transformation of useless city space to a splendid garden satisfies readers every time they watch it happen.

When this book appeared in 1997, I thought it a wonderful re-creation of the Depression era for children. Now it seems to me an even more important book. With children who might well identify with a parent out of work or having little money, the book speaks to the true American can-do spirit. Make beauty where none exists; plant victory gardens; transform useless landscapes into those that produce food and joy; reuse and recycle. *The Gardener* can be used to talk about all of these contemporary issues. It continues to send its readers off to find that "bit of earth," whether in vacant lots, window boxes, or well-laid-out garden beds.

APRIL 18

Happy Birthday Mitchell Sharmat (Nate the Great series) and Barbara Reid (*Fox Walked Alone*).

It's the birth date of Evelyn Sibley Lampman (1907–1980), *The Shy Stegosaurus of Cricket Creek.*

Happy Birthday to the original **Yankee Stadium**, first opened in The Bronx, New York City, in 1923. The facility, known as "The House that Ruth Built" was demolished in 2010. Read *Ballpark: The Story of America's Baseball Fields* by Lynn Curlee.

In 1924 the first crossword puzzle book was published. Read *The Puzzling World of Winston Breen* and *The Potato Chip Puzzles*, both by Eric Berlin.

A massive earthquate hit San Francisco, measuring 8/25 on the Richter scale, on this day in 1906. Read *Earthquake!* by Milly Lee.

APRIL 19

Happy Birthday Jon Agee (*Terrific; Palindromania!*), Javaka Steptoe (*In Daddy's Arms I Am Tall: African Americans Celebrating Fathers, Hot Day on Abbot Avenue*), and Melissa Sweet (*River of Words, Tupelo Rides the Rails*).

It's the birth date of Jean Lee Latham (1902–1995), *Carry On, Mr. Bowditch.*

It's National Garlic Day. Read *Onions and Garlic* by Eric A. Kimmel, illustrated by Katya Arnold; *Vampire Boy's Goodnight* by Lisa Brown; *Vampire State Building* by Elizabeth Levy, illustrated by Sally Wern Comport; and *A Vampire is Coming to Dinner: 10 Rules to Follow* by Pamela Jane, illustrated by Pedro Rodriguez.

PAUL REVERE'S RIDE: THE LANDLORD'S TALE

By Henry Wadsworth Longfellow
Illustrated by Charles Santore

For those attuned to sports, around this time of year the Boston Marathon occurs. But for those who delight in the details of America's hard-won independence as a nation, April 19 remains sacred: the beginning of the American Revolution. Many in the Boston area wake long before dawn to stand on the Lexington Green and watch British and American reenactors face each other in a reconstruction of the Battle of Lexington. Usually an all-you-can-eat pancake breakfast rounds out this engaging event.

Since April is also Poetry Month, the two events can be celebrated with one spectacular book, *Paul Revere's Ride: The Landlord's Tale* by Henry Wadsworth Longfellow, illustrated by Charles Santore. Certainly many of us memorized Longfellow as part of our elementary school experience. Poetry has changed since this nineteenth-century classic, but to my ears these Longfellow lines bring back memories of devoted teachers: "Listen, my children, and you shall hear / Of the midnight ride of Paul Revere, / On the eighteenth of April, in Seventy-five; / Hardly a man is now alive / Who remembers that famous day and year." Paul Revere waits for his signal in the old North Church, and then heads out to alert the citizens in the towns like Medford, Lexington, and Concord. He travels "To every Middlesex [Massachusetts County] village and farm" to deliver "the midnight message of Paul Revere."

Many artists have illustrated Longfellow's words, but in 2003 Philadelphia artist Charles Santore created a highly realistic version that shows the uniforms, faces, and landscapes in exact detail. If any artist can be said to be the descendant of the great American illustrator and artist educator Howard Pyle, Santore would be chosen for this accolade. Certainly one of the finest realistic draftsman working in children's books today, he knows how to render every nuance of a horse and rider in motion. Readers view the landscape in detail as Revere might have, and they move along in time with Longfellow's stirring beat.

I know historians remind us that the British did capture Revere, and he did not ride alone. Longfellow re-created the spirit of the Revolution but missed some of its exact history. Fortunately, Santore has taken greater care with accuracy in his visual rendition of events.

So, if you aren't able to be in Lexington and Concord for pancakes to celebrate Patriots' Day this year, you can at least feel as if you have helped set the Revolution in motion by picking up *Paul Revere's Ride.*

ALL THE SMALL POEMS AND FOURTEEN MORE

By Valerie Worth

Illustrated by Natalie Babbitt

For Poetry Month I'd like to celebrate one of the twentieth century's finest poets for children, Valerie Worth.

After graduating from Swarthmore College, Worth moved to Clinton, New York, and met fellow author and artist Natalie Babbitt. Babbitt, who is known for classic novels such as *Tuck Everlasting*, began contributing simple line drawings to Worth's poetry volumes, beginning with *Small Poems*, published in 1972. In 1994 all of Worth's small poem volumes were pulled together in a glorious edition, *All the Small Poems and Fourteen More*. If you do not own this gem, run—don't walk—to your nearest bookstore. For any poetry library, I would list it as one of the first volumes any family should own.

In this elegant and simply designed volume, Worth brings her love of nature that began in her childhood in Pennsylvania to each offering. She looks at common animals, plants, and objects through her particular poetic lens: "Under a maple tree / The dog lies down / Lolls his limp / Tongue, yawns / Rests his long chin / Carefully between / Front paws." In Worth's free verse, every word counts. Everything is stripped to bare minimum so that the text creates exquisite and simple "word pictures."

Many of the poems can be used at various times of the year, such as ones about pumpkins or Christmas lights. For Earth Day on April 22, Worth's poetry provides a simple yet effective way for children to look at all creatures great and small. Like haiku, the poems naturally encourage children to try their own free verse forms and to explore their world through poetry.

Shortly before her death in 1994, Valerie Worth wrote an essay for *Children's Books and Their Creators* about her own goals and dreams as a poet. She writes, "[I'm] trying to catch hold of things and put them into poems; poems that would somehow express the essential qualities of an object or an experience, so that somebody else could read what I'd written and think, 'Yes, that's right. I've seen that myself.' So many poets have done this for me. I've tried to do the same for others, especially children, who are encountering so much for the first time and are responding to what they see so directly and intensely."

Now more than fifteen years later, her poetry still helps children and adults see the world around them in fresh language and striking images. After reading a poem by Worth, I also find myself thinking, "Yes, that's right. I've seen that myself."

APRIL 20

Happy Birthday Peter S. Beagle (*The Last Unicorn, Tamsen*) and Mary Hoffman (*Amazing Grace, Princess Grace*).

It's the birth date of Dinah Craik (1826–1887), *The Little Lame Prince*.

Best birthday wishes to Fenway Park, home of the Red Sox, opened on this day in 1912. Read *The Prince of Fenway Park* by Julianna Baggott and *The Fenway Foul-Up* by David A. Kelly, illustrated by Mark Meyers.

In 1916 the Chicago Cubs played their first game in Weegham Park, now called Wrigley Field. Read *The Story of the Chicago Cubs* by Tyler Omoth.

Billie Holiday recorded the haunting anti-lynching song "Strange Fruit" in 1939. Read *Becoming Billie Holiday* by Carole Boston Weatherford, illustrated by Floyd Cooper.

APRIL 21

Happy Birthday Jane Breskin Zalben (*Paths to Peace: People Who Changed the World*; *Four Seasons*) and Tim Jacobus (*It Came from New Jersey!: My Life as an Artist*).

It's the birth date of Charlotte Brontë (1816–1855), *Jane Eyre*.

John Muir (1838–1914) was born on this day. Read *Squirrel and John Muir* by Emily Arnold McCully; *John Muir: America's First Environmentalist* by Kathryn Lasky, illustrated by Stan Fellows; and *John Muir: America's Naturalist* by Thomas Locker.

According to legend, twins Romulus and Remus founded Rome in 753 BC. Read *Romulus and Remus* by Anne Rockwell and *Roman Myths* by Geraldine McCaughrean, illustrated by Emma Chichester Clark.

JUNIE B. JONES AND THE STUPID SMELLY BUS

By Barbara Park
Illustrated by Denise Brunkus

Today we celebrate Kindergarten Day, observed on the birthday of Friedrich Froebel, who founded the first kindergarten in Blankenburg, Germany, in 1837. Froebel believed that play, toys, and music formed the building blocks of children's education. Certainly the most famous kindergartner in the canon of children's books, Junie B. Jones, does not initially believe that going to school is a good idea. She particularly dislikes riding on that stupid, smelly bus. In fact, she will do anything, even hide in the supply closet, to avoid it.

Welcome to the very real and very funny world of Junie B. Jones, created by comic genius Barbara Park. Reading expert Jim Trelease has always claimed that the books in Junie's series, which first appeared in 1992, are the most stolen books in the United States. One teacher in Washington, D.C., records having 800 Junie B. Jones books swiped from her classroom in one year. She happily replenishes them—because after all a stolen book is one that a child can't live without.

The saga begins in *Junie B. Jones and the Stupid Smelly Bus*. Junie starts kindergarten in her own manner—driving the teacher, principal, and her mother a bit crazy on her first day. She says what she thinks; she talks when she wants. She acts up, and she murders the English language. Most readers in the six- to eight-year-old age range identify with Junie B. immediately. I've known children who read only Junie B. Jones books while they are in kindergarten—one after another.

Not only do adults misunderstand Junie B., she frequently misinterprets them, as well. In the second book, *Junie B. Jones and a Little Monkey Business*, Junie hears her grandmother describe her newborn baby brother as a cute little monkey—and Junie takes Grandma literally. Now Junie B. believes she will have a pet monkey to play with.

With twenty-seven volumes that take Junie B. from kindergarten to first grade—and with around twenty-five million copies in print—this series provides the perfect way to keep kindergarteners entertained as the year progresses. With her energy, screwball logic, and true-to-life behavior, Junie B. Jones has won over one reader after another. Although adults don't always comprehend the behavior of Junie B., her readers know beyond a shadow of a doubt that Barbara Park completely understands them.

IN THE SMALL, SMALL POND

By Denise Fleming

Since 1970 Earth Day has been celebrated worldwide on April 22. With an emphasis on the resources of the planet and renewable energy, Earth Day reminds us to take a closer look at the world around us.

Today I'd like to take a look at a book that focus on the environment and the creatures of the earth. Since Denise Fleming's *In the Small, Small Pond,* a Caldecott Honor book, first appeared in 1993, I have always thought it one of the best ways to explain an ecosystem to young children ages two through eight. In bold, graphic double-page spreads, Fleming shows a small boy examining all the life forms that can be found in a freshwater pond. She uses light verse—"waddle, wade, geese parade"—and vibrant artwork to bring the inhabitants of this world to life. Tadpoles, dragonflies, turtles, herons, and beavers all strut across the stage, showing their shapes and movement.

Fleming created the art by pouring colored cotton pulp through stencils—the resulting images are both childlike and child-friendly. Although the book allows a very young child to simply enjoy the sounds of language and the activity of the creatures, it also shows the life forms in this contained ecosystem. Anyone wanting to present a small lesson on Earth Day about how ponds teem with life can do no better than to pick up this classic book for the very young.

As a child growing up in Toledo, Ohio, Denise Fleming was always making things—clothespin Pilgrims or treasure eggs. When not involved in crafts, she and her sister spent time putting on plays. By the third grade Denise had been selected to study at the Toledo Museum of Art. Training to be an artist, at first she found nothing in the advertising world to excite her. But then by a happy coincidence, she enrolled in a papermaking class and began to experiment with her own method of making pulp paper. In the 1990s she started publishing a series of very exciting children's books that explore the natural world from a child's perspective.

On Earth Day I hope all children have a chance to think about our planet, our need to preserve it, and its fabulous inhabitants. Happy Earth Day.

APRIL 22

Happy Birthday William Jay Smith (*Birds and Beasts*), Paula Fox (*The Slave Dancer, One-Eyed Cat*), Ron Koertge (*Shakespeare Bats Cleanup, Stoner & Spaz*), Eileen Christelow (*Letters from a Desperate Dog, Five Little Monkeys Jumping on the Bed*), and Kathy Stinson (*Red is Best, 101 Ways to Dance*).

It's the birth date of Henry Fielding (1707–1754), *Tom Jones*; and Kurt Wiese (1887–1974), *Five Chinese Brothers, The Story about Ping*.

In 1976 Barbara Walters became the first female nightly network news anchor on the ABC Evening News with Harry Reasoner.

In 1993 the Holocaust Memorial Museum was dedicated in Washington, D.C. Read *The United States Holocaust Memorial Museum: America Keeps the Memory Alive* by Eleanor H. Ayer.

APRIL 23

Happy Birthday **William Shakespeare**. Read *William Shakespeare & the Globe* by Aliki, *The Bard of Avon* by Peter Vennema, co-authored and illustrated by Diane Stanley, *Shakespeare's Secret* by Elise Broach, and *Shakespeare Stories* by Leon Garfield, illustrated by Michael Foreman.

It's the birth date of James Buchanan (1791–1868), the 15th president of the United States.

In 1635 Boston Latin School, first public school in what will become the United States, was founded. Read *The Secret School* by Avi and *Schooled* by Gordon Korman.

It's Take a Chance Day. Read *Take a Chance, Gramps* by Jean Davies Okimoto and *Cloudy with a Chance of Meatballs* by Judi Barrett, illustrated by Ron Barrett.

THE SHAKESPEARE STEALER
By Gary Blackwood

Today marks both the probable birthday and death day of the most famous author in the English language, William Shakespeare (1564–1616) of Stratford-upon-Avon. In honor of the bard, April 23 has been designated Talk Like Shakespeare Day. Call any tormentor a "jackanapes" or "white-livered canker-blossom." Instead of *you*, say "thou" or "thee." And end verbs with the letters -*eth*. Anyone with a little imagination will have a very good time today, unless you find yourself melancholy, pondering "to be or not to be."

Methinks the best book about Shakespeare, for nine- to fourteen-year-olds, to be Gary Blackwood's *The Shakespeare Stealer*, published in 1998. Blackwood knows how to capture all of the excitement, villainy, emotion, and action of a Shakespeare play. Young Widge, orphaned at birth in 1587, spends seven years in an orphanage and then the next seven as an apprentice to an apothecary. His master, Dr. Bright, has devised a type of shorthand, which he teaches Widge. Consequently, the young boy can capture any conversation and then render it in long hand. This skill seals his fate—Simon Bass, a shady character connected to the London theater, needs a boy with just such a talent. Simon has a bold plan—to copy the lines of Shakespeare's new play *Hamlet* and then make it available for another acting company to perform.

Purchased from Dr. Bright by Bass and transported to his new home by an evil character called Falconer, Widge sets out to copy every line of *Hamlet* as it is being performed. He has never really questioned his masters; he follows blindly. Copying down every phrase of *Hamlet* proves more difficult than he thinks, particularly because he gets swept up in the play. Then Widge is invited to join Shakespeare's company as an understudy. All the while Falconer stalks him, telling him to steal the official play book and threatening his life. As Widge gains competence as a player, he begins to think for himself. How can he betray these people who have become a family to him? But how can he break away from Bass and Falconer?

With great scenes of swordplay, chases, and duels, *The Shakespeare Stealer* brings the world of Elizabethan theater and the street life of London alive for young readers. In a book where Shakespeare makes only cameo appearances, Widge performs for Queen Elizabeth herself, who encourages the young man in his choice of career. Blackwood knows how to keep a taut plot line and introduce unfamiliar elements so that anyone can understand them. He has, in short, paid a great tribute to the bard.

So happy Talk Like Shakespeare Day. I hope you have half as much fun celebrating the bard as you will reading about his world in *The Shakespeare Stealer*.

THE COUNTRY BUNNY AND THE LITTLE GOLD SHOES

By DuBose Heyward

Illustrated by Marjorie Flack

Happy Birthday Lynn Hall (*Barry the Bravest Saint Bernard*) and Bert Kitchen (*Whoo Goes There?*).

It's the birth date of Robert Penn Warren (1905–1989), *Remember the Alamo!*; and Evaline Ness (1911–1986), *Sams, Bangs, and Moonshine.*

Best birthday wishes to the Library of Congress, established by John Adams in 1800. Read *American Treasures in the Library of Congress: Memory, Reason, Imagination* by Margaret E. Wagner and *Presidents: A Library of Congress Book* by Martin W. Sandler.

The celebration of Easter in April contains both religious and secular components. Although hundreds of books have been published for Easter, for me the best was published seventy-two years ago: DuBose Heyward's *The Country Bunny and the Little Gold Shoes.* Although much has changed in our society, this timeless book still works beautifully for young readers.

"We hear of the Easter Bunny who comes each Easter before sunrise to bring eggs for boys and girls, and we think there is only one," begins master storyteller Heyward. Not so, he tells readers. There are five Easter Bunnies, and each must cover vast territories. They must be the kindest, swiftest, and wisest bunnies in the whole wide world. One day a country bunny with brown fur dreams of becoming one of these fine Easter Bunnies. But when she grows up, she has no less than twenty-one babies, and she temporarily stops thinking about hopping all over the world as an Easter Bunny. Instead she raises her babies, trains them to be productive, and keeps everything in order.

Lo and behold, one fine day the old, wise, and kind Grandfather Rabbit needs to replace one of the Easter Bunnies and ends up choosing our heroine—because he is so impressed by how well turned out all her children have become. In the second part of the story, the little country bunny gets tested on Easter Day—and finally delivers the most beautiful Easter egg of all.

Heyward told a version of this rabbit story to his eight-year-old daughter Jennifer. A frequent visitor to the McDowell Writing Colony in Peterborough, New Hampshire, Heyward narrated the story there in the summer of 1938. Illustrator Marjorie Flack, also a frequent visitor to McDowell, asked him to write it down so that she could add art to it. It only took Heyward two hours to do so. Heyward's proper Boston editor insisted the country bunny have a husband—although he does not make any appearance in the book. For all intents and purposes, the country bunny remains a single mother. Most often remembered for her art in *The Story about Ping*, Marjorie Flack drew her inspiration for this book from Japanese prints. She shifts between wonderful domestic scenes, with the bunnies engaged in activities, to broad panoramas of the Country Bunny delivering eggs.

The story stresses the importance of hope, determination, and courage. Not only was the book a feminist statement in a time when this perspective was rarely shown, it also celebrates the achievements of a brown bunny rather than a white one. Yet at no point does the reader ever feel as if they are being given a polemic—Heyward has created a totally satisfying world.

Over seventy years after the book was originally published, this little country bunny continues to delight. Some books, like old wine, just get better over time; such is the case with *The Country Bunny and the Little Gold Shoes.*

APRIL 25

Happy Birthday June Behrens (*Fiesta!*), Stuart J. Murphy (MathStart series), George Ella Lyon (*Borrowed Children*), Melvin Burgess (*Junk*), Marie G. Lee (*Finding My Voice*), and David Kirk (Miss Spider series).

It's the birth date of Walter de la Mare (1873–1956), *The Turnip*, *The Lord Fish*; Maud Hart Lovelace (1892–1980), the Betsy-Tacy series; and Alvin Schwartz (1927–1992), *Scary Stories to Tell in the Dark*.

New York became the first state to require car license plates in 1901. Read *The Way Cool License Plate Book* by Leonard Wise.

In 1954 Bell Laboratories announced the first solar battery in Murray Hill, New Jersey.

Today is World Penguin Day. Read *Mr. Popper's Penguins* by Richard Atwater, illustrated by Florence Atwater.

THE INCREDIBLE JOURNEY
By Sheila Burnford

In April, we celebrate Pets Are Wonderful Month. For all pet owners the concept is self-explanatory. Fifty years ago, in 1961, a book appeared that celebrates the bond between humans and their pets—Sheila Burnford's *The Incredible Journey*. In this story, ideal for seven- to twelve-year-olds, three pets—an old bull terrier, a Siamese cat, and a young Labrador retriever—attempt a treacherous 250-mile journey through the Canadian wilderness. Having been left with a friend of their owners, the three head back home to their own family. They battle the elements, face starvation and illness, and fight wild animals. The third-person, omniscient voice of the novel allows readers to watch the actions of the animals but avoids anthropomorphizing them. With characters based on Burnford's own three pets, the narrative contains lots of action and adventure and leaves readers smiling at the end.

Emilie McLeod of the Atlantic Monthly Press instantly loved this novel written by an unknown Canadian writer. But in the 1960s, the Atlantic and Little, Brown shared publishing operations, and McLeod needed to have the approval of Little, Brown's children's book publisher Helen Jones. Jones was a no-nonsense straight shooter, who said what she thought and took no prisoners. Emilie and Helen became embroiled in a heated controversy over whether the house should publish this book—and both refused to back down. Eventually the higher levels of management in both companies intervened. The publisher of the Atlantic's adult list claimed the book—his counterpart at Little, Brown agreed to the acquisition. Hence one of the great children's books of the 1960s appeared as an adult book, even though no one thought it was written for them. Such are the vagaries of publishing, then and now. After all, it is a business conducted by very "human" beings. Things might be better if our pets ran publishing houses. Certainly everyone would get more treats!

Today I'm going to spend some quality time with my own canine sweethearts and savor, once again, the fabulous storytelling in *The Incredible Journey*.

OKAY FOR NOW

By Gary D. Schmidt

On April 26, 1795, John James Audubon, naturalist and painter, was born on his father's sugar plantation in Haiti. He would become famous in his adopted country, the newly formed United States, for setting out to paint, catalogue, and gain an encyclopedic understanding of its winged creatures. A copy of Audubon's *Birds of America* recently made auction history, selling for more than 11.5 million dollars to become the most expensive book in the world.

Many books for children have featured Audubon. But I think Gary D. Schmidt's *Okay for Now* may do more to explain the enduring appeal of Audubon's work to fifth through eighth graders than anything else ever written about him. In this historical novel set in 1968, Doug Swieteck (who made an appearance in Schmidt's *The Wednesday Wars*) moves to a small town in upstate New York. With a brother in Vietnam, an incredibly abusive father, and an older brother who torments him and seems intent on a life of crime, Doug faces more problems than your average child.

APRIL 26

Happy Birthday Patricia Reilly Giff (*Pictures of Hollis Woods*, *Lily's Crossing*) and Marilyn Nelson (*A Wreath for Emmett Till*, *Sweethearts of Rhythm*).

In 1986 an explosion at the Chernobyl nuclear power plant in Ukraine sent radioactive fallout over a wide geographic area, including Europe. Read *The Chernobyl Disaster: Legacy and Impact on the Future of Nuclear Energy* by Wil Mara and *Meltdown: A Race Against Nuclear Disaster at Three Mile Island* by Wilborn Hampton.

It's National Pretzel Day. Read *Pretzel* by Margret Rey, illustrated by H. A. Rey, and *My Daddy Is a Pretzel: Yoga for Parents and Kids* by Baron Baptiste, illustrations by Sophie Fatus.

But he also possesses an incredible spirit. He is a good kid caught in a very bad situation. Over the course of the novel he convinces everyone in the town—including himself—that he, not his father or brothers, will determine his own fate. Schmidt is a master at describing absolutely believable young boys who readers grow to care for and to cheer on. As the novel evolves, readers slowly understand some of the demons in Doug's life and why he acts the way he does. Even more important, they watch him change and become stronger, more true to himself.

Right after Doug arrives in town, he discovers a copy of Audubon's *Birds of America* in the library. With the help of a staff member he starts to copy the illustrations in the book. Doug becomes obsessed with these birds. Each chapter presents a black-and-white reproduction of one of Audubon's masterpieces—along with Doug's understanding of it. Schmidt weaves plot threads together with consummate grace so that the bird also signifies some of the events in Doug's life. He deftly works in the historical issues of the era—the Vietnam War and an Apollo 11 moon shot—in a way that makes them understandable for young readers.

If you love baseball, you'll learn a lot about the Yankees in the 1960s. If you are interested in art, you'll find some brilliant composition analysis. If you are a literature nut, you will be able to see *Jane Eyre* through Doug's eyes. If you enjoy watching a writer weave story, plot, and language together, you can savor this brilliant book by a master at the top of his craft. And if you simply enjoy a heartwarming, compelling story, you will have a fabulous time reading *Okay for Now*.

APRIL 27

Happy Birthday John Burningham (*Mr. Gumpy's Outing*), Nancy Shaw (*Sheep in a Jeep*), and Betty G. Birney (*The World According to Humphrey*).

It's the birth date of Wende Devlin (1918–2002), *Cranberry Thanksgiving*; Jan Hudson (1954–1990), *Dawn Rider*; and Ludwig Bemelmans (Madeline series).

It's the birth date of Ulysses S. Grant (1822–1885), the 18th president of the United States.

 Coretta Scott King (1927–2006), author of *My Life with Martin Luther King, Jr.*, was also born on this day. Read *Dare to Dream: Coretta Scott King and the Civil Rights Movement* by Angela Medearis, illustrated by Anna Rich.

In 1810 Beethoven composed *Für Elise*. Gazillions of children play it on the piano to this day. Read *Beethoven Lives Upstairs* by Barbara Nichol, illustrated by Scott Cameron.

MADELINE
By Ludwig Bemelmans

Born on April 27, 1898, Ludwig Bemelmans came to the United States when he was sixteen, after having been raised in Austria. As a child he lived in a hotel that his father ran; later he worked in a New York hotel to pay his bills. His true love, drawing and painting, had always been something he did only for pleasure.

In 1938 while bicycling on a small island off the coast of France, Bemelmans ran into a car and spent part of the summer in a local hospital. In the next room was a little girl who had just had an appendectomy. A crack in the ceiling over his bed looked like a rabbit. "I remembered the story my mother had told me of life in a convent school . . . and the little girl, the hospital, the room, the crank on the bed, the nurse . . . all fell into place." Creativity happens in the empty places in a writer's life—in Bemelmans's case he needed the time spent in a hospital to think through his masterpiece.

Returning to New York to write the book, Bemelmans observed a French teacher who taught a class of small girls and gave them daily walks around Gramercy Park. His story begins with rhyming couplets: "In an old house in Paris / that was covered in vines / lived twelve little girls in two straight lines." The youngest and cheekiest of these girls, Madeline, fearlessly faces the removal of her appendix. The operation turns out to be such a joyous event that the other girls in the convent want an operation, too.

Legendary Viking Press editor May Massee had encouraged Bemelmans to create his first children's book *Hansi* (1934), but she though this new story too sophisticated for young readers and turned it down. Hence the new publisher on the block, Simon and Schuster, ended up releasing *Madeline* in 1939. Although the book won a Caldecott Honor, Simon and Schuster put it out of print in 1950. Massee immediately snatched it up for the Viking list and asked Bemelmans to craft sequels, beginning with *Madeline's Rescue* in 1953. From then on, a growing group of devoted fans eagerly awaited each new volume. First Lady Jacqueline Kennedy read *Madeline* to her children and corresponded with Bemelmans. Child after child has fallen under its spell. Judy Blume, one of the most beloved children's book writers of our era, hid her library copy of *Madeline* because she could not endure having it returned. As she said in *Everything I Need to Know I Learned from a Children's Book*, "Many years have passed since I hid that copy of *Madeline* . . . but I can still recite the story by heart. . . . Some books you never forget. Some characters become your friends for life."

Millions of children would agree with her; they are so happy to have a friend like Madeline. Happy Birthday Ludwig Bemelmans—your hospital stay resulted in a book that has brought joy to generations of readers.

BRONTORINA

By James Howe
Illustrated by Randy Cecil

During the last week of April we celebrate National Dance Week, a time to reflect on the benefits and beauty of dance and its ability "to enrich our lives, our bodies, our spirits and our culture." Dance, dancers, and ballet have always proved fertile ground for children's book creators. Brontorina, a recent picture book by James Howe, allows young readers to learn about dance and laugh at the same time. In more than eighty books, including the famous vampire bunny *Bunnicula*, author James Howe has proved himself a comic master. He knows how to tell a very funny story that also motivates readers to keep turning the pages. His books often win awards selected by children. His text for *Brontorina* stands with the best of his work. Not only has he found a funny premise for a book, he has delivered it on point.

Brontorina Apatosaurus has a dream—a dream shared by many youngsters. She wants to dance, and so she appears, somewhat timidly, at Madame Lucille's Dance Academy for Girls and Boys. Madame Lucille quickly spots a problem—Brontorina is a dinosaur, a large dinosaur. "But in my heart," our heroine says, "I am a ballerina." So with a command, "Please try not to squash the other dancers," Madame Lucille begins her training—*plie, releve, arabesque,* and *jete.* The students become enamored of Brontorina. One of the other dancers' mothers fashions special shoes for her. And Madame Lucille decides to find a larger space, so her star pupil can dance. When they go outdoors, to perform en plein air, other dinosaurs, cows, and hippos join the ranks. The final page, which shows Brontorina being held overhead in a ballet pose, ends with the words, "And it all began with a dream".

Like the best picture book texts, *Brontorina* provides ample opportunity for an illustrator to add magic. Randy Cecil plays that humor to full advantage, as he shows the dinosaur in all the poses. On each page he uses Brontorina's circular shape to balance his composition. In this book both the author and illustrator have executed some flawless dance steps themselves, moving in perfect unison.

The entire performance makes readers want to reread the book and/or head to the next ballet in town. If you do, this book provides a perfect fantasy line—"Do you think Brontorina will perform today?"

APRIL 28

Happy Birthday Antonio Frasconi (*Elijah the Slave*), Lois Duncan (*I Know What You Did Last Summer, Hotel for Dogs*), Ben Shecter (*The Hating Book, Great-Uncle Alfred Forgets*), Brett Harvey (*My Prairie Year*), Diane Hoh (*Nightmare Hall* series), Marvin Terban (*In a Pickle: And Other Funny Idioms*), Terry Pratchett (*Nation*), and Amy Hest (*When Jessie Came Across the Sea*).

It's the birth date of Palmer Cox (1840–1924), *The Brownies*; and Barbara Juster Esbensen (1925–1996), *Swing around the Sun*.

It's also the birth date of **James Monroe** (1758–1831), the fifth president of the United States.

Best birthday wishes to Harper Lee (*To Kill a Mockingbird*). Read *I Am Scout: The Biography of Harper Lee* by Charles J. Shields.

Happy Birthday Maryland, which became the seventh U.S. state on this day in 1788.

APRIL 29

Happy Birthday Jill Paton Walsh (*The Green Book*, *The Emperor's Winding Sheet*), Ron Roy (A to Z Mysteries series), and Nicole Rubel (*Rotten Ralph*).

Today marks the anniversary of the Zipper patent, granted to inventor Gideon Sundback in 1913.

In 1968 the musical *Hair* opened on Broadway. Read *Crazy Hair* by Neil Gaiman, illustrated by Dave McKean, *Crazy Hair Day* by Barney Saltzberg, *This Is My Hair* by Todd Parr, *Hair Dance* by Dinah Johnson, photographs by Kelly Johnson, and *The Hair of Zoe Fleefenbacher Goes to School* by Laurie Halse Anderson, illustrated by Ard Hoyt.

RED-EYED TREE FROG

By Joy Cowley
Photographs by Nic Bishop

April 29 has been designated Save the Frogs Day, a day of amphibian education. The organizers encourage people to recognize the day in their own communities. Their website contains lesson plans and activities that can be adapted by teachers and parents to help children become aware that frogs are disappearing in great numbers.

There are, of course, a plethora of great books on conservation and ecology for children. For young children ages two through eight I would begin with a book published in 1999: Joy Cowley's *Red-Eyed Tree Frog* with photographs by Nic Bishop. With the simplest language, the author brings us into the text: "Evening comes to the rain forest." Then we are treated to brilliant photos of rain forest birds like the macaw and toucan before we meet the hero of the book, the sleepy red-eyed tree frog. Set against a red leaf that really make his eyes pop, the tree frog looks like a movie star, so brilliant are his colors and features. As he hunts for food, he encounters other fascinating creatures of the rain forest—the iguana, katydid, poisonous caterpillar, and boa constrictor. All are displayed in breathtaking color photographs that show their markings and movements. Readers watch the snake's tongue flick out of its mouth as our hero hops away. Finally, landing on a leaf with a moth, the red-eyed tree frog enjoys his dinner and shuts his eyes "as morning comes to the rain forest."

With endnotes that round out the story, the book presents an ecological community to the youngest of viewers in simple words and images. The red-eyed tree frog jumps and leaps through the story. Cowley's text, spare and simple, leaves room for Nic Bishop to employ all his strengths as a photographer. Bishop roamed the rain forests with a camera and lots of high-speed film to record the inhabitants in all their glory.

Winner of a *Boston Globe–Horn Book* Award, this book works well with readers of all ages and those who speak English as a second language because the story is perfectly told through the pictures. After reading and rereading this book, I, as well as many others, would be willing to go to any length to save this frog. That, of course, is what truly great books about the natural world do—they make children and adults care about the diverse creatures on this planet.

CHARLIE PARKER PLAYED BE BOP

By Chris Raschka

On April 30, 1941, the first commercially recorded work of Charlie Parker was cut at Decca Records. Born in 1920 in Kansas City, Kansas, Charlie Parker began playing the saxophone at age eleven without formal training. In 1939 he headed to New York City, where he teamed up with Dizzy Gillespie and Thelonious Monk—a group that helped invent a new type of jazz, be bop. "We wanted a music that they [white band leaders] couldn't play." Nicknamed "the Bird," Parker set new standards for his instrument, the alto saxophone.

Chris Raschka's *Charlie Parker Played Be Bop* doesn't include any of this information about "the Bird," but it does contain language that captures the rhythm, sound, and spirit of the be bop Parker created. Sometimes, you can hear a book read once and remember it almost word for word decades later. *Charlie Parker Played Be Bop* contains such an original and exciting text that I could quote it word for word when I picked it up today—yet I hadn't looked at the book since it was published in 1992.

Raschka had already established himself as a promising young illustrator with *Yo! Yes?* when he turned his hand to creating art for the text of *Charlie Parker Played Be Bop*, which is only around a hundred words. Most picture book writers would have provided a brief biography of Parker—but Raschka approached the book in another way. He captures the feeling of playing music, its syncopation and sound. In the first illustration Parker looms large, filling the entire page with his saxophone. The mesmerizing, intriguing text begins, "Charlie Parker played be bop. / Charlie Parker played saxophone. / The music sounded like be bop. / Never leave your cat alone."

With a fabulous combination of text and art, the book delights readers ages three to eight with its rhythm, rhyme, and unusual imagery. *Charlie Parker Played Be Bop* can be used to inspire creative writing or for music education. The book sends everyone, adults and children alike, off to learn more about "the Bird." I'm glad that Charlie Parker made his first recording and very grateful to Chris Raschka for celebrating his music.

APRIL 30

Happy Birthday Harriet Langsam Sobol (*We Don't Look Like Our Mom and Dad*), Kirkpatrick Hill (*Do Not Pass Go*, *The Year of Miss Agnes*), Dorothy Hinshaw Patent (*When the Wolves Returned*, *Saving Audie*), Joan Sandin (*The Long Way to a New Land*), Kit Pearson (*A Handful of Time*), Janet Morgan Stoeke (*A Hat for Minerva Louise*).

Happy Birthday Louisiana, which became the 18th U.S. state on this day in 1803. Read *Today Is Monday in Louisiana* by Johnette Downing, illustrated by Deborah Ousley Kadair, *Little Pierre: A Cajun Story from Louisiana* by Robert D. Dan Souci, illustrated by David Catrow, and *My Louisiana Sky* by Kimberly Willis Holt.

In 1789 George Washington was inaugurated as the first U.S. president.

It's *El día de los niños, El día de los libros* (Children's Day, Book Day), the family literacy initiative.

MAY 1

Happy Birthday Bobbie Ann Mason (*In Country*) and Robert Bender (*Lima Beans Would Be Illegal*).

It's the birth date of Charles G. Shaw (1892–1974), *It Looked Like Spilt Milk*; Louisa Shotwell (1902–1993), *Magdalena*; and Elizabeth Marie Pope (1917–1992), *The Perilous Gard*.

It's Mother Goose Day, a day to appreciate nursery rhymes of yore. Read *My Very First Mother Goose* and *Here Comes Mother Goose*, both edited by Iona Opie, illustrated by Rosemary Wells.

It's also School Principals' Day. Read *Report to the Principal's Office* by Jerry Spinelli, *A Fine, Fine School* by Sharon Creech, illustrated by Harry Bliss, and *Mr. Lincoln's Way* by Patricia Polacco.

THE ARRIVAL

By Shaun Tan

May 1, International Workers' Day, was originally established to commemorate the 1886 Haymarket Strike in Chicago when dozens of demonstrators were killed. It was first celebrated in 1890; over the years the day has been adapted for other causes. Around 140 countries use May 1 as Labor Day, a workers' holiday. For the last ten years the day has been acknowledged as Immigration Day in Los Angeles. Except for American Indians, the United States is a nation of immigrants; consequently, hundreds of books for children explore the experience of our ancestors from different perspectives. But few enable readers to understand the emotions an immigrant to a strange country might feel as well as Shaun Tan's *The Arrival*.

In this brilliant graphic novel readers follow the story, presented without words, of a lone immigrant who leaves his wife, daughter, and home, and travels by steamship to a new land. Huddled together with other passengers, he eventually sees his destination, but everything looks bizarre. Even the pets look like they might best be avoided. The language used on buildings and signs perplexes both the immigrant and the reader. Eventually he obtains a job hanging posters, but turns them upside down until corrected. Since readers view the scene from the immigrant's eyes, they experience this strange new land just as the man does.

With kindness from strangers and his own determination, the man makes his way through this surreal landscape and manages to piece a life together. Finally, in an emotional double-page spread, the family is reunited—they are shown as small specs in a large, overwhelming world. This entire saga has been rendered in sepia-colored drawings in panels of varying sizes. The drawings dictate the pace and emotional impact of the story: the small panels move the action forward; the single or double-paged panels cause the reader to pause.

The Arrival allows viewers to imagine visually how the world appeared to immigrant ancestors, and it unfolds history in an immediate and striking way. Some fifth- through eighth-grade teachers have integrated the title into immigration units; others have pulled the book into writing classes, so students can tell their own interpretations of the story. Since the entire narrative occurs in the art, there are as many versions of what is happening as there are readers. Like Art Spiegelman's graphic novel *Maus*, *The Arrival* can be appreciated both for its artistry and for its social and political content.

If you have missed the books of Australian genius Shaun Tan, winner of an Oscar and the Astrid Lindgren Memorial Award, often called the "Nobel Prize for Children's Literature," run, do not walk, to the nearest bookstore or library to pick up *The Arrival*.

SHARK VS. TRAIN

By Chris Barton

Illustrated by Tom Lichtenheld

In May we celebrate Children's Book Week. First noted in 1919, this event is now sponsored by the Children's Book Council and brings attention to children's books and those who create them. Since 2008 the council has been hosting a gala celebrating books and reading. During the event the much-coveted Children's Choice Book Awards are presented.

Children enthusiastically endorse the book of the day, *Shark vs. Train*, which explores the imaginative life of children. Author Chris Barton, who also wrote *The Day-Glo Brothers*, a fascinating biography of the Switzers, shows just how inventive he can be in *Shark vs. Train*. The ever-creative artist Tom Lichtenheld adds the other half of the equation with illustrations that enhance the humor of the story and make it even more appealing.

Our two boy protagonists meet, even before the story begins, over the toy box. As they rummage through it, one picks out a plastic shark and the other a train. And then the battle begins. As it asks on the title page: "Who will win?" Immediately the toys begin to trade insults, often including bad puns: "I'm going to Fin-ish you, mackerel-breath," Train warns. Then these two antagonistic toys compete in a variety of settings where one obviously dominates. Train's furnace doesn't work in the ocean; Shark has trouble on a seesaw. Shark can eat more pies, but Train can belch louder. Essentially, the two toys behave like rowdy young boys who try to one-up each other. If they go trick-or-treating, Shark has an advantage; at the carnival Train's lines go around the page. Neither, it turns out, can play the piano or video games because they lack thumbs. When the boys get called for lunch, they throw the toys back in the box and run out—although Shark and Train continue to hurl insults at each other.

Perfect for two- through eight-year-olds, the book can be acted out with puppets. It naturally can be used for writing exercises: What other contests would be appropriate for Shark and Train? It shows a profound understanding of childhood imaginative play and creates a lot of laughs when read aloud. Funny, original, exciting, *Shark vs. Train* demonstrates that the picture book format has endless possibilities; creative people can find new and exciting ways to use it all the time.

MAY 2

Happy Birthday Susan Richards Shreve (*Trout and Me*) and Mary Quattlebaum (Jackson Jones series).

It's the birth date of Dr. Benjamin Spock (1903–1998), whose book *Baby and Child Care* was first published in 1946. On a related note, it's Baby Day! Read *The Boss Baby* by Marla Frazee, *Baby Cakes* by Karma Wilson, illustrated by Sam Williams, and *Everywhere Babies* by Susan Meyers, illustrated by Marla Frazee.

In 1885 *Good Housekeeping* magazine went on sale. Read *Chores Chores Chores!* by Salina Yoon and *Why Do I Have to Make My Bed?* by Wade Bradford, illustrated by Johanna van der Sterre.

MAY 3

Happy Birthday Karen Heywood (*The Saddlebag Hero*), Mavis Jukes (*Blackberries in the Dark*), and Joe Murray (*Who Asked the Moon to Dinner?*).

It's the birth date of Suekichi Akaba (1910–1990), *Suho's White Horse: A Mongolian Legend*; and John Ney (1923–2010), *Ox: The Story of a Kid at the Top*.

It's also the birthday of Pete Seeger, the iconic American folksinger and songwriter. Read *Abigoys* by Pete Seeger, illustrated by Michael Hays.

Margaret Mitchell's epic *Gone with the Wind* won Pulitzer Prize in 1937. Read *The Wind Blew* by Pat Hutchins.

In 1960 the Anne Frank House opened in Amsterdam. Read *The Diary of a Young Girl* by Anne Frank and *Anne Frank's Tales from the Secret Annex: A Collection of Her Short Stories, Fables, and Lesser-Known Writings*.

HOLES
By Louis Sachar

For Children's Book Week, I pose the question: What book of the last fifteen years seems poised for classic status? Whenever I ask audiences this question one title leads all the rest: Louis Sachar's *Holes*. A rare winner of the Triple Crown in prizes (National Book Award, Newbery Medal, *Boston Globe–Horn Book* Award), *Holes*, has gained a devoted readership among the ten through fourteen crowd. After all, it is hard to resist a book with a character called Armpit.

Louis Sachar began his career as a lawyer but went on to create a body of appealing, light, and funny middle-grade novels, with titles such as *Sideways Stories from Wayside School* and *There's a Boy in the Girls' Bathroom*. *Holes*, however, broke the mold of his earlier work: funny, but also weighty, profound, and meticulously crafted, it established Sachar as one of the most important children's book writers of the twentieth century.

For his masterpiece, Sachar drew inspiration from something he knew very well first hand: hot Texas summers. He has said, "Anyone who has ever tried to do yard work in Texas in July can easily imagine Hell to be a place where you are required to dig a hole five feet deep and five feet across day after day under the brutal Texas sun." In *Holes* the protagonist Stanley Yelnats—whose name is a palindrome—get sentenced to a boot camp for juvenile delinquents. At Camp Green Lake, a misnomer because nothing actually grows there and no lake exists, he and his fellow inmates have to dig a five-foot-round hole each day while supervised by a terrible warden who has venom-tipped fingernails. Buried treasure, yellow-spotted lizards, and outlaw Kissin' Kate Barlow all add to the flavor of this adventure, survival novel, and tall tale.

At first many critics seemed surprised that such a sophisticated novel could come from the pen of someone known for lighthearted titles. But Sachar's editor, Frances Foster, was not surprised when she read the manuscript. She had always known that Sachar had a great book in him and realized, while working on *Holes*, that he had written such a book. The manuscript went through at least five complete revisions, with both author and editor making sure all the elements of this complex plot fit together. The attention to detail and the author and editor's commitment to making the book as perfect as possible made a difference with *Holes*. It would always have been a good book, but it became a great one. Fortunately for fans of the book, Sachar himself worked on the screenplay for a highly successful movie that remains true to the original novel. Sachar has summed up the moral or lesson of *Holes* quite simply: "Reading is fun." There can be no better slogan to celebrate Children's Book Week than that one.

MISS SPITFIRE: REACHING HELEN KELLER

By Sarah Miller

The first week in May has been earmarked Teacher Appreciation Week—to celebrate some of the most important work going on in our society. Perfect for sharing with third through fifth grades, Sarah Miller's *Miss Spitfire: Reaching Helen Keller* chronicles the first month in the most recorded teacher-pupil relationship of all time—Annie Sullivan and Helen Keller.

In this remarkable first novel based on material from Sullivan's letters, readers meet the young Helen Keller. Willful, physically violent, deaf and blind, living in a world without language, Helen fights her young teacher like a wild animal. An orphan who attended the Perkins School for the Blind, Annie writes in a letter, "the greatest problem I shall have to solve is how to discipline and control her without breaking her spirit."

As readers experience the ensuing battle between these two forces of the universe, they grow to appreciate this young teacher, who fights her own battles with loneliness and longing to be loved. Then, one day, Annie finds a way to break in to the silence of Helen's world—she stands at the water pump and teaches Helen the signs for "w-a-t-e-r." In the end Annie proves more stubborn than her charge—the "Miss Spitfire" of the title had been bestowed as a nickname not on Helen but on Annie.

Sarah Miller had a love affair with the written word from early childhood on. In first grade she became a published author for a poem about a unicorn. By fifth grade she set out to write an entire book; in fact, she carried a spy notebook just like her favorite character, Harriet the Spy. While working in an independent children's bookstore, Miller wrote *Miss Spitfire*, her first published book for children.

More than anything, the book demonstrates the incredible bond between teacher and pupil. So rather than giving an apple to the teacher in your life this week, you might want to pick up a copy of *Miss Spitfire*. Because in the end, all teachers want to accomplish miracles with their students—just as Miss Spitfire did when she arrived at Helen Keller's home in Alabama in 1887.

MAY 4

Happy Birthday Patricia Hooper (*A Bundle of Beasts*), Don Wood (*King Bidgood's in the Bathtub*), Doug Cushman (*Aunt Eater Loves a Mystery*), Dom Lee (*Baseball Saved Us*).

It's the birth date of Clara Ingram Judson (1879–1960), *Abraham Lincoln: Friend of the People*.

Alice Pleasance Liddell (1852–1934), **Lewis Carroll**'s inspiration for *Alice in Wonderland*, was born on this day. Read *The Annotated Alice* by Lewis Carroll, edited by Martin Gardner, illustrated by John Tenniel.

It's International Firefighters Day. Read *Firefighters A to Z* by Chris L. Demarest, *The Little Fire Engine* by Lois Lenski, and *Fire! Fire!* by Gail Gibbons.

MAY 5

Happy Birthday Alice Low (*The Witch Who Was Afraid of Witches*) and Todd Strasser (*Boot Camp*).

It's the birth date of Leo Lionni (1910–1999), *Swimmy*.

Happy Birthday Carnegie Hall. The grand opening of this midtown Manhattan concert venue, originally called The Music Hall, featured guest conductor Tchaikovsky, in 1891. Read *Tchaikovsky Discovers America* by Esther Kalman, illustrated by Laura Fernandez and Rick Jacobson.

 In 1925 an arrest warrant was served to **John Scopes**, for teaching evolution, a violation of Tennessee's Butler Act. Read *The Evolution of Calpurnia Tate* by Jacqueline Kelly and *Life on Earth: The Story of Evolution* by Steve Jenkins.

It's Cinco de Mayo.

MISS RUMPHIUS
By Barbara Cooney

During the first week of May, we celebrate National Wildflower Week, created by the Lady Bird Johnson Wildflower Center, to "encourage the observations, cultivations and study of native wildflowers." *Miss Rumphius* by Barbara Cooney completely embodies the spirit of this week. In this story a spinster librarian travels around the world and eventually returns to a home by the sea. Wanting to make the world a more beautiful place, she decides to scatter lupine seeds wherever she goes.

Published in November of 1982, when Barbara Cooney lived in Damariscotta, Maine, *Miss Rumphius* was one of more than two hundred books that Cooney, a two-time winner of the Caldecott Medal, illustrated in her lifetime. By the time she worked on *Miss Rumphius*, she had over forty years of experience in children's book illustrations. For this project Cooney drew on the life of her great-grandfather. He painted pictures and allowed his young daughter, Cooney's grandmother, to help. "I see that little girl—painting away, making yards and yards of fluffy clouds and sunsets and storms with lightning and rainbows." Cooney also based the character of Alice Rumphius on a historical figure who traveled the world planting flower seeds. Probably even more important, Alice became what Cooney described as her "alter ego." She later mused, "Perhaps she had been that right from the start."

What makes *Miss Rumphius* memorable for many young readers, however, is the exquisite artwork, executed in the purples, pinks, and blues of the lupines—breathtaking landscapes marked by their beauty and soft color. With its positive and idealistic message of making the world a more beautiful place, this book has captivated both young readers and the parents and teachers who share the book with them. It reminds all of us that with just a little effort we can add beauty to our world.

If you are planting wildflower seeds this week, pick up a copy of *Miss Rumphius*, a great read aloud for kindergarten through third grade, and share it with children and adult friends—both will love it. Not only does Alice Rumphius make the world a more beautiful place by scattering lupines in the story, but Barbara Cooney also enhances our visual world by giving us breathtaking picture books that we can return to again and again.

RASCAL

By Sterling North

National Pet Week occurs during the first week of May. Desiring a pet is almost a universal experience of childhood. Usually, the term *pet* brings to mind dogs, cats, fish, hamsters, or other domesticated animals. But, of course, a pet can be any animal that forms a bond with a human—and that is the case in Sterling North's *Rascal.*

In this autobiographical story that takes place during World War I in rural Wisconsin, young Sterling North collects a menagerie of pets—a Saint Bernard named Wowser, cats, four skunks, and Poe, a crow. Very lonely because his mother has died and his father is often absent, Sterling relies on these animals for company. Then one day he finds a baby raccoon.

During the course of a year, that raccoon, Rascal, shares Sterling's life. Sterling takes Rascal everywhere by placing him on the front of his bicycle. They go on fishing expeditions and share meals together. As is true to his species, Rascal washes all his food—in a hilarious episode, he discovers sugar cubes, only to watch them dissolve when he cleans them. But, of course, the raccoon is a wild creature destined for another life. In one of the great three-handkerchief endings in children's books, Sterling realizes that Rascal needs to go back to live in the forest.

> "Do as you please, my little raccoon. It's your life," I told him.
>
> He hesitated for a full minute, turned once to look back at me, then took the plunge and swam to the near shore. He had chosen to join that entrancing female somewhere in the shadows. I caught only one glimpse of them in a moonlit glade before they disappeared to begin their new life together.
>
> Sterling never saw Rascal again.

Sterling North had a very distinguished career as a critic and publisher, editor of the North Star books series for Houghton Mifflin. But he is best remembered for his Newbery Honor book *Rascal*—the biography of an unusual but beloved pet.

So go play with your dog, pat your cat, feed your goldfish, and think about the role pets play in your life.

MAY 6

Happy Birthday Ted Lewin (*Peppe the Lamplighter, Stable*), Susan Terris (*The Latchkey Kids*), Giulio Maestro (*A More Perfect Union: The Story of Our Constitution*), and Barbara McClintock (*Dahlia*).

It's the birth date of Randall Jarrell (1914–1965), *The Gingerbread Rabbit*; and Judy Delton (1931–2001), Pee Wee Scouts series.

Sigmund Freud (1856–1939), founder of the psychoanalytic school of psychiatry, was born on this day. Read *Sigmund Freud* by Kathleen Krull.

It's National No Homework Day. Read *No More Homework! No More Tests!* by Bruce Lansky, illustrated by Stephen Carpenter, and *The Homework Machine* by Dan Gutman.

MAY 7

Happy Birthday Nonny Hogrogian (*Always Room for One More, One Fine Day*), Peter Carey (*The Big Bazoohley*), and Erik Craddock (*Stone Rabbit* series).

It's the birth date of Robert Browning (1812–1889), *The Pied Piper of Hamelin*; and Angela Carter (1940–1992), *Sea-Cat and Dragon King*.

It's also the birth date of the Russian Composer, Pyotr Ilyich Tchaikovsky (1840–1893).

 In 1429 **Joan of Arc** ended the Siege of Orléans. Read *Joan of Arc* by Diane Stanley.

On this day in 1945 Germany signed an unconditional surrender in France, ending World War II. V-Day or Victory in Europe Day, is celebrated on May 8 to commemorate the Allies' official acceptance of the German surrender.

IVY + BEAN TAKE CARE OF THE BABYSITTER

By Annie Barrows
Illustrated by Sophie Blackall

On the Saturday before Mother's Day we celebrate National Babysitters Day. Almost every child has had the experience of being taken care of by a babysitter—many later even become one themselves. The protagonists of today's book, two irrepressible seven-year-old girls, have to deal with babysitter problems in *Ivy+Bean Take Care of the Babysitter*. BFFs Bean and Ivy can get into more mischief while egging each other on than the proverbial barrel of monkeys. At the beginning of the story, they and their friends have taken over a pile of dirt and fashioned a volcano with a lava flow from a hose. Nothing is ever boring for this twosome because they possess so much imagination.

Then a potential tragedy strikes. Bean's parents are going out for a few hours. Horror of all horrors, they have decided to leave Bean's mean older sister, Nancy, age eleven, in charge. She even gets twenty dollars—and will keep Bean in the house, or in jail, depending on the perspective. Bean believes she has been left with the meanest babysitter in history and that action needs to be taken. By the time that her parents come back, Bean and Ivy have managed to secure some of Nancy's money and have definitely convinced this older sister that she is much too young to be a babysitter. Just your average exploit in the lives of two very devoted, very resourceful seven-year-olds.

Author Annie Barrows hits one comic high note after another and has made her series about these two girls a favorite of seven- to nine-year-olds. With illustrator Sophie Blackall's lively art, rendered in Chinese ink, the text breezes by. Great chapter books—perfect for kids who are starting to read on their own—are extremely difficult to create. Authors and illustrators need to know how to make exciting stories out of the everyday lives of young children. In *Ivy+Bean Take Care of the Babysitter*, the common experience of having a babysitter is transformed into laugh-out-loud comedy.

For those who fall in love with one of the books, the two talented creators have extended their winning formula in a series that keeps young readers enthralled. Ivy+Bean=BFFs rule!

A CHAIR FOR MY MOTHER

By Vera Williams

On the second Sunday in May we celebrate Mother's Day, a time to remember all of the sacrifices and kindnesses of our mothers. Vera Williams grew up in a household where her mother had a full-time job. As a child, she often wished her mom stayed at home, like others in the neighborhood. But later when Vera herself became a working mother, she realized what a wonderful gift she had been given: not only shelter and food but also an example of a woman who balanced family and work. Fortunately, authors can write from their own experiences or they can rewrite history, imagining a childhood they would have liked to have had. In the case of Vera Williams, she created Rosa, the daughter she wished she had been, to narrate *A Chair for My Mother*. She writes, "I now had the power, as a writer and an illustrator, to change the past into something I liked better and to make it as a kind of gift to my mother's memory."

In this beautiful example of a mother/daughter relationship, the little girl Rosa says, "My mother works as a waitress for the Blue Tile Diner." A fire has left the family without any good furniture, particularly a sofa and comfortable chairs. And so all the tips that her mother makes, the coins that her grandmother saves when she gets a bargain, or anything Rosa can contribute go into a large glass jar. In the end, they go shopping and finally find a plump rose-covered chair mother and daughter can snuggle in together. Although the family is poor, they are very rich in community and in loving relationships. Hence each illustration in this book is framed with a lush border that indicates the rich emotional life these three women share with one another and with their neighbors.

Besides being a wonderful book to use with very young readers ages three through eight, this is a book parents enjoy just as much as children. *A Chair for My Mother* reminds us why we have Mother's Day—to be thankful for everything our mothers do for us, every day of our lives.

MAY 8

It's the birth date of Milton Meltzer (1915–2009), *Tough Times*; and Mary Q. Steele, who sometimes used the pen name Wilson Gage (1922–1992), *Journey Outside*.

It's the birth date of **Harry S. Truman** (1884–1972), the 33rd president of the United States.

In 1886 Atlanta pharmacist John Pemberton invented Coca-Cola.

It's World Red Cross Day. Henry Dunant (1828–1910), born on this day, inspired the creation of the International Red Cross, as well as the Geneva Convention. He received the first-ever Nobel Peace Prize in honor of his efforts.

Best birthday wishes to the Westminster Kennel Club Dog Show, first held on this day in 1877. Read *A Dog's Way Home* by Bobbie Pyron.

On this day in 1933 Mahatma Gandhi began a hunger strike to protest British rule in India. Read *Gandhi* by Demi.

MAY 9

Happy Birthday Richard Adams (*Watership Down*).

It's the birth date of **Sir James M. Barrie** (1860–1937), *Peter Pan*; Keith Robertson (1914–1991), Henry Reed series; William Pène du Bois (1916–1993), *The Twenty-One Balloons*, *Williams Doll*; Roger Hargreaves (1935–1988), Mr. Men series; and Eleanor Estes (1906–1988), *Ginger Pye*, *The Middle Moffat*, *Rufus M.*, *The Hundred Dresses*.

In 1887 Buffalo Bill Cody's Wild West Show opened in London. Read *Buffalo Bill's Wild West: Celebrity, Memory, and Popular History* by Joy S. Kasson and *Bull's-Eye: A Photobiography of Annie Oakley* by Sue Macy.

It's Lost Sock Memorial Day. Read *A Pair of Socks* by Stuart J. Murphy, illustrated by Lois Ehlert.

THE HUNDRED DRESSES
By Eleanor Estes
Illustrated by Louis Slobodkin

Born on May 9, 1906, in West Haven, Connecticut, Eleanor Estes worked in the New York Public Library until her first book, *The Moffats*, was published in 1941. Although she won the Newbery Medal for *Ginger Pye* in 1951, Estes's earlier book, *The Hundred Dresses*, has emerged as one of our most unusual and powerful classics.

In print since 1944, this eighty-page novel addresses one of our current societal concerns: bullying. Even when approaching this serious subject, Estes does so with a lightness of touch that has caused *The Hundred Dresses* to be used in classrooms from elementary through high school. Estes also tackles the subjects of social class and money. In spot art and occasionally double-page illustrations, Louis Slobodkin, winner of a Caldecott Medal for James Thurber's *Many Moons*, draws a mere suggestion of the characters allowing readers to imagine the faces on them.

In *The Hundred Dresses* a group of fourth, grade girls tease and torment one of their classmates, a poor Polish girl named Wanda Petronski who wears the same dress to school every day. But Wanda claims to have a hundred dresses. Peggy, a wealthy, cruel bully, encourages her sidekick, Maddie, to torment Wanda. Insecure and depending on Peggy's hand-me-down clothes, Maddie acts in ways not consistent with her own sense of morality. She knows that harassing Wanda is wrong, but she does not want to alienate Peggy. Rather than telling the book from Wanda's point of view, Estes focuses on Maddie. Consequently, readers see the effect of bullying on those who engage in it.

In the end, Wanda does possess a hundred dresses—ones she has drawn herself. And Maddie, feeling tremendous remorse, does not have a chance to apologize and make her actions right. She must now live with what she has done and her sense that she has not treated others as she herself would like to be treated. The reader feels remorse along with the main characters making this title a first choice for guidance counselors when addressing the issue of bullying.

The Hundred Dresses reminds us that childhood bullying is not a new phenomenon—and that those who seem different can become easy targets in classrooms. After all these years, it remains a three-handkerchief book—one that touches children emotionally as they confront its important and significant content.

TOM SWIFT SERIES
By Victor Appleton II

Eighty-one years ago on May 10, 1930, Edward Stratemeyer, author and empire builder, died. He began his career as a ghostwriter for the Horatio Alger series, then fashioned his own adventures about the Rover Boys. In 1906 Stratemeyer began to hire freelance writers to develop his ideas. He created nothing less than a literary assembly line—in the end about 65 series, 1,300 books that sold more than 200 million copies. In his day he was considered the equal of Ford and Rockefeller, only he mass-produced books for children.

The gatekeepers and critics vilified Stratemeyer—articles like "Blowing the Boy's Brains Out" claimed that his books actually crippled readers' imaginations. They were called "tripe" and the "devices of Satan." But young readers did not agree with those trying to protect children from these mass-produced wares. They found characters they loved and page-turning adventures in the best of the Stratemeyer creations—Tom Swift, the Bobbsey Twins, Nancy Drew, and the Hardy Boys. So successful was the syndicate that in the twenties through the fifties, the majority of the books purchased by children in America, often with their allowance money, had been created by the Stratemeyer Syndicate.

Stratemeyer's death by no means ended his enterprise. It was ably taken over by his daughters for a few years until Edna Stratemeyer Squier sold her share to her sister. Harriet Stratemeyer Adams continued to run the syndicate until her death in 1982. She focused much of her attention on the development of the girl detective Nancy Drew.

When I interviewed society leaders for *Everything I Need to Know I Learned from a Children's Book*, I discovered many enjoyed Stratemeyer offerings. Steve Wozniak, who invented Apple I and Apple II, fell under the spell of the Tom Swift books. The books made him realize that he wanted to become an inventor—he created his first computer at age twelve. So the pseudonym for the writer of Tom Swift, Victor Appleton II, may well have been memorialized by one of his greatest fans.

Although many of the Stratemeyer books have been updated and changed, they eventually lost their place as the most popular reading in America—upstaged by newer heroes like Harry Potter. But in the first six decades of the twentieth century, Edward Stratemeyer and his syndicate ruled the reading lives of children. His success reminds us that although as adults we want to move children to complex stories, series that foster a love of books keep a child on the reading path.

MAY 10

Happy Birthday Palmer Brown (*Beyond the Pawpaw Trees*), John Rowe Townsend (*The Intruder*), Mel Glenn (*Who Killed Mr. Chippendale?*), Bruce McMillan (*The Problem with Chickens*), Caroline B. Cooney (*The Face on the Milk Carton*), Christopher Paul Curtis (*The Watsons Go to Birmingham—1963, Bud, Not Buddy*), and Linda Glaser (*Our Big Home: An Earth Poem*).

It's the birth date of Amabel Williams-Ellis (1894–1984), *Arabian Nights*.

In 1869 the last spike was driven into the tracks at Promontory Summit, Utah, marking the completion of the first Transcontinental Railroad. Read *Dragon's Gate* by Laurence Yep, *Coolies* by Yin, illustrated by Chris Soentpiet, and *The Journal of Sean Sullivan: A Transcontinental Railroad Worker* by William Durbin.

In 1773, to keep the troubled East India Company afloat, British Parliament passes the Tea Act, taxing all tea in the American colonies.

MAY 11

Happy Birthday Zilpha Keatley Snyder (*The Egypt Game*), Francine Jacobs (*Sam, the Sea Cow*), Juanita Havill (*Jamaica's Find*), Peter Sìs (*Tibet Through the Red Box*), and Jane Sutton (*Don't Call Me Sidney*).

It's the birth date of Sheila Burnford (1918–1984), *The Incredible Journey*.

 Painter Salvador Dalí (1904–1989) was also born on this day. Read *The Mad, Mad, Mad World of Salvador Dalí* by Angela Wenzel.

Happy Birthday Minnesota, which became the 32nd U.S. state on this day in 1858. Read *V is for Viking: A Minnesota Alphabet* by Kathy-jo Wargin, illustrated by Karen Latham and Rebecca Latham.

BALLET FOR MARTHA: MAKING APPALACHIAN SPRING

By Jan Greenberg and Sandra Jordan
Illustrated by Brian Floca

On May 11, 1894, Martha Graham was born in Pittsburgh, Pennsylvania. At the age of sixteen, she saw her first dance performance "and that night my fate was sealed." In her early twenties Graham moved to Greenwich Village, New York, and joined the Follies, with assorted animal acts and chorus girls. In 1926 she started her own dance company and began a new type of dance based on "emotion, breathing, and spare, angular forms." The Martha Graham Company also became the first racially integrated dance company in the United States.

Of all art forms, dance, which depends on movement, remains the hardest to convey in a book—particularly a book for children. Jan Greenberg and Sandra Jordan took on this task in *Ballet for Martha: Making Appalachian Spring* and succeeded brilliantly. At the beginning of the book, they write that though art is sometimes created by one artist, other times "it is the result of artists working together—collaborating—to forge something new." Then they introduce three fabulous artists: Martha Graham, who created the dance; Aaron Copland, who fashioned the music; and Isamu Noguchi, who constructed the stage setting. Readers watch each of them work on their contribution to the ballet. Noguchi carves marble, granite, and wood to create a stage. Copland chooses the Shaker hymn "Simple Gifts" as the melody for the "Ballet for Martha." Graham trains the dancers. Not all goes smoothly; at one point she has a tantrum, screams, yells, and even throws a shoe.

But on October 30, 1944, in Washington, D.C., the first performance of *Appalachian Spring* occurs. Up until this point in the book, many passages of text are needed to explain the development of the dance. Then the authors cut back their words, allowing artist Brian Floca to work his magic. Using small vignettes and double-page spreads he brings both the dancers and the dance to life. They jump and leap and dominate the stage. Floca's strong portraits of the individual dancers allow readers to feel, for several pages, as if they are witnessing this historic event.

These three artists, Greenberg, Jordan, and Floca, themselves a triumvirate, show how creative people work together to fashion something new. If you love the arts, dance, or simply creative information books for young readers ages six through twelve, you will not want to miss this performance. Bravo! All three deserve a standing ovation.

ESPERANZA RISING

By Pam Muñoz Ryan

In an ongoing effort to promote books by Latinos, the Association of American Publishers has designated May as Latino Book Month. During May they hope booksellers, librarians, and teachers will encourage people in their communities to read books by and for Latinos in both English and Spanish. Today's book, *Esperanza Rising* by Pam Muñoz Ryan, perfectly fits this mission.

Like many authors hunting for inspiration, Muñoz Ryan pulled from the stories told in her family, particularly those of her *abuelita* (grandmother), Esperanza Ortega. Even late in her life, when Esperanza talked about first coming to the United States from Mexico as a teenager, she would cry. Pam began to fashion a protagonist based on her grandmother, weaving in other family experiences and some of her own, as well.

Right before her thirteenth birthday, Esperanza faces a terrible tragedy—the death of her beloved father. Suddenly she and her mother find their fortunes reversed. Once wealthy land owners in Mexico, they must now rely on former servants to help them immigrate to the United States and find work in a migrant camp in California. At first Esperanza can barely tolerate the cramped conditions and lack of autonomy. She naturally misses the feasts, the dresses, the accoutrements of being a privileged young girl. But because she loves her mother, she begins performing manual labor even though she has to be taught how to hold a broom. Eventually, when her mother grows ill and must stay in a hospital, Esperanza does backbreaking work in the fields, in hopes of saving enough money to bring her grandmother to America.

For a novel to be truly satisfying, the character needs to change in a believable way over the course of the narrative. Esperanza becomes a kinder, more appreciative, more caring individual. Rather than hoarding her own few possessions, she gives away a beloved doll to help another little girl in pain. In 1930, when Mexicans went on strike for better wages but often got deported for doing so, Esperanza learns to look beyond politics to the human issues—everyone is simply trying to feed their family. In the end, Esperanza finds someone to love, a former servant of her father's.

As Pam Muñoz Ryan states in a superb author's note, *Esperanza* means "hope" in Spanish. The hopes of immigrants to this country, their dreams, and their triumphs are clearly captured in this book. It is small wonder that *Esperanza Rising* has moved into the curriculum for fourth through ninth grade. It reminds all its readers that human beings can live with dignity, no matter the conditions, as long as family and community remain intact.

Few who read this powerful book forget it. The final line gives me inspiration every day: "Do not ever be afraid to start over."

MAY 12

Happy Birthday Farley Mowat (*Never Cry Wolf*), Caroline Feller Bauer (*My Mom Travels a Lot*), Betsy Lewin (*Click, Clack, Moo*), Janice Lee Smith (*Adam Joshua Capers* series), and Jennifer Armstrong (*Shipwreck at the Bottom of the World*).

It's the birth date of Edward Lear (1812–1888), *The Owl and the Pussycat*. In honor of Mr. Lear, it's Limerick Day, celebrating the humorous and witty five-line poem. Read *Limericks* by Valerie Bodden, *Pocketful of Nonsense* by James Marshall, and *Lots of Limericks* by Myra Cohn Livingston, illustrated by Rebecca Perry.

Florence Nightingale (1820–1910) was born on this day. It's International Nurses Day. Read *Heart and Soul: The Story of Florence Nightingale* by Gena K. Gorrell.

MAY 13

Happy Birthday Bernadette Watts (*Ugly Duckling*).

It's the birth date of Norma Klein (1938–1989), *Mom, the Wolf Man and Me.*

In 1958 velcro was trademarked. Read *Mistakes that Worked* by Charlotte Foltz Jones, illustrated by John O'Brien.

It's Leprechaun Day. Read *That's What Leprechauns Do* by Eve Bunting, illustrated by Emily Arnold McCully.

LILLY'S PURPLE PLASTIC PURSE

By Kevin Henkes

During the second week of May, Reading Is Fundamental celebrates Reading Is Fun Week. Nothing will guarantee the reading success of children more than if they find enjoyment in reading. Kevin Henkes's *Lilly's Purple Plastic Purse* has been delighting young readers since it appeared in the 1990s. Lilly, a young mouse, absolutely loves everything about school—pointy pencils, squeaky chalk, her own desk, and her teacher Mr. Slinger. At home Lilly pretends to be Mr. Slinger, giving instruction to her baby brother, Julius. Every class has a student like Lilly—one with lots of ideas, always raising his or her hand, and even staying after school to help.

But even in this idealized universe, conflict arises. One day, when Lilly comes to school for show-and-tell, she brings a noisy plastic purple purse that plays a jaunty tune. Mr. Slinger is not amused. In this picture book where every piece of art is accompanied by a funny, spot-on aside, Lilly and Mr. Slinger finally reconcile. In the end Lilly still wants to be a teacher, "That is, when she didn't want to be a dancer or a surgeon or an ambulance driver or a diva or a pilot or a hairdresser or a scuba diver."

From the age of ten, Kevin Henkes knew that he wanted to draw and write picture books. At nineteen, while still a student at the University of Wisconsin at Madison, he took his art portfolio to New York City. In preparation for the trip, he had studied recently published picture books and made a list of his favorite publishers, setting up appointments in the order of his preference. At his first meeting, Susan Hirschman of Greenwillow, quite impressed by what she saw, asked why he had come to the Greenwillow offices. After he told her about his systematic approach, she asked, "Where is your next appointment?" Then she assured Henkes that he did not need to go to this rival house—he would be a Greenwillow author. But Susan did hope that he would call his mother, as he looked so young.

Many years later, Kevin Henkes won a Caldecott Medal for *Kitten's First Full Moon.* Appropriately, his mentor and friend, Susan Hirschman, now retired from the industry, had traveled to Madison to be with him when he received the news. People often ask the question: What do great editors do? They spot talent, nuture it, and support it—just as Susan did.

With just the right balance of pictures and text, humor and insight, emotion and intellect, *Lilly's Purple Plastic Purse* provides reading pleasure for all who pick it up. It always sends young readers in search of another book, or specifically another book by Kevin Henkes, the greatest tribute that can be paid to a creator of children's books.

THE MYSTERIOUS BENEDICT SOCIETY

By Trenton Lee Stewart

For Reading Is Fun week, I surveyed young readers in grades four through six about what books they adore reading, and one title kept coming up—Trenton Lee Stewart's *The Mysterious Benedict Society*.

Most end-of-the-world, dystopian novels for children and teens share a basic plot—the world as we know it will soon, or has already, come to an end, and children are going to have to save the planet. Although *The Mysterious Benedict Society* relies on this idea, it has emerged as one of the sunniest of the fantasy/science fiction offerings in recent years, combing a lot of humor as well as edge-of-the-seat adventure.

At the beginning of the book eleven-year-old Reynie Muldoon, an orphan, responds to an advertisement seeking gifted children. After passing a series of tests, Reynie, "Sticky" Washington, Kate, and Constance Contraire form the Mysterious Benedict Society. Trained by Mr. Benedict and his assistants, the four embark on a top-secret mission to the Institute for the Very Enlightened. There, the mastermind Mr. Curtain has been using children at this school to lay the groundwork for his bid for world domination. Working together, using their special abilities, the Mysterious Benedict Society children must determine what he is doing—and how they can stop him.

With lots of twists, turns, puzzles, even Morse codes, the book engages readers' minds. It does not merely serve up escapist reading, although the over-five-hundred-page book certainly provides many hours of entertaining adventure. The book explores larger issues like the power of the media and the need for teamwork in overcoming obstacles.

In this book for ten- to sixteen-year-olds, the happy ending satisfies but still leaves room for sequels. The children seem quite vulnerable and real—not superheroes or heroines, but children who have their share of problems. They use ropes and marbles to solve dilemmas, not magic swords. Recently I saw an essay from Jerod, a sixth grader from Winesburg, Ohio, who said the book made him think "about how important family is, and . . . how everyone is special in their own little way."

So if you and the children in your life want to enjoy reading, pick up *The Mysterious Benedict Society*. You may even want to learn Morse code after you do.

MAY 14

Happy Birthday Eoin Colfer (Artemis Fowl series).

It's the birth date of Hal Borland (1900–1978), *When the Legends Die*, and George Selden Thompson (1929–1989), *The Cricket in Times Square*.

Best birthday wishes to Mark Zuckerberg, cofounder of Facebook. Read *It's a Book* by Lane Smith.

It's also the birthday of George Lucas, film director and producer of *Star Wars*.

It's National Chicken Dance Day. Read *Chicken Joy on Redbean Road: A Bayou Country Romp* by Jacqueline Briggs Martin, illustrated by Melissa Sweet, and *Chicken Dance* by Tammi Sauer, illustrated by Dan Santat.

MAY 15

Happy Birthday Nancy Garden (*Annie on My Mind*), G. Clifton Wisler (*Red Cap*), David Almond (*Skellig*), and Kadir Nelson (*We Are the Ship*).

It's the birth date of Florence Crannell Means (1891–1980), *The Moved-Outers*; L. Frank Baum (1856–1919), the Oz series; Ellen MacGregor (1906–1954), Miss Pickerell series; Norma Fox Mazer (1931–2009), *When She Was Good*; and Paul Zindel (1936–2003), *The Pigman*.

In 1869 Susan B. Anthony and Elizabeth Cady Stanton formed the National Woman Suffrage Association. Read *Susan B. Anthony* by Deborah Hopkinson, illustrated by Amy June Bates, and *Elizabeth Leads the Way: Elizabeth Cady Stanton and the Right to Vote* by Tanya Lee Stone, illustrated by Rebecca Gibbon.

THE WONDERFUL WIZARD OF OZ

By L. Frank Baum

Today marks the birthday of the American author Lyman Frank Baum. He worked in a variety of jobs—journalist, actor, theater manager, salesman. In fact, he may well have been the inspiration for his most famous character: the Wizard of Oz. In 1900 Baum released the first book about Oz, *The Wonderful Wizard of Oz*, a highly original, imaginative, and enduring fantasy.

Like so many of our now-classic authors, Baum had trouble getting a publisher to take a chance on him. So he and W. W. Denslow, the illustrator, paid for all the costs of printing their book, agreeing to split the profit, if there were any, with the publisher. With author and illustrator willing to self-publish the saga, this enduring American fantasy was launched and became part of the cultural heritage of almost every adult and child in the nation.

Even if you've never read the Oz books, you probably have encountered Baum's creations in the 1933 film starring Judy Garland. The characters of Dorothy and Toto, Aunty Em and Uncle Henry, the Scarecrow who needs a brain, the Cowardly Lion who needs courage, and the Tin Woodman who needs a heart—these inventions of Baum's mind have become cherished friends for generations of readers. Recently, Gregory Maguire's clever reinterpretation of Baum's world, *Wicked*, became a hit Broadway musical.

While working on *Everything I Need to Know I Learned from a Children's Book*, I found a statement by Dr. William C. DeVries, the cardiothoracic surgeon who implanted the first artificial heart, that speaks to the impact of Baum's work. DeVries says, "One of the first books my mother introduced me to was *The Wizard of Oz*. . . . In the book, the Wizard of Oz talks to the Tin Woodman about whether or not he really wants a heart. The Wizard believes that having a heart is not such a good thing: 'It makes most people unhappy.' But the Tin Woodman says, 'For my part, I will bear all the unhappiness without a murmur, if you will give me a heart.' In my work, I have thought about those lines many, many times."

Happy birthday L. Frank Baum—his books continue to influence, and even change, lives. Although, like his famous character, he may have been a flimflam artist at one point in his life, in the end he worked true and lasting magic when he created *The Wizard of Oz*.

THE CIRCUIT: STORIES FROM THE LIFE OF A MIGRANT CHILD

By Francisco Jiménez

May has been designated both Personal History Month and Latino Book Month. Both experiences can be found in one of the most remarkable autobiographies of the last twenty years, Francisco Jiménez's *The Circuit: Stories from the Life of a Migrant Child*. Now a university professor, Jiménez began his journey toward United States citizenship as a child when he and his family were illegal immigrants and migrant workers in California.

In the *The Circuit*, he explores his own story, showing it through the eyes of young Francisco. That life begins as he enters the United States, "Under the Wire," and ends with the immigrant guard (INS) removing him from his eighth-grade classroom for deportation. In between, the family constantly moves around searching for work. Francisco struggles with English and has to repeat first grade because he does not understand anything his teacher says.

Yet nothing in these chapters, which work independently as single stories, even hints at bitterness or anger. All contain moments of grace, where good things happen to the family. Francisco begins to work at age six. Despite his manual labor responsibilities, he finds himself fascinated with books—and he ultimately masters English. Francisco, his parents, and seven siblings live in tents or shacks. Yet even in these cramped conditions, he enjoys the simple things of life like playing guessing games or listening to ghost stories.

These dozen stories set in the 1940s have often been described as *The Grapes of Wrath* told from the Mexican-American point of view. When Jimenez read Steinbeck's masterpiece in college, he felt it was the first book that he could truly relate to: "For the first time, I realized the power of the written word, that an artist can write creatively and make a difference in people's lives."

Francisco continued his saga in *Breaking Through* and *Reaching Out*. Eventually, his family returned legally to the United States and he became the embodiment of the American dream. Perfect for use with ESL students, *The Circuit* explores the migrant experience and showcases an appealing young boy with a strong work ethic. For thoughtful ten- to fourteen-year-old readers as well as adults, this book can alter the way they look at current headlines and even their own lives.

MAY 16

Happy Birthday Betty Miles (*The Real Me*), Caroline Arnold (*The Terrible Hodag and the Animal Catchers*), Deborah Nourse Lattimore (*Cinderhazel*), and Bruce Coville (*Jeremy Thatcher, Dragon Hatcher*).

It's the birth date of Margret Rey (1906–1996), Curious George series.

In 1866 U.S. Congress eliminated the half dime coin and replaced it with the five-cent piece, or nickel. Read *The Buffalo Nickel* by Taylor Morrison.

It's Love a Tree Day. Read *A Tree is Nice* by Janice Udry, illustrated by Marc Simont.

MAY 17

Happy Birthday Eloise Greenfield (*Honey, I love and Other Poems*), Nancy Polette (*Eight Cinderellas*), Gary Paulsen (*Hatchet*), and Jeanne M. Lee (*I Once Was a Monkey*).

 It's the birth date of the **New York Stock Exchange**, formed in 1792. Read *Six Days in October: The Stock Market Crash of 1929* by Karen Blumenthal.

In 1954 the U.S. Supreme Court unanimously ruled for school integration in *Brown v. Board of Education*.

In 1939 the Columbia Lions and Princeton Tigers played in the first televised sporting event in the U.S., a collegiate baseball game. Read *Library Lion* by Michelle Knudson, illustrated by Kevin Hawkes, and *Riding the Tiger* by Eve Bunting, illustrated by David Frampton.

It's Pack Rat Day. Read *The Return of Pete Pack Rat* by Robert Quakenbush.

THE CARROT SEED
By Ruth Krauss
Illustrated by Crockett Johnson

In May of 1945—around the time of Victory in Europe Day in World War II—a small book appeared on the list of Harper and Brothers. A quirky, offbeat title, it was not advertised that year and did not seem a likely candidate for celebrity status in the picture book world. But sometimes truly brilliant books overcome all the obstacles the market places in their way. When it comes to children's books for the very young (those one to three years old), simplicity often makes a winning book, and *The Carrot Seed* exemplifies simplicity.

The creation of writer Ruth Krauss, this small gem actually began as a manuscript of ten thousand words. A testament to revision, the final book stands at 101 words. When asked how long it took her to write *The Carrot Seed*, Krauss always said "her whole life." She had to pare the story down, again and again, until she got its essence.

In this saga, a young child plants a seed. Everyone else believes it won't grow (or as they say, "come up") except the child. "And then one day, / a carrot came up / just as the little boy had known it would." A statement about childhood belief and faith, the book—sometimes called "the little book with the big idea"—has become one of our most cherished American picture books.

Krauss could be quite acerbic when she wanted to, and even her editor Ursula Nordstrom addressed her in letters as "Dear Ruthless." Krauss often terrorized her illustrators. On one notable occasion she took some drawings offered her by a frightened, young illustrator and deposited them in a wastebasket. But she pronounced the drawings for *The Carrot Seed* "perfect."

Of course, Krauss was married to the illustrator of this book, David Johnson Leisk, who worked under the pen name Crockett Johnson. But it would be hard to image any other rendition of this book or of the child in the drawings. Johnson, who was himself bald, always drew bald characters or, in the case of *The Carrot Seed*, a child with a single hair. He maintained that bald heads were easier to render than ones with hair.

Happy birthday to *The Carrot Seed*. For all these years, children have been absorbing its subtle message about the power of positive thinking.

THE RELATIVES CAME

By Cynthia Rylant

Illustrated by Stephen Gammell

May 18 has been designated Visit Your Relatives Day. The idea of a trip to see family members can bring many different images to mind. For Cynthia Rylant, who grew up in Appalachia, West Virginia, visiting relatives is the topic of one of her best books, *The Relatives Came*, which has been in print for almost thirty years and won a Caldecott Honor.

Although she had many rich childhood experiences, Cynthia Rylant did not encounter her first children's book until she was an adult. Then, while working as a children's librarian, she began to voraciously read all the titles she had missed. Largely raised by her grandparents in Cool Ridge, West Virginia, Rylant began to understand that the experiences of those who lived in that area rarely got presented in books for children. So she set out to write about the people she knew—and how they interacted—in her books.

In *The Relatives Came*, after traveling all day and all night from Virginia, a carload of relatives arrives to visit those they love during the summer. They stay for weeks, have picnics, pose for pictures, share the bed and floor of a humble house, play music, and hug. Oh how they hug. Eventually they have to leave for their own home. When they get back, they fall asleep, dreaming about next summer. This wonderful account of a family reunion has been written in simple but poetic language and extended by Stephen Gammell's evocative watercolors. Although this family may be poor in possessions—they are very rich in love and community.

In her career as an author, Cynthia Rylant has crafted many great titles: *When I Was Young in the Mountains*, *Missing May*, and the Henry and Mudge series. But the book you should bring on your next family vacation is *The Relatives Came*. Then you can all enjoy it—and the hugs—together.

MAY 18

Happy Birthday Gloria D. Miklowitz (*Secrets in the House of Delgado*), Barbara Ann Porte (*Beauty and the Serpent*), Ron Hirschi (*Ocean Seasons*), Diane Duane (*So You Want to be a Wizard*), Deborah Guarino (*Is Your Mama a Llama?*), and Debbie Dadey (Bailey School Kids series).

It's the birth date of Irene Hunt (1907–2001), *Across Five Aprils*; and Lillian Hoban (1925–1998), *Bread and Jam for Frances*.

In 1897 *Dracula*, a novel by Irish author Bram Stoker, was published. Read *Dick and Jane and Vampires* by Laura Marchesani, illustrated by Tommy Hunt, and *Vampire Kisses* by Ellen Schreiber.

On this day in 1980 the Mount Saint Helen volcano erupted in Washington State. The catastrophe left fifty-seven people dead or missing.

It's International Museum Day. Read *From the Mixed-up Files of Mrs. Basil E. Frankweiler* by E. L. Konigsburg.

MAY 19

Happy Birthday Pauline Clarke (*Return of the Twelves*), Peter J. Lippman (*Archibald: Or, I was Very Shy*), Judith Hendershot (*In Coal Country*), Arthur Dorros (*Abuela*), Sarah Ellis (*Odd Man Out*), Elise Primavera (*Auntie Claus*), and Kimberly Bulcken Root (*Birdie's Lighthouse*).

It's the birth date of Mary V. Carey (1925–1994), the Three Investigators series; Tom Feelings (1933–2003), *The Middle Passage*; and Lorraine Hansberry (1930–1965), *A Raisin in the Sun*.

 Malcolm X (1925–1965) was also born on this day. Read *Malcolm X: By Any Means Necessary* by Walter Dean Myers and *Malcolm X* by Arnold Adoff, illustrated by Rudy Gutierrez.

In 1536 Anne Boleyn was beheaded on Town Green in the Tower of London.

It's May Ray Day. Read *The Day Ray Got Away* by Angela Johnson, illustrated by Luke LaMarca.

JAMBO MEANS HELLO: SWAHILI ALPHABET BOOK

By Tom Feelings and Muriel Feelings

On May 19, 1933, Tom Feelings was born in Brooklyn, New York. An African American, he chose to spend many years of his adult life in Africa, seeking to understand his heritage. As an artist and picture book illustrator, he presented what he discovered about African culture and history.

While in Africa in the 1960s, Feelings found himself stunned by the physical beauty of the people and the landscape. During this period he created books for the government of Ghana. Even in his early work, Feelings excelled in portraits and faces; the human spirit can be seen in so many of his drawings. He tried to show what he saw in people. As he wrote about his subjects, "[I saw] a glow that came from within, from a knowledge of self, a trust in life, or maybe from a feeling of being part of a majority in your own world. I had seen the same glow in the faces of very young black children in America, the ones who hadn't yet found out that they were considered 'ugly.'"

When he returned to the United States, he sought to illustrate the works of black writers. He added his luminous artwork to Julius Lester's *To Be a Slave* (1968), Eloise Greenfeld's *Daydreamers* (1981), Nikki Grimes's *Something on My Mind* (1978), and Maya Angelou's *Soul Looks Back in Wonder* (1994). Then from 1970 to 1974 he worked with his wife, Muriel, to create picture books about their experience in Africa.

Two of their books, *Jambo Means Hello: Swahili Alphabet Book* and *Moja Means One: Swahili Counting Book*, were without a question a couple of the finest picture books of the decade. Both won Caldecott Honors, although Feelings, like so many extraordinary black artists, never won the medal itself.

What these books do so brilliantly is focus on all the things that Feelings loved about Africa—the beauty of the people, the verdant land, food, animals, and customs. Rarely have those from another country been treated with such respect in a book for American children. While harsh rhetoric and riots engulfed American cities over civil rights, *Moja Means One* and *Jambo Means Hello* demonstrated peace, love, and the integrity of a culture.

Tom Feelings died in 2003 at seventy years old, much too young. He left a small body of books—unique, authentic, intense, and transcendent—that still stand as some of the great works of their time.

SWINDLE

By Gordon Korman

Today has been designated Be a Millionaire Day. Oddly enough, the topics of money and becoming rich rarely find their way into the plots of children's books. Still the preoccupation of being richer than you are must be a universal childhood fantasy. The book of the day, Gordon Korman's *Swindle*, focuses on some children who almost become rich—but actually end up solving many of their problems without obtaining a million dollars.

Griffin Bing, The Man with The Plan, thinks big and drags his friends along with him on his various schemes. While sleeping overnight in a house about to be destroyed by a wrecking crew, Griffin finds a baseball card, one featuring Babe Ruth wearing a Boston Red Sox uniform. Griffin has been worried about money; his family may have to leave their neighborhood because they can't afford to live there. Attempting to get money for the card, he foolishly permits a local trader to swindle him—it turns out the card may actually fetch more than a million dollars at auction.

Since no one will listen to him because he is a kid, Griffin organizes a group of middle schoolers to get the card back. These students can climb, act, calm vicious dogs, hack computers, and provide muscle. So the dream team, filled with school misfits, works to pull off a dramatic heist—and they have only a few hours before the card vanishes forever.

MAY 20

Happy Birthday Shirley Rousseau Murphy (Joe Grey Cat Mystery series), Carol Carrick (*Patrick's Dinosaur*), Carolyn Croll (*What Will the Weather Be?*), and Mary Pope Osborne (Magic Tree House series).

It's the birth date of Sorche Nic Leodhas (1898–1987), *Always Room for One More*; and Don Lawson (1917–1990), *An Album of the Vietnam War*.

In 1609 Shakespeare's sonnets were first published in London. Read *Under the Greenwood Tree: Shakespeare for Young People* edited by Barbara Holdridge, illustrated by Robin and Pat DeWitt, and *Seeing the Blue Between: Advice and Inspiration for Young Poets*, compiled by Paul B. Janeczko.

On this day in 1927 Charles Lindbergh became the first man to complete a nonstop flight from New York to Paris. And on this day in 1932, Amelia Earhart landed near Londonderry, Ireland, and became the first woman to fly solo across the Atlantic.

Gordon Korman was himself a Man with a Plan in middle school. In seventh grade, he wrote his first children's book. Since he collected the money for the Scholastic book club, he submitted this novel to Scholastic Canada, where it was published as *This Can't Be Happening at Macdonald Hall*. His plan ever since, some sixty novels into his career, seems to be to keep children reading—particularly those who may not even believe that they like books. His dialogue is spot-on; his characters, intriguing and funny; and his pacing and dramatic tension so good that no reader wants to put down a Gordon Korman book before it is finished. Today, I don't think I'm actually going to celebrate Be a Millionaire Day, but I would love to raise a cheer for Gordon Korman. He should have a holiday just for himself—and after you read *Swindle,* you will understand why.

MAY 21

Happy Birthday Beverley Naidoo (*Journey to Jo'burg*), Erica Silverman (*Cowgirl Kate and Cocoa*), and Bonnie Bryant (Saddle Club series).

It's the birth date of Virginia Haviland (1911–1988), *The Fairy Tale Treasury*.

On this day in 1881 the American Red Cross was established by **Clara Barton**. Read *Clara Barton: Founder of the American Red Cross* by Christin Ditchfield.

TANGERINE
By Edward Bloor

On May 21, 1904, the Fédération Internationale de Football Association (FIFA) was founded in Paris. Today the Fédération administers the World Cup. What the rest of the world calls "football" has been renamed soccer in the United States. Over the last decade, because of soccer's obvious advantages—an exciting game, team play, and inexpensive equipment—the sport has been embraced by American children. Consequently, a lot of books about this sport have been published.

But if I could choose only one, it would have to be Edward Bloor's 1997 masterpiece, *Tangerine*. Bloor brilliantly explores so many things in this book—sibling relationships, sports drama, the environment, and the tensions of race and economic class. He also creates Paul Fisher, one of the most endearing sports heroes in the children's literature canon. In the seventh grade Paul and his family move to Tangerine, Florida—once a citrus paradise. But the groves of trees have been burned and new housing developments placed over them. However, because of destruction to the native environment, these new residential areas face severe problems like muck fires that constantly burn, or termites that eat their way out of tree roots. Torrential rains happen every afternoon; lightning strikes all the time, sometimes even killing children. Into this disordered landscape, Paul and his highly dysfunctional family immediately begin to add to the chaos.

Paul's father pursues the Eric Fisher Football Dream, doing everything in his power to advance the career of Paul's high-school-age sibling, Eric. Paul's mother butts her nose into everyone's business, but ignores what goes on in her own family. Eric, a truly evil older brother, continues to make Paul's life hell. Paul himself just wants to fit in and find a community. Soccer has always been Paul's saving grace, even though he borders on being legally blind. Special goggles have made it possible for him to play the goalie position despite his poor eyesight.

When part of Paul's school literally disappears into a sinkhole, he uses the situation as an opportunity to gain admittance to another middle school in a rougher neighborhood. That school possesses a superior soccer program, and Paul's tenacity gains the team's approval. Now he plays with a group who sees soccer as war—war against all opposing teams, particularly those of their more privileged neighbors.

Magnificent scenes take place in tangerine groves, and the soccer action will keep all sports fans happily turning the pages. But the mystery behind the story—how Paul lost his sight—and the consequences of ignoring the devastation to the environment allow this book to work on many different levels for young readers ages twelve through fourteen.

In short Bloor has written an unforgettable literary sports novel—great content, great characters, and great sports action. Readers love Paul's tenacity and his eventual triumph over adversity. As he says, "Maybe I am just a sub, maybe I am just along for the ride, but this is the greatest thing that has ever happened to me."

IMOGENE'S LAST STAND

By Candace Fleming
Illustrated by Nancy Carpenter

In England, May has been designated Local and Community History Month to "increase awareness of local history, promote history in general in the local community, and encourage all members of the community to participate." This is such a great concept that I want to advocate that we celebrate local history month in America as well. All of us live in communities rich with history—we just have to champion it.

That message lies at the heart of the book of the day, Candace Fleming's *Imogene's Last Stand*. Imogene Tripp, the heroine of the story, lives in Liddleville, New Hampshire, a town so small it "wasn't even a speck on the state map." Imogene loves history, and she constantly quotes from great historical speeches. As a kindergartner, she used show-and-tell to deliver the words of important women from the past. When older, she discovers the Liddleville Historical Society, an old house filled with antiques, "unloved and unwanted until Imogene pushed open its creaky front door." After restoring the society to order, Imogene discovers that the mayor intends to tear the building down—but unfortunately for him, Imogene proves a worthy opponent, one who repeats John Paul Jones's line "I have not yet begun to fight!"

As Imogene works to have the house declared a national landmark, the book emphasizes that important events in history often occur in the smallest of towns. Although it addresses the serious topic of historical preservation, the book is executed with humor and panache. This picture book combines a delicious text that is expanded and made even funnier by Nancy Carpenter's energetic pen-and-ink illustrations. She extends the role of Imogene's father—we see him supporting his daughter, taking her on motorcycle trips, up in an airplane, and finally putting himself in stocks along with her on the porch of the house to keep it from being demolished.

As Imogene says of her own adventure—"That was totally fun!" Celebrate local history by sharing this great read-aloud book with the budding historians that you know. After you do, you will probably agree with the words of an eight-year-old boy who loved the book—"Wouldn't it be great if everyone had at least a little Imogene in them?"

MAY 22

Happy Birthday Ruth Young (*Who Says Moo?*) and Nancy Krulik (*How I Survived Middle School* series).

It's the birth date of Sir Arthur Conan Doyle (1859–1930), *Sherlock Holmes*; and Arnold Lobel (1933–1987), *Frog and Toad*.

In 1804 the Lewis and Clark Expedition, or Corps of Discovery, officially began when it departed from St. Charles, Missouri.

In 1906 the Wright brothers were granted a patent for their "Flying-Machine." Read *My Brothers' Flying Machine: Wilbur, Orville and Me* by Jane Yolen, illustrated by Jim Burke, and *The Wright Brothers* by Russell Freedman.

In 2002 a Birmingham, Alabama, jury convicted a former Ku Klux Klan member of the September 15, 1963, murders of four girls in the bombing of a baptist church. Read *The Watsons Go to Birmingham—1963* by Christopher Paul Curtis, and *Birmingham, 1963* by Carole Boston Weatherford.

MAY 23

Happy Birthday Susan Cooper (The Dark Is Rising series), Peter Parnall (*Everybody Needs a Rock*), and Jeanne Titherington (*Pumpkin Pumpkin*).

It's the birth date of Scott O'Dell (1898–1989), *Island of the Blue Dolphins*; and Oliver Butterworth (1915–1990), *The Enormous Egg*.

Happy Birthday to the New York Public Library, dedicated on this day in 1911. Read *I'm Going to New York to Visit the Lions* by Margot Linn, illustrated by Tanya Roitman.

Happy Birthday South Carolina, which became the eighth U.S. state on this day in 1788.

It's World Turtle Day. Read *Yertle the Turtle* by Dr. Seuss, *The Turtle* by Cynthia Rylant, illustrated by Preston McDaniels, and *Old Turtle* by Douglas Wood, illustrated by Cheng-Khee Chee.

GOODNIGHT MOON
By Margaret Wise Brown
Illustrated by Clement Hurd

Today marks the birthday of one of the greatest children's book creators of the twentieth century, Margaret Wise Brown. Although she died suddenly of an embolism at the age of forty-two, Brown wrote more than one hundred books, including *The Runaway Bunny* and the classic *Goodnight Moon*. Born in Brooklyn, New York, Brown grew up on Long Island and attended the Dana Hall School and Hollins College, where she was encouraged to write. Later the teacher-training program of Bank Street in New York changed her life.

Flourishing under the mentorship of Lucy Sprague Mitchell, founder of Bank Street, Brown began to study early childhood development and write stories for very young children. Mitchell believed that children under the age of six wanted stories that reflected the reality of their own lives. Brown embraced Mitchell's ideals and crafted individual works of genius for babies, toddlers, and preliterate children.

For a period of time, Brown became an editor for William R. Scott, publishing books like *Caps for Sale* by Esphyr Slobodkina, Gertrude Stein's *The World Is Round,* and her own titles such as *The Noisy Book*. Eventually, with the publication of *The Runaway Bunny* in 1942, Brown began to write full time, penning one classic after another—*The Color Kittens* (1949), a Golden Book that deals with color theory, *The Little Island* (1946) under the pseudonym of Golden MacDonald, and *Mister Dog* (1952).

Today Brown is best remembered for a book that took almost twenty years to establish itself as a classic. Upon awakening one morning in 1945, she wrote down the entire text of *Goodnight Moon*, telephoned her editor, Ursula Nordstrom, and read it aloud. Nordstrom accepted it immediately for publication. In a melodic, rhythmic text a young bunny says goodnight to all the objects in the room. Brown waited for Clement Hurd to return from the Pacific, where he was fighting in World War II, to work his illustration magic. She had loved his art for *The Runaway Bunny*. But when she saw the first draft of the art, Brown hated it. Hurd portrayed an old white grandmother sitting in the chair, with a young black boy in bed. Brown insisted the story had always been about bunnies, and she wanted bunnies! Nordstrom backed her.

The resulting book seemed a bit unexciting and overpriced for most customers. Critics found it sentimental. However, in the end children established it as a classic. A timeless book, almost like a child's evening prayers, *Goodnight Moon* has lulled millions of children to sleep over the decades.

So happy birthday Margaret Wise Brown. She taught us, and still teaches us, how to communicate with the youngest children.

THE GREAT BRAIN

By John D. Fitzgerald

Today has been designated Brother's Day—a celebration of brotherhood for biological brothers, fraternity brothers, and brothers bonded by union affiliation or lifetime experience. As you might expect, children's books frequently focus on sibling relationships, both brothers and sisters. After all, in childhood these relationships loom large in our lives.

When I think of brothers in children's books, to my mind the best series was published more than forty years ago, beginning with John D. Fitzgerald's *The Great Brain*. In the 1950s Fitzgerald had written adult fiction, *Uncle Will and the Fitzgerald Curse*, *Papa Married a Mormon*, and *Mama's Boarding House*. But then he began writing about the children of Adenville, Utah, at the turn of the twentieth century. For these eight novels, he drew loosely on his own childhood experience.

In *The Great Brain*, narrated by young John Dennis Fitzgerald, we see his two older brothers through his eyes. Sweyn Dennis (all the boys have Dennis as a middle name) makes a cameo appearance. But Tom Dennis, aka the Great Brain, is the focus of the novel. For Tom is a smooth-talking, silver-tongued con artist—and loves to find any scheme that he can to relieve the children, and even parents, of Adenville, of their hard-earned money. Whether Tom is charging the children a penny to look at the family's indoor water closet (the first indoor toilet in the neighborhood) or negotiating deals to breed John's dog, he always finds a way to come out on top—usually at John's expense. But Tom can also be compassionate. He helps a Greek immigrant assimilate into the community and shows a boy who has lost part of a leg how to recover emotionally and physically from his disability. The books bring to life the community of Adenville, Utah. Most people are Mormon but some are Catholics and Protestants. Religious tension and conflict rarely get explored in children's books, but the Great Brain books continually discuss this reality—even showing how religious prejudice brings about the death of an itinerant Jewish peddler.

In the end, these books, ideal for seven- to ten-year-olds, celebrate brothers—caring, scraping, devoted brothers. So celebrate Brother's Day by acknowledging the brothers in your life—and by picking up *The Great Brain* and its sequels.

MAY 24

Happy Birthday Diane DeGroat (*Roses Are Pink, Your Feet Really Stink*) and Candace Fleming (*Imogene's Last Stand*).

It's the birth date of Martha Alexander (1920–2006), *A, You're Adorable*; and Elizabeth Foreman Lewis (1892–1958), *Yong Fu of the Upper Yangtze*.

Best birthday wishes to singer Bob Dylan. Read *Forever Young* by Bob Dylan, illustrated by Paul Rogers, *Man Gave Names to All the Animals* by Bob Dylan, illustrated by Jim Arnosky, and *When Bob Met Woody: The Story of the Young Bob Dylan* by Gary Golio, illustrated by Marc Burckhardt.

In 1830 *Mary Had a Little Lamb* by Sarah Josepha Hale was first published.

In 1844 **Samuel Morse** tapped out the first telegraph message.

MAY 25

Happy Birthday Robert Froman (*Angles Are Easy as Pie*), Audrey Smith (*The Halloween Misfits*), Ivy Ruckman (*Night of the Twisters*), Ann McGovern (*Stone Soup*), Joyce Carol Thomas (*The Blacker the Berry: Poems*), and Barbara Bottner (*Bootsie Barker Bites*).

In 1961 President John F. Kennedy announced the project to put a "man on the moon." Read Brian Floca's *Moonshot*.

It's National Tap Dance Day, celebrating this American art form. Read *Tap-Dance Fever* by Pat Brisson, illustrated by Nancy Cote, *Savion!: My Life in Tap* by Savion Glover and Bruce Weber, and *Rap a Tap Tap* by Leo Dillon and Diane Dillon.

FIRST THE EGG
By Laura Vaccaro Seeger

May has been designated Egg Month—dedicated to the versatility, convenience, and good nutrition of "The incredible edible egg."™ Children's book writers and illustrators have always been bullish on eggs—at least as the subject matter for books. Just think of classics like Dr. Seuss's *Horton Hatches the Egg* or Oliver Butterworth's *The Enormous Egg*. But my favorite egg book of recent years—by our most innovative and versatile creator of books for the preschool set—is Laura Vaccaro Seeger's *First the Egg*.

Laura Vaccaro Seeger grew up on Long Island, New York, and began drawing at the age of two. Fortunately for the world she never stopped. After getting a BFA at the State University of New York, she moved to Manhattan and began a career as an animator and designer for network television. She brought her sense of graphic design and knowledge of children to a career in children's books. Her concept books for one- to four-year-olds are never tired or formulaic; for those just learning to enjoy books, she has created one inspired book after another—*One Boy*; *Lemons Are Not Red*; *Black? White! Day? Night!* As a creator, she does not repeat herself and finds new ways to use the picture-book format each time she publishes.

In *First the Egg*, Seeger explores the age-old question: Which came first, the chicken or the egg? On double-page spreads, she shows us "First the EGG / then the CHICKEN." Each cutout in the book leads to a mature form of the first picture. In a book about transformation, a tadpole becomes a frog, a caterpillar a butterfly, and a word becomes the story. At the end of the book, the lines "First the CHICKEN / then the EGG!" turns the story around for a satisfying conclusion. This Caldecott Honor book is illustrated with brilliantly colored paintings. Each page is designed with great care, using type and art to draw the reader in again and again. Laura has taken a familiar subject and made it uniquely her own.

If I were building a library for a new baby right now, I'd first purchase all the books by Laura Vaccaro Seeger, and then add in some of the classics. Her books are both contemporary and timeless. Perfect for new readers, they also engage adults who have read hundreds of books. In a few short years, Laura has become the master of the concept book—someone we can rely on to give us one brilliant book after another.

DUCK ON A BIKE

By David Shannon

Organizers of National Bike Month—established to celebrate bicycling for fun, fitness, and transportation—estimate that five million people will participate in biking activities across the country during May. Certainly for many people, nothing says "good weather" and "good times" as much as a bike trip, however long or short. I just wish the National Bike Month organizers would expand their anticipated population—after all, many animals might like to take a spin as well!

This delightful premise lies behind David Shannon's *Duck on a Bike*, first published in 2002. Shannon consistently crafts practically perfect picture books telling fascinating stories through a great balance of text and art. With unusual perspectives in the illustrations that are drenched with bright, sunny color, *Duck on a Bike* showcases all of his talents.

On the title page, we meet our hero: Duck

MAY 26

Happy Birthday Ann Schlee (*Ask Me No Questions*), Sheila Greenwald (Rosy Cole series), Adrienne Kennaway (*Greedy Zebra*), Lisbeth Zwerger (*Gift of the Magi*), and Raina Telgemeier (*Smile*).

Jazz musician Miles Davis (1926–1991) was born on this day. Read *Lookin' for Bird in the Big City* by Robert Burleigh, illustrated by Marek Los.

It's the birth date of astronaut Sally Ride (1951–2012), the first American woman to travel into space. Read *Mission: Planet Earth* by Sally Ride and Tam O'Shaughnessy. And by the way, it's Sally Ride Day!

looks at a huge bicycle and strokes his chin. What is he thinking? On the first page readers learn that Duck has a wild idea: he wants to ride a bike! So he waddles over to a boy's bike, jumps aboard, and then wobbles away. Soon Duck gets his bike legs and realizes just how much fun he can have.

In a repetitive-pattern story, Duck rides past typical barnyard creatures and says hello. Although all the cow does is moo and the sheep baa, they each have negative thoughts about biking. The dog chases Duck and the cat "wouldn't waste my time riding a bike!" but none of this fazes our hero who moves jauntily along, enjoying a wonderful day. Goats, pigs, mice, and a horse all weigh in with their opinions, until a group of kids race down the road. They park their bikes beside a house and go inside. The next wordless double-page spread shows only the animals, with their faces quite animated. Then they all jump on a bike and ride around the barnyard. In a humorous end to the tale, all bikes get returned, with their owners none the wiser. On the last page we see our hero again—sizing up a tractor.

As funny and lighthearted as this book is, it also explores some serious ideas. A fourth grader in Ohio named Kerri felt that the book encouraged her not to be disheartened by others' negative comments. Since Duck doesn't care what others think, his approach to life gave her a way to respond differently. "When my brother teases me," she said, "I won't care."

Personally, I would cheer for Duck if he ever took on the Tour de France. But in the meantime parents and children, ages one through ten, can enjoy reading and rereading about Duck's escapades in this totally satisfying picture book.

MAY 27

Happy Birthday M. E. Kerr (*Deliver Us from Evie*), Lynn Sweat (*Amelia Bedelia* series), and Trenton Lee Stewart (*The Mysterious Benedict Society*).

It's the birth date of **Rachel Carson** (1907–1942), author of *Silent Spring*, credited with starting the U.S. environmental movement. Read *Rachel Carson: Clearing the Way for Environmental Protection* by Mike Venezia and *Rachel: The Story of Rachel Carson* by Amy Ehrlich, illustrated by Wendell Minor.

In 1933 Walt Disney released the cartoon *Three Little Pigs*, with the song "Who's Afraid of the Big Bad Wolf?" Read *The Three Pigs* by David Wiesner, and *The Three Little Wolves and the Big Bad Pig* by Eugene Trivizas, illustrated by Helen Oxenbury.

In 1937 San Francisco's Golden Gate Bridge opened. Read *Pop's Bridge* by Eve Bunting, illustrated by C. F. Payne.

YOU FORGOT YOUR SKIRT, AMELIA BLOOMER!

By Shana Corey
Illustrated by Chesley McLaren

On May 27, 1818, Amelia Jenks was born in Homer, New York. She married an attorney named Dexter Bloomer, who encouraged her to write for his paper, the *Seneca Falls Country Courier*. Amelia became a strong voice for both temperance and women's rights. She also had the good fortune of having a piece of clothing that she popularized named after her. Recently, Amelia has gotten renewed attention because of a book and a project inspired by her.

The picture book, *You Forgot Your Skirt, Amelia Bloomer!* by Shana Corey, focuses on Amelia's rebellious nature. Not a proper lady, Amelia thought the trappings of femininity silly—with the voluminous skirts that swept up trash and the corsets that made women faint. She believed that a woman should have a job and vote. Hence, Amelia became the first woman to own, operate, and edit a newspaper, *The Lily*. She used her bully pulpit to advocate against drinking and for women's rights. When she spied Elizabeth Cady Stanton's cousin Libby wearing a costume that was not a dress—but pantaloons with a skirt over them—Amelia made one, wore it, sold patterns to her readers, and used the power of the press to advocate for what became known as the "bloomer." This style did go out of fashion but, fortunately, dress reform continued—and women and girls today can wear clothes to suit their active lifestyles.

Since 2002, the Amelia Bloomer Project—administered by the Feminist Task Force of the American Library Association's Social Responsibilities Round Table—has been selecting books notable for their feminist content, quality writing, and appeal to young readers. In 2010, the Amelia Bloomer List included fifty-four books—a notable year in the task force's estimation, partly because of Hillary Clinton running for president. For more information and book suggestions, you can visit their website.

So thank you Amelia Bloomer for passion and spirited advocacy of comfortable clothes. And thank all of those on the Bloomer Project for finding books that show women taking action and fighting for their rights.

CHITTY CHITTY BANG BANG: THE MAGICAL CAR

By Ian Fleming

Today marks the 103nd birthday of British writer, journalist, and Naval Intelligence Officer Ian Fleming. If his name sounds unfamiliar, you're sure to know "Bond. James Bond," the character he created. Like many authors who distinguished themselves writing for adults—E. B. White or Esther Forbes—Fleming also created a beloved children's book, *Chitty Chitty Bang Bang: The Magical Car.* Based on a story he told to his son and published in 1964, the year Fleming died, the book brought a fantasy car to life, one that any child would love to own.

The title character is a once-beautiful automobile that has become a pile of junk, ready to be towed off and destroyed. Fortunately, Commander Caractacus Potts, an inventor, sees possibility in this machine. He lovingly restores her, in his garage in secret. When the commander, his wife Mimsie, and their two children, Jeremy and Jemima, finally take her out for a spin, they name her "Chitty Chitty Bang Bang" because of the sound she makes. Only later, on a vacation day to the beach, do they discover that she can sprout wings and fly, turn into a motor boat, and hone in on a gangster getaway car. She even exhibits independent actions and thinking. Lights appear on her dashboard that provide instructions—simple statements such as "PULL IDIOT." In the end, Chitty Chitty Bang Bang foils some gangsters' plan to rob a French candy store, and then heads off into the stratosphere with the Potts family along for the ride.

For those who love this book, in 2012 a sequel, *Chitty Chitty Bang Bang Flies Again,* was published by Frank Cottrell Boyce. Boyce caught the spirit of Fleming's creation and created a saga with more madcap nonsense about the magical car. Devotees of the Fleming's book will not be disappointed as they read about Chitty's new adventures.

May has been designated Get Caught Reading Month by the American Association of Publishers. During this month various celebrities pose for posters that show them reading a book. I have no doubt that James Bond himself would be caught reading *Chitty Chitty Bang Bang.* It is just the type of story that any spy in training—or first- to sixth-grade reader—would want to pick up.

MAY 28

Happy Birthday Isabella Leitner (*The Big Lie*), Lynn Johnston (*Farley Follows His Nose*), and Debby Atwell (*Barn*).

Today also marks the birth date of the Dionne quintuplets. They were the first quintuplets to survive infancy and were born in Canada in 1934.

In 1859 sixteen horses pulled a carriage carrying Big Ben from the Whitechapel Bell Foundry to the Palace of Westminster. Read *B is for Big Ben: An England Alphabet* by Pamela Edwards, illustrated by Melanie Rose, and *Ben and the Big Balloon* by Sue Graves and Helen Jackson.

In 1984 a state funeral was led by President Ronald Reagan at Arlington National Cemetery for an unidentified American soldier who died in the Vietnam War. Read *The Wall* by Eve Bunting, illustrated by Ronald Himler, and *Arlington: The Story of Our Nation's Cemetery* by Chris Demarest.

MAY 29

Happy Birthday Brock Cole (*The Goats*), Stephen T. Johnson (*Alphabet City*), and Andrew Clements (*Frindle*).

It's the birth date of Mary Louisa Molesworth (1839–1921), *Tell Me a Story*; T. H. White (1906–1964), *The Sword in the Stone*, *The Once and Future King*; and Eleanor Coerr (1922–2010), *Sadako and the Thousand Paper Cranes*.

 It's also the birth date of **John F. Kennedy** (1917–1963), the 35th president of the United States. Read *Jack's Path of Courage* by Doreen Rappaport, illustrated by Matt Tavares, and *When JFK Was My Father* by Amy Gordon.

In 1953 Edmund Hillary and Tenzing Norgay became the first explorers to reach the top of Mount Everest.

Happy Birthday to both Rhode Island and Wisconsin. Rhode Island became the 13th U.S. state on this day in 1790, and Wisconsin became the 30th state in 1848.

THE SCHWA WAS HERE
By Neal Shusterman

Get out your party clothes! Today those in the know celebrate National Paper Clip Day. The modern version of this lowly but extremely useful object was patented on November 9, 1899, by William D. Middlebrook of Waterbury, Connecticut. But during World War II the paper clip became the symbol of national unity in Norway. Forbidden by the occupying Nazis from wearing buttons imprinted with their king's initials, Norwegians wore paper clips on their lapels as a show of opposition. Citizens wearing this object could, and did, get arrested.

Paper clips keep all kinds of valuable papers connected, and one of the heroes of the book of the day, Neal Shusterman's *The Schwa Was Here*, collects them. He owns the paper clip that held together the Nuclear Arms Treaty signed by Reagan and Gorbachev. Just as paper clips usually go unnoticed, so does Calvin Schwa. He is the kid that blends in and that no one pays attention to.

Eighth grader Anthony (Antsy) Bonono can't remember when he first met the Schwa. As he says: "You couldn't even think about him without losing track of your own thoughts—like even in your head he was somehow becoming invisible." But the Schwa can go places and do things without anyone seeing him, like to the faculty lounge at school, for instance. So Antsy becomes the Schwa's agent, placing bets and collecting the money for the two of them as Calvin pulls off one stunt after another.

All goes well until Antsy stretches too far. He wagers that the Schwa can enter the apartment of the rich local misanthrope, Old Man Crowly, a Howard Hughes–type character, and get away with it. And when Calvin fails, suddenly both Antsy and the Schwa find themselves up against someone who can outthink and outwit them. Old Man Crowly insists they walk his fourteen Afghans every day as well as take care of his blind granddaughter.

This extremely funny but true-to-life story has been executed with great humor. All the characters are wonderfully eccentric but seem as real as any that can be found in children's books. Yet the book takes a very serious look at the way some children slip between the cracks. Winner of the *Boston Globe–Horn Book* Award for Fiction, *The Schwa Was Here* appeals to those eleven- to fourteen-year-olds who love not only a funny, realistic, entertaining story with appealing characters but also one that makes them think as well.

Today I'm going to notice all the ways I use the paper clip—and pay more attention to the people I see during the day.

TOM'S MIDNIGHT GARDEN

By Philippa Pearce

On the last Monday of May we celebrate Memorial Day to honor those who have served their country. In the minds of many, Memorial Day weekend signifies not only lovely barbecues, but also the beginning of summer. And for children summer often means more unstructured time when they can enjoy their own activities.

Tom Long is the hero of our book of the day, Philippa Pearce's *Tom's Midnight Garden*. Tom has been looking forward to his summer idyll with his brother, Peter. But Peter comes down with the measles, and Tom gets sent off to stay with relatives even though he doesn't want to go. Fortunately Tom finds unusual attractions in their home. At midnight, after the clock downstairs rings thirteen times, he can enter a magical garden. There he encounters an enchanting girl named Hatty. They build a tree house together and ice skate for miles over a river. Hatty begins to grow older during these nighttime vigils. Slowly Tom comprehends that although Hatty lives in the same house that he does, she comes from another era.

In the summer of 1951, Philippa Pearce lay in a hospital bed recovering from tuberculosis. She spent the summer thinking of her parents' old mill house and garden, which stood near the River Cam. When she had recovered enough to work, she used this setting for *Tom's Midnight Garden*. After she had finished the manuscript, she provided many photographs and sketches for the illustrator, so the drawings actually reflected details from Pearce's childhood home.

Considered by British critics as the finest fantasy of the twentieth century after *The Hobbit*, *Tom's Midnight Garden* has never been as well known in America as it is in England. Yet, like *The Wind in the Willows*, *Tom's Midnight Garden* can be appreciated by adults, as well as children, and seems even more profound with each reading. As Pearce explores how present experience has been influenced by the past, she manages to weave an absolutely perfect time-travel fantasy novel that surprises me every time I come to the end, even though I know what will happen.

If you don't know it or simply want to experience the story again, *Tom's Midnight Garden* makes a fabulous beginning for a summer of reading. On Memorial Day, as we honor our heroes and heroines of the past, we can also reflect on the profound way that our past intersects with the present.

MAY 30

Happy Birthday Frances Barnes-Murphy (*The Fables of Aesop*) and Kevin Eastman (*Teenage Mutant Ninja Turtles*).

It's the birth date of Cornelia Otis Skinner (1901–1979), *Our Hearts Were Young and Gay*; Countee Cullen (1903–1946), *The Lost Zoo*; and Millicent E. Selsam (1912–1996), *Greg's Microscope*.

In 1783 the first American daily newspaper, *The Pennsylvania Evening Post*, began publishing in Philadelphia.

On this day in 1859 Westminster's Big Ben rang for the first time in London. Read *Ben, the Bells and the Peacock* by Rhoda Trooboff, illustrated by Cecile Bucher.

Happy 100th birthday to the Indianapolis 500 auto race, first held in 1911. Read *The Wheels on the Race Car* by Alex Zane, illustrated by James Warhola.

It's Water a Flower Day. Read *Alison's Zinnia* by Anita Lobel.

MAY 31

Happy Birthday Harry Mazer (*A Boy at War*), Ron Goor (*Insect Metamorphosis*), Elaine Moore (*Get That Girl Out of the Boys' Locker Room!*), Phillip Hoose (*Claudette Colvin: Twice Toward Justice*), and Will Hillenbrand (*Sleep, Big Bear, Sleep!*).

 It's the birth date of **Walt Whitman** (1819–1892), *Leaves of Grass*; Elizabeth Coatsworth (1893–1986), *The Cat Who Went to Heaven*; and Jay Williams (1914–1978), *Everyone Knows What a Dragon Looks Like*.

In 1927 the last Model T Ford rolled off the assembly line after a production run of over fifteen million vehicles. Read *Tin Lizzie* by Allan Drummond and *Mama and Me and the Model T* by Faye Gibbons, illustrated by Ted Rand.

Turn down the music and take care of your ears on National Save Your Hearing Day.

HALF MAGIC
By Edward Eager

"It began one day in summer about thirty years ago, and it happened to four children." So begins the book of the day, a perfect story about summer for the beginning of summer reading. This book holds a unique place in the children's book canon. It is the only one I know where the author admitted to copying, shamelessly, from another in style and spirit. But in the case of Edward Eager, he always claimed that *Half Magic*, and other books in the series, stood as a way to lead young readers back to the master, E. Nesbit.

Whatever he owes to Nesbit, Edward Eager invented a unique and intriguing premise for a fantasy novel. Four children—Jane, Mark, Kathleen, and Martha—find a magical coin that grants wishes. What could be better? Except this coin proves to be tricky: it grants only half a wish. The children quickly learn that wishes have to be carefully framed or they lead to a lot of difficulties. Young Martha, for instance, wishes for the cat to talk, but it only manages a flow of meaningless words. But one thing is certain: the coin provides a lot of excitement for the summer.

Eager produced a play so successful that he left Harvard to write dramas and songs for theater, radio, and television. It wasn't until he had a son that he began to read the books of English fantasy writer E. Nesbit. These books were grounded in "everyday" magic, things that could occur in the lives of ordinary children living normal lives. Eager drew from Nesbit's structure and ideas for all seven books in his series. By combining realism with exciting magical adventures, a child doesn't have to be attending Hogwarts for interesting events to happen. He or she can just live on an average block in an average city—like Toledo, Ohio, Eager's hometown—and fabulous events occur.

Although Eager's work went out of print for a short period, the fantasy craze brought about by Harry Potter brought it quickly back into favor. Plot-driven, with a huge dollop of humor and inventiveness, *Half Magic* and its sequels appeal greatly to those in second to fourth grades hunting for a accessible fantasy novel.

Even if you don't find a magic coin this summer, *Half Magic* will allow you to think about what you would wish for—divided by half.

FLIPPED

By Wendelin Van Draanen

Today has been designated Flip a Coin Day. The word *flip* immediately reminds me of one of the funniest, and yet most true-to-life romances written for the ten- to fourteen-year-old set, Wendelin Van Draanen's *Flipped*.

The two protagonists, Julie and Bryce, alternate narrating chapters. In second grade, when Bryce moves in across the street, Julie falls in love at first sight: "The first day I met Bryce Loski, I flipped. Honestly, one look at him and I became a lunatic." Handsome, with brilliant blue eyes, Bryce becomes Julie's love obsession for six long years.

Passionate and intense, Julie lets Bryce know, along with everyone else, how she feels about him. When another girl in fifth grade gets near him, a cat fight ensues. Julie follows him around, smells his hair in class, and generally makes herself a nuisance. Bryce, on the other hand, tries to blend in, get along, and not create waves. He remains aloof but polite to Julie. Their relationship is exacerbated by the socioeconomic standings of both families. Julie lives in a rented house, the eyesore of the neighborhood. Her father scrapes to get by because he also provides economic support for his brother. Bryce's father, on the other hand, believes in keeping up appearances and displaying his wealth.

Readers follow along—through a "he said, she said" storytelling approach—until Bryce and Julie reach eighth grade. Then, as is true in the lives of adolescents everywhere, things begin to tilt. When Julie battles to save a neighborhood sycamore tree from being chopped down and Bryce does not come to her defense, she begins to suspect that he may be much more superficial than she has realized.

But Bryce changes too and slowly comes to realize that the girl he considered an annoying neighbor could actually be someone special. As her ardor cools, his expands. Finally, he flips, too—and chases her around, hoping for a kiss. The book leaves the romance unresolved; they agree to sit down and actually talk to each other, something that has not happened in all six years. In the meantime readers have been taken on a roller-coaster ride of misunderstanding and laughter. One of the funniest chapters in the book revolves around a dinner where the two families sit down to get to know each other.

Made into a motion picture and beloved by readers for a decade, *Flipped* is perfect for summer reading, particularly for those wondering about a certain boy or girl in their lives. Young love in all its phases—from insecurity to insanity—is brilliantly explored in this breezy, easy-to-read novel.

JUNE 1

Happy Birthday Leah Komaiko (*Annie Bananie*).

It's the birth date of John Masefield (1878–1967), *The Midnight Folk*, *The Box of Delights*; James Daugherty (1889–1974), *Andy and the Lion*; and Doris Buchanan Smith (1934–2002), *A Taste of Blackberries*.

Happy Birthday to both Kentucky and Tennessee. Kentucky became the 15th U.S. state on this day in 1792, and Tennessee became the 16th state in 1796.

More to read on Flip a Coin Day: *Flip* by David Lubar, *Flip-Flop Girl* by Katherine Paterson, and *The Gold Coin* by Alma Flor Ada, illustrated by Neil Waldman.

JUNE 2

Happy Birthday William Loren Katz (*Black Women of the Old West*), Helen Oxenbury (*We're Going on a Bear Hunt*), Jack Gantos (*Joey Pigza* series), and Michael Emberley (*It's Perfectly Normal*).

It's the birth date of Paul Galdone (1914–1986), *The Three Billy Goats Gruff.*

 Martha Washington (1731–1802), the first first lady of the United States, was born on this day. Read *The Escape of Oney Judge: Martha Washington's Slave Finds Freedom* by Emily Arnold McCully.

On this day in 1924 President Calvin Coolidge signed the Indian Citizen Act of 1924, also known as the Snyder Act. This document granted citizenship status to all Native Americans who previously had not obtained citizenship rights by other means.

THE PHANTOM TOLLBOOTH

By Norton Juster
Illustrated by Jules Feiffer

Today marks the birthday of Norton Juster, a man who should be named the patron saint of all who put pen to paper. One of the things that all writers do, on almost a daily basis, is avoid writing. If most creators put as much energy into writing as they put into not writing, the world would simply be flooded with books!

Creative procrastination can sometimes lead to great things—that is what writers constantly tell themselves. Norton Juster proved this point several decades ago. An architect by trade, he received a Ford Foundation grant to write about how people experience cities. To avoid work on this project, he began spinning a tale about a very bored boy, Milo, who travels in an electric car to the Kingdom of Wisdom. In this land, with its tension between words and numbers, Milo encounters an array of fascinating characters: giant insects (Humbug and the Spelling Bee) and a watchdog, Tock, whose body contains a large alarm clock. Even the minor characters in this book have names that can be savored: Duke of Definition, Minister of Meaning, Earl of Essence, Count of Connotation, and Undersecretary of Understanding. In this story that might remind readers of Lewis Carroll's *Alice's Adventures in Wonderland,* Milo attempts to rescue the twin sisters Rhyme and Reason and goes from one fantastic region of this madcap world to another.

As luck would have it, Juster lived in the same apartment building as cartoonist Jules Feiffer in Brooklyn Heights, New York. So as Juster wrote the book, Feiffer made drawings of these incredible creatures. The story became a kind of competition between the two; the author attempted to describe things that would be difficult for Feiffer to draw. The whole exercise became a game, inventive, free-flowing—a fabulous example of thinking and writing out of the box.

Evidentially, when the Ford Foundation received a copy of the manuscript, they did not respond. But children have absolutely adored *The Phantom Tollbooth* since it appeared in 1961. To celebrate Norton Juster's birthday, I'm going to engage in some good old procrastination—and see what creativity comes from it.

JENNY AND THE CAT CLUB

By Esther Averill

June has been designated Adopt a Shelter Cat month. In the 1940s and 1950s author Esther Averill brought us Jenny Linsky, one of the most engaging cats in children's books. Poor Jenny. Found as a stray, she's taken into the home of the kindly Captain. But she desperately wants to become a member of the Cat Club that meets in her neighborhood. To gain admittance, she must demonstrate a special talent. Not until the Captain fashions ice skates for Jenny so she can show the other cats her prowess does she finally become a member of the club. In *Jenny and the Cat Club*, which contains five stories about our intrepid heroine, Jenny goes to her first party (where she shows off her ability to dance the sailor's hornpipe), acquires some brothers, loses a scarf, and gets her brothers admitted to the Cat Club.

Although all the stories about Jenny Linsky stay true to cat behavior, they rely on the realities of childhood—wanting to fit in, jealousy over siblings, losing a valued object. All the cat characters have names and personalities, are rendered in black line with spots of color, and engage in clever dialogue. In Jenny, young readers see both their beloved pet and themselves. Perfect for readers ages five through eight who have moved up from picture books but are not yet ready for longer novels, the stories about Jenny contain a great deal of humor, and each chapter works independently so they can be read in several sittings.

Throughout her career Esther Averill pursued many lines of work. A graduate of Vassar in the 1920s, she wrote for *Women's Wear Daily*. She went to Paris and in 1931 established her own press, where she specialized in superb reproductions of the artwork of some of the most gifted European artists of the time. Because of the Nazi invasion of Paris, Averill returned to the United States and worked for the New York Public Library. Then she studied art and began creating stories about Jenny set in Greenwich Village, where Averill lived.

Although immensely popular in their day, the thirteen volumes about Jenny the cat began to vanish from print in the later part of the twentieth century. However, in 2003, *The New York Review of Books* started reissuing them. These editions are commendable not only because they put Jenny back in circulation but also because of the attention given to design and production. All the Averill reissues are elegant books, perfect to give as gifts. It seems so fitting that Averill, who cared deeply about book production, received the kind of care and attention for her books she once lavished on the books of others.

If there are any cat lovers out there who have not discovered or reread these books for years, you will be delighted when you pick up these sagas that work beautifully for young readers and cat lovers of all ages.

JUNE 3

Happy Birthday Anita Lobel (*On Market Street, No Pretty Pictures*).

It's the birth date of Robert Newman (1909–1988), *The Case of the Baker Street Irregular*.

In 1888 "Casey at the Bat" by Ernest Lawrence Thayer was published in the *San Francisco Examiner*. There are several current picture book editions of *Casey at the Bat* in print, illustrated by Christopher Bing, Joe Morse, Barry Moser, Leroy Neiman, C. F. Payne, and Patricia Polacco.

JUNE 4

Happy Birthday Joyce Sidman (*Dark Emperor and Other Poems of the Night, Red Sings from Tree Tops*).

 In 1917 the first Pulitzer Prizes were awarded according to the will of media giant **Joseph Pulitzer**. Read *Joseph Pulitzer and the Story of the Pulitzer Prize* by Susan Zannos.

In 1919 the U.S. Congress approves the 19th Amendment, allowing women to vote. Read *You Want Women to Vote, Lizzie Stanton?* by Jean Fritz, illustrated by DyAnne DeSilvo-Ryan.

JUMANJI
By Chris Van Allsburg

The first Saturday in June has been designated Drawing Day or Pencil Day. Today we are encouraged to create art and to remember the joy we had when we first picked up a pencil and drew. If I ask myself what is the most amazing book that was created by a pencil, the answer comes in a flash: Chris Van Allsburg's now-classic *Jumanji*.

Appearing on April 27, 1981, *Jumanji* was Chris's second book, following his highly successful *The Garden of Abdul Gasazi*. Chris was trained as a sculptor at the University of Michigan but taught himself to draw. His super-realistic but otherworldly black-and-white illustrations came to the attention of Walter Lorraine at Houghton Mifflin, who encouraged Chris to create picture books.

The reception to Chris's artwork was not immediately favorable. Paul Heins of the *Horn Book* criticized *The Garden of Abdul Gasazi* for being too sophisticated—Paul later apologized in print. By the time *Jumanji* came on the scene, adults and children alike were watching what this extraordinary newcomer to the field might do. He had wowed everyone with amazing scenes, one-point perspective, and aerial views. So realistic did his pictures appear that many children remembered his first two books as being in color rather than black and white.

Jumanji rests on an age-old premise: the parents leave home, the children start to entertain themselves, and chaos ensues. Before the parents' return, order has to be restored. In this story, the children, Judy and Peter, pull out a board game, Jumanji, which warns them that once started it must be finished. They don't pay much attention to the instructions and suddenly find the game come to life in their home—a lion on the piano, monkeys in the kitchen, rhinos charging into the dining room, and a snake on the mantle. All of these images from Van Allsburg's brilliantly created fantasy world have been rendered in pencil. All show detail, shading, patterns, perspective, and drama. The rhinos burst out of the picture frame. Readers look down from the ceiling as Judy and Peter play this game with increased frenzy.

Because the drawings carry so much of the book, Chris finished them first. He wanted to make sure that every detail, every nuance was right. I still have the selling sample prepared for sales conference—only the drawings are in place because the words still needed to be finalized. Even without a line of text, you can "read" the story in the art, all of it created with the lowly pencil.

Chris won his first won his first Caldecott Medal for *Jumanji*. It became a successful movie and it stands as an important part of the picture book canon for its inventiveness and execution. It encourages all budding young artists to pick up a pencil and see what happens.

HURRICANE DANCERS

By Margarita Engle

This month marks the beginning of the Atlantic, Caribbean, and Gulf hurricane season. June also marks Caribbean-American Heritage month. Both events are celebrated in the book of the day, Margarita Engle's *Hurricane Dancers*. In a powerful, 145-page poetic novel, Engle presents a fresh and unusual look at Cuba, its history from 1509 to 1510, and its people.

After winning a Newbery Honor for *The Surrender Tree*, Engle turned to an absolutely fascinating subject for her next book: the real pirates of the Caribbean. Readers meet pirate captain Bernardino de Talavera, an impoverished conquistador who has worked the native Indians on his land to death. To avoid debtors' prison he steals a ship, takes some hostages, and becomes the first pirate of the Caribbean. One of those hostages, Alonso de Ojeda, had been governor of Venezuela and was known for selling the native people for profit. Another, Quebrado, called "the broken one," claims a Taino mother and Spanish father as his ancestors. Although this makes him an outcast, it gives him the ability to communicate in two languages.

In the first part of the book, "Wild Sea," Engle re-creates the effect of a hurricane on water. The ship tosses, tears apart, and eventually spills out its passengers and cargo on the ocean. Then each of the three main characters make their way to the nearest land, off the south coast of Cuba. Although the two conquistadors ultimately are banished, Quelbrado finds a home in Cuba and provides help for two star-crossed lovers, Nairdo and Caucubu.

Engle expertly weaves details of the culture of the native people and sixteenth-century Cuban life into her story that keeps readers breathlessly turning the pages to find out what will happen. The sparseness of the text and the beauty of the poetry mean that every word carries weight and meaning. I didn't linger over the text on my first reading because I was so fascinated by the story. Only in going back for a second reading did I savor words like these: "So I work alone, / catching silvery marsh fish / in tapered baskets, / chasing swift river fish / into stone traps / and wrapping the sea's / great gold-belly fish / in nets that fly out / over the waves / like wings."

An extraordinary book on so many levels, this brilliantly crafted poetic novel presents subject matter completely absent from existing children's and young adult books. *Hurricane Dancers* makes an excellent choice for summer reading, classroom teaching, or book discussion groups. And, of course, if you enjoy talking about books, few plots sound more intriguing than the real story of the pirates of the caribbean.

JUNE 5

Happy Birthday Ilse-Margret Vogel (*Bad Times, Good Friends*), Franklyn M. Branley (*Down Comes the Rain*), Alice Low (*The Witch Who Was Afraid of Witches*), Irene Haas (*A Summertime Song*), Allan Ahlberg (*Each Peach Pear Plum*), Louise Lawrence (*Dream-Weaver*), Caroline Binch (*Amazing Grace*), and Rick Riordan (*Percy Jackson & the Olympians* series).

It's the birth date of Richard Scarry (1919–1994), *Richard Scarry's Cars and Trucks and Things That Go*.

On this day in 1851 Harriet Beecher Stowe's antislavery serial, *Uncle Tom's Cabin or, Life Among the Lowly* started a ten-month run in the *National Era* abolitionist newspaper. Read *Harriet Beecher Stowe and the Beecher Preachers* by Jean Fritz.

JUNE 6

Happy Birthday Maxine Kumin (*What Color Is Ceasar?*, *The Microscope*), Peter Spier (*People*, *The Fox Went Out on a Chilly Night*), Cynthia Rylant (*The Relatives Came*, *When I Was Young in the Mountains*), and Geraldine McCaughrean (*The White Darkness*, *Peter Pan in Scarlet*).

It's the birth date of Will James (1892–1942), *Smoky*, *The Cowhorse*; Verna Aardema (1911–2000), *Why Mosquitoes Buzz in People's Ears*; and Miriam Schlein (1926–2004), *Year of the Panda*.

It's National Yo-Yo Day. Read *Knots in My Yo-Yo String* by Jerry Spinelli, *Yo-Yo Man* by Daniel Pinkwater, illustrated by Jack Davis, and *Yo? Yes!* by Chris Raschka.

It's National Applesauce Cake Day. Read *Applesauce Season* by Eden Lipson, illustrated by Mordicai Gerstein.

WHEN MY NAME WAS KEOKO

By Linda Sue Park

Today in Korea there are Memorial Day celebrations to pay tribute to those who died in war. Although very few books for children are set in Korea, Linda Sue Park's extraordinary novel *When My Name Was Keoko*, published in 2002, explores World War II as seen by Korean citizens.

For this powerful novel, Linda Sue Park, winner of the Newbery Medal for *A Single Shard*, interviewed members of her Korean family for details about their experience during World War II. Set in Korea right before the Japanese attack on Pearl Harbor, the novel is narrated by two engaging protagonists, Sun-hee, age ten, and her older brother Tae-yul, age thirteen. Forced to give up their Korean names and abandon the Korean language, the two struggle to deal with the Japanese occupation of their homeland. Sun-hee studies hard, hoping to become a scholar like her father. Tae-yul rebels, hating the Japanese history lessons forced down his throat.

Their uncle becomes a member of the Korean resistance. Eventually he leaves home to escape capture. Their father tries to survive passively. Toward the end of the war, Tae-yul signs up for the Japanese army and receives training to become a Kamikaze pilot. In one of the most chilling chapters in children's fiction, he and other young men prepare for their suicide flight.

Park weaves history and culture, family and friendship, deprivation and life's joys together seamlessly in this novel. Although she does not avoid the horrors of the situation, she brings the events to a hopeful and happy conclusion—a free Korea where the young people can have their own names and customs. *When My Name Was Keoko*, in fact, ends with two young people practicing the once-forbidden Korean language.

The book explores the tremendous upheaval of war, the fate of minority people in times of crisis, and the power of language to shape identity. For any adult or child ages ten through fourteen seeking information about the significance of Korean Memorial Day, *When My Name Was Keoko* brings these historic events alive and makes readers understand why this day in history needs to be celebrated.

ONE MORNING IN MAINE

By Robert McCloskey

"I scream, you scream, we all scream, for ice cream," goes the old ditty, and today marks National Chocolate Ice Cream Day. What a wonderful idea—two of the world's most popular foods, chocolate and ice cream, celebrated together. For me, chocolate ice cream in June conjures up wonderful summer days, the ocean, sea gulls wailing, walks on the beach, clamming. In short, it brings to mind the plot of Robert McCloskey's *One Morning in Maine*.

Robert McCloskey's classic picture books of the late forties and early fifties are firmly grounded in details of the Maine coast and life in a small Maine community. These titles include two Caldecott Honor books, *Blueberries for Sal* (1948) and *One Morning in Maine* (1952), and the Caldecott Medal–winning *Time of Wonder,* which made McCloskey the first artist to win the Caldecott Medal twice.

In an interview, McCloskey once said that he always had one foot planted firmly midair—and the other on a banana peel. But rather than creating an absurdist or fantasy world, his Maine books are firmly grounded in reality. *One Morning in Maine* is an intensely personal picture book. In it, Sal, McCloskey's daughter, discovers that she has a loose tooth. She's afraid she won't be able to sail to Buck's Harbor with her father as planned. But her mother talks to her and then sends Sal to help her father dig clams. Sal tells everyone she meets—the fish hawk, the loon, and the seal—about her loose tooth. As she helps father, she talks and talks about her tooth, only to discover that it is missing and has fallen in the mud. They find a gull feather for her to make a wish on, and Robert, Sal, and baby sister Jane head out on the boat while their mother makes clam chowder. At the local store, Sal's wish comes true—she gets a chocolate ice cream cone. And in the final line of the book the three head off for "CLAM CHOWDER FOR LUNCH!"

In print for sixty years, *One Morning in Maine* shows the details and beauty of the Maine coast. McCloskey renders this slice-of-life picture book so realistically that you can almost hear the gulls crying. Readers for decades have been invited into a day of the McCloskey family's life, one that is both special and very normal. Let's all raise an ice cream cone today—one chocolate and one vanilla—in honor of the genius of Robert McCloskey.

JUNE 7

Happy Birthday Nikki Giovanni (*Rosa*) and Louise Erdrich (*The Birchbark House*).

It's the birth date of Patricia Lynch (1891–1972), *Tales of Irish Enchantment*; John Goodall (1908–1996), *Creepy Castle*; and Gwendolyn Brooks (1917–2000), *Bronzeville Boys and Girls*.

In 1982 Priscilla Presley opened Graceland to the public. Read *Elvis Presley* by Wilborn Hampton, *Ten Little Elvi* by Duffy Grooms, illustrated by Dean Gorissen, and *Amy and Roger's Epic Detour* by Morgan Matson.

Other books to read for National Chocolate Ice Cream Day are *Ice Cream: Including Great Moments in Ice Cream History* by Jules Older, illustrated by Lyn Severance and *Ice Cream: The Full Scoop* by Gail Gibbons.

JUNE 8

Happy Birthday Carolyn Meyer (*The True Adventures of Charley Darwin, White Lilacs*), Judy Sierra (*Wild about Books, Tell the Truth, B.B. Wolf*), and Penny Dale (*Ten in the Bed, The Jamie and Angus Stories*).

It's the birth date of Ivan Southall (1921–2008), *Ash Road*.

In 793 the Vikings began to invade England. Read *Viking Ships at Sunrise* by Mary Pope Osborne, illustrated by Sal Murdocca and *Yo, Vikings!* by Judy Byron Schachner.

In 1949 George Orwell's *1984* was published. Read *George Orwell: Battling Big Brother* by Tanya Agathocleous.

It's World Ocean Day. Read *The Day the Ocean Came to Visit* by Diane Wolkstein, illustrated by Steve Johnson and Lou Fancher, and *Hello Ocean* by Pam Muñoz Ryan, illustrated by Mark Astrella.

11 BIRTHDAYS
By Wendy Mass

Today marks Best Friends Day, a time to celebrate the BFF in your life. Nothing can be so wonderful in the life of a child as a best friend. And, conversely, nothing can be so terrible than a rift between them. I still wince with pain when I think about my "break up" with my BFF in seventh grade. The exploration of best friends—and what happens when you stop speaking to each other—forms the premise of the book of the day, Wendy Mass's *11 Birthdays*.

Born on the same day, Amanda and Leo first meet in the hospital nursery. Then, a year later, they accidentally celebrate their first birthday together when both of their parents rent the same hall. From then on, the two form an incredible bond and they delight in having joint birthday parties. Until they turn ten. Then, in a horrible incident, Amanda hears Leo tell some boys that she has no friends. She flees the party, and for an entire year the two do not talk.

All this background forms the prelude of what seems, at first, like a simple saga of friendship gone awry. Amanda narrates her eleventh birthday, horrible from beginning to end. She and Leo are not speaking so they have planned separate birthday events. And everything that can go wrong in Amanda's day does: she tries out for but doesn't make the gymnastics team; her mother gets fired; and all her friends leave her house early so that they can attend Leo's much ritzier affair. But as her mother assures her, you only turn eleven once in your life.

Then both the reader and Amanda get a big surprise. The next day, she turns eleven again, with a repeat of the events. In fact, Amanda is going to turn eleven eleven times. And so does Leo. As Amanda makes choices for the do-over day, she begins to see how some produce better results. But the main choice involves Leo. Not until our two protagonists start talking, join forces, bury the wounds of the past, and become BFFs again does their curse lift. (An old woman, a fairy godmother of sorts, has been involved all along.) In the process of learning to be true friends to each other, they also learn how to take the right action for themselves.

With great humor and profound understanding of the emotions of eleven-year-olds, Wendy Mass spins a page-turning story. Absolutely beloved by readers eight through twelve and the recipient of many awards selected by children, including Vermont's Dorothy Canfield Fisher Award, *11 Birthdays* combines realistic fiction with a touch of magic and provides a totally satisfying ending. Readers have no doubt now that Amanda and Leo with be BFFs forever—if only not to repeat their birthday again and again.

I hope you have time for your best friend today—and to read, or reread, this delightful novel.

THE RISE AND FALL OF SENATOR JOE MCCARTHY

By James Cross Giblin

On June 9, 1954, a lawyer from Boston, Joseph Welch, confronted the most feared man in the United States with the cry "Have you left no sense of decency?" These words marked the beginning of the end of Senator Joe McCarthy, a man who had ruined the careers and lives of countless Americans, and his sway over American politics. The fearful fifties, as they are sometimes called, can be difficult to describe to young people who have not grown up believing that Communism is the greatest threat to America.

In *The Rise and Fall of Senator Joe McCarthy,* James Cross Giblin brilliantly re-creates this period and the complex and disturbing character of McCarthy for readers ages eleven through eighteen. He makes it possible for the young to understand the meaning of the word *McCarthyism*—guilt by association and unfounded accusation.

From an initial cartoon of the period—showing McCarthy signing legislation in the White House while President Eisenhower looks on—to the final notes about what happened to those covered in the book, Giblin provides an in-depth analysis of the events and personalities. In his final chapter for young readers, he poses the question, "Another McCarthy?"—Can another dangerous leader rise up in the American landscape? Because of the thoroughness of the coverage, *The Rise and Fall of Senator Joe McCarthy* is ideal for thoughtful young readers trying to understand the politics of another era.

James Cross Giblin came to writing books after many years as a very distinguished editor of children's books. He began writing books such as *Chimney Sweeps* and *The Truth about Santa Claus.* But over time the subject matter of his narrative nonfiction became more serious and darker.

I was fortunate to work with Jim Giblin for many years, and he is truly one of the nicest people I've ever known as a colleague. Yet in his books, he has presented some of the darkest characters in history, including Adolf Hitler. I am thankful this thoroughly decent author is willing to analyze these complex and dark characters and write about them in a way that young people can understand. Today we can celebrate the courage of both Joseph Welch and of James Cross Giblin, who is willing to tackle difficult subjects and write about them with intelligence and passion.

JUNE 9

Happy Birthday Gregory Maguire (*What-the-Dickens, Confessions of an Ugly Stepsister*).

It's the birth date of Patricia Clapp (1912–2003), *Jane-Emily, The Tamarack Tree.*

In 1959 Queen Elizabeth II officially opened the London Gatwick Airport. Read *A Plane Goes Ka-Zoom!* by Jonathan London, illustrated by Denis Roche and *This Is London* by Miroslav Sasek.

In 1934 the cartoon character Donald Duck makes his debut in *The Wise Little Hen.* Hence, it is Donald Duck Day. Read *The Life and Times of Scrooge McDuck* by Don Rosa, *Donald Duk* by Frank Chin, and *Duck* by Randy Cecil.

JUNE 10

Happy Birthday Aranka Siegal (*Memories of Babi, Upon the Head of a Goat: A Childhood in Hungary 1939–1944*), and Charlotte Herman (*My Chocolate Year, Max Malone Makes a Million*).

It's the birth date of Chap Reaver (1935–1993), *Bill*; and actress Judy Garland (1922–1969), best known for her role as Dorothy in *The Wizard of Oz*.

In 1829 the first boat race between the universities of Cambridge and Oxford took place in England. Read *Busytown Boat Race* by Richard Scarry.

It's National Iced Tea Day. Read *Ice* by Sarah Beth Durst, *Ice* by Arthur Geisert, *Ice* by Phyllis Reynolds Naylor, *Ice Magic* by Matt Christopher, *Miss Spider's Tea Party* by David Kirk, and *The Tiger Who Came to Tea* by Judith Kerr.

WHERE THE WILD THINGS ARE
By Maurice Sendak

Today we celebrate the birthday of someone who might best be described as the grandfather of the American picture book. When Maurice Sendak published his masterpiece, *Where the Wild Things Are*, in 1963, he changed the content of the picture book for every artist to come after him. He gave shape to the imagination and fantasies of children, and he became the friend of millions of young readers who knew he understood them.

In all of his books, Sendak explored his own inner landscape, one that is idiosyncratic and personal. Because of his honesty and because he never forgot the feelings and emotions of childhood, children can identify with his characters. As Sendak once wrote, "children live on familiar terms with disrupting emotions. . . . They continually cope with frustration as best they can. And it is through fantasy that children achieve catharsis. It is the best means they have for taming Wild Things." For almost sixty years Sendak created books that portrayed the children he saw in the streets of Brooklyn where he grew up—immigrants from Poland and other countries, squat, solid, individual beings.

After illustrating more than fifty books for other writers, in November of 1955 Sendak began his own story, initially called "Where the Wild Horses Are." Unfortunately, he couldn't draw horses and had to find another subject. Then the phrase "Wild Things" came to him. Sendak threw memories of King Kong into the story cauldron. As he drew and redrew his creatures, the skinny beings gained weight and density. In the resulting story the hero Max rages against his mother for being sent to bed without supper. Max's bedroom becomes a forest where he meets, tames, and becomes king of the Wild Things. Through his fantasy, Max works out his anger against his mother and returns to the real world, at peace with himself.

Sendak used a mere 338 words to tell the story; the pictures, which allow children to build their own fantasy, fill all the rest of the narrative. As Max's emotions swell, the art takes up more and more space on each page until the center of the book where a double-page spread shows Max parading as king of the Wild Things. Sendak's editor, Ursula Nordstrom, always said that he created art with the "hand of God." Winner of the Caldecott Medal in 1964, *Where the Wild Things Are* has become part of the American conscience, the birthright of every child.

When Sendak died in 2012 an outpouring of grief rose from so many segments of society. But the books remain. When it comes to picture books, Maurice Sendak remains in a class by himself.

CURIOUS GEORGE

By H. A. Rey and Margret Rey

In 1941, three days before Hitler's army marched into Paris, two German Jews who had come to the city on a honeymoon and stayed for a couple of years found themselves trapped in Paris. Although Hans and Margret Rey had secured railroad tickets, the trains stopped running. So Hans scoured bicycle stores, but found all the bicycles had already been sold. He purchased spare parts and fashioned something for them to ride that *resembled* a bicycle. On June 12 they headed out of Paris, with only some book manuscripts and their winter coats, in an attempt to evade the Germans.

For about a week they stayed two days ahead of the invading troops—peddling by day, sleeping in the fields at night. At one point, a border guard stopped them and asked the man what he did. "I create children's books," Hans Rey said. Asking to see one of the books, the guard smiled at the manuscript presented to him: "My children would like this . . . you can continue." That day Hans and Margret Rey's lives were spared because of a story about a mischievous monkey named Curious George. To be accurate, their lives were saved by a monkey named Fifi, whom Margret Rey served as the model for and who was later renamed "George."

Brazilian passports got them out of France and America's Good Neighbor Policy made it possible for them to come to New York. Without resources, they frantically contacted their British editor, Grace Hogarth, who as luck would have it was currently directing the children's book department of Houghton Mifflin in Boston. To help these struggling refugees, Hogarth gave them a four-book contract—thereby paying $250 in advance for a book that still sells millions of copies every year. With endless capacity to get into trouble, Curious George serves as the alter ego for many preliterate children who would love to behave just like George does. Fortunately, George is always rescued by the man in the yellow hat.

I had the privilege of working with both the Reys. Margret lived to be ninety, and I would sit with her, in her home in Cambridge, Massachusetts, decorated as a shrine to George—with books, stuffed toys, and various replicas in all forms. She would look in wonder around her and say, "It is so hard to believe that all of this came from that manuscript we brought from Paris so many years ago." No story demonstrates the miracle of children's books as much as Curious George. No matter how, where, and when great children's books begin, or their trials on the way to publication—they can reach across generations, across time and history, to speak to children.

JUNE 11

Happy Birthday Robert Munsch (*Paper Bag Princess, Mud Puddle*) and Satoshi Kitamura (*Sheep in Wolves' Clothing, UFO Diary*).

In 1776 the Continental Congress appointed Thomas Jefferson, John Adams, Benjamin Franklin, Roger Sherman, and Robert Livingston to the Committee of Five to draft the Declaration of Independence. Read *Signers: The 56 Stories Behind the Declaration of Independence* by Dennis Brindell Fradin, illustrated by Michael McCurdy, and *Rissa Bartholomew's Declaration of Independence* by Linda B. Comerford.

It's Corn on the Cob Day. Read *Corn Is Maize* by Aliki and *The Life and Times of Corn* by Charles Micucci.

JUNE 12

ANNE FRANK: HER LIFE IN WORDS AND PICTURES FROM THE ARCHIVES OF THE ANNE FRANK HOUSE

Edited by Menno Metselaar and Ruud van der Rol, translated by Arnold J. Pomerans

On June 12, 1929, a young German girl was born. Had history played out differently, she might well have been celebrating her birthday today. Anne Frank lived in extraordinary times—and in recording those times, she became the world's most famous young writer.

Scores of books providing supplementary reading for *The Diary of Anne Frank* have appeared over the years. One of the best, a translation of a book that first appeared in the Netherlands, is an elegantly designed edition of about 210 pages—*Anne Frank: Her Life in Words and Pictures* looks and feels like a photo album. And it is just that. The album opens with a photo of one of Anne's best presents, the diary she received on her thirteenth birthday.

With frequent quotations from that diary, the book shows readers a wedding picture of the Franks and photos of Anne and Margot as babies. Because we know the end of the story, every photograph seems poignant and haunting.

After the Franks left Germany for Holland because of persecution of the Jews, the photographs document how year by year Anne ages, plays with friends, has parties, or goes to the seashore. As the text reminds readers, soon these simple pleasures will be denied all Jews. A series of photos show the annex that Otto Frank constructed; pictures display the daily living quarters. Excerpts from Anne's diary tell us how much she longs to walk outside, to breathe fresh air, to have a normal life again.

On August 4, 1944, when Anne and her family are captured in the annex, readers of this photo album experience the intense emotions of realizing these people they now know intimately will be sent to concentration camps. The photos have brought Anne Frank to life as a real girl.

No book written by a young writer has ever had the impact of *The Diary of Anne Frank*. *Anne Frank: Her Life in Words and Pictures* extends the *Diary*, elucidates it, and adds to readers' understandings. Produced in cooperation with the Anne Frank House, this small volume can be appreciated by those who tour the house and those who only can do so by visiting the house website.

On Anne Frank's birthday and through her diary and books like *Anne Frank: Her Life in Words and Pictures*, we remember the cost of hatred and prejudice.

HIS SHOES WERE FAR TOO TIGHT

By Edward Lear with Daniel Pinkwater

Illustrated by Calef Brown

Today in Australia, Belize, the Cayman Islands, and Fiji they celebrate the "Queen's Official Birthday." Queen Elizabeth II actually was born on April 21. Celebrating the Queen's Official Birthday on a day when she wasn't born would be just the kind of corkscrew logic that our English author of the day, Edward Lear, would enjoy. A self-taught artist, Lear even gave drawing lessons to Queen Victoria and no doubt celebrated many of her birthdays, official or real.

Edward Lear's writing, not art, would become his claim to fame. In 1845 he published *The Book of Nonsense* under the pseudonym Derry Down Derry. The youngest of twenty children, Lear had faced years of hardship and sadness in his youth, and he wanted to bring joy and amusement to children in his writing. For almost 160 years his work has done exactly that. But in the last decade of so, much of it was unavailable in the United States. Hence, I cheered the minute I saw a copy of Daniel Pinkwater and Calef Brown's *His Shoes Were Far Too Tight by Edward Lear.*

On the title page, Pinkwater is credited with being the mastermind, Brown the illustrator. Pinkwater has written a short introduction. Then in large double-page spreads Calef Brown brings his quirky vision to the poetry of Edward Lear. "The Owl and the Pussycat," "The Jumblies," "The Quangle Wrangle's Hat," "The Nonsense Alphabet," and other Lear gems are given plenty of space, sometimes several pages, so that Brown can provide a plethora of inventive creatures that give readers even more reasons to laugh. Even nuts and oysters are rendered with distinct personalities.

Best of all, of course, Lear's language, alliteration, and humor sing out on these pages. When I first saw *His Shoes Were Far Too Tight*, I immediately went to my favorite lines from childhood: "They dined on mince, and slices of quince, which they ate with a runcible spoon; / And hand in hand, on the edge of the sand, / They danced by the light of the moon, / The moon, / The moon," They danced by the light of the moon.

Beautifully produced, with exuberant endpapers and heavy pages that display the full range of Brown's intense palette, the book can be read with a child on the lap, in story hour, or all alone to provide hours of fun.

JUNE 13

Happy Birthday Niki Daly (*Pretty Salma: A Little Red Riding Hood Story From Africa*) and Alexandra Sheedy (*She Was Nice to Mice*).

In 1927 a ticker-tape parade in honor of aviator Charles Lindbergh was held on Fifth Avenue in New York City. Read *Charles Lindbergh: A Human Hero* by James Cross Giblin and *Parade* by Donald Crews.

On this day in 1967 U.S. President Lyndon B. Johnson nominated **Thurgood Marshall** to the Supreme Court. Marshall became the first black U.S. Justice. Read *A Picture Book of Thurgood Marshall* by David A. Adler, illustrated by Robert Casilla.

In 1920 the U.S. Post Office Department ruled that children may not be sent by parcel post. Read *Henry's Freedom Box* by Ellen Levine, illustrated by Kadir Nelson, and *Flat Stanley* by Jeff Brown.

JUNE 14

Happy Birthday Judith Kerr (*When Hitler Stole Pink Rabbit*), Janice May Udry (*A Tree Is Nice*), Lensey Namioka (*Ties That Bind, Ties That Break*), Bruce Degen (*Jamberry, The Magic School Bus* series), Penelope Farmer (*Charlotte Sometimes*), Laurence Yep (*Dragonwings*), and James Gurney (*Dinotopia*).

It's the birth date of John Bartlett (1820–1905), *Bartlett's Familiar Quotations*; Nicolas Bentley (1907–1978), *The Wind on the Moon*; Harriet Beecher Stowe (1811–1896), *Uncle Tom's Cabin*.

 It's Flag Day! In 1893 the city of Philadelphia was the first to observe this holiday commemorating the adoption of the U.S. flag.

Happy Birthday, Superman! In 1938 Action Comics issue #1 released, introducing the now-iconic character. Read *Boys of Steel: The Creators of Superman* by Marc Tyler Nobleman, illustrated by Ross MacDonald, and *Superman: The Story of the Man of Steel* by Ralph Cosentino.

ANNE OF GREEN GABLES
By L. M. Montgomery

In June of 1908, *Anne of Green Gables* appeared on the list of a small Boston firm, L. C. Page and Company. Then-unknown Canadian author L. M. Montgomery had found it difficult to find a publisher, and so she did what so many new authors do today: she submitted to a small press hoping it might be easier to get published.

As luck would have it, a young editorial assistant from Prince Edward Island read the manuscript and fell in love with it. The owners of the firm seemed less enthusiastic. When they wrote the author, they suggested that the book might not do very well, and so they wanted to make a deal with her. She would get a flat fee of $500, and the firm would retain all rights to the book in perpetuity. As Montgomery later admitted, she now had to make one of the hardest decisions in her life. In 1908, $500 was a lot of money. But she had such belief in her character—she could not give Anne away even for $500. In the end, she negotiated a reduced royalty on each book sold, a mere $.09 a copy.

Although the firm created less than two thousand copies for the first print run, the book met with immediate acclaim. *Anne of Green Gables* would go through six printings in six months, selling nineteen thousand copies. At the end of that period, the now much more famous author received her first royalty check—for $1,730. She had been right about her character, one whom Mark Twain believed to be the most lovable child in fiction to follow Alice in Wonderland.

Anne Shirley, a redheaded, determined orphan, realizes the minute she arrives at the farmhouse called Green Gables that she wants to stay forever. But she fears that the Cuthberts will send her away because they wanted a sturdy boy to help with the farm work. Anne ultimately charms her new family, the neighborhood, and readers—and her exploits continue in other volumes. The author so brilliantly re-creates the landscape and people of Prince Edward Island that today millions of families travel there to see the house that inspired Green Gables, run by the Canadian Park Service and the L. M. Montgomery Museum.

Anne always called her special friends "kindred spirits." Today there are legions of them, all over the world. Happy birthday *Anne of Green Gables*. It is hard to imagine the children's book world without this glorious book.

REDWALL
By Brian Jacques

Born on June 15, 1939, Brian Jacques grew up in Liverpool and went to the same school as Paul McCartney and George Harrison. But the author always claimed that he received his education "in the University of Life." At fifteen he became a merchant seaman; he worked in a variety of positions including longshoreman, truck driver, police officer, postmaster, stand-up comic, milk-truck driver, and radio announcer. Nothing up to this point in his life indicated that Jacques would ultimately become one of the world's best loved children's book writers.

As is true of so many of our classic authors, he began to tell and then write a story for a child, actually several children, in the Royal School for the Blind, Wavertree, Liverpool, where he delivered milk. Because they could not see, he needed to create vivid pictures of scenes for them. He emphasized action and adventure. In the process he came up with the winning concept that sustained over twenty-some books, which have been translated into twenty-nine languages, and have sold twenty million copies worldwide.

The peaceful members of Redwall Abbey suddenly find their lives changed when attacked by Cluny the Scourge and his horde of villainous followers. A young novice of the abbey named Matthias mobilizes the defenses of his beloved refuge and attempts to become a hero. While this plot is not unusual Jacques gives it his own twist. The residents of the abbey in Redwall are mice; the villains, rats. A colorful cast of characters—Constance the Badger, Basil Stag Hare, Warbeak the Sparrow—all join forces to save the abbey. Not only does the plot boil over with excitement and daring, it contains a strong sense of right and wrong.

Jacques traveled extensively in the United States to introduce each of his books and meet his fans. He was always a fabulous performer to watch—he loved to create characters, set scenes, and hold audiences enthralled as he brought to life his book and his characters. Many who had become bored with reading were inspired to pick up a Redwall book after hearing Brian Jacques speak. Then they read volume after volume of his saga.

Although Brian Jacques died in 2011, we can all be grateful that we have the books of this generous, creative, and engaging writer for young people.

JUNE 15

Happy Birthday Betty Ren Wright (*The Dollhouse Murders*) and Loreen Leedy (*Measuring Penny*).

In 1752 **Benjamin Franklin** proved that lightning is electricity. Read *Ben Franklin and His First Kite* by Stephen Krensky, illustrated by Bert Dodson.

Happy Birthday Arkansas, which became the 25th U.S. state in 1836. Read *The Painters of Lexieville* by Sharon Darrow and *Summer of My German Soldier* by Bette Greene.

On this day in 1215 King John signed the Magna Carta.

It's Smile Power Day. Read *Smile* by Raina Telgemeier, *Smile!* by Leigh Hodgkinson, *Smiles To Go* by Jerry Spinelli, and *Grandma's Smile* by Randy Siegel, illustrated by DyAnne DiSalvo.

JUNE 16

Happy Birthday Paul Rogers (*Jazz ABZ*), Jennifer L. Holm (*Turtle in Paradise*), and Joyce Carol Oates (*Big Mouth & Ugly Girl*, *After the Wreck*, *I Picked Myself Up*, *Spread My Wings*, *and Flew Away*).

It's the birth date of Zachary Ball (1897–1987), *Bristle Face*; and Isabelle Holland (1920–2002), *The Man Without a Face*.

It's Bloomsday, a commemoration and celebration of the life of Irish writer James Joyce because his seminal novel *Ulysses* took place on June 16, 1904.

For National Fudge Day also read *Peeny Butter Fudge* by Toni Morrison and Slade Morrison, illustrated by Joe Cepeda, and *The Chocolate Fudge Mystery* by David A. Adler.

TALES OF A FOURTH GRADE NOTHING

By Judy Blume

Today marks National Fudge Day. For children's books aficionados, fudge not only conjures up delicious sweets but also one of Judy Blume's most original characters, Fudge, the younger brother of Peter, hero of *Tales of a Fourth Grade Nothing*.

When I entered the children's book field in the seventies, Judy Blume reigned as the most controversial writer of the time. She talked about menstruation in *Are You There God? It's Me, Margaret*. She discussed sex in *Forever*. She was frank and forthright, believing that children deserved the truth in books. Hence, she spent decades defending First Amendment rights for books for children, an accomplishment that has been recognized by various groups.

In the early nineties, when critic Zena Sutherland wrote her passionate defense of Judy Blume for *Children's Books and Their Creators*, she claimed that "in her books for younger readers . . . Blume is at her amusing best." And that analysis was quite accurate. Blume's comic masterpieces have stood the test of time.

In *Tales of a Fourth Grade Nothing*, Peter informs us in the first chapter: "My mother isn't my biggest problem. Neither is my father. . . . My biggest problem is my brother, Farley Drexel Hatcher. He's two and a half years old. Everyone calls him Fudge." Filled with episodic chapters, the book shows how easily Fudge brings chaos into Peter's life. Never has a younger brother terrorized an older one more effectively. In the final chapter, Fudge even swallows Peter's pet turtle.

Based on Blume's own children, and filled with her wit, humor, insight into childhood emotion, and spot-on dialogue, *Tales of a Fourth Grade Nothing* and its four sequels have become sure-fire hits with the emerging reading crowd. At least two publishers, including Blume's own Bradbury Press, turned the first book down, and early reviews, like the one in *Booklist,* claimed that "Fudge is too exaggerated to be very believable." Fortunately Ann Durrell of Dutton was an editor who delighted "when a character in a Judy Blume book peed on the rug at a birthday party." In fact, Durrell convinced Blume to change the manuscript from a picture book to a novel and provide more stories about this hysterically funny family. Blume's most popular title with nine million copies in print, the book has gone through countless editions and been translated into more than twenty languages.

Today let's raise a piece of fudge to Judy Blume. She deserves praise for keeping faith with children, for years of defending the right of authors to be honest and true in their books, and for this fabulously funny book and its sequels that have convinced children that "reading can be fun."

THE WALL: GROWING UP BEHIND THE IRON CURTAIN

By Peter Sís

On June 17, 1969, in Prague, Czechoslovakia, ten months after the Soviet Union invaded the city with tanks, the Beach Boys gave a concert in Lucerna Hall. Although police with dogs waited nearby, in this dark time the American band provided "a glimmer of hope."

Peter Sís, recipient of a MacArthur genius grant, captured these events, the history of his native country, and his own journey as an artist in the 2007 title *The Wall: Growing Up Behind the Iron Curtain*. Both a Caldecott Honor book and winner of the Sibert Award, this incredible book begins with endpapers showing the map of the world, filled in with red to indicate Communist countries. The first page has a picture of a baby, with pen and pencil in hand, with the caption, "As long as he could remember, he had loved to draw."

JUNE 17

Happy Birthday Marie-Louise Gay (Stella series).

It's the birth date of James Weldon Johnson (1871–1938), *The Creation*; and Robbie Branscum (1937–1997), *The Murder of Hound Dog Bates*.

In 1775 the British took Bunker Hill outside of Boston, after a costly battle.

It's also Eat Your Vegetables Day (perhaps a follow up to yesterday's Fresh Veggies Day). Read *The Ugly Vegetables* by Grace Lin, *Growing Vegetable Soup* by Lois Ehlert, *Vegetable Garden* by Douglas Florian, and *The Vegetables We Eat* by Gail Gibbons.

In intricate black-and-white sketches, occasionally marked with red, Sís shows his development as a child and an artist, as well as what life was like for those who lived in Czechslovakia. Some of the incidents, like collecting scrap metal, would not have been experienced by American children during this period. Others, like hiding under the desk in preparation for a nuclear attack, happened in the U.S. as well. In the book Sís grows up to be an adolescent when "everything from the West seems colorful and desirable." He loves American music and he and his friends make their own electric guitars. In the spring of 1968, everything seems possible under the new, enlightened leadership of Alexander Dubek. Then the Soviet tanks invade, and Sís finds that the content of his drawings could be used against him. But as the book ends, "Sometimes dreams come true. On November 9, 1989, the wall fell."

This extraordinary book presents a social studies lesson of the Cold War in forty-eight pages. Any student from fourth grade through high school who wants to understand not only the events of the Cold War but the emotional effect of growing up behind the Iron Curtain can do no better than begin their reading here.

Even in the United States, Peter Sís has followed his own direction and vision by creating illustrated books that work for a wide range of readers. After picking up *The Wall*, those who did not know his struggle will simply be grateful that he persevered in what he wanted to do. Although the events that he describes took place in Europe years ago, they remind us to fight against censorship, in all of its forms, here and now in America.

PICTURE BOOK, MEMOIR, Elementary School, Middle School, High School

JUNE 18

Happy Birthday Pat Hutchins (*The Wind Blew*), Chris Van Allsburg (*The Polar Express*), Vivian Vande Velde (*Heir Apparent*), Connie Roop (*Keep the Lights Burning, Abbie*), Angela Johnson (*Toning the Sweep*), and Philip Stead (*A Sick Day for Amos McGee, A Home for Bird*).

It's the birth date of Pam Conrad (1947–1996), *The Tub People*.

The War of 1812 began on this day when the United States declared war against Great Britain.

 In 1983 astronaut **Sally Ride** became the first U.S. woman in space on board the shuttle *Challenger*. Read *To Space and Back* by Sally Ride with Susan Oakie, and *Exploring Our Solar System* and *Mission: Planet Earth*, both by Sally Ride and Tam O'Shaughnessy.

It's Go Fishing Day. Read *Go Fish* by Mary Stolz, illustrated by Pat Cummings, *Going Fishing* by Bruce McMillan, and *Piggy and Dad Go Fishing* by David Martin, illustrated by Frank Remkiewicz.

THE CAT IN THE HAT
By Dr. Seuss

June is Adopt a Shelter Cat Month and there is no more famous cat in all of children's books than the Cat in the Hat. The Cat in the Hat's story of conception begins at 2 Park Street in Boston which served as the headquarters for Houghton Mifflin Publishers. In this Beacon Hill landmark, a rickety brass elevator cage took employees up and down, shuddering and whining as it did. This elevator required the care of an operator—and for many years this operator was Mrs. Williams. During much of her tenure she served as the only black employee of the firm.

Every day she decorated the elevator with fresh flowers. She wore impeccably clean white gloves. She loved her work and always greeted people with a Cheshire cat smile and lots of information about who was in the building. "Roger Tory Peterson is with Mr. Olney today," she would say as employees entered the elevator, often showing a book signed for her personally.

One day, she conveyed William Spaulding, head of the Houghton Mifflin Reading Division, to his office with his guest, an army buddy by the name of Theodore Geisel. That day Spaulding made the man we call "Dr. Seuss" an intriguing book offer. Wanting to outstrip his competitor, Scott Foresman, who published the bestselling Dick and Jane series, Spaulding believed there was another way to approach the teaching of reading. He told Seuss that if he could wed what he knew—how to entertain children—with words that children knew in first and second grade, reading instruction in the United States could be revolutionized.

So Seuss rode down in the elevator again with Mrs. Williams. Working from a list of a few hundred words, Seuss always maintained that the resulting book was the toughest assignment he ever accepted. "It was like trying to make strudel without any strudel." But he finally settled on two rhyming words, *cat* and *hat*, and began to doodle. Seuss always built his best books out of character, and as he sketched his cat, he remembered Mrs. Williams. Her white gloves. Her Cheshire cat smile. Her black skin. Slowly *The Cat in the Hat* took form under the pen of Dr. Seuss.

The Cat, who surely would wreak havoc in a shelter, saves the day for two bored children—and provides a lot of raucous entertainment. Anyone interested in more publishing history about this revolutionary book can find it recorded in Phil Nel's *The Annotated Cat: Under the Hats of Seuss and His Cats*. And tip the hat to Mrs. Williams, one of the unsung heroines of the children's book world.

MY FATHER'S DRAGON

By Ruth Stiles Gannett

Illustrated by Ruth Chrisman Gannett

On June 19, 1910 the first Father's Day was celebrated in Spokane, Washington. As a rule, children are not particularly excited to read a book about an adult, even if they love their fathers. They would rather read about children they relate to. But one of the best children's books of all time (perfect for reading to children at the end of first grade or independent reading in second and third), focuses on a father—and a dragon. In *My Father's Dragon* by Ruth Stiles Gannett, nine-year-old Elmer Elevator travels a long distance to Wild Island to save a baby dragon. After stowing items he may need in a backpack (a lollipop, hair ribbons, rubber bands, a toothbrush, and chewing gum), Elmer must outwit a tiger, a gorilla, and crocodiles before he completes his quest. In fact, he needs every item he has carried with him.

When Ruth Stiles Gannett was young, she found herself out of work and went to her father's home at Cream Hill in West Cornwall, Connecticut. In a couple of weeks she spun out *My Father's Dragon*. Her father, Lewis Stiles Gannett, the daily book critic of the *New York Herald Tribune*, happened to be one of the most influential figures in the publishing industry, and he connected her to a publisher, Random House. Her stepmother, Ruth Chrisman Gannett, had her own skills—she'd just won a Caldecott Honor that year and provided magnificent illustrations for this new book. Ruth's husband-to-be, Peter Kahn, an artist and typographer, helped with the maps of Wild and Tangerine Islands as well as the book design. A few weeks after this little family project was published on April 12, 1948, it won the *Herald Tribune*'s children's book award—it never hurts an author, then or now, to have friends in high places.

Actually these *Herald Tribune* judges made a prescient choice, because this delightful and whimsical book has enchanted children for decades. As Nick Clark, Director of the Eric Carle Museum of Picture Book Art, says in *Everything I Need to Know I Learned from a Children's Book*, "From *My Father's Dragon* I learned that you have to use your noodle—and that the underdog can triumph in the end." So if you want to use your noodle today, pick up a copy of *My Father's Dragon* and celebrate Father's Day with Elmer Elevator and the magnificent creators of Wild Island.

JUNE 19

Happy Birthday Elvira Woodruff (*Dear Austin: Letters from the Underground Railroad*).

For Father's Day read *A Perfect Father's Day* by Eve Bunting, illustrated by Susan Meddaugh, and *Father's Day* by Anne Rockwell, illustrated by Lizzy Rockwell.

In 1846 the New York Knickerbocker Club played the New York Club in the first baseball game at Elysian Field, Hoboken, New Jersey.

It's World Sauntering Day, so slow down and enjoy the world around you! Read *All the World* by Liz Garton Scanlon, illustrated by Marla Frazee, *Crinkleroot's Guide to Walking in Wild Places* by Jim Arnosky, and *Ramona's World* by Beverly Cleary.

JUNE 20

Happy Birthday Vikram Seth (*Arion and the Dolphin*).

It's the birth date of Edward Eager (1911–1964), *Half Magic*.

 In 1837 Victoria becomes Queen of England. Read *Queen Victoria* by Robert Green and *In the Days of Queen Victoria* by Eva March Tappan.

Happy Birthday West Virginia, which became the 35th U.S. state on this day in 1863. Read *Blue-Eyed Daisy* by Cynthia Rylant.

It's Ice Cream Soda Day. Read *Soda Jerk* by Cynthia Rylant.

It's American Eagle Day. Read *Soaring with the Wind* by Gail Gibbons, *The Eagle* by Cynthia Rylant, illustrated by Preston McDaniels, and *Eagle Song* by Joseph Bruchac, illustrated by Dan Andreasen.

FROG AND TOAD ARE FRIENDS

By Arnold Lobel

In June of 1970, over forty years ago, one of the best children's books about friendship was published, Arnold Lobel's *Frog and Toad Are Friends,* a Caldecott Honor book.

Lobel, who studied at the Pratt Institute to become an illustrator, made the most important connection of his creative career when he walked into Harper & Row one day to show his portfolio. The young Susan Carr Hirschman immediately recognized Lobel's talent and asked him to illustrate one of the I Can Read books that Harper had been developing. Hirschman also quickly sensed that Lobel could both write and illustrate; his first solo I Can Read title, *Lucille*, appeared in 1964.

To escape the heat of New York City in the summer, the Lobel family, Arnold, his wife Anita, and their two children, vacationed on Lake Bomoseen in Vermont. A city boy, Lobel was terrified by living in the country, where marauding raccoons created noises. When a bat flew into the cabin, Lobel dove under the bed. But for the children, everything seemed pure bliss. Exploring a nearby swamp, they brought home a large slimy frog and two dour and dyspeptic toads.

Back in New York, searching for the subject matter for a new book, Lobel thought back to the summer, now more wonderful in reflection than it had been in experience. He wrote the words, "Frog ran up the path to Toad's house," and the story began to pour forth. Lobel was a master at crafting narrative. His handwritten manuscript for *Frog and Toad Are Friends*, housed in the Kerlan Collection of the University of Minnesota, is remarkably close to the final text and needed only a few changes before it appeared in print.

Known for his close ties to other illustrators such as Maurice Sendak and Jim Marshall, Lobel could write about friendship brilliantly. In five short stories two unlikely companions, a cheerful green frog and a dour brown toad, are bound by friendship and understanding. They experience the simple joys of life: Toad makes Frog a cup of tea when he looks sick; Frog helps Toad hunt for a lost button. With kindness and sensitivity to each other's needs, they make each other's lives better and inspire children to think about the needs of their own friends.

Happy birthday Frog and Toad—may they stay with us for at least another forty decades.

THE LIGHTNING THIEF

By Rick Riordan

Around June 21 we celebrate the longest day of the year, the summer solstice, which also marks the first day of summer. This date looms large for the hero of our featured book, a kid who just can't get a break. He's never seen his father and lives with an odious and repellent stepfather when not away at boarding school for disturbed kids. He's ADHD, hyperactive, always in trouble, and to make matters worse, he gets kicked out of school, again. Even those who like him say, "you are not normal." And weird things happen to him; on a field trip to the Metropolitan Museum of Art, one of his teachers turns into a monster. Before she can kill him, he slays her with a ballpoint pen that miraculously turns into a sword.

Welcome to the world of Percy Jackson. In *The Lightning Thief*, the first volume of a series of gripping books, he discovers that he is a demigod, the offspring of a mortal and a Greek god. His only safe haven turns out to be Camp Half Blood, where other demi-gods who are kids his age learn survival skills. To avoid a war among the Greek gods, Percy, son of Poseidon, must locate Zeus's stolen thunderbolt and deliver it to the annual family get-together on the solstice. An inventive plot, engaging characters, non-stop action, and an unpredictable ending have helped make the stories of Percy Jackson by Rick Riordan some of the most beloved reading for ten- to fourteen-year-olds in the last few years. As young readers devour Percy's saga, they also learn a lot about Greek mythology.

Much like Harry Potter's Hogwarts, Camp Half Blood sounds like so much fun that everyone wants to attend. Since 2006 the good folk at BookPeople, an amazing independent bookstore in Austin, Texas, where Rick Riordan lives, have hosted several summer sessions of Camp Half Blood, a day camp where participants act out their roles as demi-gods. Not only do they study history, mythology, and literature, but they also practice chariot racing, archery, and lava wall climbing. But if you can't attend this summer, you can at least curl up with *The Lightning Thief* and its sequels. It is good that this is the longest day of the year—it makes a perfect time for a Percy Jackson readathon.

JUNE 21

It's the birth date of Robert Kraus (1925–2001), *Leo the Late Bloomer, Whose Mouse Are You?*

Happy Birthday New Hampshire, which became the ninth U.S. state on this day in 1788. Read *The Trouble with Jeremy Chance* by George Harrar and *Lucy's Summer* by Donald Hall, illustrated by Michael McCurdy.

On this day in 2000 NASA reported evidence of possible ancient water on Mars. Read *Destination Mars* by Seymour Simon.

It's Go Skateboarding Day. Read *Skateboard Tough* by Matt Christopher.

It's also World Handshake Day. Read *Sterkarm Handshake* by Susan Price and *Hands: Growing Up To Be an Artist* by Lois Ehlert.

JUNE 22

It's the birth date of Margaret Sidney (1844–1924), *Five Little Peppers and How They Grew*.

It's also the birth date of the British explorer, George Vancouver (1757–1798), who explored territories from the southwest coast of Australia to Alaska.

In 1873 Prince Edward Island joined Canada. Read the Anne of Green Gables series by L. M. Montgomery.

In 1970 eighteen-year-olds in the United States were granted the right to vote in national elections. Read *Vote!* by Eileen Christelow, *If I Ran for President* by Catherine Stier, illustrated by Lynne Avril, and *See How They Run: Campaign Dreams, Election Schemes, and the Race to the White House* by Susan E. Goodman, illustrated by Elwood H. Smith.

It's National Chocolate Éclair Day.

PINK AND SAY
By Patricia Polacco

In April of 2011 the five-year-long Sesquicentennial of the Civil War began. We have hundreds, probably thousands, of resources to use with children to explore the War Between the States. But if I were going to start observing this milestone in American history, I would first share *Pink and Say* by Patricia Polacco with children four through twelve.

Patricia Polacco is a writer who always goes for the heart. Because she weaves her stories out of her love for family and history, they resonate emotionally. Since her first book in the eighties until today, she has crafted dozens of great titles. Many readers adore *Thank You, Mr. Falker*. Others love *The Keeping Quilt*. But for me, if I could only have one Patricia Polacco title, I'd scoop up *Pink and Say*.

Based on a true story passed down in her family, Polacco tells the saga of her ancestor, a Yankee soldier who was rescued after a battle in Georgia and nursed back to health by a young black soldier of the 48th Regiment Infantry U.S. Colored Troops. For a time, Say (Sheldon Russell Curtis) stays with Pink (Pinkus Aylee) and his mother. After her death at the hands of Confederates, they flee—only to be captured and sent to Andersonville. There Pink is hanged, hours after arriving; Say returns to his Ohio home and his ancestors keep alive the story of this remarkable friendship. Pink, of course, has no living descendants. Polacco ends the book, "When you read this, before you put this book down, say his name out loud and vow to remember him always."

There should be a statute of limitations on the number of times that you cry when reading a book. My first encounter with *Pink and Say* came in 1994 when I first read it in my office at Horn Book; I closed the door and sobbed. I have used this book with classes many times in the last seventeen years. And yet, each time, even though I know what will happen, the text has the same effect.

In forty-eight pages Patricia Polacco brings children into the loss and heartache of the Civil War. She shows the devastation of that war on U.S. citizens. She brings to life two human boys who seem so real they might live near us. How do we make the Civil War come alive for young readers? By re-creating the human beings who experienced these events—just as Patricia Polacco does in *Pink and Say*.

CLICK, CLACK, MOO: COWS THAT TYPE

By Doreen Cronin

Illustrated by Betsy Lewin

On June 23, 1868, the first American typewriter was patented by Luther Sholes. Beginning in 1937 the dairy industry has dedicated June as National Dairy Month, a time to call attention to the important role that milk and milk products play in our diets and the outstanding contributions made by dairy farmers.

So how do these seemingly unrelated topics—typewriters, dairy farmers, and cows—connect to children's books? In *Click, Clack, Moo: Cows That Type* author Doreen Cronin, a lawyer by training, weaves these three elements together so perfectly that once you read the book, cows and typing will become intertwined forever.

Farmer Brown is dumbstruck when his cows discover an old typewriter in the barn and begin pecking away at it. "All day long he hears click, clack, moo. Click, clack, moo. Clickety, clackety, moo." Typing gives the cows a means to communicate. Rather than placidly chewing their cuds, they take up a mission. "Dear Farmer Brown, The barn is very cold at night. We'd like some electric blankets. Sincerely, The Cows." When he refuses to comply with their requests, they go on strike and post a note on the door: "No milk today." Fortunately for Farmer Brown, he finds a mediator, a duck, but the final page suggests that his troubles may not be over.

Communication skills. Negotiating. Conflict resolution. These heavy matters rarely get presented in a picture book, particularly one that keeps readers laughing from the first page to last. Cronin's text exemplifies two qualities of great picture book writing: lightness of touch and showing rather than telling. Some of the best moments in this Caldecott Honor book occur in Betsy Lewin's comic watercolor illustrations, from Farmer Brown with straw in his hat to the expressive faces of the cows as they set out on their course of passive resistance. Both the text and art in *Click, Clack, Moo* come together perfectly to create a small gem that has readers ages two through eight turning the pages to find out how everything gets resolved.

So if you want to celebrate both National Dairy Month and the invention of the typewriter, pick up *Click, Clack, Moo: Cows That Type.*

JUNE 23

It's the birth date of Theodore Taylor (1921–2006), *The Cay.*

Olympic athlete **Wilma Rudolph** (1940–1994) was born on this day. Read *How Wilma Rudolph Became the World's Fastest Woman* by Kathleen Krull, illustrated by David Diaz.

In 1860 the U.S. Secret Service was created to arrest counterfeiters and protect the president. Read *The President's Daughter* by Ellen Emerson White.

In 1972 Title IX, an amendment to the Civil Rights Act of 1964, was enacted, ensuring equality for girls in education. Read *Let Me Play: The Story of Title IX: The Law That Changed the Future of Girls in America* by Karen Blumenthal.

It's National Pink Day. Read *The Pink Refrigerator* by Tim Egan and *Pink Me Up!* by Charise Mericle Harper.

JUNE 24

Happy Birthday Leonard Everett Fisher (*The Great Wall of China*), Kathryn Lasky (The Guardians of Ga'Hoole series), and Jean Marzollo (I Spy series).

It's the birth date of John Ciardi (1916–1986), *You Read to Me, I'll Read to You.*

In 1997 the U.S. Air Force reported on the "Roswell Incident," stating it was life-sized dummies, not aliens from a UFO, witnesses saw in 1947.

MY LOUISIANA SKY

By Kimberly Willis Holt

Around this time of year the Squire Creek Louisiana Peach Festival is held—with a rodeo, parades, and a cooking contest. If you are in the area and want some local culture, head on over. But if you aren't, I have an alternative: Kimberly Willis Holt's *My Louisiana Sky*, for young readers ages ten through fourteen.

The daughter of a naval officer, Holt became an observer of cultures other than her own at an early age. But after growing up in Louisiana and now living in West Texas, the south has always been home. She has crafted a series of unique, emotionally moving, and beautifully written novels that resonate with a Southern voice. She has said, "I don't think I've ever really gotten over being twelve," and her young protagonists all bear witness to the fact that she remembers, in exquisite detail, what it feels like to be a young child.

I personally fell in love with her voice in 1998, shortly after the publication of her first novel, *My Louisiana Sky*, a *Boston Globe–Horn Book* Honor Book. In this unusual book, Tiger, a twelve-year-old girl living in a small Louisiana community, has a mother and father who have both been described as "simple" or "retarded," and yet Tiger herself is smart as a whip and quite responsible. Her grandmother cares for Tiger and her parents. When she was young, Tiger could play with her mother as a friend, but now Tiger has grown older and her mother has remained developmentally around six years old.

Holt shows Tiger's consternation about the actions of her parents—and how they affect her social standing. But Holt also presents both parents with dignity. Tiger's father provides reliable work at a local plant farm; he even helps save the stock by correctly reading the weather signs of an approaching hurricane. Her mother's love is simple and deep; a gentle soul, she supports Tiger completely. When her grandmother dies, Tiger must make the choice of whether she should leave what she knows to live with her aunt in Baton Rouge.

Although this story requires a reader who enjoys depth and complexity in novels, for the right child at the right time, it can be amazingly rewarding. These readers often say *My Louisiana Sky* is the best book they have ever read. I love the honesty of the story, and the portrayal of how families and small communities can care for the disabled with love and charity.

Kimberly Willis Holt always gets family dynamics and human relationships right. She is one of those writers I have always wished I could have coffee with in the morning. The next best thing is savoring her novels, including *When Zachary Beaver Came to Town* and *Keeper of the Night*. With an attractive new paperback cover, *My Louisiana Sky* makes a wonderful starting point for those who might have missed this singular writer.

ALVIN HO: ALLERGIC TO CAMPING, HIKING, AND OTHER NATURAL DISASTERS

By Lenore Look
Illustrated by LeUyen Pham

During the month of June, the National Wildlife Federation has been promoting the joys of camping. Although they advocate camping on any day this month, on the fourth Saturday in June they hold the Great American Backyard Campout. They want everyone to participate in the pleasures of singing songs around an open fire, toasting s'mores, looking at the stars at night, and experiencing the joys of camping.

The hero of our book for this day, *Alvin Ho: Allergic to Camping, Hiking, and Other Natural Disasters*, is going camping with his father. But Alvin isn't wildly enthusiastic. Born scared, young Alvin doesn't have any pleasant associations with the idea of camping. He bears an amazing resemblance, in fact, to Mélanie Watt's Scaredy Squirrel. He can always see what might go wrong in any situation—flash floods, meteorites, pit toilets. He writes notes: "How to avoid a bear attack. Don't go camping. Don't go anywhere near a camp. Don't even think of camping." However, his father persists in camping enthusiasm, so Alvin turns to his older brother Calvin and his uncle Dennis for help in assembling equipment that will save him from disaster—generators, GPS machines, and loads of dangle traps. But Alvin hasn't planned for everything: his sister Anibelly gets included at the last minute; they forget the food and can openers; and the wonderful dangle trap captures Alvin's father hanging him upside down from a tree.

In *Alvin Ho: Allergic to Camping, Hiking, and Other Natural Disasters*, comic genius Lenore Look shows readers a slightly different side of camping than the one advocated by the National Wildlife Federation. However, at the end of the day, Alvin and his family do spend a magic night under the stars and exchange some important words: "I love you, son" and "I love you, Dad." Now that makes even natural disasters worthwhile.

Before you celebrate the Great American Backyard Campout, you might want to get some tips from Alvin Ho. Reading the book, ideal for six- to ten-year-olds, will make your own campout experience seem mild in comparison.

JUNE 25

Happy Birthday Eric Carle (*The Very Hungry Caterpillar, Brown Bear, Brown Bear, What Do You See?*).

It's the birth date of Elizabeth Orton Jones (1910–2005), *Prayer for a Child*.

In 1788 Virginia became the tenth state to ratify the United States Constitution. Read *Blood on the River* by Elise Carbonne.

In 1903 Marie Curie announced her discovery of radium. Read *Something Out of Nothing: Marie Curie and Radium* by Carla Killough McClafferty.

In 1950 North Korea invaded South Korea, beginning the Korean War.

In 1967 The Beatles performed a new song, "All You Need Is Love," during a live international telecast.

It's National Catfish Day. Read *Kidnap at the Catfish Café* by Patricia Reilly Giff, illustrated by Lynne Cravath, and *Catfish Kate and the Sweet Swamp Band* by Sarah Weeks, illustrated by Elwood Smith.

JUNE 26

Happy Birthday Nancy Willard (*A Visit to William Blake's Inn*) and Robert Burch (*Ida Early Comes Over the Mountain*).

It's the birth date of Walter Farley (1915–1989), *The Black Stallion*; and Lynd Ward (1905–1985), *The Biggest Bear*.

Athlete Babe Didrikson Zaharias (1911–1956) was born on this day. Read *Babe Didrikson Zaharias: The Making of a Champion* by Russell Freedman and *Babe Didrikson: The Greatest All-Sport Athlete of All Time* by Susan E. Cayleff.

It's National Chocolate Pudding Day. Read *The Magic Pudding* by Norman Lindsay and *The Roly-Poly Pudding* by Beatrix Potter.

MR. RABBIT AND THE LOVELY PRESENT

By Charlotte Zolotow
Illustrated by Maurice Sendak

Today marks the birthday of Charlotte Zolotow, legendary publisher, editor, and writer. Sometime in the late seventies I first met Charlotte and from that day on, I suddenly had a new goal—I wanted to grow up to be Charlotte Zolotow. Her grace, intelligence, sparking eyes, sly sense of humor—and her talent—simply won me over.

In her career, Charlotte excelled as both an editor and a writer. As an editor for one of the great children's imprints in the history of publishing, Harper & Row during the forties through eighties, she made her mark by encouraging writers and bringing books into print that otherwise would not have existed. Louise Fitzhugh's *Harriet the Spy* was drawn from the author by conversations with Charlotte and Ursula Nordstrom, the latter then head of the department. *Harriet the Spy* did not arrive as a book, but became one under Charlotte's direction. She helped find talent for the emerging young adult arena, often locating writers who were doing other kinds of work, such as playwright Paul Zindel. His *My Darling, My Hamburger* is dedicated simply to "My Darling, My Charlotte Zolotow."

When the brilliant group of Harper illustrators needed new picture book texts, Charlotte wrote them. Examples include *The Park Book* for H. A. Rey and *The Storm Book* for Margaret Bloy Graham. In *William's Doll*, illustrated by William Pène du Bois, she took a stand against gender stereotypes. Gentleness, a sense of the joy of life, and a beauty of phrasing exist in these texts—qualities very difficult for picture book writers to achieve.

Best known for a book that won a Caldecott Honor for Maurice Sendak, *Mr. Rabbit and the Lovely Present*, Charlotte wrote the text when she became aware that her three-year-old daughter was attempting to locate the perfect birthday present for her mother. Charlotte started to think about the Pulitzer Prize–winning play, Harvey, about a six-foot invisible rabbit, who was the companion of a good-hearted inebriate. If the rabbit were visible, he could help a little girl find the perfect present for her mother. As Charlotte has said about the writing process, "All children's books, really, are made up of double and triple exposures, pieces of this and that that you carry around. . . . One day they take shape and become a book."

I can think of no better words to celebrate Charlotte Zolotow's birthday than a quote from one of the great Harper classics, E. B. White's *Charlotte's Web*: "She was in a class by herself. It is not often that someone comes along who is a true friend and a good writer. Charlotte was both."

CAMP BABYMOUSE

By Jennifer L. Holm and Matthew Holm

June has been designated the Great Outdoors Month, to celebrate our nation's natural beauty and renew our commitment to protecting the environment. In June many people and families head to the great outdoors, often to camp out. Many children go to camp for a week or two, giving them experiences that they might not have at home.

What if you do not naturally appreciate a camp of any kind? Enter our heroine of the day, Babymouse. She's signed up for two weeks of sleepaway camp, and she's not exactly the camping type. Even garden hoses and sticks remind her of snakes. Dropped off at Camp Wild Whiskers with enough cupcakes to feed an army, Babymouse tries to make a good first impression on her camp mates, flinging her arms out wide and yelling, "HI EVERYONE! I'M BABYMOUSE." Unfortunately, none of her cabinmates—including a skunk, cat, and dog—seem impressed.

From there things just go downhill. Babymouse constantly racks up demerits for her cabin, the Buttercups. She's a camping disaster and creates havoc whether she makes bracelets or tries to find her way home out of the woods. She tries everyone's patience to the point that her camp mates wish she'd go home. Finally, even her active imaginative life where she stars as a superhero and always saves the day doesn't keep her going, and she's ready to bail on the outdoor experience. At the last minute she finds a way to become a team player and bring at least small success to her newfound friends.

In their series of graphic novels about Babymouse, brother and sister team Jennifer L. and Matthew Holm have created one masterful book after another. From attractive pink covers through page after page of action rendered in black, white, and pink, young readers just whiz through these ninety-page books. Once readers age four through ten find one of the sagas about this endearing protagonist, they long for more. Fortunately, this talented duo continues to create one great book after another.

If you haven't yet met this incredibly popular heroine, *Camp Babymouse* will make you a convert. I myself am just grateful that no one is sending me to any sleepaway camp this year, but if they were, I'd definitely bring Babymouse—not to mention scores of cupcakes—with me.

JUNE 27

Happy Birthday James Lincoln Collier (*My Brother Sam Is Dead*) and Christina Björk (*Linnea in Monet's Garden*).

It's the birth date of **Helen Keller** (1880–1968). Read her autobiography, *The Story of My Life*, and *Miss Spitfire* by Sarah Miller.

In 1922 the Newbery Medal is first awarded, named for the eighteenth-century British bookseller John Newbery. It's given annually to an author considered to have written the "most distinguished contribution to American literature for children" by the Association for Library Service to Children (ALSC), a division of the American Library Association (ALA).

JUNE 28

Happy Birthday Bette Greene (*Summer of My German Soldier*) and Dennis Haseley (*A Story for Bear*).

It's the birth date of Esther Forbes (1891–1967), *Johnny Tremain*.

In 1914 Austria's **Archduke Francis Ferdinand** was assassinated in Sarajevo, Serbia, an event which precipitated the start of World War I. And in 1919 Germany signed the Treaty of Versailles ending the War.

In 1973 a lawsuit in Detroit challenges the "no girls" rule in Little League. Read *Catching the Moon: The Story of a Young Girl's Baseball Dreams* by Crystal Hubbard, illustrated by Randy Du-Burke, *Mama Played Baseball* by David A. Adler, illustrated by Chris O'Leary, and *The Girl Who Threw Butterflies* by Mick Cochrane.

It's Paul Bunyan Day. Read *Paul Bunyan* by Steven Kellogg and *Paul Bunyan: My Story* by David L. Harrison, illustrated by John Kanzler.

OLD POSSUM'S BOOK OF PRACTICAL CATS

By T. S. Eliot
Illustrated by Edward Gorey

In the 1930s, an author who called himself "Old Possum" sent his godchildren (Tom Faber, Alison Tandy, Susan Wolcott, and Susanne Morley) a series of poems about cats. Playful, irreverent, and brilliantly written, these fourteen poems (a fifteenth, "Cat Morgan Introduces Himself," appeared in 1952) were published in England by Faber and Faber in September of 1939. The author was not your average godparent, but the great modern writer T. S. Eliot. We are celebrating Adopt a Shelter Cat Month in June, and no volume has ever made me want to own a cat, possibly even several cats, more than *Old Possum's Book of Practical Cats*.

Children ages four and up respond to the cadence and the language, bubbling over with fantasy and fun, long before they can even understand the meaning of the words. Therefore *Old Possum's Book of Practical Cats* is ideal for a parent, librarian, or teacher to read aloud; the poems provide equal enjoyment for all listeners. These cats all have distinct personalities; the poems celebrating them introduce readers and listeners to one individual, idiosyncratic cat after another. For instance: "Macavity's a Mystery Cat: he's called the Hidden Paw— / For he's the master criminal who can defy the Law. / He's the bafflement of Scotland Yard, the Flying Squad's despair: / For when they reach the scene of crime—*Macavity's not there!*"

In 1982 Harcourt made an edition available with illustrations by Edward Gorey. No one can make cats more droll or more sinister than he did. As maniacal as these cats look, the humans seem a good deal more bizarre.

The inspiration for Andrew Lloyd Weber's musical *Cats, Old Possum's Book of Practical Cats* can be savored again and again for its language and charm. Hours of reading pleasure can be found, for both adults and children, in this slim volume of fifty-six pages, one of the finest volumes of poetry ever written for young people.

JUNE 29, 1999

By David Wiesner

Today is June 29, a day synonymous with the most decorated contemporary children's book illustrator, three-time winner of the Caldecott Medal David Wiesner. David began his work at Rhode Island School of Design, a student of David Macaulay. Even as a boy, David knew that he wanted to be an artist, and his family supported his dream. As a student at RISD, he was searching for a way to create a different kind of picture book for children—one that would rely much more on the pictures than the words. He wanted to see how few words he could use in a book.

To establish himself as an illustrator, he took whatever work came his way. Trina Schart Hyman, art director of *Cricket Magazine*, asked him to illustrate the cover of an issue with frogs; others gave him covers or interior art assignments. But like so many truly talented people, David did not really fashion his best books until an editor, in his case Dorothy Briley, had enough faith in him to allow him to take over the whole book—text and art. His first solo attempt, *Freefall*, a Caldecott Honor book, uses no words at all. In the dream sequences of the book, characters walk, float, fly, and ride through metamorphosing landscapes. By following illustration clues, young viewers can create their own stories from the pictures.

In 1992 David published *June 29, 1999*—an interesting exploration of a school science project. Holly Evans has been sending seeds into the ionosphere to test the effects of extraterrestrial conditions on vegetables. Suddenly the skies fill up with gigantic vegetables. "Cucumbers circle Kalamazoo. / Lima beans loom over Levittown. / Artichokes advance in Anchorage. / Parsnips pass by Providence." But some of these species have not been initially launched by Holly. So what is going on? On the final pages, David brings science and extraterrestrials together in a completely unexpected way.

David Wiesner makes the perfect candidate for an author study because from his student years to his three Caldecott Medal books—*Tuesday*, *The Three Pigs*, and *Flotsam*—he has created one brilliant picture book after another. But sometimes even fans of Wiesner have missed *June 29, 1999*. If you have, too, once you discover it you may find yourself looking up at the sky from time to time, attempting to see if any giant cauliflowers are floating near you.

JUNE 29

It's the birth date of Antoine de Saint-Exupéry (1900–1944), *The Little Prince*.

In 1949 South Africa began implementing apartheid. Read *No Turning Back: A Novel of South Africa* and *Journey to Jo'Burg*, both by Beverley Naiddo.

The Civil Rights Act passed after an eighty-three-day filibuster in the U.S. Senate on this day in 1964. Read *A Tugging String* by David Greenberg, *Child of the Civil Rights Movement* by Paula Young Shelton, illustrated by Raul Colón, and *The Civil Rights Act of 1964* by Robert H. Mayer.

In 1995 the U.S. Satellite *Atlantis* docked with the Russian space station *Mir* to create the largest man-made satellite to orbit the Earth.

On this day in 2007 the Apple iPhone first went on sale.

JUNE 30

Happy Birthday David McPhail (*Edward and the Pirates, Pigs Aplenty, Pigs Galore*) and Mollie Hunter (*A Stranger Came Ashore*).

In 1859 French acrobat Charles Blondin crossed Niagara Falls on a tightrope to an audience of five thousand. Read *Mirette & Bellini Cross Niagara Falls* by Emily Arnold McCully and *Yours Till Niagara Falls, Abby* by Jane O'Connor, illustrated by Margot Apple.

The forty-hour workweek was established in 1936. Read *The Bobbin Girl* by Emily Arnold McCully.

Happy Birthday to the National Organization of Women/NOW, founded on this day in 1966. Read *Lives of Extraordinary Women: Rulers, Rebels (and What the Neighbors Thought)* by Kathleen Krull, illustrated by Kathryn Hewitt.

OFFICER BUCKLE AND GLORIA
By Peggy Rathmann

June has been designated National Safety Month to promote safety at work, at home, on the road, and in our communities. Safety might seem a bit dull as a topic for a book for children, but the book of the day, *Officer Buckle and Gloria* by Peggy Rathmann, demonstrates that highly creative people can make seemingly mundane topics into fascinating reading. Winner of the Caldecott Medal, *Officer Buckle and Gloria* has been delighting young readers for more than fifteen years. Beginning and closing with endpapers that show a variety of safety tips, the book uses humor to convey many rules about safe behavior.

Friendly Officer Buckle knows more safety tips than anyone in his town and appears at schools to share them. Unfortunately, his appearances generate little enthusiasm from the students. No one, in fact, listens to him at all, no matter what wisdom he imparts. Fortunately, he begins to take his new police dog Gloria with him. Gloria can do more than sit; she can act out the very safety lesson he describes—cleaning up spilled liquids, tying shoelaces, or avoiding thumbtacks. Since Officer Buckle doesn't see Gloria's actions, his speech looks like a funny play, and this pas de deux gets rave reviews from the children. Only after he watches himself on television does the good police officer realize that Gloria has been hamming it up for applause.

At first hurt, he grows to realize that the two can do together what neither of them can do alone. With one of the best final picture book lines of all time, the officer gives safety tip number 101: "ALWAYS STICK WITH YOUR BUDDY!"

In this perfect picture book, author Peggy Rathmann creates tension on every page between what is said in the text and what is revealed in the art. With a multitude of real safety tips throughout the story, this book demonstrates that learning about anything—even safety—can be fun. So during National Safety Month, remember to look both ways before you cross the street, buckle your seat belt, obey all traffic signs, and read, at least once, *Officer Buckle and Gloria*. You will be glad that you have followed this sound advice.

ZOO-OLOGY

By Emmanuelle Grundmann
Illustrated by Joëlle Jolivet

On July 1, 1874, the first zoo in the United States opened its doors to visitors in Philadelphia. A quarter for adults and a dime for children allowed visitors to view 813 animals housed there. Three thousand people traveled by foot, horse and buggy, or steamboat to look at the wonders.

Thousands of books about zoos or zoo animals have been published for children since 1874, but if I had only one of them to pack in a trunk and take to an island, it would be an easy choice for me. Admittedly, I'd need a big trunk; the oversize volume stands almost a foot and a half tall. From the minute you spot its reddish-orange cover across the room, *Zoo-ology* begs to be opened. Joëlle Jolivet, a brilliant French illustrator, crafted the art. Emmanuelle Grundmann, Zoology Consultant of the French National Museum of Natural History, provides fabulous notes.

Every double-page spread features mammals,

JULY 1

Happy Birthday Emily Arnold McCully (*Mirette on the High Wire*) and Diane Hoyt-Goldsmith (*Cinco De Mayo: Celebrating the Traditions of Mexico*).

Best birthday wishes also go to choreographer Twyla Tharp. Read *To Dance: A Ballerina's Graphic Novel* by Siena Cherson Siegel and Mark Siegel.

It's the birth date of French aviator Louis Blériot (1872–1936). Read *The Glorious Flight: Across the Channel with Louise Blériot* by Alice and Martin Provensen.

It's the birthday of the zip code, inaugurated in 1963. Hence, it's Zip Code Day.

insects, fish, or amphibians, grouped sometimes by climate (hot, cold), form (feathered, horned), habitat (in the seas, in the trees, underground), or color (black and white, spots and stripes). All have their name close to their images, except for the chameleon that moves from page to page and changes color. Children love finding him in each double-page spread as he ambles through the book. Each page has been so imaginatively constructed that you can spend hours studying the creatures and testing your knowledge of zoology. After your eyes have feasted on the book, you can go to the endnotes. Here we learn that the beluga whale was once called the "canary of the sea" because of its song or that the civet's liquid for marking its territory is used in making perfume. Each sentence contains a fascinating fact, conveyed in minimal words.

The images serve as models of graphic design and can be used to inspire students artistically. In short, whether at school or as a beloved treasure at home, this is a book every child in the United States, even preschoolers, should pick up. Not only does it make readers want to quickly head to a zoo, but it also inspires its viewers to immediately research a creature that has caught his or her fancy.

So happy birthday, Philadelphia Zoo. I can't get there today for a visit—but I will do the next best thing and pick up *Zoo-ology* one more time.

JULY 2

Happy Birthday Jack Gantos (Joey Pigza series, Rotten Ralph series, *Dead End in Norvelt*).

It's the birth date of Thurgood Marshall (1908–1993), the first African American to serve on the United States Supreme Court. Read *A Picture Book of Thurgood Marshall* by David A. Adler, illustrated by Robert Casilla.

In 1698 the steam engine was patented in England. Read *Mike Mulligan and His Steam Shovel* by Virginia Lee Burton.

In 1777 Vermont became the first American territory to abolish slavery. Read *Alec's Primer* by Mildred Pitts Walter, illustrated by Larry Johnson.

 Aviator **Amelia Earhart** disappeared over the Pacific Ocean on this day in 1937. Read *Amelia Earhart: The Legend of the Lost Aviator* by Shelley Tanaka, illustrated by David Craig, and *Amelia Lost: The Life and Disappearance of Amelia Earhart* by Candace Fleming.

In 1964 President Lyndon Johnson signed the Civil Rights Act into law.

MY SIDE OF THE MOUNTAIN
By Jean Craighead George

On July 2, 1919, Jean Craighead George was born in Washington, D.C. In a life filled with travel and adventure, she also wrote two beloved classics—*My Side of the Mountain* and *Julie of the Wolves*—and scores of other great books.

Admittedly, her family gave her a good start. As she wrote, "I was lured into natural history by my father." He took Jean and her two brothers, who both became distinguished scientists, into the wilderness outside the city, and taught them the names of plants and animals. For Jean Craighead George exploring the natural world was a lot of fun: "Each day is filled with excitement. I watch a pond or a tree or a rain forest, talk to scientists, observe my parrot, and listen to my children and grandchildren. After that writing comes easy."

In the fifties she began to work on a manuscript that combined her love of the natural world with an experience from childhood. She once declared that she was going to run away from home—but returned forty minutes later. In *My Side of the Mountain* Jean's alter ego, Sam Gribley, actually manages to run away from his family. Sam makes a new home for himself in a hemlock tree hollow in the Catskills. Slowly he develops his survival skills, even learning how to make delicious acorn pancakes. For a companion Sam captures and trains a peregrine falcon, Frightful. As he makes insightful observations about the world he now lives in, Sam creates a life of freedom and joy.

At first Jean's publisher balked at the idea of the novel. They were afraid that it might encourage young readers to flee their families for the nearest hemlock tree. However, when the book was finally released in 1959, it merely caused children to read the novel, cover to cover, because of the compelling story. Because of Sam's resilience and ingenuity, he remains one of the best-remembered children's book characters of the twentieth century.

My Side of the Mountain encouraged many to pursue careers in environmental studies. As Robert Kennedy Jr. wrote in *Everything I Need to Know I Learned from a Children's Book*, "*My Side of the Mountain* has inspired countless children, as it did me, to take up ecological stewardship in their adult years."

I can think of no more fitting summer read than *My Side of the Mountain*. It still inspires children to explore the natural world—even if only in their imaginations.

ROLL OF THUNDER, HEAR MY CRY

By Mildred D. Taylor

July has been designated both Family Reunion Month and National Black Family Month. We all need to take time to celebrate the strengths and virtues of our families. For some writers, their family and their family stories provide the necessary ingredients for great books. Such is the case of our author of the day, Mildred D. Taylor.

Turning to family legends of her childhood, Taylor created a proud black family, the Logans, who own their land in Mississippi in the 1930s. The children suffer from inadequate schooling, and they see the nightriders who terrorize their community. In her most famous novel, the Newbery Medal–winning *Roll of Thunder, Hear My Cry*, Taylor depicts the family so vividly that readers immediately love and respect the Logans and are drawn into their story. In the end, no matter what your racial background, you identify with their plight and want to battle prejudice with them. Taylor continues to follow these characters—Cassie, Stacey, Little Man, and David—through her series.

JULY 3

Happy Birthday Dave Barry (Starcatcher series).

Happy Birthday Idaho, which became the 43rd U.S. state on this day in 1890. Read *Potato: A Tale from the Great Depression* by Kate Lied, illustrated by Lisa Campbell Ernst.

In 1962 Jackie Robinson became the first African-American player inducted into the Baseball Hall of Fame. Read *In the Year of the Boar and Jackie Robinson* by Bette Boa Lord, illustrated by Marc Simont.

It's National Eat Beans Day. Read the Ivy and Bean series by Annie Barrows, illustrated by Sophie Blackall, the Clarice Bean series by Lauren Child, and the Harriet Bean series by Alexander McCall Smith, illustrated by Laura Rankin.

Published in 1976 at the height of the civil rights movement, *Roll of Thunder, Hear My Cry* is one of the most important children's novels of the twentieth century. It enables children to understand a period of time unknown to them and to think about and feel what children of another era might have experienced. Often young readers who have never thought about discrimination admit this book helped them understand what it would be like to be hated for your race. In one powerful scene, Taylor simply describes the inside front cover of a textbook. There is a list recording its owners and the quality of the book. It shows that when the textbook has been judged to be in poor condition, it then became the property of a black child.

Roll of Thunder, Hear My Cry depicts the story of one remarkable family and in doing so changes the way children and adults look at their own society—the true testament of a great book. It celebrates the strength of families and their importance—no matter your race or religion.

JULY 4

Happy Birthday Jamie Gilson (*Thirteen Ways to Sink a Sub*).

It's the birth date of Nathaniel Hawthorne (1804–1864), *The House of the Seven Gables*.

Birthday greetings to Koko the gorilla, born on this day in 1971. Read *Koko's Kitten* by Dr. Francine Patterson, photographs by Ronald Cohn.

It's also the birth date of Calvin Coolidge (1872–1933), the 30th president of the United States.

In 1776 the Declaration of Independence was approved and signed. Read *The Signers: The 56 Stories Behind the Declaration of Independence* by Dennis Brindell Fradin, illustrated by Michael McCurdy.

While it's the anniversary of the birth of the United States, it's also the death date of two of the founding fathers. Thomas Jefferson and John Adams both died on this day in 1826.

In 1845 Henry David Thoreau began his twenty-six-month stay at Walden Pond.

It's Sidewalk Egg Frying Day. Read *Sidewalk Circus* by Paul Fleischman, illustrated by Kevin Hawles, *The Egg* by M. P. Robertson, and *How to Eat Fried Worms* by Thomas Rockwell.

AMERICA THE BEAUTIFUL
By Katharine Lee Bates
Illustrated by Wendell Minor

Today we celebrate Independence Day in the United States with fireworks and patriotic songs. The best-loved melody about America does not happen to be our national anthem, which even trained singers perform with difficulty. Most Americans prefer an easier and more haunting song, first published a hundred years ago: "America the Beautiful."

The words for this celebration of the American landscape first appeared on July 4, 1895, in the *Congregationalist*. Written by Wellesley College professor Katharine Lee Bates, this poem was inspired by a trip to Pikes Peak in Colorado. She continued to revise the words for several years, to make it easier to sing. In 1888 music composer Samuel Ward, traveling on a steamboat ride from Coney Island, started humming a tune, one that he had to write down on a friend's shirt cuff because he had no paper at hand. Finally, in 1910, the words and music of the song we know today were published together.

Following in the tradition of N. C. Wyeth, Edward Hopper, and Norman Rockwell, Wendell Minor stands as the most accomplished re-creator of American history and natural life in the twenty-first century. In *America the Beautiful*, he depicts magnificent scenes from across the country—the alabaster cities, patriot dreams, and amber waves of grain. In double-page spreads showing the hill country of Texas, a lighthouse in Massachusetts, and Mount Rushmore, Minor infuses each glorious painting with light, dignity, beauty, and love. Each double-page image serves as a reminder of the natural and human-made wonders of the United States.

At the back of the book Minor identifies all the locations depicted in his art, and he also places each on a map of the United States. Background notes about Katharine Lee Bates and Samuel Ward round out this volume, which includes a CD narrated by Minor and a recording of this beloved song. So pick up a copy of *America the Beautiful* for the Fourth of July. It brilliantly showcases what all Americans can joyfully celebrate—"from sea to shining sea."

REX ZERO AND THE END OF THE WORLD

By Tim Wynne-Jones

Around this time of year the annual Kimberley International Old Time Accordion Championship take place in Kimberley, B.C., Canada. Family dances, jam sessions, and pancake breakfasts occur. What family in children's books would be fun to take there? I would select the Norton-Nortons of *Rex Zero and the End of the World*.

Few authors treat the topic of the end of the world with humor. But Canadian writer Tim Wynne-Jones pulls that task off with panache in a book that demonstrates his great ability to turn a phrase and create fascinating and idiosyncratic characters. The wildly eccentric Norton-Nortons move to Ottawa, Canada, just as young Rex is about to turn eleven. Every single child in the Norton-Norton family seems more eccentric than the next. Neighbors build bomb shelters out of concrete; Rex and his sister build one out of *Punch* magazines. Rex's sister Annie Oakley breaks into the local convent because she believes it contains nuns who act as Communist spies.

As Rex tries to fit into his new community and find some new friends, he discovers all sorts of odd things. A strange creature lurks nearby in Adams Park, and a group of children stalk it, believing it to be an escaped panther. The End of the World Man proclaims that all will cease on October 23. Endearing, charming, confused, Rex just tries to get by in a world gone mad. The issues of the Cold War in 1962 are explored in the book, but in this character-driven story history is woven seamlessly into the plot. With a profound understanding of novel structure, Tim brings multiple plot lines together in the totally satisfying ending.

Tim Wynne-Jones came to children's books as a detour from being an architect. Although he excels in writing all forms, as his powerful young adult novel *Blink & Caution* demonstrates, he began to win awards in the States for his short story collections such as *Some of the Kinder Planets* and *Lord of the Fries*. Tim not only writes fabulous books, but as a long-time member of the Vermont College MFA in Writing for Children staff, he also generously helps other writers, both novice and seasoned. Like Rex Zero he endears himself to those who know him.

If you can't attend the Old Time Accordion Championship, pick up *Rex Zero and the End of the World* today. It provides its own kind of Canadian fun.

JULY 5

Happy Birthday Jill Murphy (Worst Witch series).

It's the birth date of John Carl Schoenherr (1935–2010), *Owl Moon*.

Showman P. T. Barnum (1810–1891) was born on this day. Read *The Great and Only Barnum* by Candace Fleming, illustrated by Ray Fenwick.

Happy Birthday Spam, the mysterious meat not the annoying e-mail clutter. The Hormel Food Corporation introduced this iconic product in 1937. Though not specifically a children's book, you may enjoy reading *SPAM: A Biography—The Amazing True Story of America's "Miracle Meat"!* by Carolyn Wyman.

It's Bikini Day. Happy birthday to the post–World War II swimsuit, launched in 1946. Read *The Last Night on Bikini* by Patricia MacInnes.

In 1996 a sheep named Dolly was created, the first-ever cloned animal. Read *The Clone Codes* by Patricia, Fred, and John McKissack.

JULY 6

Happy Birthday Cheryl Harness (*Three Young Pilgrims, Remember the Ladies*) and Kathi Appelt (*The Underneath*).

Happy Birthday George W. Bush, the 43rd president of the United States.

 It's the birth date of artist **Frida Kahlo** (1907–1954). Read *Frida* by Jonah Winter, illustrated by Ana Juan, *Me, Frida* by Amy Novesky, illustrated by David Diaz, and *Casa Azul: An Encounter with Frida Kahlo* by Laban Carrick Hill.

In 1189 Richard I (The Lionheart) was crowned King of England.

On this day in 1885 Dr. Louis Pasteur successfully treated a patient with his rabies vaccine. Read *Old Yeller* by Fred Gipson.

Happy Birthday to Garrison Keillor's radio show "A Prairie Home Companion," which made its debut on this day in 1974.

It's National Fried Chicken Day. Read *Peiling and the Chicken-Fried Christmas* by Pauline Chen.

JOHN'S SECRET DREAMS: THE LIFE OF JOHN LENNON

By Doreen Rappaport
Illustrated by Bryan Collier

On July 6, 1957, in Saint Peter's Parish Church in Woolton, England, a young musician performed with his band, The Quarrymen. Another young guitarist attended the event. As Elizabeth Partridge writes in *John Lennon: All I Want Is the Truth*, the guitarist "was dressed to kill. He'd come to the garden fete hoping to pick up girls. His white sports jacket was shot through with metallic threads that sparked in the sunlight, his black drainies were tight, his hair was carefully greased back." He arrived just in time to hear the singer of The Quarrymen break into a rendition of the Del Viking hit, "Come Go with Me." And that is how the guitarist, Sir Paul McCartney, met John Lennon.

While Partridge's *John Lennon: All I Want Is the Truth* has been written for fourteen- to eighteen-year-olds, in a book for children eight through ten, Doreen Rappaport explores Lennon and his songwriting in *John's Secret Dreams: The Life of John Lennon*, magnificently illustrated by Bryan Collier.

The book begins and ends with Lennon's words: "I like to write about me, because I know about me," and "War is over, if you want it." In the book key phrases and words from Lennon's music form the backdrop, the accompaniment as it were, to the details of his life. Born in the Penny Lane district of Liverpool, raised by his aunt and uncle, the bright young boy got swept up in the rock-and-roll movement that was taking America by storm. Lennon and McCartney brought in two other performers, Ringo Starr on drums, and George Harrison on guitar, to form the Beatles. By the age of twenty-four Lennon and this group had gone to the top of the charts, again and again.

Rappaport deals honestly with the details of Lennon's life—his drug use, leaving his wife for Yoko Ono, the pressures of being so famous at such a young age, and his untimely death. In the end the text simply reads, "John Lennon was murdered when he was only forty years old." Brian Collier's collages, which rely on circle compositions, bring both the images and words of John Lennon to life.

Grandparents, who may well have seen the Beatles on the *Ed Sullivan Show*, might want to share this book with their grandchildren. It can be used to explain the question: Who were the Beatles? Their journey began over fifty years ago when John Lennon met Paul McCartney.

HALF BROTHER

By Kenneth Oppel

Canada Day is celebrated at the beginning of July, and one Canadian writer who has won my affection in the last few years is Kenneth Oppel.

I first encountered his work with the Airborn series and loved his voice, imagination, and ability to write page-turning science fiction. A newer book, *Half Brother*, for ten- to fourteen-year-olds, extends the range of what Oppel has attempted in fiction. In it, he demonstrates that he can also create realistic fiction that delves into important issues yet still keep his story character- and plot-driven.

In *Half Brother*, when Ben turns thirteen his parents bring home a new baby. This scenario, of course, is often fraught with problems. In Ben's case, however, the problems are magnified tenfold; his new brother is a hairy chimp, an experiment for his behavioral scientist father. Mr. Tomlin wants to discover how fast an animal raised in a normal family situation can learn communication and sign language. At first, like any normal thirteen-year-old, Ben resents this intrusion into the family. But as he begins working in sign language with Zan, he grows to love the chimp. In doing so, he realizes that although he cares for this being, his father views the chimp as only an experiment. When Ben's father loses funding for his project, Ben tries to find a happy ending for the creature he has grown to love.

Set in Victoria, British Columbia, in the seventies, this story examines the inexplicable and often unexplainable bond between humans and animals. Although Oppel raises questions about animal rights and scientific experimentation, he presents no easy answers. As it deals with important issues, *Half Brother* presents a very real young boy—trying to fit into a new school, developing his first crush, and dealing with tensions in his family.

Animal nut that I am, I fell in love with Zan! I kept thinking how much fun it would be to have a chimp around the house. Fortunately, the ending convinced me of the waywardness of this idea. But anyone hunting for well-written, well-crafted, thought-provoking books will be delighted with the work of Kenneth Oppel. I myself am eager to see what he accomplishes next.

JULY 7

Happy Birthday Harriet Ziefert (*Sleepy Dog*).

It's the birth date of Gian Carlo Menotti (1911–2007), *Amahl and the Night Visitors*.

Baseball player Satchel Paige (1906–1982) was also born on this day. Read *Satchel Paige* by Lesa Cline-Ransome, illustrated by James E. Ransom, *Satchel Paige: Striking Out Jim Crow* by James Sturm, illustrated by Rich Tommaso, and *Satchel Paige: Don't Look Back* by David Adler, illustrated by Terry Widner.

Best birthday wishes to Dr. John H. Watson (1852), fictional sidekick of Sherlock Holmes, created by Sir Arthur Conan Doyle. Read *Mercy Watson Goes for a Ride* by Kate DiCamillo, illustrated by Chris Van Dusen.

In 1456, twenty-five years after she was executed, heresy charges against Joan of Arc were annulled by Pope Calixtus III. Read *Joan of Arc* by Josephine Poole, illustrated by Angela Barrett, and *Joan of Arc: Heroine of France* by Ann Tompert, illustrated by Michael Garland.

In 1981 Sandra Day O'Connor became the first woman to serve on the Supreme Court.

It's Tell the Truth Day. Read *Nothing But the Truth* by Avi.

JULY 8

Happy Birthday Jerry Stanley (*Children of the Dustbowl*), Raffi (*Baby Beluga*), and James Cross Giblin (*The Life and Death of Adolf Hitler, The Rise and Fall of Senator Joe McCarthy*).

 In 1776 the bell now known as the **Liberty Bell** rang out in Philadelphia, to call the city's population together for the first public reading of the Declaration of Independence. Then, on this day in 1835, the Liberty Bell cracked. Read *Saving the Liberty Bell* by Megan McDonald, illustrated by Marsha Gray Carrington.

Happy Birthday Paris, founded in 951 AD. Reread *Madeline* by Ludwig Bemelmans.

In 1941 Nazi Germany required all Jews in Baltic States to wear a six-pointed star. Read *Number the Stars* by Lois Lowry.

It's Video Game Day. Read *Game On!: The Adventures of Daniel Book, Loud Boy* by D. J. Steinberg, illustrated by Brian Smith.

THE EVOLUTION OF CALPURNIA TATE

By Jacqueline Kelly

Today marks the birthday of Étienne de Silhouette, the French finance minister. In 1759, because of France's credit crisis during the Seven Years War, he had to impose severe economic demands on the country, particularly on the wealthy. He was also something of an artist and enjoyed making cut-paper portraits. Eventually Silhouette's name became synonymous with these creations. After all, they could be made of anything and executed cheaply.

Although we often say "you can't judge a book by its cover," authors, publishers, critics, and readers focus a lot of their attention on book jackets. It serves as the first advertisement for the book, either drawing in the reader or repelling them. Recently, the silhouette has been getting a lot of front-cover exposure in children's books.

One remarkable silhouette adorns the jacket for *The Evolution of Calpurnia Tate*, a novel for ages ten through fourteen by Jacqueline Kelly. In cover art created by Beth White, the portrait of a young girl with a butterfly net behind her absolutely begs readers to open the cover. And they are glad when they do.

Living in Fentress, Texas, in 1889, eleven-year-old Callie Vee doesn't excel in sewing or cooking, but she has a passion for science. This is not really an acceptable calling for a girl in the nineteenth century, but her penchant truly makes her crotchety grandfather happy. He delights in providing Callie with information from a controversial book, Darwin's *On the Origin of Species*. In their outdoor explorations, the two even discover a new plant, which they have scientifically verified by the Smithsonian. Callie's voice, feisty and engaging, draws readers into this saga, one that makes science seem like the most exciting passion a girl, or a grandfather, could ever have. The tension between what society and her mother expect of Callie and what she herself longs to do underscores the action of the novel. Callie emerges as an engaging young girl, whom readers want to succeed.

I think Callie Vee would be happy to celebrate Finance Minister de Silhouette's birthday today. Just like Callie Vee, he demonstrated that unlikely contributions can come from people whom society expects to act differently. Both Silhouette and Callie Vee remind us to hold on to our passions and our dreams.

THE BFG

By Roald Dahl
Illustrated by Quentin Blake

On July 9, 1982, Queen Elizabeth II woke up in Buckingham Palace to find a stranger sitting at the end of her bed. Wearing jeans and a T-shirt, the intruder had actually planned to commit suicide in the queen's bedroom, but then decided that wasn't "a nice thing to do." Instead he simply wanted to say hello and discuss his problems with the queen. Needless to say, the incident raised concern about the security of England's monarch. In an even more bizarre twist, an author had already written about—but not yet published—a scene about another intruder to Buckingham Palace who also needed to talk to the queen about her problems. Her name was Sophie, the protagonist of one of the funniest children's books ever written, Roald Dahl's *The BFG*.

Initially told as a story to Dahl's granddaughter Sophie, the book begins with a young girl unable to fall asleep. She sees a giant blowing something into the windows down the street. This benevolent monster, the Big Friendly Giant, takes her to his home and introduces her to his strange life. With his huge ears, he hears dreams and sends them with a blowpipe into the bedrooms of children. He also catches nightmares, bottling them up. Because he doesn't eat humans, he must subsist on food like the revolting "snozz-cumber" or drink "frobscottle," a fizzy concoction that unfortunately causes flatulence, what he calls "whizzpoppers." Since the human-devouring giants need to be stopped, the BFG prepares a doozy of a dream for the queen of England and leaves Sophie on the queen's windowsill to help her interpret it.

The BFG contains all of Dahl's best qualities as a writer—inventive word play, nasty villains, lots of action, and a large dose of nonsense. Dahl had a genius for fashioning unforgettable characters like the Big Friendly Giant. Most readers of the book think that the BFG would be even more fun to hang out with than the queen of England, and in the story they get to enjoy his company for two hundred pages. So rather than visiting the queen today, you should pick up *The BFG* and other delightfully funny books by Roald Dahl. And raise a "frobscottle" in his honor!

JULY 9

Happy Birthday Nancy Farmer (*House of the Scorpion*, *A Girl Named Disaster*).

On this day in 1804 **Alexander Hamilton** was mortally wounded by Aaron Burr in a duel.

In 1872 the doughnut cutter was patented in Maine. Read *Homer Price* by Robert McCloskey.

The first successful open heart surgery was performed in 1893. Read *Hope Is an Open Heart* by Lauren Thompson.

In 1962 Bob Dylan recorded "Blowin' in the Wind." Read *The Wind Blew* by Pat Hutchins, *A Wind in the Door* by Madeleine L'Engle, and *The Wind in the Willows* by Kenneth Grahame.

It's National Sugar Cookie Day. Read *Sugar Cookies: Sweet Little Lessons on Love* by Amy Krouse Rosenthal, illustrated by Jane Dyer and Brooke Dyer.

192

JULY 10

It's the birth date of Martin Provensen (1916–1987), *The Year at Maple Hill Farm*; and Mary O'Hara (1885–1980), *My Friend Flicka*.

Arthur Ashe (1943–1993) was also born on this day. Read *Game, Set, Match: Champion Arthur Ashe* by Crystal Hubbard, illustrated by Kevin Belford, and *Arthur Ashe: Against the Wind* by David Collins.

Happy Birthday to Dublin, Ireland, founded in 988 AD. Read *Patrick: Patron Saint of Ireland* by Tomie dePaola.

Happy Birthday Wyoming, which became the 44th U.S. state on this day in 1890. Read *Green Grass of Wyoming* by Mary O'Hara (who also celebrates her own birthday today).

It's Don't Step on a Bee Day, as is every day. Read *The Bee Tree* by Patricia Polacco, *Bee-Bim Bop* by Linda Sue Park, illustrated by Ho Baek Lee, and *Quilting Bee* by Gail Gibbons.

LITTLE HOUSE IN THE BIG WOODS
By Laura Ingalls Wilder
Illustrated by Garth Williams

Around this time of year the annual Laura Ingalls Wilder Pageant takes place in De Smet, South Dakota. In the town made famous by Mrs. Wilder, the festival includes an outdoor pageant depicting scenes from her life and books. Published in the thirties and called the "books that the Depression could not stop," Laura Ingalls Wilder's fictionalized account of the events of her own life were published and immediately became popular at a time when many families had to do without necessities, not to mention books. She celebrated the dignity and the resilience of the American pioneer. Nothing was too small to be recycled and reused. Even a pig's bladder could be blown up to become a balloon toy for young Laura. As writer Emily Bazelon states in *Everything I Need to Know I Learned from a Children's Book*: "Every scrap mattered. That seemed enviable to me, somehow, as a child—it made the ease and carelessness of our throwaway culture seem dull and thoughtless by comparison."

By the fifties Ursula Nordstrom of Harper thought the books needed redesigning for modern times. She brought illustrator Garth Williams in to work his usual charm, and he gave the books the look and feel that they have today. The newly illustrated books fascinated children who lived in cities; they had no sense of small, farm communities—the life of most Americans just a couple of generations before them.

In nine books, the Wilder family moves from Lake Pepin, Wisconsin, to De Smet, South Dakota, and Laura grows up to have children of her own. One of these children, Rose Wilder Lane, was a ghostwriter by trade. In looking over the original manuscripts for the books, scholars have determined that Rose had a hand in helping her mother craft this magnificent series. She typed, edited, and probably even wrote some sections of the books we have today. One of the greatest mother/daughter collaborations of all times, this effort was not acknowledged during the publication years. Dual-author books were considered substandard. Today both women would appear on talk shows and discuss how they work together!

No matter how the books initially came to be, *The Little House in the Big Woods* stands as a great testament to American strength, fortitude, family, and community. In the end, the Little House series reminds us that having a loving family and friends constitutes true wealth for both an individual and a nation.

HISTORICAL FICTION, Elementary School

STUART LITTLE

By E. B. White
Illustrated by Garth Williams

On July 11, 1899, Elwyn Brooks White, known to his friends as Andy and the literary world as E. B., was born in Mount Vernon, New York. He would eventually become a Mainer, where he lived with his wife, Katharine.

White published his first article in *The New Yorker* in 1925 and continued to write witty and beautifully crafted pieces for the magazine for six decades. With James Thurber he published *Is Sex Necessary?* He also updated *The Elements of Style* by William Strunk—a book now commonly called simply *Strunk and White*.

As brilliant an adult writer as he was, White became even more renowned when he turned to writing novels for children. In October of 1945 his first effort, *Stuart Little*—a droll story about a small mouse born to a family living in Manhattan—was published by Harper and Brothers. White had begun *Stuart Little* in the twenties, planning to share his mouse stories with family members, and eventually expanded his ideas into a novel. Although *Stuart Little* did receive some favorable reviews—the venerable *Horn Book Magazine* said it was "full of wit and wisdom and amusement"—other children's book critics were not so amused. Anne Carroll Moore, the New York Public Library's fierce defender of the proper content for novels for children ages ten and up, read the book before it appeared. She sent no less than a fourteen-page handwritten letter to White, insisting that the book was "non-affirmative, inconclusive, unfit for children" and would harm White's reputation.

Children, however, found the book hilarious. In this episodic and picaresque adventure, a two-inch-tall hero, who "looks very much like a mouse," engages in a series of adventures—loosening stuck piano keys, fetching a ring from a drain, and getting rolled up in a window shade. I find that many adults who read this book as a child particularly remember Stuart's magical ride on a sailboat in Central Park. Eventually, Stuart takes up a quest to rescue a beautiful bird named Margalo.

All of White's novels provide the best read-aloud experiences any family or any classroom can have. His books have garnered an enthusiastic audience of readers from eight to one hundred. Today I am thankful that E. B. White ignored his critics and persevered as a writer of books for children.

JULY 11

Happy Birthday Patricia Polacco (*Thank You Mr. Falker*) and James Stevenson (*What's Under My Bed?*).

It's the birth date of E. B. White (1899–1985), *Stuart Little, Charlotte's Web, The Trumpet of the Swan*.

It's also the birth date of John Quincy Adams (1767–1848), son of President John Adams and himself the sixth president of the United States.

In 1914 **Babe Ruth** made his Major League Baseball debut, as a pitcher for the Boston Red Sox. Read *Home Run: The Story of Babe Ruth* by Robert Burleigh, illustrated by Mike Wimmer; *Babe Ruth Saves Baseball* by Frank Murphy, illustrated by Richard Walz; and *Babe Ruth and the Baseball Curse* by David A. Kelly, illustrated by Tim Jessell.

To Kill a Mockingbird by Harper Lee was published on this day in 1960.

In 1975 the ancient Terra Cotta Warriors were discovered by farmers in Xi'an, China. Read *The Emperor's Silent Army* by Jane O'Connor and *Terra Cotta Warriors: Guardians of China's First Emperor* by Jane Portal.

JULY 12

Happy Birthday Joan Bauer (*Rules of the Road, Sticks*).

It's the birth date of Johanna Spyri (1827–1901), *Heidi*.

It's also the birth date of Pablo Neruda (1904–1973), Chilean poet and political activist. Read *The Dreamer* by Pam Muñoz Ryan and Peter Sís.

In 1859 a paper bag manufacturing machine was patented in Massachusetts. Read *The Paper Bag Princess* by Robert Munsch, illustrated by Michael Martchenko.

 It's Simplicity Day, in honor of **Henry David Thoreau** who was born on this day in 1817.

It's Different-Colored Eyes Day. Read *Kaleidoscope Eyes* by Jen Bryant, *Edward's Eyes* by Patricia MacLachlan, and *Through My Eyes* by Ruby Bridges.

HENRY HIKES TO FITCHBURG

By D. B. Johnson

On July 12, 1817, Henry David Thoreau, American author, poet, naturalist, historian, and philosopher, was born in Concord, Massachusetts. Neighbor to other radical thinkers of his day—Ralph Waldo Emerson, Bronson Alcott (the father of Louisa May Alcott), and Nathaniel Hawthorne—Thoreau believed in living simply. He built a small cabin near Walden Pond, where he lived alone, and then described his experience in his most famous work, *Walden*. In this book, Thoreau argues that rather than riding thirty miles on a train, and having to earn the money to do so, a person would be better walking that distance. "I have learned that the swiftest traveler is he that goes afoot." This concept, developed by artist and storyteller D. B. Johnson, forms the basis of *Henry Hikes to Fitchburg*.

Johnson tried for almost a decade to get one of his picture books published. Finally, when he turned to his idol Henry David Thoreau for inspiration, he found the story that he needed. In this absolutely charming saga, Henry, depicted as a bear, and a friend make a wager: Henry will walk; his friend will work and then take the train. Who will get to Fitchburg, a community thirty miles outside of Boston, first? On one side of each double-page spread, readers see Henry's friend complete a task, on the other they watch Henry enjoy the countryside as he travels. Henry's friend works at the Alcott, Hawthorne, and Emerson homes. Henry carves a walking stick, presses ferns and flowers, rafts down the river, swims, and stops to eat blackberries. Although his friend arrives before him and insists the train was faster, Henry simply replies, "I know. I stopped for blackberries."

Perfect for four- through eight-year-olds, the book introduces the philosophy of the transcendentalists to the very young and raises questions about the best way to spend one's day and live one's life. Cubist-inspired paintings, filled with detail, bring Henry's world vividly to life. In *Henry Hikes to Fitchburg*, Johnson both educates and delights with a simple and powerful story—the perfect way to honor Thoreau and celebrate simplicity.

WORDS TO MY LIFE'S SONG

By Ashley Bryan

Today marks the birthday of author and illustrator Ashley Bryan. Born in Harlem and raised in the Bronx, Ashley has lived on an island off the coast of Maine for many years. He gets to stay there less than he might like, because he is in so much demand as a speaker. Not only has Ashley created his own work, he has championed the work of black poets, such as Paul Laurence Dunbar and Eloise Greenfield. Anyone who has ever heard Ashley perform other poets' words comes away with an entirely new appreciation for them. When I pick up these poets' books, I often hear Ashley's voice. I am sure there are hundreds of readers of the Almanac who have had the same experience.

A few years ago, Ashley published his life story in *Words to My Life's Song.* Growing up in the Bronx during the Depression, he always drew and painted. A World War II veteran who landed on Omaha Beach, Ashley ultimately received degrees from two art schools, Cooper Union and Columbia. After teaching in New York at Queens College and the Dalton School, he headed to New England and became chair of the art department at Dartmouth. In the sixties he began to work with Jean Karl of Atheneum on a series of books. Karl was famous in the industry for her great taste and Ashley Bryan was certainly one of her greatest discoveries.

Ashley initially produced books based on African legends or African-American songs, such as *The Ox of the Wonderful Horns and Other African Tales*, *Walk Together Children: Black American Spirituals*, and *Beat the Story-Drum, Pum-Pum.* While he built up his own canon, he toured throughout the United States, presenting the literature of black writers to thousands of listeners.

Ashley ends *Words to My Life's Song* with this sentence: "This is my story. Whether it be bitter or whether it be sweet, take some of it elsewhere and let the rest come back to me." What I hope will come back to Ashley today, on his birthday, will be lots of love letters, like this one, to him from all his many admirers and fans.

JULY 13

Happy Birthday Marcia Brown (*Stone Soup, Once a Mouse . . . , Shadow*) and Ashley Bryan (*Beautiful Blackbird*).

Best birthday wishes to Ernö Rubik, the Hungarian architect who invented the Rubik's Cube.

Goal! The first-ever FIFA World Cup soccer competition began on this day in 1930 in Montevideo, Uruguay. Read *Tangerine* by Edward Bloor.

It's International Puzzle Day. Read *The Calder Game* by Blue Balliett, illustrated by Brett Helquist, and *From the Mixed-Up Files of Mrs. Basil E. Frankweiler* by E. L. Konigsburg.

It's National French Fries Day. Read *My Mother Is a French Fry and Further Proof of My Fuzzed-Up Life* by Collen Sydor and *French Fries Up Your Nose* by Margaret Ragz.

MEMOIR, PICTURE BOOK, Elementary School, Middle School

JULY 14

Happy Birthday Brian Selznick (*The Invention of Hugo Cabret*) and Laura Numeroff (*If You Give a Mouse a Cookie*).

It's the birth date of Peggy Parish (1927–1988), the Amelia Bedelia series.

It's also the birth date of Gerald R. Ford (1913–2006), the 38th president of the United States.

 Woody Guthrie (1912–1967) was born on this day. Read *This Land Was Made for You and Me: The Life and Songs of Woody Guthrie* by Elizabeth Partridge.

In 1946 Dr. Benjamin Spock's *Common Sense Book of Baby and Child Care* was published. Read *Everywhere Babies* by Susan Meyers, illustrated by Marla Frazee, *Owl Babies* by Martin Waddell, illustrated by Patrick Benson, and *Princess Baby* by Karen Katz.

Happy Bastille Day to our French friends. Read *The Queen of France* by Tim Wadham, illustrated by Kady MacDonald Denton.

THE SATURDAYS
By Elizabeth Enright

July has been designated Make a Difference to Children month. All involved with children's books celebrate this cause year round. Nothing can make more of a difference than the right book for the right child at the right time. In *Everything I Need to Know I Learned from a Children's Book*, both movie critic Roger Ebert and Newbery winner Linda Sue Park have written about Elizabeth Enright's *The Saturdays* as the book that most influenced their lives. The niece of architect Frank Lloyd Wright, Enright studied dance with Martha Graham and illustration at the Art Students League of New York and Parsons The New School for Design. The multitalented Enright discovered she actually liked writing books more than she liked illustrating them. In 1939 when she won the Newbery Medal for *Thimble Summer*, she became one of the youngest writers to receive the honor. She is remembered today not for that Newbery but for the series of books called the Melendy Quartet, which begins with *The Saturdays*.

The four Melendy children—Mona, Rush, Miranda, and Oliver—live with their widowed father and a housekeeper in a New York City brownstone. Quite inventive, the group decides to pool their allowance money. That way one Saturday every month, each of them can do something quite unusual and special. Although the children must practice economy, they can enjoy New York in all its opulence. Randy goes to the art museum; Rush attends the opera; Oliver experiences the circus; Mona goes to the hairdresser. Enright excels at telling details in her work. For instance, when she describes Randy's tea at the hotel she writes, the petit fours have "frilled paper collars . . . with silver peppermint buttons on top." Now, who wouldn't want to have one of those? One of their adventures ultimately leads to a wealthy patron asking them to spend the summer at a lighthouse she just happens to own. A wonderful blend of realism and wish fulfillment, *The Saturdays* and its sequels feature four protagonists that children want either to be or have as friends. As Enright herself wrote, the books have been crafted out of "wishes and memory and fancy."

In *Everything I Need to Know I Learned from a Children's Book*, film critic Roger Ebert says that the Melendy Quartet taught that stories could be wonderful; and many who have encountered these books over the years agree. The series was recently given attractive new covers for the paperback editions. So if you want to make a difference in the life of a child, pick up these books—or any of the others that you favor—to share with them this summer.

LITTLE WOMEN

By Louisa May Alcott

On July 15, 1868, an author who had been known for worthy adult writing—a novel called *Moods* and a Civil War memoir called *Hospital Sketches*—finished the first half of a book that would secure her literary immortality. This was not an adult book but a girl's story. Louisa May Alcott had actually bristled when her editor suggested she write such a manuscript; she had no interest in creating books for girls at all. In her diary she mentions that besides her three sisters she knew very little, if anything, about young women. In the end, however, she had the authority to write for children because she had once been a child.

Always in desperate need of money to support her family, Alcott decided that she and her three sisters might, indeed, provide some intriguing content for a children's book. Beginning in May of 1868, she turned out the first half of *Little Women* in a mere ten weeks. In it she relates the story of the four March girls—beautiful Meg, determined Jo, saintly Beth, and artistic Amy—who struggle with the Civil War, its aftermath, and their poverty. With a modest printing of two thousand copies, the first half of *Little Women*, which appeared in the fall of that year, became an immediate sensation. Alcott finished the rest of the manuscript a few months later, and it was published in March of 1869. The book we know today contains both volumes.

By the time she wrote the rest of the book, Alcott had already heard from enough of her readers to know they universally wanted—much as readers often do today—Jo March to marry the wealthy Laurie, her best friend who loves her. But Alcott, who always claimed that she wanted to paddle her own canoe, had no patience for pat solutions for her beloved female character. Jo would take another, more unconventional, path.

Because of this artistic decision, Jo March may have inspired more women over the years—including Hillary Clinton and French philosopher Simone de Beauvoir—than any other character in a children's book. As actress Julianne Moore says in *Everything I Need to Know I Learned from a Children's Book*, "From Jo I learned that a woman could choose . . . that she has a choice about her career."

I'm glad Louisa May Alcott decided to write this American classic, for it has encouraged readers to think outside the box for over 140 years.

JULY 15

It's the birth date of Clement C. Moore (1779–1863), *The Night Before Christmas*; and Walter Edmonds (1903–1998), *Drums Along the Mohawk*.

The artist Rembrandt (1606–1669) was also born on this day. Read *What Makes a Rembrandt a Rembrandt?* by Richard Mühlberger.

In 1922 the first duck-billed platypus was publicly exhibited in the United States at the New York Zoo. Read *Platypus* by Chris Riddell, *Platypus!* by Ginjer L. Clarke, illustrated by Paul Mirocha, and *A Platypus, Probably* by Sneed B. Collard III, illustrated by Andrew Plant.

It's I Love Horses Day. Read *The Black Stallion* by Walter Farley and *National Velvet* by Enid Bagnold.

JULY 16

Happy birthday Arnold Adoff (*black is brown is tan*), Richard Egielski (*Saint Francis and the Wolf*), and Shirley Hughes (*Alfie* series).

It's the birth date of Eve Titus (1922–2002), *Anatole* series.

 Journalist and newspaper editor **Ida B. Wells** (1862–1931) was born on this day. Read *Ida B. Wells: Mother of the Civil Rights Movement* by Judith Bloom Fradin and Dennis Brindell Fradin; *Ida B. Wells Let the Truth Be Told* by Walter Dean Myers, illustrated by Bonnie Christensen; and *Yours For Justice, Ida B. Wells: The Daring Life of a Crusading Journalist* by Philip Dray, illustrated by Stephen Alcorn.

Happy Birthday Washington, D.C. Congress approved its creation on this day in 1790.

In 1945 the first U.S. atomic bomb test was conducted at Los Alamos, New Mexico. Read *The Green Glass Sea* by Ellen Klages.

J. D. Salinger's *Catcher in the Rye* was first published on this day in 1951.

MY FRIEND RABBIT
By Eric Rohmann

The third week of July has been designated National Rabbit Week. What is it about rabbits that so inspire children's book authors and illustrators? Ever since Peter Rabbit went lippety, lippety down the road, rabbits in children's books have multiplied like—well—bunnies. In *My Friend Rabbit*, winner of the Caldecott Medal, Eric Rohmann introduces one very memorable rabbit to readers ages one through six. Right away on the title page, the tension of the story begins. A large enthusiastic white rabbit stands next to a small mouse, who is seated in an airplane just removed from a beribboned box. Mouse narrates the story: "My friend Rabbit means well. But whatever he does, wherever he goes, trouble follows." Sometimes authors write pages and chapters to develop narrative tension, but Eric Rohmann builds his story with only a few words. In the art, Rabbit sends his friend airborne, in his toy.

A truly visual book, *My Friend Rabbit* develops only a fraction of the story in the text—the rest of the action occurs in the hand-colored, strong black outline relief prints that dominate each page. Like a master stage director, Rohmann draws readers across each page and makes them want to turn it to see what happens. In a series of illustrations Rabbit helps his small friend retrieve the plane now stuck in a tree. Commandeering several large animals, Rabbit piles them on top of each other so that Mouse can reach his toy. Pandamonium ensues when the animals crash to earth—"The animals were not happy." But Rabbit and Mouse go sailing off into the sky . . . until they get stuck once more.

With his glorious images and just a few words, Eric Rohmann allows readers to predict what will happen next. The book has even inspired an animated children's television show based on the characters. Behind the story lies a common dilemma of childhood friendship—what if your slightly larger and older friend has so many good ideas that he or she causes chaos in your life? Randolph Caldecott himself would delight in this energetic and original picture book by one of our most talented author-artists working today.

Just be prepared, when the story finishes for children to say, "Let's read it again." And again. And again.

THE RUNAWAY BUNNY

By Margaret Wise Brown

Illustrated by Clement Hurd

National Rabbit Week would not be complete without one of the most memorable rabbits in picture books: Margaret Wise Brown's *The Runaway Bunny*. Margaret Wise Brown, a graduate of Bank Street College in New York, became one of the first talented writers to focus on the needs of very young children, believing that they wanted to see objects familiar to them in books—the "here and now" philosophy of children's books. She also had a touch of magic and the gift of a poet.

In *The Runaway Bunny*, illustrated by Clement Hurd, a young bunny describes how he will run away and his mother responds with her plans to find him. They go through scenario after scenario until the bunny decides, finally, to stay. For Brown's spare text in this picture book ideal for one- to four-year-olds, Clement Hurd creates watercolors and pencil sketches that provide a perfect visual counterpoint.

Hurd studied painting in Paris under Frederick Leger after Hurd graduated from Yale. For a period of time after he came back to the United States he created public murals. But in the late 1930s he enrolled in the Writer's Laboratory at Bank Street College. There he met his wife Edith Thatcher and was given one of his first books to illustrate by then-editor Margaret Wise Brown. Hurd became one of Brown's favorite illustrators and a collaborator on her most successful books. *The Runaway Bunny*, combining two great talents, attests to a mother's love and devotion. It has never been out of print, or out of favor.

Margaret Wise Brown used rabbit characters to explore human traits and actions. In doing so she created an exciting, funny, and totally satisfying book for preliterate readers. Before they meet Peter Rabbit, young children can master *The Runaway Bunny*.

JULY 17

Happy Birthday Chris Crutcher (*Staying Fat for Sarah Byrnes*).

It's the birth date of Karla Kuskin (1932–2009), *The Philharmonic Gets Dressed*.

In 1861 printing paper money was authorized by Congress to supplement coin shortages in the face of looming Civil War costs.

In 1867 Harvard School of Dental Medicine, the first dental school in the U.S., was established. Read *Doctor De Soto* by William Steig.

In 1897 the first ship arrived in Seattle carrying gold from the Yukon, a Canadian territory. Read *Children of the Gold Rush* by Claire Rudolf Murphy and Jane G. Haigh.

On this day in 1955 Disneyland opened in Anaheim, California.

JULY 18

Happy Birthday Felicia Bond (*If You Give a Mouse a Cookie*) and Ai-Ling Louie (*Yeh-Shen: A Cinderella Story From China*).

 It's Mandela Day. Best birthday wishes to South African peacemaker **Nelson Mandela**. Read *Nelson Mandela: "No Easy Walk to Freedom"* by Barry Denenberg, *Tree Shaker: The Story of Nelson Mandela* by Bill Keller, and *Peaceful Protest: The Life of Nelson Mandela* by Yona Zeldis McDonough, illustrated by Malcah Zeldis.

Adolf Hitler published the first volume of his manifesto, *Mein Kampf,* on this day in 1925. Read *Hitler Youth: Growing Up in Hitler's Shadow* by Susan Campbell Bartoletti.

In 1932 the United States and Canada signed a treaty to develop St. Lawrence Seaway. Read *Paddle-to-the-Sea* by Holling Clancy Holling.

THE STORY OF FERDINAND

By Munro Leaf
Illustrated by Robert Lawson

On July 18, 1936, General Francisco Franco led an uprising of army troops in North Africa against the elected government of Spain. So began the Spanish Civil War, sometimes called "the first media war" because foreign correspondents and writers became involved—people like Ernest Hemingway and George Orwell. One would not expect this event to have much effect, if at all, on American children's books. However, timing is everything and the Spanish Civil War looms large as the defining publicity event for one of our classic picture books, *The Story of Ferdinand.*

This seventy-page saga, illustrated with black-and-white drawings, began as something of a lark. Munro Leaf felt that bunnies and kittens had been done to death in picture books, and he wanted a more memorable protagonist—so he chose a bull. Robert Lawson, who also lived in New York City at the time, delighted in incorporating visual puns and references into his art. For this Depression era book, their publisher Viking printed just around fifteen hundred copies.

Because of the Spanish Civil War, people began to look for political messages in this story about a Spanish bull. Some thought it was Fascist, some Socialist, and some Communist. It was banned in Spain and in Germany as degenerate propaganda. But many opinion makers—including Franklin and Eleanor Roosevelt, Thomas Mann, and H. G. Wells—rose to the book's defense. In children's books, any censorship attempt always sells a lot of books. As a society, we simply don't want anyone telling us what our children should or should not read. The next year, eighty thousand copies were sold, and *The Story of Ferdinand* became a staple on the bestseller list.

Censorship can get books started, but not keep books going. What has sustained *The Story of Ferdinand* over the years is the wonderful interplay between the Leaf's text and Lawson's art. The book does have a message—but not one about the Spanish Civil War. Pete Wentz of the rock group Fall Out Boys recently wrote about *The Story of Ferdinand*: "The book provides an amazing metaphor for how people can be. There's something really honorable about following your own path and not doing what's expected of you. . . . When we are ninety years old and on our deathbeds, it will matter to us that at least we took chances and followed our own path."

Decades after Munro Leaf wrote *The Story of Ferdinand*, young readers still respond to its gentle humor, its advocacy of taking one's own direction, and its happy ending. Just as Leaf and Lawson believed, the book tells the story of a bull that, in the end, was very happy.

RABBIT HILL

By Robert Lawson

For National Rabbit Week, pick up one of our timeless classics. The Newbery Medal winner *Rabbit Hill* has been much loved from the time it was published in 1944 during the height of World War II, at least in part because it seems very contemporary in its concerns.

Robert Lawson was one of those rare creators who could write and illustrate with equal finesse. We have had only a few of these gifted individuals—people like William Steig or Kevin Henkes. Lawson's editor May Massee prodded him for some time to write a rabbit story about the house where he lived, "Rabbit Hill," near Westport, Connecticut. Lawson chose to tell the story from the point of view of the animals who live on the property. New owners are arriving, and Little Georgie, our rabbit hero, along with a woodchuck, fox, squirrel, fieldmouse, mole, skunk, deer, and other woodland creatures, find themselves both excited about the possibilities and worried about the consequences. In the final chapter, "There Is Enough for All," Lawson outlines an early message of ecological interdependence. The simple story explores the complex idea of ecological diversity. It emphasizes how people need to share, get along with others, and cooperate.

As Lawson wrote about the rabbits on his property, he began to notice them behaving in peculiar ways. In fact, any time good news occurred about the book, a rabbit seemed to herald its arrival. One time a rabbit hopped with him to the mailbox where he found a letter accepting the book. Later, he saw a rabbit sitting on the lawn, staring at him through the window. It had been months after the publication of the book, and Lawson thought nothing more could be happening to the book. How wrong he was. That day he received a letter congratulating him on the Newbery Medal!

Lawson had won the Caldecott Medal for his 1941 book, *They Were Strong and Good*. To this day, he remains the only person to win both the Newbery and Caldecott Medals.

JULY 19

It's the birth date of Eve Merriam (1916–1992), *The Inner City Mother Goose*; and John Newbery (1713–1767), *The History of Little Goody Two-Shoes, A Little Pretty Pocket Book*.

Artist Edgar Degas (1834–1917) was also born on this day. Read *Dancing with Degas* by Julie Merberg and Suzanne Bober.

In 1799 the Rosetta Stone, a tablet with hieroglyphic translations into Greek, was found in Egypt.

In 1692 five women were accused of witchcraft and hung in Salem, Massachusetts. Read *The Witch of Blackbird Pond* by Elizabeth George Speare.

The first Women's Rights convention in the U.S. was held on this day in 1848, at Seneca Falls, New York. The convention was attended by Amelia Bloomer, who wore and advocated for long loose trousers for women, which came to be known as Bloomers. Read *You Forgot Your Skirt, Amelia Bloomer* by Shana Corey and Chesley McLaren.

In 1954 J.R.R. Tolkien's *Lord of the Rings* (Book 1) was published.

JULY 20

Happy Birthday Mark Buehner (*The Escape of Marvin the Ape, My Life with the Wave*).

It's the birth date of explorer Sir Edmund Hillary (1919–2008). Read *Mount Everest and Beyond: Sir Edmund Hillary* by Sue Muller Hacking and *The Top of the World: Climbing Mount Everest* by Steve Jenkins.

 In 1881 Sioux leader **Sitting Bull** surrendered to U.S. troops. Read *Sitting Bull Remembers* by Ann Turner, illustrated by Wendell Minor.

It's Moon Day! In 1969 Apollo 11 was the first manned spacecraft to land on the moon. Read *Moonshot: The Flight of Apollo 11* by Brian Floca.

It's also National Lollipop Day. Read *Big Red Lollipop* by Rukhsana Khan, illustrated by Sophie Blackall; *Lady Lollipop* by Dick King-Smith, illustrated by Jill Barton; *Many Luscious Lollipops: A Book about Adjectives* by Ruth Heller; and *Amanda Pig and Her Best Friend Lollipop* by Jean Van Leeuwen, illustrated by Ann Schweninger.

LOST & FOUND
By Shaun Tan

For National Rabbit Week a book by Shaun Tan, *Lost & Found*, takes an entirely original look at this furry creature. Containing three separate books that were previously unavailable in the United States, *Lost & Found* presents *The Red Tree*, *Lost & Found*, and *The Rabbits*.

The last story was written by Australian writer John Marsden. For my money the books in Marsden's Tomorrow When the War Began series happen to be among the best dystopian novels written for children. In *The Rabbits*, Marsden found inspiration in both Australian and American history, drawing on Allan W. Eckert's history of Tecumseh, *A Sorrow in Our Heart*.

In this incredibly disquieting story, the rabbits arrive by water and keep coming and coming. They crowd out the original settlers and decimate the landscape. In a desolate ending Marsden asks, "Where is the smell of rain dripping from the gum tree? Where are the great billabongs, the river-swollen lakes, alive with long-legged birds? Who will save us from the rabbits?"

The Rabbits—with its exploration of history, colonization, and ecology—is made even more powerful by Tan's surreal illustrations. Tan opens the saga with a beautiful spread of long-legged birds, which at the end become small flecks against the dark, heading out from the land. The art becomes darker in palette as the story moves to its sad conclusion.

A great book for discussion, *Lost & Found* was adapted for an animated short film that won Tan an Oscar. With imagery that might well have come from the fevered imagination of Hieronymus Bosch, Tan creates picture books with philosophical, historical, or emotional issues at their core. Each story causes the reader to pause, think about the issues raised, and then go back and pore over the pictures because so much detail has been incorporated in the art.

I am simply in awe of Shaun Tan's talent. He is an artist's artist, who in the twenty-first century is changing our vision of what can be accomplished in a picture book.

BULL RUN

By Paul Fleischman

From 2011 to 2015 the sesquicentennial of the Civil War is celebrated. Although the war began 150 years ago, many contemporary issues can be discussed with children using the Civil War as a starting place.

July 21 marks the first battle in the war—the South called it the Battle of First Manassas and the North, the First Battle of Bull Run. Picnickers came from Washington, D.C., with hampers of food and champagne to watch the grand spectacle. Untrained Union and Confederate troops experienced brutal conflict for the first time.

In 1993 Newbery winner Paul Fleischman published an amazing work of fiction, *Bull Run*. Winner of the Scott O'Dell Award for Historical Fiction, the story is narrated by sixteen different characters who experience the events that day. Union and Confederate, black and white, male and female, from alternating points of view they reveal their hopes for the battle, and its grim realities. Ideal for readers' theater, the book works best if read independently by those who know something of Civil War history and the details of the battle. One of Fleischman's finest pieces of writing, *Bull Run* is powerful, beautifully crafted, spare, and haunting; it captures how individuals experienced the horrors of the Civil War.

While Fleishman's *Bull Run* is best for a more knowledgeable reader, Michael Hempill and Sam Riddleburger's 2009 book, *Stonewall Hinkleman and the Battle of Bull Run*, is perfect for the average young reader who knows little of the Civil War. The son of fanatic Civil War reenactors, Stonewall Hinkleman finds himself carted around by his parents to various events. He hates having to wear hot scratchy uniforms and being deprived of contemporary electronic games. At Bull Run, he finds himself transported back to the real battle, where he needs to keep another reenactor from changing history forever. Hemphill and Riddleburger provide a lot of action, excitement, and details of the actual battle. The book makes a great introduction to the Civil War for any third through seventh grade child you might be dragging to a Civil War battlefield this summer.

If you haven't ever gone to see some of the hallowed ground of the Civil War, both books together might convince you that you should. Only then do you truly understand the fragility and the importance of the phrase, "The United States of America."

JULY 21

It's the birth date of John Gardner (1933–1982), *A Child's Bestiary*.

Ernest Hemingway (1899–1961), author of the classics *The Old Man and the Sea*, *The Sun Also Rises*, and *A Farewell to Arms*, was also born on this day. Read *Ernest Hemingway: A Writer's Life* by Catherine Reef and *Turtle in Paradise* by Jennifer L. Holm.

On this day in 1969 **Neil Armstrong** was the first person to walk on the moon. Read *One Giant Leap: The Story of Neil Armstrong* by Don Brown and *Neil Armstrong Is My Uncle and Other Lies Muscle Man McGinty Told Me* by Nan Marino.

In 2007 *Harry Potter and the Deathly Hallows* by J. K. Rowling, the last volume in the wizard series, went on sale.

It's National Tug-of-War Day. Read *The Great Tug of War* by Beverley Naidoo, illustrated by Piet Grobler.

JULY 22

Happy Birthday S. E. Hinton (*The Outsiders, Rumble Fish*) and Carole Byard (*Working Cotton*).

It's the birth date of Margery Williams (1881–1944), *The Velveteen Rabbit*.

Emma Lazarus (1849–1887), the American poet whose words are on the Statue of Liberty, was born on this day. Read *Liberty's Voice: The Emma Lazarus Story* by Erica Silverman, illustrated by Stacy Shuett.

Also born on this day was artist **Edward Hopper** (1882–1967). Read *Edward Hopper: Painter of Light and Shadow* by Susan Goldman Rubin.

In 1620 a group English religious dissenters now known as the Pilgrims boarded a ship named the *Mayflower* and set sail for what they considered to be the New World. Read *. . . If You Sailed on the Mayflower in 1620* by Ann McGovern and Anna DiVito.

Happy Birthday to the city of Albany, New York, chartered in 1686. Read *River of Dreams: The Story of the Hudson River* by Hudson Talbott and *Hudson River: An Adventure from the Mountains to the Sea* by Peter Lourie.

It's Hammock Day. Read *The Terrible, Wonderful Tellin' at Hog Hammock* by Kim Siegleson, illustrated by Ereic Velasquez, and *Moxie Maxwell Does Not Love Stuart Little* by Peggy Giffors, photographs by Valorie Fisher.

LIZZIE BRIGHT AND THE BUCKMINSTER BOY

By Gary D. Schmidt

July has been designated Make a Difference in the Life of a Child Month. One of the most powerful books of the last decade, Gary Schmidt's *Lizzie Bright and the Buckminster Boy* has been changing the lives of children since it was published.

In a story that begins in July of 1912, Turner Buckminster III, the son of the new Congregational preacher in a small Maine town, believes that when he looks through the number at the end of his name, he is glancing through prison bars. Coming from the city, he doesn't know how to play the local brand of baseball, or plunge into the swimming hole, or say or do anything right. Everyone in the small town of Phippsburg tells his father everything Turner does and their opinion about it. But he finally finds a friend: Lizzie Bright Griffin, a smart and adventurous girl who lives in the poor community founded by former slaves on Malaga Island. In this well-researched and beautifully written historical novel, which explores Northern racial prejudice after the Civil War, the residents of the town don't want a white boy and black girl to be friends—they don't even want African Americans to be living on the island of Malaga.

The true and heart-wrenching story of Malaga Island is successfully woven into a story of a young boy trying to find an acceptable place in a community and a friend he can trust. Gary D. Schmidt offers no happy solutions—nor did history. The book explores so many important themes: the difference between the words Christians preach and their actions, the right of individuals to be different, and how God can be found in nature.

In this poignant coming-of-age story, Gary Schmidt magnificently re-creates the Maine landscape and the characters of two sensitive young people. If you can't get to Maine in July, pick up *Lizzie Bright and the Buckminster Boy*—you will feel like you are visiting this rare and special state when you do.

THE PIGEON FINDS A HOT DOG!

By Mo Willems

Today is National Hot Dog Day, and July is National Hot Dog Month. So it seems a good time to focus on hot dogs, one of America's favorite and "most patriotic" foods according to promoters.

Although the book of the day seems like a natural for publication, Mo Willems's first book, *Don't Let the Pigeon Drive the Bus*, was rejected again and again. Fortunately, he had an agent who believed in him: Marcia Wernick of Wernick & Pratt Agency. She thought he had all the right stuff to be "a hot dog" in the children's book world. Finally, she found a just-hired editor, hunting for projects, who was willing to take a chance on this funny and offbeat story.

Once Mo Willems got published, wild enthusiasm for his books took over. Some of his titles such as *Don't Let the Pigeon Drive the Bus*, *Knuffle Bunny*, and the book of the day, *The Pigeon Finds a Hot Dog!*, seem destined to sit alongside Dr. Seuss on the picture book classics shelf.

The Pigeon Finds a Hot Dog! opens with endpapers depicting multiple hot dogs in a style reminiscent of Andy Warhol's Campbell's soup cans. A pigeon and a duckling spy a hot dog, but Pigeon picks it up first, ready to chomp into his discovery. "Is that a hot dog?" whispers the ducking. And so the two battle each other for the treat—"Each morsel is a joy! A celebration in a bun!" shouts Pigeon. As Pigeon struggles with his conscience, he gets louder and louder, but the duck remains softly persistent. In the end, they both discover the joy of sharing.

JULY 23

Happy Birthday Margaree King Mitchell (*Uncle Jed's Barbershop*), Robert Quackenbush (*Henry's Awful Mistake*), and Patricia Coombs (*Dorrie and the Haunted Schoolhouse*).

In 1881 the Fédération Internationale de Gymnastique was founded, the world's oldest international sports federation. More than a hundred years later, in 1996, the U.S. Women's Gymnastics Team, known as "The Magnificent Seven," won a team gold for the first time ever. Read *The Greatest Gymnast of All* by Stuart J. Murphy, illustrated by Cynthia Jabar.

On this day in 1914 Austria and Hungary issued an ultimatum to Serbia after the assassination of Archduke Ferdinand, sowing the seeds of World War I. Read *Leviathan* by Scott Westerfeld, illustrated by Keith Thompson.

In 1973 President **Richard Nixon** refused to release tapes of White House conversations relevant to the Watergate investigation. Read *So You Want to Be President?* by Judith St. George, illustrated by David Small.

Mo Willems brings his years of television animation work to developing a clear story and dynamic action from page to page in this book for young readers ages two through six. He utilizes all parts of this fabulously funny work to extend the story. On the back cover Pigeon holds up his reviews for *Don't Let the Pigeon Drive the Bus* and comments on them—"Can those guys at *The Horn Book* review or what?"

Reading the book of the day will make everyone want to celebrate National Hot Dog Day.

JULY 24

It's the birth date of Esther Averill (1902–1992), *The Fire Cat*.

It's also the birth date of aviator Amelia Earhart (1897–1939). Hence, it is Amelia Earhart Day. Read *Amelia and Eleanor Go for a Ride* by Pam Muñoz Ryan, illustrated by Brian Selznick.

Happy Birthday to Detroit, which was founded in 1701 in what would eventually become the state of Michigan. Read *Antoine de la Mothe Cadillac: French Settlements in Detroit and Louisiana* by Anders Kundsen and *These Hands* by Margaret H. Mason, illustrated by Floyd Cooper.

It's Tell an Old Joke Day. Read *Old Turtle's 90 Knock-Knocks, Jokes, and Riddles* by Leonard Kessler.

SKELLIG
By David Almond

July has been designated Make a Difference in the Life of a Child Month. The right book for the right child has and always will change lives. The book of the day is one that can be very powerful when it gets in a child's hands at the right moment.

Ideal for ten- to fourteen-year-olds, *Skellig* tells the story of ten-year-old Michael, who is moving with his family into a new house in England. There's a baby, yet unnamed, in the family, but she has been in and out of the hospital, hanging tentatively on to life. So besides the normal moving worries, Michael must deal with a loving but preoccupied mother and father who have to focus on taking care of a sick infant.

In the new house's dilapidated, collapsing garage, Michael stumbles upon an old man, half dead, who the boy secretly begins to feed and care for. Eventually he tells his friend, Mina—she is the only person he trusts with his secret. For Skellig, as the man calls himself, may not be a mortal man at all. At one point, Mina and Michael discover that he has wings—and in a magical scene he takes them flying. Owls also feed Skellig, although he seems to prefer Michael's Chinese takeout. He mumbles and rants, but he also makes sense in a prophetic and illogical way.

The book alternates between the almost dreamlike sequences where Michael deals with Skellig, and the realistic chapters focusing on his school and the baby's declining health. During the day-to-day events, Mina tells Michael about William Blake. Skellig is just the kind of creature Blake would invent.

Finally, the two parts of the story intertwine, when Michael's mother dreams of Skellig visiting the baby in the hospital. The baby begins to mend—and Skellig bids farewell to his friends who have brought him back to life.

A book of magical realism, *Skellig* does not read like any other novel written for children. It explores the healing power of love and a sense of spiritual wonder. Although it can be enjoyed for independent reading, it begs for a book discussion group so that everyone can talk about their own understanding of its contents. My sense of the book changes each time I read it. However the reader experiences *Skellig*, it remains one of those haunting, amazing novels for children that can be appreciated by the adults who find it as well.

TAR BEACH

By Faith Ringgold

July has been designated National Black Family Month, a month for black Americans "to invest in their families as well as themselves." The organizers hope that participants will have family reunions, dinners, or network with each other.

Today I want to focus on one of the most magical family dinners ever portrayed. Faith Ringgold created her first children's book, *Tar Beach*, winner of a Caldecott Honor, not from pencil and paper but from one of the story quilts that made her famous. In 1988, she finished five story quilts, part of the "Woman on a Bridge" series, now owned by the Guggenheim Museum. As a descendant of Southern slaves, Ringgold decided to use one of their artistic formats, the patchwork quilt, to tell modern stories based on her own childhood.

Cassie, the narrator of *Tar Beach*, dreams of being free and flying over New York City and the George Washington Bridge, which she can see from her Harlem apartment. Her fantasy of flying stands in juxtaposition to the reality of her life in a crowded apartment and busy city. On this evening in 1939, Cassie and her mother, father, and brother have a sumptuous dinner with Mr. and Mrs. Honey on the rooftop of their building, which they call tar beach. As the adults play cards, the children stretch out on the tiny rooftop with views of stars and skyscrapers and look at floodlights in the sky: "I owned all that I could see. The bridge was my most prized possession."

JULY 25

It's the birth date of Ruth Kraus (1901–1993), *The Carrot Seed, A Hole Is to Dig*.

Early twentieth-century illustrator **Maxfield Parrish** (1870–1966) was also born on this day. Read *The Knave of Hearts* and *Maxfield Parrish: A Treasury of Art and Children's Literature* edited by Alma Gilbert.

It's the anniversary of the first flight from France across the English Channel in 1909. Read *The Glorious Flight: Across the Channel with Louise Bleriot* by Alice and Martin Provensen.

In 1952 Puerto Rico became a self-governing commonwealth of the United States. Read *Puerto Rico in American History* by Richard Worth and *The Song of el Coqui and Other Tales of Puerto Rico* by Nicholasa Mohr and Antonio Martorell.

It's Merry-Go-Round Day. Read *Merry-Go-Round: A Book about Nouns* by Ruth Heller and *Up and Down on the Merry-Go-Round* by Bill Martin Jr. and John Archambault, illustrated by Ted Rand.

Although the book explores how wonderful everyday life can be with enough imagination, it also contains a somber note: Cassie's father can't join the workers' union because of his racial heritage. But in the end, the book celebrates a family dinner of roasted peanuts, fried chicken, and watermelon, made even more delectable by the setting. In short, this is perfect summer's evening caught forever in one of Faith Ringgold's quilts—and also in this lyrical children's book.

Wherever you head for family dinner, be sure to bring along *Tar Beach*. For all families it celebrates the small moments of life and the strength of family ties and community.

JULY 26

Happy Birthday Jan Berenstain (Berenstain Bears series).

In 1775 the U.S. Postal service was established. Benjamin Franklin served as the first postmaster general. Read *Ben and Me* by Robert Lawson.

In 1788 New York was the 11th state to ratify the U.S. Constitution.

Happy Birthday to the Federal Bureau of Investigation (FBI), established in 1908. The Central Intelligence Agency (CIA) was also established on this day in 1947 by the U.S. National Security Act. Read *Al Capone Does My Shirts* by Gennifer Choldenko and *Deterring and Investigating Attack: The Role of the FBI and CIA* by Jennifer Keeley.

It's All or Nothing Day. Read *Nothing At All* by Wanda Gág and *How to Do Nothing with Nobody All Alone by Yourself* by Robert Paul Smith, illustrated by Elinor Goulding Smith.

MISTY OF CHINCOTEAGUE

By Marguerite Henry
Illustrated by Wesley Dennis

Around this time of year the annual pony-penning contest takes place on Chincoteague Island. Since 1925, around fifty thousand people gather each year to watch 150 wild ponies herded off Assateague Island. The horses swim across the channel, are rounded up, examined, and auctioned. If you aren't in Virginia at this time, you can watch some clips from the event on YouTube.

Or, even better, you can read Marguerite Henry's *Misty of Chincoteague.* Henry's editor encouraged her to write about the pony penning on the island, and Henry and her illustrator Wesley Dennis headed to Virginia to make sketches, take photographs, and get a sense of the place. She visited the Beebe Ranch and saw one of their horses with white markings that looked like a map of America on her coat. Because Henry desperately wanted this animal to come stay with her in Illinois, she bargained with Mr. Beebe, offering to make his children the two main characters in her novel. Henry kept her word and wrote a story about Maureen and Paul Beebe who long for one of the wild ponies, descendants of a stallion named Fire Chief who was traveling on a Spanish ship that went down in a gale. The children eventually manage to raise enough money to buy Misty.

After Henry returned to her home, Misty came to stay in her household. When Henry wrote, she brought Misty into her studio and even allowed the horse access to the living room. Once the story was finished, Henry took the horse on book tour, and Misty sold a lot of copies. Henry visited schools, libraries, and book shows. In 1948, when Henry won the Newbery Medal for *King of the Wind*, she even brought Misty to the American Library Association Annual Convention in Grand Rapids, Michigan, where Misty was made an honorary member of the ALA—probably the only horse to become one. Modern children's book authors often consider themselves quite clever when it comes to book promotion—but I have never seen any idea as brilliant as touring with Misty of Chincoteague.

Misty eventually returned to the Beebe farm, had colts, and lived to the age of twenty-six. Because some of the ranch has been preserved, those who visit the island can still see it. In fact, most of the people who now travel to Chincoteague to witness pony-penning days will be coming to these events because of this beloved book, one of the greatest horse stories ever told.

WHALES ON STILTS!
By M. T. Anderson

It is amazing how many holidays exist, and what strange ones some of them are. Today is National Walk on Stilts Day. According to those who observe this day, walking on stilts allows you to build coordination and have a lot of fun at the same time. The holiday organizers want you to get out, give stilts a try, and enjoy acting like a clown for a day.

If taking up stilts seems a bit farfetched as a sport, you might want to read *Whales on Stilts!* But that book may be even more bizarre than National Walk on Stilts Day. Here's the first sentence of M. T. Anderson's amazing story: "On Career Day Lily visited her dad's work with him and discovered he worked for a mad scientist who wanted to rule the earth through destruction and desolation." From that opening line the story careens from one strange event to another.

The mad scientist Larry—part whale and part human, who keeps a bag over his head and douses himself with brine—hates the earth and wants to dominate it. So he has invented electronic gear to control all the whales on the planet, equipped them with laser-beam eyes, and made stilts for them to use in an invasion. Unfortunately for Larry, who is smarter than your usual half human and half whale, Lily and her two friends Katie Mulligan, the star of a mystery book series, and Jasper Dash, Boy Technonaut, devise endless ways to foil his plot. But not before the whales on stilts create a lot of havoc in their hometown.

Virtually every line in this book is hilarious—even the author's note jokes that Anderson divides his time between the sofa and the floor. The book spoofs thirties and forties series fiction like the Hardy Boys and Nancy Drew, but it works, in itself, as a funny, page-turning adventure. Anderson wrote the book during a Canadian vacation and admits that he had a blast doing it; he says it was "an expression of pure joy." He only hopes that readers have as much fun with the book as he had writing it—and they do!

If you like these characters—and what's not to like about them?—you can continue their exploits in other Pals in Peril books, like *Jasper Dash and the Flame-Pits of Delaware* and *Agent Q, or the Smell of Danger*. I wonder if there is a National Jump into a Flame Pit day? If not, you don't really need a holiday to have a great time with a Pals in Peril story by M. T. Anderson. You just have to be ready to laugh.

JULY 27

Happy Birthday Paul B. Janeczko (*A Poke in the I: A Collection of Concrete Poems, A Kick in the Head: An Everyday Guide to Poetic Forms*).

It's the birth date of Paul Laurence Dunbar (1872–1906), *Jump Back, Honey.*

On this day in 1931 thousands of acres of crops in Iowa, Nebraska, and South Dakota were destroyed by grasshopper swarms. Read *Storm in the Barn* by Matt Phelan.

For Walk on Stilts Day, you might want to also read *The King's Stilts* by Dr. Seuss.

JULY 28

Happy Birthday Jim Davis (*Garfield* series), Jon J. Muth (*Zen Shorts*), and Natalie Babbitt (*Tuck Everlasting*).

Best birthday wishes to the city of Miami, Florida, established in 1886. Read *It's Hot and Cold in Miami* by Nicole Rubel and *Miami-Nanny Stories* by Linda Milstein, illustrated by Oki S. Han.

In 1914 World War I begins when Austria-Hungary declares war on Serbia. Read *The War to End All Wars: World War I* by Russell Freedman.

It's National Milk Chocolate Day. Read *Charlie and the Chocolate Factory* by Roald Dahl and *The Chocolate War* by Robert Cormier.

THE TALE OF PETER RABBIT

By Beatrix Potter

On July 28, 1866, one year after the end of the American Civil War, a baby girl was born into an affluent English family. She would eventually create the world's bestselling picture book. As a child Helen Beatrix Potter loved drawing both images of the natural world and of the multitude of pets her family kept—rabbits, mice, newts, and a hedgehog named Mrs. Tiggy-Winkle.

In 1893 she sent a letter to a sick child, telling a story about one of those rabbits, Peter. In 1901, at age thirty-five, she decided to fashion that story into a small book for children. In this story, Peter disobeys his mother, loses his way, and nearly loses his life in Mr. McGregor's garden. The English publishers she consulted turned the project down, so Potter drew on her family resources and self-published 250 copies. Because the book was immediately a hit in bookshops, one of the publishers who had turned her down, Frederick Warne, offered her a contract.

As Potter and her editor worked on the book, it became tighter. At Warne's insistence, every piece of art was printed in full color. When *The Tale of Peter Rabbit* was released in the fall of 1902, it sold 56,000 copies in England in the next year, a remarkable sale then—a good one even now. In exquisite artwork, Peter is portrayed as a real rabbit, one who goes "lippety-lippety" when he walks, and has strong hind legs and sensitive whiskers.

Potter would follow her success with other fabulous titles over the next few years—*The Tale of Squirrel Nutkin*, *The Tailor of Gloucester*, and *The Tale of Two Bad Mice*. Almost the entire Potter canon, twenty-four books, has remained in print for around a century, a record that no other children's book creator can even approach. One can study her books for so many things: animal behavior, realistic drawing, superb vocabulary, and concise writing. In *Everything I Need to Know I Learned from a Children's Book*, author Ken Follett discusses how *The Story of a Fierce Bad Rabbit* is the shortest thriller on record: "In just 141 words it presents suspense, crime, gunplay, and retributive justice. . . . It still teaches me how to write."

Happy birthday to Beatrix Potter. It is impossible to imagine picture books for children without the ones that she created.

BLUEBERRIES FOR SAL

By Robert McCloskey

July has been designated National Blueberry Month, to alert the public that this is the best time for fresh blueberries. One of the most beloved children's books of all time celebrates this delicious fruit: Robert McCloskey's *Blueberries for Sal*. McCloskey was allowed to use only one color in the book. Most artists would have selected black, but he chose a dark blueberry ink for his art, totally appropriate for the story he wanted to tell. Just like *One Morning in Maine*, *Blueberries for Sal* presents another personal look at the McCloskey family in their home setting.

Sal and her mother travel up Blueberry Hill to pick enough fruit to preserve. However, Sal can never quite fill her pail, because the berries taste so good. They both independently encounter a mother bear and cub who are also hunting for their own sweet food. Readers hear the berries "*kuplink, kuplank, kuplunk!*" as they hit the pail; they can see the berries and almost taste them. McCloskey draws on all the senses as he weaves this simple but totally satisfying story of daily life. The endpapers extend the text, showing Mother and Sal as they preserve blueberries in an old-fashioned kitchen with a Garmen stove. Inevitably, this book brings a request to "read it again." Parents and teachers have been reading and rereading McCloskey's Caldecott Honor book *Blueberries for Sal* for more than six decades.

JULY 29

Happy Birthday Sharon Creech (*Walk Two Moons, Love That Dog*) and Kathleen Krull (*Lives of the Musicians*).

In 1914 transcontinental telephone service began with the first phone conversation between New York and San Francisco. Read *Telephone* by Kornei Chukovsky, illustrated by Vladimir Radunsky, translated by Jamey Gambrell, and *Tingleberries, Tucketubs and Telephones* by Margaret Mahy, illustrated by Robert Staermose.

Happy Birthday NASA, the U.S. National Aeronautics and Space Administration, established in 1958. Read *Orbit: NASA Astronauts Photograph the Earth* by Jay Apt, Michael Helfer, and Justin Wilkinson and *Team Moon: How 400,000 People Landed Apollo 11 on the Moon* by Catherine Thimmesh.

The last Friday in July is National Talk in an Elevator Day. Read *Charlie and the Great Glass Elevator* by Roald Dahl.

In 1991 Robert McCloskey made a rare foray away from his Maine home to tour and celebrate the Fiftieth anniversary of *Make Way for Ducklings*. Because I was editor of *The Horn Book Magazine* at the time, I had a chance to spend most of a day with him in Boston, interviewing him for a radio program. He had been my hero since my childhood—and I was equally enchanted as an adult. I still feel that having time to talk to this amazing and gentle individual was one of the highlights of my career.

Blueberries, by the way, are believed to improve memory. Even if you don't have the memory of meeting Robert McCloskey, you can share some time with him and his family in Maine, just by picking up a copy of *Blueberries for Sal*.

JULY 30

Happy Birthday Marcus Pfister (*The Rainbow Fish*).

It's the birth date of Emily Brontë (1818–1848), *Wuthering Heights*.

It's also the birth date of **Henry Ford** (1863–1947). Read *Driven: A Photobiography of Henry Ford* by Don Mitchell.

Happy Birthday to Baltimore, Maryland, founded in 1729. Read *Goliath: Hero of the Great Baltimore Fire* by Claudia Friddell, illustrated by Troy Howell, and *Anna All Year Round* by Mary Downing Hahn, illustrated by Diane de Groat.

In 1942 WAVES (Woman Appointed for Volunteer Emergency Services), the women's section of the U.S. Navy, was established. Read *Women Heroes of World War II* by Kathryn J. Atwood.

It's National Cheesecake Day. Read *The Cheese* by Margie Palatini, illustrated by Steve Johnson and Lou Fancher, and *Who Made This Cake?* by Chihiro Nakagawa, illustrated by Junji Koyose.

NUMBER THE STARS
By Lois Lowry

On July 30, 1935, the modern paperback revolution began when Sir Allen Lane published the first Penguin paperback. I have always been grateful that he was knighted for this achievement—and that in the United States, beginning in the sixties, paperback books for children became a staple of publishing lists. Although I love hardcover books, I must admit that today's paperbacks often look just as nice as the original—and, of course, their price allows many more children to have access to these books. This is true of the book of the day, Lois Lowry's *Number the Stars*.

In 1989 Lois Lowry, who has distinguished herself by the range and quality of her writing for children, tackled the subject of the Holocaust in a book for fourth through seventh graders. One of the hallmarks of the Lowry canon rests in her ability to bring complex subjects into the emotional and intellectual range of children. For years Lois had listened to the stories of her friend Annelise Platt, who experienced World War II as a youngster in Denmark. By creating an engaging and sympathetic Danish child, Annemarie, Lowry found a way to depict the events of World War II in Denmark as a child would experience them.

Ten-year-old Annemarie Johansen and her Jewish friend Ellen are inseparable, and their mothers are also best friends. When Nazi soldiers begin the round up of the Jews, Annemarie's family hides Ellen and gets the girl and her parents to Uncle Henrik, who runs a fishing operation near Sweden and can take them to freedom. Because part of the plan goes awry, Annemarie must travel, in the dark of night, with a basket for her uncle—one that contains a handkerchief that will confuse the Nazi dogs' sense of smell.

Each chapter has been beautifully crafted. From the first moments when Annemarie encounters Nazi soldiers to the final page when Denmark has been freed, readers stay with her and hope that she makes the right choices. The life of her best friend rests on the thin shoulders of this child. Ultimately, *Number the Stars* explores the issue of taking political action, even if to do so might mean death. The book also shows Denmark at one of its finest hours in history—a time when the citizens banded together, forgetting religious differences.

In a recent paperback edition, Lowry provides an introduction to her classic. She says that ten "is an age when young people are beginning to develop a strong set of personal ethics. They want to be honorable people. They want to do the right thing." Used in many schools, read independently, shared in families, *Number the Stars* shows one of the darkest periods of world history and brings light and beauty into the landscape.

HARRY POTTER AND THE SORCERER'S STONE

By J. K. Rowling

Today marks the birthday of the world's best-known literary character. He has taken his place along with Sherlock Holmes and Winnie the Pooh as a household name. And he's only been around since 1998.

Harry Potter emerged in the mind of his creator J. K. Rowling on a train trip. Today everyone wants to be like J. K. Rowling. Celebrities and people who never thought of writing a children's book are all enticed by her wealth and notoriety. I doubt that many would choose her early path as a novelist. Almost every publisher in England rejected the manuscript of *Harry Potter*; she had to persevere for years with a story that seemed to be only of interest to her. Finally, she found a recently-hired editor new to the field in a small publishing house: Barry Cunningham of Bloomsbury Press was willing to take a chance on her book. For around a thousand dollars he acquired the rights to publish the first book about Harry Potter, and when he called her in for an editorial meeting, he told her that she needed to get a job, because "Nobody, absolutely nobody, ever makes any money in children's books."

Why does Harry intrigue so many people? His saga combines an orphan story, a school story, magic, adventure, and page-turning drama. Certainly the seven books about him are among the most child-friendly volumes of the last two decades. Not only does Harry have loyal and wonderful friends like Ron and Hermione, but he also encounters interesting adults like Albus Dumbledore and Professor Snape. After I read *Harry Potter*, I had a new life goal—some day I want to teach Defense Against the Dark Arts at Hogwarts. Millions of other readers have projected themselves into the stories in entirely different roles.

In very short order after the publication of the first book, the world became wild about Harry Potter. Now there are more than four hundred million copies of Harry Potter books in print. So happy birthday, Harry. For a couple of decades you have fought and won a battle against "you know who" and also convinced millions of young children, who thought they didn't like to read, that books can be exciting. Also happy birthday to J. K. Rowling; by some strange coincidence she shares this birthday with her most famous literary character.

JULY 31

Happy Birthday Muriel Feelings (*Jambo Means Hello*), Robert Kimmel Smith (*The War with Grandpa*), J. K. Rowling (Harry Potter series), and Lynne Reid Banks (*The Indian in the Cupboard*).

In 1790 the first U.S. patent was granted. Read *So You Want to Be an Inventor* by Judith St. George, illustrated by David Small.

Shredded Wheat, now considered a breakfast cereal, was invented by Henry Perky in 1893. Read *Quirky, Jerky, Extra Perky* by Brian P. Cleary, illustrated by Brian Gable, and *A Plump and Perky Turkey* by Teresa Bateman, illustrated by Jeff Shelly.

AUGUST 1

Happy Birthday Michael Martchenko (*The Paper Bag Princess*), Gail Gibbons (*The Vegetables We Eat*, *The Reasons for Seasons*), Bill Wallace (*The Backward Bird Dog*, *A Dog Called Kitty*), and Sheila Hamanaka (*All the Colors of the Earth*, *I Look Like a Girl*).

It's the birth date of Herman Melville (1779–1843), *Moby Dick*.

 Also born on this day was **Francis Scott Key** (1779–1843), composer of "The Star-Spangled Banner." Read *The Star-Spangled Banner* illustrated by Peter Spier and *Francis Scott Key and "The Star-Spangled Banner"* by Lynea Bowdish, illustrated by Harry Burman.

Happy Birthday Colorado, which became the 38th U.S. state on this day in 1876. Read *Hard Gold: The Colorado Gold Rush of 1859* by Avi.

Anne Frank's last diary entry was written on this day in 1944.

In 1872 the first long-distance gas pipeline in the U.S. was completed. Designed for natural gas, the two-inch pipe ran five miles from Newton Wells to Titusville, Pennsylvania.

It's Get Ready for Kindergarten month. Read *Miss Bindergarten Gets Ready for Kindergarten* by Joseph Slate, illustrated by Ashley Wolff.

TUCK EVERLASTING
By Natalie Babbitt

"If you had to choose only one children's book, which one would it be?" I am often asked that difficult question. Fortunately, I have not yet been marooned on a desert island with only one book to last me for the rest of my life. But I do have a book to offer up as an answer. This book begins during the first week of August: "The first week of August hangs at the very top of summer, the top of the live-long year, like the highest seat of a Ferris wheel when it pauses in its turning." In *Tuck Everlasting*, a novel published in 1975 and only 139 pages long, Natalie Babbitt explores a question she had been concerned about as a child: What if you could live forever?

In this story, eleven-year-old Winnie Foster decides to explore the woods her family owns. There she finds a strange family, the Tucks, who have discovered a source of water that will give the drinker immortality. Rather than counting this a blessing, the Tucks have found living forever a hard burden for eighty-seven years. They have to keep moving. They cannot form relationships with people outside their family because other people grow old and they don't. And they must foil their enemy, an evil man in a yellow suit who lurks around the woods, sensing that it contains a secret.

After Winnie discovers the Tuck family, she is swept up in a kidnapping, a murder, and an escape from jail. More important, handsome seventeen-year-old Jesse wants her to drink the water when she turns seventeen, so the two of them can have a life together. Immortality or a normal life. To drink or not to drink. That is the question posed to this eleven-year-old girl. Only at the end does the reader learn Winnie's answer.

So in these dog days of August, pick up *Tuck Everlasting* for some refreshment. Although it may not make you immortal, it will definitely remind you of just how precious our days on earth can be.

PADDLE-TO-THE-SEA

By Holling Clancy Holling

Today marks the birthday of one of America's greatest authors and illustrators. Holling Clancy Holling worked on developing his signature style for forty years before the release of his classic, *Paddle-to-the-Sea*, in 1941. For this book he drew on his years as a Michigan farm boy, a sailor on the Great Lakes, an anthropological researcher in New Mexico, and a muralist in Montana—along with his training at Chicago's Art Institute and Field Museum of Natural History. Holling camped on Native American reservations and attended tribal ceremonies. In fact his *The Book of Indians* was hailed by the U.S. Indian Service as one of the few books for children that they could whole-heartedly recommend, because it contained no misstatements in either text or art.

In *Paddle-to-the-Sea* Holling brought all of his interests together to tell the story of a Native American boy who launches a tiny carved Indian in a canoe as the snows melt on Lake Superior. Bearing the inscription, "Please put me back in the water," this canoe makes its way through the Great Lakes and down the St. Lawrence River to the Atlantic. It survives the perils of fishing nets, saw mills, and Niagara Falls. Holling provided spectacular full-color art for each step of the journey; his wife, Lucille, added detailed line drawings that helped clarify the discussions in the text. The book is both story and information in equal parts.

Holling created several other gems in his lifetime: *Seabird*, about the life cycle of a seagull; *Minn of the Mississippi*, an exploration of the life of a snapping turtle; and *Tree in the Trail,* which focuses on the Sante Fe Trail. The best teaching tool to use with Holling's books is a set of four maps for the regions covered, printed on sturdy ivory paper, which can be secured from Beautiful Feet Books. The maps are designed so children can follow the narrative and draw their own map, learning geography, ecology, biology, and history as they do.

Whether for school or pleasure, the books of Holling Clancy Holling can be visited again and again. Holling knew how to create heartwarming stories, communicate exciting information, and deliver spectacular artwork. He set standards of excellence in nonfiction books for children—and all of us are much richer because of him.

AUGUST 2

Happy Birthday James Howe (Bunnicula series, *Brontorina*).

It's the birth date of James Baldwin (1924–1987), *Go Tell It on the Mountain, Notes of a Native Son.*

In 1610 Henry Hudson sailed into what is now known as Hudson Bay and mistakes it for the Northwest Passage entry for the Pacific Ocean. Read *Beyond the Sea of Ice: The Voyages of Henry Hudson* by Joan Elizabeth Goodman, maps by Bette Duke.

Happy Birthday to the United States Census, first held in 1790. Read *Tricking the Tallyman* by Jacqueline Davies, illustrated by S. D. Schindler.

In 1870 the first underground tube railway opened in London. Read *The London Underground* by Elaine Pascoe and *Underground* by David Macaulay.

Scientists **Albert Einstein** and Leo Szilard wrote to U.S. President Roosevelt asking to start the Manhattan Project on this day in 1939. Their work led to the creation of the first atomic bomb. Read *The Ultimate Weapon: The Race to Develop the Atomic Bomb* by Edward T. Sullivan.

AUGUST 3

Happy Birthday Mary Calhoun (*Hot-Air Henry, Henry the Christmas Cat*), and Steve Sanfield (*The Adventures of High John the Conqueror, Bit by Bit*).

It's the birth date of Juliana Horatia Ewing (1841–1885), *Jacknapes, Daddy Darwin's Dovecot, and Other Stories*.

On this day in 1914 Germany declared war on France. Read *The War to End All Wars: World War I* by Russell Freedman.

In 1936 African-American Jesse Owens won the hundred-meter dash at the Berlin Olympics, as Nazi Germany watched. Read *Jesse Owens* by Jane Sutcliffe, illustrated by Janice Lee Porter, and *Jesse Owens: Fastest Man Alive* by Carolyn Boston Weatherford, illustrated by Eric Velasquez.

Happy Birthday to the National Basketball League (NBA), founded in 1949. Read *Basketball: A History of Hoops* by Mark Stewart and *Great Moments in Basketball History* by Matt Christopher.

It's Watermelon Day. Read *War & Watermelon* by Rich Wallace, *Watermelon Wishes* by Lisa Moser, illustrated by Stacey Schuett, and *Watermelon Day* by Kathi Appelt, illustrated by Dale Gottlieb.

AN AMERICAN PLAGUE: THE TRUE AND TERRIFYING STORY OF THE YELLOW FEVER EPIDEMIC OF 1793

By Jim Murphy

On August 3, 1793, a young French sailor in Philadelphia, Pennsylvania, contracted a virulent fever, which worsened before he died. Newspaper accounts in the new nation's capital did not even give his name, and everyone went about their usual business in the City of Brotherly Love. But from that moment on, an invisible killer stalked the streets of the city.

As more and more people died, the local doctors, who included Dr. Benjamin Rush, could not agree about the cause of the deaths. No one knew how to treat the patients. When scores began to die, they started to remove the barely living to a makeshift hospital away from the city. Everyone with means and money fled. The death count mounted daily. Because the city lacked sufficient medical personnel, the Free African Society, composed of former black slaves, became nurses for the patients. Then their members also began to sicken and die. When George Washington finally left the capital a couple of months later, he placed Secretary of War Henry Knox in charge of the country.

In *An American Plague: The True and Terrifying Story of the Yellow Fever Epidemic of 1793* Jim Murphy brings an absolutely gripping account of these events to young readers ages ten through fourteen. How does a plague get started? How effective is government in responding? How much do doctors really know about diseases they have rarely seen? If these sound like modern questions, think again: they all apply to the epidemic of 1793.

An American Plague allows the reader to be swept up in events, breathlessly turning the pages. I first read it, unfortunately, on a hot summer night. Mosquitoes (the cause of the plague) flew in droves over the Vermont countryside outside my window. Because I couldn't stop reading, by the morning I was convinced I had contracted a rare case of yellow fever. That is what great books do for you—they take you away to another place, another reality.

Jim Murphy has been given the Margaret A. Edwards award for his exciting information books—including *Blizzard, A Boy's War, The Long Road to Gettysburg,* and *The Great Chicago Fire.* If you don't know his titles, *An American Plague* makes an excellent first choice. Just stay away from mosquitoes while you read it.

THE DIARY OF A YOUNG GIRL

By Anne Frank

On August 4, 1944, a fifteen-year-old girl wrote what would be the last entry in a diary she had been keeping since June 14, 1942. Her outpourings in this diary over the course of more than two years were remarkable. In this final entry, she talked about her character, striving to become a better human being. "I've already told you before that I have, as it were, a dual personality. One half embodies my exuberant cheerfulness, making fun of everything. . . . I have another side, a finer and better side. I'm afraid they'll laugh at me, think I'm ridiculous and sentimental, not take me seriously." Today no one laughs at the character of this young woman; she has become the most widely read and most widely revered teenager of all time.

Shortly after this entry on August 4, 1944, Nazi troops discovered the location of Anne Frank and her family, who had been hiding in the secret annex of an office building on Prinsengracht Canal in Amsterdam. Although all the human inhabitants of the annex disappeared that day, taken to the Bergen-Belsen concentration camp, Anne's diary remained behind. When Anne's father Otto Frank returned the next year, the only one of the eight in hiding to survive, he found her diary in a desk. Surprised by the complexity and depth of Anne's writing, he typed a copy, cutting about a third of the content, and circulated it among friends.

AUGUST 4

Happy Birthday Joyce McDonald (*Swallowing Stones, Shades of Simon Gray*), Nancy White Carlstrom (Jesse Bear series, *This Is the Day*), and Laurence Anholt (*Leonardo and the Flying Boy, Chimp and Zee*).

It's the birthday of 44th president of the United States, President Barack Obama (*Of Thee I Sing: A Letter to My Daughters*).

It's the birth date of poet Percy Bysshe Shelley (1792–1822). Read *Wildly Romantic: The English Romantic Poets: The Mad, the Bad, and the Dangerous* by Catherine M. Andronik.

Jazz musician **Louis Armstrong** (1901–1971) was born on this day, as was mathematician John Venn (1834–1923), inventor of the Venn diagram. Read *When Louis Armstrong Taught Me Scat* by Muriel Harris Weinstein, illustrated by R. Gregory Christie, and *That Is Not My Hat* by Cecilia Venn, photographs by Dorothy Handelman.

At first German publishers turned down the project, but eventually one took a chance on it in 1947, issuing only fifteen hundred copies. Five years later, after several U.S. publishers passed on the book, Doubleday released an edition in the United States with a stirring introduction by Eleanor Roosevelt. Adults expressed concern that the content would be too emotionally difficult for teens and children, but young readers disagreed. In Anne they found a kindred spirit. In many ways an exceptional teenager, Anne lived in extraordinary times. Her diary shows not only the plight of those threatened with death, but also domestic life and squabbles, common adolescent problems, and an examination of moral issues. And, in the end, it shows her idealism triumphing over despair.

Today a complete edition of the diary exists, made available in 1995 by the Anne Frank Foundation. Whatever version you read, *The Diary of a Young Girl* can be shared in the classroom, with family, or for independent reading. With more than fifteen million readers worldwide, the diary eventually fulfilled one of Anne's dreams: "I want to go on living even after my death."

AUGUST 5

Happy Birthday Neil Armstrong, the first man to walk on the moon.

It's the birth date of Guy de Maupassant (1850–1893), *The Necklace, When Chickens Grow Teeth*; Conrad Aiken (1889–1973), *A Little Who's Zoo of Mild Animals*; Maud Petersham (1889–1971), *The Rooster Crows*; and Robert Bright (1902–1988), *Georgie*.

In 1620 the *Mayflower* departed from Southampton, England, on its first attempt to reach North America. Read *The Mayflower and the Pilgrims' New World* by Nathaniel Philbrick.

The cornerstone for the **Statue of Liberty** was laid on Bedloe's Island (now Liberty Island) on this day in 1884. Read *The Story of the Statue of Liberty* by Betsy and Giulio Maestro.

Cleveland, Ohio, is the home of the first electric traffic light, installed in 1914. Read *Red Light, Green Light* by Anastasia Suen, illustrated by Ken Wilson-Max.

THE RESCUERS
By Margery Sharp
Illustrated by Garth Williams

Around this time of year the Norway Cup takes place in Oslo. More than fourteen hundred international youth soccer teams travel from different countries to compete.

Well, our book of the day doesn't have much to do with soccer. But it is about a Norwegian poet who is being kept prisoner in the dreadful Black Tower. Nils, one of the book's three heroes, is summoned to help because he speaks the language. Nils is a true Norwegian, proud of his country and its heritage, and he also happens to be a mouse, just like all the other main characters in Margery Sharp's fabulously funny tale of great adventure, *The Rescuers*.

According to the book, mice have always been the companions of prisoners, and the mice Prisoners' Aid Society plans to rescue the poet. Led by Miss Bianca, a privileged, pampered mouse who lives in a cage with a pagoda, the team needs a Norwegian-speaking mouse to enter the Black Castle to talk to the prisoner. That's when Nils enters the story.

If this seems a bit far-fetched, it all makes perfect sense as the plot plays out. Nils, Miss Bianca, and Miss Bianca's love interest Bernard set out for the Black Castle to free the poet and bring him home alive. How they outsmart the jailer, his evil cat Mamelouk, and all the people in prison makes for an exciting tale. Readers watch Miss Bianca change from a pampered princess to a resourceful and daring espionage agent. For those who fall under her spell and are captivated by her charm, Margery Sharp penned eight more volumes.

For some years, *The Rescuers* had been out of print. But the *New York Review of Books* rescued this gem and republished it with all the original Garth Williams's illustrations drawn at the height of his craft. During the fifties and early sixties Williams lent his genius to the reissue of Wilder's Little House books, *Charlotte's Web*, *The Cricket in Times Square*, and *The Rescuers*. His details of the cozy homes that Miss Bianca fashions—one uses Wrigley chewing gum wrappers for wallpaper—are infinitely satisfying.

Good luck to all the participants of the Norway Cup. I am sure Nils would be proud of all his fellow countrymen.

LING & TING: NOT EXACTLY THE SAME!

By Grace Lin

At the beginning of August in Twinsburg, Ohio, twins from around the world come for festivities that include contests, talent shows, and fireworks. In past years this assembly has made the *Guinness Book of World Records* for being the largest gathering of twins at one time. Twins have always fascinated children, and literature for children has been rich with them ever since Lucy Fitch Perkins's Twins series.

A new entry into the twins canon presents some very fresh and exciting material. *Ling & Ting: Not Exactly the Same!* written and illustrated by Grace Lin features twin girls in a chapter book ideal for emerging readers ages six through eight. The opening segment about these two Chinese-American twins shows them visiting a barber. Ting sneezes at an inopportune moment, and she gets a chunk cut out of her bangs. Consequently, it is easy for readers to tell them apart for the rest of the book. Just as young viewers look for George's gold tooth in each panel of James Marshall's *George and Martha*, readers of these stories have an easy visual way to identify the two girls.

The book's six chapters present episodes in the lives of Ling and Ting. Because the girls look alike, people assume they are alike—but in fact they are quite different. These young girls go about their activities—making dumplings, playing magic tricks, going to the library—and enjoy being together and having a close relationship. However, they also insist on celebrating their unique qualities.

For anyone now in Twinsburg looking for a great book for the younger set, *Ling & Ting* fills the bill. For the rest of us, this Geisel Honor book simply reminds us of what an accomplished writer Grace Lin has become over the last few years. With a range of books from *Where the Mountain Meets the Moon* to *Ling & Ting*, she has demonstrated that she knows how to craft beautifully written books—with great appeal for the intended audience.

AUGUST 6

Happy Birthday Frank Asch (Moonbear series, *Milk and Cookies*).

It's the birth date of Barbara Cooney (1917–2000), *Ox-Cart Man*, *Miss Rumphius*, *Eleanor*; and Roger Lea MacBride (1929–1995), *Little Farm in the Ozarks*, *In the Land of the Big Red Apple*.

The Japanese city of Hiroshima was bombed on this day in 1945. Thus, it is Hiroshima Day. Read *Hiroshima* by Laurence Yep, *Hiroshima: The Story of the First Atomic Bomb* by Clive A. Lawton, *Hiroshima No Pika* by Toshi Maruki, illustrated by Ed Young, and *Sadako and the Thousand Paper Cranes* by Eleanor Coerr, illustrated by Ronald Himler.

It's National Fresh Breath Day. Read *Squids Will Be Squids: Fresh Morals, Beastly Fables* by Jon Scieszka, illustrated by Lane Smith, and *Calvin Coconut: Zoo Breath* by Graham Salisbury, illustrated by Jacqueline Rogers.

AUGUST 7

Happy Birthday Betsy Byars (*Summer of the Swans*) and Garrison Keillor (*Daddy's Girl, Cat, You Better Come Home*).

It's the birth date of Maia Wojciechowska (1927–2002), *Shadow of a Bull*; and Colleen Salley (1929–2008), *Epossumondas* series.

In 1974 Philippe Petit performed a high-wire act between the twin towers of the World Trade Center, 1,368 feet (417 m) in the air. Read *The Man Who Walked Between the Towers* by Mordicai Gerstein and *Mirette on the High Wire* by Emily Arnold McCully.

It's National Lighthouse Day. Read *Birdie's Lighthouse* by Deborah Hopkinson, illustrated by Kimberly Bulcken Root, *Lighthouse Cat* by Sue Stainton, illustrted by Anne Mortimer, *The Abandoned Lighthouse* by Albert Lamb, illustrated by David McPhail, and the Lighthouse Family series by Cynthia Rylant, illustrated by Preston McDaniels.

DOG AND BEAR
By Laura Vaccaro Seeger

Since 1935, the first Sunday in August has been celebrated as Friendship Day. The organizers of the event often quote Albert Camus on the subject: "Don't walk in front of me, I may not follow. Don't walk behind me, I may not lead. Walk beside me and be my friend."

Some of our most long-lasting and cherished children's books celebrate friendship: James Marshall gave us George and Martha; Arnold Lobel, Frog and Toad. Recently two characters have been created by a talented young author-illustrator that deserve to stand next to these classics—Laura Vaccaro Seeger's Dog and Bear. Humor and emotion often prove to be the most difficult qualities to create in a picture book since emotion can so quickly degenerate into sentimentality. But in *Dog and Bear: Two Friends, Three Stories*, Laura combines funny stories with a great deal of heart as she explores the friendship between a stuffed bear and a playful dachshund. Each of the stories contains its own tension and resolution. Every page has a unique design, and the illustrations, with black ink outlines, add humor to the text. Combining simplicity with panache, emotion with graphic brilliance, this saga of two BFF's can be read again and again with pleasure.

Laura Vaccaro Seeger has been an artist since the age of two. By fifth grade she knew she wanted to create picture books, but spent time as a television animator before she pursued her childhood dream. One day when editor Neal Porter was visiting her home, he spied a multicolored stuffed bear perched on a tall chair in the living room. Standing there, holding the bear, Neal said to Laura, "Write a book about this!" As she worked on the text, she realized that she based the characters of Dog and Bear on herself and Neal and their working relationship.

What children can appreciate in the book are the ways the two buddies help each other and delight in each other's company. When Bear is unable to get out of the high chair, Dog, a long dachshund, offers his back as a slide. When Dog wants to change his name because it is so boring, Bear helps with the problem. Perfect for emerging readers ages two through six, this book and its sequels, *Dog and Bear: Two's Company* and *Dog and Bear: Three to Get Ready*, bring the concept of friendship alive in the stories of two engaging and wonderful characters.

Celebrate Friendship Day with Dog and Bear. They remind us why friends are so precious.

THE YEARLING

By Marjorie Kinnan Rawlings

Today we celebrate the birthday of a writer who had no intention of crafting a book for children—nor was her classic published as one. Marjorie Kinnan Rawlings's *The Yearling* appeared on the Scribner adult list in 1938. Edited by the legendary Maxwell Perkins who also worked with Hemingway, Fitzgerald, and Thomas Wolfe, *The Yearling* became the bestselling adult title in 1939 and also won the Pulitzer Prize. A year later an exquisitely illustrated edition with art by N. C. Wyeth helped shift the readership of the book—it became a staple of family reading, ideal to share with ten- to fourteen-year-olds.

To create the book, Rawlings drew on the history, flora, and fauna of North Florida, where she moved after leaving her husband. She learned that in 1876, Reuben and Sara Long set up a homestead on Pat's Island, now part of the Ocala National Forest, and that their son Melvin found and adopted a fawn. Rawlings incorporated the actual setting of this homestead and a few facts about the Longs into her book.

In *The Yearling*, the Baxter family struggles to survive in Florida scrub country, often with barely enough to eat. All of the Baxter children have died, except Jody who finds the natural landscape a kind of paradise. He hunts, fishes, and rambles through this world, alive to all of its beauty. On one of his trips, Jody finds an infant fawn and convinces his parents to let him adopt the animal, now named Flag. This lonely child and unusual pet become inseparable. Realistic in its treatment of the poverty and dignity of the family, the novel does not provide a happy ending. When Flag dies, Jody, stoically, faces his life going forward: "He did not believe he should ever again love anything, man or woman or his own child, as he had loved the yearling. He would be lonely all his life. But a man took it for his share and went on."

Acclaimed children's book writer Lois Lowry commented on *The Yearling* in *Everything I Need to Know I Learned from a Children's Book*: "It was the first book that allowed me to see how the writer could elicit an emotional reaction—she made my mother cry. . . . *The Yearling* made me understand what fiction could accomplish and what a writer could do with words."

If by any chance you are headed to North Florida, you can actually visit the remains of the homestead and the setting of the book. Otherwise, you can go there simply by reading *The Yearling*.

AUGUST 8

Happy Birthday Jan Pienkowski (*Little Monsters, Haunted House*) and Candy Dawson Boyd (*Daddy, Daddy, Be There, Forever Friends*).

In 1945 the United Nations Charter was signed by the United States, the third nation to join. Read *We Are All Born Free: The Universal Declaration of Human Rights in Pictures* by Amnesty International.

In 1974 U.S. President Richard Nixon announced his resignation. Read *The Watergate Scandal* by Kathleen Tracy.

It's Sneak Some Zucchini onto Your Neighbor's Porch Day/Night. Read *Zucchini* by Barbara Dana, illustrated by Eileen Christelow, *The Accidental Zucchini: An Unexpected Alphabet* by Max Grover, and *I Heard It from Alice Zucchini: Poems about the Garden* by Juanita Havill, illustrated by Christine Davenier.

It's also Happiness Happens Day. Read *The Garden of Happiness* by Erika Tamar, illustrated by Barbara Lambase, *The Wonderful Happens* by Cynthia Rylant, illustrated by Coco Dowley, and *Happy Birthday, Little Pookie* by Sandra Boynton.

AUGUST 9

Happy Birthday Seymour Simon (*Weather*), Jose Aruego (*Leo the Late Bloomer, Gregory, the Terrible Eater*), and Patricia C. McKissack (*Mirandy and Brother Wind, The Dark-Thirty: Southern Tales of the Supernatural*).

It's the birth date of Izaak Walton (1593–1683), *The Compleat Angler*; and P. L. Travers (1899–1996), *Mary Poppins*.

 In 1173 construction began on what would become the **Leaning Tower of Pisa**. Read *The Diary of Melanie Martin: Or How I Survived Matt the Brat, Michelangelo, and the Leaning Tower of Pizza* by Carol Weston, and *Galileo's Leaning Tower Experiment* by Wendy Macdonald, illustrated by Paolo Rui.

In 1483 the Sistine Chapel in Rome opened with the celebration of a Mass. Read *Michelangelo* by Diane Stanley and *The Tiger Rising* by Kate DiCamillo.

Walden by Henry David Thoreau was published on this day in 1854. Read *Thoreau at Walden* by John Porcellino, illustrated by D. B. Johnson, and *Walden Then and Now* by Michael McCurdy.

In 1945 an atomic bomb was dropped on the Japanese city of Nagasaki. Read *Mop, Moondance, and the Nagasaki Knights* by Walter Dean Myers.

COMET IN MOOMINLAND

By Tove Jansson

If you spent your childhood in Europe, particularly Scandinavia or England, you will be more familiar with the book of the day than if you grew up in the United States. Unfortunately, this gem has never gained the popularity in America that it enjoys abroad.

Born on August 9, 1914, Tove Jansson, a Swedish-speaking Finnish novelist, grew up in an artistic family in Helsinki. As someone who studied art and design, she worked as an illustrator and cartoonist for a variety of magazines. At the end of the Second World War, Jansson began publishing a series of books about her most successful cartoon characters, the Moomins. Depressed by the events of the war, Jansson chose to write about an idealized, harmonious family of furry, rotund trolls who look a bit like hippopotami. Moomintroll, Moominpappa, and Moominmamma love and support each other completely.

In the first volume, *Comet in Moominland*, Moomintroll and his best friend Sniff, sensing that an approaching comet threatens their peaceful valley, set out to visit an observatory to find out what is going on. Along the way, Moomintroll falls in love with the beautiful Snork Maiden, and they discover that water has been disappearing from the earth, placing the world in distress. Scandinavian critics often focus on the political content of these stories. The comet serves as a metaphor for the threat of a nuclear war; the disruption of the weather and the natural landscape can be viewed as ecological imbalance on our planet. Although these deeper issues underscore the text, this story works completely as an adventure saga that keeps readers turning the pages to see what will happen when the comet strikes the earth on October 7.

Jansson treats her tale with an amazingly light touch. She excels in exploring childhood emotion and fantasy. So many eccentric and unusual creatures populate her fantasy world that readers long to go back and visit them again and again. Their dialogue has a ring all its own; the all-white Moomintroll likes to say, "Well, strike me pink!" Jansson, who won the Hans Christian Andersen Award for her body of work, manages to stay true to her Scandinavian sensibility and yet be completely universal in the eight volumes of the series.

To celebrate Tove Jansson's birthday. I'm going to exclaim several times today, "Well, strike me pink!"

HIDDEN

By Helen Frost

Around this time of year families and children start wrapping up summer activities and begin to prepare for a new school year. All those summer camps come to an end. The book of the day, Helen Frost's *Hidden*, takes place at summer camp but is unlike any camp novel I've ever read.

When I picked up *Hidden*, I had only a few minutes and lots of deadlines. I was merely going to scan a chapter to get a sense of the book. Do not make this mistake with *Hidden*! Unable to do anything else until I found out how the story ends, I finally put the book down several hours later.

In *Hidden*, Helen Frost works in free-verse format to relate the story of Wren Abbott. In first person, Wren narrates how as a happy eight-year-old girl in a pink dress she waits for her mother in the family minivan. But in one of those terrible twists of fate a robber seizes the van for a getaway and drives the car to his home. Wren finds herself alone, in a dangerous position, and must use her wits to survive. She is aided, in part, by the man's daughter Darra, who brings food to the girl now held captive in their garage. Wren escapes and helps the police locate the criminal. Darra's world is now turned upside down; she doesn't understand what happened that day and wonders if she is to blame for her father's incarceration.

When they are fourteen, Wren and Darra end up at the same month-long summer camp in Michigan's Upper Peninsula. What should have been a wonderful camping experience for Wren becomes a nightmare. Suddenly she must relive the events from six years earlier and come to terms with her past. Darra must face her own guilt, her feelings about her father who is now divorced from her mother, and her unanswered questions about the events of that fateful day.

Told in alternating sections by Darra and Wren, the book moves to a breathtaking finish. Showing how childhood trauma can shape character and give strength, the story presents two totally believable and likable young girls, struggling to make sense of their past.

For my taste, Helen Frost has emerged as our greatest living craftsperson of poetic novels. *Hidden* maintains her reputation in that arena. In the end she shows readers how they can revisit the verse and find other details contained in it. After reading the book in one gulp, both adults and children ages eleven through fourteen will want to go back to this complex book and learn more about the characters.

AUGUST 10

Happy Birthday Tony Ross (*I'm Coming to Get You!*; *Wash Your Hands!*).

It's the birth date of Margot Tomes (1917–1991), *Homesick: My Own Story*, *Phoebe the Spy*; and Thomas J. Dygard (1931–1996), *Infield Hit*, *Second Stringer*.

It's also the birth date of **Herbert Hoover** (1874–1964), the 31st president of the United States.

In 1793 the Musée du Louvre opened in Paris, France. Read *Louvre Up Close* by Claire d'Harcourt.

Happy Birthday Missouri, which became the 24th U.S. state on this day in 1821. Read *Missouri Boy* by Leland Myrick.

The Civil Liberties Act of 1988 was signed by President Ronald Reagan on this day, providing reparation payments to Japanese Americans who were interned by the United States during World War II. Read *A Place Where Sunflowers Grow* by Amy Lee-Tai, illustrated by Felicia Hoshino, and *Baseball Saved Us* by Ken Mochizuki, illustrated by Dom Lee.

AUGUST 11

Happy Birthday George Sullivan (*Helen Keller: Her Life in Pictures*), Joanna Cole (The Magic School Bus series), and Sally Keehn (*I Am Regina, The First Horse I See*).

It's the birth date of Enid Blyton (1897–1968), Famous Five series; and Steven Kroll (1941–2011), *Jungle Bullies, The Biggest Pumpkin Ever*.

In 1929 Babe Ruth became the first baseball player to hit five hundred home runs. Read *Home Run: The Story of Babe Ruth* by Robert Burleigh, illustrated by Mike Wimmer, and *Cam Jansen and the Mystery of the Babe Ruth Baseball* by David A. Adler.

The first prisoners arrived at Alcatraz Island in 1934. Read *Children of Alcatraz: Growing Up on the Rock* by Claire Rudolph Murphy and *Al Capone Does My Shirts* by Gennifer Choldenko.

CORDUROY

By Don Freeman

On August 11, 1908, Don Freeman was born in San Diego, California. Freeman showed early skills as both a musician and an artist. In the late twenties he moved to New York City to make a living. He arrived a few days before the stock market crash and always carried a guilt complex about the event. Of course, work became hard to find. While playing jazz trumpet at music gigs, he took art lessons with John Sloan at the Art Students League and drew character sketches wherever he went. One night on the subway, Don, who had been sketching, left his trumpet on the train. He always said that was the night he decided he would stick to drawing.

In the fifties, with help from his wife, Lydia, Freeman began to fashion children's books for their son Roy—*Pet of the Met, Norman the Doorman*, and *Mop Top*. Freeman started a book based on his son's nickname "Corduroy" called *Corduroy, the Inferior Decorator*, the story of a young boy who drove his parents nuts by painting the walls of their apartment. But several years later Freeman began to develop a story about a character who wanders around a department store at night. He was trying to explore the difference between the luxury of the store and the simple life that most people live. Then the image of a stuffed bear, wearing corduroy overalls and missing a button, came into Freeman's mind, and he knew he had the character he'd been looking for.

In this heartwarming story, no one wants to buy Corduroy the bear from the department store because his overalls are missing a button. So one night he goes hunting for a new button. He doesn't find one, but discovers lots of other exciting things outside the toy department. Fortunately, a young girl named Lisa does want to buy Corduroy and provides him with both a home and a button. This story is perfectly pitched for a four- or five-year-old point of view. Corduroy experiences everything in an excited and wonderful way. As he climbs onto the escalator he exclaims, "Could this be a mountain? . . . I've always wanted to climb a mountain."

As art director of Viking, Barbara Hennessy had the privilege of working with Freeman on *A Pocket for Corduroy*. She was always amazed that Freeman—a large man, full of life, energy, enthusiasm, and warmth—could contain himself enough to work in scratchboard, a technique that requires patience and precision. Characters often serve as alter egos: Don, according to Barbara, was much like Corduroy; and his wife, Lydia, exactly like the lovely and charming Lisa.

Happy birthday to Don Freeman. Fortunately he left his trumpet on that subway train and dedicated his creative life to making books for children.

BAD BOY

By Walter Dean Myers

Today marks the birthday of a man who called his autobiography *Bad Boy*. But for the past forty years the children's book field has considered Walter Dean Myers a "Good and Great Man." Possibly that should be the title of the second volume of his autobiography. Indeed, he was selected in 2012 as the third National Ambassador for Children's Books.

Myers initially made his mark in the seventies, as part of a group of authors who brought an African-American conscience to the world of children's books—creators like Jerry Pinkney, Tom Feelings, Julius Lester, Ashley Bryan, and Mildred Taylor. Of that talented pool, Myers would prove the most versatile in terms of the number of genres he excels in: cutting-edge young adult novels such as *Monster*; inspired nonfiction like *Malcolm X*, *The Greatest: Muhammad Ali*; poetry (*Brown Angels*); and short stories (*145th Street*).

Anyone who wants to gain a greater appreciation of Walter Dean Myers will want to read *Bad Boy*, his account of Harlem during the forties and fifties. Gifted in both athletics and school, Myers struggled with a quick and violent temper that caused a lot of trouble. In his memoir he examines being black in America and his realization that his best friend, who was white, had opportunities that he did not have. Walter also dealt with a serious speech impediment and learned that he could write what he could not say. In the end, he took the prescient advice of a teacher, "Whatever happens, don't stop writing."

AUGUST 12

Happy Birthday Ruth Stiles Gannett (*My Father's Dragon*), Mary Ann Hoberman (*You Read to Me, I'll Read to You, The Seven Silly Eaters*), Frederick McKissack (*Christmas in the Big House: Christmas in the Quarters*), Tim Wynne-Jones (*Rex Zero series, The Maestro*), Ann M. Martin (*Baby-Sitters Club series, A Corner of the Universe*), and Audrey Wood (*The Napping House*).

It's the birth date of Katharine Lee Bates (1859–1929), *America the Beautiful*; Edith Hamilton (1867–1963), *Mythology, The Roman Way*; Mary Roberts Rinehart (1876–1958), *Tish*; Zerna Sharp (1889–1981), *Dick and Jane*; and Deborah Howe (1946–1978), Bunnicula series.

It's International Youth Day, an initiative of the United Nations to improve the situation of young people around the world.

Happy Birthday Chicago, founded in 1833. Read *The Coast of Chicago* by Stuart Dybek and *A Long Way from Chicago* by Richard Peck.

On this day in South Dakota in 1990 Susan Hendrickson discovered the largest known *Tyrannosaurus rex* skeleton.

Sharon Creech's *Love That Dog* contains a fan letter from a young boy to Walter Dean Myers that describes him quite well: "And when you laughed / you had the / best best BEST / laugh I've ever heard in my life / like it was coming from way down deep / and bubbling up and / rolling and tumbling / out into the air."

Today in honor of Walter Dean Myers, read *Bad Boy*. Thank goodness he took the advice of his teacher—"Whatever happens, don't stop writing!"

AUGUST 13

It's the birth date of Walter Crane (1845–1915), *Household Stories from the Collection of the Brothers Grimm, The Baby's Own Aesop.*

 Also born on this day was sharpshooter **Annie Oakley** (1860–1926). Read *Bull's-Eye: A Photobiography of Annie Oakley* by Sue Macy, *Annie Oakley* by Charles Wills, and *Annie Oakley Saves the Day* by Anna DiVito.

On this day in 2008 U.S. swimmer Michael Phelps set the Olympic record for the most gold medals (eight in Beijing and six in Athens) won by an individual in Olympic history. Read *Stotan!* and *Staying Fat for Sarah Byrnes,* both by Chris Crutcher.

It's International Left-Handers' Day. Read *The Case of the Left-Handed Lady* by Nancy Springer.

THE MAN WHO WALKED BETWEEN THE TOWERS

By Mordicai Gerstein

Born in France on August 13, 1949, Philippe Petit became a high-wire artist best remembered for an event that took place on August 7, 1974. That day he walked on a tightrope between the two World Trade Center skyscrapers in New York City. In the air for around an hour, he danced and performed tricks—as New Yorkers and the police looked on. He even lay down on the high wire and took a rest. No stranger to this kind of acrobatic performance, Petit had walked above the skies of Paris on a wire strung between the towers of Notre Dame.

Author and artist Mordicai Gerstein had long been fascinated with Petit's life and his daring act that August day. Gerstein finally made Petit the subject of a picture book, *The Man Who Walked Between the Towers*, after the tragic events of September 11, 2001. The book first shows Petit's daily routine as a New York City street performer. He juggles, rides a bike, and walks across a rope between two trees. Readers watch Philippe plan his next bold act of accessing the World Trade Center site late at night, and then stringing a cable from one building to the other with the help of friends. Most of this thirty-two-page picture book shows incredible aerial views of New York as Petit walks and performs above the city with a feeling of complete freedom. Two folded pages open out to give a sense of the panorama that Petit sees as well as an idea of how he appears from the ground. Safely on the other side, Petit is arrested. His sentence is to perform for children in the city.

Every line of this meticulously laid out picture book, winner of the Caldecott Medal, celebrates Petit's industry and daring, his joy at practicing his artistry and pulling off this incredible feat. It is only the last two pages that bring this picture book, stunningly, to another level: "Now the towers are gone. But in memory, as if imprinted on the sky, the towers are still there. And part of that memory is the joyful morning, August 7, 1974, when Philippe Petit walked between them in the air."

In *The Man Who Walked Between the Towers* Mordicai Gerstein created a way to introduce September 11, 2001, to children who had yet to be born. What he accomplished is remarkable—a book that makes adults cry and children ask questions. For all readers, he establishes that memory of a beautiful August day when the Twin Towers still stood—and a human being walked between them while spectators looked on with wonder.

CODE TALKER

By Joseph Bruchac

In 1982 the United States Senate designated August 14 as National Code Talkers Day. In his address that day, Dennis DeConcini, an Arizona senator, said, "Since the Code Talkers' work required absolute secrecy, they never enjoyed the national acclaim they so much deserved. I do not want this illustrious yet unassuming group of Navajo marines to fade into history without notice." The Navajo Nation Council has also marked this day as a tribal holiday.

Although unacknowledged until 1969, the Navajo Code Talkers invented an unbreakable military code for relaying information on the Pacific front in World War II. Hundreds of these brave marines went into battle in some of the fiercest fighting of the war. They successfully conveyed military intelligence without the Japanese ever deciphering their transmissions, which were based on the complex nature of the Navajo language. These soldiers, who as children had often been punished for speaking Navajo in government schools, used their native tongue to help save America.

The best book on this topic, Joseph Bruchac's novel *Code Talker*, presents the account of a young Navajo boy, Ned Begay, who tells his story years later in a narrative addressed to his grandchildren. In early scenes, readers witness Ned's experiences at boarding school where everything is stripped away from him: his possessions, his hair, and even his name. He learns how to thrive in this environment, but never gives up his Navajo identity or the use of his language. When World War II begins, Ned is just the kind of educated young man that the marines need in their new unit, the Navajo Code Talkers. At sixteen, he heads to the Pacific, to take part in all the major battles—from Guadalcanal to Iwa Jima.

Told in straightforward and precise language, the book does not glorify war, but it does convey the bravery and endurance of the marines as they fought the Japanese. In this fictional account, Bruchac includes a vast amount of historical information—all of it worked into the narrative. To research the book, he talked to former Code Talkers about their experiences. Sometimes earmarked as a young adult book, *Code Talker* is completely accessible to ten- to twelve-year-olds both in narrative style and content and stands as one of our best novels for children about the events of World War II.

Anyone age ten to one hundred, who wants to understand this chapter in American history, will be riveted by Joseph Bruchac's powerful novel. It has often been adopted for one-city reads because it works for such a wide range of people. In the end, the story of the Code Talkers stands as a testament to the power of language—and why all languages should be respected and kept alive.

AUGUST 14

Happy Birthday Alice Provensen (*A Glorious Flight, A Year at Maple Hill Farm*), Gary Larson (The Far Side comic series), and Steve Martin (*Late for School*).

It's the birth date of Ernest Thayer (1863–1940), *Casey at the Bat*.

In 1848 the Oregon Territory was created by act of the U.S. Congress. Read Joshua's Oregon Trail Diary series by Patricia Hermes.

On this day in 1945 Japan announced its unconditional surrender in World War II.

In 1967 the United Kingdom Marine Broadcasting Offences Act declared participation in offshore "pirate radio" illegal. Read *Radio Radio* by Graham Marks.

It's National Creamsicle Day. Read and/or play with *Ice Cream Truck* by Peter Lippman.

AUGUST 15

Happy Birthday Jane Resh Thomas (*Daddy Doesn't Have to Be a Giant Anymore*) and Theresa Nelson (*Ruby Electric*).

It's the birth date of Edith Nesbit (1858–1924), *The Book of Dragons*.

French Emperor Napoleon Bonaparte (1769–1821) was also born on this day. Read *Napoleon: The Story of the Little Corporal* by Robert Burleigh.

In 1824 freed American slaves founded Liberia, on the west coast of Africa. Read *Head, Body, Legs: A Story from Liberia* by Won-Ldy Paye and Margaret H. Lippert, illustrated by Julie Paschkis; *Koi and the Kola Nuts* by Verna Aardema, illustrated by Joe Cepeda; and *Why Leopard Has Spots: Dan Stories from Liberia* by Won-Ldy Paye and Margaret H. Lippert, illustrated by Ashley Brown.

Stadium rock was born on this day in 1965, when the Beatles played to nearly sixty thousand fans at New York City's Shea Stadium. Read *Arthur, It's Only Rock 'n' Roll* by Marc Brown.

In 1969 the Woodstock Music and Art Festival opened. Read *Max Said Yes! The Woodstock Story* by Abigail Yasger and Joseph Lipner, illustrated by Barbara Mendes, and *My Hippie Grandmother* by Reeve Lindbergh, illustrated by Abby Carter.

THE CABINET OF WONDERS
By Marie Rutkoski

Today marks National Relaxation Day. We are encouraged to leave our stress-filled lives, kick back, put our feet up, and enjoy something. To me that sounds like an invitation to read an engrossing book.

For a relaxing day, I would recommend picking up Marie Rutkoski's series ideal for ten- to fourteen-year-olds that begins with *The Cabinet of Wonders*. One of its protagonists, John Dee, was a real person, born in 1527, who straddled the world of science and magic. He worked as a mathematician, astronomer, navigator, occultist, and advisor to Queen Elizabeth I. As he amassed one of the largest libraries in Europe, this extraordinary scientist spent the last decades of his life attempting to communicate with angels. These fascinating details have made Dee a darling of the literary establishment; writers as diverse as H. P. Lovecraft, William Shakespeare, and Umberto Eco have all woven him into their fiction.

Rutkoski sets *The Cabinet of Wonders* in sixteenth-century Bohemia, in a society that wavers between science and magic. Mikhail Kronos, who has a gift for molding metal, has his eyes removed by the Prince of Bohemia. Mikhail had constructed an extraordinary clock that now sits in the town square of Prague; his blindness ensures he will never be able to replicate it. Using magic the prince can now wear Mikhail's eyes. Mikhail's twelve-year-old daughter, Petra, the protagonist of the story, embarks on a journey to retrieve his eyes and is swept up in a magical and scientific world. John Dee, a spy on assignment from Queen Elizabeth I, helps in her quest, as does a young boy Petra befriends, a member of the Roma tribe, called Gypsies, who live surreptitiously on the prince's land. Whether Petra is helping manufacture a new primary color or looking into the future for John Dee, she demonstrates grit and determination.

Fans of Philip Pullman's His Dark Materials trilogy will love *The Cabinet of Wonders*. Petra has her own constant companion, a tin spider who can talk and read and lives in her hair. Fantasy, steam punk, folklore, and the political and social landscape of the Renaissance all meld into a spellbinding story. Fortunately for those who fall in love with Petra and this setting, *The Celestial Globe* and *The Jewel of the Kalderash* continue the saga of Petra and John Dee.

So I hope you get to relax today—and pick up a great book like *The Cabinet of Wonders*.

THE PENDERWICKS
By Jeanne Birdsall

Many head out for summer vacation in August. If a trip could be taken with a children's book character, who would it be? I myself long to travel with a family that Jeanne Birdsall created for *The Penderwicks*. The book takes place in three weeks in August in a perfect vacation spot: Massachusetts's Berkshire Mountains.

Meet the Penderwicks. As the subtitle states, this is *A Summer Tale of Four Sisters, Two Rabbits, and a Very Interesting Boy.* Having lost their mother to cancer, the four Penderwick sisters work together and support their father, an absent-minded but loving botanist. Because their vacation reservations on Cape Cod fell through, they take a chance on a cottage in the Berkshires and find that it's located on the grounds of the Arundel estate, a seemingly magical place with an evil owner and her very attractive son, Jeffrey.

All of the sisters have distinct personalities—Rosalind is the caretaker; Skye, the math expert; Jane, the writer; and Batty, the youngest who loves her dog, Hound. Hound feels equally enthusiastic about Batty. With secret hand signals, the Penderwick code of honor, and ties that bind them together, the girls quickly pull everyone on the estate—including Jeffrey—into their activities and mayhem.

Although their escapades seem innocent enough—interrupting a garden party with a soccer match, for instance—the book provides just enough intrigue, romance, excitement, and adventure to keep readers enthralled with this summer vacation. Those who have read Louisa May Alcott, E. Nesbitt, Eleanor Estes, and Edward Eager will see similarities to beloved books by these masters. But Birdsall has managed to make her family thoroughly modern and believable. With no tricks or flimflam, just good old-fashioned character development and writing, she builds a book that many readers list as one of their favorites of the last decade.

How I wish I could be there with them in Arundel. So I'll see if the Penderwicks will stuff me into the back of the car with Hound. And in the meantime, I'm going to reread this glorious book and its sequels—*The Penderwicks on Gardam Street* and *The Penderwicks at Point Mouette*—which are just as exciting as the original book.

AUGUST 16

Happy Birthday Beverly Brodsky (*Buffalo*) and Eileen Spinelli (*The Best Story, Somebody Loves You, Mr. Hatch*).

It's the birth date of Marchette Chute (1909–1994), *Stories from Shakespeare, The Wonderful Winter*; Beatrice S. de Regniers (1914–2000), *May I Bring a Friend?*; Matt Christopher (1917–1997), *The Kid Who Only Hit Homers*; and Diana Wynne Jones (1934–2011), *Howl's Moving Castle, Castle in the Air.*

British Intelligence officer, **T. E. Lawrence** (1888–1935), known as Lawrence of Arabia, was born on this day.

In 1896 gold was discovered in the Klondike in Canada's Yukon Territory, setting off the Klondike Gold Rush.

In 1954 the first edition of the magazine *Sports Illustrated* was published. Read *Bring Your "A" Game: A Young Athlete's Guide to Mental Toughness* by Jennifer L. Etnier.

It's National Tell a Joke Day. Read *Pearl and Wagner: One Funny Day* by Kate McMullan, illustrated by R. W. Alley.

AUGUST 17

Happy Birthday Ariane Dewey (*The Last Laugh*, *Herman the Helper*).

It's the birth date of Gene Stratton-Porter (1863–1924), *A Girl of the Limberlost*; and Myra Cohn Livingston (1926–1996), *Celebrations*.

 Davy Crockett (1786–1836) was also born on this day. Read *Davy Crockett: His Own Story* and *Davy Crockett: A Life on the Frontier* by Stephan Krensky, illustrated by Debra Bandelin and Bob Dacey.

In 1907 Pike Place Market, the longest continuously running public farmers market in the U.S., opened in Seattle. Read *Salt and Pepper at the Pike Place Market* by Carol A. Losi, illustrated by Amy Meissner.

It's National Thrift Shop Day. Read *The Old Curiosity Shop* by Charles Dickens.

THE GOLDEN COMPASS
By Philip Pullman

August has been designated Audio Book Appreciation Month. Certainly one of the great changes in children's book publishing during my career has been the increase in superb audio recordings of novels. Since many families spend time in the car going to and from vacation spots in August, today's book is a sophisticated novel that will provide a lot of listening pleasure for everyone in the family.

In 1999 Listening Library issued a nine-disc recording of Philip Pullman's novel, *The Golden Compass*, unabridged, narrated by Pullman and a cast of actors. Pullman proves to be just as graceful a narrator as he is a writer, and the assembled cast brings all his characters to life.

In *The Golden Compass* readers encounter a parallel world—it seems like our own but it is Victorian in its details, and all humans possess a daemon, a companion, who takes the form of an animal and stays with them at all times. In childhood the daemon can change shapes; when adulthood comes, it settles on a form. Eleven-year-old Lyra Belacqua and her daemon, Pantalaimon, live in Jordan College at Oxford, under the care of the master of the college. But in Oxford and other areas around England, children have been disappearing. When Lyra's friend Roger vanishes, she gets swept up in a mission to save him and others—taking her on a journey to the far north. Along the way, she must come to terms with her father, her mother (the evil Mrs. Coulter), and an armored bear, who becomes a trusted friend.

The entire book has been written with grace and finesse. Pullman knows how to create tension in each chapter, and shows the gradual change of Lyra from a wild child to one with a conscience and purpose. Throughout her journey, her daemon, Pantalaimon, provides some pretty snappy observations to keep her on track.

Action, adventure, mystery, intrigue—Pullman writes beautifully descriptive scenes and creates fascinating characters. I've listened to the audio book twice over the years and always find I hear details in the story that I have missed. So even if everyone in the family has read *The Golden Compass*, which works for ten-year-olds on up, this audio version will keep you at the edge of your seat.

Be sure to keep a copy of the book nearby. You will probably want to savor some of the passages after you hear them read.

CLEMENTE!

By Willie Perdomo
Illustrated by Bryan Collier

On August 18, 1934, one of the most revered National League baseball players of all times, Roberto Clemente, was born in Carolina, Puerto Rico. Considered something of a saint in his native land, Clemente made his fame in America after being drafted in 1954 by the Pittsburgh Pirates. He brought new life to the team and excitement to the ballpark, ultimately spurring the Pirates on to become World Series champions. As good as Clemente was on the ball field, his activities off the diamond became a critical part of his legend. He built a sports complex in Puerto Rico for children and gave large sums to charity. While delivering aid to earthquake victims in Nicaragua in 1972, Clemente died when the plane with these supplies plummeted into the ocean.

In *Roberto Clemente: Pride of the Pittsburgh Pirates*, Jonah Winter stresses Clemente's genius as a ball player as well as the discrimination that he faced from newspaper writers who called him lazy, mocked his Spanish, and dubbed him a hothead.

But in *Clemente!* Willie Perdomo provides a different perspective on the first Latin-American player inducted into the National Baseball Hall of Fame. A young boy, named Clemente in honor of his father's favorite ball player, narrates a text that moves frequently from English to Spanish to celebrate Clemente's accomplishments. Both the boy's father and uncle regale him with information about their idol. Bryan Collier, one of the most talented illustrators working today, has created strong and compelling portraits of Clemente as well as striking and dramatic baseball stadium scenes to make every page of this book visually compelling.

Both books work well together to honor Clemente. Although he died almost three decades ago, he remains a hero for our time—a brilliant baseball player who gave his resources and ultimately his life to help others.

AUGUST 18

Happy Birthday Sonia Levitin (*The Cure, Journey to America*) and Joan Carris (Bed and Biscuit series).

It is also the birthday of Percy Jackson, star of Rick Riordan's Lightning Thief series.

It's the birth date of Louise Fatio (1904–1993), *The Happy Lion*; and Paula Danziger (1944–2004), *Can You Sue Your Parents for Malpractice?*, Amber Brown series.

In 1868 French astronomer Pierre Jules César Janssen discovered helium. Read *The Twenty-One Balloons* by William Pène Du Bois, *Emily's Balloon* by Komako Sakai, and *The Red Balloon* by Albert Lamorisse.

On this day in 1920 the 19th Amendment to the United States Constitution was ratified, enabling all U.S. citizens to vote, regardless of gender. Read *A Long Way to Go: A Story of Women's Right to Vote* by Zibby Oneal and *Elizabeth Leads the Way: Elizabeth Cady Stanton and the Right to Vote* by Tanya Lee Stone, illustrated by Rebecca Gibbon.

In 1939 the film *The Wizard of Oz* opened in New York City.

It's Bad Poetry Day. Read *Teen Angst: A Celebration of Really Bad Poetry* edited by Sara Bynoe.

PICTURE BOOK, BIOGRAPHY, Elementary School

AUGUST 19

Happy Birthday Barbara Wersba (*Walter: The Story of a Rat*) and Vicki Cobb (*We Dare You!: Hundreds of Science Bets, Challenges, and Experiments You Can Do at Home*).

It's the birth date of Ogden Nash (1902–1971), *The Tale of Custard the Dragon*, *The Adventures of Isabel*; and Frank McCourt (1931–2009), *Angela and the Baby Jesus*.

 Happy Birthday **William Jefferson Clinton,** the 42nd president of the United States.

It's also the birth date of Gabrielle "Coco" Chanel (1883–1971), fashion designer. Read *Different Like Coco* by Elizabeth Matthews.

It's Aviation Day, in honor of the birthday of Orville Wright (1871–1948). Read *To Fly: The Story of the Wright Brothers* by Wendy Old, illustrated by Robert Parker, and *The Wright Brothers: How They Invented the Airplane* by Russell Freedman.

In 1839 Jacque Daguerre's new photographic process is presented to the French Academy of Sciences. Read *Snowflake Bentley* by Jacqueline Briggs Martin, illustrated by Mary Azarian.

In 1934 the first All-American Soap Box Derby is held in Dayton, Ohio. Read *Babymouse Burns Rubber* by Jennifer L. Holm and Matthew Holm.

WEMBERLY WORRIED
By Kevin Henkes

For some children, the end of August means preparing to go to school for the very first time. For them August has been designated Get Ready for Kindergarten Month. If you are hunting for a book that might help the very young overcome some of their anxieties about school, Kevin Henkes's *Wemberly Worried* works perfectly.

First published in 2000, *Wemberly Worried* appears to be one of the many Kevin Henkes titles headed for classic status. As a young artist, Kevin always knew he wanted to write and illustrate books, and he got his foot in the door of a publisher when he was nineteen. Since then, he has crafted one fabulous book after another.

Although Kevin is now married with children of his own, he is one of those gifted creators who has never forgotten what it feels like to be small and young and vulnerable. His books always have insight into the way children think and feel.

Kevin opens the story with these words: "Wemberly worried about everything." And readers get to see all the things that concern our mouse heroine—such as shrinking in the bathtub. Although everyone in her family tries to tell her not to worry—including her hip grandma mouse sporting a "Go with the Flow" T-shirt—Wemberly just can't help the thoughts that go through her mind. The radiator might contain a snake; the tree might fall on their house. So when school looms, she worries about the beginning of school. On a two-page spread her worries are even listed in large type: a mean teacher, a smelly room, finding the bathroom.

But of course, in Kevin Henkes's universe, everything turns out for the best. Wemberly finds a friend and discovers that her teacher, Mrs. Peachum, may not be so bad. By the end of the first day, she jauntily walks out of the room, telling everyone she'll return. "I will," she said. "Don't worry."

By creating a character full of neuroses, Kevin Henkes allows children to laugh at their own fears and feel that, in the end, going to school just might not be so bad after all. So to relieve your children's anxiety—and your own—about the beginning of a new school year, pick up *Wemberly Worried*.

KINDERGARTEN DIARY

By Antoinette Portis

For Get Ready for Kindergarten Month Antoinette Portis's *Kindergarten Diary* explores what a young child might think and experience each day in a new school. Portis, the very creative author of *Not a Box*, completely understands the imaginative and emotional landscape of young children. In *Kindergarten Diary* she gives us a child's-eye view of the first month of school.

At first new kindergartener Anna focuses on dressing her best—although she definitely doesn't want to wear socks. Rather than having a scary teacher, the children in Room 2 K find Ms. Duffy, who seems mild and friendly. The monkey bars on the playground suggest problems for our young girl—underneath lurk pretend alligators who just might eat you if you fall. As Anna practices sharing, writing her name, and jumping rope with a new friend, she discovers that she loves certain activities such as show-and-tell. By September 30, our heroine is "Too Busy to Write Any More! P.S. We are room 2 K. We are fine!"

As in her other books, Portis conjures up the extensive fantasy world of her young heroine as it plays against the real world. Monkey bars "were on a spaceship and you had to hold on or you would float away forever." The strong black line and bold art complements the simple story that shows the journey of a fearful child as she becomes engaged in her new world. Anna may well graduate from kindergarten with a "major in finger painting and a minor in show-and-tell"—not unlike Portis herself.

So if you have a kindergartener still tentative about what will happen in the coming weeks, pick up *Kindergarten Diary*. It will help any child understand that new experiences don't have to be frightening—they can lead to friendships and exciting adventures. *Kindergarten Diary* reassures young readers that, one day at a time, they can go to school and end up triumphant.

AUGUST 20

Happy Birthday Belinda Hurmence (*A Girl Called Boy*), Mélanie Watt (*Scaredy Squirrel*), Judy Schachner (*Skippyjon Jones*), and Margaret Bloy Graham (*Harry the Dirty Dog*).

It's the birth date of H. P. Lovecraft (1890–1937), *Dreams in the Witch House: And Other Weird Stories*; Jeff Brown (1926–2003), Flat Stanley series; and Sue Alexander (1933–2008), *Behold the Trees*.

It's also the birth date of Benjamin Harrison (1833–1901), the 23rd president of the United States.

In 1775 the Spanish establish a presidio (fort) in the town that will become Tucson, Arizona. Read *The No Place Cat* by C. S. Adler.

Charles Darwin first published his theory of evolution through natural selection in *The Journal of the Proceedings of the Linnean Society* of London on this day in 1858. Read *Life on Earth: The Story of Evolution* by Steve Jenkins.

In 1882 Peter Ilyich Tchaikovsky's *1812 Overture* made its debut in Moscow. Read *Jeremy's War 1812* by John Ibbitson.

In 1920 the first commercial radio station, 8MK (WWJ), began operations in Detroit, Michigan. Read *Radio Fifth Grade* by Gordon Korman.

PICTURE BOOK, Preschool, Elementary School

AUGUST 21

Happy Birthday X. J. Kennedy (*Talking Like the Rain*, *Elefantina's Dream*), Arthur Yorinks (*Hey, Al*), and Claudia Mills (*Gus and Grandpa* series, *Being Teddy Roosevelt*).

It's the birth date of Christopher Robin Milne (1920–1996), inspiration for his father, author A. A. Milne's, Winnie-the-Pooh stories.

In 1770 Captain James Cook claimed eastern Australia for Great Britain, naming it New South Wales. Read *Riding the Black Cockatoo* by Jack Danalis and *Bittangabee Tribe: An Aboriginal Story from Coastal New South Wales* by Beryl Cruse.

In 1831 Nat Turner led a slave revolt in Southampton County, Virginia, that killed close to sixty white people, the largest slave rebellion experienced in the American South.

In 1911 the *Mona Lisa*, a famous painting by Leonardo da Vinci, was stolen by a Louvre employee. Read *Who Stole the Mona Lisa?* by Ruthie Knapp, illustrated by Jill McElmurry.

Happy Birthday Hawaii, which became the 50th U.S. state on this day in 1959. Hence, it's Hawaii Admission Day. Read *High Tide in Hawaii* by Mary Pope Osborne and *Pig-Boy: A Trickster Tale from Hawai'i* by Gerald McDermott.

SALLY GOES TO THE BEACH
By Stephen Huneck

August has been designated National Beach Month and during this time people are encouraged to make one more trip to their local beach and enjoy the scenery and warm weather before it vanishes.

If you have small children ages two through eight and you want to take them on a beach trip, two recent picture books make wonderful beach companions. For anyone who loves canine companions, New England artist Stephen Huneck was the patron saint of dogs. He even built a chapel dedicated to them. He fashioned mesmerizing wood sculptures of different breeds, and he wrote and illustrated several picture books starring his black Labrador retriever Sally. In *Sally Goes to the Beach*, readers view a perfect beach trip through the eyes of a dog. Although people accompany her, Sally only thinks about other dogs. When they board the Island Ferry, Sally doesn't see a line of cars but a line of black and yellow labs. A seagull and a whale greet Sally as she heads to the island; there she finds a beach, a boat ride, and sand to dig. As she says at the end, "I cannot wait until tomorrow."

The bold woodcuts of Sally contain a lot of humor and exude the pure, simple joy of living. Perfect to use along with this book is Huy Voun Lee's *At the Beach*, which provides a multilingual beach party. In the book, Xiao Ming is learning to write Chinese. Because many Chinese characters are like pictures, his mother draws pictures in the sand on their day at the beach, describing the sites they see. By the end of the story both Xiao Ming and the reader have learned several Chinese words and gained an understanding of how this picture language works. A glossary at the end provides an easy reference for what has been covered. A perfect learning exercise, *At the Beach* has been illustrated using cut-paper collages with stunning boarders. This unusual picture book inspires children to gain some knowledge while they enjoy beach time.

Wherever you live, landlocked or otherwise, I hope you get to plan one more trip to the beach this summer. If you can't, enjoy these books about a glorious day at the beach.

BATS AT THE BEACH

By Brian Lies

August serves as National Beach Month, reminding us to get out and enjoy this environment before the summer season ends. When most of us think of beaches, bats don't instantly come to mind. But what if creatures we don't normally associate with it inhabited the beach?

Incongruity can be one of the most powerful tools in the hands of a creative artist. Brian Lies, who has added his illustrative charm to a plethora of children's books, brought together the beach and an unusual visitor. While his second grade daughter was getting ready for the school bus one December morning, she pointed to a bumpy frost pattern on the window and said, "Look, Daddy. It's a bat, with sea foam." As soon as she was on the bus, he pulled out a yellow legal pad and started writing and drawing. *Bats at the Beach* begins with an enticing bat, surfing the waves. This version of the frost pattern on the window serves as Lies's way of thanking his daughter for the idea behind the book.

Against a dark blue night background, when "the moon is just perfect for bats at the beach," the bats prepare for their outing just as human families do. Buckets, trowels, banjoes, blankets, books, and towels get strapped to their backs and under their wings before they fly off. The bats have all of the appropriate accoutrements—including moon-tan lotion—and they make creative use of what has been left behind by people that day. Bats fly each other as kites; they play volleyball; they slip notes in a bottle to go out to sea; and they use discarded cardboard cartons for boat races. Admittedly, most of their gastronomic fare sounds a bit repulsive—beetles, ants, moths, pickled slugs. But Lies remains true to bat behavior, even in fantasy. Certainly one of the most inventive picnic treats ever invented, bug-mallows toasted on slender sticks, looks familiar, although I don't think I would eat one. When they head to the snack bar, they hang upside down and chase moths for desert. And, before the sun rises, these happy creatures head home, to sleep and dream about their experiences.

If you go to the beach today, daylight hours will probably be best. But take along a copy of *Bats at the Beach*. This celebration of bats enjoying the simple pleasures of beach living will keep children ages three through eight laughing, turning the pages, and asking for it to be read again.

AUGUST 22

Happy Birthday Ray Bradbury (*The Halloween Tree, Switch On the Night*) and Will Hobbs (*Downriver*).

In 1864 twelve European nations signed the First Geneva Convention, establishing laws for the care and treatment of prisoners of war. Read *Summer of My German Soldier* by Bette Greene.

On this day in 1902 **Theodore Roosevelt** became the first president of the United States to ride in an automobile. Read *Bully for You, Teddy Roosevelt!* by Jean Fritz, illustrated by Mike Wimmer, and *The Great Adventure: Theodore Roosevelt and the Rise of Modern America* by Albert Marrin.

Althea Gibson became the first black competitor in international tennis on this day in 1950. Read *Nothing but Trouble: The Story of Althea Gibson* by Sue Stauffacher, illustrated by Greg Couch, and *Playing to Win* by Karen Deans, illustrated by Elbrite Brown.

It's Be an Angel Day. Read *Green Angel* by Alice Hoffman and *How Angel Peterson Got His Name* by Gary Paulsen.

AUGUST 23

Happy Birthday Melvin Berger (*Germs Make Me Sick!*).

In 79 AD Mount Vesuvius, in what is now Italy, began stirring on the feast day of Vulcan, the Roman god of fire. Read *Bodies from the Ash: Life and Death in Ancient Pompeii* by James M. Deem, *Pompeii Lost and Found* by Mary Pope Osborne, illustrated by Bonnie Christensen, and *Danger! Volcanoes* by Seymour Simon.

In 1966 Lunar Orbiter 1 took the first photograph of Earth from orbit around the Moon. Read *Earth: Our Planet in Space* by Seymour Simon.

It's National Sponge Cake Day. Read *Good Work, Amelia Bedelia* by Peggy Parish, illustrated by Lynn Sweet.

THE PEOPLE COULD FLY

By Virginia Hamilton
Illustrated by Leo and Diane Dillon

August 23 of each year has been designated by UNESCO as the International Day for the Remembrance of the Slave Trade and Its Abolition. This date was chosen because from August 22 to 23, 1791, an uprising began on the island of Saint Domingue, now Haiti, which helped bring about the end of the slave trade. If you want to introduce children ages eight through twelve to the topic of the day, pick up a classic, Virginia Hamilton's *The People Could Fly*.

Certainly the most awarded writer of her generation, Hamilton received two Newbery Medals, the first McArthur Genius grant to a children's book writer, the Hans Christian Anderson Award, the Laura Ingalls Wilder Award, and the National Book Award. The list got longer every year of her life. As a student at Antioch College, she met Janet Schulman, who became publisher of Random House's children's book department. Hamilton had just had an adult novel rejected and mentioned this to Janet, who suggested that she go back to a story of a Watutsi princess, written in college, for the subject of a children's novel. That book, *Zeely*, would launch Hamilton's career in 1967.

During the eighties, Schulman observed that there were no anthologies of African-American folktales for children. She knew that Hamilton had always been interested in the stories that grew out of slavery and suggested that she pull together a large volume of these, making them accessible to children and families. In *The People Could Fly*, Hamilton gathered slave stories and rewrote them in her own beautiful literary style.

In this attractive volume, oversize and illustrated by Leo and Diane Dillon, two dozen slave stories are arranged according to theme: animals; the real, the extravagant, and the fanciful; the supernatural; and freedom. Certainly one of the most successful books about African-American culture during the eighties, the book attracted a lot of attention in the press and became a staple of almost every library.

I always think *The People Could Fly* is one of the best ways to introduce Virginia Hamilton to those who may have missed this singular author. I am so sorry that I can no longer hear her tell her spellbinding tales. No one could hold an audience in the palm of her hand as easily as Virginia Hamilton. But collections like *The People Could Fly* allow readers to hear her voice in narrative.

POMPEII: LOST AND FOUND

By Mary Pope Osborne

Illustrated by
Bonnie Christensen

On this day in 79 AD an active volcano in southern Italy, Mount Vesuvius, erupted and destroyed the Roman cities of Pompeii and Herculaneum. Escaping the disaster, Pliny the Younger wrote: "[B]lack and horrible clouds, broken by sinuous shapes of flaming winds, were opening with long tongues of fire." What a stylist! Modern authors can rarely do better.

Our book of the day, Mary Pope Osborne's *Pompeii: Lost and Found*, illustrated by Bonnie Christensen, brings this disaster alive for young readers. In a very clear text, Mary Pope Osborne provides the historical background of the events of almost two thousand years ago. For eighteen hours poisonous gasses filled the air and hot ash poured down on the city, completely burying it. Not until 1763 did archaeologists identify Pompeii, and since then two-thirds of the village has been uncovered. Osborne provides information about the town that has been gleaned from artifacts and engages in speculation about various objects located in the ruins. She encourages young readers to put themselves in the place of the archaeologists themselves.

The Romans were masters of creating frescoes and used these lush paintings to decorate Pompeii. So Bonnie Christensen also learned how to create frescoes and designed one for every part of this book: the endpapers, the jacket, and each large double-page spread. Her attention and dedication not only made it possible to depict everything discussed in the text, but also allowed her to create a book completely authentic in feeling and tone. All parts of this once-vibrant city—the public baths, the theater, the children playing, even the election posters—have been believably re-created. Not only do you learn about Pompeii in this book, you also feel that you are truly walking its streets, getting to know its citizens.

I am grateful that artists with Bonnie's talent have turned their hand to illustrating informational texts for the young. Not only do children benefit—so do the adults who read with them.

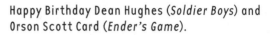

AUGUST 24

Happy Birthday Dean Hughes (*Soldier Boys*) and Orson Scott Card (*Ender's Game*).

In 1456 printing of the **Gutenberg** Bible was completed. Read *Johann Gutenberg and the Amazing Printing Press* by Bruce Koscielniak.

Alaska became a United States territory in 1912. Read *Under Alaska's Midnight Sun* by Deb Vanasse, illustrated by Jeremiah Trammell, and *Diamond Willow* by Helen Frost.

In 1932 Amelia Earhart became the first woman to fly across the United States nonstop (from Los Angeles, California, to Newark, New Jersey). Read *A Picture Book of Amelia Earhart* by David A. Adler, illustrated by Jeff Fisher.

It's Pluto Demoted Day, because in 2006 the International Astronomical Union (IAU) redefined the term *planet* such that Pluto was no longer considered one. Read *Pluto: From Planet to Dwarf* by Elaine Landau, *When Is a Planet Not a Planet?* by Elaine Scott, and *The Planet Hunter: The Story Behind What Happened to Pluto* by Elizabeth Rusch, illustrated by Guy Francis.

It's also National Waffle Day. Read *Everything On a Waffle* by Polly Horvath.

AUGUST 25

Happy Birthday Virginia Euwer Wolff (*Make Lemonade*), Charles Ghigna (*Mice Are Nice*), Ian Falconer (*Olivia*), and Lane Smith (*It's a Book*, *Grandpa Green*, *The Stinky Cheese Man and Other Fairly Stupid Tales*).

It's the birth date of Bret Harte (1836–1902), *The Queen of the Pirate Isle*; and Walt Kelly (1913–1973), *Pogo*.

In 1835 the *New York Sun* newspaper perpetrated the Great Moon Hoax. Read *The Great Moon Hoax* by Stephan Krensky, illustrated by Josee Bisaillon.

Best birthday wishes to the United States National Park Service, created in 1916. Read *M Is for Majestic* by David Domeniconi, illustrated by Pam Carroll.

Other books to read in honor of the 1944 liberation of Paris from the Nazis by the Allies include *Eloise in Paris* by Kay Thompson, illustrated by Hilary Knight, and *Dodsworth in Paris* by Tim Egan.

It's Kiss and Make Up Day. Read *Counting Kisses* by Karen Katz and *Funny You Should Ask: How to Make Up Jokes and Riddles with Wordplay* by Marvin Terban, illustrated by John O'Brien.

THIS IS PARIS
By Miroslav Sasek

At dawn on August 25, 1944, the Second French Armored Division entered Paris, ending the German occupation. Charles de Galle led a parade that day down the Champs Elysees. Although Hitler had ordered the destruction of this amazing city, the occupying German officer ignored that decree and surrendered instead.

The book of the day, *This Is Paris* by Miroslav Sasek, focuses on none of these amazing, historic events. What it presents, in full glorious color, is a tribute to the City of Light. But certainly the author had been a witness to many of the events in Europe during World War II and immediately afterward.

After the Communist takeover of Czechoslovakia, Sasek left his homeland and studied first in Paris before eventually settling in Munich. While he worked for Radio Free Europe, he noticed that tourists were often ill prepared for sightseeing. So he wrote his first travel guide for families in 1959, *This Is Paris*. Because of the book's success, Sasek created a series with thirteen additional titles, on places such as London, Rome, and New York.

Sasek renders the buildings of Paris in images pleasing to the eye, but he also focuses on the people of the city. He incorporates stamps, currency, flags, costumes, and customs. This oversize volume is perfect for presenting a grand city. Although adults can enjoy everything about the books, Sasek always focused on details of interest to children. *This Is Paris* begins by introducing readers to the cats of the city and then shows street artists, the bird market, and the cemetery for dogs. In sixty pages he presents the highlights of Paris, providing just enough information to entice readers to explore other sources.

But like all nonfiction, Sasek's titles became inaccurate over time. After forty years *This Was Paris* would have been a better title for our book of the day. By the time I published *Children's Books and Their Creators* in the midnineties I had to say, sadly, that these gems were out of print. Fortunately, the art book publisher Rizzo brought *This Is Paris* back into print in 2004. They retained the large size of the book, captured the color and quality of the artwork, and printed the images on a beautiful cream paper. Using an asterisk to indicate facts that have changed, the publisher provides an updated "This is Paris . . . Today" section on current facts.

Now "it's your turn to see Paris" Sasek writes at the end of his book. For anyone traveling to the city, or anyone who wants to provide lessons in culture and geography, no finer book exists than this one.

THE ASTONISHING LIFE OF OCTAVIAN NOTHING: THE POX PARTY

By M. T. Anderson

For Audio Book Month, M. T. Anderson's *The Astonishing Life of Octavian Nothing: The Pox Party* makes an excellent choice for listening with the entire family. Although the book has had a profound effect on good seventh- and eighth-grade readers, it may be most appreciated by high school students and adults. If you are trying to hook middle schoolers—or anyone—into this title, I suggest picking up the audio recording of it.

In the first chapter readers meet Octavian Nothing, an elegant and refined eighteenth-century Boston resident, who boasts knowledge of the classical subjects and lives with his mother in the Novanglian College of Lucidity. But the first section of this book ends with a shocking revelation: Octavian is a slave, the subject of experiments by scientists and philosophers of the Age of Reason to determine how well Africans can learn and think. During a Pox Party, where they inoculate everyone against the dreaded smallpox, Octavian's beloved mother dies, leaving him senseless and speechless, unable even to compose descriptions in his diary. Although most of the book is narrated from Octavian's point of view, letters, newspaper clippings, and scientific studies pick up the narrative when he cannot talk. In this two-volume work Octavian eventually becomes a soldier in the American Revolution—but for the British in Lord Dunmore's army.

With shifting points of view and understanding, language that comes out of the eighteenth century, and a profound vision of hypocrisy and evil, *Octavian Nothing* shows the American Revolution in a different light: What did the fight for freedom mean for those who were enslaved? Were Anderson merely interested in philosophy, of course, the novel would fail. But he has brought Octavian and an entire cast of characters vividly to life. He has crafted a story that has haunted me as a reader from the first minute that I picked up this incredible book until today.

If you love books for children, M. T. Anderson's work is simply too good to miss. It sets new standards for writing and treats readers with the ultimate respect. For anyone who has felt intimidated by this book, try the audio version—it helps listeners understand the cadence and rhythm of the language. Just be sure to have a copy of the book close by. You will definitely find yourself going back—or forward—to read more.

AUGUST 26

It's the birth date of Patricia Beatty (1922–1991), *Turn Homeward, Hannalee, Lupita Manana.*

In 1789 the Declaration of the Rights of Man and of the Citizen was approved by the National Constituent Assembly of France. Read *The Red Necklace: A Novel of the French Revolution* by Sally Gardner.

On this day in 1920 the 19th Amendment to United States Constitution took effect, giving women the right to vote.

It's National Dog Day. Read *Dog Day* by Sarah Hayes, illustrated by Hannah Broadway, *Dog Days* by Jeff Kinney, and *Good Dog, Carl* by Alexandra Day.

It is also National Cherry Popsicle Day. Read *The Kid Who Invented the Popsicle* by Don L. Wullfson.

AUGUST 27

Happy Birthday Ann Rinaldi (*A Break with Charity*, *The Secret of Sarah Revere*), Suzy Kline (Horrible Harry series, *Herbie Jones*), Suzanne Fisher Staples (*Shabanu*, *Under the Persimmon Tree*), and Sarah Stewart (*The Gardener*, *The Library*).

It's the birth date of Arlene Mosel (1921–1996), *Tikki Tikki Tembo*.

 It's also the birth date of **Lyndon Baines Johnson** (1908–1973), the 36th president of the United States.

Charles Rolls (1877–1920), cofounder of Rolls-Royce, was also born on this day. Read *Shapes That Roll* by Karen Nagel, illustrated by Steve Wilson.

THE MAGIC SCHOOL BUS AT THE WATERWORKS

By Joanna Cole

Illustrated by Bruce Degen

Children around the country have either headed back to school or are about to do so. Much of the drama of these first days centers on the teacher: Who will she be? Will he be nice or mean? Will she be easy or hard?

The best I can wish for these children is that they might end up with the real-life equivalent of my second favorite fictional teacher: Ms. Frizzle. (My favorite remains Albus Dumbledore.) When Ms. Frizzle's students arrive in class, they feel they have bad luck because they have the strangest teacher in the school. Ms. Frizzle wears bizarre dresses and shoes with snakes and frogs on them and keeps a pet iguana named Liz in the classroom. She makes her class conduct science experiments and read five science books a week. And while other classes get to go to the zoo, Ms. Frizzle plans to take her students to the waterworks, assigning them to gather facts about water before they do.

When it comes time to leave for the class trip, rather than a real bus driver, the Frizz herself sits at the wheel of a school bus that miraculously changes into an airplane! The children embark on an adventure that will teach them about science and water in a completely amazing way. Every page of this funny information book has been filled with facts about water, as well as banter between the children and Ms. Frizzle. At the end of the book when the students learn they will be studying volcanoes next, they know to prepare for some pretty strange things.

In *The Magic School Bus at the Waterworks*, Joanna Cole's text for ages four through eight is a perfect balance of understatement and irony, as Ms. Frizzle leads her students on one of the most exciting field trips of all time. Bruce Degen adds a great deal of humor and information in the drawings. From the first Magic School Bus book in 1986 to a television series based on the books, Ms. Frizzle has been leading students through all kinds of science trips—from exploring the solar system to going inside a beehive. All the Magic School Bus books demonstrate that science can be fun, exciting, and entertaining. And they also remind us that it might not be so bad to get the strangest teacher in school this year.

Fasten your seat belt. You are going to love traveling with the Frizz, wherever she takes you.

MAKE WAY FOR DUCKLINGS
By Robert McCloskey

In August of 1941 a picture book appeared that has become synonymous with the city of Boston for millions of readers. While he was an art student there, Robert McCloskey got the idea for *Make Way for Ducklings* from a true story that appeared in the newspaper. However, he developed the book in New York while living in a small Greenwich Village apartment with illustrator Marc Simont.

Unfortunately, although he had a great story about Mr. and Mrs. Mallard and their search for a safe home for their ducklings, McCloskey didn't know how to draw ducks. He went to the park and the Museum of Natural History—and made hundreds of duck drawings. Finally, in an act of desperation, he bought some ducks and put them in his bathtub. But the ducks still moved too quickly for McCloskey to capture them in detail.

Finally, one night as he and Simont were having dinner, a solution occurred to the frustrated artist: McCloskey gave the ducks some of the red wine he was enjoying that evening, and the ducks slowed down. McCloskey later apologized for his youthful misdemeanor. If you look closely to the page where a boy goes speeding by on a bicycle, you will notice a male mallard back on his wings. I have always believed that this picture was drawn from a drunken duck.

In the final picture for *Make Way for Ducklings*, the reader sees Mr. Mallard waiting for his family on a safe island, one without turtles and foxes. Because the book was published during World War II, the first children who read it often had fathers away from home. It sent a subtle, but powerful message: that the family would be reunited in a safe place.

However unorthodox McCloskey's methods, they always remind me that a great book requires an author and artist to be willing to go the extra mile to complete a classic. And for over seventy years, children have delighted in the adventures of Kack, Lack, Mack, Nack, Ouck, Pack, Quack, and their parents as they explore the city of Boston.

AUGUST 28

Happy Birthday Phyllis Krasilovsky (*The Cow Who Fell in the Canal*), Allen Say (*Grandfather's Journey*), Kevin Hawkes (*Library Lion*, *The Wicked Big Toddlah*), and Brian Pinkney (*The Faithful Friend*, *Duke Ellington*).

It's the birth date of Roger Duvoisin (1904–1980), *Petunia, Veronica, White Snow, Bright Snow*; Roger Tory Peterson (1908–1996), *Backyard Birds*; Tasha Tudor (1915–2008), *1 is One, A Time to Keep, Corgiville Fair*; and F. N. Monjo (1924–1978), *The Drinking Gourd*.

In 1845 the first issue of *Scientific American* magazine was published. Read *Investigating the Scientific Method with Max Axion, Super Scientist* by Donald Lemke, illustrated by Tod Smith.

In 1961 Motown released what would be its first number one hit, "Please Mr. Postman" by The Marvelettes. Read *The Jolly Postman* by Janet and Allan Ahlberg.

On this day in 1963 **Martin Luther King Jr.** gave his famous "I Have a Dream" speech during the March on Washington for Jobs and Freedom. Reread *Martin's Big Words* by Doreen Rappaport, illustrated by Bryan Collier.

In 2003 the planet Mars made its closest approach to Earth in nearly sixty thousand years. Read *Destination: Mars* by Seymour Simon and *You Are the First Kid on Mars* by Patrick O'Brien.

AUGUST 29

Happy Birthday Karen Hesse (*Out of the Dust*).

It's the birth date of Joseph Jacobs (1854–1916), *English Fairy Tales*.

In 1758 the first American Indian Reservation was established at Indian Mills, New Jersey. Read *The Absolutely True Diary of a Part-Time Indian* by Sherman Alexie.

Shays' Rebellion began on this day in 1786. Read *The Bar Code Rebellion* by Suzanne Weyn.

It's More Herbs, Less Salt Day. Read *Herb the Vegetarian Dragon* by Jules Bass, illustrated by Debbie Harter.

JOURNEY TO THE RIVER SEA

By Eva Ibbotson
Illustrated by Kevin Hawkes

If you are trying to squeeze in one more great book for summer reading, our book of the day, Eva Ibbotson's *Journey to the River Sea*, would be a wonderful choice. Born in Austria, Eva Ibbotson traveled between homes in Edinburgh and Berlin as a child. While attending school at Cambridge University, she met and married Alan Ibbotson, a professor and entomologist who kept an ant nest under his bed. After he died, she wrote *Journey to the River Sea* in honor of him and his love of the natural world.

For this book she chose a fearless and sensitive orphan, Maia, as her protagonist. In 1910, accompanied by a fierce governess, Miss Minton, Maia gets sent to live with her aunt and uncle in Brazil. Although she imagines wild adventures on the Amazon, she finds that this family has done everything in its power to live like Englishmen in the midst of a jungle.

But everything changes when Maia follows a mysterious young boy and gets swept up into the adventure of her dreams. This boy, Finn, actually is a British heir who would rather live in the wild than be captured and sent back to his English estate. Maia also befriends Clovis, a young actor traveling in Brazil, and helps him find a home of his own. With lots of wicked characters and saintly figures, the book lovingly captures the flora and fauna of the Amazon. Maia adores the natural world around her, and every time she escapes to it readers feel they have entered paradise. She sounds, actually, a great deal like naturalist and explorer Baron von Humboldt did in his journal as he described the wonders of this very region in 1800.

Grounded in fine historical research, the book reads like an adventure and survival novel. Ideal for eight-year-olds and up, the book can be used as a read aloud for families and in the classroom, or can be enjoyed in book discussion groups. Like all of Ibbotson's books, *Journey to the River Sea* relies on a plot- and character-driven story that keeps readers enthralled until the final pages. And, of course, this queen of happy endings does not disappoint anyone as she wraps up the story.

Reading *Journey to the River Sea* is the next best thing to a trip down the Amazon. Pick it up if you enjoy an old-fashioned story, well told.

LIFE STORY

By Virginia Lee Burton

Today is the birthday of an artist who was born into a cultured family in Newton, Massachusetts, in 1909. Virginia Lee Burton could draw, write, and dance with equal skill. She favored the latter as a career; in fact, she was headed to New York to pursue that dream when her father broke his leg. She stayed to help him recover, a fortuitous moment for children's books.

Her sons, Aris and Michael, have always delighted in telling the story of how their parents met. Wanting to take art classes from the renowned sculptor George Demetrios, Ginnee showed up one day at his door. He took one look at this New England beauty—and fainted. Shortly after that, they got married.

While working as a newspaper artist, she drafted a book for children, "The Trials and Trails of Jonnifer Lint," the story of a dust bunny who had some interesting adventures. Editors all turned it down, but Lovell Thompson of Houghton Mifflin told her that he loved her drawing and thought she needed to work on finding material that children would enjoy. Ginnee read "Jonnifer Lint" to Aris, who promptly fell asleep. Then she asked herself, "What kinds of books would keep Aris from nodding off?" Well, he liked trains, and snow plows, and steam shovels. By focusing on the needs of her sons, Virginia Lee Burton invented one picture book after another, including *Mike Mulligan and His Steam Shovel* and *The Little House*, that would keep them, and other children, eagerly following the story.

AUGUST **30**

Happy Birthday Sesyle Joslin (*What Do You Say, Dear?*), Laurent de Brunhoff (*Babar* series), Helen Craig (*Angelina Ballerina*), and Donald Crews (*Freight Train*).

It's the birth date of Mary Wollstonecraft Shelley (1797–1851), *Frankenstein*; and John Gunther (1901–1970), *Death Be Not Proud*.

Happy Birthday Melbourne, Australia, founded in 1835. Read *The Lost Day* by Judith Clarke.

In 1909 the Burgess Shale fossils were discovered by Charles Doolittle Walcott. Read *Fossils Tell of Long Ago* by Aliki.

Thurgood Marshall was confirmed as the first African-American Justice of the Supreme Court of the United States on this day in 1967. Read *A Picture Book of Thurgood Marshall* by David A. Adler, illustrated by Robert Casilla.

In 1984 the Space Shuttle *Discovery* took off on its maiden voyage. Read *Onboard the Space Shuttle* by Ray Spangenburg, illustrated by Kit Moser.

To celebrate Burton's birthday I would suggest picking up her last book, *Life Story*. While not as well known as her two classics, it provides a stellar example of her genius. In this book Burton presents the history of the world in seventy-seven pages, a stunning display of her artistic and literary talents. She moves through the creation of the world to the age of dinosaurs to modern times with finesse, presenting an amazing amount of information along the way. The book ends with these optimistic and empowering words. "And now it is your Life Story and it is you who play the leading role. The stage is set, the time is now, and the place wherever you are."

Unfortunately, I never got a chance to meet Virginia Lee Burton, but I spent long and happy hours with her sons Aris and Mike Demetrios. Today I am thankful for her life, her sons, and those incredible books.

AUGUST 31

Happy Birthday Dennis Lee (*Alligator Pie*), Deborah Kogan Ray (*Dinosaur Mountain: Digging into the Jurassic Age*), and Kenneth Oppel (*Airborn*).

It's the birth date of William Saroyan (1908–1981), *The Human Comedy*.

 Also born on this day was educator **Maria Montessori** (1870–1952).

In 1803 Lewis and Clark left Pittsburgh, Pennsylvania, starting their expedition to the West. Read *Lewis & Clark* by Nick Bertozzi.

It's National Trail Mix Day. Read *Sheep Take a Hike* by Nancy Shaw, illustrated by Margot Apple.

MISS NELSON IS MISSING!

By Harry Allard and James Marshall

As August comes to a close, many children head back to or have already started school. Today I'm recommending one of my favorite stories about school, one that some teachers like to use at this time. It not only tells a great story, but also sends a subtle message.

For a few years James Marshall taught French and Spanish in high school, but in his spare time he loved to doodle. That talent eventually secured his first children's book contract for *Plink, Plink, Plink* by Byrd Baylor. By the time James Marshall created *Miss Nelson Is Missing!* he was at the height of his craft. Having worked out picture-book pacing and timing in the George and Martha series, he was now able to take a story, run it over thirty-two pages, and arrive at the end of a perfect arc. The idea of Miss Nelson was given to Jim by his friend Harry Allard, who called in the middle of the night and said to Jim: "Miss Nelson Is Missing!" And then Harry hung up the phone. Jim couldn't reach him, couldn't get back to sleep, and began to wonder about this Miss Nelson. In Jim's sketchbooks at the University of Connecticut, Storrs, you can follow his progress as he develops the idea for the book.

Miss Nelson presides over the worst-behaved class in school—they are rude during story hours and refuse to do their lessons. One day, rather than Miss Nelson, a substitute teacher—"a woman in an ugly black dress stood before them." Looking a bit like Maria Callas with a fake nose and long sharp fingernails, Miss Viola Swamp rules the class with an iron hand. She loads them down with homework and works them to death, and days go by without a sign of Miss Nelson. When the teacher finally returns, her students behave like angels. Only on the last pages do readers comprehend the true identity of Miss Nelson and Viola Swamp.

Of course, when read in class, it can always be followed by that question, "Who do you want, Miss Nelson or Viola? The choice is yours!" In this book, and so many others, Marshall shows that stories that make us laugh together are good for our spirits. James Marshall crafted some of the best characters ever created for children. In *Miss Nelson Is Missing!* he also explores with heart and wit the relationship between teachers and students—and the need to appreciate a good teacher when we find one.

ME . . . JANE

By Patrick McDonnell

September 1 has been set aside to celebrate International Primate Day. I can think of no better way to mark this day than to look at the life of Jane Goodall, who has devoted herself to the study and the conservation of chimpanzees.

Patrick McDonnell's *Me . . . Jane* is an exquisite picture book distinguished by writing, art, and design. The title page displays a girl clutching a stuffed chimpanzee, and the text introduces them as Jane and Jubilee. Jane loves the natural world and explores it; she makes drawings and notes of all she observes. She stays in the barn to watch how chickens lay eggs—all with her companion Jubilee. And she reads in trees—wonderful sagas of Tarzan, Jane, and the jungles of Africa. In a magical sequence, McDonnell shows Jane going to bed, saying her prayers, and dreaming of being in Africa working with animals. And then one day she wakes as an adult—and all her dreams have come true.

Two drawings from Jane Goodall herself have been incorporated into this story along with actual ornamental engravings from nineteenth- and twentieth-century texts. McDonnell has seamlessly woven these elements into his own India-ink-and-watercolor drawings. Everything about the book has been chosen with care: the pleasing and era-appropriate font type, which has been distressed to look old. The cream-colored, weighty paper feels wonderful to touch. This is one of those rare picture books where every element has been given care and attention.

But what is most remarkable is McDonnell's ability to re-create Jane Goodall as a child, in a way that any child can appreciate. She and Jubilee seem totally real and believable. And he perfectly shows the relationship of a child and a beloved stuffed toy. Jubilee at times appears to be alive in the art—just as stuffed toys do to children.

The final note, in which McDonnell talks about Goodall's accomplishments as an adult, seems inevitable given what she cared about as a child. This message that your childhood dreams can, and do, come true will be welcomed by both parents and children. This original, fresh, and exciting picture book is destined for a long life of its own.

SEPTEMBER 1

Happy Birthday to Gail Gibbons (*The Reasons for the Seasons, The Vegetables We Eat*), Jim Arnosky (Crinkleroot series), and Jane Hissey (Old Bear series).

It's also the birth date of Edgar Rice Burroughs (1875–1950), author of *Tarzan of the Apes*.

The Boston subway, the first underground public transportation system in North America, opened on this day in 1897.

In 1914 it was the last day of life for the last known passenger pigeon, Martha (named after Martha Washington), who lived in the Cincinnati Zoo. Read *Grandmother's Pigeon* by Louise Erdrich, illustrated by Jim LaMarche.

On this day in 1939 Germany invaded Poland starting World War II.

It's National No Rhyme (Nor Reason) Day! Read Norton Juster's *The Phantom Tollbooth*.

PICTURE BOOK, BIOGRAPHY, Elementary School

SEPTEMBER 2

Happy Birthday to Demi (*The Empty Pot, One Grain of Rice*), Ellen Stoll Walsh (*Mouse Paint*), and John Bierhorst (*Latin American Folktales*).

It's the birth date of Eugene Field (1850–1895), who wrote *Wynken, Blynken, and Nod* as well as other classic children's poems, and Lucretia Peabody Hale (1820–1900), author of *The Peterkin Papers*.

On this day in 1901 at the Minnesota State Fair, vice president Theodore Roosevelt was reported to have first said, "Speak softly and carry a big stick." For a glimpse at Roosevelt's childhood, read *Teddie: The Story of Young Teddy Roosevelt* by Don Brown.

In 1944 Anne Frank was sent to Auschwitz, the infamous Nazi death camp. For the autobiography of a girl who survived this camp and the end of the war, read *Hello, America: A Refugee's Journey from Auschwitz to the New World* by Livia Bitton-Jackson.

It's also National Blueberry Popsicle Day. Bon appétit!

FIRST PITCH: HOW BASEBALL BEGAN

By John Thorn

On September 2, 1850, Albert Goodwill Spalding was born on a farm in Byron, Illinois. As a boy he began to play baseball in boarding school, and as an adult he became one of the great pitchers in America. Spalding brought four pennants to his Boston Red Stockings club before he headed to the Midwest to play for the Chicago White Stockings. But today, of course, he is best remembered for his role as a sporting-goods king, which made him a millionaire, and the Spalding baseball.

In *First Pitch: How Baseball Began* baseball historian John Thorn describes Spalding and a lot of other baseball legends to debunk the prevailing story that Abner Doubleday is the inventor of baseball. In 1905, Spalding appointed an elite group of baseball old-timers to determine the origins of the game. Unfortunately, the Special Commission on the Origin of Baseball made a mess of this assignment—they accepted the completely false story of a man named Abner Graves who credited Civil War General Abner Doubleday with inventing the national pastime.

Thorn continues the saga, providing evidence of the early origins of baseball and showing young readers how real research can be accomplished. It really doesn't matter if you like baseball or not, this book presents a scholar's journey to find the truth. Thorn takes readers through a score of primary documents, including a handwritten 1791 law from Pittsfield, Massachusetts, that states "For the Preservation of Windows in the New Meeting House . . . no Person or Inhabitant of said town shall be permitted to play at any game called . . . Base Ball." In the end, Thorn argues that the 1845 New York Knickerbockers might best be called the fathers of American baseball, as they put in place so many of the rules of the game we know today. Curses! New York triumphs over Massachusetts in baseball once more!

As Thorn builds his evidence, he weaves in information about American colonial life, the Civil War, even references to baseball in Jane Austen. The forty-page paperback published by Beach Ball Books has been beautifully produced with full-color art, sidebars, and a heavy paper cover with elegant flaps. Now the Official Historian of Major League Baseball, Thorn goes a long way in this book to entice young readers to think about baseball—and to think about the process of historical research. Anyone who wants to share the best narrative nonfiction with young readers will want to pick up a copy of *First Pitch*.

PINKERTON, BEHAVE!

By Steven Kellogg

September has been designated Adopt a Shelter Dog Month. Possibly September should also be designated Steven Kellogg Appreciation Month. Steven has given so much to the field of children's books—both in the great picture books he has created and the hours he has spent talking to children. There was a time in his life when he traveled forty weeks out of the year to visit classrooms and libraries.

Anyone thinking of adopting a shelter dog should pick up a story inspired by Steven's own Great Dane, *Pinkerton, Behave!* It focuses on the dog's training, because like every puppy he needs to learn how to behave. At first the patient family tries to train Pinkerton at home, but he quickly develops some peculiar habits. "Come" sends him jumping out the window, and "fetch" causes him to eat the newspaper. So like dog owners the world over, the family calls in some professional help and sends Pinkerton to dog school.

Unfortunately, Pinkerton affects the dog school much as my puppy Lancelot did—he still doesn't get commands but causes the other dogs to disobey. Pinkerton proves to be particularly clueless on the "Get the burglar!" command and acts as if he has just met his new best friend. But, of course, even misbehaving Great Danes have a role to play. When a real burglar arrives in the house, Pinkerton saves the day! As a proud owner says in the end, "I love you, Pinkerton."

In this book as in all of his work, Steven combines a totally satisfying story with drawings filled with energy and exuberance. In fact, Steven Kellogg has never stopped having fun making picture books that are child-friendly and filled with humor. So if you know anyone who needs to laugh a bit about an ill-behaved puppy, get them a copy of *Pinkerton, Behave!* And treat yourself to other books by Steven Kellogg. You'll be glad that you did.

SEPTEMBER 3

Happy Birthday to Aliki (*Digging Up Dinosaurs, Mummies Made in Egypt, Feelings*) and Anita Silvey (*I'll Pass for Your Comrade: Women Soldiers in the Civil War, The Plant Hunters*).

It is the birth date of American author Sarah Orne Jewett (1849–1909), best known for *The Country of the Pointed Firs.* Jewett's children's book *Play Days* was published in 1878.

Happy Birthday also to Barkley the Dog on Sesame Street.

This day in 1752 never did happen, nor did the next six! England adopted the Gregorian calendar, and jumped from 9/2 to 9/9 to get in synch with other nations who had already switched to this arithmetical calendar. Read *A Child's Calendar* by John Updike, illustrated by Trina Schart Hyman.

It's Skyscraper Day! Visit your nearest high rise and read *Skyscraper* by Susan E. Goodman and Michael J. Doolittle or *Unbuilding* by David Macaulay.

SEPTEMBER 4

It's the birth date of Syd Hoff (1912–2004), *Danny and the Dinosaur*.

It's also the birthday of cartoon character Beetle Bailey, created by Mort Walker.

The city of Los Angeles was founded on this day in 1781.

Ten-year-old Barney Flaherty was hired as the first newsboy by the *New York Sun* on this day in 1833. Hence, it's Newspaper Carrier Day! Read *Henry and the Paper Route* by Beverly Cleary and *Paperboy* by Dav Pilkey.

In 1888 George Eastman trademarked Kodak and patented his roll film camera in 1888. Read *It's a Snap!: George Eastman's First Photo* by Monica Kulling, illustrated by Bill Slavin.

Beatrix Potter told the tale of Peter Rabbit in a picture and story letter to five-year-old Noel Moore in 1893.

THE WOLVES OF WILLOUGHBY CHASE

By Joan Aiken

On September 4, 1924, Joan Aiken was born in Rye, East Sussex, England. She was the newest member of a family of authors. Her father, Pulitzer Prize–winning poet Conrad Aiken, was just one of the creative people in Joan's life. Homeschooled by her mother, Joan Aiken decided at age five that she, too, wanted to be a writer. After working for the BBC and United Nations Information Office, she was able, after the publication of her first novel in 1962, to become a full-time author, sometimes producing two or three books a year.

When critics talk about comparisons to J. K. Rowling, they often mention Dianna Wynne Jones or Ursula K. Le Guin, because they created schools for wizards long before Hogwarts. But I have always thought that Rowling's most obvious kindred spirit, in terms of style, approach, and inventiveness, is Joan Aiken. Although Aiken's books are beautifully written and executed with a vocabulary that would impress any adult, they are plot and character driven and contain one exciting scene after another. Don't pick up one of her books late at night if you need to get sleep—she keeps the story going nonstop until the end.

The Wolves of Willoughby Chase, like the rest of the books that followed in the Wolves Chronicles, takes place in an alternate nineteenth-century England during the reign of James III. Aiken makes use of some real historical material, but the books are chock full of wild exaggerations, melodrama, and improbable events. They read as if they might have been written by Charles Dickens.

The owners of Willoughby Manor, the Greens, set off for a vacation and leave their plucky, resourceful, and outspoken daughter Bonnie with a new governess. Bonnie's cousin Sylvia comes from London to keep Bonnie company. This might seem like an innocent enough beginning, but things quickly grow menacing for the two girls. Bands of ferocious wolves roam the countryside, ready to tear apart anyone they capture, and Sylvia narrowly escapes them before she arrives at the manor. And the new governess isn't quite what the Greens envisioned—she fires the servants, burns wills and valuable documents, and locks the children in a closet without food. Aiken once said that her books "are concerned with children tackling the problems of an adult world," but good always triumphs over evil.

For many years when I was editor of *The Horn Book*, I brought Aiken books as gifts at parties or for overnight visits to friends who had children from ten to fourteen. Today young people in their twenties and thirties, many of them with children themselves, come up to me and say, "You gave me the Joan Aiken books!" *The Wolves of Willoughby Chase* is one of those unforgettable children's books.

BREAD AND ROSES, TOO

By Katherine Paterson

The first Monday of September marks Labor Day. A well-known poster proclaims, "The Labor Movement. The Folks Who Brought You the Weekend." But almost nothing exists in books for children to help explain the events of the first part of the twentieth century, when workers fought for fair pay and rights. Katherine Paterson's *Bread and Roses, Too*, will help young readers understand the historical background of this holiday.

Centered around the events of the Lawrence, Massachusetts, labor strike in the textile mills, which became known as the "Bread and Roses, Too" strike, the book brilliantly re-creates the life of workers in this era—the poverty, hunger, bad conditions, and early death. The story alternates between two protagonists, Rosa, whose mother and sister work in the mills as she tries to get an education, and Jake Beale, who has faked papers to labor in the mills so that he can support his drunken father.

SEPTEMBER 5

Happy Birthday Paul Fleishman (*Bull Run, Joyful Noise: Poems for Two Voices, Seedfolks*).

It's the birth date of the Wild West outlaw **Jesse James** (1847–1882).

On the Road by Jack Kerouac was published on this day in 1957.

The first ever Labor Day parade was held in New York City on this day in 1882. Read *Parade* by Donald Crews.

It's Be Late for Something Day.

It's also, officially, Cheese Pizza Day. Read William Steig's *Pete's a Pizza*.

As cries of "Short pay, all out" inspire the workers, they sing and chant, "We shall not be moved." Both Rose and Jake get swept up in the labor strike. Rosa frets over what will happen to their already impoverished family. Jake considers becoming a scab but manages to stay away from the mills and from the wrath of his father. However, in one particularly chilling scene, when Jake manages to get enough money to bring his father liquor, his father beats Jake until blood seeps all over his clothes.

Eventually, because the International Workers of the World, the Wobblies, get behind the strike and provide money and food, the families are able to send their children to New York, Philadelphia, and Barre, Vermont, to be cared for by other Labor Union members. Rosa boards a train to Barre, only to find Jake stowed away there. His father is now dead, and Jake fears that he will be sent to an orphanage or even accused of killing him. Fortunately for these two scarred children, a loving Italian family takes them into their hearts and home and helps them heal from the trauma caused by the strike.

In *Bread and Roses, Too*, Katherine Paterson makes the poverty of these children, their lack of food and clothing, palpable and real. She also shows what can happen when human beings band together and help one another. In a three-handkerchief ending, Rosa heads back to the family she loves—and Jake has a future that gives him reason to hope. Grounded in superb historical research, which Paterson shares in the end, the book goes a long way to explaining why we celebrate Labor Day weekend.

SEPTEMBER 6

It's the birth date of Felix Salten (1869–1945), *Bambi*; and Jessie Willcox Smith (1863–1935), *The Water Babies*, *The Everyday Fairy Book*, and *The Jesse Willcox Smith Mother Goose*.

In 1628 Puritans settled in Salem, Massachusetts. Read *Tituba of Salem Village* by Ann Lane Petry and *Witches!* by Rosalyn Schanzer.

In 1839 Cherokee leaders drafted a constitution for the Cherokee Nation. This followed a yearlong forced evacuation of Native Americans from their homes in the southern United States to Oklahoma, known as the Trail of Tears. Read *Only the Names Remain* by Alex W. Bealer, illustrated by Kristina Rodanas, and *Sequoyah: The Cherokee Man Who Gave His People Writing* by James Rumford.

It's Fight Procrastination Day, which must be the anecdote to yesterday's Be Late for Something Day.

It's Read a Book Day (though every day is a day to read a book!). Read *A Book* by Mordicai Gerstein.

AMOS AND BORIS
By William Steig

"On the sixth of September, with a very calm sea, he waited till the high tide had almost reached his boat; then, using his most savage strength, he just managed to push the boat into the water, climb on board, and set sail." Who is our sailor with savage strength? A mouse named Amos; his boat, the *Rodent*.

In *Amos and Boris*, legendary storyteller William Steig provides a yarn that will please all sailors, animal enthusiasts, and children and adults alike. Steig always had fabulous premises for his books. In *Amos and Boris* he explores this idea: What if a mouse, lost at sea, gets saved by a whale? Hence Amos finds himself a passenger on the back of Boris, who speaks in exquisite phrases like "Holy clam and cuttlefish!"

But long after Boris has gone back to sea and Amos returned to land, there comes a day when the small mouse must help the great whale. The ending of this picture book for ages six through ten rounds out a totally satisfying story. In this celebration of friendship—of the small and the large—Amos is finally able to bring their saga full circle. "They knew they might never meet again. They knew they would never forget each other." Playful and profound, the book also deals with serious questions: "Would his soul go to heaven? Would there be any mice there?"

Once described as "a sublime doodler," a phrase that pleased Steig, he created artwork from these doodles that has always delighted young readers. But his books have also been graced with beautiful language. Steig never talks down to children nor does he dumb down the language of his books. Words like *luminous* or *phosphorescent* appear in the text; there is a beauty and cadence to the prose. As is typical of Steig books, adults and children can savor each page and follow a unique story.

So, on September 6 take a sail with an unforgettable rodent and his friend. Because of recent movies, William Steig may best be known for *Shrek!*, now celebrating more than twenty years of publication. But *Amos and Boris* stands along with *Doctor De Soto* and *Sylvester and the Magic Pebble* as one of his greatest triumphs in book form. First published in 1971, it remains one of those stories that linger in the memory long after the book itself has closed.

THE LIBRARY

By Sarah Stewart
Illustrated by David Small

Over the years I have collected a list of titles, shared by teachers and librarians, to use for the beginning of school. One favorite choice of school and public librarians for the start of classes is Sarah Stewart's *The Library*, illustrated by David Small. Published in 1995, *The Library* begins with endpapers showing, appropriately, a library. Even before the first line, a young redheaded girl can be seen with her face behind a book, sitting on a park bench and walking through the rain.

Elizabeth Brown doesn't like to skate or play with dolls—but she loves to read. "She always took a book to bed, / With a flashlight under the sheet. / She'd make a tent of covers / And read herself to sleep." And so we follow our heroine through school and through her early attempts to lend out her books to friends. She settles down, tutors students, and buys any book that she can locate. She even reads while practicing yoga. In a house that becomes increasingly chaotic because of books, Elizabeth uses them as furniture and keeps them in piles stacked up to the ceiling.

In a wonderful end to the saga, readers see Elizabeth donate all her books to the Elizabeth Brown Free Library, move in with a friend, and read her way to the last page. Never has the *joie de livre* (joy of books) been captured so well. David Small's watercolors perfectly depict the library as it grows. He also moves a series of cats across that landscape, a detail that delights children. One of those great picture book texts with a pleasing beginning, middle, and end, *The Library* allows all of us who love books to acknowledge that we have a kindred spirit in Elizabeth Brown.

So whether you use David Wiesner's *Tuesday*, on the first Tuesday of school, or James Marshall's *Miss Nelson Is Missing!*, or Sarah Stewart's *The Library*, I hope you get the school year off to a good start by letting your students, or your children, know that they are going to find a lot of books that they will love this year. Just like Elizabeth Brown.

SEPTEMBER 7

Happy Birthday Sandra Louise Woodward Darling, pen name Alexandra Day, (*Good Dog, Carl*) and Eric Hill (*Where's Spot?*).

It's the birth date of C. B. Colby (1904–1977), *Strangely Enough, World's Best "True" Ghost Stories*; and Elmer Hader (1889–1973), *The Big Snow*.

Teeny tiny newborn Edith Eleanor McLean was the first baby placed in an incubator, called a "hatching cradle," in 1888. Read *Hatching Magic* by Ann Downer.

Philo Farnsworth transmitted the first TV image, a straight line, at his laboratory in San Francisco, with his image dissector camera tube, on this day in 1927. Read *The Boy Who Invented TV: The Story of Philo Farnsworth* by Kathleen Krull, illustrated by Greg Couch.

It's Neither Rain Nor Snow Day. Read *Cloudy with a Chance of Meatballs* by Judi Barrett and Ron Barrett and *Tuesday* by David Wiesner.

It's also Salami Day. Read *Go Hang A Salami! I'm a Lasagna Hog!: And More Palindromes* by Jon Agee.

SEPTEMBER 8

Happy Birthday to Jack Prelutsky, the first U.S. Children's Poet Laureate (*The New Kid on the Block, It's Raining Pigs and Noodles*), Jon Scieszka, the first National Ambassador for Young People's Literature (*The Stinky Cheese Man,* Time Warp Trio series, *The True Story of the Three Little Pigs*), Byron Barton (*Dinosaurs, Dinosaurs, Machines at Work*), Jeanie Adams (*Pigs and Honey*), and Michael Hague (*A Child's Book of Prayers*).

Richard Drew invented Scotch tape on this day in 1930.

Ellis Island Historical Site in New York opened to the public in 1990, providing access to the starting point of many families' American Journey. Read *I Was Dreaming to Come to America: Memories from the Ellis Island Oral History Project* by Veronica Lawlor, *Coming to America: The Story of Immigration* by Betsy Maestro, illustrated by Susannah Ryan, and *When Jesse Came Across the Sea* by Amy Hest, illustrated by P. J. Lynch.

It's International Literacy Day, highlighting efforts to provide the opportunity for all people, all over the world, to learn to read. Read *Booktalking Around the World: Great Global Reads for Ages 9–14* by Sonja Cole.

It's Pardon Day—a time for seeking forgiveness (because we all make mistakes) and remembering to say "Excuse me!" Read *Excuse Me, But That Is My Book* by Lauren Child.

DAVID GOES TO SCHOOL
By David Shannon

For some children, the beginning of school may be a bit of a challenge. For teachers, these children can often prove trying. David Shannon celebrates the reluctant learners in the perfect book, *David Goes to School.*

Many readers may have met young David in an earlier book, *No, David!* David Shannon actually wrote the first draft of this book when he was a child. His mother saved it and sent it to him years later. After looking at it, David decided that with a little alteration it would make a very good picture book. He writes, "The text consisted entirely of the words *no* and *David*—they were the only words I knew how to spell—and it was illustrated with drawings of David doing all sorts of things he wasn't supposed to do."

In *David Goes to School* our hero, or antihero, finds himself in trouble again. Only this time, the teacher tells him no—no yelling, no pushing, and no running in the halls. The teacher also gives David a new set of commands: sit down, don't chew gum, raise your hand, and pay attention. But David, unwilling and unable to obey the rules, acts out continually. When David has been told to pay attention, for instance, the illustration shows him gazing at the sky, where a large cloud shaped like a dinosaur lurks. In the end our bad boy has to stay after school and clean the desks. But the final lines give the reader—if not young David—some hope. "Good job, David! Yes, David. . . . You can go home now."

While adult readers might find themselves exhausted, feeling sorry for this poor teacher, children will see a bit of themselves—or at least enjoy watching a book character do what they might like to do. And the book functions as a way to introduce basic school rules. For this very reason many teachers love to open the school year with it because the ending makes quite clear that although bad behavior will be scolded, good behavior will be praised.

Both in *No, David!* and *David Goes to School,* David Shannon has executed picture books that keep readers laughing from the first page to the last. He has clearly never forgotten what it feels like to be a child.

THEODOSIA AND THE SERPENTS OF CHAOS

By R. L. LaFevers

Many states observe Archaeological Month during September, with activities to get children to think about this profession as a career. Even to me as an adult, the lure of going on an archaeological dig remains one of my unfulfilled fantasies.

The book of the day, R. L. LaFevers's *Theodosia and the Serpents of Chaos*, definitely flames those dreams. In a story that begins on December 17, 1906, eleven-year-old Theodosia introduces readers to her rather unusual living arrangements. Her father oversees the Museum of Legends and Antiquities, and her mother frequently travels by herself to Egypt to bring back artifacts for this London establishment. Although there is some tension about taking Egypt's treasures out of the country, the British and Germans have few qualms about doing so.

But although Theodosia shares her parents' passion for ancient objects, she has a gift they lack. She can tell when an object contains an evil curse—and she has perfected ways to remove them. Because her parents are so absorbed in their work, they have not made arrangements for Theodosia to attend school or be managed by a governess. She lives most of the time in the museum and has found a cozy sarcophagus to sleep in.

When her mother returns from her latest archaeological dig, she brings a rare object called "The Heart of Egypt," which is an amulet from an ancient tomb. And because it contains a curse far more devastating than any other, Theodosia actually gets swept up in a plot to return it to its rightful owners—before Britain is destroyed. That quest ultimately leads to her first trip to Cairo and her first chance to actually find some archaeological treasures. That is if she can get out alive—for by now a band of very evil characters trace her every move.

SEPTEMBER 9

Happy Birthday to Kimberly Willis Holt (*My Louisiana Sky, When Zachary Beaver Came to Town*).

It's the birth date of Aileen Fisher (1906–2002), *The Story of Easter*; and Phyllis Whitney (1903–2008), who wrote children's mysteries from the forties through the seventies. She lived to age 104!

Happy Birthday California, which became the 31st U.S. state on this day in 1850.

In 1945 the first computer bug was identified. While working on the Mark II Aiken Relay Calculator, a primitive computer at Harvard University, Grace Murray Hopper discovered a moth in the works and wrote in a logbook "first 'actual' case of bug being found." The terms *bug* and *debug* become part of computer programmers' language.

Chrysanthemum Day (*Kiku no Sekku*) started in Japan in 910 AD. Read *The Sign of the Chrysanthemum* by Katherine Paterson.

It's Wonderful Weirdos Day! The folks in Austin, Texas, created this holiday to celebrate wacky and eclectic people. Try *Weird Friends: Unlikely Allies in the Animal Kingdom* by Jose Aruego and Ariane Dewey.

Celebrate Teddy Bear Day by reading *Corduroy* by Don Freeman.

A plucky, clever heroine, fascinating material, and a page-turning plot all help make *Theodosia and the Serpents of Chaos* delightful for the ten to fourteen set. Even if it doesn't convince them to become archaeologists, it will completely convince them that reading can be fun.

SEPTEMBER 10

Happy Birthday Babette Cole (*Dr. Dog, Princess Smartypants*).

It's the birth date of Robert M. McClung (1916–2006), *Lost Wild America: The Story of Our Extinct and Vanishing Wildlife, The True Adventures of Grizzly Adams*.

Also born on this day was Marie Laveau (1801–1881), a famous New Orleans voodoo queen. Read *Voodoo Queen: The Spirited Lives of Marie Laveau* by Martha Ward.

The first Negro League All-Star Game was held in Chicago's Comiskey Park on this day in 1933. Read *We Are The Ship: The Story of the Negro League Baseball* by Kadir Nelson.

 It's Sewing Machine Day! On this day in 1846 Elias Howe patented the **sewing machine**. Read *Queen of Inventions: How the Sewing Machine Changed the World* by Laurie Carlson.

SWIMMY
By Leo Lionni

September has been set aside as a month to "Be Kind to Authors and Editors." Authors and editors are the people who make our best books possible, who work to provide quality content for children, and they deserve kindness and praise every day of the year.

I have always been amazed that creators of books, people who could consider themselves competitors, show amazing kindness to one another. A graphic artist and designer, Leo Lionni not only made fabulous books like *Swimmy*, but also cared about others who wanted to work in the field.

Lionni was born in Holland, the product of a mixed religious marriage, Christian and Jewish. His family moved frequently during his younger years—and by the time they moved to Italy, young Leo had mastered five languages. He left Europe in 1938 and managed to get his wife and children out right before Hitler invaded Poland. As someone devoted to the fine arts and graphic arts, Lionni worked in the advertising industry for a variety of clients, including the Museum of Modern Art, where he designed one of the great books of the era, *The Family of Man*. Eventually, he settled into a job as Art Director of *Fortune* magazine.

His children's book career came about by accident. One day he was attempting to amuse his grandchildren, Pippo and Annie, by tearing out scraps from *Life* magazine, telling the story of "Little Blue and Little Yellow," which he invented on the spot. When one of his friends, Fabio Coen, came to dinner, Fabio saw the book and said he'd like to publish it.

Lionni began to craft a series of books, using cut-paper collage, which explored issues important to him. In *Swimmy*, a Caldecott Honor book, a small group of red fish form a cooperative, and Swimmy becomes the eye of the group. Because they have come together, they can support one another, travel the ocean, and chase away larger fish. For these creatures, strength comes out of unity and working together.

Throughout his life Lionni supported other artists, giving them work and encouragement. When a young German refugee came to Lionni in the early fifties asking for work, Lionni looked at Eric Carle's portfolio and alerted him to a perfect position available at the *New York Times*. Carle, author of *The Very Hungry Caterpillar*, has remained grateful throughout his career for Lionni's kindness and mentorship. A new Lionni statue at the Eric Carle Museum of Picture Book Art commemorates the special bond between these two amazing men.

So cooperate, work together, and be kind to authors and editors. These are lessons we not only need to teach our children—we need to remember them ourselves.

GRANDPA GREEN

By Lane Smith

Since 1978 the first Sunday after Labor Day has been celebrated as National Grandparents Day to encourage grandchildren to tap into the wisdom and heritage of their grandparents. Encapsulating both the spirit and the intent of this holiday, our book of the day is *Grandpa Green* by Lane Smith.

As editor of *The Horn Book Magazine* I watched the beginning of Lane Smith's career. First he contributed art to some highly original works, such as Eve Merriam's *Halloween ABC*. And then he made his mark by teaming up with Jon Scieszka on fresh and funny books like *The True Story of the Three Little Pigs*, *The Stinky Cheese Man and Other Fairly Stupid Tales*, and *Baloney (Henry P.)*. Since his first book, Lane Smith has taken risks, he never does the same book twice, and he clearly sides with young readers rather than adult critics. Whether playing with the ISBN notice on the back of *The Stinky Cheese Man* or challenging readers to think about computers in *It's a Book*, Lane Smith creates very sophisticated art that makes children laugh and return to his books again and again.

Grandpa Green draws from a different side of this artist. Although touches of humor can be found in all the art, this book pulls at the heartstrings. As Lane Smith traces the life story of Grandpa Green, the art, using a muted palette of brown and green, displays magnificent topiary creations that blend in with the ideas explored in the text. Readers watch Grandpa Green grow up on a farm, get chicken pox, and entertain himself while sick. One of the best spreads shows *The Wizard of Oz* characters presented as topiary constructions. Grandpa Green fights in a war, meets his wife, and settles down to a life of horticulture. About halfway through the book, the identity of the narrator is revealed: he is Grandpa Green's great-grandchild. And although Grandpa Green has grown old and forgetful, the garden helps him remember important things. This book is as subtle as *The Stinky Cheese Man* was bold and brash. From the opening illustration of a topiary trimmed like a crying baby, to the final picture of Grandpa Green being depicted in a topiary by his grandson, every detail of this book is engaging and original.

On Grandparents Day, I can think of no better way to celebrate lives, memories, and creativity than with *Grandpa Green*.

SEPTEMBER 11

Happy Birthday Anthony Browne (*Gorilla*), Alfred Slote (*Finding Buck McHenry*), and Philip Ardagh (Eddie Dickens series, *High in the Clouds*).

It's the birth date of William Sydney Porter, pen name O. Henry (1862–1910), *The Four Million*, *The Gift of the Magi*; and D. H. Lawrence (1885–1930).

After sixteen hours and nineteen minutes in the water, Florence Chadwick became the first woman to swim the English Channel in 1951. Read *Maisy's Pool* by Lucy Cousins and *Get Set! Swim!* by Jeannine Atkins, illustrated by Hector Viveros Lee.

Reading *America Is Under Attack* by Don Brown and *Fireboat: The Heroic Adventures of the John J. Harvey* by Maira Kalman is one way to remember the attacks of September 11, 2001. It's also Libraries Remember Day, started by the Bensenville, Illinois, Public Library, to encourage libraries to stay open for twenty-four hours on this day, to commemorate the anniversary of 9/11.

Today is Make Your Bed Day. Read *Time for Bed* by Mem Fox and *There's an Alligator Under My Bed* by Mercer Mayer.

PICTURE BOOK, Preschool, Elementary School

SEPTEMBER 12

Happy Birthday Valarie Tripp (American Girl series).

Publisher Alfred A. Knopf (1892–1984) was born on this day.

In 1624 the first submarine was tested on London's Thames River.

 Elizabeth Barrett eloped with Robert Browning on this day in 1846. Read about these poets in *Elizabeth Barrett Browning & Robert Browning* by Martin Garrett.

In 1940 four teens followed their dog down a hole near Lascaux, France, and discovered what are now known as the 17,000-year-old Lascaux Cave Paintings. Read *Discovery in the Cave* by Mark Dubowski, illustrated by Bryn Barnard, and *The Secret Cave: Discovering Lascaux* by Emily Arnold McCully.

It's Chocolate Milkshake Day.

DOG HEAVEN
By Cynthia Rylant

September is World Animal Remembrance Month. One of life's most heart-wrenching experiences, both for children and adults, is the death of a beloved pet.

I wasn't able to have a dog until I was long past childhood. He first arrived as a photo—a small, amazingly beautiful Bernese mountain dog, who in time became my best friend, Merlin. As a writer, I was particularly dependent on him. When I worked on projects, he would sit next to my desk, watch me steadily, and turn his head knowingly when I asked myself a question. Although born lame, with the full use of only three legs, he thumped around the house to be with me at all times, monitoring my writing progress and alerting me to important times of the day—such as walks, meals, and bedtime. Even with all his health problems, Merlin lived to be nine and a half, an impressive age for this large breed. And then I had to deal with the absence of my beloved companion.

In my grief, I posted news of his death on Facebook; many of my friends had met him over the years at local conferences and bookstore signings. Hundreds of messages came back, providing comfort and kindness. Many people gave the same advice—"Have you read *Dog Heaven* by Cynthia Rylant?"

Rylant both wrote and illustrated this three-tissue tribute to canines. In her vision, dogs don't have wings in heaven, but fields and fields where they can run. Angel children play with the dogs; God and angels dispense biscuits in all shapes for them; they sleep on fluffy clouds. And, from time to time, the dogs get to visit their old homes, to make sure everything is all right. They will be in heaven "when old friends show up. They will be there at the door. Angel dogs."

Using simple, poetic language, Rylant creates such a wonderful vision of the next journey for dogs that readers smile and cry along with her. The book provides both joy and comfort in equal measure. It is the perfect gift for anyone struggling with the lost of their own beloved friend.

So if you know someone who is grieving the loss of a dog or cat, by all means get them a copy of *Dog Heaven* or *Cat Heaven* by Cynthia Rylant. She truly understands how all of us who miss our pets feel. Everytime I read it, I feel happy thinking about Merlin sleeping on a fluffy cloud.

LITTLE BEAR

By Else Holmelund Minarik
Illustrated by Maurice Sendak

Born in Denmark on September 13, 1920, Else Holmelund Minarik came to the United States when she was four. At first she hated English, the new language that she had to learn, but she became devoted to it—and to teaching first graders how to read words that had once perplexed her.

As she observed her students, Minarik realized that at the point when they had mastered basic reading skills, they wanted a book a bit more sophisticated than a picture book. But most novels fell outside their range. She worked on a prototype for such a book and brought it to Susan Carr Hirschman, then Ursula Nordstrom's assistant at Harper. Minarik believed that her manuscript, some stories about a character called Little Bear and his mother, was perfect for students at the end of first grade or beginning of second.

Hirschman took the manuscript "What Will Little Bear Wear" immediately to Nordstrom. For some time Nordstrom had been trying to interest some of the Harper authors in the same

SEPTEMBER 13

Happy Birthday Carol Kendall (*The Gammage Cup*) and Mildred D. Taylor (*Roll of Thunder, Hear My Cry*).

It's the birth date of **Roald Dahl** (1916–1990), *James and the Giant Peach, Charlie and the Chocolate Factory, Matilda, The BFG.*

In 1788 New York City became the first United States capital.

It's International Chocolate Day.

It's National Celiac Awareness Day. Read *Everybody Bakes Bread* by Norah Dooley, illustrated by Peter J. Thornton, but not everyone can eat bread made with wheat. Also read *Everyone Cooks Rice* by the same author and illustrator.

kind of idea—and they all had turned it down. Now here was a real teacher, with experience, who could help frame the books. Although Minarik's role was not acknowledged at the time, she, in fact, became the consultant for the entire I Can Read series, as these books were called. She helped establish character counts for each line (no more than forty), the spacing between the lines of text, and made sure the subjects of the books remained appropriate for first- and second-grade students.

For the truly lovable character that Minarik created, Nordstrom had no trouble choosing her favorite illustrator, Maurice Sendak. Sendak's Little Bear has heft and weight as he interacts with his mother in a warm, respectful, and playful way. In one story Little Bear pretends to fly to the moon, and his mother plays along. However, when he tires of the game he says, "You are my Mother Bear / and I am your Little Bear / and we are on Earth, and you know it." The four stories in the first Little Bear book, which would be followed by others, attest to the universal need for love, acceptance, and independence.

With more than six million copies in print, the Little Bear books have beguiled children since 1957, convincing them that they really enjoy this new skill called reading.

SEPTEMBER 14

Happy Birthday Diane Goode (*When I Was Young in the Mountains*), Elizabeth Winthrop (*The Castle in the Attic*), and Holly Meade (*Hush! A Thai Lullaby, On the Farm*).

It's the birth date of William H. Armstrong (1911–1999), *Sounder*; and John Steptoe (1950–1989), *Mufaro's Beautiful Daughters*.

In 1716 the first lighthouse in what will become the United States was lit in Boston Harbor. Read *Birdie's Lighthouse* by Deborah Hopkins, illustrated by Kimberly Bulcken Root, and *The Lighthouse Cat* by Sue Stainton, illustrated by Anne Mortimer.

Composer George Handel completed *The Messiah* in 1741. Read *Handel, Who Knew What He Liked* by M. T. Anderson.

In the British Isles it is Nutting Day and time to pick the hazelnuts. Read *Nuts to You!* by Lois Ehlert.

JOEY PIGZA SWALLOWED THE KEY

By Jack Gantos

September has been designated Attention Deficit Hyperactivity Disorder (ADHD) Month to educate everyone about effective treatments for the disease. In 1998 Jack Gantos published a book called *Joey Pigza Swallowed the Key* that not only became a National Book Award finalist but also goes a long way in educating young readers about ADHD. Joey Pigza is an endearing and sympathetic protagonist who is also both distracted and hyperactive. As he tells us in the first paragraph, "At school they say I'm wired bad, or wired mad, or wired sad, or wired glad, depending on my mood and what teacher has ended up with me. But there is no doubt about it. I'm wired."

Joey has had some rough times: his alcoholic father has abandoned him and he has been raised by his grandmother. When his mother returns, things don't really get better for him. He can't sit still. He can't pay attention. He always says the wrong thing. He just says, and does, whatever comes to his mind. His medication doesn't seem to work at certain times of the day. He swallows his house key; he hurts his finger when he sticks it into the pencil sharpener. Eventually Joey causes a serious accident that hurts another student. Throughout all of these events, Gantos keeps the story moving along at record speed, as Joey processes what happens in his own first-person voice.

Eventually, Joey gets sent off to a special educational center, where they send him to the hospital to scan his brain, do a lot of psychological analysis, and adjust his medication. And finally readers cheer as, much more in control, Joey goes back to his own school. It's impossible not to root for him. He's basically a good kid who always does the wrong thing. He's funny and dear and enraging all at the same time.

Jack Gantos began his career with a series of books about a badly behaved cat, Rotten Ralph. His own autobiography, *Hole in My Life*, tells about Gantos's scrapes with the law as a young boy. In fact, no one describes rowdy, out-of-control boys better than Jack. But Joey Pigza may well be his finest creation. For this character, Jack blended elements of his friends, kids he saw in school visits, and, of course, Jack himself as a boy. Joey's adventures continue in *Joey Pigza Loses Control*, *What Would Joey Pigza Do?* and *I Am Not Joey Pigza*. If you know young readers ages eight through twelve who want to understand ADHD—or who just want to laugh a lot about a badly behaved boy—share these books with them.

STREGA NONA

By Tomie dePaola

On September 15, 1934, in Meriden, Connecticut, a boy who would become one of the world's best storytellers was born. Tomie dePaola always credited his Irish and Italian family for providing him with the material for many of his sagas. I don't know if he came out of the womb spinning tales, but he claims that at age four he knew he wanted to draw pictures for books and "sing and tap-dance on the stage." Tomie sharpened his artistic talents at Pratt—where he danced the Charleston for benefits—and then the California College of Arts and Crafts. For a time he studied in a Benedictine monastery, but silence did not seem the best path for this ebullient young man. By the time I met him in the early seventies, Tomie could weave a web of words as well as any creative person in the field—both in writing books and while speaking to an audience.

Although any of Tomie's 250 titles could be featured in the Almanac, my favorite remains his Caldecott Honor book, *Strega Nona*, published thirty-five years ago. Drawing on the magic cooking pot theme in folklore, Strega Nona features a grandmother with a magic touch. But when her assistant Big Anthony tries to duplicate her pasta-making spell, he overwhelms the town with a flood of spaghetti. Fortunately, Strega Nona returns in time—and then dishes out an appropriate punishment for Big Anthony. Executed in acrylic paints and colored pencil, with dark brown outlines, the art captures dePaola's characteristic playfulness and silliness—just right for this story.

In general our humorists get fewer major awards than their more serious counterparts. Such has been the case with Tomie. Recently the American Library Association presented Tomie with the Wilder Award for his body of work—and as would be expected, he kept the audience enthralled. He has kept children laughing and adults equally amused for four decades. Even more important, he has reminded us not to take ourselves so seriously—but still pay great attention to what we put into the hands of children.

SEPTEMBER 15

It's the birth date of James Fenimore Cooper (1789–1851), *The Last of the Mohicans*; and Robert McCloskey (1914–2003), *Make Way for Ducklings*.

It's also the birth date of William Howard Taft (1857–1930), the 27th president of the United States.

In 1835 Charles Darwin and the HMS *Beagle* reached the Galápagos Islands. Read *"Galápagos" Means "Tortoises"* by Ruth Heller.

In 1928 Scottish bacteriologist Alexander Fleming discovered, by accident, that the mold penicillin has an antibiotic effect.

On this day in 1963 the bombing of the **Sixteenth Street Baptist Church** in Birmingham, Alabama, killed four little girls. Read *The Watsons Go to Birmingham—1963* by Christopher Paul Curtis and *Birmingham, 1963* by Carol Boston Weatherford.

It's Make a Hat Day. Reread *The Cat in the Hat* by Dr. Seuss and *A Three Hat Day* by Laura Geringer, illustrated by Arnold Lobel.

SEPTEMBER 16

Happy Birthday Joanne Ryder (*Bear of My Heart, Little Panda, The World Welcomes Hua Mei at the San Diego Zoo*).

It's the birth date of H. A. Rey (1898–1977), Curious George series.

In 1620 the good ship *Mayflower* set sail from Plymouth, England, to America. Hence, it is Mayflower Day. Read *Mayflower 1620: A New Look at a Pilgrim Voyage* by the Plimoth Plantation, with Peter Arenstam, John Kemp, and Catherine O'Neill Grace.

In 1630 the Village of Shawmut changed its name to Boston. Read *A Million Miles from Boston* by Karen Day.

It's Stepfamily Day. Read *Out of Order* by Betty Hicks and *Wait Till Helen Comes* by Mary Downing Hahn.

WHERE'S SPOT?

By Eric Hill

September has been designated World Animal Remembrance Month—and today I'm going to talk about one of the dogs most loved by the preschool set, Eric Hill's Spot. It is hard to believe that this pooch has only been around over thirty years. The ongoing saga of Spot began not with Spot himself, but his mother Sally. In *Where's Spot?* published in 1980, Sally goes searching for her son. As this yellow dog, with brown spots and a distinctive brown-tipped tail, looks around the house, she opens a door to find . . . a bear. Young readers lift several flaps in the book to see what Sally sees: a hippo in the piano, a monkey in the closet, and a turtle under the rug. Only in the end does Sally find the adorable Spot—nicely nestled in a basket.

Like many classics the book came about because of a child. Although never formally trained in art school, at fifteen Eric Hill studied informally with a cartoonist. While Hill was working as a freelance artist and designer, he noticed that his two-year-old son Christopher loved lifting flaps on the advertising pieces that Hill was creating. Hill had always been intrigued by the question of what his beloved dog actually did when the family left the house. He imagined that the dog had a secret life, never seen by owners. So in *Where's Spot?* he explored the idea of dogs at home with no human intervention and an imaginative lift-the-flap game. The book became such an immediate success that Hill was able to create children's books full time.

As a book for very young children, *Where's Spot?* does so many things right. It helps with place identification and animal identification. It provides a repetitive story pattern and a guessing game. And using very few words, the book presents a small story arc—a beloved son is lost and finally found in under a hundred words. The art itself—clear and clean, with strong black outline and bright colors—is showcased on bright thick paper, making it durable for the youngest reader. All the paper engineering details have been worked out brilliantly. Even on the first page, the flap can be lifted to put in the child's name in "This book belongs to." Perfect for shower gifts or the first book on a child's bookshelf, the Spot series has been translated into sixty languages and sold over fifty million copies worldwide.

BAD KITTY GETS A BATH

By Nick Bruel

September has been designated Happy Cat Month. But the cat featured in our book of the day isn't really happy. In fact, her owners have found a way to make her extremely miserable—by giving Bad Kitty a bath. I believe, however, that Nick Bruel, Bad Kitty's creator, must certainly be laughing as he works on Bad Kitty's saga. For in titles like *Bad Kitty Gets a Bath* and *Bad Kitty Meets the Baby*, Nick has developed a winning formula, making these books among the most popular graphic novels for children.

Bad Kitty actually made her debut in a picture book. With years as a children's bookseller at New York's Books of Wonder, Nick knew that good chapter books, that first step into reading, were hard to find. And so rather than taking Bad Kitty and making her the star of a board book, as others might have, Nick brought his character into a book for older children, those just learning to read. The combination of Bad Kitty, with her electric energy and zany antics, and a longer format to extend his story made the perfect combination. It also allowed Nick to create a book of "128 pages of pure Kitty-induced mayhem."

In *Bad Kitty Gets a Bath*, our feline friend gets very dirty and needs a bath. In the first chapter, the text tells readers that cats hate baths. Another chapter gives instructions to the person who is going to administer the bath—it recommends having an ambulance waiting with the engine running. Then the narrator tries different approaches—pleading, reverse psychology, and cajoling—to get Bad Kitty in the bath. None of the strategies work. Finally, Bad Kitty gets deposited in the bathtub. Humorous notes from Nick's editor Neal Porter sprinkle the text—"what Kitty says is so horrible and repulsive that we could all go to jail for the rest of our lives if this was printed."

Children love the mayhem created by Bad Kitty. Of course, the personality of this character is basically that of a little kid. Laugh-out-loud funny, with energetic drawings, this book invites many readings. It might also deter any parent or child from giving a cat a bath. Consequently your cat will be more likely to have a Happy Cat Month after you read this book!

SEPTEMBER 17

Happy Birthday Gail Carson Levine (*Ella Enchanted*), Elizabeth Hall (*Child of the Wolves*), and David McRobbie (*A Whole Lot of Wayne*).

It's the birth date of Elizabeth Enright (1909–1968), *Thimble Summer, Gone-Away Lake*.

In 642 AD the Library of Alexandria was destroyed. Read *The Library of Alexandria* by Kelly Trumble, illustrated by Robina MacIntyre Marshall.

The United States constitution was adopted in 1787. Hence, it is Constitution Day and the start of Constitution week. Read *The U.S. Constitution* by Kathy Allen.

On this day in 1796 the first U.S. president, George Washington, delivered his farewell address. Read *George Washington's Socks* by Elvira Woodruff and *George Washington's Breakfast* by Jean Fritz, illustrated by Paul Galdone.

SEPTEMBER 18

Happy Birthday to the *New York Times*, first edition published in 1851 and sold at two cents a copy.

The Fugitive Slave Act declaring that all runaway slaves were to be returned to their masters was passed on this day in 1850.

In 1977 the U.S. Voyager I took the first space picture of Earth and Moon together. Read *From the Earth to the Moon* by Jules Verne.

On this day in 1990 a six-foot-tall, five-hundred-pound Hershey Kiss was displayed in Times Square.

TREASURE ISLAND
By Robert Louis Stevenson

Today I want to prepare for one of the best days on the calendar—tomorrow is International Talk Like a Pirate Day. I am a firm believer that before you can talk like a pirate, you have to read about them.

Pirates remain fascinating for children, and in *Treasure Island* Robert Louis Stevenson brings together pirates, maps, and one-legged seamen with parrots on their shoulders. *Treasure Island* began, as do so many children's books, as a story told to a single child: Robert Louis Stevenson's stepson.

Robert Louis Stevenson's father believed his son should follow the family profession and design and build lighthouses. Although Stevenson loved hanging about in harbors and visiting isolated islands, writing was the only profession that truly appealed to him. After trying to be a barrister, he settled into a life of traveling and crafting essays about the people and places he saw. He made his name as a travel writer before he began creating the books that would ensure his immortality.

Published in 1881, *Treasure Island* moves from one tense moment to another, from the opening scene when a mysterious seaman, Billy Bones, arrives at the Admiral Benbow Inn. Young Jim Hawkins narrates the tale, and Long John Silver serves as the arch-villain, a character who now stands as the archetypical pirate. Eventually a band of heroes find the island, discover its treasure, and escape, foiling the pirates in the process.

Without a doubt, the best version of the book remains the Scribner classic edition, with art by N. C. Wyeth. He creates characters, sets scenes, and makes it possible to visualize Stevenson's masterpiece. In *Everything I Need to Know I Learned from a Children's Book* Andrew Wyeth says the illustration of "Blind Pew tapping up and down the road" from this volume set him on his path to become an artist, and the actor Robert Montgomery says it inspired him to become an actor.

But back to Talk Like a Pirate Day. An old pirate tune appears in the book: "Fifteen men on the dead man's chest— / Yo-ho-ho, and a bottle of rum! / Drink and the devil had done for the rest— / Yo-ho-ho, and a bottle of rum!"

As a child, I had no idea what these words meant but I couldn't resist the sound of them. So get reading and start salting away some catchy phrases for tomorrow.

LARKLIGHT

By Philip Reeve

It's International Talk Like a Pirate Day! What an inspired idea for a celebration. Pirate lore for children, however, can be a bit formulaic. After Robert Louis Stevenson's *Treasure Island* and James Barrie's *Peter Pan* set the parameters, most pirate books have followed a similar script. But not our book of the day: *Larklight* by Philip Reeve. In the fertile mind of the man who wrote The Hungry Cities chronicles, pirates have been combined with some surprising elements. In a nutshell, Reeve's romp in the park explores the premise: What if space travel had been invented when the British Empire was in full swing? Then nineteenth-century Britains, and not those upstart Americans, would start colonizing space. This idea allows Reeve to combine alternate history, steam punk, real historical events, adventure, travel, and yes, pirates—not on the high seas but in space.

At the beginning of the saga, Art and his sister Myrtle, the two narrators, live with their scientist father at Larklight, a space outpost just beyond the moon in the reign of Queen Victoria. When giant spiders attack their home and appear to have killed their father, Art and Myrtle flee— only to be rescued by Jack Havock, a space pirate who saves them from the vicious Potter moth. Jack has a grudge against the British Empire and travels with a makeshift crew of creatures from various locations in the solar system. But no peg leg for our boy; he even develops a crush on Myrtle.

From there, the story careens from one exciting Star Wars–type chase to another until the band ends up trying to foil a mad scientist, intent on destroying much of the universe. They get separated and are brought back together again in a smashing finale! Literally smashing. For it turns out that the Crystal Palace of the 1851 Great Exhibition can walk and is being controlled by the scientist.

Everything in this imaginative work of fantasy and science fiction is not only fun but also makes the reader long to explore space with Jack's band. In *Larklight* the combination of death-defying adventure and Victorian propriety is both hilarious and completely satisfying. Before going on to the sequel, our hero Art sits down to a "hot buttered muffin and a nice cup of tea."

However you celebrate International Talk Like a Pirate Day, pick up this gem. In the children's book field Philip Reeve is one of our most creative contemporary wordsmiths. You don't want to miss him.

SEPTEMBER 19

Happy Birthday Vicki Cobb (*Science Experiments You Can Eat*) and Libby Gleeson (*Half a World Away*).

Birthday greetings to fictional characters Hermione Granger of the Harry Potter series and Slimey the Worm from *Sesame Street*.

It's the birth date of Rachel Field (1894–1942), *Hitty, Her First Hundred Years*, *Prayer for a Child*, *Calico Bush*; Arthur Rackham (1867–1939), *Arthur Rackham Fairy Book*; Jim Haskins (1941–2005), *Get on Board: The Story of the Underground Railroad*; and William Golding (1911–1993), *The Lord of the Flies*.

In 1783 the first hot-air balloon was sent aloft in Versailles, France.

Mickey Mouse made his screen debut in *Steamboat Willie* at Colony Theater, New York City, in 1928.

SEPTEMBER 20

Happy Birthday Arthur Geisert (*Ice*; *Oops!*) and Donald Hall (*The Ox-Cart Man*).

It's the birth date of Miska Petersham (1888–1960), *The Rooster Crows*.

Author **Upton Sinclair** (1878–1968) was also born on this day. Read *Muckrakers: How Ida Tarbell, Upton Sinclair, and Lincoln Steffens Helped Expose Scandal, Inspire Reform, and Invent Investigative Journalism* by Ann Bausum.

In 1663 Galileo Galilei was tried before the Congregation for the Doctrine of the Faith for teaching students the Earth orbits the Sun. Read *Starry Messenger* by Peter Sís.

In 1848 the American Association for the Advancement of Science was created. Read *Science Verse* by Jon Scieszka, illustrated by Lane Smith.

GO, DOG. GO!
By P. D. Eastman

For World Animal Remembrance Month, I'd like to discuss a book with some canine heroes that do not have names. But the protagonists in P. D. Eastman's *Go, Dog. Go!* are some of the fastest, and funniest, dogs to appear in a children's book.

After the success of Dr. Seuss's *The Cat in the Hat*, Bennett Cerf of Random House convinced Seuss, his wife, Helen, and Cerf's wife, Phyllis, to form an editorial board that would shape stories suitable for children just learning to read, the Beginner Books series. Seuss would not only write two other very successful books for the series, *Green Eggs and Ham* and *One Fish Two Fish Red Fish Blue Fish*, but he would also publish P. D. Eastman's *Are You My Mother?* Philip Dey Eastman followed up this great book with an even more exciting title, *Go, Dog. Go!*

In a mere seventy-five words, Eastman portrays a group of dogs engaged in high-speed activities and madness. "Dogs in cars again. / Going away. / Going away fast. / Look at those dogs go. / Go, dog. Go!" These dogs drive around in cars and finally meet at a party. Three times a pink poodle asks a yellow dog, "Do you like my hat?" And he doesn't! Then on her fourth try, the dog adores the poodle's outrageous party hat—and they drive off into the sunset together.

As an antidote to the boring Dick and Jane stories found in school readers, the text engages young readers with a small vocabulary. Who wouldn't want to read about speeding dogs rather than slow children. As our first National Ambassador for Children's Books, Jon Scieszka, wrote in *Everything I Need to Know I Learned from a Children's Book*: "At school I was trying to learn to read by deciphering stories featuring two lame kids named Dick and Jane. They never did much of anything exciting. And they talked funny. If this was reading, I wondered why anyone would bother.

"Then I found *Go, Dog. Go!* . . . The book seemed so much more real to me (so much more like my family of five brothers) than the books about those strange kids with funny speech patterns.

"And that hat. That hat may mean more than we ever know."

Well, even if this book saved only Jon Scieszka as a reader, we would owe Eastman a debt of gratitude. But, of course, *Go, Dog. Go!* continues to convince millions of children that books can contain wild and crazy stories. And you can even learn punctuation from the title—a comma, period, and exclamation point. *Go, Dog. Go!*

THE HOBBIT

By J.R.R. Tolkien

On September 21, 1937, a children's book appeared in England that, like other English classics such as Stevenson's *Treasure Island*, Potter's *Peter Rabbit*, or Grahame's *The Wind in the Willows*, began as a story told to children. Actually, the idea for the book came when the author, correcting 286 school exams, found a blank page in one of them. He wrote simply, "In a hole in the ground there lived a hobbit," and then J.R.R. Tolkien set out to discover what hobbits actually were. He started telling his three sons stories about a small being with furry feet and small imagination but great courage—the kind of courage he had seen in the trenches in World War I. In the story, Bilbo Baggins, a comfort-loving hero, sets out from his home with a band of dwarfs to seek the treasure guarded by a dangerous, fire-breathing dragon. Over a period of nearly three years, Tolkien developed this unlikely hero's journey, crafting one of the greatest fantasies ever written.

The Hobbit experienced a charmed life in terms of publication. Even before Tolkien had finished the book, the editors at Allyn and Unwin knew of its existence and pursued the author. Raynor Unwin, the ten-year-old son of the chairman of the firm, was paid a shilling for reading the manuscript and giving his opinion. He wrote what is believed to be the first child's response to the book: "This book with the help of maps does not need any illustrations . . . it is good and should appeal to all children between the ages of 5 to 9." Obviously, young Raynor thought himself a bit superior to the contents. Today *The Hobbit* usually gets classified as a novel for children ages ten through fourteen. Tolkien himself believed the book needed both maps and illustrations, and he also designed a book jacket decorated with runes, a language that he invented.

The book quickly became a bestseller in England, as well as in the United States when it appeared in 1938. A mere month after the publication, Stanley Unwin discussed the idea of a sequel with the author—and Tolkien set to work. But it would not be until 1951 that he completed his thousand-page extension of on this saga: the Lord of the Rings trilogy. At one point in *The Hobbit*, Gandalf the wizard says to Bilbo, "You are a very fine person, Mr. Baggins, and I am very fond of you; but you are only quite a little fellow in a wide world after all." But this little fellow has found millions and millions of fans in the wide world since he first appeared over seventy years ago.

SEPTEMBER 21

Happy Birthday Stephen King (*The Girl Who Loved Tom Gordon*), Hans Wilhelm (*I'll Always Love You*), and Hazel Edwards (*Stickybeak*).

It's the birth date of H. G. Wells (1866–1946), *The War of the Worlds*; Taro Yashima (1908–1994), *Crow Boy, Umbrella*; and Alexander Key (1904–1979), *Escape to Witch Mountain*.

In 1897 the *New York Sun* ran an editorial response to a girl's letter about the existence of a Jolly Man in Red. Read *Yes, Virginia, There Is a Santa Claus* by Frances P. Church, illustrated by Joel Spector.

In 1981 **Sandra Day O'Connor** became the first woman to serve as a U.S. Supreme Court Justice. Read her semiautobiographical picture book *Finding Susie*, illustrated by Tom Pohrt.

It's World Alzheimer's Day. Read *The Graduation of Jake Moon* by Barbara Park, and *Figuring Out Frances* by Gina Willner-Pardo.

The United Nations has declared today an International Day of Peace. Read *Peace One Day* by Jeremy Gilley and Karen Blessen.

SEPTEMBER 22

It's the birth date of Esphyr Slobodkina (1908–2002), *Caps for Sale*.

Happy Birthday to fictional character Bilbo Baggins from J.R.R. Tolkien's *The Hobbit*. Hence, it is Hobbit Day.

Hope you enjoy celebrating National White Chocolate Day!

THE WORLD'S GREATEST ELEPHANT

By Ralph Helfer

Illustrated by Ted Lewin

Today, Elephant Appreciation Day, has been set aside to celebrate the "earth's largest, most interesting, and most noble endangered land animal." Certainly elephants have always had enormous appeal for children. In fact, circus founder P. T. Barnum once said, "When entertaining the public, it is best to have an elephant."

In 2006 Ralph Helfer, wild-animal trainer, and Ted Lewin, known for his realistic artwork for children, teamed up to tell a fascinating story about an elephant. Their book, *The World's Greatest Elephant*, is a forty-eight-page picture book with an extensive text and introduces Modoc, a very remarkable elephant, indeed.

When she is born in Zezeldorf, Germany, on the same day and almost same hour as the elephant trainer's son, named Bram, the trainer hopes that the boy and the elephant will always be together. In fact, they become best friends. By the age of five, Modoc weighs two thousand pounds; at ten, she weighs four thousand, making her the world's biggest elephant. She and Bram perform in the circus together, he a diminutive figure who stands on her head.

Tragedy strikes when a new owner named Jay North buys the circus and decides to ship it to New York—but refuses to take Modoc's trainer. Bram stows away on the boat with his beloved friend. When the boat gets swamped by water, the boy and elephant get separated but find each other in the waves. Rescued by a maharajah, the two friends recover in India. Unfortunately, Jay North has not forgotten about his property, and he gathers up both Modoc and Bram, who come to New York.

At this point in the story, readers long for a quiet life for the elephant—because of the trials Modoc has already undergone. But her problems continue. A circus fire scars the giant performer, and North sells her off in the middle of the night. So Bram begins to search for his friend.

Narrated by Ralph Helfer, who owned Modoc for the last twenty years of her life, the book celebrates the tenacity of this incredible animal and attests to the wonderful relationship that can exist between a human being and an elephant. Helfer witnessed this relationship firsthand—he was there when Modoc and Bram were finally reunited. Through Ted Lewin's dramatic and moving paintings, readers also feel as if they witness this remarkable friendship. Modoc comes to life on the page. She dances and performs and trumpets her way through the book.

I can think of no better way to celebrate Elephant Appreciation Day than to read this book and discuss Modoc's incredible life story with children.

ART DOG

By Thacher Hurd

Today for World Animal Remembrance Month, I'd like to look at a highly original and amusing protagonist, Thacher Hurd's Art Dog. In terms of children's books, Thacher Hurd has lived a charmed life. He was the son of not only one, but two great children's book creators—writer Edith Thacher Hurd and artist Clement Hurd, who illustrated many classics including *Goodnight Moon*. As a child Thacher met Margaret Wise Brown, Maurice Sendak, and Don Freeman, all friends of his parents. Sometimes this led to not-so-desirable situations. Margaret Wise Brown once wanted Thacher to sleep in an all-fur room that she had made for him, but Thacher didn't want to.

But just as his father was known for his gentleness and quietness in books, Thacher went on to create titles that have been described as zany, high octane, and fast paced. In 1996 Thacher presented the saga of Arthur Dog, guard of the Dogopolis Museum of Art by day—where he protects masterpieces created by Pablo Poodle, Henri Muttisse, and Vincent Van Dog—but a crime fighter and graffiti artist by night. He drives the Brushmobile, with a tank that gets filled up with bright colors at the Acme Paint Company. Rather than exclaiming "Bam" or "Pow" like other superheroes, Art Dog is more likely to say "Touché" or "Paint!" When Dog Vinci's painting *Mona Woofa* is stolen, Art Dog sets out to find the culprit—because he himself has been accused of its theft.

While working on the book, Thacher turned to Maurice Sendak for advice. He also received input from his wife, Olivia, who has been at his side as critic for many years and reads all the dummies for his books. Both encouraged Thacher to revise the original story and make the plot tighter. Often editors get credit, and should, for helping shape a book. But in the case of *Art Dog* a childhood mentor and Thacher's wife helped him create a book that has thrilled critics and children alike. In fact, *Art Dog* has won the Vermont Red Clover Award, selected by children of the state.

Art Dog naturally lends itself to learning activities like identifying the painters spoofed in the book or even having children take their favorite paintings and replace the main character with a dog. In short, it's a great way to remember not only dogs but also great works of fine art.

SEPTEMBER 23

Happy Birthday Jan Ormerod (*Lizzie Nonsense*) and Gary Crew (*Memorial*).

Neptune, the first planet in our solar system found by mathematic prediction rather than observation, was discovered in 1846. Read *Next Stop Neptune* by Alvin Jenkins, illustrated by Steve Jenkins.

In 1962 the **Lincoln Center for the Performing Arts** in New York City opened with the completion of the Philharmonic Hall, home of the New York Philharmonic. Read *The Philharmonic Gets Dressed* by Karla Kuskin, illustrated by Marc Simont.

It's also Dogs in Politics Day. Read *My Senator and Me: A Dog's Eye View of Washington, D.C.* by Senator Edward M. Kennedy, illustrated by David Small, and *First Dog* by J. Patrick Lewis and Beth Zappitello, illustrated by Tim Bowers.

SEPTEMBER 24

Happy Birthday Jane Cutler (*Guttersnipe*).

It's the birth date of Harry Behn (1898–1973), *The Faraway Lurs*; Wilson Rawls (1913–1984), *Where the Red Fern Grows*; and L. Leslie Brooke (1862–1940), *Johnny Crow's Garden*.

It's also the birth date of Jim Henson (1936–1990), the puppeteer who created the Muppets in 1954 and television's *Sesame Street*.

Happy Birthday to the United States Post Office, established in 1789. Read *Dear Mr. Blueberry* by Simon James.

And it's the birth date of F. Scott Fitzgerald (1896–1940), author of the classic *The Great Gatsby*.

In 1906 U.S. President Theodore Roosevelt proclaimed **Devil's Tower** in Wyoming the first National Monument. Read *A Blizzard Year* by Gretel Ehrlich.

PUNCTUATION TAKES A VACATION

By Robin Pulver

Illustrated by Lynn Rowe Reed

What if we had the English language as we know it, but no punctuation had been invented? The sentences you are reading now would be nearly impossible to comprehend. The importance of punctuation in communication lies at the heart of today's holiday, the annual National Punctuation Day. For the organizers, today serves as a "celebration of the lowly comma, correctly used quotation marks, and other proper uses of periods, semicolons, and the ever-mysterious ellipsis."

If you want to get children ages five through ten thinking about the importance of commas and semicolons, pick up Robin Pulver's *Punctuation Takes a Vacation*, illustrated by Lynn Rowe Reed. Day after day, reliable punctuation marks show up in Mr. Wright's classroom—even though they get erased and ignored. So in a move to get more respect, the question mark, exclamation point, comma, period, colon, quotation marks, and apostrophes head out the door. Now the class is in big trouble—absolutely nothing makes sense without these lowly creatures. Soon postcards start to be delivered from Take-a-Break Lake. "Do you miss us? . . . Guess who?" a typical one reads.

As they ride on water tubes and eat picnic lunches, each punctuation mark sends an appropriate greeting, challenging the students and reader to guess who created it. Although the students can figure out who sent the postcards, they can't write anything back that makes sense. Eventually returning to a much more grateful group of kids, the punctuation marks pose some difficult questions like "Who did you miss the most?"

In a totally lighthearted and funny manner, the book explores the importance of punctuation in all of our lives. A list of punctuation rules rounds out a book that reads aloud beautifully and works both in school and home settings. I know of one kindergarten girl who insisted that this be read as a bedtime story every night. I wonder what punctuation mark she liked best.

PICTURE BOOK, Elementary School

HAROLD AND THE PURPLE CRAYON

By Crockett Johnson

September 25 has been designated National Comic Book Day. From Jennifer L. and Matthew Holm's Babymouse series to Jeff Kinney's Wimpy Kid offerings, comic books (sometimes called graphic novels) have been the hottest publishing phenomena of the past few years. But like everything under the sun that seems new, comic books and children's books go way back as both use words and pictures to tell a story. The author of our book of the day, Crockett Johnson, under the nom de plume of David Johnson Leisk, created the very popular Barnaby newspaper series. But he also was married to children's book writer Ruth Krauss and was inevitably drawn into the children's book world. This comic book master fashioned two enduring classics, *The Carrot Seed* and *Harold and the Purple Crayon*.

Today *Harold and the Purple Crayon* has sold two million copies and has never gone out of print, but it failed to impress Johnson's editor Ursula Nordstrom when she first saw it. "It doesn't seem like a good children's book to me," the ever-frank Nordstrom quipped. Later, Nordstrom apologized for her initial unenthusiastic response and published the book in 1955.

In both his comic strips and children's books Johnson distilled figures and landscape to their bare essentials. Harold sets out for a walk, and with a worn, stubby purple crayon draws an entire adventure and world for himself—including a picnic with the nine types of pie he loves best.

SEPTEMBER 25

Happy Birthday Cooper Edens (*If You're Afraid of the Dark, Remember the Night Rainbow*), Jim Murphy (*An American Plague: The True and Terrifying Story of the Yellow Fever Epidemic of 1793*), James Ransome (*Uncle Jed's Barbershop*), and Andrea Davis Pinkney (*Duke Ellington*, *Let It Shine*).

It's the birth date of Shel Silverstein (1930–1999), *The Giving Tree*, *Where the Sidewalk Ends*, *A Light in the Attic*.

In 1639 the first printing press in what will become the United States of America opened in Cambridge. Read *The Printing Press* by Milton Meltzer.

On this day in 1957 United States Army troops integrated Central High School in Little Rock, Arkansas. Read *Remember Little Rock* by Paul Robert Walker, *The Little Rock Nine* by Marshall Poe, illustrated by Ellen Lindner, and *The Lions of Little Rock* by Kristin Levine.

For National Comic Book Day read *Understanding Comics: The Invisible Art* by Scott McCloud.

A celebration of the creative spirit and the power of imagination, *Harold and the Purple Crayon* has appealed to a legion of artists over the years. In *Everything I Need to Know I Learned from a Children's Book*, both the grandfather of the American picture book, Maurice Sendak, and the father, Chris Van Allsburg, discuss the influences of this book on their work. As Sendak notes, the book "is just immense fun. Harold does exactly as he pleases." Van Allsburg states, "I believe that the empowerment of Harold appealed to me as a reader—I loved the idea that I could be in control and create my own world."

Celebrate National Comic Book Day with a classic: *Harold and the Purple Crayon*. And then practice drawing your own universe. As Harold discovers, anything is possible with crayon and paper.

SEPTEMBER 26

Happy Birthday Mark Haddon (*The Curious Incident of the Dog in the Night-Time*).

It's the birth date of Libby Hathorn (1943–2003), *Way Home*, *Sky Sash So Blue*; T. S. Eliot (1888–1965), *Old Possum's Book of Practical Cats*; and Jane Taylor (1783–1824), author of the poem "Twinkle, Twinkle, Little Star."

Johnny Appleseed (1774–1845), born on this day as John Chapman in Leominster, Massachusetts, was a pioneer nurseryman and American legend. Read *Johnny Appleseed* by Reeve Lindbergh, illustrated by Kathy Jakobsen, *Johnny Appleseed* by Jane Kurtz, illustrated by Mary Haverfield, and *Johnny Appleseed* by Steven Kellogg. It also happens to be Johnny Appleseed Day.

THE AGONY OF ALICE
By Phyllis Reynolds Naylor

In the last week of September the American Library Association celebrates Banned Books Week. Often your local public library will display some famous banned books. I am always surprised to see what makes the list of "top banned/challenged books" of the decade. Harry Potter leads the list—possibly Harry Potter is going to lead all lists (sales, censorship, and box office). But number two seems to me almost impossible: Phyllis Reynolds Naylor's series about Alice McKinley.

Phyllis won a Newbery Medal for her much beloved *Shiloh* in 1991. But before that, in 1985, she published *The Agony of Alice*, the first in a series of popular titles. We first meet Alice in sixth grade, after she has moved to a new neighborhood. She has a loving father, a single parent because her mother died when Alice was five, and an older brother, Lester. Like many middle schoolers, Alice thinks and worries about everything. She is often mortified by her own behavior—including bad poetry that she wrote in third grade. Overly sensitive, she tries to fit in at her new school. But she does not like her teacher and even tries to get her classroom changed to be with the teacher she admires more. A refreshing blend of daring and cringing, Alice successfully bumps her way along until the end of sixth grade, when she comes to adore her teacher and has gained a boyfriend.

Relationships and feelings stand at the core of these books. But Naylor is completely frank about details of life such as getting a first bra and having your first kiss. Since Alice goes through high school in the series, she encounters more and more complex issues. All the issues have been woven easily into the narrative, but these books give young readers a place to go for information in the event that they feel that they can't ask certain kinds of questions at school or at home.

I suppose this honesty about the human body has caused the books to be banned. All I know is that if a young girl needs some answers to life's questions, she can gain a lot of wisdom from one of the great ladies of the book world, Phyllis Reynolds Naylor. Naylor, in fact, has said that to her Alice is the daughter she always wanted.

Young readers age eleven to fourteen love these books because they identify with Alice—her awkwardness, her hopes, her dreams—and they also appreciate the wise advice about personal issues. For those who haven't read these books, pick them up during Banned Books Week and make your own decision about their merit. In my forty years of experience, the children's books one group bans are the books that another group cherishes.

LYLE, LYLE, CROCODILE
By Bernard Waber

Today is the birthday of one of the nicest human beings on the planet, Bernard Waber. A quiet, unassuming man, Bernie has a gentle sense of humor—one that he relied on for books like *Ira Sleeps Over* and *Lyle, Lyle, Crocodile*.

Born in Philadelphia, Bernie moved frequently during his childhood years; during the Depression, his family often fled just before the bill collectors arrived. In each new town Bernie located two things: the public library and the movie theater. In *Children's Books and Their Creators*, he wrote that during his childhood he was "a hopeless, chronic daydreamer. Everyone told me it was bad—bad, bad, bad—to daydream. . . . I tried everything to cure myself of the pernicious affliction . . . The problem deviled me all through my maturing years. Even in the army, sergeants constantly bellowed at me to wake up."

He did not set out to be an author of children's books. Trained in commercial art, he designed and illustrated magazines. But several art directors looked at his portfolio and told him that his illustrations would be perfect for books for the young. As a father of three, he read aloud to his children, often inventing stories. Once again Bernie found himself hanging out in the children's section of the library. Consequently, he began writing and illustrating his own stories and, after some rejections, Houghton Mifflin started publishing his work in the early sixties.

In 1965 Bernie took a character that had appeared in another book, *The House on East 88th Street*, and starred him in his own story: *Lyle, Lyle, Crocodile*. Lyle, a very well-behaved crocodile, lives with the Primm family on East Eighty-Eighth street. But because of an unfortunate episode, Lyle finds himself incarcerated in the Central Park Zoo—and he just doesn't cotton to all those other crocodiles. Fortunately, the Primms find a way to bring him back home.

Even though Bernie became highly successful as an author, he never left his day job designing magazines. He always maintained that he would create better and more thoughtful books if he did not have to rely on them for income. It meant he could polish material for as long as he needed and even abandon a project if it wasn't coming together.

Happy birthday to Bernard Waber whose books teach us to laugh! I'm going to celebrate by letting myself daydream about living with a chivalrous crocodile.

SEPTEMBER 27

Happy Birthday Paul Goble (*The Girl Who Loved Wild Horses*), Martin Handford (*Where's Waldo?*), and G. Brian Karas (*Atlantic, Saving Sweetness*).

In 1905 the physics journal *Annalen der Physik* published Albert Einstein's paper "Does the Inertia of a Body Depend Upon Its Energy Content?" which introduced $E=mc^2$. Read *Odd Boy Out: Young Albert Einstein* by Don Brown and *Ordinary Genius: The Story of Albert Einstein* by Stephanie Sammartino McPherson.

In 1908 the first Model T Ford automobile left the factory in Detroit, Michigan. Read *Tin Lizzie* by Allan Drummond.

The first Santa Claus Training School opened in Albion, New York, in 1937. Read *Santa Claus: The World's Number One Toy Expert* by Marla Frazee.

It's Ancestor Appreciation Day. Read *The Ancestors Are Singing* by Tony Johnston, illustrated by Karen Barbour.

SEPTEMBER 28

It's the birth date of Kate Douglas Wiggin (1856–1923), *Rebecca of Sunnybrook Farm*.

Confucius (551–479 BC), the Chinese philosopher, was born on this day. Read *Confucius: The Golden Rule* by Russell Freedman, illustrated by Frederic Clement.

In 1678 *Pilgrim's Progress* by John Bunyan was published. Read *Pilgrim's Progress* retold by Gary D. Schmidt, illustrated by Barry Moser.

In 1850 the United States Navy abolished flogging as punishment. Read *The Whipping Boy* by Sid Fleischman.

BOOTLEG: MURDER, MOONSHINE, AND THE LAWLESS YEARS OF PROHIBITION

By Karen Blumenthal

On September 28, 1839, Frances Elizabeth Caroline Willard was born in Churchville, New York. She would become the first corresponding secretary of the Women's Christian Temperance Union; later as its president she became one of the most effective crusaders for two Constitutional amendments: the 18th (Prohibition) and the 19th (Women's Suffrage).

Willard is only one of the many reformers discussed in *Bootleg: Murder, Moonshine, and the Lawless Years of Prohibition* by Karen Blumenthal. The book begins with the Valentine's Day Massacre in Chicago, an event certain to get the attention of readers aged eleven to fourteen.

In this well-written, thoroughly researched volume, Blumenthal explores how America came to embrace the 18th Amendment and why the country abandoned it less than fourteen years later—the only part of the Constitution ever to be reversed. As she moves along the journey, she brings fascinating historical details into the text.

We learn that President George Washington spent more than forty-seven pounds buying drinks for those who voted for him for the House of Burgesses; President Woodrow Wilson vetoed the 18th Amendment but it was passed anyway; and one of President F. D. Roosevelt's first acts was to sign into law a bill that made beer legal again. Blumenthal also tells how prohibition began. While World War I raged, moral crusaders seized hold of the government and managed to get the 18th Amendment ratified by the states. Of course, a government trying to enforce "morality" always stands on shaky ground. In the end, because no one liked the law, everyone began to violate it—including those in Washington who had voted for it. Rum-running and bootlegging became popular; gangs, organized to supply liquor to eager customers, gained tremendous strength.

In the process of talking about the issues, Blumenthal brings to life a cast of very colorful characters like Frances Willard, Carrie Nation, and Al Capone. Certainly, as the author discusses, the most enduring legacy of the 18th Amendment was how it galvanized women—a movement that ultimately led to their voting rights. And she shows how the use of automobiles for outrunning the police eventually led to the formation of NASCAR.

In the final chapter, Karen Blumenthal discusses present-day youth pledges about drinking and drugs as well as school awareness programs about drugs and alcohol. Anyone using the book with young readers will easily be able to transition from the fourteen-year experiment of Prohibition to many of the arguments heard in Washington today.

If any of my adult readers love history well told, you will want to pick up this book. It makes an excellent introduction to Prohibition; you know how the story turns out, but it will keep you riveted.

IT'S PERFECTLY NORMAL: CHANGING BODIES, GROWING UP, SEX, AND SEXUAL HEALTH

By Robie H. Harris
Illustrated by Michael Emberley

In the last fifteen years, only one children's book has officially ever been challenged in the town where I live: Robie H. Harris's *It's Perfectly Normal*. Even though the sticker on the second edition boldly says "for age 10 and up," books about sex for young people routinely bring out the censors.

But if you want a book that answers young people's questions about sex, no better book has been written. Harris has been a passionate advocate for providing children with the information they need as they go through life's difficult passages. The tenth anniversary edition is even better than the first edition, with information on AIDS and STDs.

Michael Emberley's artwork includes the dialogue between a bird and a bee—the bird wants to know more, and the bee is less than eager for information. Emberley's art brings humor and illustrates many of the points with a variety of people who certainly have less than perfect bodies. The book provides information in a gentle, nonjudgmental, and engaging way.

Robie Harris never planned to be a children's book author. But she always loved making books and created her first in kindergarten. After graduate school, she became a teacher at the Bank Street School for Children in New York City, teaching children how to write. Asked by an editor in the 1980s if she would be interested in crafting a children's book on HIV/AIDS, Robie realized that she would want to make such a book more comprehensive—to look at the issues of sexual health and how the body changes in puberty. In the end she crafted *It's Perfectly Normal,* making sure to vet it with experts who confirmed it was scientifically and psychologically accurate.

To First Amendment advocate Robie Harris, a nod in appreciation and in recognition of how she has spent the last two decades of her life. Children need information, all kinds of information, and Robie has worked tirelessly to make sure that subjects like sex and childbirth get communicated to the young in a clear way. This goal has landed her work on the banned books lists, year after year—but she has made it possible for children to live better lives, because they have the information that they need.

SEPTEMBER 29

Happy Birthday Marissa Moss (*Amelia's Notebook*).

It's the birth date of Stan Berenstain (1923–2005), Berenstain Bears series.

In 1916 **John D. Rockefeller** became the world's first billionaire. Read *John D. Rockefeller: Oil Baron and Philanthropist* by Rosemary Laughlin.

It's National Attend Your Grandchild's Birth Day. Read *Zero Grandparents* by Michelle Edwards and *Grandparents Song* by Sheila Hamanaka.

It's also National Coffee Day. Read *The Bug in the Teacher's Coffee and Other School Poems* by Kalli Dakos, illustrated by Mike Reed, and *All Because of a Cup of Coffee* by Geronimo Stilton.

SEPTEMBER 30

Happy Birthday Nette Hilton (*Andrew Jessup*) and Elie Wiesel (*King Solomon and His Magic Ring*).

It's the birth date of Edgar D'Aulaire (1898–1986), *Abraham Lincoln*, *D'Aulaires' Book of Trolls*; Alvin Tresselt (1916–2000), *White Snow, Bright Snow, Hide and Seek Fog*; and Carol Fenner (1929–2002), *Yolanda's Genius*.

The protagonist of Daniel Defoe's *Robinson Crusoe* was shipwrecked on a tropical island on this day.

On this day in 1791 Mozart's last opera, *The Magic Flute*, premiered in Vienna. Read *Polo and the Magic Flute* by Règis Faller.

In 1947 baseball's World Series was televised for the first time. Read *First Pitch* by John Thorn.

Hello. *Hola. Hallo.* It's International Translation Day! Read *Inkheart* written and translated by Cornelia Funke.

THE RABBITS' WEDDING
By Garth Williams

Sometimes, after a controversy has swarmed around a book, it is almost impossible to see it as the author intended. That is true of today's banned book for Banned Books Week, Garth Williams's *The Rabbits' Wedding*—one of the next major picture books, after *The Story of Ferdinand,* to create an incredible ruckus. At its heart, *The Rabbits' Wedding* is a simple love story with spectacular art, executed in black, white, and yellow. A creator who crafted iconic illustrations for some of our great novels—such as *Charlotte's Web* and the Little House books—Williams could also pull off a picture book with dexterity and grace.

In *The Rabbits' Wedding* two rabbits, who live in a forest, hop, skip, jump, and play games. The male rabbit is thoughtful and pensive; the female rabbit more playful and happy. He keeps thinking about how he wants them to be together always, and he asks her to wed. Then they have a celebration where all the other animals come to dance in a circle around the newly married bunnies. Sunlight, dandelions, pastures—all is bliss in this book. Trained as a sculptor, Williams brings weight and texture to his art creating characters that seem three-dimensional and ready to come off the page.

So why the controversy over this seemingly innocent title? Published first in 1958, *The Rabbits' Wedding* features black and white rabbit protagonists. The artist most likely chose these colors to help delineate the two characters in a limited-color book, but adults interpreted this lovely romp in the forest as an endorsement of interracial marriage. As Leonard Marcus recounts the controversy in *Minders of Make-Believe, The Montgomery Home News* condemned the book, then Alabama politicians rallied against the book and spoke out against the director of the Alabama Public Library Service Division, Emily Reed. She had held her ground in ordering copies of this racy title to circulate to Alabama libraries.

I believe *The Rabbits' Wedding* is simply a sweet idyll about two rabbits that fall in love. But take a look yourself. Times have definitely changed; if you want to provide a lovely gift for an interracial couple, you definitely would want to consider *The Rabbits' Wedding*. But it works for any romantic—after all, our protagonist only wants to be with his loved one "forever and always."

THE SAILOR DOG

By Margaret Wise Brown
Illustrated by Garth Williams

On October 1, 1942, a brave new experiment in publishing was launched as collaboration between Simon & Schuster and Western Printing and Lithograph Company. The project was described as "a new series of 25 cent books for children," with an initial print run of 600,000 copies each. Carried in independent bookstores, these volumes also made their way into department stores like Marshall Field's, Macy's, and Gimbels, before becoming a staple at corner grocery stores across the country where they were purchased by millions.

The philosophy behind Golden Books—and they were indeed golden for their publisher—was to provide parents and children with books by the best artists and writers of the day at a very affordable price. So successful was the imprint at attracting talent (people like Margaret Wise Brown, Ruth Krauss, the Provensens, Garth Williams, and Richard Scarry among others) and at getting the books distributed, that most home libraries of the fifties consisted entirely of Golden Books. Each had a bookplate with "This Little Golden Book Belongs to" printed on the interior front cover where the young baby-boom generation enthusiastically inscribed their names. That first list saw the publication of the all-time bestselling picture book in the United States, *The Poky Little Puppy*. Other classic titles soon followed: *The Color Kittens*, *Mister Dog*, and Rojankovsky's *The Three Bears*. Although the paper might have been a bit thin, the art itself was glorious.

Over years of speaking with audiences across the country, I've noticed that one title seems to have attracted more long-term devotees than most of the others: Margaret Wise Brown's *The Sailor Dog*. Grown men often want to discuss it; sometimes their wives say simply, "He's Scuppers, you know!" Written toward the end of Brown's career and with artwork by Garth Williams, the book seems to have inspired a desire to sail among many young boys. Scuppers the Sailor Dog loves being out at sea; he keeps everything in its place in his snug bunk. When he is shipwrecked, he builds a hut, patches his boat, finds more supplies in a foreign land, and heads out: "And here he is where he wants to be—a sailor sailing the deep green sea."

Happy birthday to Golden Books. For over seventy years these titles have enchanted young readers.

OCTOBER 1

Happy Birthday Julie Andrews Edwards (*Mandy*).

Happy Birthday **Jimmy Carter**, the 39th president of the United States.

Happy Birthday to *National Geographic* magazine, first published in 1888.

It's National Book Month sponsored by the National Book Foundation.

During Squirrel Awareness Month, read the Scaredy Squirrel series by Melanie Watt.

It's Fire Pup Day. Read *The Fire Pup* by Esther Averill.

OCTOBER 2

Happy Birthday T. Ernesto Bethancourt (*The Dog Days of Arthur Cane*) and Jeanne Betancourt (*My Name is Brain Brian*, Pony Pal series).

It's the birth date of Dirk Zimmer (1943–2008), *In a Dark, Dark Room and Other Scary Stories*.

In 1950 the first *Peanuts* comic strip ran in nine newspapers. Read *How to Draw Peanuts* by Charles Schultz and *Peanuts: The Art of Charles Schultz*.

Thurgood Marshall was sworn in as the first African-American Supreme Court justice on this day in 1967. Read *A Picture Book of Thurgood Marshall* by David A. Adler, illustrated by Robert Casilla.

It's Name Your Car Day. Read *The Old Woman Who Named Things* by Cynthia Rylant, illustrated by Kathryn Brown.

It's Phileas Fogg's Wager Day. Read *Around the World in Eighty Days* by Jules Verne.

ON THE FARM

By David Elliott
Illustrated by Holly Meade

Since the 1980s the birthday of Mahatma Gandhi has been honored with World Farm Animals Day. If I were to pick a single book that celebrates living farm animals, it would have to be *On the Farm*, an inspired collaboration between poet David Elliott and illustrator Holly Meade.

David once actually worked on a farm—although he claims that he had little aptitude and actually made the animals a bit nervous. He became a writer and poet instead, and is known for his ability to hold audiences—of both adults and children—spellbound as he explains poetry and poetic form.

In *On the Farm* he takes familiar creatures and helps us look at them in new ways. In very simple and approachable verse, David presents thirteen poems about creatures who can be found on a farm—from cows and horses to snakes and rabbits. "The Sheep / began his woolly life / as gentle as a / lamb. Too bad / he turned / into a / ram. BAM!" Or "The Bees / Tell their story, / sweet and old, It begins in clover; / it ends with gold."

Each poem has been given a generous double-page spread, which allows illustrator Holly Meade to showcase the animals but also delineate their surroundings. On the copyright page, a double-page spread of the farm with familiar animals sets the scene. Then in woodblock and watercolor prints with bold outlines each animal struts, or runs, or simply stands to be recognized. Artist and writer work in complete harmony in this book. When these lines appear about the pig, "Some look at her and see a sow;/I see a beauty queen," the illustration showcases a truly lovely creature. Some pig, indeed! The exquisitely executed watercolors, the large trim size, and the heavy paper stock all make this book incredibly attractive—one of those titles you might pick up to read even if you had no interest in farm animals.

On the Farm can be used to introduce any study on farm animals or any poetry unit. The poems encourage young readers to see if they can craft some short pieces of their own. And this book works brilliantly as a read aloud for the very young from sixteen months on. Since it appeared in 2008, *On the Farm* has become one of the poetry volumes that teachers and parents most enjoy using—for providing information or pure pleasure.

MIKE MULLIGAN AND HIS STEAM SHOVEL

By Virginia Lee Burton

The first week of October has been designated Great Books Week to remind us to use our time well by picking up excellent books. By asking questions such as "If stranded on an deserted island, what five books would you want?" or "What books do you read over and over?" the organizers hope to get us all to focus on the books that really matter in our lives.

On top of my great books list stands Virginia Lee Burton's *Mike Mulligan and His Steam Shovel,* which explores one of Burton's favorite themes—how the old order must make way for the new and still survive. A steam shovel, Mary Anne, originally named Bertha in the manuscript, "who could dig as much in a day as a hundred men could dig in a week," finds her jobs taken away by newer, faster steam shovels. But with her champion, Mike Mulligan, at the helm, Mary Anne proves her worth. After digging a cellar for the town hall in Popperville, she stays there and becomes the furnace for the building.

Before Burton committed herself to any project, she read the story for at least a month to her two sons, Aris and Michael. If they didn't want to hear it after that period of time, she felt it not worthy of moving to book form. An early lesson in reusing and recycling, Burton's text found ready listeners in her sons and their friends.

When she read the children *Mike Mulligan and His Steam Shovel*, however, she struggled to find a satisfying end to the story. Then one of her sons' friends, Dickie Berkenbush, presented her with the idea of installing Mary Anne as the town hall furnace. Children often help writers during the artistic process, but Burton did something extraordinary and generous. She credited him in the book. Hence after Richard Berkenbush became an adult, he was able to claim credit for his contribution to this classic. During his life he was always present at events for *Mike Mulligan*, enjoying the praise that Burton made it possible for him to receive.

Published in 1939, at the beginning of World War II, *Mike Mulligan and His Steam Shovel* remains one of the most frequently read, and reread, books of childhood and has become a cultural icon.

OCTOBER 3

Happy Birthday Marilyn Singer (*Mirror Mirror, Tallulah's Tutu*).

It's the birth date of Natalie Savage Carlson (1906–1997), *The Family Under the Bridge.*

In 1872 Bloomingdale's department store opened in New York City. Read *Amy Elizabeth Explores Bloomingdale's* by E. L. Konigsburg and *Ruby, the Red-Hot Witch at Bloomingdale's* by Marlene Fanta Shyer.

Disney's variety show, the *Mickey Mouse Club*, first aired on ABC on this day in 1955.

On the day in 1990 East and West Germany were united after forty-five years of post–World War II division.

It's Virus Appreciation Day. Read *Iris Has a Virus* by Arlene Alda, illustrated by Lisa Desimini.

OCTOBER 4

Happy Birthday Karen Cushman (*Catherine, Called Birdy*).

It's the birth date of Edward Stratemeyer (1862–1930), The Rover Boys series; Robert Lawson (1892–1957), *The Story of Ferdinand*, *Rabbit Hill*; and Julia Cunningham (1916–2008), *Dorp Dead*.

 It's also the birth date of **Rutherford B. Hayes** (1822–1893), the 19th president of the United States.

Happy Birthday Dinosaur National Monument in Colorado and Utah, established in 1915. Read *Dinosaur Mountain: Digging into the Jurassic Age* by Deborah Ray.

The first public elevator, in London's Earl's Court metro station, began operation in 1911. Read *Charlie and the Great Glass Elevator* by Roald Dahl.

In 1957 Sputnik I, the first artificial satellite to orbit Earth, was launched by the U.S.S.R. Read *Laika* by Nick Abadzis.

It's Ten-Four Day, in reference to radio operators' affirmative utterance. Read *10 Minutes Till Bedtime* by Peggy Rathmann and *Four Perfect Pebbles* by Lila Perl and Marion Blumenthal Lazan.

ENCYCLOPEDIA BROWN: BOY DETECTIVE

By Donald Sobol

Born on October 4, 1924, in New York City, Donald Sobol served in the Army Corps of Engineers in World War II and then attended Oberlin College. There he became interested in writing and worked as a reporter for the *New York Sun* and the *New York Daily News*. In the late fifties Sobol began creating a syndicated series called "Two-Minute Mysteries."

But in 1963, shortly before his fortieth birthday, Sobol published the first of the books that would make his legacy, *Encyclopedia Brown: Boy Detective*. This book, like the sequels that would follow, contains ten short but exciting stories about Leroy Brown, son of the police chief of Idaville, Florida. Leroy is nicknamed "Encyclopedia" because of his vast knowledge, and receives help or hindrance from Sally Kimball, his Watson, or Bugs Meany, his nemesis. In each story the reader is asked to solve a mystery or question by logic, observation, or deduction. Ideal for readers not always enthusiastic about books, the stories have some of the same appeal as the Sherlock Holmes sagas. They are fun but tricky at the same time. In the back of the book, the solutions are presented so the child can test his or herself against the author's conclusions.

Chapter 3, The Case of the Civil War Sword, is particularly appropriate for the sesquicentennial of the Civil War, beginning in 2011. A boy wants Encyclopedia to verify that a sword really belonged to Thomas Jonathan "Stonewall" Jackson. It is inscribed: *"To Thomas J. Jackson, for standing like a stone wall at the First Battle of Bull Run on July 21, 1861. The sword is presented to him by his men on August 21, 1861."* No problem for Encyclopedia.

In *Everything I Need to Know I Learned from a Children's Book*, sports writer Rick Reilly talked about the charms of the Encyclopedia Brown books. "I loved the fact that all the clues for the mystery were right there in the story, and the answer was waiting in the back. How cool was that? Of course, I never got any of the answers right at first, but I started to learn."

The most important thing that any reader starts to learn in these books is just how much fun can be had in the pages of a book. For almost fifty years young readers have been drawn back to Donald Sobol's books again and again.

THE THREE BILLY GOATS GRUFF

By Paul Galdone

For Great Books Week, I want to look at the work of Paul Galdone. In his lifetime, Paul received very little critical praise for his books, although he did garner two Caldecott Honors for Eve Titus's *Anatole* and *Anatole and the Cat*. Beginning in the fifties, he illustrated the work of others for many years, including Ellen MacGregor's fabulous *Miss Pickerell Goes to Mars*.

But Paul would become loved for his renditions of classic nursery rhymes and fairy tales. At a time when such books formed the backbone of all publishing lists, Paul's basic retellings of classic tales stood out as the most popular in a very crowded field. By the midnineties publishers began to drop these titles from their lists.

But not Paul Galdone's. He retold his work in a straightforward manner, going for the essence of the stories. Hence when *Children's Books and Their Creators* appeared in 1995, the essay on Galdone talked about how these tales have "aged well and remain the old reliables of folk literature." Sixteen years later they are still the old reliables. If you are hunting for a version of a folktale as you remember it, you can do no better than to pick up a Galdone retelling. I have always thought that *The Three Billy Goats Gruff* is a great place to begin when looking at the Galdone canon.

"Once upon a time there were three Billy Goats. They lived in a valley and the names of all three Billy Goats was 'Gruff.' " On a double-page spread, readers are greeted with three winsome goats, each with distinct personalities, coats, markings, and horns. All look directly at the viewer. Then the three goats try to get to the meadow across a bridge, guarded by a very ugly troll. The text is spare; action occurs on every page; the language is repetitive; and the essence of the story is captured. This Galdone rendition relies on sound storytelling principles. You can read the text a hundred times if necessary—and if the children in your life have anything to say about it, you might have to.

Paul Galdone created books at a time when "high art" picture books received all the accolades. But his enduring legacy, in books like *The Three Billy Goat Gruff*, is to remind us that children always love a good story, well told, that cuts to the heart of the matter.

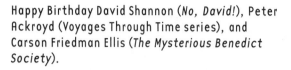

OCTOBER 5

Happy Birthday David Shannon (*No, David!*), Peter Ackroyd (Voyages Through Time series), and Carson Friedman Ellis (*The Mysterious Benedict Society*).

It's the birth date of Louise Fitzhugh (1928–1974), *Harriet the Spy*; and Gene Zion (1913–1975), *Harry the Dirty Dog*.

It's the birth date of **Chester Alan Arthur** (1829–1886), the 21st president of the United States.

In 1582 this day never happened in Italy, Poland, Portugal, and Spain due to the Gregorian Calendar. Read *The Story of Clocks and Calendars* by Betsy Maestro and Giulio Maestro.

In 1921 baseball's World Series was broadcast on radio for the first time. Read *The World Series* by Matt Christopher.

It's Do Something Nice Day. Read *Mr. Rabbit and the Lovely Present* by Charlotte Zolotow, illustrated by Maurice Sendak, and *A Tree Is Nice* by Janice Udry, illustrated by Marc Simont.

PICTURE BOOK, CLASSIC, Elementary School

OCTOBER 6

Happy Birthday Lee Kingman (*Pierre Pigeon*).

It's the birth date of Elizabeth Janet Gray Vining (1902–1999), *Adam of the Road*.

 Happy Birthday American Chess Association, formed in 1857. Read *Alex and the Wednesday Chess Club* by Janet Wong, illustrated by Stacy Schuett.

Happy Birthday also to the American Library Association, founded in Philadelphia, 1876. Read *The Library Card* by Jerry Spinelli.

It's Mad Hatter Day, inspired by John Tenniel's illustration of the Mad Hatter in *Alice in Wonderland* by Lewis Carroll.

It's also Come and Take It Day. Read *Here Comes the Garbage Barge* by Jonah Winter, illustrated by Red Nose Studio, *Come Back, Amelia Bedelia* by Peggy Parish, illustrated by Wallace Tripp, and *If You Take a Mouse to School* by Laura Numeroff, illustrated by Felicia Bond.

MIRROR MIRROR

By Marilyn Singer
Illustrated by Josée Masse

October is National Poetry Month in the United Kingdom and the first Thursday of the month is set aside as National Poetry Day. In the U.S. we set aside the month of April to celebrate poetry, but I actually think children's poetry should be honored at least once a month. Even for children who think they don't like to read, a poem can be a magical entry into the literary world. I once saw Canadian poet Dennis Lee work with a group of "hard case" nonreaders. In the end they wanted to copy his poems down, letter by letter, because they had enjoyed them so much.

Our book of the day, Marilyn Singer's *Mirror Mirror*, not only helps celebrate poetry—it will help children play games with words as well. For this book Marilyn created fourteen "reversos." Read down the page and the poem sounds one way; read up, with punctuation changes, and it conveys a completely different meaning. The form would have been a great deal of fun no matter what Marilyn wrote about, and she focused on some well-known fairy tales, which often have two points of view. So the book works not only as a way to play with language, but also to examine folklore characters.

Hence we see the story of Hansel and Gretel told first from the point of view of the witch: "Fatten up, boy! / Don't you / like prime rib? / Then your hostess, she will roast you / goose. / Have another chocolate. / Eat another piece of gingerbread."

And then we see the story from the point of view of Gretel, talking to her brother: "Eat another piece of gingerbread, / have another chocolate – / Goose! / Then your hostess, she will roast you / like prime rib. / Don't you / Fatten up, boy!"

Not only will children enjoy reading these reversos, they will also be able to play around writing them. And there are a lot of fairy-tale characters not explored by Marilyn. She has written one inventive book of poetry after another, and *Mirror Mirror* provides a fabulous place to get a sense of her craft.

ARTHUR'S NOSE

By Marc Brown

Today for Great Books Week, I'd like to look at a modest picture book that launched an empire: Marc Brown's *Arthur's Nose*. In 1976 a failed television weatherman, Marc Brown, published his first picture book under the astute guidance of Emilie McLeod of *Atlantic Monthly*. Emilie, one of those most respected editors working in Boston publishing, had exquisite taste and an eye for new talent. She published Sid Fleischman and Eleanor Cameron, fought for *The Incredible Journey,* and took a chance on Marc's first attempt to both write and illustrate a book.

When Marc's son Tolan requested a bedtime story about a weird animal, Marc started to go through the alphabet, and for the letter *A* he came up with *Aardvark*. As he developed the plot, though, he discovered that his hero was simply a young child who looked like an aardvark. In other words, Arthur is an aardvark, but he faces the same dilemmas of every young child in school. To write the books, Marc recorded what he observed with his own children, Tucker, Tolan, and Eliza. Over the years the book grew in popularity; eventually PBS picked up this popular series and made Arthur recognizable worldwide.

Those who only know the PBS series or later Arthur books might be quite surprised when they pick up the original volume. Arthur worries about his nose—he has an anteater-sized schnoz and looks much different on TV than he does in his first book. In this volume, when he plays hide-and-seek, his nose always gives him away. So Arthur goes to a rhinologist, but after trying out various possibilities, he decides to stay with the nose nature has given him. In the twenty-fifth anniversary of the book, Marc Brown shows Arthur's nose as it has evolved over the years—Arthur gains glasses but loses his aardvark nose.

The series has worked so well over the years not because of a nose but because Arthur has become friends with children everywhere. In him they see reflections of themselves; he has an entire cast of friends, many who also become the stars of their own books, and he's funny and approachable and gentle. Much like Marc Brown himself.

Arthur's Nose ends with the words, "There is a lot more to Arthur than his nose." And indeed with more than fifty million copies of the Arthur books in print, Arthur has demonstrated his attraction to children for several decades. In that time Arthur has moved from the star of a modest picture book to becoming a household name.

OCTOBER 7

Happy Birthday Susan Jeffers (McDuff series), Sherman Alexie (*The Absolutely True Diary of a Part-Time Indian*), and Diane Ackerman (*Animal Sense, Bats: Shadows in the Night*).

It's the birth date of Alice Dalgliesh (1893–1979), *The Courage of Sarah Noble, The Bears of Hemlock Mountain*; James Whitcomb Riley (1849–1916), *When the Frost Is on the Pumpkin*; and Robert Westall (1929–1993), *The Machine Gunners, The Scarecrows.*

In 1955 Allen Ginsberg read his epic "Howl" for the first time at a poetry reading in San Francisco. Read *The Mysterious Howling* by Maryrose Wood, illustrated by Jon Klassen.

The musical *Cats* opens on Broadway in 1982, beginning an almost eighteen-year run. Read *Old Possum's Book of Practical Cats* by T. S. Eliot, illustrated by Edward Gorey.

It's National Frappe Day. Read *Oliver's Milk Shake* by Vivian French, illustrated by Alison Bartlett.

PICTURE BOOK, Preschool, Elementary School

OCTOBER 8

Happy Birthday Barthe DeClements (*Nothing's Fair in the Fifth Grade*), Edward Ormondroyd (*David and the Phoenix*), R. L. Stine (Goosebumps series), Faith Ringgold (*Tar Beach*), and Mike Thaler (Black Lagoon Adventure series).

In 1775 officers barred slaves and free blacks from the Continental Army. Read *Forge* by Laurie Halse Anderson and *The Astonishing Life of Octavian Nothing* by M. T. Anderson.

In 1871 the Great Chicago Fire began in southwest Chicago, possibly in a barn owned by Patrick and Katherine O'Leary, and ultimately destroyed one-third of the city. Read *The Great Fire* by Jim Murphy.

In 1971 former Beatle John Lennon released "Imagine." Read *John's Secret Dream* by Doreen Rappaport, illustrated by Bryan Collier.

It's American Touch Tag Day. Read *Tag!* by Ann Bryant, illustrated by Kirsteen H. Jones, and *Jamaica Tag-Along* by Juanita Havill, illustrated by Anne Sibley O'Brien.

THE MIDNIGHT FOX
By Betsy Byars

Another offering for Great Books Week, Betsy Byars's *The Midnight Fox* was published in 1968. In her career, Betsy wrote picture books, easy readers, historical fiction, and fantasies, and she won the Newbery Medal for *The Summer of the Swans*. But *The Midnight Fox*, a book about a young city boy who finds himself in the country for the summer, stands as her most enduring work.

While Tom's parents are taking a vacation in Europe, he is sent to live with his aunt and uncle for a month on their farm. He likes nothing about this idea, as he wants to spend summer with his friend Petie. At first, everything seems boring. "The first three days were the longest, slowest days of my life." Then, after writing Petie a letter, Tom looks up to see a black fox, tinged with some white, moving through the grass. A wild creature in her habitat, the fox mesmerizes him.

Suddenly, Tom has a cause and a mission: to follow the fox, find her den, and see her as often as he can. He manages to spot her fifteen times, and he locates her single cub in the den. But then Tom's world, in which he and this creature of nature stand in harmony, and the harsh reality of the farm life come in sharp conflict. When one of Aunt Millie's turkeys gets taken by the fox, Tom's uncle goes out hunting for him.

I am not a big fan of dead dog or dead animal books. It has always seemed to me that the author has other choices for the plot. Hence I admire the way Betsy Byars pulls this novel together. While keeping her characters true to themselves, she manages to find a plausible ending without killing any living creature. Throughout most of the book, Tom has been a victim of circumstance. But, finally, when his beloved creature is threatened, he takes decisive action that makes a difference.

Betsy Byars's great strength as a writer is in creating young people that the reader cares about. For eight- to twelve-year-olds, Tom makes a wonderful companion. It is easy to relate first to his boredom and then to his fascination with life on a farm. One of those books that children often remember with fondness well into their adult years, *The Midnight Fox* demonstrates how an author can take simple elements—a boy and a wild animal—and create a spellbinding, page-turning story.

THE STINKY CHEESE MAN AND OTHER FAIRLY STUPID TALES

By Jon Scieszka

Illustrated by Lane Smith

Today we celebrate Moldy Cheese Day. Molds play an important part in the production of delicious—but often stinky—blue cheeses like Roquefort and Gorgonzola. Even the milder Brie and Camembert get created by the introduction of a mold, a member of the *Penicillium* genus.

In 1992 when I was editor in chief of *The Horn Book Magazine*, the most talented new duo of the decade, Jon Scieszka and Lane Smith, published their second book, one deliciously entitled *The Stinky Cheese Man and Other Fairly Stupid Tales*. In it the creators play with everything from the title page to the bar code, and they give us fractured versions of classic fairy tales. "Little Red Riding Hood" becomes "Little Red Running Shorts" with quite a few liberties taken, and "The Gingerbread Man" becomes "The Stinky Cheese Man." As the introduction announces with pride: "The stories in this book are almost Fairy Tales. But not quite. The stories in this book are Fairly Stupid Tales."

The Stinky Cheese Man completely divided the *Horn Book* review staff. Some thought this book too sophisticated for children, as it relies on an understanding of the story being spoofed. Others thought it hilarious on every page and spot-on for the audience. At that time, we held review meetings where everyone came to the office to argue about which books would appear in the next issue. I sent people back to their libraries and classrooms, to try out the book with children. Those who were dubious to begin with said children found it confusing. Those who loved the book found a ready audience. As is so often true, research with children sometimes tells us more about the researcher than the child. At that point I realized that I was witnessing the kind of controversy that greets classic children's books as they come into the world.

The Stinky Cheese Man and Other Fairly Stupid Tales would make a great impact on children's books in the nineties, solidify the position of Jon Scieszka and Lane Smith as children's book geniuses, and keep children laughing for decades. Every part of the book entertains; as a whole, it works brilliantly in its combination of design, art, and text.

On Moldy Cheese Day, you can do no better than pick up a slice of Stilton and read *The Stinky Cheese Man and Other Fairly Stupid Tales*.

OCTOBER 9

Happy Birthday Johanna Hurwitz (*Busybody Nora*).

On the day in 1547 Miguel de Cervantes (1547–1616) was baptized in Alcala de Heraves, Spain. Read *Don Quixote*.

The **Washington Monument** opened to the public in 1888. Read *Mystery at the Washington Monument* by Ron Roy, illustrated by Timothy Bush.

It's Curious Events Day. Read *Curious George* by H. A. Rey.

OCTOBER 10

Happy Birthday Daniel San Souci (*The Legend of Scarface*) and Robert D. San Souci (*The Talking Eggs*).

It's the birth date of James Marshall (1942–1992), *Miss Nelson Is Missing, George and Martha*.

In 1854 the Naval School, later named the United States Naval Academy, opened in Annapolis. Read *Piper Reed, Navy Brat* by Kimberly Willis Holt, illustrated by Christine Davenier.

 In 1978 the United States Congress approved the **Susan B. Anthony** dollar coin. Read *Susan B. Anthony: Fighter for Women's Rights* by Deborah Hopkinson, illustrated by Amy Bates.

The cornerstone dedication for Holocaust Museum in New York City was held on this day in 1996. Read *Tell Them We Remember: The Story of the Holocaust* by Susan D. Bachrach.

It's National Angel Food Cake Day. Read *The High Rise Glorious Skittle Skat Roarious Sky Pie Angel Food Cake* by Nancy Willard, illustrated by Richard Jesse Watson.

MORNING GIRL
By Michael Dorris

On the first Monday of October we celebrate Columbus Day. Every now and then a book not only educates you but changes the way you view history. Once you have read it, you cannot see things quite the way you once did.

That is how I think about the book of the day, Michael Dorris's *Morning Girl*. Published in 1992, and now a classic, the book first came to me when I was editor of *The Horn Book Magazine*. I had admired Michael Dorris for his adult writing, *A Yellow Raft in Blue Water* and *The Broken Cord*, but writing beautifully for adults does not necessarily mean an author has a voice that speakers to children. But in this seventy-four-page novel that works for grades three through five, Dorris immediately convinced me he had something very important to say to children, and adults will find his voice compelling too.

Of mixed racial background—French, Irish, and Modoc—Dorris spent time on various Native-American reservations in the Pacific Northwest. With a degree from Yale, he founded the Native American Studies program at Dartmouth. While writing his own adult book on Columbus, he began to explore the history of the Taino people, the first to greet Christopher Columbus in the New World.

As a child, Dorris had found only stereotypical Indians in books; so he set out to craft a story with authentic Native-American characters that children would want to read about and get to know. In a narrative told in two voices, readers meet both twelve-year-old Morning Girl and ten-year-old Star Boy—brother and sister. She loves the day and he, the night. In simple language, they revel in the natural world and all its delights. But they also face universal tragedies—their mother's miscarriage and a tropical storm that almost destroys Star Boy. Independent, strong, curious, devoted, these two children make ideal friends for any young reader.

In one of the most heart-wrenching epilogues in a children's book, readers find out that Christopher Columbus once wrote, "They should be good and intelligent servants," of the young people of the island. Within a year of Columbus's arrival, entire tribes of these characters readers have grown to love are exterminated by the diseases carried by the Spanish troops.

Morning Girl provides a different lens for history. As the saying goes, history gets written by the winners. But in this slim book, Michael Dorris makes it possible to view events in 1492 from the point of view of the people already living in the Americas, sailing no oceans. It casts an entirely different light on Columbus Day.

ELEANOR ROOSEVELT: A LIFE OF DISCOVERY

By Russell Freedman

Today marks the birthday of both Russell Freedman and Eleanor Roosevelt. Originally a West Coaster, Russell was born in San Francisco and studied at the University of California at Berkeley. Russell's long-time editor Dorothy Briley once said that he was the perfect dinner guest. He could make intelligent conversation about any topic with anyone she brought to the table. Indeed, he has often been called a Renaissance man, because of the range and depth of his knowledge in a variety of topics.

Russell began writing books for young readers in the science and social studies arena—books like *How Animals Learn* and *Sharks*. But when his editor Ann Troy asked him to write a biography, something he had never done, he turned to his childhood hero Abraham Lincoln and wrote *Lincoln: A Photobiography*. He won the Newbery Medal for this book and found a new direction and purpose: writing quality narrative nonfiction for young readers.

As Russell wrote in *The Essential Guide to Children's Books and Their Creators*: "Nonfiction is supposed to be utilitarian. It's expected to do its duty—to inform, instruct, enlighten. And yet a hard-working, nose-to-the-grindstone nonfiction book should be just as absorbing as any imaginary story, because it is, in fact, a story, too."

Perfect for ten- to fourteen-year-olds, Russell's biography of Eleanor Roosevelt reveals little-known aspects of the first lady. A shy child, with absent parents, Eleanor only began to bloom when she was sent away to London for schooling. She married her distant cousin and was given away as a bride by her uncle Theodore, the president of the United States. "Well, Franklin, there's nothing like keeping the name in the family," the president quipped.

But as Eleanor Roosevelt began to find the causes of her life—the plight of minorities, the poverty of the disadvantaged—she turned from a shy person into a firebrand and became the conscience of Franklin D. Roosevelt. Russell captures this complex marriage—its betrayals and its strength. He shows the final years of Eleanor Roosevelt as she worked in the United Nations and became, as President Harry Truman called her, "the First Lady of the World."

Happy birthday to both Russell Freedman and Eleanor Roosevelt. Both have been crusaders for their passions and dedicated to telling stories the world needs to hear.

OCTOBER 11

It's the birth date of Eleanor Roosevelt (1884–1962). For further reading about this great first lady try *Eleanor* by Barbara Cooney and *Our Eleanor: A Scrapbook Look at Eleanor Roosevelt's Remarkable Life* by Candace Fleming.

In 1864 slavery was abolished in Maryland. Read **Frederick Douglas**: *The Last Day of Slavery* by William Miller, illustrated by Cedric Lucas, and *Stealing Freedom* by Elise Carbone.

If you can prove you're a descendent of someone who helped achieve the United States's independence and you happen to be female, you can apply to become a member of the Daughters of the American Revolution (DAR), formed on this day in 1890. Read *Independent Dames* by Laurie Halse Anderson.

In 1922 Alaska Davidson became the first woman appointed to the Federal Bureau of Investigation (FBI) as a "special investigator." Read *The History of the FBI* by Sabrina Crewe.

In 1984 Dr. Kathryn D. Sullivan became the first woman to take a space walk. Read *Almost Astronauts* by Tanya Lee Stone.

OCTOBER 12

Cease and desist! A letter from Massachusetts Governor William Phips dated 1692 ended the Salem Witch Trials. Read *The Witch of Blackbird Pond* by Elizabeth George Speare.

In 1792 the first Columbus Day celebration in the United States of America was held in New York. One hundred years later, in 1892, the Pledge of Allegiance was first recited by public school students to commemorate the 400th anniversary of Columbus's voyage and arrival to what was considered by Europeans to be "The New World."

"Executive Mansion" is a mouthful! President Theodore Roosevelt renamed his home "**The White House**" in 1901. Read *Our White House: Looking Out, Looking In* created by the N.C.B.L.A.

In 1999 the six billionth living human was born, and thus it's proclaimed The Day of Six Billion. The current estimates of human population (as of this writing) are just under seven billion. Read *People* by Peter Spier.

THE THIEF LORD
By Cornelia Funke

On October 12, 1797, Napoleon signed the Treaty of Campo Formio, handing Venice over to Austria. In one of the best children's books of the last decade, the city of Venice comes so alive that it almost seems like a character itself.

In *The Thief Lord*, the first novel by German author Cornelia Funke translated into English, the canals, the streets, the abandoned buildings, and the small islands outside of Venice provide an amazing setting for a gripping novel. After his mother dies, twelve-year-old Prosper's aunt wants to separate him from his brother, and so Prosper runs away to Venice with five-year-old Bo. In Venice they find other children supporting themselves—a girl named Hornet, Mosca, and Riccio—who live in an abandoned movie theater. These children get taken care of by the mysterious Thief Lord, a fifteen-year-old boy named Scipio, who shows up with items that they can hock for food and clothing.

However unconventional this arrangement, it works quite well for all the children. But Prosper's aunt and uncle trace the boys to Venice and hire a detective to find them. As the boys try to escape this man, they get swept up in another mystery—finding a missing part for a magical merry-go-round that can turn a child into an adult and an adult into a child. Conte Renzo hires the Thief Lord and his band to locate the missing wing that will restore this carousel to its original glory. In an unforgettable chapter, some of the characters mount the wooden animals to test whether the legend of the merry-go-round is true.

These Dickensian characters inhabit the city of Venice; they go on moonlit rides in its canals and explore its abandoned and decaying properties. Strong brotherly loyalty, a community of children who take care of each other, a fast-paced plot, eccentric adult characters, and the city of Venice all weave together in *The Thief Lord* for an unforgettable reading experience. Teachers have used this book successfully as a read aloud for third through sixth grades; readers ages ten to adult have loved it for independent reading. Fortunately, many other books by Cornelia Funke are now available in English (*Inkheart*, *Dragon Rider*), making her one of the few children's writers in translation to appear on the *New York Times* bestseller lists for children.

So if you want to go to Venice, just pick up *The Thief Lord*. You will find it hard to put down.

LUNCH LADY AND THE CYBORG SUBSTITUTE

By Jarrett J. Krosoczka

During the second week of October America celebrates National School Lunch Week. And as that old ditty goes: "Teachers come and teachers go, It's the lunch lady who you get to know." But how well do you really know the lunch lady? Do you know what she does when she leaves the school? In our book of the day, an inquiring group of kids ask these questions and discover some amazing answers. For in their school, the lunch lady is someone to be feared. She serves both lunch—and justice—in equal measure.

When author-illustrator Jarrett J. Krosoczka went back to visit his own elementary school as an adult, he saw the same lunch lady who had been working there when he was a child. After some time drawing and thinking about a book, he transformed her into a cafeteria worker by day, superheroine by night. She speeds on a motorcycle to stop robbers and enters abandoned warehouses to find criminals. In 2009 she took on one of her most difficult cases yet in *Lunch Lady and the Cyborg Substitute*.

When Mr. Pasteur, a substitute teacher, shows up to take over the class of someone who hasn't been sick in twenty years, the Lunch Lady gets suspicious. After she monitors school activities on a huge computer system, she decides to follow her suspect home. Unbeknownst to her, some students are tracking her as well—to discover what she actually does at night. Shocked to find the real answer to their question, they help her foil the evil plan of the science teacher Mr. Edison, who wants to replace the teaching staff with robots. The entire story is told in comic book format, perfect for first through third graders who like action-packed adventure mixed with fantasy.

In the past few years, Jarrett J. Krosoczka has become one of our most popular authors with children. His Lunch Lady series demonstrates why. He remembers what he thought about as a child and knows how to entertain children and keep them laughing.

So happy School Lunch Week. What does your lunch lady do when she isn't dishing out sloppy joes?

OCTOBER 13

Happy Birthday David Greenberg (*A Tugging String, Don't Forget Your Etiquette, Enchanted Lions*).

The infamous Nero became emperor of Rome in 54 AD. Read *Nero Corleone* by Elke Heidenreich, illustrated by Quint Buchholz.

In 1307 hundreds of Knights Templar in France were arrested by agents of King Phillip the Fair. It may also have been the birth date of Jaques de Molay (1244–1314), the last Grand Master of the Knights Templar. Read *A Templar's Apprentice: The Book of Tormod* by Kat Black.

The **Whirlpool Galaxy**, one of the most famous galaxies and easily observable by even amateur stargazers, was discovered in 1773 by French astronomer Charles Messier. Read *Galaxies* by Seymour Simon, *NightWatch: A Practical Guide to Viewing the Universe* by Terence Dickinson, and *Henry and Mudge and the Starry Night* by Cynthia Rylant.

It's International Skeptics Day. Read *The Magician's Book: A Skeptic's Adventures in Narnia* by Laura Miller.

OCTOBER 14

Happy Birthday Miriam Cohen (*Will I Have a Friend*) and Elisa Kleven (*Ernst, Abuela*).

It's the birth date of Lois Lenski (1893–1974), *Strawberry Girl*; and poet e. e. cummings (1894–1962), *Fairy Tales, Little Tree*.

It's also the birth date of Dwight D. Eisenhower (1890–1969), the 34th president of the United States.

Happy Birthday Pooh! In 1926 *Winnie-the-Pooh* by A. A. Milne was published.

Live! From Apollo 7 in space! The first live telecast with people on it beamed to earth from a spacecraft in 1968.

So sorry for the extra keystrokes! In 2009 Sir Tim Berners-Lee, World Wide Web creator, apologized for the unnecessary "//" in URLs.

GREGORY, THE TERRIBLE EATER

By Mitchell Sharmat

Illustrated by Jose Aruego and Ariane Dewey

October has been designated Vegetable Awareness Month and today also marks National Dessert Day. The book of the day, *Gregory, the Terrible Eater* by Mitchell Sharmat, brings these two holidays together in a humorous and totally satisfying story.

Like many children, Gregory was a fussy eater; he wants only fruits, vegetables, eggs, fish, bread, and butter. He sounds, of course, like many a parent's dream. But such is not the case—mainly because Gregory is a young goat. His parents want him to eat normal food like tin cans and rubber tires. When he refuses, they excuse him from the table, and then eat the newspaper in silence. The next day they take Gregory to the knowing Dr. Ram, who has some age-old wisdom to share. Just introduce one new food each day until Gregory eats everything!

So crafty parents that they are, they throw a shoelace into the spaghetti or a rubber heel in the string beans. And slowly Gregory develops a species-appropriate taste. Gregory, in fact, takes the term *omnivore* to a whole new level. After his parents go to the dump for food, he consumes eight flat tires, a barber pole, a violin, and half of a car. The latter gives him so much trouble that he reverts to his old vegetable meals—but with some wax paper thrown in for good measure.

Jose Aruego, an American born in the Philippines, and his former wife, Ariane Dewey, have taken this very clever text and added wonderful details of Gregory thinking about and consuming all kinds of food. Collaborators on many titles, Jose designs the page layout and creates the strong and energetic line drawings, while Ariane fills them in with color washes. This method has worked for them, and in books like *Gregory, the Terrible Eater* their partnership has worked for millions of children.

But what about dessert? Well, when Gregory asks Father Goat what they are having for dessert he answers, "Ice cream . . . But you have to eat the box, too."

So if you have a picky eater who you want to entertain, or you just want to laugh at the antics of Gregory and his goat family, pick up this book today.

BALLET SHOES

By Noel Streatfeild

October has been designated Reading Group Month, organized by the Women's National Book Association. I am always interested in the books that people remember from childhood—children read so many books but which ones stay with them into adulthood? When I talk to young women in their twenties and thirties, one title that comes up again and again is Noel Streatfeild's *Ballet Shoes*.

The daughter of an English country vicar, Noel Streatfeild first distinguished herself as an actress; then she tried a short stint as an adult writer. But she was to make her most important mark on the field of children's books. Noticing that books for children did not show young people as professionals or pursuing a career, Streatfeild published England's first career novel in 1936: *Ballet Shoes*.

In this somewhat misnamed book—because only part of it actually concerns ballet—three adopted orphan girls, Pauline, Petrova, and Posy, live in a large ramshackle house in London. The family takes in a group of boarders to make ends meet, but eventually the girls need to work to help the family. Pauline longs to be an actress; Petrova, a mechanic; and Posy, a ballerina. The novel abounds in exact details of how they go about their professional training, the joys and difficulties that they face, and the financial life of a young performer. You could even use sections of the book to teach math, so concerned is Streatfeild with getting all the financial details exactly right. Each year on their birthdays, the girls vow to accomplish something so special that it will get their names in history books. By the end, you have no doubt that they will achieve their goal.

OCTOBER 15

Happy Birthday Barry Moser (*Appalachia, Jump!, Hogwood Steps Out*) and Katherine Ayres (*Macaroni Boy; Up, Down, and Around*).

In 1764 historian Edward Gibbon observed a group of friars singing in the ruined Temple of Jupiter in Rome. This inspired him to begin work on the now-classic *The History of the Decline and Fall of the Roman Empire*.

"Dear Mr. President . . ." In 1860 eleven-year-old Grace Bedell writes to Lincoln suggesting he grow a beard. Read *Abe Lincoln: The Boy Who Loved Books* by Kay Winters, illustrated by Nancy Carpenter, and *Lincoln Tells a Joke* by Kathleen Krull and Paul Brewer, illustrated by Stacy Innerst.

Comedian Lucille Ball's famous TV show, *I Love Lucy*, made its debut on CBS in 1951. Read *Lucy Goosey* by Margaret Wild, illustrated by Ann James.

In 1964 Martin Luther King, Jr. was awarded the Nobel Peace Prize. Reread *Martin's Big Words* by Doreen Rappaport, illustrated by Bryan Collier.

Sesame Street's Oscar the Grouch is the inspiration for National Grouch Day celebrated today.

Ballet Shoes met immediate success in England and Depression era America when it was published. In the thirties women and girls who worked outside the domestic sphere could rarely be found in books for children. Hence any adult who wanted more literary fare than Nancy Drew often led young readers to Streatfeild. A wonderful story about orphans who ban together and make a family, *Ballet Shoes* still works its charm over seventy-five years after publication. It continues to inspire many young women to find their own way and their own career.

OCTOBER 16

Happy Birthday Joseph Bruchac (*Code Talker, Keepers of the Earth*) and Peter McCarty (*Little Bunny on the Move*).

It's the birth date of Edward Ardizzone (1900–1979), *Diana and Her Rhinoceros*; and Cecile de Brunhoff (1903–2003), cocreator of *The Story of Babar* and subsequent books in the series.

It's also the birth date of American lexicographer Noah Webster (1758–1843), considered the Father of the American Dictionary. Hence, it is Dictionary Day. Read Andrew Clements's *Frindle*.

The library of ancient Alexandria was the largest and best library in the ancient Roman world. In 2002 Bibliotheca Alexandrina, the commemoration of the lost library of Alexandria, was inaugurated on the shores of the Mediterranean Sea in Egypt. Read *The Library* by Sarah Stewart, illustrated by David Small.

Donating to your local food pantry or volunteering to serve community meals are ways to help alleviate hunger on World Food Day today. Read *Dim Sum for Everyone* by Grace Lin.

It's also Sweetest Day.

THE SUMMER I LEARNED TO FLY

By Dana Reinhardt

Some books just beg to be discussed with others, and our book of the day for Reading Group Month, Dana Reinhardt's *The Summer I Learned to Fly*, is perfect for mother/daughter groups.

When we first meet the protagonist of the book, she tells us that some smells draw us back to childhood—like her grandfather's aftershave lotion. But the scent that reminds her of the most important summer of her life, between age thirteen and fourteen, is the smell of Limburger, Camembert, or Stilton cheese. Narrated by Birdie when she is eighteen, she explains a lot about cheese—her mother has opened up a gourmet cheese shop—and what it feels like to be an outsider without friends.

Birdie makes up for her lack of a social life by helping her mother in the shop. She likes working at the counter or making pasta with her mother's assistant, the dreamboat Nick. Her other companions, not really friends, are away for the summer. In fact, her one true friend appears to be a pet rat that she carries around in her backpack.

Then one day, out behind the shop, Birdie meets Emmett. He knows a lot about rats and a good deal about human misery. Slowly she begins to understand that he has no real home; piece by piece she puts his story together. When he finally confides all the details to her, he asks her to go with him on a journey—a quest to find healing and a miracle. Although they quickly return home, the book opens up questions about honesty in the mother/daughter relationships. For neither Birdie nor her mother have been completely candid with each other.

Although the premise of the novel, that transitional summer between being a girl and growing up, is as old as Maureen Daly's *Seventeenth Summer,* the voice, approach, and quirkiness of *The Summer I Learned to Fly* is completely original. Birdie is honest and compassionate and struggling to find her own place in the world. For those who love books of gentle romance like *Flipped*, for those who love a great first-person voice, for those who enjoy an intriguing protagonist, *The Summer I Learned to Fly* will be totally satisfying. But a word of warning: it will make you hungry for cheese!

AL CAPONE DOES MY SHIRTS

By Gennifer Choldenko

On October 17, 1931, Al Capone, known as Scarface and the most notorious outlaw in the United States, was finally convicted for tax evasion, a rather dull offense amid his many crimes. Eventually, when a new, completely secure federal penitentiary was completed, Capone, known as prisoner AZ 85, went to live on Alcatraz Island, off the coast of San Francisco, for four and a half years.

Now, Al Capone and Alcatraz don't seem obvious subjects for one of the best novels for children of the past ten years—but, in fact, they form the core of Gennifer Choldenko's *Al Capone Does My Shirts*. Alcatraz not only housed some of the most vicious criminals of the time, but it also served as the home for fifty to sixty families who provided services in the prison. They lived on the island around the clock.

The hero of *Al Capone Does My Shirts*, Moose Flanagan, a twelve-year-old baseball nut, finds himself taken from the school and friends he loves because his father accepts a job as an Alcatraz prison guard. Not only does Moose have to get used to a new school but he must also adjust to the realities of this bizarre and tight-knit community. On Alcatraz the daughter of the prison warden, Piper, cows all of the children with her recklessness and deceit. Since Al Capone works in the laundry, Piper sets up a clothes-cleaning service for children at their off-island school—she tells them they can brag forever that Al Capone did their laundry. Meanwhile, Moose has problems all his own. His older sister, Natalie, suffers from a form of autism. Living with a disease undiagnosed at the time of the story, Natalie has driven their mother to the brink of insanity. Moose often is the only member of the family able to care for her.

The historical novel, taking place over six months from January through June of 1935, develops a cast of characters that children want to hang out with and an unusual setting that often provides the tension for the plot. Although the relationships of the children take up most of the narrative, readers learn a great deal about Al Capone, as well—his favorite colors, that he likes silk underwear, and that he opened the first soup kitchen in Chicago. And, in the end, the infamous Mr. Capone actually helps Moose get Natalie into a school that may help her.

A Newbery Honor book published in 2004, *Al Capone Does My Shirts* exemplifies the best qualities of historical fiction for children—a sense of story, a sense of place, and a sense of history. It stands at the top of my list of recent books with a great chance to become literary classics—one of those books you can savor again and again.

OCTOBER 17

Happy Birthday Alan Garner (*The Owl Service*).

It's the birth date of Robert Jordan (1948–2007), *The Hunt Begins*.

Scientist Albert Einstein fled Nazi Germany and moved to the United States in 1933. Read *Albert Einstein* by Kathleen Krull, illustrated by Boris Kulikov.

Created by the United Nations, this is the International Day for the Eradication of Poverty. Read *The Family Under the Bridge* by Natalie Savage Carlson, illustrated by Garth Williams.

It's Wear Something Gaudy Day.

You get a do-over on Mulligan Day. Give someone, or yourself, a second chance! And read *Mike Mulligan and His Steam Shovel* by Virginia Lee Burton.

OCTOBER 18

Happy Birthday Nancy Winslow Parker (*The Jacket I Wear in the Snow*), Joyce Hansen (*I Thought My Soul Would Rise, Which Way Freedom?*), and Susan Jeschke (*Perfect the Pig*).

Poet **Phillis Wheatley** was freed from slavery on this day in 1775. Read *Phillis's Big Test* by Catherine Clinton and Sean Qualls.

The United States bought Alaska from Russia in 1867, at the cost of a mere $7.2 million. Hence it's Alaska Day, to commemorate the transfer of the territory. Read *The Call of the Wild* by Jack London and *Diamond Willow* by Helen Frost.

Also in 1867, the rules for American football were formulated at a meeting in New York among delegates from Columbia, Rutgers, Princeton, and Yale universities.

In 1898 Puerto Rico became a United States territory. Read *The Golden Flower: A Taino Myth from Puerto Rico* by Nina Jaffe and Enrique O. Sanchez.

It's National Chocolate Cupcake Day—indulge in a celebration!

DANNY AND THE DINOSAUR
By Syd Hoff

October is International Dinosaur Month. Few creatures are as appealing to children as dinosaurs. In fact, to have a dinosaur as a pet must be one of the great childhood fantasies, an idea explored by Oliver Butterworth in *The Enormous Egg*.

Our dinosaur of the day isn't exactly a pet. He lives in the museum. But when young Danny stands in front of this large creature and says he'd like to play with a dinosaur, the dinosaur responds, "And I think it would be nice to play with you." In Syd Hoff's *Danny and the Dinosaur*, the beginning of an I Can Read picture book series, Danny gets the thrill of a lifetime when he climbs on board the dinosaur's neck and heads out into the world.

Born in 1912, Syd Hoff began his career as a cartoonist. A high school dropout, at sixteen he attended the National Academy of Design in New York. At eighteen he sold his first cartoon to *The New Yorker* and became a frequent contributor to the magazine. He created two syndicated comic strips, "Tuffy" and "Laugh It Off." But in the midfifties Hoff was struggling to keep his sick daughter from focusing on her medical treatments. He began to make some drawings and tell her stories with them. They turned into *Danny and the Dinosaur*, published in 1958.

This book works brilliantly as a way to chase the blues away for all children. Walking outside with a dinosaur proves quite a challenge for Danny. His friend gets caught in clotheslines. Danny needs to watch out for the dinosaur's tail. But a companion of this size, it turns out, can be quite useful in the city by serving as a bridge over traffic, carrying passengers, and providing water transport. Admittedly, he does have trouble playing hide-and-seek. It's hard for a dinosaur to find a place to hide! Hoff always maintained that the best humor springs from the familiar. *Danny and the Dinosaur* can make children laugh from the first page to the last through familiar settings transformed by an uncommon creature.

Danny and the Dinosaur has been enticing children ages two through eight into reading for more than forty years. There's no moral or message—just humor and fun and excitement. Syd Hoff was one of those comic geniuses who never received enough accolades for his work during his career. Except, of course, from children. They know that anyone who can write a book like *Danny and the Dinosaur* has to be a friend of theirs.

HORTON HATCHES THE EGG

By Dr. Seuss

In October 1940 a new children's book author and illustrator published his fourth book, one destined to become a classic. Since he had been rejected some twenty times for his first book, and then only been picked up by a small press, Vanguard, he did not necessarily seem to be poised to become America's best-known and bestselling children's book creator. But our book of the day definitely improved the trajectory of his career.

The beauty of children's books, of course, is that we come to them at many moments in our lives—first in our own childhoods and then when we share them with children. When I touch the green-and-red cover of this seventy-year veteran, I am instantly transported back years. This book was a surefire staple when I babysat as a teenager. It never ceased to please whatever little rascals I had charge of for the evening. And although I have forgotten what I did yesterday, I can remember its refrain: "I meant what I said / And I said what I meant. . . . / An elephant's faithful / One hundred per cent!"

Dr. Seuss's *Horton Hatches the Egg* takes a sly look at the nature versus nurture debate. Seuss presents a less than ideal parent in the lazy Mayzie bird. She abandons her nest after she coaxes slow but steady Horton the Elephant to take care of her egg. And egg sit he does—

OCTOBER 19

Happy Birthday Ed Emberly (*The Wing on a Flea, One Wide River to Cross, Drummer Hoff*), Dan Gutman (*Honus and Me*), and Phillip Pullman (*The Golden Compass*).

What a view they must've had! In 1874 Mary Walsh and Charles Colson were the first couple married in a hot air balloon. Read *Hot Air* by Marjorie Priceman, *Hot-Air Henry* by Mary Calhoun, illustrated by Erick Ingraham, and *Sally's Great Balloon Adventure* by Stephen Huneck.

Now often played at graduations, Edward Elgar's "Pomp and Circumstance March" premiered in Liverpool on this date in 1901. Read *Oh, the Places You'll Go* by Dr. Seuss and *Yay, You!* by Sandra Boynton.

In 1941 Anna Lee Wiley became the first female jockey in North America. Read *National Velvet* by Enid Bagnold.

In 1988 the United States Senate passed a law limiting ads during children's television shows. Read *Arthur's TV Trouble* by Marc Brown.

through snow, sleet, and lightning, and even capture in a cage. With an ending that still makes me cheer, Horton does get his reward—an offspring who adores him!

So many different interpretations exist for *Horton Hatches the Egg*. In *Everything I Need to Know I Learned from a Children's Book*, Karen Hesse writes, "I met my first genuine humanitarian in the elephant Horton. . . . I wanted to be like Horton. I wanted the world to be populated by Hortons. I wanted all the children of the world to be treated with the same loving devotion with which Horton treated the egg." Others perceive a different message: Even if your mother might not love you or want to stay with you, you can find someone who will. Someone important. Someone as fabulous as Horton.

Persistence, honor, devotion—all these traits form the character of our hero. May Horton live another seven decades. Since the publication of this book, the name Dr. Seuss has become synonymous with laughter; *Horton Hatches the Egg* shows us why.

OCTOBER 20

Happy Birthday Nikki Grimes (*Bronx Masquerade*).

It's the birth date of Crockett Johnson (1906–1975), *Harold and the Purple Crayon*; and Wylly Folk St. John (1908–1985), *The Ghost Next Door*.

It's also the birth date of American philosopher and educator John Dewey (1859–1952). Read *Dewey: There's a Cat in the Library!* by Vicki Myron and Bret Witter, illustrated by Steve James.

Due to the onset of World War II, cheese was rationed in the Netherlands starting on this day in 1940. Read *The Stinky Cheese Man and Other Fairly Stupid Tales* by Jon Scieszka, illustrated by Lane Smith.

Fact or hoax? On this day in 1967 Roger Patterson and Robert Gimlin supposedly filmed Bigfoot, a large unidentified creature walking on two legs. Read *Bigfoot and Other Legendary Creatures* by Paul Robert Walker, illustrated by William Noonan, and *Uncle Bigfoot* by George O'Connor.

It's the National Day on Writing, brought to you by the National Council of Teachers of English. All kinds of writing is celebrated on this day. Submit your writing to their online gallery.

CARL GOES SHOPPING
By Alexandra Day

In October 1992, the board book edition of a title that had already gained a devoted following of picture book fans appeared: Alexandra Day's *Carl Goes Shopping*. Publishers eager for titles for the very young frequently republish material that had appeared as standard picture books in board book form. For the Carl books, wordless except for a sentence at the beginning and at the end, the board book format allowed the preliterate set to get to know a character they would love, Carl the Rottweiler, without the danger of ripping the pages.

Left to take care of the baby while mother goes on an errand, Carl takes his charge on a wild ride through a department store. In a modern version of *Corduroy*, Carl hits the elevator button with his paw, carries the baby on his back, and begins to explore department after department. They visit toys, books (*Rottweilers I Have Known*), hats, and electronics. Carl really gets into the act in the rug, food, and pet departments. And then they race back to the place where the baby's mother left them and are greeted with, "Good dog, Carl!"

Day excels in telling a completely understandable story, which can be embellished by both the child and adult. The oil paintings are so precise and full of realistic detail that they make this fantasy shopping trip seem completely real. And what child wouldn't want Carl as a caretaker?

Alexandra Day founded Green Tiger Press with her husband. Her first book, *Good Dog, Carl*, was published by their press. Day used her own Rottweiler as a model; as the success of the books grew, she began to travel with a dog, who could execute a variety of tricks and commands. In fact, her canine companions on speaking trips were so well trained that one could even imagine them acting out the detailed tour of a department store shown in *Carl Goes Shopping*.

If you have not yet introduced your young readers to this fabulous dog, don't hesitate. All of the Carl books demonstrate how brilliantly art can tell a story—and how delightful it would be to ride around on Carl, anywhere, anytime.

HARRIET THE SPY

By Louise Fitzhugh

On October 21, 1964, a book appeared that critics consider to be the beginning of modern fiction for children. Before that day, it had been controversial even in its own publishing house. After all, its protagonist wrote and said bad things about people, broke into New York City apartments, and didn't really change her ways over the course of the narrative. She was called "one of the most fatiguing, ill-mannered children imaginable."

The book of the day is none other than Louise Fitzhugh's *Harriet the Spy*. Harriet was different than the characters in the books of the sixties, and she remains a quirky protagonist even today. The book began as a series of diary entries. By asking Fitzhugh questions such as "Why was Harriet angry?" Charlotte Zolotow and Ursula Nordstrom of Harper helped her flesh out the story. In the end, they helped her craft a book that children would love, and adults, for a short time, would hate. Susan Hirschman, who worked in the offices of Harper at the time, believed that Nordstrom, having set picture books on a different path by publishing *Where the Wild Things Are*, had decided that she was also going to change children's fiction. Certainly by the end of the sixties a new wave of realism had swept over children's books.

In the story eleven-year-old Harriet M. Welsch always carries a spy notebook and records her observations. Stuck with two of the most feckless parents in all of children's literature, young Harriet dresses like a spy—dark hooded sweatshirt and blue jeans—and eavesdrops in dumbwaiters or listens through doors. She writes brutally honest observations about her classmates. Unfortunately, her diary ends up being read by them—and Harriet's life begins to spin out of control. Any child who has ever felt a victim of cruelty can identify with Harriet.

After the publication of the book, children began forming spy clubs; they hid under tables in schools, taking notes. Harriet inspired many readers to realize that they could dress or act differently than their peers. And, as Perri Klass writes in *Everything I Need to Know I Learned from a Children's Book*, decades of writers have learned from the book: "From *Harriet the Spy* I discovered the pleasure, even the addictive pleasure, of having a notebook and writing things down."

Happy birthday *Harriet the Spy*. She may not be the most well-behaved character in literature, but the world is a richer place because she was allowed to pick up her pen.

OCTOBER 21

Happy Birthday Ursula K. Le Guin (*A Wizard of Earthsea*) and Ann Cameron (*The Stories Julian Tells*).

It's the birth date of Janet Ahlberg (1944–1994), *Each Peach Pear Plum*, *The Jolly Postman*; and Samuel Taylor Coleridge (1772–1834), *The Rime of the Ancient Mariner*.

It's also the birth date of Alfred Nobel (1833–1896), who instituted the Nobel Prizes. Read *The Man Behind the Peace Prize: Alfred Nobel* by Kathy-Jo Wargin, illustrated by Zachary Pullen.

Ferdinand Magellan discovered a channel of water between the Atlantic and Pacific oceans in 1520, now known as the Strait of Magellan in South America. Read *To the Edge of the World* by Michele Torrey and *MVP: Magellan Voyage Project* by Douglas Evans, illustrated by John Shelley.

In 1879 Thomas Edison tested the first practical electric lightbulb, which lasted thirteen and a half hours. Read *The Lightbulb* by Joseph Wallace, illustrated by Toby Wells.

It's Count Your Buttons Day. Read *Corduroy* by Don Freeman.

OCTOBER 22

In 1836 **Sam Houston** became president of the Republic of Texas. Read *Make Way for Sam Houston* by Jean Fritz, illustrated by Elise Primavera, and *Armadillo Rodeo* by Jan Brett.

The Metropolitan Opera House opened in New York City on this day in 1883. Read *The Dog Who Sang at the Opera* by Marshall Izen and Jim West, illustrated by Erika Oller, and *Pet of the Met* by Lydia and Don Freeman.

In 1907 the Ringling Brothers Greatest Show on Earth bought Barnum & Bailey circus. Read *Ballet of the Elephants* by Leda Schubert, illustrated by Robert Parker.

In 1926 J. Gordon Whitehead sucker punched Harry Houdini in the stomach. Read *Escape!* by Sid Fleischman.

ROBIN HOOD
By Paul Creswick
Illustrated by N. C. Wyeth

Born in 1882 in Needham, Massachusetts, Newel Convers Wyeth was raised on a family farm that dated from 1730. As a young man he fell under the tutelage of Howard Pyle, the great children's book illustrator of his era, and became the advocate of the principles of book illustration taught at Pyle's Brandywine School in Chadds Ford, Pennsylvania. It did not take Wyeth long to distinguish himself. By the time he was twenty he created a piece of art featured on the cover of the *Saturday Evening Post*. Wyeth settled in the Chadds Ford area and began his career as a very successful magazine illustrator in a time when those talents were much in demand. However, Wyeth's method of working remained that of a painter; he created enormous canvases with oils. His scenes made dramatic use of light and shadow; many were executed with the "golden triangle" composition so beloved by Pyle.

Beginning in 1911, Wyeth created art for a group of illustrated classics published by Charles Scribner's Sons. With ten to fifteen visual pieces per book, Wyeth brought a visual intelligence to the classics—titles included Stevenson's *Treasure Island* and *Kidnapped* and Rawlings's *The Yearling*. In their heyday the Scribner volumes represented the best of the "book beautiful" for children. They were also sophisticated enough that they became reading for the entire family.

In 1917 Wyeth added his art to Paul Creswick's *Robin Hood*. Today an abridged version of the text remains in print, showcasing Wyeth's glorious art. Larger than the original Scribner volumes in size, the book is dominated by Wyeth's paintings. He brings readers into the sun-dappled Sherwood Forest and presents a beguiling Maid Marian. Wyeth, who always had an eye for women, knew how to capture their subtlety and seduction very well. In one of his most interesting artistic choices, Wyeth does not focus the art on the hero—Robin Hood is often to the side or in shadows throughout the book. But in the last spread readers see him at the center of the composition as he lies in his deathbed. And so it is the villages, forests, and people of this medieval story who become its stars.

Anyone seeing original Wyeth work understands immediately that he could have made a career as a fine artist—as his son Andrew did. But he chose instead to be an artist whose work was displayed in classic volumes for children. Generations of families and children owe him a debt of gratitude for that decision and for his productive career.

APPLES AND PUMPKINS

By Anne Rockwell

Illustrated by Lizzy Rockwell

In New England, as in many other states of the country, October is the perfect time to harvest and eat two crops—apples and pumpkins. Our book of the day, *Apples and Pumpkins* by Anne Rockwell, celebrates that idea. For years I have admired Anne Rockwell's ability to render the complex simple in her picture books for the very young. Rockwell was one of the pioneers in the area of books for very young readers, ages birth to three. She studied art at Pratt Institute and began to write and illustrate picture books after her children were born. In the seventies Anne created a series of groundbreaking books in collaboration with her husband Harlow—*The Toolbox*, *My Doctor*, *My Dentist*—that explained these topics to preliterate children.

Rockwell's touch has always been light, never preaching, never overexplaining. More than twenty years ago she began working with her daughter Lizzy to extend the range of her nonfiction picture books. Our book of the day, *Apples and Pumpkins*, explores two of October's most visible foods. A young child tells the story of the annual fall visit to Comstock Farm to pick apples and pumpkins. Barnyard animals accompany everyone around the orchard. When the family has picked enough apples, they go in search of the best pumpkin. Then the story continues at home where the pumpkin is carved and the apples given out for Halloween.

City children often have no idea where their food comes from. In *Apples and Pumpkins* Anne Rockwell takes them out to the farm and captures the activities of a perfect fall day. Clear and clean drawings spell out exactly what is described in the text. In this one book young readers learn about farms, food cycles, and a major holiday. Quite remarkable for a mere thirty-two pages, but that is what Anne Rockwell has always been able to accomplish in her work.

I'm grateful that we have writers like Anne Rockwell and artists like Lizzy Rockwell who can explain the world so well to very young readers.

OCTOBER 23

Happy Birthday Laurie Halse Anderson (*Speak, Wintergirls*), Elizabeth Cody Kimmel (*Balto and the Great Race, Glamsters*), and Lydia Dabcovich (*The Polar Bear Son*).

It's the birth date of Marjorie Flack (1897–1958), *The Story about Ping*.

In 2001 Apple released the first iPod. Hence, it is iPod Day.

It's Mole Day! Not in honor of the four-footed mammal, but the basic unit of measuring in chemistry known as Avogadro's number (6.02×10^{23}). But you might still want to read *Mole Music* by David McPhail, *Naked Mole Rat Gets Dressed* by Mo Willems, and the Mouse and Mole series by Wong Herbert Lee.

OCTOBER 24

Happy Birthday Meilo So (*Moonbeams, Dumplings & Dragon Boats*) and Barbara Robinson (*The Best Christmas Pageant Ever*).

 It's the birth date of **Sarah Josepha Hale** (1788–1879), magazine editor and poet whose book *Poems for Our Children* included "Mary Had a Little Lamb."

On this day in 1939 the Nazis began requiring Jewish Germans to wear the Star of David on their clothes. Read *Number the Stars* by Lois Lowry.

It's United Nations Day! Happy Birthday to the United Nations, founded in 1945.

If you are in the mood to celebrate lunch meat, it's National Bologna Day. And that's no baloney! Read *Baloney (Henry P.)* by Jon Scieszka and Lane Smith.

On your mark, get set, fold! Join the international community of origami for the kick-off (or fold-off) of World Origami Days (October 24 through November 11). Read *The Strange Case of Origami Yoda* by Tom Angelberger.

PETE'S A PIZZA
By William Steig

Today we celebrate an event everyone can enjoy. October is National Pizza Month, a perfect time to engage in America's favorite pastime: eating a scrumptious pie. As a nation, we consume 350 slices of pizza each second! According to a recent Gallop poll, children three to eleven prefer pizza over any other food for lunch and dinner. But before you head out to snatch up your favorite kind, pick up one of the funniest, most original books written about the subject: William Steig's *Pete's a Pizza*.

Poor Pete. He's having a bad day. But his father knows just what to do to cheer up his son. Dad sets Pete down on a kitchen table, starts kneading him like dough, stretches him out, and tosses him back and forth with his mother. Then Dad begins to cover him in pizza ingredients. Although he pretends to pour on oil and flour, these substances are really water and talcum powder. Checkers come out next, substituting for tomatoes, and already Pete can't control his giggling. Kids will be laughing long before then. Eventually, Pete the Pizza runs away, gets hugged, and heads out to play with his friends, happy at last. The story, accompanied by Steig's watercolor-and-ink illustrations, is perfectly paced. Even the layout of the text, set in capital letters, makes it look like a printed recipe.

William Steig was eighty-one years old when he published this contemporary classic, which works both for independent reading and as an activity for a family or class. Sometimes teachers use a storyboard with felt to tell this saga, and families love to act out the book with their children. At some library events the reading is concluded with the best of all possible endings: pizza for the participants.

The book also stands as a tribute to octogenarians. There is no rule that our greatest children's books need to be written and conceived by young writers—the authors just need to be young in spirit. Fortunately, William Steig remained true to his childlike spirit all of his creative life. Consequently in his eighties, he knew a great book idea when he discovered it, and he executed his concept flawlessly.

SADAKO AND THE THOUSAND PAPER CRANES

By Eleanor Coerr

For two and a half weeks, from October 24 through November 11, we celebrate World Origami Days. *Sadako and the Thousand Paper Cranes* is perfect for the celebration. Published in 1977, shortly after the end of the Vietnam War, Eleanor Coerr chose the time period of another conflict, World War II in the Pacific, to deliver her thoughts about the effects of war on children and her message of peace. As a journalist Coerr visited Japan for the first time in 1949 and spent three years interviewing the citizens about their post–World War II experience. After marrying a career diplomat and ambassador, she returned to Japan in the 1960s. At the Hiroshima Peace Park, she saw a new statue honoring Sadako Sasaki (1943–1955). Decorated with thousands of paper cranes, the memorial was engraved with these words: "This is our cry, / this is our prayer: / for building peace in the world."

When she returned to the United States, Coerr became a children's librarian and wrote books as well. For her eighth children's book, she went back to Sadako's letters, collected in an autobiography called *Kokeshi*, and presented the material in a straightforward manner so it could be read by children ages seven to ten.

Sometimes called the "Anne Frank of Hiroshima," twelve-year-old Sadako was the star of the school running team, but her athletic prowess did not save her from contracting leukemia, "the atomic bomb disease." Sadako had once heard that paper cranes might cure illness: "If a sick person folds one thousand paper cranes, the gods will grant her wish and make her healthy again." So she set out to fold that many, but died before they were finished. Her classmates completed the task for her and buried Sadako with a thousand paper cranes. In American schools, reading Coerr's *Sadako and the Thousand Paper Cranes* is often accompanied by the folding of origami birds—instructions are included in the book. In Japan on Peace Day, August 6, children place thousands of paper cranes on Sadako's statue.

October 25 marks the anniversary of Sadako's death. This slim book of eighty pages, written in very simple language, presents her heart-wrenching story. A three-handkerchief story, it will always work for those readers who request "a sad book." By showing the effect of a war on the life of a vibrant and attractive child, Eleanor Coerr wrote a powerful book that advocates for peace.

OCTOBER 25

Happy Birthday Stephanie S. Tolan (*Surviving the Applewhites*).

It's the birth date of Carolyn Sherwin Bailey (1875–1961), *Miss Hickory*; Fred Marcellino (1938–2001), *Puss in Boots*; and Hardy Boys ghostwriter Leslie McFarlane (1902–1977), pseudonym Franklin W. Dixon.

John Steinbeck received the Nobel Literature Prize in 1962. His major works include *The Grapes of Wrath*, *Of Mice and Men*, *Travels with Charlie*, and *The Pearl*.

It's time for spaghetti silliness and macaroni mayhem on World Pasta Day. Read *The Story of Noodles* by Ying Chang Compestine and YoungShen Xuan and *Pino and the Signora's Pasta* by Janet Pedersen.

OCTOBER 26

Happy Birthday Steven Kellogg (*Johnny Apple-seed*, *Pecos Bill*), Ellen Showell (*The Trickster Ghost*), and Eric Rohmann (*My Friend Rabbit*).

Happy Birthday also to Hillary Rodham Clinton. Read *Dear Socks, Dear Buddy: Kids' Letters to the First Pets* by Hillary Rodham Clinton and *Hillary Rodham Clinton: Dreams Taking Flight* by Kathleen Krull, illustrated by Amy June Bates.

The Erie Canal opened in 1825. Read *The Amazing Impossible Erie Canal* by Cheryl Harness and *The Erie Canal* by Martha E. Kendall.

The Pony Express mail service ended in 1861. Read *Pony Express!* by Stephen Kroll, illustrated by Dan Andreasen, *Black Storm Coming* by Diane Lee Wilson, and *Whatever Happened to the Pony Express?* by Verla Kay, illustrated by Kimberly Bulken Root and Barry Root.

It's Worldwide Howl at the Moon Night. Read *Big Bad Wolves at School* by Stephen Krensky, illustrated by Brad Sneed, and *The Incorrigible Children of Ashton Place: The Mysterious Howling* by Maryrose Wood.

SARAH, PLAIN AND TALL

By Patricia MacLachlan

October is Family History Month, celebrated by genealogists and family historians who believe in actively searching for information about ancestors. For children's book writers, one reason to explore family history is the possibility of discovering stories that can be transformed into books. Our book of the day by Patricia MacLachlan, *Sarah, Plain and Tall*, began as a story passed down in her family.

Patty MacLachlan had already written many books for children when she crafted this masterpiece for seven- to nine-year-olds. After taking her family to North Dakota to show them the farm where her father was born in a humble sod house, she was inspired to preserve his history. To do this she turned to a story that her mother had often told about a mail-order bride who went to live on the plains.

Anna, a young girl in the nineteenth century, narrates the story about her father, Jacob Witting, a widowed farmer. He places a newspaper ad to ask a wife to come to his prairie home and become a mother for his children. After they exchange a series of letters, Sarah Wheaton leaves Maine to visit Jacob and his family. The children, Anna and her brother Caleb, grow to love Sarah and long for her to love them in return and stay, rather than go back to Maine. In a spare, economical style, the novel of a mere fifty-eight pages explores the feelings of the children and Sarah's developing love for all members of the family. *Sarah, Plain and Tall* celebrates family life and how a cohesive unit can be formed by those not related by blood.

MacLachlan wrote two other books about these characters: *Caleb's Story* and *Skylark*. All were adapted for Hallmark television specials featuring Glenn Close. The book has become a staple of second- and third-grade classrooms across the country. Now a quarter of a century after its publication, this beautiful story and its evocative language has become part of the literary heritage of American children: "I will come by train. I will wear a yellow bonnet. I am plain and tall. Tell them I sing."

MY BROTHER SAM IS DEAD

By James Lincoln Collier and Christopher Collier

October has been designated Reading Group Month by the Women's National Book Association. All kinds of reading groups have become popular over the last couple of decades: teen book groups, mother and daughter groups, parents and children groups.

An ideal pick for book groups and classroom discussions is our book of the day, *My Brother Sam Is Dead* by James Lincoln Collier and Christopher Collier. First published in 1974, the book was released at the end of the war in Vietnam. Unlike Forbes's *Johnny Tremain* the book might best be described as an antiwar Revolutionary War book. Until the publication of M. T. Anderson's *The Astonishing Life of Octavian Nothing*, I always considered *My Brother Sam Is Dead* the darkest Revolutionary War novel in the children's literature canon.

Narrated by Tim Meeker, the novel, set in Redding, Connecticut, describes the effect of the war on a typical family in a small, New England community. Right after the skirmish at Lexington and Concord, Sam Meeker leaves Yale and marches to fight with the Patriots. But his father, who owns a tavern, considers himself a Tory, as do many others in Redding, and argues with Sam before he goes off to join the battle. Because Sam needs a gun, he steals one from the house—and in doing so takes the family's only means of protection.

Tim has always idolized his older brother, and now he must live with his father's anger and the uncertainty of what will happen to his hero. Based on superb historical research, this Newbery Honor book shows the terrible price that families paid during the war. Largely focusing on Connecticut's role in the Revolution, the book contains some very compelling scenes when Tim and his father travel through Westchester County in New York—a lawless area where Patriots and Tories formed renegade groups and attacked those they believed to be on the other side. The hunger, the shifting positions of neighbors, and the brutality of both the British and the Americans toward average citizens gets full play in the book. Even more important, the novel shows that the American Revolution was the first Civil War in this country. For many readers, this revelation will be one they did not encounter in history textbooks.

For those who dislike unhappy endings, the title alone should tell you all you need to know. In an ironic twist, Mr. Meeker actually dies while in custody of the British, and Sam is killed by the Patriots for a crime he did not commit. Fortunately the narrator, Tim, who readers have grown to care for, lives and thrives in the new country—one born out of violence and bloodshed.

Riveting storytelling and a powerful commentary on war help make *My Brother Sam Is Dead* ideal for group discussions. For almost forty years it has reminded its readers of the brutality of war.

OCTOBER 27

Happy Birthday Constance C. Greene (*Beat the Turtle Drum*) and Lillian Morrison (*Yours Till Niagara Falls*).

It's the birth date of Enid Bagnold (1889–1981), *National Velvet*.

It's also the birth date of Theodore "Teddy" Roosevelt (1858–1919), the 26th president of the United States, and Isaac Merrit Singer (1811–1875), who invented the first practical home sewing machine.

In 1916 the word *jazz* appeared in *Variety* magazine, the first published reference to this uniquely American music. Read *Jazz* by Walter Dean Myers and Christopher Myers, *This Jazz Man* by Karen Ehrhardt and R. G. Roth, and *Jazz on a Saturday Night* by Leo and Diane Dillon.

OCTOBER 28

Happy Birthday Leonard P. Kessler (*Mr. Pine's Mixed-up Signs*).

You're not going anywhere! A British proclamation on this day in 1775 forbid residents from leaving Boston. Read *Johnny Tremain* by Esther Forbes.

Harvard College, the oldest institution of higher learning in the United States, was founded in Cambridge, Massachusetts, in 1636.

 In 1793 **Eli Whitney** patented the cotton gin, an invention separating cotton fibers from seeds at a much faster rate than can be done by hand. Read *Up before Daybreak: Cotton and People in America* by Deborah Hopkinson.

With Halloween just a few days away, get a head start on National Chocolate Day. Read *Charlie and the Chocolate Factory* by Roald Dahl and *Chocolate Fever* by Robert Kimmel Smith, illustrated by Gioia Fiammenghi.

GRANDFATHER'S JOURNEY
By Allen Say

On October 28, 1886, Frédéric Auguste Bartholdi's sculpture *Liberty Enlightening the World*, was officially dedicated on Bedloe's Island in New York. A sonnet by Emma Lazarus was inscribed on the pedestal: "Give me your tired, your poor, / your huddled masses yearning to breathe free, / the wretched refuse of your teeming shore. / Send these, the homeless, tempest-tost to me." Certainly many great children's books have been written about the statue itself, including Lynn Curlee's *Liberty*. But the Statue of Liberty signifies more than just the journey of those who came through Ellis Island to America. We are, after all, largely a nation of immigrants, descendants of those who arrived from a variety of places, at different times, to begin their life here.

Grandfather's Journey, written and illustrated by Japanese-American author Allen Say, is one of the most powerful books about the immigrant experience published in the past twenty years. With a spare text, this winner of the Caldecott Medal tells the story of Say's grandfather, who left Japan as a young man to travel around the world. In luminous watercolors, filled with sunlight and deep shadows, Say pictures the America that his grandfather saw—deserts with magnificent rock sculptures and fields of endless wheat. Returning to Japan, his grandfather married and then came to California to live and raise a daughter. But he went back to Japan before World War II and was never able to return to California, although he told his grandson stories about it. Bringing the book full circle, the text reads, "After a time, I came to love the land my grandfather had loved, and I stayed on and on until I had a daughter of my own . . . I think I know my grandfather now: I miss him very much."

In a mere thirty-two pages Allen Say brings his grandfather to life. Even more important, the book speaks to the experience of those who have known two homes in their lifetime—"the moment I am in one country, I am homesick for the other."

The dedication of the Statue of Liberty celebrates the American experience: people from many nations, with many different stories, come to this land, still missing the place they came from. Allen Say's loving tribute to his grandfather resonates for readers because he conveys a universal story, even though the one he tells is so very personal. Emma Lazarus's poem ends with the words, "I lift my lamp beside the golden door!" In *Grandfather's Journey* readers witness just how special, how golden, this land can be for its immigrants.

THE SECRET GARDEN
By Frances Hodgson Burnett

On October 29, 1924, England and America's bestselling children's book writer died in New York. After leaving her native land, she lived for many years in the United States, and a *New York Times* obituary mourned the passing of this beloved figure. She was, by way of an easy comparison, the J. K. Rowling of her day—she was read with equal enthusiasm by adults and children. Her works had been successfully adapted for theater and for a then-new media, motion pictures.

She is still, today, a household name—but not for the books mentioned in that obituary. Frances Hodgson Burnett's classic works, *The Secret Garden* and *The Little Princess*, were considered of minor importance in her lifetime, but long ago people stopped reading what her contemporaries felt to be her masterpiece, *Little Lord Fauntleroy*.

Sometimes called the first modern novel for children, *The Secret Garden* features two sickly, unlikable protagonists. In the process of the narrative, however, Colin Craven and Mary Lennox undergo personal transformations, as they set out to revive a languishing garden at Misselthwaite Manor. Burnett excelled in the telling detail. A gardener could learn how to prune roses from the book. In fact, Burnett once said, "It is not enough to mention they have tea, you must specify the muffins."

In Everything I Need to Know I Learned from a Children's Book, Katherine Paterson writes about the sense of wonder she feels when she reads *The Secret Garden*: "that a shriveled brown bulb can produce a tulip, that dead sticks can give birth to roses, and that even people shriveled by illness and deadened by grief can still blossom. Her book helped me to see the miracle of new life bursting forth from apparent death." Recently, an eleven-year-old Texan girl told me that *The Secret Garden* was her favorite book because it showed her that no matter how hurt or damaged a child has become, she can still be healed. Both of these comments cut to the heart of this timeless and magnificent story.

Next to my desk I keep a first edition of *The Secret Garden*. It was purchased by my mother's great-aunt, born in 1865 at the end of the Civil War. She read it and passed it on to my mother, who gave it to me. When I look at the book, I am connected to all the members of my family back to the time of the Civil War. To me *The Secret Garden* demonstrates how great children's books transcend history and bring generations together. No matter what Frances Hodgson Burnett's contemporaries thought, I believe *The Secret Garden*, now over a hundred years old, to be one of the greatest children's books of all time.

OCTOBER 29

It's the birth date of Valerie Worth (1933–1994), *All the Small Poems and Fourteen More*.

In 1945 the first ballpoint pens went on sale for $12.50 each! Read *The Bronze Pen* by Zilpha Keatley Snyder, *Ellie McDoodle: Have Pen, Will Travel* by Ruth McNally Barshaw, and *A Pen Pal for Max* by Gloria Rand, illustrated by Ted Rand.

On this day in 1969 the U.S. Supreme Court ruled segregation must end. Read *The Story of Ruby Bridges* by Robert Coles, illustrated by George Ford, *Rosa Parks: My Story* by Rosa Parks with Jim Haskins, and *Satchel Paige: Striking Out Jim Crow* by James Sturm and Rich Tommaso.

It's Hermit Day, so spend some time alone, thinking, writing or reading. Try *Kermit The Hermit* by Bill Peet.

OCTOBER 30

Happy Birthday Eric Kimmel (*Hershel and the Hanukkah Goblins*), Vivian Walsh (*Olive, the Other Reindeer*), and Rudolfo Anaya (*The Farolitos of Christmas*).

It's the birth date of Sydney Taylor (1904–1978), *All-of-a-Kind Family*.

It's also the birth date of John Adams (1735–1826), the second president of the United States.

On this evening in 1938 Orson Welles narrated a radio broadcast of the story *The War of the Worlds*, frightening listeners who believed space invaders had landed. Read *War of the Worlds* by H. G. Wells or *Captain Underpants and the Invasion of the Incredibly Naughty Cafeteria Ladies from Outer Space* by Dav Pilkey.

It's National Candy Corn Day. Read *Candy Corn: Poems* by James Stevenson.

THE CRICKET IN TIMES SQUARE

By George Selden
Illustrated by Garth Williams

The Cricket in Times Square celebrates its birthday in the month of October. More than fifty years ago George Selden, a down-on-his-luck New York City playwright who had graduated from Yale, wandered into the Times Square subway station late at night and heard a cricket chirp. It reminded him of his childhood in Connecticut when his life had been more optimistic and innocent. Because he knew how to write scenes and create characters as a playwright, he began crafting a book about a little cricket from the country in a big city subway station and the boy who finds him there. The book's proceeds would lift George Selden out of poverty and despair.

To write *The Cricket in Times Square*, a funny and intriguing story, Selden drew on what he knew—a love of music, particularly opera, and the longing of city dwellers for the simple country life. Children and adults find themselves falling in love with Selden's characters—both human and animal. They include Chester, a cricket who adores liverwurst; Mario Bellini and his parents, running an unsuccessful newspaper stand in the Times Square subway; Tucker, an amiable scavenger mouse; and Harry, the warm-hearted cat. Chester arrives in the Times Square subway station from his home in Connecticut via a picnic basket. After Chester befriends Mario, the singing insect uses his operatic talents to bring customers to the newsstand. But in the end, Chester leaves fame, fortune, and the city behind so that he can return to his country home.

Like *Charlotte's Web*, the book explores enduring friendships and community between unlikely protagonists. The two books, in fact, often appeal to the same readers. Both were illustrated by Garth Williams, who uses satire to delineate characters and plays up the humor of the book through his artwork. Although Williams and Selden were paired by their publisher, they went on to develop a friendship of their own and worked together on sequels such as *Tucker's Countryside* and *Chester Cricket's New Home*.

We have every reason to be grateful that George Selden took the advice given to him by Noel Coward at a party: "Press on!" Selden did, and today we can celebrate over fifty years of a comic masterpiece for children because he persevered.

BONE DOG

By Eric Rohmann

Tonight we celebrate All Hallows Eve, or Halloween, a time of carved pumpkins, parties, or door-to-door canvassing in costume for treats. Eric Rohmann's *Bone Dog*, the book of the day, isn't a Halloween book per se. Although a scene occurs on Halloween, the book really focuses on other subject matter.

Gus and his dog Ella have been friends for a long time. One night Ella said, "I'm an old dog and won't be around much longer. But no matter what happens, I'll always be with you . . . A promise made under a full moon cannot be broken." Dejected after Ella dies, Gus goes about his life without enthusiasm—he doesn't even get excited about heading out to trick or treat on Halloween.

But on the way home from trick or treating he finds himself attacked by a group of skeletons in the graveyard. Suddenly Ella comes to his defense as a bone dog! Although she does not scare the skeletons, the two of them call up a pack of real dogs—who know exactly what they want from those skeletons. Finally in a very touching ending, Gus asks Ella, "Will I see you again?"

Eric Rohmann has managed to craft a story that is both just a bit scary and also a tearjerker. This is a hard combination to pull off. The book can work as a Halloween story or as a book to reassure youngsters who have lost a beloved pet. As he does in all his work, Eric uses the full page for text and art; he balances compositions of the skeletons running on one double-page spread with that of a lone dog carrying a bone. With minimum words he conveys an exciting story and makes readers care for Gus. With the genius that allowed Eric to show a special friendship between two animals in *My Friend Rabbit*, he showcases that special bond between children and their pets in *Bone Dog*. The pets of our childhood always do remain with us.

OCTOBER 31

Happy Birthday Helen Griffith (*Grandaddy and Janetta Together*) and Katherine Paterson (*Bridge to Terabithia, Jacob Have I Loved, The Great Gilly Hopkins*).

It's the birth date of Juliette Gordon Low (1860–1927), founder of the Girl Scouts of America.

Happy Birthday Nevada, which became the 36th U.S. state on this day in 1864.

In 1517 Martin Luther nailed his Ninety-five Theses to the door of the church at Wittenberg in Germany. Luther's theories and writings calling for Reformation in the Catholic church inaugurated Protestantism. Thus, it's Reformation Day.

On this day in 1941 after fourteen years of work, the Mount Rushmore National Memorial was completed.

Practice your tricks and read about magicians and illusionists on National Magic Day, created in honor of the great **Harry Houdini** who died on this day in 1926. Read *Escape! The Story of the Great Houdini* by Sid Fleischman.

It's UNICEF Day, a tradition started in 1950 to raise money for medicine, clean water, food, education, and emergency relief to children in over 150 countries. UNICEF stands for United Nations International Children's Emergency Fund.

NOVEMBER 1

Happy Birthday Nicholasa Mohr (*El Bronx Remembered and Other Stories*) and Hilary Knight (*Eloise, Mrs. Piggle-Wiggle*).

It's the birth date of Symeon Shimin (1902–1984), *Onion John*; and Stephen Crane (1871–1900), *The Red Badge of Courage*.

 Seabiscuit defeated War Admiral in a horse-racing upset in 1938, becoming a symbol of hope for Depression Era Americans. Read *A Horse Named Seabiscuit* by Mark Dubowski and *Seabiscuit vs War Admiral* by Kat Shehata.

In 1952 the first U.S. hydrogen bomb was tested in the Marshall Islands.

It's *El Día de los Meurtos*, a holiday for celebrating deceased relatives and friends. Read *The Day of the Dead: El Día de los Muertos* by Bob Barner.

IT'S A BOOK
By Lane Smith

In 1929 the General Federation of Women's Clubs adopted a holiday that became generally observed in the country by 1949 as National Author's Day. The resolution for the holiday reads: "by celebrating an Author's Day as a nation, we would not only show patriotism, loyalty, and appreciation of the men and women who have made American literature possible, but would also encourage and inspire others to give of themselves in making a better America." I like the idea that authors make a better country and society by their attention to words and ideas.

But what do authors actually do? That is besides sit around in a bathrobe when the rest of the world is dressed and in meetings. Or stare at computer screens or typewriters with the hope of transferring something in their brain to that blank page. And since authors create books, what is a book in this day and age of electronic media?

With the kind of corkscrew humor that has made him famous, Lane Smith explores this question in *It's a Book*. On the title page, Smith introduces his three characters—a mouse, a jackass, and a monkey. The ever-patient monkey attempts to read his book, while the jackass peppers him with questions: Does it scroll? Do you blog with it? Can it text or tweet? Finally the jackass picks up the book in question—and finds himself lost in its adventure. As monkey heads out the door to the library to find another book for himself, he delivers his final, cutting line: "It's a book, jackass."

With strong black line and bold shapes, the artwork was first executed in oil, dry brush, and black ink, and then tweaked on the computer. Everything from the title page to the note about the author gives the child reader a chance to think about what makes books so special. No matter the distractions of the world, books take us to another place, another reality. And they do this without electricity, passwords, or being recharged.

Even in this media-saturated world, books and stories still have the ability to take us away and beguile us. Using humor, story, and character, Lane Smith reminds us why we pick up a book when we could turn to other distractions—and he tells a story that makes us laugh out loud!

So happy National Author's Day to Lane and to all who create a unique and special item—a book.

SO YOU WANT TO BE PRESIDENT?

By Judith St. George
Illustrated by David Small

On the first Tuesday of November, Americans vote in national elections. The events of this day generate a lot of discussion and passion in many households. In general, we stay away from both politics and religion in children's books—a good thing. But every now and then an author manages to enter the political arena in a way that helps educate and entertain young people.

Winner of the 2001 Caldecott Medal for David Small's expressive and extremely funny illustrations, *So You Want to Be President?* by Judith St. George (revised in 2004) explores the backgrounds and personal characteristics of our nation's presidents. Using telling details and fascinating quotes, St. George reveals one drawback of the job—people get mad at the president. Someone once threw a cabbage at William Howard Taft, who quipped, "I see that one of my adversaries has lost his head." But St. George also points out why someone would want to be president. One of the perks is living in the White House—with its own swimming pool, movie theater, and bowling alley.

In this book we learn that our nation has a propensity for electing those born in a log cabin and how presidents come with a variety of personalities. Calvin Coolidge, shy and quiet, had a dinner guest bet that she could get him to say more than two words. "You lose," he retorted. Clearly he also possessed a dry sense of humor. Presidents can be handsome or homely; Warren Harding may have been our best-looking president, but he once said, "I am not fit for this office and never should have been here." In this extremely witty and clever text, St. George shows the quirks and eccentricities of those who've occupied the Oval Office.

Even readers who consider themselves quite savvy about American history will find a lot of surprises. Abraham Lincoln, a poor dancer, once said to his future wife, Mary, "Miss Todd, I should like to dance with you in the worst way." She later said to a friend, "He certainly did." One day while the very distinguished John Quincy Adams swam naked in the Potomac River, a female reporter sat on his clothes and refused to give them back until he granted an interview.

If on election day you are eager for some humor and lightheartedness, pick up *So You Want to Be President?* It will give you, and the seven- to twelve-year-olds that you share it with, a lot of reasons to laugh.

NOVEMBER 2

Happy Birthday Natalie Kinsey-Warnock (*The Canada Geese Quilt*).

It's the birth date of **James Knox Polk** (1795–1849), the 11th president of the United States, and Warren G. Harding (1865–1923), the 29th president of the United States.

Happy Birthday North and South Dakota, which became the 39th and 40th U.S. states on this day in 1889.

On this day in 1983 President Ronald Regan signed a bill creating Martin Luther King Jr. Day.

People living in space! The first crew arrived at the International Space Station in 2000. Read *Space Station Rat* by Michael Daley.

It's Look for Circles Day so see how many you can find! Read *So Many Circles, So Many Squares* by Tana Hoban and *Pond Circles* by Betsy Franco and Stefano Vitale.

NOVEMBER 3

Happy Birthday Janell Cannon (*Stellaluna*).

It's the birth date of Gyo Fujikawa (1908–1998), *Babies*, *Baby Animals*.

In 1507 Leonardo da Vinci was commissioned to paint Lisa Gherardini (*Mona Lisa*). Read *Art Dog* by Thacher Hurd.

What has become the world's largest circulated English daily newspaper was founded on this day in 1838. It was *The Bombay Times and Journal of Commerce*, now *The Times of India*. Read *Landry News* by Andrew Clements, illustrated by Brian Selznick.

IN THE YEAR OF THE BOAR AND JACKIE ROBINSON

By Bette Bao Lord
Illustrated by Marc Simont

On November 3, 1938, Bette Bao was born in Shanghai, China. By the age of eight she came to the United States with her father and mother and one sister. When Mao Zedong and his Communist party won the Chinese civil war, the Boas were stranded in America. Bette's youngest sister Sansan had been left behind with relatives. The family struggled to get her out of China, a process that took over a decade.

In 1964 Bette Bao Lord published her first book, *Eighth Moon: The True Story of a Young Girl's Life in Communist China*, the saga of her sister Sansan. Twenty years later, Bette Bao Lord turned to her own childhood, that of a Chinese immigrant educated in American schools, and crafted one of our best auto-biographical novels for children, *In the Year of the Boar and Jackie Robinson*.

The book began as a magazine article, but then Bao Lord decided to change the perspective of her story to tell it from a child's point of view. In 1947 Chinese-born Bandit Wong, age ten, must shift from being a pampered child in a very affluent family to an American immigrant, struggling to fit into Brooklyn P.S. 8. Her family still observes their Chinese customs, while she tries to understand the new American ones. As Bandit struggles with English, she finally realizes that the best way to connect with these strange Americans may well be through the sport of baseball—more exactly, with her classmates' love of the Brooklyn Dodgers.

And though Bandit (now renamed Shirley Temple Wong) has some rough times, in the end she triumphs and demonstrates that America can truly be a home for immigrants. Expressively illustrated by Caldecott Winner Marc Simont, the book works both as a read aloud and read alone for second through fourth graders. This honest but funny account shows how someone born in another country becomes assimilated into the United States. If you happen to be a baseball fan it captures how a community can be brought together because of a group of players. Even if those players are called "the bums"!

Although published in 1984, the book addresses issues as contemporary as today's headlines. Bette Bao Lord devoted her life to writing novels for adults like *Spring Moon* and engaging in ambassadorial work around the world. In *In the Year of the Boar and Jackie Robinson* she gave the children of this country a portrait of one very engaging child's process of becoming an American.

TUTANKHAMUN: THE MYSTERY OF THE BOY KING

By Zahi Hawass

In Luxor, Egypt, on November 4, 1922, the English archaeologist Howard Carter, funded by the wealthy Lord Carnarvon, discovered a pharaoh's tomb that had not yet been plundered by grave robbers. This tomb contained more than five thousand artifacts of Tutankhamun from ancient Egypt. For children, King Tut, as he became known, is naturally interesting, because he ascended to the throne when he was a child of eight or nine, and died as a teenager at about nineteen. Also since King Tut's story is surrounded in mystery, the curious can invent scenarios about what might have happened in his life.

To explore the boy king with the children in your life, I would first pick up David Macaulay's *Pyramid*. In this book, readers watch a pyramid rise step by step from the sands of Egypt and observe a mummy being prepared for the tomb.

Then you will want to read a book written by the head of Egypt's Supreme Council of Antiquities, Zahi Hawass. In *Tutankhamun: The Mystery of the Boy King*, Dr. Hawass provides a unique perspective on both the events of the tomb's discovery and what has been learned in subsequent years. He personally interviewed Sheikh Ali, who worked at the Tut archaeological dig and described the scene: "We sang all the time. My cousin was in charge of transporting the water jars to the site. . . . On the morning of November 4, 1922, my cousin came with the water and began to dig a hole for the first jar. With his hand, he uncovered the top of a step cut into the rock . . . he ran back to the tent to tell Carter." Just that line, "We sang all the time," changes my vision of the event. I had always imagined the tomb was unearthed with hushed awe. Dr. Hawass also discusses events he has personally witnessed—such as the CT scanning of King Tut. With magnificent full-color images, *Tutankhamun: The Mystery of the Boy King* brings young readers front and center into the activities of archaeologists today.

So thank you Howard Carter and Sheikh Ali's cousin. On this November day, you gave us a story that has fascinated the world for almost a century.

NOVEMBER 4

Happy Birthday Gail E. Haley (*A Story, a Story, The Post Office Cat*).

It's the birth date of Sterling North (1906–1974), *Rascal*.

Birthday greetings to librarian and former First Lady **Laura Bush**, who established Washington, D.C.'s annual National Book Festival in 2001.

Poet T. S. Eliot won the Nobel Prize for Literature in 1948. Read *Old Possum's Book of Practical Cats* with illustrations by Edward Gorey.

On this day in 2008 Barack Obama was elected the 44th president of the United States, the first African American to hold that position.

In honor of the tomb of Tutankhamun's discovery in Egypt's Valley of the Kings, it's King Tut Day.

PICTURE BOOK, NONFICTION, Elementary School, Middle School

NOVEMBER 5

Happy Birthday Marcia Sewall (*Pilgrims of Plimoth*) and Raymond Bial (*A Handful of Dirt*).

In 1872 American women couldn't legally vote, but suffragist Susan B. Anthony did anyway and was fined $100. Read *Susan B. Anthony: Fighter for Freedom and Equality* by Suzanne Slade.

In 1895 the state of Utah granted women the right to vote. Read *You Want Women to Vote, Lizzie Stanton?* by Jean Fritz.

A woman's right to vote is affirmed by Arizona, Kansas, and Wisconsin in 1912. Read *Elizabeth Leads the Way* by Tanya Lee Stone.

THE STRANGE CASE OF ORIGAMI YODA

By Tom Angleberger

Perfect for celebrating World Origami Days (October 24–November 11), our book of the day was published in 2010 and has delighted young readers by the score. The ancient Japanese art of origami does not seem an obvious premise for a trendy, funny, contemporary novel, but then great children's writers always find new slants on old topics.

In *The Strange Case of Origami Yoda* writer Tom Angleberger, who works on the staff of the *Roanoke Times* (Virginia), uses the book design and illustration as well as the text itself to bring to life a great cast of eccentric and misfit sixth graders. Tommy opens and closes the story with a discussion of how an origami finger puppet, which looks like Yoda of *Star Wars*, alters the lives of those in his class. Origami Yoda's owner, Dwight, does strange things all the time—says "purple" as his only answer to questions, for instance—and carries around his paper puppet. As the members of the class begin to ask Origami Yoda questions, they find a screwball logic to his bizarre sayings: "The Twist you must learn," he tells them one day, referring to the 1960s dance craze. Or "Likes you he does. Kissing you he wants."

Each chapter is a case file in Tommy's narrative and is told by a different student who describes his or her experience with Dwight and Origami Yoda. After each file, Tommy and his friend Harvey comment on the contents. In this way the book functions as a great way to teach point of view to fifth to seventh graders. But, more important, it provides a funny, rich reading experience. As his classmates wonder whether Dwight is smarter or dumber than he seems—is he giving the advice or is the finger puppet really clairvoyant and wise?—they get carried along in a series of events that wrap up in a perfectly satisfying ending.

Complete with lessons on folding an origami Yoda, this book is also a perfect follow-up for readers of the Wimpy Kid series. The author happens to be a pretty savvy Yoda himself, knowing how to be true to child behavior and language while crafting an engaging story filled with wisdom. Origami Yoda does say, "Read a book should you. . . . *The Hobbit*." But young readers might want to pick up *The Strange Case of Origami Yoda* first. As he might say, "Read about me. Happy you will be."

For those who fall in love with these characters, the sequel, *Darth Paper Strikes Back*, will continue to make them happy.

WINTER'S TALE

By Robert Sabuda

Today we celebrate the birthday of one of the most original creators of children's books, Lothar Meggendorfer, born in Munich in 1847. Meggendorfer did not want the images of a book to lie flat on the page—he thought they should move. Decades before motion pictures or interactive computer graphics, he experimented with paper engineering to create exquisite pop-up books. Rather than reproducing the crude prototype of the day, Meggendorfer created pages that contained many movements, made possible by rivets and levers. His early books were hand-colored, although later works relied on the process of chromolithography. Given the age and fragility of these items, they remain prized and rare. Both the University of North Texas and the University of Virginia house Meggendorfers as does the Mazza Museum at the University of Findlay in Ohio.

Although always valued in Europe, particularly Germany, pop-ups remained rare in the United States until the end of the twentieth century. The most accomplished artist in the genre, Robert Sabuda, began creating pop-up books in 1994 with *The Christmas Alphabet* and has gone on to publish one title after another that both delights young viewers and amazes adults.

If you want to purchase a book appropriate for the winter season, pick up Sabuda's *Winter's Tale*. I suggest buying your own copy because the fragility of this book often makes it difficult for libraries to circulate. In *Winter's Tale*, readers see, in 3-D pop-up versions, several creatures—owl, bears, mice, foxes, rabbits, deer, and moose—responding to the change of season. The final double-page spread shows the natural world in all its wonder, with a tiny house tucked into the woods.

Children and adults naturally wonder how Sabuda manages to get paper to move. His website www.RobertSabuda.com contains valuable information about both his process and paper engineering in general, providing a template, so that amateur paper engineers can try their hand at the craft. He also explains his fascination with pop-up books, a passion he shares with Lothar Meggendorfer.

NOVEMBER 6

It's the birth date of **John Philip Sousa** (1854–1932).

Mary Ann Evans, pen name George Eliot, submitted her first work, *Scenes of Clerical Life*, for publication in 1856.

On this day in 1935 Elizabeth "Lizzie" Magie Phillips agreed to sell Parker Brothers the patent for her version of the board game Monopoly.

Today marks two presidential elections: Abraham Lincoln was elected the 16th U.S. president in 1860, whereas Jefferson Davis was elected president of the confederacy the following year.

It's Marooned Without a Compass Day. Read *Marooned: The Strange but True Adventures of Alexander Selkirk* by Robert Kraske and *The Golden Compass* by Philip Pullman.

On Saxophone Day, read *Saxophone Sam and His Snazzy Jazz Band* by Christine Schneider and *Charlie Parker Played Be Bop* by Chris Raschka.

NOVEMBER 7

It's the birth date of Armstrong Sperry (1897–1976), *Call It Courage.*

In 1874 Thomas Nast's cartoon in *Harper's Weekly* was the first use of an elephant as the symbol for the Republican party. Read *When Elephant Goes to a Party* by Sonia Levitin and Jeff Seaver.

It is also the birth date of scientist and Nobel Prize winner Marie Curie (1867–1934). Read *Borrowed Names* by Jeannine Atkins.

On this day in 1917 the Bolshevik Revolution started in Russia.

Duck and cover! In 1957 the Gaither Report called for more Americans to build backyard fallout shelters. Read *Gemini Summer* by Iain Lawrence and *Beyond Mayfield* by Vaunda Micheaux Nelson.

TO FLY: THE STORY OF THE WRIGHT BROTHERS
By Wendie C. Old
Illustrated by Robert Andrew Parker

In November we recognize National Aviation History Month. There have been endless treatments and biographies of the Wright brothers over the years. But one of the best for second through fourth graders appeared in 2002: Wendie C. Old's *To Fly*, containing magnificent watercolor illustrations by Robert Andrew Parker. In a forty-eight-page picture book, Old provides just enough detail to interest readers in the Wrights, without overwhelming them with too much material. She begins in Dayton, Ohio, as young Orville lay in bed at night, imagining what it would be like to swoop through the sky. By second grade he whittled a flying machine out of a piece of wood. He and his brother Wilbur experimented with flying kites—Orville built the best ones in Dayton and learned about how to curve wings. Although the brothers were diverted for a period of time with a printing business, they moved on to fixing bicycles and began experimenting with building gliders.

Old takes the readers through all of the Wrights' flight attempts at Kitty Hawk, from 1900 on. As Wilbur sails off of Kill Devil Hill, Parker's breathtaking art shows the aviator in flight, with a magnificent panorama of the sea and sky around him. Readers cheer the Wright brothers on as they try and try again, through periods of depression and doubt. In this brief text, the author manages to show the difficulties the brothers overcame, and how their final success rested on perseverance, tenacity, and amazing ingenuity.

A full timeline rounds out this glorious exploration of two of America's most famous inventors. A French newspaper once asked if the Wrights were "flyers or liars." As the author discusses in the Epilogue, these two bicycle repairmen managed to build an airplane when scientists failed to do so. In the end, they achieved their childhood dreams and became the most famous figures in aviation history.

A great story to share with the next generation of American inventors, *To Fly* helps readers understand Beverly McLoughland's poem, "Crazy Boys," which opens the book and would be an appropriate way to begin honoring National Aviation History Month: "Watching buzzards, / Flying kites, / Lazy, crazy boys / The Wrights. They / Tried to fly / Just like a bird. / Foolish dreamers / Strange. Absurd. We / Scoffed and scorned / Their dreams of flight. / But we were wrong / And they were Wright."

HATCHET

By Gary Paulsen

In the second week of November we celebrate National Young Readers Week, an event created in 1989 by the Center for the Book of the Library of Congress to help schools recognize the joys and benefits of reading. To start out the week with a surefire hit, pick up one of the greatest survival stories of all times.

Gary Paulsen actually dedicated *Hatchet* "To the students of the Hershey [Pennsylvania] Middle School." While on a visit there, the young people encouraged him to write this story—one he had wanted to create all his life. An outdoorsman with a love of nature, Paulsen drew on his own experiences as he crafted the story of thirteen-year-old Brian, a city boy who finds himself alone in the Canadian wilderness after a plane crash. Fortunately, Brian brought along a hatchet, his only tool to use in this hostile landscape.

Filled with harrowing escapes and breathless action, Brian's story keeps readers turning the pages to see if this engaging hero will be able to stay alive. Paulsen wanted to make sure each incident Brian experiences was based on reality, so the author wrote about things he had done—or could accomplish. Paulsen started a fire with a hatchet and rock, something that took four hours. He even attempted to eat turtle eggs, because he wanted to ask his character Brian to do this.

Paulsen's editor for the book, Barbara Lalicki, postponed publication of the novel so they could strive to get every sentence right. Lalicki knew she was working with a very special book. This editor, with great attention to detail, and a writer willing to go the extra mile together crafted one of the classics of the 1980s.

Forget your television survival shows! *Hatchet* is more compelling and believable than any of them. It is a great way to celebrate National Young Readers Week and to remind children in grades three through six how exciting a book can be.

NOVEMBER 8

Happy Birthday Marianna Mayer (*Pegasus*) and Gloria Rand (*Salty Dog*).

Happy Birthday Montana, which became the 41st U.S. state on this day in 1803.

In 1519 the Aztec emperor Montezuma II welcomed Spanish explorer Cortez to the ancient capital city of Tenochtitlan. Read *The Lost Temple of the Aztecs* by Shelley Tanaka and *The Sad Night* by Sally Schofer Mathews.

Art for everyone! In 1793 the French Revolutionary government opened the Louvre Museum to the public. Read *Louvre in Close-up* by Claire d'Harcourt.

In 1895 Wilhem Röntgen discovered the X-ray, a wavelength of electromagnetic radiation. Hence, it's X-Ray Day. Read *The Head Bone's Connected to the Neck Bone* by Carla Killough McClafferty.

NOVEMBER 9

Happy Birthday Benjamin Banneker. I'd like to celebrate this day by recognizing all the grandparents who have kept literacy alive in their family. They have truly made a difference, not only in their own families but also to the world.

Happy Birthday Pat Cummings (*Clean Your Own Room, Harvey Moon!*) and Lois Ehlert (*Chicka Chicka Boom Boom*).

It's the birth date of Kay Thompson (1909–1998), *Eloise.*

 Mary Robinson was elected Ireland's first female president in 1990. Read *Madam President* by Lane Smith and *Madam President: The Extraordinary, True (and Evolving) Story of Women in Politics* by Catherine Thimmesh.

It's Chaos Never Dies Day. Read *Absolutely Normal Chaos* by Sharon Creech and *Theodosia and the Serpents of Chaos* by R. L. LaFevers.

World Freedom Day commemorates the fall of the Berlin Wall. Read *The Wall: Growing Up Behind the Iron Curtain* by Peter Sís.

MOLLY BANNAKY

By Alice McGill
Illustrated by Chris Soentpiet

On November 9, 1731, American astronomer, mathematician, clockmaker, and surveyor, Benjamin Banneker, called "the first black man of science," was born in Elliott's Mills, Maryland. Banneker published an almanac, becoming the first black man to do so. His life has been frequently presented in books for children, including Andrea Davis Pinkney's *Dear Benjamin Banneker.*

When I was Publisher of Children's Books at Houghton Mifflin, one day I picked up a small manuscript, just three pages in length, which literally sent a chill down my spine. It presented the story of Benjamin Banneker in a way that I had not encountered, told by African-American storyteller and author Alice McGill.

The finished book, *Molly Bannaky*, still gives me chills. Molly Walsh, a servant girl in England, spills her lord's milk and is sentenced in a court of law. Because she can "take the book," or read from the Bible, she is not executed but sent as an indentured servant to the colonies. There Molly works hard, becomes a free woman, and heads out to start her own farm close to the wilderness. But she needs help and, consequently, she buys an African slave, promising to free him after a period of time. After they fall in love, Molly once again breaks the law by marrying a black man. However, the couple gains the acceptance of their community; they help neighbors and raise their children and grandchildren. In the final scene, we see Molly teaching her grandson how to read and recording his name in the family Bible—Benjamin Banneker.

By telling Molly's story, Alice McGill examines an aspect of Colonial America that rarely gets discussed in children's books, the life of an interracial couple. As the grandson of a slave, Benjamin Banneker would have been denied access to books. But because of his grandmother, he received the gift that he needed to become an intellectual—the ability to read.

Artist Chris Soentpiet extends the story in his luminous watercolors. In this large-format book, the characters seem bigger than life, their story bold and important. Chris delights in historic research, the telling detail of a composition. The book makes it possible for children to feel they have walked back into Colonial America. A spare, lyrical text, lush and vibrant artwork, and an important story from a different point of view all add to the power of *Molly Bannaky.*

THE GOATS
by Brock Cole

Today for National Young Readers Week I am going to look at one of the most powerful books ever written for twelve- to fourteen-year-olds. Like all books that change us and make us different people, I remember exactly where I was and how I felt the first time I read it. I was editor of *The Horn Book*, completed the entire book in my office, and then was just grateful that the door was closed because of my emotional response. In rereading Brock Cole's *The Goats*, I once again had the visceral feeling that I had been punched in the stomach. *The Goats* has lost none of its power over the last twenty-four years.

Two young people, Howie and Laura, are attending summer camp and find themselves the subjects of a cruel action: both are stripped of their clothes, and then left stranded together on an island. Their plight has been engineered as part of a camp ritual to mock the outsiders, "the goats," who other campers don't like. But rather than remain victims, Howie figures out a way to get the two of them to the shoreline. At first he has to keep a survival scenario going, but in the end Laura will save them both. They wander making things up as they go, breaking into a house to steal some clothes and food, traveling and trying to stay out of camp. Both understand that under no circumstances will they go back to the camp and people who have bullied them.

By the time Brock Cole wrote *The Goats* he had created a body of picture books. Certainly in control of the craft of writing, he depicts two totally believable characters and a horrible situation; slowly he shows the growth and change of Laura and Howie as they move from victims to young people who carry themselves with dignity. They do so in a world where the adults are either absent or uncaring. One of the things that Brock accomplishes so brilliantly is their feeling of being utterly alone, of needing to find solutions for themselves in a hostile world.

Although the book has been controversial since publication, many young readers have found comfort in it. In the end *The Goats* suggests that no matter how horrific the situation you find yourself in, there is a solution, which you can work toward. For anyone who is going or has gone through difficulties with peers and family, *The Goats* can provide a light in a dark world. For as Laura says at the end: "Hold on. . . . Hold on."

NOVEMBER 10

Happy Birthday Neil Gaiman (*The Graveyard Book*).

Happy Birthday to the United States Marine Corps, first formed on this day in 1775. Read *The Journal of Patrick Seamus Flaherty* by Ellen White.

Can you hear me now? Direct-dial coast-to-coast telephone service began in the United States in 1951. Read *Telephone* by Kornei Chukovsky.

In 1958 the allegedly cursed Hope Diamond was donated to the Smithsonian National Museum of Natural History in Washington, D.C. Read *The Robbery at the Diamond Dog Diner* by Eileen Christelow.

Happy Birthday *Sesame Street*. The television show debuted on this day in 1969.

NOVEMBER 11

Happy Birthday Diane Wolkstein (*The Magic Orange Tree and Other Haitian Folktales, Esther's Story*) and Bob Barner (*Dem Bones, Dinosaur Bones*).

Happy Birthday Washington, which became the 42nd U.S. state on this day in 1889.

 The **Mayflower** Compact, the first governing document of Plymouth Colony, was signed on this day in 1620. Read *On the Mayflower* by Kate Waters, *Across the Wide Dark Sea* by Jean Van Leeuwen, and *The Mayflower and the Pilgrims' New World* by Nathaniel Philbrick.

In 1954 the Armistice Day holiday officially changed to Veterans Day in the United States, and Remembrance Day in British Commonwealth countries. Read *Truce* by Jim Murphy, *The Wall* by Eve Bunting, and *I Remember Korea* by Linda Granfield and Russell Freedman.

CROSSING STONES
By Helen Frost

On this day in history, the eleventh hour of the eleventh day of the eleventh month, World War I ended in 1918. America's involvement came late in the conflict, and, in fact, most of the books written about World War I for young readers have originated in England.

But *Crossing Stones* by Helen Frost, an extraordinary novel written entirely in verse, is the story of the effect of the war on two midwestern families who send sons away to fight. Muriel, Emma, Ollie, and Frank each tell their stories in language so precise and beautiful that the reader gets swept up in the events of the time—fighting the war, the flu pandemic, and the suffragette movement. Although from another era, these characters emerge as very real and relatable in their passion for life and their moral conflicts. To create such living, breathing figures, Helen Frost drew on family history and personal memories from her childhood in Brookings, South Dakota.

Frost's poetry is so fluid and immediate that only after breathlessly reading until the end of the story did I even become aware of the strict poetic structure used for each character's voice. In *Crossing Stones* Helen Frost alternates between free verse and cupped-hand sonnets to add dimension to each character. Consequently, the literary craft of this novel is as brilliant as any we have for young readers. This book demonstrates the same attention to word choice as Karen Hesse's *Out of the Dust*.

If you want young readers grades five through eight to truly understand what Armistice Day means, introduce them to *Crossing Stones*. History, poetry, human relations, the sadness of war, the resilience of the human spirit—all are conveyed in a novel that runs just under two hundred pages. From my point of view, *Crossing Stones* stands as one of our finest literary novels for children written in the first decade of the twenty-first century.

MASTERPIECE

By Elise Broach
Illustrated by Kelly Murphy

The second week of November is National Young Readers Week. A great book for young readers and a novel of mystery and suspense, Elise Broach's *Masterpiece* also presents the work of Albrecht Durer, painter and printmaker, to young readers in grades three through six. Precocious as a child because of his drawing skill, Durer became known for his meticulous, true-to-life pencil sketches, etchings, and woodcuts. Today Durer is considered the greatest artist of the Northern Renaissance. Obviously, an original Durer drawing could be worth an immense amount of money. But could anyone successfully forge a drawing by this master?

This question lies at the center of a story that brings to mind several children's classics—*From the Mixed-up Files of Mrs. Basil E. Frankweiler*, *The Westing Game*, *The Cricket in Times Square*—and then adds just a trace of Kafka. The unusual, though very likable, protagonist of this novel happens to be a beetle—one who lives with young James Pompaday in a Manhattan apartment building. After James receives a pen-and-ink drawing set for his eleventh birthday, Martin the beetle discovers that he can use it to craft museum-quality miniatures of existing artwork. Being small and agile, Martin can actually forge a believable copy of a Durer drawing. Hence he and James are drawn into the art-smuggling world, trying to be of service to the Metropolitan Museum of Art.

However farfetched this plot may sound, the author presents the entire saga in such a believable way that readers get swept up, cheering for Martin and James, and learn a lot about the art world and Albrecht Durer in the process. With suspense, mystery, and humor, *Masterpiece* is perfect to read alone or aloud to a fifth- or sixth-grade classroom. Memorable characters, great drama, and beautiful writing have helped establish this book as a classic in the making. The friendship between a beetle and this young boy tugs at one's heartstrings. It even makes you wish you could have a beetle like Marvin as a friend in your own home!

In short, the book is a masterpiece—and a perfect way to celebrate National Young Readers Week.

NOVEMBER 12

Happy Birthday Marjorie W. Sharmat (*Nate the Great*) and Neal Shusterman (*The Schwa Was Here, Unwind*).

It's the birth date of Elizabeth Cady Stanton (1815–1902), who started the U.S. women's suffrage movement by presenting her Declaration of Sentiments at the first women's rights convention in Seneca Falls, New York.

He flew through the air with the greatest of ease! Jules Leotard, designer of the leotard, performed first flying trapeze circus act in Paris in 1859.

It's National Pizza with the Works Except Anchovies Day. Read *Pete's A Pizza* by William Steig, *Pizza the Size of the Sun* by Jack Prelutsky, and *The Princess and the Pizza* by Mary Jane and Herm Auch.

NOVEMBER 13

Happy Birthday Jez Alborough (*Duck in the Truck*).

 It's the birth date of **Robert Louis Stevenson** (1850–1894), *Treasure Island, The Strange Case of Dr. Jekyll and Mr. Hyde.*

The Montgomery Bus Boycott ended in 1956. Read *Freedom Walkers* by Russell Freedman, *Walking to the Bus-Rider Blues* by Harriet Gillem Robinet, and *Rosa* by Nikki Giovanni and Bryan Collier.

In 1982 the Vietnam Veterans Memorial is dedicated in Washington, D.C. Read *Always to Remember: The Story of the Vietnam Veterans Memorial* by Brent Ashabranner and *The Wall* by Eve Bunting.

MARY POPPINS
By P. L. Travers

On November 13, 1926, a short story appeared in an Australian newspaper, the *Christchurch Sun*, by a young writer who had emigrated to England but frequently published material in her native land. It recounted the saga of an "underneath nurse" age seventeen, and her charges Jane, Michael, Barbara, and John. On a day out, she puts on gloves, tucks a parrot-headed umbrella under her arm, and meets Bert, a pavement artist. This story eventually became part of a book published eight years later—P. L. Travers's now-classic *Mary Poppins*.

If you know Mary only through her interpretation in the Walt Disney movie, you have missed one of the great characters in children's literature. Conventional wisdom says that young readers focus only on the children in their fiction, having little interest in adults' lives. But Mary Poppins is one of the exceptions to that rule. Salty, mysterious, vain, sharp of tongue, and independent in the extreme, Mary makes life in the Banks household very exciting for her young charges. They encounter an ancient candy storeowner, whose self-regenerating fingers happened to be made of barley sugar; she levitates everyone so that they have tea parties on the ceiling; and she can speak to the animals and interpret animal speech. In fact, she supports anarchy and defies authority every moment of her life as a nanny. In *Everything I Need to Know I Learned from a Children's Book*, Anita Diamant, author of *The Red Tent*, reveals that she was just one of many children inspired by Mary Poppins: "I never wanted Mary Poppins to be my nanny. I wanted to be Mary Poppins when I grew up."

A serious writer and journalist for adults, P. L. Travers grew up in Australia and then settled in England. She became a protégée of George Russell, who wrote under the pen name AE, and in the 1930s even traveled to the Soviet Union. Later Travers became a devotee of the spiritual mystic Gurdjieff, and Eastern religion worked its way into her writing for both adults and children.

I actually met P. L. Travers on her last tour to America, and I am happy to report that she herself was as sharp-tongued and eccentric as her beloved character. "I don't write for children at all. I turn my back on them," she once said. Fortunately, young readers have never agreed with her. So happy birthday Mary Poppins—may you have many, many more.

PIPPI LONGSTOCKING

By Astrid Lindgren

Born on November 14, 1907, Astrid Lindgren grew up on a farm just outside Vimmerby, Sweden. *Pippi Longstocking*, the book for which she became world renowned, published in the United States more than sixty years ago, arose from stories she told her seven-year-old daughter. Sick in bed with pneumonia, the young girl asked for a story about Pippi Longstocking. Lindgren loved the name and gave her daughter a finished manuscript of the story for her tenth birthday. Lindgren always claimed that Pippi "was just waiting for someone to pick her up and write about her."

After the manuscript was rejected by many publishers, Lindgren decided to enter Pippi's story into a contest held by a Swedish publishing house. She won first prize! When Lindgren submitted the final version, she added a note: "In the hope that you won't notify the Child Welfare Committee."

Pippilotta Delicatessa Windowshade Mackrelmint Ephraim's Daughter Longstocking, or Pippi for short, lives without parents. Pippi dictates her own rules and nags herself about going to bed at night. With endless money, time, and freedom, she certainly fulfills the fantasy of most children who often think about what life would be like if they had no one to boss them around. Her friends Tommy and Annika live a more traditional life, but enjoy the antics of Pippi.

The book became highly controversial in Sweden, particularly after it was read on the radio; "totally antisocial rubbish," its critics declared. But Lindgren, rather than those critics, would triumph. Years later, she won the Hans Christian Anderson Award for her body of work. She and Pippi became celebrities in Sweden. A theme park in Lindgren's hometown celebrates *Pippi Longstocking* and its characters. In her lifetime, Lindgren was consistently mentioned as a contender for the Nobel Prize in Literature, an honor never yet bestowed on a children's book writer. In recent years, Pippi became the inspiration for the Swedish international bestselling series that began with *The Girl with the Dragon Tattoo*. Author Stieg Larsson believed that his protagonist, Lisbeth Salander, was simply a grown-up version of Pippi.

From a devoted mother to an international icon, Astrid Lindgren symbolizes what can happen when an author creates original, fascinating books for the young and defends these stories and characters, even when the going gets rough.

NOVEMBER 14

Happy Birthday Nancy Tafuri (*Have You Seen My Duckling?*).

It's the birth date of Patricia Miles Martin, pen name Miska Miles (1899–1986), *Annie and the Old One*; William Steig (1907–2003), *Sylvester and the Magic Pebble*, *Shrek*; and William H. Hooks (1922–2008), *Pioneer Cat*, *Moss Gown*.

It's also the birth date of French Impressionist painter Claude Monet. Read *Linnea in Monet's Garden* by Christina Björk and Lena Anderson.

Happy Birthday *Moby Dick* by Herman Melville, published in 1851.

Bon voyage! Journalist **Nellie Bly** began her "Around the World in 80 Days" trip in 1889. Read *The Daring Nellie Bly: America's Star Reporter* by Bonnie Christensen and *Nellie Bly's Book* edited by Ira Peck.

English nobleman John Montagu, the fourth Earl of Sandwich, was born on this day in 1718. Legend has it he once instructed his servants to bring him meat between two pieces of bread. To celebrate this expeditious occasion, it's National Sandwich Day.

NOVEMBER 15

Happy Birthday Daniel Pinkwater (*Adventures of a Cat-Whiskered Girl*, *The Big Orange Splot*) and Maira Kalman (*Fireboat*, *Smartypants*).

Chickens, chickens, and more chickens! The first U.S. poultry show opened in Boston in 1849. Read *Chickens to the Rescue* by John Himmelman and *Louise, the Adventures of a Chicken* by Kate DiCamillo and Harry Bliss.

It's Clean Your Refrigerator Day, perhaps in preparation for Thanksgiving when it will be filled up with leftovers. Read *The Pink Refrigerator* by Tim Egan.

It's America Recycles Day. Read *50 Ways to Get Your CartOn* by Ellen Warwick.

THE SCRAMBLED STATES OF AMERICA
By Laurie Keller

The third week in November marks Geography Awareness Week. To celebrate, in the month of November schools participate in the National Geographic Bee, an annual contest sponsored by the National Geographic Society. Since 1989, participants from fourth through eighth grades have competed in this annual event for scholarships, based on their knowledge of world geography.

During my own elementary school years I was fascinated with geography. Sensing a convert to reference books, my school librarian allowed me to lug home the huge school atlas every night, so that I could meticulously copy maps of Portugal or China or whatever captured my fancy. Possibly because I have always needed a GPS chip implanted in my brain, I worked to figure out how all the countries and states fit together.

Children like me—and even some who have no interest in geography—will love Laurie Keller's *The Scrambled States of America*. First published in 1998, perfect for the three- to eight-year-old crowd, the story opens with a terrible dilemma—Kansas is "not feeling happy at all." Sitting in the middle of the country, Kansas never gets to go anywhere, do anything, or meet any new states. And so Kansas and BFF Nebraska plan a party and invite the other states so they can make friends, laugh, dance, and sing. When it's time to go home, all the states swap spots on the map to be closer to their new friends—and create mass chaos. In the end they decide that there is no place like home. With lots of humor, not to mention information about each state worked into the text and art, *The Scrambled States of America* will help any child—including those who need a GPS chip—remember where each state sits on the map.

The winning question in the 2009 National Geographic Bee focused on a country of Europe. What country contains a Timiş County? The winner, Eric Yang, seventh grader from Texas, correctly identified Romania. I would have missed it. But now, thanks to the best book about geography for children, *The Scrambled States of America*, I will always remember, as will all readers, that Nebraska sits on top of Kansas!

AND THEN WHAT HAPPENED, PAUL REVERE?

By Jean Fritz

On November 16, 1915, Jean Fritz was born to American missionaries in Hankow, China. She spent the next thirteen years there—and observed another culture while "wondering what it was like to be an American." Fritz would write about that childhood for her compelling autobiography, *Homesick: My Own Story*, a Newbery Honor book, as well as *China Homecoming* and *China's Long March*.

In the seventies Fritz began a series of chapter book biographies for children grades one through four that revolutionized writing about American history for children. Showing the foibles of our founding fathers in *And Then What Happened, Paul Revere?* Fritz demonstrated that one of the best ways to get children to read and understand history is to get them laughing. "I realized when I started doing research for my first book that history wasn't what I'd been taught in school. History is full of gossip; it's real people and emotion. I kept being surprised by the real people I met in the past. They all had their foibles and idiosyncrasies."

A genius at picking out the telling details of history, she lets children know that Paul Revere, a secret agent, also made false teeth. In such a hurry to make his secret ride, he forgot his spurs and sent his dog on a mission to get them.

Fritz keeps a light hand while telling these incidents of American history, but her search to understand the past had a very serious purpose in her life. Since she was raised in another country, she wanted to understand her native land and comprehend its history. Because she had not been inundated with the romanticized versions of stories taught during this time period in American schools, she was able to take a fresh look, to reflect on what she found, and to present her recent discoveries to children. So in books that present our heroes—from the Revolutionary War to Teddy Roosevelt—she creates flesh-and-blood human beings, who accomplished great things and yet are completely human and believable. So popular did these biographies become in the seventies and eighties that they encouraged all nonfiction writers to take a more honest, less idealized approach to writing history for children.

Intelligent, witty, and charming Jean Fritz has convinced generations of readers that history can be fun.

NOVEMBER 16

Happy Birthday Ann Blades (*Mary of Mile 18, A Salmon for Simon*), Robin McKinley (*The Hero and the Crown, The Blue Sword*), Carolyn Reeder (*Shades of Gray, Moonshiner's Son*), Stephanie Spinner (*Aliens for Breakfast*), Angela Shelf Medearis (*The 100th Day of School*).

Happy Birthday Oklahoma, which became the 46th U.S. state on this day in 1907.

Missouri trader William Becknell arrived in Santa Fe, New Mexico, on this day in 1821. His route became known as the Santa Fe Trail. Read *Tree in the Trail* by Holling C. Holling and *All the Stars in the Sky* by Megan McDonald.

It's Button Day. Read *Bone Button Borscht* by Aubrey Davis, illustrated by Dušan Petričić.

NOVEMBER 17

Happy Birthday Christopher Paolini (*Eragon*).

 England's **Queen Elizabeth I** began her reign on this day in 1558. Read Jane Resh Thomas's *Behind the Mask: The Life of Queen Elizabeth I.*

It's Homemade Bread Day. Read *Everybody Bakes Bread* by Norah Dooley and Peter Thorton, *Tony's Bread* by Tomie DePaola, and *Loaves of Fun* by Elizabeth Harbison.

It's Take a Hike Day. Read *Henry Hikes to Fitchburg* by D. B. Johnson and *Alvin Ho: Allergic to Camping, Hiking, and Other Natural Disasters* by Lenore Look.

MY SEASON WITH PENGUINS: AN ANTARCTIC JOURNAL

By Sophie Webb

On November 17, 1820, Nathaniel Palmer and his men on the *Hero* became the first Americans to set foot on the Antarctic Peninsula. He was a young man, twenty-two, when he accomplished the act for which he has been immortalized.

When I think of young Americans journeying to Antarctica, the book that instantly comes to mind is Sophie Webb's *My Season with Penguins: An Antarctic Journal*, published over ten years ago. Webb is a biologist and an artist who specializes in nature drawings. This forty-eight-page picture book, ideal for second through fourth graders, presents entries about her trip to McMurdo, one of the U.S. Antarctic Program's bases. As she describes the base, it is "devoted to scientific research and exploration. An international treaty designates the Antarctic as a continent used only for peaceful purposes.... There are no territorial borders and no part of the Antarctic is owned by a country."

Webb shows the extensive preparation required for a trip to the Antarctic: picking up clothing, finding the necessary gear, and attending survival school. In December the sun shines twenty-four hours a day, something hard for Webb to adjust to. As she and her fellow scientists set up camp, she shows the layout and gives the details children will want to know about like how bathrooms work in freezing temperatures! All of these steps in the process have been illustrated by Webb's precise watercolor, gouache, and graphite illustrations.

Then we come to my favorite part of this fascinating journal—pages and pages of drawings of Adélie Penguins, the true dwellers of the Antarctic. We see them in ecstatic display, tobogganing, incubating eggs, and greeting each other. Because Webb can control all aspects of the illustrations, these birds seem much more alive on the page than any photo or movie of them I have witnessed. Animated and vibrant, her illustrations make you feel as though you can actually reach out and touch these penguins.

The journal is both a record of what the scientists are doing, and of their subject, the penguins. A glossary provides more information and terms about the birds. Outside of the admirable Scientists in the Field series, it is difficult to find books that actually show what scientists do. This book provides a glimpse into the life of someone dedicated to science. It pleases penguin fanciers everywhere, and it shows a young woman making a contribution to our understanding of the natural world.

If you can't travel to Antarctica in the next couple of months, pick up *My Season with Penguins*. It will make you feel as if you have been there.

ALMOST ASTRONAUTS: 13 WOMEN WHO DARED TO DREAM

By Tanya Lee Stone

For National Aviation Month, I've chosen a book honoring women who loved flying. When Lieutenant Colonel Eileen M. Collins became the first woman to command a spacecraft that orbited the earth, a group of women pilots was invited to sit in the coveted VIP spots at Cape Canaveral to watch the launch. This group included women air force service pilots, pioneering air race champions, and members of the Mercury 13 team. "T minus six seconds!" someone in the crowd yelled. "Try T minus thirty-eight years," Jerri Sloan Truhill responded. She and her fellow Mercury 13 team members believed they could have made the trip into space in 1961.

Tanya Lee Stone opens *Almost Astronauts: 13 Women Who Dared to Dream* with this thrilling scene. With extensive research into the period and interviews with the Mercury 13 women—who thought they might actually get to travel into space during a time when only men were considered fit to do so—Stone explores little-known events of the NASA space program. In *Almost Astronauts* she brings to life the sixties, a time when women had to think and act outside the box if they wanted to do something other than be a housewife.

Randy Lovelace, chairman of NASA's Life Science Committee, favored placing women in space, and he devised a program called Women in Space Earliest or Project WISE. In this program some of the most qualified women pilots in America were subjected to brutal testing, including submersion in the isolation tank for hours, which was thought to simulate conditions in outer space.

Readers follow these women as they sign up for the project, learn about their dreams, and watch them go through rigorous ordeals. When officials at NASA decided not to back the program anymore, some of the women decided to plead their case to Congress. The rigors of being an astronaut, the disappointment and anger felt by these brave pioneers, and their tenacity and grit all emerge in a book written with passion and eloquence.

Pilot Amelia Earhart wrote: "Women must try to do things as men have tried. When they fail, their failure must be but a challenge to others." By the end of the book, no reader feels these women failed even though their own dream of space flight did not come true. In 2007 the House of Representatives passed a resolution honoring their achievements. In 2009 Tanya Lee Stone made their stories available to young readers in a compelling work of nonfiction that keeps readers turning the pages.

NOVEMBER 18

Happy Birthday Nancy Van Laan (*Possum Come a-Knockin'*), Margaret Atwood (*Up in the Tree*), and Alan Dean Foster (*Dinatopia Lost*).

It's the birth date of Miroslav Sasek (1916–1980), *This Is Paris*.

Happy Birthday Mickey Mouse, who appeared in the 1926 Disney release of *Steamboat Willy*.

As punishment for not bowing to a nobleman's hat, William Tell shoots an apple off his son's head in 1307. Read *William Tell* by Leonard Everett Fisher and *The Apple and the Arrow* by Mary and Conrad Buff.

NOVEMBER 19

Happy Birthday Margaret Musgrove (*Ashanti to Zulu*) and Ann Herbert Scott (*Cowboy Country*).

 It's the birth date of **James Garfield** (1831–1881), the 20th president of the United States.

It's "play ball" not "work ball." In 1953 the U.S. Supreme Court ruled baseball is a sport, not a business. Read *The Boy Who Saved Baseball* by John Ritter.

It's Have a Bad Day Day, an antidote to the phrase "Have a good day." Read *Alexander and the Terrible, Horrible, No Good, Very Bad Day* by Judith Viorst, illustrated by Ray Cruz.

World Toilet Day was started by the World Toilet Organization to improve toilet and sanitation conditions around the globe. Read *Captain Underpants and the Attack of the Talking Toilets* by Dav Pilkey and *Flush* by Carl Hiaasen.

Toymaker Morris Michtom named teddy bears after President Theodore Roosevelt on this day in 1902.

ABRAHAM LINCOLN
By Ingri and Edgar Parin d'Aulaire

On November 19, 1863, President Abraham Lincoln helped dedicate seventeen acres of the Civil War battlefield at Gettysburg, Pennsylvania. Orator Edward Everett delivered the main speech that day. He spoke for two hours; Lincoln's short address lasted about two minutes. Although contemporaries thought little of the president's address, today we consider the "Gettysburg Address" one of the most eloquent speeches in the English language.

When Ingri and Edgar Parin d'Aulaire received the third Caldecott Medal for *Abraham Lincoln*, their Norwegian families were living under Nazi occupation. In this book, first published in 1940, the d'Aulaires present Lincoln as an American folk hero—larger than life, with all the legends that had grown up around him. The book does not end with his assassination, but with him sitting down in a rocking chair to rest, having held a great nation together.

Like an old painting, allowed to gather dust before it is gloriously restored, this gem of a book had been allowed to deteriorate in quality over the years. Originally, it had been printed using stone lithography but that method became too expensive for the publisher Doubleday to execute. In 1957 they asked the d'Aulaires to redraw all the art for this book and create acetate films for printing. This new edition suffered greatly in its color and clarity and looked quite different from the book that the artists had originally created.

A few years ago Rea Berg of Beautiful Feet Books saw a first edition of *Abraham Lincoln* and realized how much of its grandeur had been lost over the years. Using that edition as her guide, Berg directed a new color separation for each page—working to restore the book to its former glory.

The 2008 edition from Beautiful Feet Books allows readers to view Abraham Lincoln as the d'Aulaires saw him. Because of the care with color reproduction and the heavy ivory paper selected for the book, contemporary audiences can finally see why the d'Aulaires and their artwork were held in awe by those who first saw it published.

Today in honor of Lincoln's great speech at Gettysburg, pick up the d'Aulaires' loving and glorious tribute to their hero. In this new edition, Lincoln is given the respect he deserved that day in Gettysburg.

THE (MOSTLY) TRUE ADVENTURES OF HOMER P. FIGG

By Rodman Philbrick

On the Saturday closest to November 19 an annual event in Pennsylvania, Remembrance Day, honors the Battle of Gettysburg with a parade of Civil War groups and organizations. One of the most dramatic events of the battle occurred on the second day when Joshua Lawrence Chamberlain, a Bowdoin College professor who commanded the 20th Maine, was sent to defend Little Round Top, at the extreme left of the Union Army. At one critical point, out of ammunition and resources, Chamberlain ordered his men to make a bayonet charge against the Confederates, an act that saved the day for the Union. At the core of the brilliant adult novel *The Killer Angels* and the film *Gettysburg*, Chamberlain and the 20th Maine also play an important role in a novel for young readers, aged eight to twelve: Rodman Philbrick's *The (Mostly) True Adventures of Homer P. Figg*, winner of a Newbery Honor.

Philbrick, a genius at creating child-friendly books such as *Freak the Mighty* and *The Last Book in the Universe*, has accomplished something extraordinary in his saga of two Maine boys, who inadvertently become soldiers in the Civil War. He has fashioned a tall tale that allows readers to turn the pages breathlessly as they absorb Civil War history. Homer, as the title suggests, has a tendency to dissemble a bit, even though he tells us at the beginning, "My name is Homer P. Figg and these are my true adventures." Like many unreliable narrators, Homer never allows the truth to stand in the way of a good story. When his brother Harold is sold by a villainous uncle to fight in the Civil War, Homer heads out to save Harold from the clutches of the Union. Abduction, robbery, and espionage in a hydrogen balloon are just a few of our hero's adventures before he and his brother end up with Joshua Lawrence Chamberlain and the 20th Maine at Little Round Top, winning the Civil War for the brave boys in blue. Or so Homer would have us believe.

One of the problems all writers of historical fiction for children face is making young readers believe these figures from the past are actual people. Although he is a terrible fibber, we still like Homer P. Figg. He's fun to hang out with—he's loyal and funny and fresh. In fact, Mr. Chamberlain was lucky to have him there at Gettysburg. Kids love this book for its lightning-quick plot, page-turning story, and plucky main character; adults appreciate how much real history kids learn as they go merrily along with Homer on his adventures.

If you can't be one of the thousands to attend Remembrance Day celebrations in Gettysburg, read *The (Mostly) True Adventures of Homer P. Figg* to appreciate what happened in this sleepy Pennsylvania town so many years ago.

NOVEMBER 20

Happy Birthday Marion Dane Bauer (*On My Honor*) and Jill Thompson (*Scary Godmother*).

It's the birth date of Peregrine White (1620–1704), the first English child born in what the Pilgrims considered the New World.

In 1820 an eighty-ton sperm whale attacked the whaling ship Essex in 1820, inspiring the book *Moby-Dick* by Herman Melville.

No way, it's Absurdity Day! Read *Gooney Bird Is So Absurd* by Lois Lowry.

Universal Children's Day is the anniversary of the United Nations Assembly's Rights of the Child Declaration (1959) and Convention (1989). Read *For Every Child* by UNICEF, adapted by Caroline Castle and illustrated by John Birmingham.

NOVEMBER 21

Happy Birthday Marlo Thomas (*Free to Be . . . You and Me*) and Mary Jane Auch (*Ashes of Roses*).

It's the birth date of Leo Politi (1908–1996), *Pedro, the Angel of Olvera Street*, *Song of the Swallows*.

Happy Birthday North Carolina, which became the 12th U.S. state on this day in 1789.

In 1783 two men in Paris made the first untethered hot air balloon flight. Read *Hot Air: The (Mostly) True Story of the First Hot-Air Balloon Ride* by Marjorie Priceman.

To celebrate World Hello Day, say hello to ten people. It's as simple as that!

It's World Television Day, created by the United Nations General Assembly to acknowledge the role of television as a mode of sharing information.

THE WITCH OF BLACKBIRD POND

By Elizabeth George Speare

On November 21, 1908, Elizabeth George Speare was born in Melrose, Massachusetts. After finishing degrees from Boston University, she taught in the Massachusetts schools, then married and moved to Connecticut. When her children entered junior high school, she began writing articles and eventually books for children. One thing that distinguishes Speare from other writers is how few books she created—and how much acclaim they all received. Four novels—*Calico Captive*, *The Witch of Blackbird Pond*, *The Bronze Bow*, *The Sign of the Beaver*—and one work of nonfiction, *Life in Colonial America*, constitute her entire output. Yet for these five books, she won two Newbery Medals and one Newbery Honor, a record of excellence unsurpassed by others.

Elizabeth George Speare found one of the great editors of children's books, Mary Silva Cosgrave of Houghton Mifflin. Mary always maintained that *The Witch of Blackbird Pond* arrived on her desk letter perfect. She merely changed one comma to a semicolon. To create this book, Speare turned to her own town of Wethersfield, Connecticut. One day while walking with her husband, Alden, she felt the presence of a solitary young woman. Chosing 1687 as the year for the novel, the time of the Connecticut Charter, Speare drew on actual testimonies from local witchcraft trials. Kit Tyler, an orphan immigrant from Barbados, arrives unexpectedly at the home of her aunt and uncle in the town. Although everything seems strange at first, Kit finds a friend in the reclusive Hannah Tupper, a Quaker who lives on Blackbird Pond. But then the town turns on Hannah, branding her as a witch.

Newbery deliberations are always kept secret, but in the case of *The Witch of Blackbird Pond*, the committee broke precedent and stated that Speare's gem had received a rare unanimous vote on the first ballot. This book, published during the McCarthy era, explored another period of time, Colonial Connecticut, and featured an innocent woman believed to be a witch. Although today readers don't think of *The Witch of Blackbird Pond* as being linked to Communist blacklisting, those of its time period would not have missed Speare's impassioned cry for justice.

I was fortunate to know and work with Elizabeth George Speare. Dignified, intelligent, softspoken but articulate, Speare was beloved not only by Mary Silva Cosgrave but by all those in the publishing house. Speare's career should encourage all writers: you don't have to write hundreds of books to get a classic—you just have to write one great book.

LEVIATHAN

By Scott Westerfeld
Illustrated by Keith Thompson

Today marks the first interracial kiss on TV, between Captain James Kirk and Lt. Uhura of Star Trek. Tomorrow in 1963 the BBC broadcasted the first episode of *Doctor Who*, the world's longest-running science fiction drama. So what science fiction books written for the young readers today are on their way to becoming classics? Certainly one of the most original recent offerings, Scott Westerfeld's *Leviathan*, for children ages ten through fourteen, provides a fascinating glimpse into a history that might have occurred.

Alternate history, a science fiction genre began by Philip K. Dick and perfected by Harry Turtledove, permits the writer to change the facts of the past and create an imagined world that is rooted in our own. In his highly inventive steampunk novel, Westerfeld conjures up a fascinating vision of the twentieth century—if history had played out with a few significant changes.

In the world of *Leviathan*, Charles Darwin continues scientific explorations and finds ways to fabricate creatures from DNA. Although opposition emerges from the Monkey Luddites, Darwinists invent scores of magnificent beasts. Many of these creatures become tools of war—like the *Leviathan*, a living, hydrogen-filled animal that serves as deadly airship. The German alliance, however, develops mechanical creatures that walk on legs—these machines look like living beasts. Hence the First World War will be played out between the Darwinists and the Clankers.

After the assassination of his parents, Prince Aleksandar attempts to flee with his tutors to safety in Switzerland. He learns to pilot one of the mechanical walking warships and survives harrowing circumstances. Meanwhile in England, Deryn Sharp, one of the most engaging heroines of recent fiction, has disguised herself as a boy so that she can become a midshipman in the British Air Service and become part of the *Leviathan*'s crew. Filled with exciting battles and fascinating details about the manufactured creatures, the story of these two engaging protagonists is almost impossible to put down. Not only is the action engaging, but Westerfeld has also used some of the best epithets in recent fiction—sayings like "barking spiders!"

If you'd like an unconventional way to get young readers excited about history, pick up Leviathan and its two sequels. The book explores a period of time when the aristocracy and commoners lived very different lives and when women had to disguise themselves as men to do what they wanted to do.

NOVEMBER 22

Happy Birthday Valerie Wilson Wesley (Willimena Rules series) and Marjane Satrapi (*Persepolis, Monsters Are Afraid of the Moon*).

It's the birth date of Mary Ann Evans, pen name **George Eliot** (1819–1880), *Silas Marner, The Mill on the Floss.*

On this day in 1963 Lee Harvey Oswald assassinated President John F. Kennedy in Dallas, Texas. Lyndon B. Johnson becomes president.

It's Go for a Ride Day. Take a ride on a horse, a bicycle, a train, a roller coaster, or whatever you fancy! Read *Roller Coaster* by Marla Frazee, *Mr. Grumpy's Outing* by John Burningham, and *Amelia and Eleanor Go for a Ride* by Pam Muñoz Ryan and illustrated by Brian Selznick.

It's Start Your Own Country Day, which itself started at the 1939 World's Fair in New York, whose theme was "Building the World of Tomorrow."

NOVEMBER 23

Happy Birthday Gloria Whelan (*Homeless Bird*).

It's the birth date of Boris Karloff (1887–1969), known for his monster portrayal in the movie *Frankenstein*, and as the narrator of recorded versions of *The Three Little Pigs* and *Just So Stories*.

 It's also the birth date of **Franklin Pierce** (1804–1869), the 14th president of the United States.

Writing about freedom of speech and expression, John Milton published *Aeropagitica*, decrying censorship, in 1644. Read *Nothing but the Truth* by Avi.

The first jukebox made its debut in San Francisco's Palais Royale Saloon in 1889. Read *The Jukebox Man* by Jacqueline Ogburn.

In 1942 the film *Casablanca* premiered in New York City.

It's *Eat a Cranberry Day*. Read *Cranberry Thanksgiving* by Wende and Harry Devlin.

THE ANNOTATED PETER PAN

Edited by Maria Tatar

On November 23, 1903, an already popular writer and playwright began the first draft of a play entitled "ANON" and set in the night nursery of the Darling family. A few years later, in 1911, he extended the ideas of that play, *Peter Pan*, into a longer novel for children, *Wendy and Peter*. From creating Nana, the best nursemaid possible, to recounting Peter Pan's adventures on a remote island with Captain Hook, James Barrie told a story that has become part of our collective conscience.

In reality no definitive edition of *Peter Pan* exists, for J. M. Barrie constantly changed it for the stage and various print formats. In *The Annotated Peter Pan*, however, Maria Tatar deftly describes all the versions of the work before examining *Wendy and Peter* in detail. Tatar masterfully re-creates Barrie's life. With an even hand, she explores Barrie's marriage and his relationships with the five sons of Arthur and Sylvia Llewlyn Davies, who served as both the inspiration for Peter Pan and an audience for early renditions. Certainly Barrie's psyche, which produced a saga about the boy who never grew up, provides a great deal of material for any writer. Rather than aiming for the sensational, or even the speculative, Tatar uses impeccable scholarship to ground the book in what can be learned from primary documents found at the Beinecke Library at Yale.

She rounds out her analysis with fascinating photos and materials such as a reproduction of Arthur Rackham's artwork for *Peter Pan in Kensington Garden*. Barrie's early rendition of the story *The Boys Castaway of Black Lake Island,* created for the Llewlyn Davies boys, has been included in its entirety. Pictures from the Walt Disney animated movie and even shots of Johnny Depp, portraying Barrie in the film *Finding Neverland*, round out the book. Rarely has such an extensive body of archival materials been pulled together to celebrate a cultural icon.

Although I have grown up since I first encountered *Peter Pan* as a child, part of me remains forever with Peter, Wendy, Nana, and the Lost Boys. With *The Annotated Peter Pan* I can relive that fantasy once again.

SAVVY
By Ingrid Law

We all have at least one talent. November 24, Celebrate Your Unique Talent Day, allows all of us to celebrate our own individual abilities. Whatever you do best, take some time today to acknowledge your gift.

What if you knew that on a certain birthday, your thirteenth, you would be given a special talent or ability just like everyone else in your family? That premise lies behind *Savvy* by Ingrid Law, one of the most original and compelling novels of the past few years. To write this book, Ingrid Law asked herself what magic would look like if it sprang up in small-town America. She wanted to create a modern American tall tale. To that mix, she adds the elements of a road trip odyssey.

Every member of the Beaumont family possesses a form of magic: Grandpa moves mountains; Fish can create hurricanes; Olive melts ice with a stare; Rocket sparks electricity. But right before Mibs's thirteenth birthday party, where she will discover her special ability, things start to go terribly wrong. Her father ends up in the hospital because of a bad accident. The day of her thirteenth birthday, she tries to visit her father by sneaking on the bus of a Bible salesman. Then her two brothers, along with two of the local pastor's children, join her. Will Junior, in fact, has a crush on Mibs but has no idea of her family's secret. Unfortunately, the bus heads in the wrong direction, and Mibs and her fellow passengers have the trip of a lifetime. That is, before the police start looking for them.

NOVEMBER 24

Happy Birthday Sylvia Engdahl (*Enchantress from the Stars*) and Gloria Houston (*The Year of the Perfect Christmas Tree*).

It's the birth date of **Frances Hodgson Burnett** (1849–1924), *The Secret Garden*; Carlo Collodi (1826–1890), *The Adventures of Pinocchio*; Yoshiko Uchida (1921–1992), *The Best Bad Thing*; and James Ramsey Ullman (1907–1971), *Banner in the Sky*.

It's also the birth date of Zachary Taylor (1784–1850), the 12th president of the United States.

Charles Darwin published *On the Origin of Species* in 1859. On a related note, it's Evolution Day. Read *The Tree of Life* by Peter Sís, *Charles and Emma* by Deborah Heiligman, and *The Evolution of Calpurnia Tate* by Jacqueline Kelly.

In 1947 *The Pearl* by John Steinbeck was published. Also read *The Black Pearl* by Scott O'Dell and *Pearl Barley and Charlie Parsley* by Aaron Blabey.

In *Savvy*, Law creates a set of unforgettable characters and a nonstop plot that she brings together seamlessly. Mibs doesn't quite get the savvy she was hoping for—but she certainly gets the birthday celebration of a lifetime! A quick pace, short chapters, an intriguing concept, and great characters keep readers turning the pages. The first chapter of the book is so compelling that even reluctant readers who give it a try admit that they can't put it down. Hence this Newbery Honor book has become a favorite of those in grades five and up—and one of those books that young adults in their twenties also adore.

What unique talent do you have—and which one would you like? You can think about both of these questions as you savor Ingrid Law's *Savvy*.

NOVEMBER 25

Happy Birthday Crescent Dragonwagon (*Alligator Arrived with Apples*, *Home Place*), Marc Brown (Arthur series), Mordicai Gerstein (*The Man Who Walked Between the Towers*), Shirley Climo (*The Cobweb Christmas*), and Jim LaMarche (*The Raft*).

It's the birth date of P. D. Eastman (1909–1986), *Are You My Mother?*, *Go, Dog. Go!*; and Elsie J. Oxenham (1880–1960), *Goblin Island*.

In 1792 Farmer's Almanac, now known as Old Farmer's Almanac, was first published. Read *Farmer George Plants a Nation* by Peggy Thomas, illustrated by Layne Johnson.

Alfred Nobel patents dynamite in 1867. Read *The Man behind the Peace Prize* by Kathy-Jo Wargin and Zak Pullen.

1621: A NEW LOOK AT THANKSGIVING

By Catherine O'Neill Grace and Margaret Bruchac

Photographs by Sisse Brimberg and Cotton Coulson

On the fourth Thursday of November Americans worship those twin pastimes of indulging in food and football. How did this day, Thanksgiving, become a holiday? *1621: A New Look at Thanksgiving* challenges a lot of our assumptions about this day by describing what happened when the fifty-two living English colonists celebrated their first successful harvest with Massasoit, the Wampanoag leader, who brought ninety of his men to the event.

The talents of author Catherine O'Neill Grace and Abenaki storyteller Marge Bruchac are combined in *1621*, with the support of the National Geographic Society and Plimouth Plantation, the living history museum in Plymouth, Massachusetts. This knowledgeable group presents the best scholarship to date about Thanksgiving. As the authors suggest, the Wampanoag and Abenaki side of the story has been basically ignored for generations. They also provide a very different version of Pilgrims from the ones children may know. The real pilgrims wore bright clothing and engaged in "butchering deer, grinding corn, plucking birds, gathering shellfish, roasting meat" for a three-day celebration. I like the idea that festivities continued for three days—possibly that is where the concept of leftovers began. The book even includes recipes of the time in case you want to bring a bit of culinary history into your celebration. Outside of turkey and pumpkin, most of our traditional Thanksgiving dishes were never even tasted by the colonists.

The book has been lavishly illustrated with photographs taken during Plimouth Plantation reenactments, and these give readers a sense of being present on this first Thanksgiving in 1621. The participants probably played games—although not football—and sang and danced. A very interesting section of the book explores the ongoing relationship of the settlers to the native people in New England. Since 1970 many Native Americans gather at the statue of Massasoit in Plymouth on Thanksgiving to remember the struggle of their ancestors.

ALICE IN WONDERLAND

By Lewis Carroll

Illustrated by John Tenniel

On November 26, 1865, a children's book was published by Macmillan in England that has remained in print ever since: the longest standing and best known of our classics, Lewis Carroll's quirky and unforgettable *Alice in Wonderland.* Although the story was clearly written and intended for children, its richness and complexity also make it appealing to adults. It has been embraced by rock groups like Jefferson Airplane, movie moguls like Tim Burton, royalty like Queen Victoria of England, and millions of college students and writers.

The book began when Oxford don and mathematician Charles Dodgson took the three Liddell daughters out on a boat trip down the River Thames and entertained them with a story. After Alice begged to have it written down, Dodgson embellished his tale, publishing it under his nom de plume Lewis Carroll. Even with its modest first printing of two thousand copies, the book quickly took hold of readers and became the darling of parents and children alike.

In *Alice in Wonderland* Alice falls down a rabbit hole into a bizarre world where all logic seems reversed. In 1871 Carroll continued Alice's story in *Through the Looking Glass, and What Alice Found There.* In this sequel, Alice discovers she is a pawn in a chess game dominated by the Red Queen. Today it is impossible to imagine either story without the artwork of Sir John Tenniel, but author and illustrator squabbled incessantly while the books were created, and Carroll considered Tenniel less than ideal for the project.

Translated into more than 125 languages, the two books brought to life an incredible cast of characters who have become part of popular culture—the March Hare, Cheshire Cat, White Rabbit, Tweedledee, Tweedledum, and the Jaberwock—to name only a few. And, of course, Alice herself has inspired legions. As Professor Alice Gopnik, of the University of California at Berkeley, wrote in *Everything I Need to Know I Learned from a Children's Book*: "I think every scientist and every child is the grave, wide-eyed little girl who fearlessly follows evidence and logic wherever it leads—even through the looking glass and down the rabbit hole."

A very happy birthday to *Alice in Wonderland.* For nearly 150 years this classic has shown us that the very best books for children just get better over time and can entertain and sustain us throughout all the stages of our life.

NOVEMBER 26

It's the birth date of Doris Gates (1901–1987), *Blue Willow*; and **Charles Schulz** (1922–2000), *Peanuts.*

In 1716 the first lion was exhibited in Boston, Massachusetts. Read *The Lion and the Mouse* by Jerry Pinkney, *Library Lion* by Michelle Knudsen, illustrated by Kevin Hawkes, and *The Happy Lion* by Louise Fatio, illustrated by Roger Duvoisin.

First step, discovery; second step, entry. In 1922 Howard Carter and Lord Carnarvon became the first people to enter the tomb of Pharaoh Tutankhamen in more than three thousand years.

NOVEMBER 27

Happy Birthday Kevin Henkes (*Lilly's Purple Plastic Purse, Owen, Olive's Ocean*).

It's the birth date of Katherine Milhous (1894–1977), *The Egg Tree*.

It's also the birth date of Anders Celsius (1701–1744), inventor of the Celsius temperature scale.

Actor/martial artist Bruce Lee (1940–1973) and musician Jimi Hendrix (1942–1970) were also born on this day. Read *The Martial Arts Book* by Laura Scandiffio and *Jimi: Sounds Like a Rainbow* by Gary Golio, illustrated by Javaka Steptoe.

It's Pins and Needles Day, to commemorate the opening of a Broadway musical in 1937. The play was produced by the International Ladies Garment Workers' Union. Read *The Bobbin Girl* by Emily Arnold McCully.

REACHING FOR THE MOON

By Buzz Aldrin

Illustrated by Wendell Minor

Buzz Aldrin's 2005 book *Reaching for the Moon*, for children ages six through ten, makes a perfect choice for National Aviation Month. He begins the book by explaining how he got his funny name. His sister called him Buzzer, rather than brother, and the family simply shortened it to Buzz. Aldrin discusses his childhood obsession with flight, which began on his first airplane ride at the age of two, and how he adored the Lone Ranger and wanted to be strong, determined, and independent like his hero.

In pursuit of his desire to fly, he became a West Point cadet, and then an air force pilot stationed in Germany. But when the Mercury flight program, America's first human space flight program, began recruiting potential astronauts, Aldrin knew he wanted to be accepted and needed to find a way to distinguish himself. With great honesty and candor he walks young readers through his process—his need for more education, his first rejection from the program, then his acceptance and training to become an astronaut. Finally, readers follow the space flight of *Apollo 11*, as Aldrin and Neil Armstrong became the first two men from earth to walk on the moon. As the plaque they placed that day states, "We came in peace for all mankind."

But the real message of the book can be found in Aldrin's final note: "Not everyone can explore space. But we all have our own moons to reach for. If you set your sights high, you may accomplish more than you ever dreamed was possible. Just as I have."

Aldrin's understated text has been brilliantly illustrated by Wendell Minor. Minor captures Aldrin as a young man and shows his steps along the way to becoming an astronaut. But it's the illustrations of the moon and space that are truly glorious; better than any photograph, they make you feel as if you are standing on the moon or traveling through space yourself. Together the text and art bring Aldrin's personal story to life—one that can inspire and challenge young readers.

If you have a budding pilot in your life, or you just want an autobiography that will inspire young readers, pick up *Reaching for the Moon*.

MOONSHOT: THE FLIGHT OF APOLLO 11

By Brian Floca

November is National Aviation Month and Brian Floca's *Moonshot: The Flight of Apollo 11* explains the *Apollo 11* mission to children ages four to eight. In 1969 families and friends gathered around small television sets in households across America to watch Neil Armstrong, Michael Collins, and Buzz Aldrin attempt to land on the moon.

Brian Floca uses a large, oversize picture book format to bring this incident of history to life. In breathtaking drawings Floca shows the preparation of the astronauts, the panels at mission control, the countdown to blastoff, and the rocket moving through space. Readers view weightless astronauts, their descent, and their historic moonwalk. Floca fills his informative text with just the type of information that children love—how to use Velcro strips to hold weightless objects down and how "after a week this small home will not smell so good. This is not why anyone wants to be an astronaut."

To create this masterpiece Brian Floca uses all of his extensive experience in illustration. Although he graduated from Brown University in Providence, Rhode Island, he took courses with David Macaulay at the nearby Rhode Island School of Design. During this time he also met Avi and created an early graphic novel with him, *City of Light, City of Darkness,* as well as illustrated Avi's *Poppy.*

In *Moonshot*, Floca also brings the human drama of this mission to a child's point of view. As a family watches these events on television, the parents and children wait, watch, worry, and finally cheer as these men successfully complete their mission. In the final spread, when the trio returns "Back to family, back to friends, to warmth, to light," readers see these children, running with their father and dog with the moon in the sky. By this wonderful sequence, Floca subtly makes the point that the heroes that day were not only those who walked on the moon—but the people who sent them there and kept vigil while history was being made also had their moment.

Moonshot is a stellar example of the information picture book, with endnotes that discuss Armstrong's famous statement "That's one small step for a man, one giant leap for mankind." If like the children in this book you watched the *Apollo* moon landing on TV forty-one years ago, *Moonshot* will bring back those memories. But it also allows children today to understand, intellectually and emotionally, what happened when these Americans became the first to walk on the moon.

NOVEMBER 28

Happy Birthday Tomi Ungerer (*The Three Robbers, Crictor*), Ed Young (*Seven Blind Mice*), and Stephanie Calmenson (*The Principal's New Clothes*).

It's the birth date of poet William Blake (1757–1827). Read *A Visit to William Blake's Inn* by Nancy Willard, illustrated by Alice and Martin Provensen.

It's Red Planet Day (referring to Mars), commemorating the launch of Mariner 4 on this day in 1964. During its voyage, the spacecraft eventually came within just over six thousand miles of Mars. Read *Cars on Mars: Roving the Red Planet* by Alexandra Siy.

NOVEMBER 29

Happy Birthday David M. Schwartz (*How Much Is a Million?*) and Maggie Stern (*The Missing Sunflowers*).

It's the birth date of **Louisa May Alcott** (1832–1888), *Little Women*; and Madeleine L'Engle (1918–2007), *A Wrinkle in Time*.

In 1910 the first U.S. patent for traffic lights was issued. Read *Go, Dog. Go!* by P. D. Eastman.

It's Square Dance Day. You're never too old for *Barnyard Dance* by Sandra Boynton!

Puppy Mill Action Week (Nov 29–Dec 5) begins, sponsored by the U.S. Humane Society. Read *The Poky Little Puppy* by Janette Sebring Lowrey, illustrated by Gustaf Tenggren, *I Am a Puppy* by Ole Risom, and *The Pigeon Wants a Puppy* by Mo Willems.

THE LION, THE WITCH AND THE WARDROBE

By C. S. Lewis

Clive Staples Lewis was born on November 29, 1898, in Belfast, Ireland. But he would live and write in Oxford, England, where he taught on the English faculty with his good friend and fellow author, J.R.R. Tolkien. C. S. Lewis died on November 22, 1963. Media coverage for him at that time was quite minimal due to the assassination that day of President John F. Kennedy and the death of English writer Aldous Huxley. But since 1963, Lewis has been written about, served as the subject of a movie, and read by millions and millions of devoted fans. Although many of his adult books about Christianity like *Surprised by Joy* have remained popular, he is best remembered for his children's fantasy series, The Chronicles of Narnia, which have sold more than a hundred million copies, been translated into forty-one languages, and established themselves as part of the canon of children's literature.

To write these books, Lewis mined images from his boyhood. When he was sixteen, he imagined a faun, carrying an umbrella in a snowy wood. Then around 1948 he began to weave a lion into this story, which he now called simply "The Lion." Lewis became swept up in the tale that poured out of him. Although he originally intended it to be a single volume, in two years he wrote five books.

In *The Lion, the Witch and the Wardrobe*, four children have been evacuated from London during the Blitz to stay with an elderly professor. By walking through a wardrobe, they find another kingdom, Narnia, under the spell of the evil White Witch. But the true king of Narnia, Aslan, has come to free this world—although to do so he will have to die and then rise again from the dead. In this series of seven books, Lewis wanted to see if he could find a way to describe Christianity so that it could be appreciated and understood by children.

But Lewis's adult friends were not so amused. As part of a writers' group called the Inklings, Lewis shared this work in progress with them. J.R.R. Tolkien, a member of the group, could not endure the Narnia tales. He considered them badly constructed and taking place in a less-than-cohesive alternate world. Although Tolkien was himself a genius at creating his own fantasy world, he failed to understand Lewis's creation. The series is ideal for young fantasy readers, ages eight to twelve, who fall in love with the talking animals, fauns, and giants.

I myself have spent a lifetime looking at armoires, hoping that they have a false back door that leads to Narnia. Since I haven't found one yet, I just pick up the books from time to time. Happy birthday, C. S. Lewis. Our real world has been a better place because of the alternate universe that he created.

DUFFY AND THE DEVIL

By Harve Zemach and Margot Zemach

One of the finest book illustrators of the twentieth century, Margot Zemach, was born on November 30, 1931. Male illustrators for children outnumber and generally receive more accolades than their female counterparts. But Margot Zemach could hold her own with the men of the field, winning the Caldecott Medal for *Duffy and the Devil*.

Zemach came to her career in children's books after studying at the Los Angeles County Art Institute and the Academy of Fine Arts in Vienna, Austria, on a Fulbright Scholarship. Collaborating with her husband, Harve, on her first book, *A Small Boy Is Listening*, she depended on his writing talents for many of her publications. Often he provided delicious language for stories; she gave them life in her animated artwork. Not only could she draw like an angel—all of her work is based on strong composition and line—but she had an impeccable sense of design. To look at her work feels like going on a walk in a well-laid-out rose garden. She knew how to combine art, text, and type to make reading a pleasure. And the white space where the paper is allowed to show around the art—she had no fear of white space.

The Zemachs often used folktales for the basis of their books. One of their best, *It Could Always Be Worse*, a Caldecott Honor, stems from a Yiddish folktale. Her Caldecott winner, *Duffy and the Devil*, was based on a Cornish folktale similar to Rumpelstiltskin. But nothing in her artwork seems borrowed or copied. Every book had freshness to the approach and liveliness in the illustration. I have always thought of Margot Zemach as a modern-day Randolph Caldecott, the great nineteenth-century English illustrator. Her characters dance and move across the page—and she always manages to bring out the humor of the text and situation.

Children's literature allows readers to bring all of their experiences to a book each time they pick it up. I was a young *Horn Book* reviewer when I first encountered Zemach's work and fell in love with *Duffy and the Devil*. To humor me, Paul Heins, editor of *The Horn Book* and a great Zemach fan, allowed me the privilege of reviewing it for the magazine because I loved the book so much. When this beautiful and spirited book won the Caldecott Medal, I felt as if I had won that medal myself. Every time I pick up the book, I read not only this story, but part of my story as well. That is what great children's books do.

In 1989 Margot Zemach died of Lou Gehrig's disease. But as with all our great creators, her books continue to delight young readers.

NOVEMBER 30

It's the birth date of Lucy Maud Montgomery (1874–1942), *Anne of Green Gables*; Jonathan Swift (1667–1745), *Gulliver's Travels*; and Samuel Clemens, pen name Mark Twain (1835–1910), *Huckleberry Finn, Tom Sawyer*.

It's also the birth date of British statesman Winston Churchill (1874–1965). Read *Winston of Churchill* by Jean Davies Okimoto.

The steam locomotive Flying Scotsman became the first to officially exceed 100 mph in 1934. Read *Steam, Smoke, and Steel* by Patrick O'Brien and *Superpower: The Making of a Steam Locomotive* by David Weitzman.

DECEMBER 1

Happy Birthday Jan Brett (*The Mitten*).

In 1913 the Ford Motor Company introduced the first moving assembly line. Read *Eat My Dust! Henry Ford's First Race* by Monica Kulling.

The first draft lottery since World War II began in 1969 to enlist soldiers for the Vietnam War. Read *10,000 Days of Thunder: A History of the Vietnam War* by Philip Caputo.

On this day in 1990 construction efforts began on the Channel Tunnel, or the "Chunnel," linking Great Britain to mainland Europe.

Today, on World AIDS Day, we raise awareness about AIDS and HIV infection.

Read a New Book Month begins today.

CLAUDETTE COLVIN: TWICE TOWARD JUSTICE
By Phillip Hoose

Today has been designated Rosa Parks Day, marking her arrest on December 1, 1955, for refusing to give up her seat on a bus. The incident sparked the yearlong Montgomery Bus Boycott and is considered the beginning of the modern civil rights movement. Because of the research of author Phillip Hoose, we can honor along with Rosa Parks another individual who changed history in Montgomery, Alabama.

A native of Birmingham, Alabama, Claudette Austin was named after the popular movie star Claudette Colbert. A rebellious teenager, she possessed a bit more courage than her peers. On March 2, 1955, in her high school in Montgomery, Alabama, she had been studying the Constitution of the United States. Going home that day, this young black woman did the unthinkable. When the bus driver yelled for her to yield her seat to a white woman, she refused to get up. "I was thinking. Why should I have to get up just because a driver tells me to, or just because I'm black? Right then, I decided I wasn't gonna take it anymore. I hadn't planned it out, but my decision was built on a lifetime of nasty experiences." Of course, in the South at this time, she was expected, even required, to defer to whites.

Even when confronted by policemen, Claudette shouted, "It's my Constitutional right to sit here as much as that lady. I paid my fare!" In *Claudette Colvin: Twice Toward Justice*, winner of the National Book Award, author Phillip Hoose presents the life story of this unsung heroine of the civil rights movement. In his fascinating account, told mainly in Claudette's own words, readers get to see the events of 1955 in Montgomery, Alabama, from a different perspective—as they were experienced by a young girl. Consequently, when Rosa Parks was arrested on December 2, 1955, readers fully comprehend why the leaflet passed around that day read: "Another Negro woman has been arrested and thrown in jail because she refused to get up out of her seat on the bus."

Since his book, *We Were There, Too! Young People in U.S. History*, Phillip Hoose has been exploring how teenagers can make a difference in the world. In *Claudette Colvin*, he brings to life one very special young woman, who truly made a difference in the civil rights movement. Today we remember the contributions of Rosa Parks and Claudette Colvin, both reminding us that individuals have the power to change history.

THE GREEN GLASS SEA
By Ellen Klages

On December 2, 1942, the Manhattan Project initiated the first self-sustaining nuclear chain reaction. Less than three years later, a group of scientists stood near Alamogordo, New Mexico, to watch the first nuclear explosion. One of them, J. Robert Oppenheimer, would later say, "We knew the world would not be the same. A few people laughed; a few people cried. Most people were silent. I remembered the line from the Hindu scripture, the *Bhagavad-Gita* . . . Now I am become Death, the destroyer of worlds."

The work of the Manhattan Project and the explosion of the first atomic bomb do not seem the most likely material for a children's book. But in one of the most original and compelling works of historical fiction published in the last ten years, Ellen Klages drew on the development of the atomic bomb for *The Green Glass Sea.* Focusing on the young people who lived in Los

DECEMBER 2

Happy Birthday David Macaulay (*Black and White*).

It's the birth date of circus owner Charles Ringling (1863–1926). Read *Ringlingville USA: The Stupendous Story of Seven Brothers and Their Stunning Circus Success* and *Tents, Tigers, and the Ringling Brothers*, both by Jerry Apps.

In 1867 **Charles Dickens** gave his first U.S. public reading at Tremont Temple in Boston. Read *A Christmas Carol.*

Alamos, the book explores the events as an entire community works on the Manhattan Project. Ten-year-old Dewey Kerrigan knows only that her father is engaged in war work—very confidential war work. But she loves the Los Alamos compound; a budding inventor, she discovers that the dump contains valuable but discarded scientific material. Unfortunately, when her father travels to Washington, D.C., Dewey is forced to move in with another girl, Suze, one of her most notorious tormentors at the compound. Slowly these two build a friendship in this unusual setting—so isolated and cut off from the rest of the world. In this novel Klages explores historical events in a way that is relatable to an eleven- to fourteen-year-old child.

San Francisco writer Ellen Klages initially developed short pieces of fiction that were published in science fiction and fantasy anthologies and magazines. For one of them, she won a Nebula Award in 2005 and was a finalist for the John W. Campbell Award. But although *The Green Glass Sea* was her first novel, she brought a well-honed sense of craft to the project.

All good historical fiction is marked by a sense of story, a sense of history, and a sense of place. This novel has all three—but Klages is particularly brilliant at re-creating the Los Alamos complex. Readers get to know the streets and the residences; you actually feel like you are walking around Los Alamos in 1945, something difficult for any writer to achieve. One young reader recently noted that she read "the book when I was thirteen, I'm fourteen now and I'm still in love with *The Green Glass Sea*! Great story." And it *is* a great story, and an important story, one that takes young people up to a moment in time after which the world was never quite the same again.

DECEMBER 3

Happy Birthday Grace Andreacchi (*Little Poems for Children*).

It's also the birth date of **Joseph Conrad** (1857–1925), *Heart of Darkness*.

Happy Birthday Illinois, which became the 21st U.S. state on this day in 1818.

In 1847 abolitionist movement leader Frederick Douglass published the first issue of the newspaper *North Star*. Read *Frederick Douglass: A Noble Life* by David Adler.

It's National Roof over Your Head Day, an opportunity to appreciate all that we have starting with shelter that protects us from the elements. Read *Let's Go Home: The Wonderful Things About a House* by Cynthia Rylant, illustrated by Wendy Halperin.

THE GIVER
By Lois Lowry

"It was almost December, and Jonas was beginning to be frightened." With these words Lois Lowry opens the best children's novel of the nineties and one of the greatest science fiction works of all time—*The Giver*.

In the early nineties Lowry found herself a frequent visitor at a nursing home. There her mother, going blind, would relate tales of her life. Although in better physical shape, her father was slowly losing his memory. He would look at pictures of Lois's sister, now dead, and ask how she was doing.

Then while taking her grandson on a Swan Boat ride in Boston Public Garden, the young boy said to her, "Have you ever noticed that when people think they are manipulating ducks, actually the ducks are manipulating people?" As she thought about this comment, her parents, and her own life, she began to wonder what kind of world the next generation of children would inherit.

In *The Giver*, Lowry began to write about what she thought was a utopia for those children of the future. This world appears to have solved all problems—poverty, inequality, loneliness, and old age. Children are carefully trained for their future occupation, chosen by the community. Families raise a controlled number of children and follow strict rules. But slowly as Lowry worked on the book, she grew to realize the dark side of this world. One of the most powerful moments of *The Giver* comes when the the story reveals to the reader the high price of this system.

The protagonist, twelve-year-old Jonas, has been given his assignment for his future work—to serve as the apprentice for The Giver, who keeps the memories of the community. In the process of receiving these memories, Jonas begins to realize that his community has made certain choices, ones that make him increasingly uncomfortable. A young man of great heart and social conscience, Jonas finally understands that he can no longer stay; he must flee and try to get himself and his brother Gabe to another community.

One of the greatest strengths of this book, perfect for the classroom or book group, has always been its ambiguous ending. The last line—"But perhaps it was only an echo"—leaves every reader with a slightly different sense of how the story ends. Although the author herself has always insisted that she provided a happy, optimistic ending, in that sentence she left room for each person to bring his or her own sensibility and opinions.

Lowry has always had the greatest respect for her audience, believing children capable of understanding complex issues. In *The Giver* she challenged them to think about the society presented in the book and their own world. This provocative and haunting book lingers in the memory of all those who pick it up—one of those rare books that changes the way its readers look at reality.

ALL-OF-A-KIND FAMILY

By Sydney Taylor

In December Hanukkah, the Festival of Lights, occurs. One of the most memorable books about Jewish life and customs ever written, *All-of-a-Kind Family* by Sydney Taylor, makes a great introduction to this celebration. When Taylor published this gem in 1951, books featuring religious Jewish children were hard to come by. To create her rare offering Taylor drew on her own personal experience. Although she also pursued a career as an actress and dancer for the Martha Graham Company, today Taylor is best remembered for the vibrant Jewish community she brought to life in this series of children's books.

Taylor set her saga in New York, in a Lower East Side tenement at the turn of the twentieth century. There a family of two loving parents and five girls experience great joy, even though they do so in the midst of poverty. For these children, finding a button while dusting or getting a piece of penny candy can be a cause for celebration. Much as Betty Smith does in *A Tree Grows in Brooklyn*, Taylor demonstrates that what people love, not what they possess, makes them rich in spirit. But for these girls the greatest pleasures come at the Jewish holidays, and these are warmly described, just as a child might experience them.

At the end of this book, a boy arrives, and then the saga of the family is continued in other volumes. These books remain one of the best representations of the Jewish faith found in children's books. They also linger in the mind of the reader well into adult years. When I ask groups of people about their favorite books from childhood, inevitably the All-of-a-Kind Family series gets mentioned. In *Everything I Need to Know I Learned from a Children's Book*, novelist Meg Wolitzer remembered a particular scene where "two of the sisters lay in bed at night eating the precious crackers and candy they had bought during the day. Because the family had very little money, they needed to make them last, and so one of the sisters instructed the other about what particular one they were allowed to eat, and how many nibbles from the edge they were allowed to take." This book gave Wolitzer "a sense of the multiple textures of the world."

So during December pick up *All-of-a-Kind Family* and its sequels. It not only provides a sense of history, but it also conveys why family and community are so important—and just how wonderful special holidays can be for children.

DECEMBER 4

It's the birth date of Munro Leaf (1905–1976), *The Story of Ferdinand*.

It's the birth date of Massachusetts Bay Colony Puritan **John Cotton** (1585–1652). Read *Mayflower 1620: A New Look at a Pilgrim Voyage* by Peter Arenstam, John Kemp, and Catherine O'Neill Grace and *Anne Hutchinson's Way* by Jeannine Atkins, illustrated by Michael Dooling.

In 1915 the Ku Klux Klan received a charter to function as a corporate fraternal order from Fulton County, Georgia. Read *Witness* by Karen Hesse and *Night Fires* by George Edward Stanley.

It's National Cookie Day. Read *Cookie's Week* by Cindy Ward, illustrated by Tomie dePaola.

DECEMBER 5

It's the birth date of Christina Rossetti (1830–1894), *Goblin Market, the Prince's Progress and Other Poems*; Harve Zemach, pen name of Harvey Fichstrom, husband of illustrator Margot Zemach (1933–1974), *Duffy and the Devil*; Ann Nolan Clark (1896–1995), *The Secret of the Andes*; and Rose Wilder Lane (1886–1968), daughter of Laura Ingalls Wilder and collaborator on the Little House books.

It's also the birth date of Walt Disney (1901–1966) and **Martin Van Buren** (1782–1862), the eighth president of the United States.

It's International Ninja Day. Read *Blue Fingers: A Ninja's Tale* by Cheryl Aylward Whitesel, *Moonshadow: Rise of the Ninja* by Simon Higgins, and *Blood Ninja* by Nick Lake.

THE TUB PEOPLE
By Pam Conrad
Illustrated by Richard Egielski

Today marks Bathtub Party Day, a time to remember, in a society that takes showers for quickness and convenience, the luxury of days gone by and a good bath. Suggestions for the day include getting candles and oils. You might also want to read *The Tub People,* a collaboration between Pam Conrad, one of the most talented writers of her era, and illustrator Richard Egielski.

A family of Tub People stands in a straight line at the edge of the bathtub, seven of them, all in order. First the father, then mother, grandmother, the doctor, the policeman, child, and dog. Very plain, made of wood, they can still smile or frown or laugh or cry. Readers follow the adventures of this group, playing games on cakes of floating soap and engaging in water races. Then when the bath is over, they always line up along the edge of the tub in order.

But into this ideal world, tragedy strikes. One day the little boy gets pulled down into the drain without a sound. The rest of them look through the grating and cannot see him; and so they line up, leaving a space for the boy, quite dejected. Although they still float in the tub, they call continually for the boy and all joy leaves their world. Fortunately, a plumber is called in and the Tub Child saved. Then all get placed on a soft bed, reunited again, and at night they line up against the windowsill, in proper order.

Although Pam Conrad died before she turned fifty, she created a wide body of fascinating work from 1985 to 1997 beginning with a historical novel, *Prairie Songs*, which won the International Reading Association's Award. Her children's book titles ranged from young adult novels to picture books; central to many of them was the experience of loss. She once wrote a fabulous book, *Call Me Ahnighito*, told from the point of view of an ancient rock, and she is just as deft with wooden toys as protagonists. Humans obviously interact with the Tub People, but we see events from the toys' point of view. The story has drama, pathos, and action—it has been perfectly paced for a picture book. And Egielski has created a family that you want to visit again and again.

So happy Bathtub Party Day—bring candles, your rubber ducky, or *The Tub People*!

THE MITTEN

By Jan Brett

December 6 marks Mitten Tree Day; to celebrate everyone is encouraged to decorate a Christmas tree with mittens (the tree and mittens can be real or cut out from brightly colored paper). Reading our book of the day, Jan Brett's *The Mitten*, is another great way to celebrate the day. While this book may not have a mitten in a tree, it certainly captures the feel and delight of this wintry article of clothing.

In a story adapted from a Ukrainian folk tale, Jan Brett relates the saga of Nikki, who wants mittens as white as snow. His grandmother Baba does not want to knit them, as they can be easily lost. But Nikki insists and finally gets his beautiful new white mittens, crafted with love and care. And, then, just as Baba predicted, he drops one of them in the snow.

What follows is a delicious repetitive sequence, in which the mitten becomes the home of many animals who crawl inside and snuggle together—rabbit, mole, hedgehog, fox, even a bear fit themselves into its warm space. To accommodate them, the mitten stretches and stretches. Finally bear's sneeze sends the mitten flying—onto Nikki's hand. In the end, although he brings both mittens back, Baba looks quizzically at one of them, now stretched to a much larger size.

A perfect cumulative tale, ideal for story hour or reading to a family, *The Mitten* features exquisite artwork that showcases Jan Brett's strengths as an artist. On many pages, scenes depicting the action of the text have been framed by borders that look like birch bark. In the border on one side, a panel shows Nikki playing and on the other side panels depict the animal that will appear next. This structure allows children to follow many stories and to anticipate the next page. Based on Ukrainian folk art, the drawings feature strong portraits of the animal characters and create a snowbound and enticing landscape.

Although for years I have used a dog-eared version of this book, I just purchased and would recommend the 20th Anniversary Edition, which has been lavishly produced and makes a very attractive present. Whatever edition you use on Mitten Tree Day or any other day in December, this totally satisfying picture book should be part of any winter celebration. It combines fantasy and reality in equal doses—the perfect offering on a cold winter's day.

DECEMBER 6

It's the birth date of Cornelia Meigs (1884–1973), *Invincible Louisa, Swift Rivers*; Jim Kjelgaard (1910–1959), *Big Red*; and Elizabeth Yates (1905–2001), *Amos Fortune, Free Man.*

In 1768 the first edition of *Encyclopædia Britannica* was published. Read the Encyclopedia Brown series by Donald Sobol.

Thomas Edison created the first human voice recording—"Mary had a little lamb"—in 1877. Read *Mary Had a Little Lamb* by Sarah Hale, illustrated by Tomie dePaola.

It's Mitten Tree Day. Read *The Mitten Tree* by Candace Christiansen, illustrated by Elaine Greenstein, and *A Mountain of Mittens* by Lynn Plourde, illustrated by Mitch Vane.

DECEMBER 7

It's the birth date of **Willa Cather** (1873–1947), *O Pioneers!*, *My Antonia*. Read *Willa Cather: Author and Critic* by Bettina Ling.

In 1941 Japanese pilots attacked Pearl Harbor. Thus, it's National Pearl Harbor Remembrance Day. Read *Boy at War* by Harry Mazer and *Pearl Harbor Is Burning* by Kathleen Kudlinksi.

Happy Birthday Delaware, which became the very first U.S. state on this day in 1787.

The microwave oven was patented in 1945. Read *Kingdom: Micro Monsters* by Nam Nguyen and *Pie's in the Oven* by Betty Birney, illustrated by Holly Meade.

It's one of two annual National Cotton Candy Days. The other is July 31. Cotton candy became popular at the 1904 St. Louis World's Fair.

THE PHILHARMONIC GETS DRESSED

By Karla Kuskin

Illustrated by Marc Simont

On December 7, 1842, the first concert of the New York Philharmonic, the first symphony orchestra founded in America, was performed. Over the years, the Philharmonic has performed more than 15,000 times. Many families attend formal events involving orchestra concerts during the holiday season and Karla Kuskin's *The Philhormonic Gets Dressed* will immediately make a child think that musicians would be a lot of fun to hang out with.

Karla Kuskin tackles the question of how do musicians prepare themselves for a concert. Presenting the 105 players of the symphony, Kuskin talks about their activities before the performance—bathing, drying themselves off, and putting on underwear and over wear. Then fully dressed in black and white they head out to take cabs, cars, subways, and buses that will deliver them to the concert hall. Finally assembled in Philharmonic Hall, the symphony waits for the conductor; after he steps on to the stand, they get to work, playing beautifully. Kuskin's text is just right, a balance of information and whimsy. But Marc Simont really steals the show in his virtuoso performance as illustrator in this book. He brings these orchestra players to life—depicting them as human beings, fat and skinny, strange and beautiful, in various stages of undress. Every page causes a chuckle from two- to eight-year-olds, as they watch these musicians getting ready for a big event. Because the book brings preparation for a concert to a child's eye view, it makes the concert hall seem more friendly and approachable. Some savvy parents even use this book as a bedtime story.

This book will make readers want to run, not walk, to the nearest concert hall so they can soak up the music. Happy birthday to the New York Philharmonic—and happy listening to concertgoers everywhere. However you listen to the music of the season, this book will make it more enjoyable for all members of the family.

THE INVENTION OF HUGO CABRET

By Brian Selznick

On December 8, 1861, Georges Méliès was born in Paris, France. He became one of the first French filmmakers, renowned for his creative development of motion pictures. Delighting in special effects, Méliès explored time-lapse photography and hand-painted color in films. His most famous movie, *A Trip to the Moon* (1902), features a scene where a spaceship lands on the eye of the man in the moon. It's reasonable to say that prior to 2007 only a handful of children or adults in America would have heard of Méliès and his work. Although today he is not exactly a household name, with *The Invention of Hugo Cabret* Brian Selznick created an awareness of his work.

In a 534-page novel every bit as revolutionary as Méliès's films, Selznick pays tribute to the French filmmaker as he takes six- to fourteen-year-old readers along on an adventure told half in text and half in pictures. The design of this book immediately catches the attention of readers. It is, in fact, one of the best designed volumes of the decade. Besides the cover, which displays the only color in the book, the story is told in a black-and-white format, one that resembles the motion pictures of the early 1900s. Our hero, twelve-year-old Hugo, orphan and thief, lives in the walls of a busy Paris train station at the turn of the twentieth century. Before Hugo's father died, he had been working on an automaton, trying to get the robot to function; Hugo also becomes obsessed with making this mechanical man work. But one day when stealing toys from a shopkeeper at the station, Hugo gets caught. Ultimately this exchange brings our birthday boy, Georges Méliès, out of hiding. Even the subplots of this sprawling novel have subplots; and because so much of the story is told in art, every reader has a slightly different version of what happens in the book.

Although *The Invention of Hugo Cabret* has 534 pages, the text is frequently broken by picture sequences. Hence it is easier to read than it looks. That has been one of the greatest advantages of this book. Even reluctant third- and fourth-grade readers find themselves swept along, many of them finishing a large book for the first time—one that can be proudly displayed to family and friends. "I read this book four times," one youngster wrote. "I was nine years old the first time I read it."

I've seen these children, often holding two or three copies of this impressive tome, standing in lines for hours to get an autograph from their hero, Brian Selznick. Already popular, the book has come to the attention of many more readers because of the award-winning film *Hugo*.

Whether you know George Méliès's films or not, read *Hugo Cabret* to celebrate his birthday. You will be awed and inspired.

DECEMBER 8

It's the birth date of Padraic Colum (1881–1972), *The Children's Homer*; and James Thurber (1894–1961), *Many Moons, The 13 Clocks*.

It's also the birthday of Roman lyric poet Horace (65–8 BC). Read *Horace* by Holly Keller and *Horace and Morris but Mostly Dolores* by James Howe, illustrated by Amy Walrod.

It's also the birth date of Eli Whitney, inventor of the cotton gin.

The first acknowledgment on national television that women sometimes are pregnant occurred in an episode of *I Love Lucy* on this day in 1952. Read *It's So Amazing!* by Robie H. Harris, illustrated by Michael Emberley and *Where Did That Baby Come From?* by Debi Gliori.

DECEMBER 9

It's the birth date of Jerome Beatty Jr. (1918–2002), Matthew and Maria Looney series; Jean de Brunhoff (1899–1937), Babar series; Joel Chandler Harris (1848–1908), Uncle Remus stories; and John Milton (1608–1674), *Paradise Lost*.

It's also the birth date of Emmett Kelly Sr. aka Weary Willy (1898–1979), a famous tramp clown known for trying to sweep a pool of light. It's Weary Willy Day, in honor of this sad-clown performer. Read *Clown* by Quentin Blake, *The Clown of God* by Tomie dePaola, and *My Friend Is Sad* by Mo Willems.

It's Anna's Day, celebrating people named Anna in Sweden and Finland, and also marking the day to start preparing lutefisk for Christmas Eve.

FRINDLE
By Andrew Clements
Illustrated by Brian Selznick

On December 9, 1793, Noah Webster established his newspaper, *American Minerva*. In 1828 Webster published *An American Dictionary of the English Language* and became the father of the American dictionary. The hero of the book of the day, Andrew Clements's *Frindle*, wants to get a new word accepted by the dictionary.

Nick Allen is smart, funny, and incredibly inventive. He always thinks outside the box and usually doesn't even know there is a box. Now in fifth grade, he finds himself in the language arts classroom of Mrs. Granger, a woman who loves words and the dictionary. While reporting on the development of this reference tool, Nick comes up with one of his fabulous ideas. He will invent a word, get everyone he knows to use it, and create a new dictionary entry. In *Frindle*, Nick takes a writing pen, renames it "frindle," and then watches as events spin out of control.

For one thing, he meets stern resistance in Mrs. Granger, who has some strong ideas about the appropriate use of language. But the students in school take up the cause of saying and writing *frindle*, as an exercise in civil disobedience. The media even gets involved. But as Shakespeare said, "All's well that ends well," and *Frindle* has a totally satisfying, even tear-producing, ending.

A staple of summer reading lists since it was published in 1996, *Frindle* can be used for a variety of classroom exercises. Author Andrew Clements knows how to keep the story going so that readers want to turn the pages. Some teachers combine reading the book with asking the class to develop its own dictionary. Everyone gets a letter of the alphabet and researches old words—and like Nick they can add a new one of their own making. As a read aloud or read alone, the book has broad appeal for third through fifth graders.

Andrew Clements attended Northwestern University, hoping to become a writer, and then received a Masters of Arts in Teaching. For about seven years, he taught in public schools north of Chicago. Then he worked as a singer-songwriter in New York before turning to publishing. While at a small press called Picture Book Studio he not only worked as editorial director, but he also began writing his own picture books. In 1990, Clements started working on *Frindle*, the book that allowed him to realize his dream of becoming a writer full time.

Still teacher at heart, Andrew Clements knows how to write funny, contemporary fiction true to children's behavior, that allows kids to think about greater issues as they enjoy the process of reading. Andrew is actually my hero of the day—even before Noah Webster and Nick Allen.

THE WIND IN THE WILLOWS

By Kenneth Grahame

Illustrated by Ernest H. Shepard

Often, with classic children's books, we remember both the writer and the illustrator. So Lewis Carroll brings to mind the illustrations of Sir John Tenniel. Contemporary readers appreciate Tenniel more than Lewis Carroll ever did—Carroll was basically disappointed with the art for *Alice in Wonderland*.

Fortunately, our birthday celebrant, Ernest H. Shepard, born in 1859, found more appreciative writers when he matched their texts with his drawings. Both A. A. Milne and Kenneth Grahame thought him amazingly sensitive to their work. Milne recommended Shepard to Grahame, who had long wanted an illustrated edition of *The Wind in the Willows*. "I love these little people, be kind to them," Grahame implored E. H. Shepard when he handed over the text for what became the 1931 edition of the book.

By that time Grahame had hunted for many years for an illustrator for his tale. Afraid that it might go out of print, Grahame thought an illustrated edition might be a good idea. He approached England's premier illustrator, Arthur Rackham, who turned him down. Many of Grahame's contemporaries didn't know quite what to think about this unusual blend of whimsy and chaos. In a few acres of English countryside, Rat, Mole, and Toad of Toad Hall get caught up in one escapade, or chase scene, after another. But each character basically longs for home.

When Grahame worked with Shepard on *The Wind in the Willows*, the author showed the illustrator the nearby river that had inspired the book. Shepard spent time there with his sketchbooks, searching for details like Rat's boathouse or holes in the ground where Mole might live. Although Grahame did not live to see the book finished, he approved the drafts that Shepard provided and knew before he died that his characters were being given the care and attention they needed.

In 1972, a few years before his death, Shepard received the Order of the British Empire. An even more important honor is that every day young readers pick up the books for which he became famous.

DECEMBER 10

Happy Birthday Cornelia Funke (*Inkheart*).

It's the birth date of Rumer Godden (1907–1988), *The Doll's House, An Episode of Sparrows*; George MacDonald (1824–1905), *Phantastes, The Princess and the Goblin*; and Mary Norton (1903–1992), *The Borrowers*.

It's also the birth date of poet Emily Dickinson (1830–1886). Read *Emily* by Michael Bedard, illustrated by Barbara Cooney, and *I'm Nobody! Who Are You?: Poems by Emily Dickinson for Young People* illustrated by Rex Schneider.

Melvil Dewey (1851–1931), creator of the Dewey Decimal classification system, was born on this day. Hence, it's Dewey Decimal Day. Read *Bob the Alien Discovers the Dewey Decimal System* by Sandy Donovan, illustrated by Martin Haake.

Happy Birthday Mississippi, which became the 20th U.S. state on this day in 1817.

DECEMBER 11

Happy Birthday Jim Harrison (*The Boy Who Ran to the Woods*) and William Joyce (*Rolie Polie Olie*).

It's the birth date of Harriet Stratemeyer Adams (1892–1982), ghostwriter for the Nancy Drew and Hardy Boys books who took over the Stratemeyer Syndicate after the death of her father, Edward Stratemeyer (1862–1930); and Marjorie Henderson Buell (1904–1993), *Little Lulu*.

Happy Birthday Indiana, which became the 19th U.S. state in 1816, and to UNICEF, established in 1946.

It's International Mountain Day. Read *Where the Mountain Meets the Moon* by Grace Lin, *When I Was Young in the Mountains* by Cynthia Rylant, illustrated by Diane Goode, and *My Side of the Mountain* by Jean Craighead George.

THE MONEY WE'LL SAVE
By Brock Cole

December has been designated Read a New Book Month. Certainly in December many people are hunting for new books both to read and to give as gifts. Well, if you are hunting for a picture book for four- to eight-year-olds and could use a good laugh, I recommend the book of the day, Brock Cole's *The Money We'll Save*. I laughed so much the first time that I read this story I started to cry.

In a saga about a dysfunctional family living in a nineteenth-century New York City tenement, Ma needs two eggs and a half a pound of flour. All the children—Bailey, Bridget, Pearl, and baby Arthur—are busy, so she sends Pa to the store. She tells him to be careful shopping, because they need every penny they have since Christmas is on the way. Well, Pa manages to avoid a lot of temptations, but the chicken man convinces him to buy a turkey poult that can be fattened up for Christmas dinner. And, so, Pa returns, pleased as punch, thinking of the money they will save.

Although by now readers have an inkling that trouble is about to ensue, Cole plays out the rest of the story brilliantly. The family puts the bird, now named Alfred, in a wooden box by the stove. Soon Alfred, who quickly becomes a mess and a glutton, has to be placed in a pen on the fire escape. They hang the pen on a clothesline for a week, and then must bring the bird into their apartment. Alfred gets the bedroom, and the family moves into the kitchen. Readers watch with delight as the home, once ordered and neat, becomes chaotic and crowded. And, of course, in the end the children have no desire to eat their friend Alfred for dinner. Fortunately, a perfect ending rounds out this romp of a tale.

Brock Cole does so many things well in this book. He uses delicious language and sentences. He develops characters in both art and text. He tells a story that you can read again and again, savoring it each time. In this holiday season, where many may have to think about economy, he reminds us of the true spirit of these days.

I'm happy to have a title that reminds me why the picture book format is so special, with its wonderful blend between text and art. And think of the money you'll save by buying a book that you can read again and again and pass down to the next generation!

SNOW

By Uri Shulevitz

In some areas of the country, the first snowfall comes in October, but depending on where you are, you may still be waiting for the first snow of the season.

In *Snow*, Caldecott winner Uri Shulevitz captures that childlike delight in even one snowflake. Upon seeing it, both a boy and his dog begin celebrating. The adults—grandfathers, men, women—of the community remain a bit more dismissive and say that the snow will melt. But our hero keeps counting snowflakes with glee. Radio and TV tell everyone there will be no snow—but snow doesn't listen to radio or watch TV. And so the snow keeps coming, floating through the air, delighting the boy and dog, and bringing the characters in the store window of Mother Goose Books out to dance and prance in the white world. The lyrical text ends simply with the words, " 'Snow,' said the boy."

For several decades Shulevitz has demonstrated a mastery of the picture-book format. In fact, his book *Writing with Pictures* remains the best book published for illustrators or those wanting to understand the picture-book form. *Snow* showcases his talents perfectly; he sets scenes, creates characters through action, utilizes every part of a double-page spread, and keeps readers turning the pages. In a Shulevitz picture book, less is more. Every page has been stripped down to its essential elements. Winner of a Caldecott Honor, *Snow*, from the title page to the final moment, reminds us just how great a classic picture book can be when it has been executed by a master.

But given all his talent, Uri Shulevitz may well be the most humble member of the children's book community. When he won the Caldecott Medal in 1970 for *The Fool of the World and the Flying Ship*, Shulevitz had not been sitting by the phone, waiting for "the call" as many authors and illustrators have over the years. A habitual night owl who usually slept late, Shulevitz had actually gotten up early the morning of the announcement. But when his editor called and said, "Congratulations," he believed she was praising him for being an early riser that day.

In *Snow* this humble creator provides a totally satisfying picture book, one that remains true to the spirit of childhood.

DECEMBER 12

Happy Birthday Barbara Emberley (*Drummer Hoff*).

It's the birth date of Ben Lucien Burman (1896–1984), Catfish Bend series.

Happy Birthday Pennsylvania, which became the second U.S. state on this day in 1787.

In 1982 thirty thousand women held hands to form a human chain around the nine-mile-perimeter fence at a Royal Air Force base, Greenham Commons, in Berkshire, England, to protest nuclear weapons. Read *The Fight for Peace* by Ted Gottfried.

It's Poinsettia Day. Read *The Miracle of the First Poinsettia* by Joanne Oppenheim, illustrated by Fabian Negrin, *The Legend of the Poinsettia* by Tomie dePaola, and *Poinsettia & Her Family* by Felicia Bond.

DECEMBER 13

It's the birth date of Leonard Weisgard (1916–2000), *The Little Island*, *The Important Book*, *The Night Before Christmas*.

 Mary Todd Lincoln (1818–1882), First Lady of the United States during her husband Abraham's presidency, was born on this day. Read *Lincolns: a Scrapbook Look at Abraham and Mary* by Candace Fleming.

Happy Birthday to *A Christmas Carol* by Charles Dickens, published in 1843.

It's National Cocoa Day. Curl up with a hot mug of the chocolaty drink and read *Cowgirl Kate and Cocoa* by Erica Silverman, illustrated by Betsy Lewin.

THE BEST CHRISTMAS PAGEANT EVER

By Barbara Robinson

Around this time of year, many families, some who do not even regularly attend church, find themselves supporting the local Christmas Pageant. This event, acted out in communities across America, allows children to play starring roles in the story of the birth of Jesus Christ. Sometimes even local animals make debut appearances in the annual event. Before you observe this ritual, you might want to pick up Barbara Robinson's incredibly funny *The Best Christmas Pageant Ever*. Narrated by a young girl whose mother is brought in at the last minute to direct the local pageant, the book introduces one of the most wicked casts of characters in a book celebrating the Christmas season: the Herdmans. They are "absolutely the worst kids in the history of the world." They smoke cigars (even the girls) and burn down property; they torment classmates and terrorize the community.

One day, on a tip that food can be found in church, the entire Herdman family shows up—just in time to volunteer for all the main parts in the local Christmas pageant. Consequently, the children who normally play these roles get shifted to the sidelines. Then chaos erupts.

The Herdmans have never heard the Christmas story, and when they begin to comprehend how badly Mary and her poor baby were treated so many years ago, they bring a whole new level of emotion to the event. Fortunately, they don't leave the stage to go off and kill Herod—although that is their first response. But what they deliver is an unusual, although authentic, rendition of the Christmas story. The narrator closes the story saying, "as far as I'm concerned, Mary is always going to look a lot like Imogene Herdman—sort of nervous and bewildered, but ready to clobber anyone who laid a hand on her baby."

One of the tasks of great children's book writers is to show characters changing in a believable way over the course of the narrative. Few have ever done this as well as Barbara Robinson as she brings the Herdmans on their journey of transformation—one that extends to everyone else in the community as well. The book depicts how a child who has never heard the Christmas story might experience it for the first time. Yet, all eighty pages remain laugh-out-loud funny.

Made into a classic TV movie, the book remains one of the greatest Christmas books ever written. Like the narrator of the story, I find myself thinking of the events of Christmas in an entirely different way each time I read the book. It makes me wish that my local Christmas pageant would forgo the sheep brought in for the event and import the Herdmans.

THE TWENTY-ONE BALLOONS

By William Pène du Bois

On December 14, 1782, the Montgolfier brothers' first balloon lifted off on its first test flight. Later they would conduct public demonstrations, taking a thirty-three-foot diameter balloon aloft for about ten minutes. From this humble beginning, humans sailing the skies in hot-air balloons became a possibility.

William Waterman Sherman, the protagonist of the Newbery Medal book *The Twenty-One Balloons* by William Pène du Bois, has been teaching arithmetic to boys in San Francisco for forty years: "Forty years of spitballs. Forty years of glue on my seat." So at the age of sixty-six, he retires, builds a hot-air balloon, and sets off to sail around the world.

But as he soon discovers, being airborne produces other problems besides spitballs. Seagulls start to eat his balloon and create a huge hole. After he plummets into the sea, he finds shelter on an island beach. This is not just any island, but the remarkable island of Krakatoa, built on the wealth of massive diamond mines. The island seems like paradise: the residents have constructed amazing homes, each one organized around the architecture of a different county, and filled them with conveniences. Their beds, for instance, have sheets that mechanically change every day and get washed, dried, and pressed. After a life of service, the professor might well have lived a life of luxury. But as is always true, timing is everything, because he has landed three days before a volcano erupts. Science, invention, fantasy, science fiction, and action all come together in a book that moves from one amazing plot detail to another.

Children's books change lives. When another great teacher, Dr. Jerry J. Mallett, took his first course in children's literature, he read *The Twenty-One Balloons* and became enchanted with Pène du Bois's pencil illustrations for the book. This led him to other picture books, and he began purchasing illustrations from those books. Today the Mazza Museum of International Art from Picture Books in Findlay, Ohio, contains this early collection as well as thousands of other pieces added over the years. As Dr. Mallett says in *Everything I Need to Know I Learned from a Children's Book*, "it is never too late to have your life changed by a children's book."

So if you want to read a ripping-good story, pick up *The Twenty-One Balloons*. Even if it doesn't change your life, it will certainly keep you engaged with its humor and panache.

DECEMBER 14

Happy Birthday John Neufeld (*Lisa, Bright and Dark*).

It's the birth date of Rosemary Sutcliff (1920–1992), *Eagle of the Ninth*; and Shirley Jackson (1916–1965), *Life Among Savages, The Lottery*.

Happy Birthday Alabama, which became the 22nd U.S. state on this day in 1819. Hence, it's Alabama Day. Read *Alabama Moon* by Watt Key.

In 1911 **Roald Amundsen**, Olav Bjaaland, Helmer Hanssen, Sverre Hassel, and Oscar Wisting become the first team to reach the South Pole. Read *Race to the South Pole: The Antarctic Challenge*, edited by Arthur M. Schlesinger Jr.

DECEMBER 15

Happy Birthday Daniel Pinkwater (*The Big Orange Splot*) and Maira Kalman (*Fireboat*).

Roman Emperor Nero (37–68) was born on this day. Read *Nero Corleone* by Elke Heidenreich, illustrated by Quint Buchholz.

 Also born on this date was Gustave Eiffel (1832–1923), engineer and architect of the **Eiffel tower**. Read *Eiffel's Tower* by Jill Jonnes and *Madeline* by Ludwig Bemelmans.

It's Bill of Rights Day. The United States Bill of Rights became law when ratified by the Virginia General Assembly in 1791. Read *A Kids' Guide to America's Bill of Rights: Curfews, Censorship, and the 100-Pound Giant* by Kathleen Krull, illustrated by Anna Divito.

MILLIONS OF CATS
By Wanda Gág

December 15 has been designated Cat Herding Day. Certainly, this impossible task deserves to be celebrated! Over eighty years ago a classic children's book demonstrated what a lot of herded cats might look like—although it left the way to accomplish this feat unexplained. In the history of picture books, men have created the vast majority of classics, but our first celebrated American picture book, *Millions of Cats*, which won a Newbery Honor because the Caldecott had not yet been established, was created by a very talented woman.

Minnesota's Wanda Gág had come to New York and was showing her bold prints in galleries when editor Ernestine Evans contacted her. Evans, just hired to create a children's book department for Coward-McCann, saw an exhibit of Gág's prints and approached her to see if she would consider creating children's books. Materials at the Kerlan Collection at the University of Minnesota indicate that Gág had started a children's book story around 1922 but had abandoned it. Encouraged by Evans, she picked it up again, focused the story, and made the refrain occur many more times: "Cats here, cats there, / Cats and kittens everywhere, / Hundreds of cats, / Thousands of cats, / Millions and billions and trillions of cats."

In *Millions of Cats* an old man goes out to find a kitten for his wife. He travels over hills and valleys and locates far too many. But after they eat each other up, only one thin scraggly kitten is left. In the end it becomes the beautiful cat the man and woman have sought. The language and feel of the story reflect Gág's German roots; in fact, she would later translate and illustrate volumes of Grimm's fairy tales for her adoring audience.

As classics go, *Millions of Cats* has one of the shortest creation times on record. Gág had only a couple of months to craft the text and art. In the end she relied on the help of others; her brother actually hand-lettered the text. In *Millions of Cats* Gág pushed the boundaries of the picture book. She developed double-page spreads, pulling the two pages together with an image. She wrapped text around the art. Using a varied layout and alternating broad vistas with intimate scenes, she developed pacing, timing, and tension. In one title, she basically invented the American picture book.

So today I'd like to honor our great-great-grandmother, as it were, of the American picture book. In 1928 she set in motion ideas about this form that others would take eight decades to explore. Considered one of the finest artists of her day, Gág also lent credibility to the emerging genre of picture books. Thousands of picture books every year—that focus on page layout, pacing, and timing—all have their beginning in *Millions of Cats*.

JUDY MOODY DECLARES INDEPENDENCE

By Megan McDonald

Illustrated by Peter H. Reynolds

On December 16, 1773, the Boston Tea Party took place. The details of the event have always sounded a bit like a college prank to me. A bunch of rebels, dressed up in disguise with faces painted, descend on a small British ship and dump some boxes of tea overboard. Of what significance would such an act be to anyone? But Sam Adams and the Sons of Liberty made their prank widely known, so that it became a symbol of the rebellion. From this moment on, the American Colonies moved inexorably toward open rebellion with England.

In Megan McDonald's *Judy Moody Declares Independence*, the spirited heroine of her own series of popular books, Judy Moody, visits Boston, the Tea Party ship, the Freedom Trail, and Paul Revere's house. In doing so she begins to get some very strong ideas about her own independence. Just like the early colonists, she draws up a list of demands. Hers include more allowance and a private bathroom. Sam Adams and the Sons of Liberty would definitely understand the allowance part, but the bathroom might leave them scratching their heads.

DECEMBER 16

Happy Birthday Quentin Blake (*The BFG*, *Matilda*, *Clown*), who served as the United Kingdom's first Children's Laureate from 1999 to 2001, and Peter Dickinson (*The Ropemaker*).

It's the birth date of Marie Hall Ets (1893–1984), *Play With Me*, *Nine Days to Christmas*.

Also born on this day were **Jane Austen** (1775–1817), *Pride and Prejudice*; and Sir Arthur C. Clarke (1917–2008), *2001: A Space Odyssey*.

It's also the birth date of Ludwig van Beethoven (1771–1827), German composer best known for his Ninth Symphony.

The last recorded eruption of Japan's Mount Fuji took place in 1701. Read *I Will Never Not Ever Eat a Tomato* by Lauren Child, because of a line referring to mashed potatoes as "cloud fluff from the pointiest peak of Mount Fuji."

It's National Chocolate-Covered Anything Day.

However, Judy continues her quest when she and her brother Stink return home. And then she discovers another cause that she can get behind when she learns that a girl, Sybil Ludington, matched the accomplishments of Paul Revere, but has been passed over by history. This situation contains just the sort of injustice that makes Judy her most creative.

Since the first book about Judy Moody, *Judy Moody Was in a Mood*, appeared ten years ago, Judy has gained a devoted audience of six- to ten-year-olds—with more than ten million books in print worldwide and translations into over twenty languages. Although few can rival author Megan McDonald when it comes to humor, word play, and snappy dialogue, Peter H. Reynolds's drawings of characters and scenes provide just as much enjoyment as the text.

If you have missed their collaboration, reading *Judy Moody Declares Independence* today will allow you to celebrate this talented duo as well as the Boston Tea Party.

DECEMBER 17

It's the birth date of Ford Madox Ford (1873–1939), *The Good Soldier*; John Kennedy Toole (1937–1969), *A Confederacy of Dunces*; and abolitionist and poet John Greenleaf Whittier (1807–1892).

It's the first flight date of the Douglas DC-3 plane (1935), whose size and range helped establish the airline industry, and of the Boeing B-47 Stratojet (1947), which led to modern jet design for airliners.

It's National Maple Syrup Day. Read *Sugaring Time* by Kathryn Lasky, illustrated by Christopher G. Knight.

THE WRIGHT BROTHERS: HOW THEY INVENTED THE AIRPLANE

By Russell Freedman

December 17 was declared Wright Brothers Day in 1963 by Presidential Proclamation. Certainly these two Buckeyes, who lived their lives in Dayton, Ohio, have inspired numerous books for children. But the best remains Russell Freedman's *The Wright Brothers: How They Invented the Airplane*, a Newbery Honor book published two decades ago.

Few in the history of children's books have ever surpassed Freedman in his ability to write intelligently and gracefully about a variety of figures—Abraham Lincoln, Eleanor Roosevelt, or Marian Anderson. Freedman begins his story with the chapter, "What Amos Root Saw." Standing in a cow pasture near Dayton, Amos, a beekeeper by trade, watched the Wright brothers fly an airplane for a minute and a half. As he later wrote, "When Columbus discovered America he did not know what the outcome would be, and no one at the time knew. . . . In a like manner these two brothers have probably not even a faint glimpse of what their discovery is going to bring to the children of men."

Freedman then goes on to present the Wrights, their family, their lack of education—neither graduated from high school—and their dreams. Like Icarus from Greek mythology, the boys wanted to fly. Many others pursued the same dream at the same time—people with money and recognition. True American icons, the Wright brothers had neither backing nor credentials, but they possessed true grit.

Freedman brilliantly takes readers through the failed attempts of the brothers in North Carolina's Kill Devil Hills, and shows what they learned at each step. They are always guided by common sense and their ability to observe the natural world. Watching buzzards glide, they made suppositions about balance and control of wings. They proceeded cautiously, step by step. Wilber once wrote to his father, "I do not intend to take dangerous chances, both because I have no wish to get hurt and because a fall would stop my experimenting." Each year they headed back to Dayton where they designed wind tunnels or changed their model. Finally, on December 17, 1903, at 10:35 a.m., the Wright Flyer achieved the world's first successful powered and controlled airplane flight—lasting all of twelve seconds.

Most of this book focuses on the Wrights' attempts to fly and then promote flight around the world. Because they knew the importance of their goal, they recorded it in photography and left three hundred glass-plate negatives. Freedman has lavishly illustrated this book with their own visual record. Hence it allows young readers to go back to the early 1900s, to watch and dream and spend time with Wilber and Orville. Give it to the budding inventors in your life—and show them how two amateurs triumphed.

NOTHING BUT THE TRUTH

By Avi

On December 18, 1956, one of the most popular long-running television shows, *To Tell the Truth*, premiered. Truth, of course, is a slippery thing. What seems true to one person does not appear that way to another. One of our best novels for ten- to fourteen-year-olds, published in 1991 and already a classic, explores the issues of what is true, what is false, and what is misleading.

In Avi's *Nothing But the Truth*, ninth grader Phillip Malloy faces problems both at school and at home. His only release comes in running and in his dreams of making the track team. But a D in English, from veteran teacher Margaret Narwin, ends his quest—although the track coach suggests that Phillip simply go to the teacher and see if he can make up work. Phillip takes another approach—goading her. In her home room, when "The Star-Spangled Banner" is played "for respectful silent attention" over the public announcement system, Phillip starts to hum. After this continues and he refuses to stop, Ms. Narwin sends him to the vice principal, who eventually suspends him for repeated incidents of disrespect. Then Phillip and his father talk to the press—about the unpatriotic nature of the school. At this point, the national media coverage causes the situation to spiral out of control.

The story itself is so suspensefully crafted that it would be a page-turner even if told as a straight narrative. But Avi has presented the differing points of view by using a variety of forms—memos, letters, conversations, interviews, and Phillip's diary. Hence readers get to see the evolving story from multiple perspectives.

Well written, well paced, and provocative, *Nothing But the Truth* works brilliantly when read by a group—because everyone will come to a slightly different understanding of the events, depending on how he or she reads the evidence. How truthful would their testimonies seem to be if Phillip or Margaret Narwin were tried in a court of law? The book also examines how accurately our media reports real incidents.

Avi's *Nothing But the Truth* is an engaging story, but it also causes readers to think about truth, lies, and their consequences.

DECEMBER 18

Happy Birthday Marilyn Sachs (*The Bear's House, A Pocket Full of Seeds*).

It's the birth date of Alison Uttley (1884–1976), *A Country Child, A Traveler in Time*.

Also born on this day was the Soviet Union leader **Joseph Stalin** (1878–1953). Read *The Inner Circle: An Inside View of Soviet Life Under Stalin*, by Andrei Konshalovsky and Alexander Lipkov.

It's New Jersey Day, in honor of this state's birthday. In 1787 New Jersey was the third state to ratify the U.S. Constitution. Read *Voices from Colonial America: New Jersey 1609–1776* by Robin Doak and *The Wizard, The Witch, and Two Girls from Jersey* by Lisa Papademetriou.

It's also Bake Cookies Day.

DECEMBER 19

Happy Birthday Eve Bunting (*One More Flight*, *Smoky Night*, *One Green Apple*).

It's the birth date of Carter Woodson (1875–1950), considered the "Father of Black History," who pioneered Negro History Week in February, which was eventually extended to Black History Month. Read *African Myths and Folk Tales* by Carter Woodson and *Carter G. Woodson* by Patricia and Fredrick McKissack.

It's Evergreen Day. Read *Mr. Willowby's Christmas Tree* by Robert Barry and *The Year of the Perfect Christmas Tree* by Gloria Houston, illustrated by Barbara Cooney.

A CHRISTMAS CAROL
By Charles Dickens

December 19 marks the anniversary of the publication of one of the most popular Christmas stories of all time. But when Charles Dickens set out to write *A Christmas Carol* in 1843, both his fortune and his reputation had hit an all-time low. "Boz [Dickens's pen name] is going down," the gossips declared, and Dickens's financial problems were known all over London. During this time the celebration of Christmas traditions in England were, as the poet Thomas Hood stated, "in danger of decay." But Dickens's short novella, written at fever pitch over a six-week period, would revive Dickens's reputation. With this small novel he also revitalized the Christmas holiday—just with the power of his pen.

Dickens drew on his own childhood and the life around him to fashion his story. Even the death of the child Tiny Tim was all too familiar to Dickens—he had lost a brother and a sister when a mere child himself. The boy Scrooge, left alone in the school during the holidays, finds children's books to be his only friend, just as Charles Dickens did. So drawing on experience and invention, Dickens locked himself in his house, excused himself from appointments, refused to see friends who dropped by, and worked all hours of the day and late into night. "No city clerk was ever more methodical or orderly than he," Dickens's eldest son Charley stated about his father.

As is often the case with groundbreaking books, Dickens met some opposition to his creation. Although he told a touching tale of the miser Ebenezer Scrooge and taught the meaning of Christmas through a series of ghostly visitors, his publisher didn't think the offering had much value. Ever the inventor, Dickens suggested the terms of his own arrangement. He would pay for the production of the book and be entitled to all profits; his publisher would get a small commission on each sale. (This is, by the way, a complete reversal of usual publishing arrangements.) Since Dickens controlled the book's production, he made some important decisions about this "Ghost Story of Christmas." The price would be kept low, only five shillings; he made the small book as handsome as possible, with a russet cloth binding and a stamp of gold on the front and spine.

Published on December 19, 1843, *A Christmas Carol* became an immediate sensation, going through several printings right away. Even the Scottish philosopher Thomas Carlyle, known to be dour, wrote, "on reading the book, sent out for a turkey, and asked two friends to dine." Thousands of editions have been issued over the years. Australian illustrator Robert Ingpen, winner of the Hans Christian Anderson Award, created an expressive and spirited rendition of the book in 2008. Today, of course, the book can be enjoyed in plays and movies, even now in a graphic novel.

Happy birthday to *A Christmas Carol*. This book reminds us that, as Scrooge's nephew Fred says, Christmas can be "a good time: a kind, forgiving, charitable, pleasant time: the only time I know of in the long calendar year, when men and women seem by one consent to open their shut-up hearts."

WRITTEN IN BONE: BURIED LIVES OF JAMESTOWN AND COLONIAL MARYLAND

By Sally M. Walker

On December 20, 1606, three small ships—*Godspeed*, *Susan Constant*, and *Discovery*—departed London, England, for Virginia. In May of the next year the men and boys on this ship founded the first permanent English settlement in America, Jamestown. Other colonists, including women, joined them in James Fort in 1608. In recent years members of the Jamestown Rediscover Project have tried to fill in gaps about our oldest settlement—by finding remnants of the fort and its surroundings and by reading the historical clues found in the bones of its skeletons.

In *Written in Bone: Buried Lives of Jamestown and Colonial Maryland*, one of the best science titles of the past few years for ten- to fourteen-year-olds, Sally M. Walker explains how modern techniques allow scientists to discover all types of details from old bones—how old the individuals were, what they ate, what type of life they lived, how they died, and even who they might be. As they watch forensic anthropologist Doug Owsley coax the stories from these skeletons, readers become familiar with how scientists work and think—and ultimately how they identify two of those first Jamestown settlers, teenage Richard Mutton and captain of the *Godspeed* Bartholomew Gosnold. In the process, Walker explains the early history of Jamestown, burying practices, and the lives of the first colonists. Then she travels to other excavations in the Chesapeake Bay area—one even reveals the murder of a young indentured servant, which took place in the 1660s. Discussing how forensic anthropology has contributed to our understanding of history, this fascinating treatise might encourage more than one reader to become part of an archaeological team. History, science, a passion for details, and a reverence for human life saturate these pages, which have been lavishly illustrated with photographs, maps, historical documents, and anatomical drawings.

Today, because of the contribution of Sally Walker, young readers can honor two of our founding ancestors—Richard Mutton and Captain Gosnold. And they can also celebrate the accomplishments of dedicated scientists like Doug Owsley.

DECEMBER 20

Happy Birthday M.B. Goffstein (*Fish for Dinner, Brookie and Her Lamb*) and Sharon Chmielarz (*Down at Angel's, The Other Mozart: Poems*).

The Louisiana Purchase was completed at a New Orleans ceremony in 1803. Read *Louisiana Purchase* by Peter and Connie Roop, illustrated by Sally Wern Comport.

On this day in 2007 Queen Elizabeth II became the oldest ever monarch of the United Kingdom. The previous record holder was Queen Victoria at eighty-one years seven months twenty-nine days. Read *A Little Princess* by Frances Hodgson Burnett, illustrated by Tasha Tudor, and *A Proud Taste for Scarlet and Miniver* by E. L. Konigsburg.

DECEMBER 21

It's the birth date of Albert Payson Terhune (1872–1942), *Gray Dawn, Lad: A Dog.*

In 1883 Royal Canadian Dragoons and The Royal Canadian Regiment are formed. Read *The RCMP Musical Ride* by Maxwell Newhouse.

In 1620 the pilgrims landed at Plymouth Rock.

It's Crossword Puzzle Day, in honor of the first crossword puzzle, created by Arthur Wynne and published in the newspaper *New York World* in 1913.

The animated film *Snow White and the Seven Dwarfs* premiered in movie theaters in 1937. Read a beautiful edition of the Brothers Grimm version of *Snow-White and the Seven Dwarfs* illustrated by Nancy Ekholm Burkert, translated by Randall Jarrell.

THE DARK IS RISING

By Susan Cooper

On December 21 or 22 we celebrate the winter solstice. On this day one of the most appealing characters in classic children's fantasy celebrates his eleventh birthday. Will Stanton, the seventh son of a seventh son, is in for some pretty big surprises during the holiday season. He learns that he is the last of the Old Ones, the Sign Seeker, who must find and gather the six signs—wood, bronze, water, fire, stone, and iron—to aid the Light in their fight against the Dark. In *The Dark Is Rising* Susan Cooper tells a saga as well as any of the contemporary plot-driven writers like Suzanne Collins and Rick Riordan. From the opening scene to the final page, she keeps readers breathlessly turning pages to see what will happen to Will and his family.

Of course, Cooper does so much more than develop a plot. She studied with the master himself, J.R.R. Tolkien, at Oxford and brings her classical British education to her work as a writer. Cooper has spent most of her career, however, in the United States because she married an American. Homesick for her own land, she turned to her hometown in Buckinghamshire for the setting for the Dark Is Rising sequence—and to the myth and folklore of her native England. Cooper's books offer a unique variation of high British fantasy, based on the legends and stories she knew as a child, woven together into a contemporary, reality-based saga. Five volumes comprise the Dark Is Rising sequence, and readers can begin with *The Dark Is Rising*, the second in the series, as it makes the best introduction.

When Will discovers that he has been given great gifts, he realizes their cost: "Any great gift or talent is a burden . . . and you will often long to be free of it. If you were born with the gift then you must serve it." And so with great danger to himself, not to mention that of his beloved family, he faces the powers of darkness over the holiday season, pulling off one amazing encounter after another. On his eleven-year-old shoulders rest the fate of the world. In Cooper's universe, characters move between centuries and across time to engage in their epic struggle.

If you and the children in your life have missed this spellbinding story, no day makes a better beginning than the solstice. An omnibus paperback edition of more than a thousand pages, *The Dark Is Rising: The Complete Sequence* brings all five books together for plenty of reading on the darkest night of the year.

JOHN HENRY

By Julius Lester
Illustrated by Jerry Pinkney

Today is the birthday of Jerry Pinkney, illustrator extraordinaire who has created more than two hundred books for children since he entered the field almost fifty years ago. Born in Philadelphia, Jerry studied at the Philadelphia Museum College of Art and then moved to Boston for work. In 1964 he published his first children's book, *The Adventures of Spider*. One of the few black illustrators in the industry at that time, even in his early books Jerry demonstrated superb artistic skills—great composition, pacing, vibrant line, and ability to delineate character. Because of this, he was offered many projects over the years, including the chance to add his artwork to classic books like Mildred Taylor's *Roll of Thunder, Hear My Cry* and Julius Lester's *The Tale of Uncle Remus*.

Over the years Julius Lester and Jerry Pinkney became frequent collaborators. Usually Julius chose the subject matter of their projects, but for *John Henry*, one of Pinkney's most brilliant picture books, Jerry suggested the idea because John Henry had been his childhood hero. When Lester realized that he could connect John Henry and Martin Luther King, Jr., he agreed to create the text. Pinkney illustrated this spirited rendition of the folk hero's life with panoramic landscapes and a John Henry so strong and vibrant that he seems to jump off the page.

I first met Jerry in 1970. He was, in fact, the first living children's book creator that I ever met, and I still have a vivid picture of him walking on Beacon Hill, carrying a portfolio of art to deliver to Little, Brown and Company publishers. Seeing Jerry and talking to him that day, I decided that children's book authors had to be the nicest people on the planet. And Jerry is still just that, after all these years. His humor, modesty, and continual kindness inform everything he creates and does.

His long career in children's books has provided great artistic satisfaction for him and a body of inspired titles for us. As he has written, his books have given him "the opportunity to use my imagination to draw, to paint, and to travel through the voices of the characters in the stories—and above all else, to touch children."

On Jerry's birthday, celebrate by reading *John Henry* or any of his other rich and wonderful books.

DECEMBER 22

It's the birth date of William O. Steele (1917–1979), *The Perilous Road*.

In 1864 Savannah, Georgia, fell to **General Sherman**, concluding his March to the Sea during the American Civil War. Read *Delivery Justice: W.W. Law and the Fight for Civil Rights* by Jim Haskins, illustrated by Benny Andrews.

Ito Hirobumi, a samurai, became the first prime minister of Japan in 1885. Read *Three Samurai Cats* by Eric Kimmel, illustrated by Mordicai Gerstein, and *Samurai* by Jason Hightman.

Beatrix Potter died on this day in 1943. Her legacy lives on in the wonderful books she wrote and illustrated, including *The Tale of Peter Rabbit* and *The Tale of Jemima Puddle-Duck*.

DECEMBER 23

Happy Birthday Avi (*Nothing But the Truth*, *The True Confessions of Charlotte Doyle*) and Erick Ingraham (*Hot-Air Henry*).

It's the birth date of Otto Soglow (1900–1975), cofounder of the National Cartoonist Society and creator of the long-running comic strip *The Little King*, which appeared in *The New Yorker*.

A few royal birthdays today: Natal anniversary greetings go to Akihito, the Emperor of Japan, and Queen of Sweden, Silvia Sommerlath. Read *The Birthday Ball* by Lois Lowry, illustrated by Jules Feiffer.

It's Festivus, a secular holiday introduced to popular culture by screenwriter Daniel O'Keefe. Read *Festivus: The Holiday for the Rest of Us* by Allen Salkin.

THE SNOWMAN
By Raymond Briggs

When winter comes around, I always think of one of my favorite books, first published in 1978, which truly captures the joy of playing in the snow. Although comic-book format picture books and graphic novels rule today, when Raymond Briggs used wordless, comic-book panels in *The Snowman*, he broke with the tradition of his time. However, the result was so magical than even adults who might have shunned comic books found themselves in love with his story.

In a book that works for preschoolers and those up to ten, a little boy wakes up to find a snow-filled landscape and goes out to build a snowman. But when the boy checks on his creation that night, it has come alive and tips its hat to the boy. Then the snowman enters the house, plays with the boy, and shares a meal with him. Finally, the two set off together on a magical flight that takes them over land and sea. In the morning, the boy goes out to find a melted snowman, an ending tinged with melancholy and loss.

As a boy, Raymond Briggs had always wanted to be a cartoonist. At fifteen, to pursue this dream, he became a student at the Wimbledon School of Art in London. Like other art students of the era, he received training in classical nineteenth-century composition and still-life and figure drawing. Eventually, he decided that he did not want to become a painter. However, when he finally returned to his childhood dream of making a comic book, he was able to bring all of his skills in draftsmanship, composition, and anatomy to *The Snowman*.

Although the landscape seems exotic, Briggs used his own home and garden in Sussex, at the foot of the South Downs, a few miles from Brighton. The snowman flies over the Downs to Brighton, and then the Royal Palace. Since Briggs wanted a feeling of childlike spontaneity in the drawings, he worked in pencil crayons to prepare the art. This medium created a book with soft color, almost as if every page has been muted by the fallen snow.

The Snowman draws on the power of a persistent childhood fantasy—what if the snowman you build could come alive? This completely satisfying and moving book was adapted quite successfully as an animated film often shown on television during the holidays. In *The Snowman* Raymond Briggs demonstrated how art alone, without any text, can convey a story that children delight in and remember.

CHRISTMAS IN THE TRENCHES

By John McCutcheon

Illustrated by Henri Sorensen

On December 24, 1818, "Silent Night" or "Stille Nacht," a Christmas carol with a beautiful melody and words of peace—one created by an Austrian priest and a headmaster—was first performed in the Church of St. Nicholas in Oberndorf, Austria.

During a concert in 1984 folksinger John Mc-Cutcheon heard a story that seized his imagination. One Christmas Eve during World War I English soldiers in the trenches sang Christmas carols to each other. Then, across the battlefield, Germans soldiers began singing "Stille Nacht," and both sides joined in, each in their own language. McCutcheon was so taken with this vignette that he wrote a song about it during the intermission of his concert, and "Christmas in the Trenches" became one of the great peace songs of the decade. Sung by an Englishman, Thomas Tolliver, the song tells of what happened that Christmas Eve in World War I and ends with the words, "on each side of the rifle we're the same."

In 2006 Atlanta-based Peachtree Press issued McCutcheon's retelling as a picture book for children with art by Henri Sorensen. Retold songs don't always make the best picture book texts, but *Christmas in the Trenches* is an exception to that rule. McCutcheon adds details that children need to the text, and Sorensen provides panoramic views of the battlefield and trenches. As the men wait for war, they hear a German singer strike up a song; soon all join in. After a flag of truce, the men exchange gifts and commodities and then head back to wait for the next day of war. A CD has been enclosed that includes McCutcheon reading the text and performing both "Stille Nacht" and his famous ballad. Together the book and CD bring this small incident of history to life and bring into focus the meaning of peace on Christmas Eve.

Together the book and CD make a perfect way to mark Christmas Eve—and one of the greatest songs of peace.

DECEMBER 24

Happy Birthday Noel Streatfeild (*Ballet Shoes*) and Stephenie Meyer (*Twilight*).

It's the birth date of Feodor Rojankovsky (1891–1970), *Over in the Meadow, Frog Went A-Courtin'*.

It's also the birth date of **Howard Hughes** (1905–1976), the aviator, inventor, filmmaker, philanthropist, and eventual recluse.

In 1851 a fire broke out at the Library of Congress and two-thirds of the collection burned. Read *American Treasures in the Library of Congress: Memory, Reason, Imagination*.

As well as Christmas Eve, it's National Eggnog Day.

DECEMBER 25

It's the birth date of Charles J. Finger (1869–1941), *Tales from Silver Lands*; and Johnny Gruelle (1880–1938), *Raggedy Ann and Raggedy Andy* stories.

Also born on this day was Clara Barton (1821–1912), founder of the American Red Cross.

Christians all over the world celebrate today as the birthday of Jesus Christ. Read *The Miracles of Jesus* by Tomie dePaola and *Jesus* by Demi.

In 1223 St. Francis of Assisi assembled the first nativity crèche. Read *The Nativity* by Julie Vivas and *Saint Francis and the Wolf* by Richard Egielski.

THE POLAR EXPRESS
By Chris Van Allsburg

In 1985 a book appeared by Caldecott-winning artist Chris Van Allsburg that would immediately become a bestseller and over the years establish itself as a picture book ritually read and enjoyed by families during the Christmas season: *The Polar Express*.

Chris came to his career as a children's book writer through his work as a sculptor. He fashioned intriguing pieces like "Sinking of the Titanic," and then drew black-and-white works in graphite and charcoal, which he exhibited in New York along with his sculpture. Every great creator needs a guardian angel to help him along, and in Chris's case that angel happened to be his wife, Lisa. She believed that her husband's drawings might be turned into a children's book and took his portfolio to editors in New York and Boston.

One of the most vivid memories of my career is of the day Lisa arrived in the Houghton Mifflin offices at 2 Park Street in Boston. Walter Lorraine, head of the children's book department and subsequently Chris's editor, asked Lisa to place these drawings along a wall so that everyone there could see them. I believed that I was looking at the work of someone who could change picture books in America. Chris incorporated so much storytelling content in a single piece that any viewer could write a short story about each one of these pictures. Many of those drawings, by the way, were later published in *The Mysteries of Harris Burdick*. That day Walter Lorraine gave Lisa the promise of a contract for any book her husband wanted to create. And the rest, as they say, is history.

His first book, *The Garden of Abdul Gasazi*, established Chris as one of the best new artists of the seventies. His second book, *Jumanji*, won the Caldecott Medal. His sixth book, *The Polar Express*, began as an image of a train standing in front of a young boy's house in the middle of the night. Where was it going? Van Allsburg thought it might be headed north, and then he decided that the train, The Polar Express, would transport children to the North Pole on Christmas Eve.

In pastel drawings on brown paper, Van Allsburg sketched out the journey of that magical train. At the North Pole, Santa and his elves greet the passengers—and he gives the young boy, who narrates the story, a bell that rings for all those who truly believe in Christmas. The book ends with a picture of the bell, one the narrator still hears ringing throughout his life.

Dedicated to Van Allsburg's sister, Karen, the book showcases a wonderful brother/sister relationship. As is true of so many classics, the story moved from the personal landscape of its author into the minds and hearts of millions of readers. It can be read as a magical adventure—or even as a statement about the nature of faith or belief.

ONE CRAZY SUMMER
By Rita Williams-Garcia

Today begins the celebration of Kwanzaa, extending through the first of January. Honoring African culture, Kwanzaa was created in 1966 to "give Blacks an alternative to the existing holidays." Today, December 26, marks the day to strive for and maintain unity in the family, community, nation, and race. But if you wanted to explain to children the beginnings of this holiday, how would you talk about the black national movement of this time period—one so different from today? If you are hunting for a Kwanzaa present or an appropriate title to explain the sixties pick up *One Crazy Summer* by Rita Williams-Garcia.

In *One Crazy Summer*, Rita has created a powerful book that explores a period in history while it pulls in young readers because of its engaging characters. In the summer of 1968, three sisters, Delphine, age eleven, Vonetta, and Fern, find themselves living for twenty-eight days with their mother, Cecile, in Oakland, California. She had abandoned all of them as children and does not seem particularly excited to see them in her living space. A poet and an activist, Cecile (called Nzila by the Black Panthers) forbids them entry to her kitchen and wants them out of the way all day.

DECEMBER 26

Happy Birthday Jean Van Leeuwen (Amanda Pig series, *Cabin on Trouble Creek*).

It's the birth date of Ella Young (1867–1956), *The Tangle-Coated Horse and Other Tales*.

In 1966 the first Kwanzaa was celebrated by Dr. Maulana Karenga, chair of Black Studies at California State University, Long Beach. Read *The Children's Book of Kwanzaa* by Dolores Johnson, *Li'l Rabbit's Kwanzaa* by Donna L. Washington, illustrated by Shane W. Evans, *Seven Spools of Thread* by Angela Shelf Medearis, illustrated by Daniel Minter.

It's National Thank-You Note Day.

It's also Boxing Day. Read *Not a Box* by Antoinette Portis.

Delphine, the oldest and the narrator of the saga, takes caring for her sisters into her own hands. In order to obtain breakfast, they spend their days at a summer camp sponsored by the Black Panthers, who provide food and education to those in the community. Although at first they are dismissive of what they hear at camp, the girls begin to comprehend the message of activism preached there. When Nzila and two Black Panthers get arrested, Delphine and her sisters go into high gear to honor their mother.

Delphine is a very engaging character; her incredible sense of responsibility for her sisters and her longing for her mother's acceptance rings true. In this character-driven novel, Rita Williams-Garcia brings to life the community of Oakland and the issues of the 1960s. She incorporates a lot of humor into these serious subjects. As the Brooklyn girls respond to utterly new teachings in day camp classes, they are not beyond letting members of the Black Panthers know that they "didn't come for the revolution. We came for breakfast."

Because the book remains so true to an eleven-year-old point of view, and because in the end, Delphine finally gets what she had traveled all those miles to find—the acceptance of her mother—the story works as a family saga with history interwoven. So whether you read *One Crazy Summer* to understand the Black Panthers, or you just want to pick up a mother/daughter saga, there is a lot of wisdom to be found in its pages.

DECEMBER 27

Happy Birthday Diane Stanley (*Leonardo da Vinci, Bella at Midnight*) and Erin Stead (*A Sick Day for Amos McGee*).

It's the birth date of Ingri Parin D'Aulaire (1904–1980), *Abraham Lincoln, D'Aulaires' Book of Norse Myths*.

In 1831 Charles Darwin embarked on his journey aboard the HMS *Beagle*, during which he began to formulate the theory of evolution. Read *Charles Darwin and the Beagle Adventure* by A. J. Wood and Clint Twist, *The True Adventures of Charlie Darwin* by Carolyn Meyer, and *The Tree of Life* by Peter Sís.

Happy Birthday to New York City's Radio City Music Hall, which opened in 1932.

It's National Fruitcake Day. Read *Junie B. Jones and the Yucky Blucky Fruitcake* by Barbara Park, illustrated by Denise Brunkus.

BREADCRUMBS
By Anne Ursu

December is Read a New Book Month; many are hunting for new books not only to read but to buy for the holidays. If you have not already found Anne Ursu's *Breadcrumbs*, you'll want to make it your new book for the month of December.

In *Breadcrumbs*, Ursu skillfully develops a friendship story between Hazel, who is adopted from India, and Jack, her neighbor. When Hazel's father leaves, her mother has to put Hazel in public school, where she and Jack ride the bus together and play at recess. Otherwise Hazel has trouble in school; she daydreams about great quests and adventures—roles that she and Jack play out in their time together. Jack is her anchor at the school, the only person who makes her feel that she fits in.

Then the story shifts. Ursu slowly brings these characters into a version of the Hans Christian Andersen story "The Snow Queen." A piece of magic mirror, falling from the sky, changes the way Jack looks at everything. He views his best friend with disdain; his heart freezes. And, finally, the Snow Queen arrives with a sled pulled by wolves to bring him into her icy kingdom.

Devastated by Jack's rejection, Hazel still hopes that someday they will be friends again. When he vanishes, she gathers all her courage to set out, entering a magical forest to bring him back home again. On this journey, she encounters many of Hans Christian Andersen's characters. And, I am happy to report that finally the Little Match Girl, under Ursu's pen, does not freeze to death! (I have hated the Andersen ending to that story my entire life!)

For anyone who knows the Andersen stories, *The Lion, the Witch and the Wardrobe*, *When You Reach Me*, or any of the other books Ursu references, *Breadcrumbs* provides a wonderful romp through children's literature. But the reader can be completely ignorant of her scaffolding and still find this story of friendship and betrayal, love and loss, compelling in its own terms. It is one of those books that readers devour to find out what happens next. And the imagery and language are sublime.

I can think of no better book to pick up on a cold winter's eve. This is one of those books that I am grateful to have read as a new title—I know I will be going back to it many times again in the future.

BEN AND ME

By Robert Lawson

On December 28, 1732, the first issue of *Poor Richard's Almanack* was advertised in the Pennsylvania Gazette. Published from 1733 to 1758, this brainchild of Benjamin Franklin has been imitated and copied many times. Franklin, like so many of the Founding Fathers, was a Renaissance man—inventor, printer, ambassador, and the delight of the French ladies. He has been the focus of countless biographies for adults, and one slightly irreverent one for young people. In Robert Lawson's *Ben and Me*, we see the great man from the point of view of the mouse who resides in his fur hat.

In the book Lawson claims to have discovered an old manuscript, lodged in a secretary desk, where Amos "with pen in paw" sets the record straight about Franklin—a man who could be overenthusiastic about himself. In this story the Revolution and its heroes get examined from a mouse-eye view. Of all the figures, Amos prefers Washington: "Not only was he a magnificent figure of a man and a soldier, but the wheat grown at Mount Vernon was of a superb quality." While he spins his tale, Amos educates readers about Philadelphia, printing presses, electricity, Franklin stoves, and the tendency of the Founding Fathers to spend excessive time in committees.

After completing the illustrations for *Mr. Popper's Penguins*, Lawson was asked by Little Brown to suggest a subject for his next book, preferably a biography that someone else could write for him. He came up with an outline for *Ben and Me*; his editor thought it was such a cockeyed story that only Lawson himself could create it. Published in 1939, the book has imparted humor, history, and wisdom to generations of American children.

In *Everything I Need to Know I Learned from a Children's Book*, Pulitzer Prize–winning historian David McCullough presents the virtues of this book: "I met my first revisionist historian when I was six. . . . Lawson understood the details of Franklin's life and the world of Franklin's travels and work, which give the book its great charm. In the writing of history and biography, one has to call on imagination. . . . This I learned early from *Ben and Me*, a book I still read for my grandchildren and for its enduring pleasure."

DECEMBER 28

It's the birth date of Carol Ryrie Brink (1895–1981), *Caddie Woodlawn*; and Emily Neville (1919–1997), *It's Like This, Cat*.

It's also the birth date of Woodrow Wilson (1856–1924), the 28th president of the United States.

In 1612 **Galileo Galilei** became the first astronomer to observe the planet Neptune, although he mistakenly catalogued it as a fixed star. Read *Starry Messenger* by Peter Sís and *Galileo: The Genius Who Faced the Inquisition* by Philip Steele.

Happy Birthday Iowa, which became the 29th U.S. state on this day in 1846.

In 1895 the Lumière brothers held the first motion picture screening for a paying audience in Paris. The presentation featured ten short films, marking the debut of the cinema. The Lumière brothers influenced Georges Méliès. Read Brian Selznick's *The Invention of Hugo Cabret*.

DECEMBER 29

Happy Birthday Molly Garrett Bang (*Ten, Nine, Eight, When Sophie Gets Angry—Really, Really Angry*).

It's the birth date of E.W. Hildick (1925–2001), *The Case of the Absent Author, Birdy Jones*.

 It's the birth date of **Andrew Johnson** (1808–1875), the 17th president of the United States.

Happy Birthday Texas, which became the 28th U.S. state on this day in 1845.

In 1851 the first American YMCA opened in Boston, Massachusetts.

It's Tick Tock Day, in reference to the days of this current year that are running out. Read *Tick Tock* by Lena Anderson, *The House with the Clock in Its Walls* by John Bellairs, illustrated by Edward Gorey, and *The Thirteen Clocks* by James Thurber.

MR. POPPER'S PENGUINS

By Richard and Florence Atwater
Illustrated by Robert Lawson

Today marks the birthday of Richard Atwater, born in 1892. He graduated with honors from the University of Chicago, where he taught Greek. But for most of his career Atwater worked as a journalist, book review editor, and columnist for newspapers. He dabbled in publishing—first he wrote an opera, then a children's book, *Doris and the Trolls*, both now long forgotten. But then after seeing a motion picture about Richard Byrd's first Antarctic expedition, Atwater wrote another story—about a man who fell in love with the birds of this snowy continent—*Mr. Popper's Penguins*.

Sometimes talented husband-and-wife teams—H. A. and Margret Rey or Crockett Johnson and Ruth Krauss—intentionally work together on a book. In the case of Richard and Florence Atwater, their collaboration grew out of necessity. After attending University of Chicago, Florence Carroll married Richard Atwater in 1921. When her husband had a stroke, she needed to support the family and published pieces in *The New Yorker* and *The Atlantic*. After two publishers turned down her husband's *Mr. Popper's Penguins* manuscript, she edited and rewrote sections, adding a bit more reality to a very fanciful story. The collaboration worked. Not only did the Atwaters find a publisher, Little Brown, but *Mr. Popper's Penguins* went on to win a Newbery Honor and has stood the test of time for seven decades.

Ideal for seven- to ten-year-old children who have just mastered reading skills, *Mr. Popper's Penguins* features a house painter—a Walter Mitty dreamer who wants to travel particularly to the North and South Poles. Mr. Popper even writes to his hero, Admiral Drake, currently exploring Antarctica. Then, unexpectedly, the admiral sends him a gift—a penguin named Captain Cook, who comes to live with the Poppers and completely transforms their lives. Although the story rests firmly on nonsense, it is related with such a matter-of-fact style that it all seems plausible. Mr. Popper remodels his house to create an ideal environment for Captain Cook. He drills holes in the refrigerator so the Captain can live there. After a female penguin arrives, and they have ten children, the troop of twelve travels the United States as a performing act.

There are no lessons or morals here, just fun and nonsense. Robert Lawson, who can delineate character brilliantly with only black line, provides fabulous drawings of all the penguins and their antics. They look so real you can almost believe these events are happening. Anyone suffering from post-holiday blues should pick up *Mr. Popper's Penguins* in honor of both Richard and Florence Atwater. No matter what is going on in reality, this book makes readers happy while they stay within these pages.

YOU NEVER HEARD OF SANDY KOUFAX?!

By Jonah Winter

Illustrated by André Carrilho

December 30, 1935, marks the birthday of Sandy Koufax, left-handed pitcher for the Brooklyn/Los Angeles Dodgers. In 1972 Koufax became the youngest player to be inducted into the Baseball Hall of Fame. But 1972 happened in the dark ages if you are six to ten. How can a baseball player of that time period be made relevant to young readers?

From the lenticular cover, where viewers watch Koufax whirl back and pitch, to the final glossary, everything in Jonah Winter's *You Never Heard of Sandy Koufax?!* strikes just the right note for young sports enthusiasts. In a story told by one of Koufax's teammates, the narrator brags about his hero: "Hittin' a Koufax fastball," says Willie Stargell, "was like tryin' to drink coffee with a fork."

As this teammate presents the life story of the prince of baseball players, readers learn that Koufax dominated pitching in Major League Baseball for six years. Koufax, who grew up in a Jewish neighborhood of Brooklyn, first became a member of the Brooklyn Dodgers and a teammate of Jackie Robinson. As one of the few Jewish ballplayers at the time, Koufax, like Robinson, knew what it meant to be a minority player and stand up to the personal slurs and attacks thrown at him. After the Dodgers moved to Los Angeles, Koufax had such a rough time it looked like his career might be over. Readers walk with him through his despair, his doubt, and his thoughts of quitting baseball. But like all good storytellers the narrator quickly moves to his moment of triumph as Koufax finds his pitching groove and begins to strike out one batter after another—becoming a human strikeout machine.

And, of course, the narrator recounts the detail for which Koufax became even more famous, sitting out the first game of the 1965 World Series because it fell on Yom Kippur, the Jewish High Holy Day. At age thirty, at the peak of his career, Koufax left the game because of debilitating arthritis. "Who was Sandy Koufax? Sandy Koufax was a guy who finally relaxed enough to let his body do the one thing it was put on this earth to do. And what a thing of beauty that was."

Not only is Winter's text spirited and lively, but André Carrilho's animated artwork is filled with movement. In illustrations on every page Koufax looks like the Greek god of baseball, just as his teammate claims. Both text and art combine in this picture book biography to bring this hero of the past vividly alive to young readers. Once they finish the book, they will definitely have heard of Sandy Koufax.

DECEMBER 30

Happy Birthday Mercer Mayer (*A Boy, a Dog, and a Frog; There's a Nightmare in My Closet*).

It's the birth date of **Rudyard Kipling** (1856–1936), *The Jungle Book*, *Rikki-Tikki-Tavi*.

The Union of Soviet Socialist Republics was formed in 1922. Read *The Endless Steppe: Growing Up in Siberia* by Esther Hautzig.

In 1940 California opened its first freeway, the Arroyo Seco Parkway. Read *Highway Cats* by Janet Taylor Lisle, illustrated by David Frankland.

It's Falling Needles Family Fest Day.

DECEMBER 31

It's the birth date of Pamela Bianco (1906–1994), *Flora*.

In 1857 Queen Victoria of the United Kingdom chose Ottawa, Ontario, as the capital of Canada. Read *Angel Square* by Brian Doyle.

Let there be light! In 1879 Thomas Edison demonstrated incandescent lighting to the public for the first time. Read *Edison's Gold* by Geoff Watson.

In 1891 a new immigration depot was opened on Ellis Island, New York. Read *If Your Name Was Changed at Ellis Island* by Ellen Levine, illustrated by Wayne Parmenter, and *The Memory Coat* by Elvira Woodruff, illustrated by Michael Dooling.

And, it's New Year's Eve! A good time to work on reading resolutions for next year.

THE LONDON EYE MYSTERY

By Siobhan Dowd

On December 31, 1999, the Prime Minister of England, Tony Blair, formally opened what was then the tallest Ferris wheel in the world, the London Eye. On the banks of the River Thames, this major landmark and tourist attraction has provided a panoramic view of the city for around 3.5 million riders each year.

In 2008 the London Eye served as the focus for one of the best new mysteries published for fifth through seventh graders, *The London Eye Mystery* by Siobhan Dowd. Readers learn a great deal about this structure from the narrator, Ted, who excels in retaining statistics because he has Asperger's Syndrome. When Ted's cousin Salim, who he has not seen for years, comes to visit London, the two head out with Ted's sister Kat to take a ride. But things don't quite turn out as Ted has hoped. Given a ticket by a stranger, Salim boards the Ferris wheel alone, and then he simply vanishes. While the adults in the story remain clueless, Ted and Kat set out to solve the mystery of what happened to their cousin.

Because of the brain difference that people with Asperger's have, Ted has unusually focused powers of observation and works on one theory after another of what actually happened. Soon he and Kat begin enlarging photographs from the scene of the crime, finding and shadowing the mysterious stranger who gave Salim his ticket, and then calling the police with discoveries. Since the adults in his life have long ago stopped listening to Ted's long explanations, they fail to notice that he, in fact, has been making the only progress on the case. Just like Sherlock Holmes and Watson, the brother and sister duo solve the mystery of what happened—and then they realize they must save their cousin's life. This book makes even better reading the second time around.

A page-turner that educates about London and its neighborhoods; a book that explores Asperger's Syndrome and brings the reader into the mind of someone with this disorder; and a very funny commentary on family life and family dynamics, *The London Eye Mystery* has been a favorite of both adults and children since it appeared. On this day when the London Eye was opened, read *The London Eye Mystery*—and get taken for a wonderful ride.

GUIDE TO MAJOR CHILDREN'S BOOK AWARDS

Boston Globe–Horn Book **Awards**—administered by *The Horn Book*, selects books in three categories: Picture Book, Fiction and Poetry, and Nonfiction.

Carnegie Medal in Literature—administered by the Chartered Institute of Library and Information Professionals in the United Kingdom, honors the writer of an outstanding book for children.

Children's Choice Book Awards—administered by the Children's Book Council and Every Child a Reader (The CBC Foundation), the only national book awards program where the winning titles are selected by children and teens of all ages.

Coretta Scott King Book Awards—administered by the American Library Association, honors African-American authors and illustrators of books that communicate the African-American experience.

Edgar Awards—administered by the Mystery Writers of America, honors the best in mystery writing including fiction for children and young adults.

Hans Christian Andersen Award—administered by the International Board on Books for Young People, honors a living author and illustrator whose complete works have made a lasting contribution to children's literature.

IRA Children's and Young Adults' Book Awards—administered by the International Reading Association, intended for newly published authors who show unusual promise in the children's and young adults' book field.

John Newbery Medal—administered by the American Library Association, honors the author of the year's most outstanding contribution to children's literature.

Kate Greenaway Medal—administered by the Chartered Institute of Library and Information Professionals in the United Kingdom, honors distinguished illustration in a book for children.

Laura Ingalls Wilder Award—administered by the American Library Association, honors an author or illustrator whose books have made a substantial and lasting contribution to literature for children.

Michael L. Printz Award—administered by the American Library Association, honors excellence in literature for young adults.

National Book Award for Young People's Literature—administered by the National Book Foundation, honors authors of books for children and young adults.

New York Times **Best Illustrated Books**—administered by the *New York Times Book Review*, honors ten best illustrated books each year.

Pura Belpré Awards—administered by the American Library Association, honors Latino writers and illustrators whose work portrays, affirms, and celebrates the Latino cultural experience.

Randolph Caldecott Medal—administered by the American Library Association, honors the illustrator of the year's most distinguished picture book.

Robert F. Sibert Informational Book Medal—administered by the American Library Association, honors the authors, illustrators, and/or photographers of the year's most distinguished nonfiction books.

Scott O'Dell Award for Historical Fiction—administered by the O'Dell Award committee, honors the author of a meritorious book of historical fiction for children or young adults.

Stonewall Children's and Young Adult Literature Award—administered by the American Library Association, honors exceptional merit in works relating to the gay/lesbian/bisexual/transgendered experience.

Theodor Seuss Geisel Award—administered by the American Library Association, honors the authors and illustrators of an outstanding book for beginning readers.

YALSA Award for Excellence in Nonfiction for Young Adults—administered by the American Library Association, honors the best nonfiction book published for young adults.

INDEX OF BOOKS AND AUTHORS FEATURED

INDEX OF BOOKS BY TYPE

Fiction

Graphic Novel

Historical Fiction

Memoir

Mystery/Thriller

Nonfiction

Novelty/Pop-up

Picture Book

Poetry

Poetic Novel

Science Fiction

Series

INDEX OF BOOKS BY AGE

Middle School

High School

All Ages

INDEX OF MAJOR HOLIDAYS

PICTURE CREDITS

2: NASA; **3:** Courtesy of the Library of Congress, LC-USZ62-74616; **5:** LOC, LC-USZ62-68483; **7:** LOC, LC-DIG-pga-02635; **9:** LOC, HABS NY,31-NEYO,151—2; **10:** LOC, LC-DIG-ppmsca-31802; **12:** LOC, LC-G3999-0049-C; **13:** LOC, LC-D401-18310; **18:** LOC, LC-H824-T01-P01-037; **19:** LOC, LC-DIG-cwpb-04830; **23:** LOC, LC-DIG-ppmsca-17519; **25:** LOC, LC-DIG-hec-23693; **27:** LOC, LC-USZ62-87246; **32:** LOC, LC-USW3-001542-D; **33:** LOC, LC-USZ62-101001; **34:** LOC, LC-USZ62-93595; **35:** LOC, LC-DIG-pga-04159; **37:** LOC, LC-USZC4-7246; **39:** Felix Nadar; **42:** LOC, LC-USZ62-98066; **43:** LOC, LC-DIG-ppmsca-19305; **45:** LOC, LC-USZ62-50927; **47:** LOC, LC-USZ62-134150; **51:** NASA; **52:** LOC, LC-USZ62-42537; **53:** United States Senate; **54:** LOC, LC-DIG-ggbain-07435; **58:** LOC, LC-USZ62-7407; **59:** self-portrait by John Tenniel; **64:** LOC, LC-USZ62-119056; **65:** LOC, LC-DIG-ggbain-04739; **69:** LOC, LC-DIG-pga-02908; **70:** LOC, LC-USZ62-14759; **75:** LOC, LC-DIG-pga-02501; **76:** LOC, LC-DIG-ppmsca-19166; **78:** LOC, LC-DIG-pga-02167; **80:** LOC, LC-USZ62-11212; **81:** LOC, LC-USZ62-68852; **86:** LOC, LC-USZ62-120742; **87:** LOC, LC-USZ62-116987; **88:** George Charles Beresford; **89:** LOC, LC-DIG-pga-01249; **91:** LOC, LC-DIG-ppmsca-31940; **93:** LOC, LC-USZ62-43573; **94:** LOC, LC-USZ62-72480; **96:** LOC, LC-USZ62-25624; **100:** LOC, LC-DIG-cwpb-04402; **104:** LOC, LC-USZ62-53985; **109:** LOC, LC-DIG-highsm-14759; **111:** LOC, LC-USZ62-116612; **112:** LOC, LC-DIG-ggbain-06861; **114:** LOC, LC-USZC4-6527; **118:** LOC, LC-DIG-highsm-14492; **119:** LOC, LC-D416-292; **125:** LOC, LC-USZ62-70064; **126:** LOC, LC-DIG-ggbain-38216; **128:** LOC, LC-USZ62-121205; **129:** Frank Gatteri, United States Army Signal Corps; **130:** LOC, LC-USZ62-89798; **132:** LOC, LC-USZ62-133965; **133:** LOC, LC-USZ62-5877; **138:** LOC, LC-USZ62-55961; **140:** LOC, LC-DIG-ppmsc-01274; **142:** LOC, LC-USZ62-75827; **143:** LOC, LC-USZ62-78454; **145:** LOC, LC-DIG-det-4a28540; **146:** NASA; **148:** U.S. Fish and Wildlife Service; **150:** LOC, LC-USZ62-117124; **152:** LOC, LC-USZ62-2884; **154:** LOC, LC-H823-1407-M-A; **156:** LOC, LC-USZ62-49254; **165:** LOC, LC-USZ62-60139; **166:** LOC, LC-DIG-highsm-04135; **167:** LOC, LC-D418-50297 <P&P> [P&P]; **170:** NASA; **172:** LOC, LC-USZ62-14976; **175:** LOC, LC-USZ62-115646; **179:** LOC, LC-DIG-ppmsca-23661; **180:** LOC, LC-DIG-ggbain-07650; **184:** LOC, LC-USZ62-20901; **187:** LOC, LC-USZ62-24466; **188:** LOC, LC-USZ62-42516; **190:** LOC, LC-DIG-hec-10415; **191:** LOC, LC-DIG-det-4a26168; **193:** LOC, LC-USZ62-98072; **194:** LOC, LC-USZ61-361; **196:** LOC, LC-USZ62-130859; **198:** LOC, LC-USZ62-107756; **200:** LOC, LC-DIG-highsm-16040; **202:** LOC, LC-USZ62-12277; **203:** NASA; **204:** LOC, LC-DIG-hec-22501; **205:** LOC, LC-USZ62-13037; **207:** LOC, LC-USZ62-105842; **211:** NASA; **212:** LOC, LC-USZ62-111278; **214:** LOC, LC-H824-T01-0523; **215:** LOC, LC-USZ62-60242; **217:** LOC, LC-USZ62-127236; **218:** LOC, LC-USZ62-49496; **220:** LOC, ABS MICH,45-GLAR,8A—2; **222:** LOC, LC-DIG-ppmsc-06581; **223:** LOC, LC-DIG-npcc-03577; **226:** LOC, LC-DIG-ppmsca-24362; **229:** British Army File photo; **230:** LOC, LC-DIG-pga-04179; **232:** Bob McNeely, The White House; **233:** LOC, LC-USZ61-104; **235:** LOC, LC-USZ62-32637; **237:** LOC, LC-USZ62-103837; **240:** LOC, LC-U91-242-2; **241:** LOC, LC-USZ62-126559; **244:** LOC, LC-DIG-ggbain-14964; **247:** LOC, LC-DIG-highsm-14719; **249:** LOC, LC-USZ62-3854; **254:** LOC, LC-DIG-npcc-20404; **255:** LOC, LC-DIG-highsm-15482; **256:** LOC, LC-DIG-ggbain-03571; **257:** LOC, LC-USZ62-120746; **259:** LOC, HABS ALA,37-BIRM,33—6; **264:** LOC, LC-DIG-ggbain-00788; **265:** LOC, LC-USZ62-86846; **267:** LOC, LC-DIG-highsm-17094; **268:** LOC, LC-USZ62-78493; **270:** H. S. Knapp; **273:** LOC, LC-USZ62-137042; **275:** LOC, LC-DIG-ppmsca-09770; **278:** LOC, LC-DIG-cwpbh-03606; **279:** LOC, LC-DIG-pga-02734; **280:** Anna Cervova; **283:** LOC, HABS DC,WASH,2—1; **284:** LOC, LC-DIG-ggbain-30126; **285:** LOC, LC-USZ62-15887; **286:** LOC, LC-DIG-ppmsca-18934; **287:** S. Beckwith (STScI) Hubble Heritage Team, (STScI/AURA), ESA, NASA; **292:** LOC, LC-DIG-ppmsca-02947; **295:** LOC, LC-USZ62-30424; **296:** LOC, LC-DIG-ppmsca-26824; **298:** James Reid Lambdin; **302:** LOC, LC-USZ62-8283; **305:** LOC, LC-USZC4-3277; **306:** Seabiscuit Heritage Foundation; **307:** LOC, LC-USZ62-1491; **309:** White House photo by Krisanna Johnson; **311:** LOC, LC-DIG-npcc-08831; **314:** U.S. Federal Government; **316:** LOC, LC-D416-28072; **318:** Albert George Dew-Smith (1848-1903); **319:** LOC, LC-USZ62-75620; **322:** LOC, LC-USZ62-47605; **324:** LOC, LC-DIG-cwpbh-00948; **327:** Samuel Laurence; **328:** LOC, LC-DIG-pga-00725; **329:** LOC, LC-USZ62-77338; **331:** LOC, LC-USZC2-6148; **334:** LOC, LC-USZ61-452; **337:** LOC, LC-USZ62-132077; **338:** George Charles Beresford; **339:** H.W. Smith; **340:** LOC, LC-DIG-det-4a26143; **342:** LOC, LC-USZ62-42538; **348:** LOC, LC-DIG-ppmsca-19219; **349:** LOC, LC-DIG-ggbain-06673; **350:** LOC, LC-USZ62-107932; **351:** LOC, LC-USZ62-103529; **353:** LOC, LC-USW33-019081-C; **357:** LOC, LC-USZ62-112190; **359:** LOC, LC-DIG-hec-24844; **363:** LOC, LC-USZ62-103175; **364:** LOC, LC-DIG-ppmsca-05704; **365:** LOC, LC-USZ62-101366.

ACKNOWLEDGMENTS

The Children's Book-a-Day Almanac was the brainchild of the brilliant Simon Boughton of Roaring Brook Press. While he was looking at one of my book proposals, Simon was also considering publishing an Almanac. He realized that the two ideas could be combined. Then as Simon and his staff worked on the basic concept, they decided that the ideal way to initially present the material would be as a blog. One of the happiest days of my life came in January of 2010 when I had dinner with Simon and Lauren Wohl, and they presented this fabulous project to me.

The day-to-day execution of both the online Almanac and this book have been in the capable hands of Katherine Jacobs. When Kate was a student in my History of Children's Book Publishing class at Simmons College, I knew she had all the right qualities to be a great editor—intelligence, perception, an ability to work with others, and sensitivity to the written word. But now she has been my editor for two years, and I am in awe of her wisdom. It has been a joy to work with her on the project—and this book owes an enormous amount to her insight.

Other Simmons students, both in the Graduate School of Library Science and the Children's Literature Program, have made significant contributions to the book. I want to particularly thank Jory Hearst, Diane Croft, Deborah St. Thomas, Christy Yaros, Jill Closter, and Kate Gagner for their research into some of the books that I have included in the Almanac.

Alison A. Ernst served as the project assistant for the online Almanac; she penned many of the entries in the sidebars. Ann McDowell tirelessly sought out holidays for me—she had a knack for finding the not-so-obvious events. It has taken a village to create both the online version of the Almanac and this book. Particular thanks to my copyeditor Patricia Egan, but also my gratitude to Beth Potter, Jill Freshney, Roberta Pressel, Miriam Frank, Desirae Freedman, Cardner Clark, and Katarzyna Lesko.

My agent Doe Coover has been behind the project every step of the way. I can call Doe with any problem, at any time. Her support has meant everything to me over the years.

I am particularly indebted to all of the readers of the online version of the Book-a-Day Almanac. Though I have not met many of them personally, all have become dear to me over the last two years. They have given me suggestions, found errors, relayed their own stories, and cheered me on. Without them, I am not sure I would have crossed the finish line and been able to complete this book.

ANITA SILVEY is a distinguished former publisher of children's books and was editor of *The Horn Book Magazine*. Her works on children's literature include *Children's Books and Their Creators*, *100 Best Books for Children*, *500 Great Books for Teens*, and *Everything I Need to Know I Learned from a Children's Book*. She teaches courses in children's literature at Simmons College in Boston and St. Michael's College in Burlington, Vermont. She lives in Westwood, Massachusetts.

More than 100 leaders from the arts, sciences, politics, business, and other fields recall a children's book they loved and its impact on their lives.

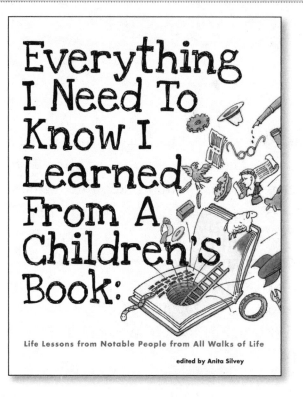

Everything I Need To Know I Learned From A Children's Book:

Life Lessons from Notable People from All Walks of Life

edited by Anita Silvey

"The more of an audience I had, the more I'd act up."
— Entertainer Jay Leno, on *Mike Mulligan and His Steam Shovel* by Virginia Lee Burton

"In the writing of history and biography, one has to call on imagination."
— Historian David McCullough, on *Ben and Me* by Robert Lawson

"A woman could choose."
— Actress Julianne Moore on *Little Women* by Louisa May Alcott

"When we give children books, we become part of their future, part of their most cherished memories, and part of their entire life. Children's books change lives."
— from the Introduction of *Everything I Need to Know I Learned from a Children's Book* by Anita Silvey